# Colonial Massachusetts Laws and Liberties and the English Commonwealth

# Legal History Library



VOLUME 68

The titles published in this series are listed at *brill.com/lhl*

# Colonial Massachusetts Laws and Liberties and the English Commonwealth

*State Formation, the Rule of Law, and the People's Welfare*

*By*

Charles Edward Smith

BRILL | NIJHOFF

LEIDEN | BOSTON

Cover illustration: Endicott cutting the cross from the king's banner, 1876–1881. Available via Getty Images.

Library of Congress Cataloging-in-Publication Data

Names: Smith, Charles Edward, 1960- author.
Title: Colonial Massachusetts laws and liberties and the English Commonwealth : state formation, the rule of law, and the people's welfare / Charles Edward Smith.
Description: Leiden ; Boston : Brill/Nijhoff, 2024. | Series: Legal history library; volume 68 | Includes bibliographical references and index.
Identifiers: LCCN 2024026316 | ISBN 9789004706330 (hardback) | ISBN 9789004706347 (ebook)
Subjects: LCSH: Law–Massachusetts–History–Colonial period, ca. 1600-1775. | Civil rights–Massachusetts–History–Colonial period, ca. 1600-1775. | Rule of law–Massachusetts–History–Colonial period, ca. 1600-1775. | Public welfare–Law and legislation–Massachusetts–History–Colonial period, ca. 1600-1775.
Classification: LCC KFM2478 .S65 2024 | DDC 349.74409/03–dc23/eng/20240614
LC record available at https://lccn.loc.gov/2024026316

Typeface for the Latin, Greek, and Cyrillic scripts: "Brill". See and download: brill.com/brill-typeface.

ISSN 1874-1793
ISBN 978-90-04-70633-0 (hardback)
ISBN 978-90-04-70634-7 (e-book)
DOI 10.1163/9789004706347



This book is printed on acid-free paper and produced in a sustainable manner.

# Contents

## PART 4
## *Transatlantic Legal Reform and Popular Sovereignty*



## PART 5
## *Imperial Ambitions*

# Preface

As an unknown independent scholar, I thought I should provide readers a sketch of my academic and professional bona fides, along with an explanation of why the work was written. It's been my good fortune for such a storied publisher as Brill to accept my manuscript. The series editors and the firm's editorial staff have been fully supportive, and extremely kind.

The work's genesis occurred thirty years ago in the University of Chicago's Department of History. I had been awarded a graduate fellowship and recruited by a center for the comparative study of legal history, with goals very similar to Brill's *Legal History Library* series. Even then, with the burgeoning group of new democracies in Eastern Europe, the need to support their development and incorporation into the international community was clear. Although the center was short-lived, I carried-on and completed the dissertation in the Fall of 1998, and presented a precis at a conference at the Sorbonne on "The Book" that November. I received my doctorate the following month.

During those months an unrelated event caught my attention and interest: the emergence of the commercial Internet. After initial on-line research for an article on that very topic I knew fundamental change in information of all types was upon us. The experience also changed how I analyzed the law: from a deductive approach, to one focusing on how legal information was disseminated through a respective jurisdiction, whether national or local. With academic interest at a minimum, I endeavored to find something in the private sector that combined my interest in the Internet with the dissertation's focus on publishing law. Luckily, I found a position with University Publications of America (UPA) just as it was formulating a publication process "without paper" to enter the on-line market; a relic of a bygone era now, but in 1999–2000 it was just what I had been looking for.

Ultimately, after canvassing a number of opportunities in the US Government, including a contractor position with the Federal Deposit Insurance Company (FDIC) where I assisted senior counsel in drafting what became policy on the Corporation's 1933 origins, the Department of Defense recruited me to lead the re-engineering of an Internet based legislative tracking system for the National Defense Authorization Act (NDAA); the largest annual piece of legislation enacted by Congress. After several years, having assisted in remedying that issue, I moved on to the office of the Assistant Secretary of Defense for Legislative Affairs where I performed the same general task, but on a far larger scale.

In my post as the Director of Legislative Operations I was responsible for assigning and tracking thousands of congressional actions (i.e., reports, hearing questions and inserts for the record, the NDAA at large). One of the more challenging aspects of the portfolio was US statute's poor organization, being split between a Code, of which only half of the titles have been enacted by Congress, and a significant number of stand-alone Acts. Moreover, the actual formatting of US statutory law itself is not standardized; since many people draft the NDAA, and there is no one "right way" to draft legislation, it does not have methodical formatting. I co-authored a report required by Congress (P.L. 115–232, sec. 874) to assist in automating the Department's responses to its statutory requirements. While well received, it was not convincing enough to prompt the implementation of our proposal: legislation's format should be standardized to be trackable. For example, we wanted to cull the Department's one thousand plus annual reporting requirements from the bill, rather than conduct line-by-line and adobe acrobat searches by staff; the latter was frustrated by the more than eighty types of reports as described in legislation.

In the last years of my career two things occurred that led me to resume my work on the Massachusetts law books. First, after responding to Professor Danielle Allen's (Harvard U.) *Washington Post* op-ed lamenting a lack of interest in civic education, to support her effort I started to review material on the colony's initiative to teach school age children to read, including its capital laws; thanks to Danielle for taking her valuable time to read the manuscript through several times to its great benefit. Since the US founding had long been utilized to celebrate and promote a number of national traits, like religion and family life, why not civic education? Before I got very far President Trump had declared an emergency on our southern border to justify redirecting military construction funds to build "the wall." Performed legally under 10 USC §2808, the provision requires DoD to report to those congressional members whose projects would be affected, either cancelled or delayed. While there are over 100 US statutes with similar emergency provisions that can be triggered by the President, it brought to mind a research topic I had left unexplored, concerning emergency powers, which turned out to be key to unlocking a great deal of both the law book's story and Revolutionary England's.

Thanks to my dissertation director Ted Cook for reading (again!) an early draft, and always taking my phone calls; and to Clemson U's Professor Rod Andrew who read a number of chapters, and assisted with advice on publication. Thanks to Jules Kirshner and Constantin Fasolt for their assistance in developing my dissertation topic; and Constantin for reading versions of the conclusion and introduction. Additionally, I was privileged to study under Lee Holcombe at the University of South Carolina (authored the first book on married women's property law); Tom Kuehn (Early Modern legal historian at Clemson U.); at Chicago I studied English legal history under Charles Gray and Gareth Jones (visiting from Cambridge U.), François Furet on Tocqueville as well as the American and French Revolutions, Robert Cooter on legal anthropology (Berkeley U.), Steven Pincus-17th century English history, and US legal history under Lawrence Friedman (Stanford U.) and Bill Novak.

I didn't get to work with Bill as much as I originally hoped, as I ultimately wrote a dissertation on the Early Modern era; however, I greatly admired his work, *The People's Welfare*, on nineteenth century US jurisprudence, and the role played by the maxim salus populi suprema lex that US judges used to justify all sorts of pro-regulatory decisions. It definitively debunks many of the dogmas that still plague us today which, with the US Supreme Court's recent "historical turn," makes Bill's work vital for providing a regulatory history of federal and state governments; I had hoped that 2007–2008's terrifying events would have been lesson enough. The quality of the work is manifest with its approaching thirtieth-year in print. We should be focusing on optimizing all parts of the legislative process to track and remedy whatever areas enacted law is not operating as intended. Too often we "walk away" from enacted legislation, but our new technological world is not long tolerant of traditional processes for their own sake. I hope this work provides effective support for Bill's thesis, despite its lateness.

*Charles Edward Smith, Ph.D.*
North Carolina, USA
February 2024

# Abbreviations

| | |
|---|---|
| Body of Liberties | William Whitmore, ed. *Colonial Laws of Massachusetts. Reprinted from the Edition of 1660, with the Supplements to 1672. Containing also, The Body of Liberties of 1641.* Boston: 1889. |
| CSP | Calendar of State Papers |
| EEBO | Early English Books Online (University of Michigan) |
| Harleian Miscellany | Thomas Osborne, ed. *The Harleian Miscellany.* 12 Vols. London: 1746. |
| Hathi Trust | Digital Online Library |
| HMSO | His/Her Majesty's Stationers Office |
| JP | Justice of the Peace |
| Laws and Liberties of 1648 | Richard Dunn, ed. *The Laws and Liberties of Massachusetts: Reprinted from the Unique Copy of the 1648 Edition.* San Marino: Huntington Library, 1998. |
| Laws and Liberties of 1660 | William Whitmore, ed. *The Colonial Laws of Massachusetts. Reprinted from the Edition of 1660, with the Supplements to 1672.* Boston: City Council of Boston, 1889. |
| Laws and Liberties of 1672 | Whitmore, William, ed. *The Colonial Law of Massachusetts. Reprinted from the Edition of 1672, with the Supplements Through 1686.* Boston: 1887. |
| MGCR | Nathaniel B. Shurtleff, ed. *Records of the Governor and Company of the Massachusetts Bay in New England.* 5 Vols. Boston: William White, 1853–1854. |
| MHS | Massachusetts Historical Society |
| MP | Member of Parliament |
| RHS | Royal Historical Society |
| Rushworth Collections | John Rushworth, ed. *Historical Collections.* 8 Vols. London: 1703–21. |
| SR | *Statutes of the Realm.* 9 Vols. London, 1810–1822. |
| Somers Tracts | Walter Scott, ed. *Somers Tracts.* 2nd ed. 13 vols. London: 1809–1815. |
| STC | Short Title Catalogue of Printed Books Microfilm Collection (1475–1640) |
| Thomason Tracts | Microfilm Collection of Civil War Tracts (1640–1661) |
| WMQ | William & Mary Quarterly |
| Wing | Early English Books on Microfilm (1641–1700) |
| Winthrop Papers | Adam Winthrop, et al., eds. *The Winthrop Papers.* 5 Vols. Boston: MHS, 1924–45. |

# Introduction

This is a study of Colonial Massachusetts' publication of laws as enacted by its legislature, the General Court, during the seventeenth century. The first enactment was a simple broadsheet listing the colony's capital punishments known as the *Capital Laws of 1642*, followed by comprehensive collections known as the *Laws and Liberties*. They were published in three major editions in twelve-year increments beginning in 1648; the series' last major edition issued in 1672, as England revoked the colonial charter when the 1684/5 iteration was in the final stages of publication. What first struck me when I picked up a copy of the initial 1648 edition was how out of place a printed collection of laws appeared in an English colony during what was long thought to be an era of "common law reception," when English practice had little use for manuscript or printed materials. Of course, parliamentary statutes were printed by the 1500s, but it was private not government printers who copy-edited and sent them to for-profit printers. Indeed, so little was the dependence on official publications for the actual practice of law that the initial government printing of the *Statutes of the Realm*, in 1810, included only laws enacted to 1714. Common law was administered in oral pleadings prepared and perfected in the Inns of Court, with statutory law incorporated into the vast corpus of English practice and traditions by the twelve common law justices at Westminster Hall. As Blackstone put it most famously,

> As to general customs, or the common law, properly so called, this is that law by which proceedings and determinations in the king's ordinary courts of justice are guided and directed … [H]ow are these customs or maxims to be known, and by whom is their validity to be determined? The answer is, by the judges in the several courts of justice. They are the depositary of the laws; the living oracles, who must decide in all cases of doubt, and who are bound by an oath to decide according to the law of the land.[1]

---

1 William Blackstone, *Commentaries on the Laws of England: 1765–1769* (Chicago: Univ. of Chicago Press, 1979), 1: 68–69. Barbara Shapiro, *Law Reform in Early Modern England: 1540–1700* (Oxford: Hart Publishing, 2019), 34, 55–61. "The printing of legal material should be included in the narrative of early modern English law reform because much of it was inspired by the desire to make the law more certain, more comprehensible and more available. Legal publications were often self-consciously offered as improvements for law often characterized as impenetrable, disorderly, and uncertain."

 DOI:10.1163/9789004706347_002

In this regard, US legal scholarship long held that the English colonies in North America had "received" English Common Law, even though a respective colony's adoption was not uniform with the rest, as each colony was thought to have implemented it on the basis of utility and practicality, according to its own needs and condition. Since the original thirteen colonies were all under British sovereignty, it's reasonable to wonder why Britain simply did not impose its common law throughout its new territories. One reason was that until the Glorious Revolution(1688–1689) England's control over its North American colonies was tenuous at best.[2]

During this era the English monarch's royal administration, commonly referred to as "the crown," largely left the colonies to their own devices under self-governing *charters.* Although Virginia was created a dominion in the early 1620's, to be ruled directly by the crown in appointing government officials and approving laws, initially it had been granted a charter in 1606. While all of these territories were in a "colonial" status, most were lightly subjugated before the 1760's. The respective colony's self-interest also played an essential role in whether it would resist what ultimately became increasing attempts by the crown to exert control. As illustrated by England's attempts to regulate colonial trade via its controversial *Navigation Acts*, American commercial activities adopted those English laws and customs that were conducive to the respective colony's interests, and naturally resisted those provisions that provoked colonial grievances. For example, the southern colonies were most closely bound to English trade as they depended on exporting "cash crops" like tobacco initially, and ultimately cotton, to English merchants who provided payment and credit in the form of finished goods to be shipped back across the Atlantic; in the future, southern plantation owners usually found themselves perpetually in debt except during their best harvest years, just as England's mercantilist system intended. Massachusetts, on the other hand, as the most prosperous and powerful New England colony could boast of a shipbuilding industry by the 1660's, and hearty international trade by the 1670's, which ultimately led to direct competition with Great Britain throughout the Caribbean. As Massachusetts balked at enforcing English trade laws, enforcement that would take money out of its own merchants' pockets and the colonial economy, it established the odd practice of allowing local juries to sit in what otherwise would be recognized as Admiralty courts; "odd" since England's Admiralty courts were presided over exclusively by judges. Bay colony juries repeatedly frustrated the crown's

2 William Stoebuck, "Reception of English Common Law in the American Colonies," *William and Mary Law Review* 10 (no. 2, 1968): 393–426.

attempt to seize goods for transfer to the royal treasury. Massachusetts and other colonies dependent on trade had far less motivation to receive English law, but no other colony achieved such a status of virtual independence to reject its uniform adoption for most of the seventeenth century.[3]

Even so, traditionally, most US legal scholars and jurists took reception of common law at face value until the latter decades of the twentieth century, as a commonsense explanation particularly valuable to the new states as they created their own legal systems.[4] However, Charles Hilkey published the earliest academic objection to the general theory over a century ago. Even while acknowledging that as the "accepted legal theory" reception had been "universally adopted by [US] courts," in reality Massachusetts colonists exhibited "a far different attitude toward the common law." Hilkey maintained that within the colony the "binding force of English law was denied, and a legal system largely different came into use." Indeed, we shall see that as late as the 1670's the colonial elected (versus royally appointed) governor John Leverett proclaimed to the English officer responsible for enforcing its customs and trade regulations that English law had *no force in the colony*, as they watched dozens of foreign flagged merchant vessels navigate in and out of Boston harbor, and even when royal credentials to supervise trade were provided in open colonial court proceedings. When Leverett was knighted by Charles II in an obvious attempt by the crown to ingratiate itself to him, he refused to acknowledge the award in fear of inflaming his colonial electorate's wrath. As to the independent stance of the colony, royal officials were unanimous upon reviewing the Massachusetts lawbooks' contents that terms such as "state" and "commonwealth" in reference to the colony must be stricken, and replaced by the appropriate citation or salutation to Charles II's prerogative.[5]

---

3 Jack Greene, *Peripheries and Center: Constitutional Development in the Extended Polities of the British Empire and the United States, 1607–1788* (New York, London: W.W. Norton, 1986). Lawrence Friedman, *History of American Law*, 3rd ed., (New York: Simon & Schuster, 2005), 2–23, 50–79. Michael Hall, *Edward Randolph and the American Colonies: 1676–1703* (New York: W.W. Norton, 1960).

4 James Kent, *Commentaries on American Law*, 7th ed., (New York: William Kent, 1851), 1: 522–27. Peter Hoffer, *Law and People in Colonial America* (Baltimore: Johns Hopkins Univ. Press, 1992), 134. "In the United States, the autonomous approach to legal history was early defended by judges greatly influenced by the English legal tradition. Typically, in the first half of the nineteenth century, James Kent's four volumes of *Commentaries on American Law* (New York, 1827–30) ... regarded the growth of the common law as a manifestation of natural law." This "internalist tradition" was carried into the twentieth century by "law professors Julius Goebel, Jr., and Joseph H. Smith."

5 Charles Hilkey, *Legal Development in Colonial Massachusetts: 1630–1686* (New York: Columbia Univ. Press, 1910), 5. Robert Wall, "The Membership of the Massachusetts General Court,"

Looking beyond the utility of having a term like common law reception to explain the legal origins of such a diverse collection of colonies along the east coast of North America, it is far more likely that any significant consolidation of legal regimes occurred after Great Britain's emergence as both a military and commercial power under the Protestant champion William III (1689–1702), as the colonies' incorporation into the nascent empire became a mandated process they necessarily adapted to Britain's mercantilist trading regime. Still, this provided the chartered New England colonies led by Massachusetts, being the oldest (besides Plymouth which ultimately was incorporated as a county) and most powerful, the opportunity to experiment with novel methods to govern themselves. While the *Massachusetts Charter of 1629* allowed the colony to enact new laws as long as they were not "repugnant" to English law, it also provided a powerful array of authorities to institute self-government; longer term, the chief importance of the *Charter* was its use by Bay colonists to defend their virtual independence, and specifically to pass laws and admit members. This did not signify a "liberal" grant by Charles I's government, but rather the aim was to provide the leadership the means to govern the colony as drawn from the example of Virginia, then considered a failed enterprise. The Bay colony was provided a great deal of leeway to create a new legal system as a result. While the colony's first governor, John Winthrop, repeatedly warned the colony's yeoman class, known as freemen, of the crown's likely reaction to a colonial legislature passing new laws (i.e., it would repeal them, bringing unwanted attention to the colony), they refused to grant colonial magistrates the authority to articulate the law via judicial decision. Instead, over a fifteen-year period these yeoman, known as "freemen," struggled to restrict the magistracy's discretion, while endeavoring to adopt the first law book in 1648.[6]

---

(Ph.D. diss., Yale University, 1965), 286–89. Leverett was governor from 1673 to 1678, and during his tenure "he refused to take the oath to support the Navigation Acts which the crown required of colonial governors." As for the award of his knighthood, "he might well have feared that it would have an adverse effect upon his political career, so opposed to concessions to the crown were the voters of the colony."

6 Max M. Edling, "Review: William E. Nelson. *E Pluribus Unum: How the Common Law Helped Unify and Liberate Colonial America, 1607–1776*," *American Historical Review* 127 (March 2022): 497–98. "In the course of the seventeenth and eighteenth centuries, the legal plurality of the American mainland colonies evolved into a reasonably cohesive common-law domain. Rather than the colonists bringing the common law with them from the motherland as their treasured birthright, it was imposed on them by the crown in a century-long process beginning with the Restoration." *The Charter of the Colony of the Massachusetts Bay in New England*, in Nathaniel Shurtleff, ed., MGCR, 1: 3–20 (March 1628/1629).

The Huntington Library holds the only known copy of the original first edition of the Massachusetts law book. In the introduction of the most recent published edition (1998), editor Richard Dunn describes its contents as "the first compilation of laws and constitutional rights to be printed in English America, and … arguably the most important statement of political, religious, and economic freedoms and obligations ever issued in the colonial era." Yet the text is largely absent in the relevant body of scholarship. In his 1989 work, *First Impressions*, Hugh Amory lamented that the lawbook remained "unread and unexamined," and had achieved the status of "a pure icon." Meanwhile, the only recent full-length monograph to cover the general topic, Edgar McManus' otherwise informative *Law and Liberty in Early New England* (1993), omits Massachusetts' printed lawbooks (which is more a reflection of the field itself than the quality of the work). When George Haskins searched for a common law precedent while writing *Law and Authority in Early Massachusetts* (1960), the now over sixty-year-old study that remains the authoritative academic text, his primary example was medieval manor custumals (or by-laws), when the actual models for the lawbooks derived from the English Commonwealth reform movement.[7] As Richard Ross has explained, the reform impulse actually derived from the sixteenth century:

> Building on Plato's concept of a res publica by way of Erasmus, English humanists such as Thomas More and Thomas Starkey championed a vision of an ideal commonwealth. The public interest of the community rather than the private interest of rulers or dominant factions was its end, the participation in governance of citizens tutored in the virtues of honesty, public-spiritedness, and godliness its foundation. The Platonic model of sound knowledge expressing itself in virtuous action made the proper education of the political nation an especially salient concern.[8]

Recently, a very useful analysis of the term "Commonwealth" was published by a group of senior scholars. Historically, it was an elastic term, as most terms

7 Richard Dunn, ed., *The Laws and Liberties of Massachusetts: Reprinted from the Unique Copy of the 1648 Edition in the Henry E. Huntington Library* (San Marino: Huntington Library, 1998); cited hereafter as the *Laws and Liberties of 1648*. Hugh Amory, *First Impressions: Printing in Cambridge, 1639–1989* (Cambridge: Harvard Univ., 1989), (intro.), 5. George Haskins, *Law and Authority in Early Massachusetts* (New York: Macmillan Co., 1960), 122–3, 169–70, 180. Edgar McManus, *Law and Liberty in Early New England: Criminal Justice and Due Process, 1620–1692* (Amherst: Univ. of Massachusetts Press, 1993).

8 Richard Ross, "The Commoning of the Common Law: The Renaissance Debate over Printing English Law, 1520–1640," *University of Pennsylvania Law Review* 146 (no. 2, 1998): 323–30.

of governance are when deployed in political discourse, but *commonwealth* or its earlier incarnation *common weal* were interchangeable until the sixteenth century and synonymous with a Republic. While commonwealth was preferred because it did not have the foreign connotations of Roman law, after its Interregnum usage it largely fell out of favor for a number of decades. Previously, the terms "common weal" or "common wealth" evolved from "being a term for the common good" for most of the fifteenth century, but in the following century they began "to denote an almost tangible entity, associated with laws, principles, consultative tradition, and denoting the welfare of the people." Ultimately, both became the "obvious translation for Cicero's res publica, and a number of early sixteenth-century usages suggest that it had been chosen with that in mind. By the sixteenth century commonweal(th) was openly defined in Ciceronian terms."[9]

While the lawbooks have been largely overlooked in the scholarship focused on early colonial legal regimes, they have received attention from a handful of more recent works that include the experiences of the freemen's deputies in the colonial assembly. These works include Francis Bremer's biography on Massachusetts first governor John Winthrop, *America's Forgotten Founding Father* (2001), David Hall's *A Reforming People* (2011), Michael Winship's *Godly Republicanism* (2012), and most recently Adrian Weimer's *Constitutional Culture* (2023). All have reincorporated at least a portion of the deputies' contest with the magistrates for control of the colony's government, and touch on colonial laws to some extent. Fortunately, this recent scholarship has begun to offer a much needed, more sophisticated understanding of the political culture between reformers across the Atlantic, and this study intends to build on these efforts. But a methodical investigation of the importance of the *Laws and Liberties* either from a domestic or cross-Atlantic perspective has yet to be written. This book aims to fill that gap. As G.B. Warden observed, however, "interpretations emphasizing cultural continuity in the transplantation of English law do not completely explain why New Englanders adopted many practices that had few or no precedents in English legal procedures."[10]

---

9 Early Modern Research Group, "Commonwealth: The Social, Cultural, and Conceptual Contexts of an Early Modern Keyword," *Historical Journal* 54 (Sept., 2011): 666.

10 Francis Bremer, *John Winthrop: America's Forgotten Founding Father* (Oxford: Oxford Univ. Press, 2003). David Hall, *A Reforming People: Puritanism and the Transformation of Public Life in New England* (New York: Alfred A. Knopf, 2011). Michael Winship, *Godly Republicanism: Puritans, Pilgrims, and a City on a Hill* (Cambridge: Harvard Univ. Press, 2012). Adrian Weimer, *Constitutional Culture: New England and the Struggle Against Arbitrary Rule in the Restoration Empire* (Philadelphia: University of Pennsylvania Press, 2023). G.B. Warden, "Law Reform in New England and England, 1620–1660," *William and*

Barbara Shapiro has recognized the array of influences that comprised the law reform movement in her recent *Law Reform in Early Modern England* (2019), summing up her career-long scholarship on the topic. In this first comprehensive study of the reform movement since Donald Veall's, *The Popular Movement for Law Reform: 1640–1660* (1970), she casts a wide perspective beyond a focus exclusively on the English legal profession or members of Parliament (MP's). This includes, for example, sixteenth-century humanist origins of law reform, as well as similarities to colonial Massachusetts' own efforts: "Little attention has been given to the similarities between English mid-century radical reformers and the emerging law of the New England colonies … [where] brief law codes," similar to those "demanded by Levellers and religious radicals, were a common feature" of daily life. Indeed, one of the leading British historians of the period, Chrisopher Hill, recognized more than fifty years ago that at the height of the reform movement during the Barebones Parliament's session of 1653 the radical parties (including the Levellers) cited the Massachusetts law book as their model for the amendment of English law: "The reformers proposed to codify the law, as had recently been done successfully in Massachusetts. That is the meaning of the oft-quoted phrase about reducing the great volumes of the law 'into the bigness of a pocket book, as it is proportionable in New England.'" But Shapiro has taken this linkage a step further based on her observation that not only did English and Massachusetts reform efforts appear to run in parallel, but also the colony sometimes took the lead in enacting specific measures. Ultimately, the most radical advocates of law reform in England cited the *Laws and Liberties* as *the* model for their reform efforts, and particularly its small size and publication in English. They hoped that by publishing the law the citizenry would be given the agency to conform to its strictures, and enforcement of the law would be more equitable as a result. This type of system would benefit the entire commonwealth. The fact that Christopher Hill's passages on the *Laws*

*Mary Quarterly* 35 (Oct., 1978): 669–70. "The Puritan Revolution had a profound, immediate effect on English law, if the term 'English' includes the legal reforms proposed and actually adopted by the English people who emigrated to New England before 1660. Curiously, most histories of the seventeenth century rarely connect events in England and New England in any detailed, comparative fashion. Yet, studies of the causes of the Puritan Revolution in England and of the reasons for establishing communities in New England make clear that both movements arose from the same set of social, economic, religious, political, constitutional, and legal conditions prevalent in England between 1558 and 1640. Like many recent social historians, analysts of law in early New England have occasionally traced legal patterns, practices, and precedents back to England … But most studies fail to appreciate the full relation of legal developments in New England to the law reform movement in England during the same period."

*and Liberties* elicited no reaction or further study by early American historians illustrates the lack of interdisciplinary work in this area, and, the necessity for undertaking a comparative study.[11]

The freedom to implement such a progressive jurisprudence during what became the colony's most dynamic and productive period of lawmaking, being 1640–1660, occurred during the same timeframe English historians term the Interregnum, featuring the execution of Charles I after his failed attempt to storm Parliament and arrest its leadership, followed by a failed attempt to establish an English Republic through parliamentary rule. Some of the most important and renowned principles of both English law and parliamentary authority were first addressed in these chaotic two decades. Moreover, it would have been hard to anticipate what constituted English law once its "fountain," as the monarch was regularly termed, was executed under a warrant signed by the remaining MPs who committed to see the shocking act through. As Member Bulstrode Whitelocke warned, "The laws of England are so interwoven with the power and practice of monarchy, that to settle a government without something of monarchy in it would make so great an alteration in the proceedings of our law, that you have scarce time to rectify, nor can we well foresee the inconveniences which will arise thereby." While royalist pamphleteers were predictably apocalyptic, "'The law lies murder'd with the King,' and 'the Gospel overthrown,'" Parliament was just as determined to govern without a monarch, as only months before the House of Commons dissolved the office of kingship and the House of Lords, its Members declared, "the People are, under God, the Original of all just power."[12]

---

11 Barbara Shapiro, *Law Reform in Early Modern England: 1540–1700*, 116–18. "Little attention has been given to the similarities between English mid-century radical reformers and the emerging law of the New England colonies ... Brief law codes, demanded by Levellers and religious radicals, were a common feature of the New England colonies. New England codes, some of them introduced before the rise of English radical movements, tended to be short, easy to understand and written in the English language." Barbara Shapiro, "Codification of the Laws in Seventeenth Century England," *Wisconsin Law Review* (1974): 428–65. Christopher Hill, *God's Englishmen: Oliver Cromwell and the English Revolution* (London: Weidenfeld and Nicolson, 1970), 140–41. Woolrych also commented on the Barebones' review of the *Laws and Liberties* a little over a decade after Hill. Austin Woolrych, *Commonwealth to Protectorate* (Oxford: Clarendon Press, 1982), 271–73.

12 Barbara Shapiro, *Law Reform in Early Modern England*, 121. "After the King's execution followed a decade of political and legal instability and bitter conflict among a sometimes bewildering number of religious and political groups, some of which wished to initiate radical alteration in the legal system." R.H. Whitelocke, ed., *Memoirs of Bulstrode Whitelocke* (London: Routledge & Warne, 1860), 296. Amos Tubb, "Mixed Messages: Royalist Newsbook Reports of Charles I's Execution and of the Leveller Uprising," *Huntington Library Quarterly* 67 (March 2004): 61–2. "[R]oyalist newsbook

Obviously, the invocation of "the people" as declarative of a popular sovereignty is more equated with the US Constitution at the end of the next century, but before Parliament had lost is legitimacy via a lack of elections, ultimately leading to the country falling under Cromwell's dictatorship as protector, there was a fervent hope that the legislature could govern the nation; chapter ten reviews John Pym's call for an independent Parliament to protect the public good, or what he termed salus populi suprema lex, from the King. Even with that initial intention, however, there was no modern example of legislative tyranny available to parliamentary leaders (similar to some of the US states that led to the call for a national constitutional convention) to alert them of the challenges. I argue that the rationales behind the enactment of the Massachusetts *Laws and Liberties*, as well as its format and contents, reveal immediate causation emanating from Christian Humanism and the Commonwealth reform movement, in tandem with the English Revolution.[13] This much larger story has hidden away in the Massachusetts lawbooks for many years, but it was essential in the implementation of republican government available to the colonists from their own history. By tracing these mutual influences our understanding of the early history of the rise of republican politics will be transformed. One of the English Revolution's primary aims, for example, as articulated by the Levellers,[14] was implementing a means to govern an

authors ... all held remarkably similar views of the consequences of the regicide, which they endlessly rehashed throughout 1649. A constant theme was that the regicide had shattered the basic institutions of both law and religion. *The Man in the Moon* summed up the royalist fears succinctly on 23 April when it proclaimed, 'The law lies muder'd with the King,' and 'the Gospel overthrown.' *Mercurius Elencticus* warned on 4 June that with its '[b]ody sever'd from the Head,' the state would spin out of control." *Settling the Government* (Jan. 4, 1649), in *Commons Journals* (London: 1803), 6: 111.

13 Jonathan Scott, "What were Commonwealth Principles?," *Historical Journal* 47 (Sept., 2004): 594. Jonathan Scott thought to successfully study this period it would be "necessary to bridge one further modern scholarly distinction ... between the classically inspired political republicanism, and the religiously inspired social radicalism ... In fact, just as the revolution can be seen as a single intellectual process, so republicanism combined radical Protestantism and anti-monarchical humanism. We will not understand it until we reintegrate our examination of the religious, social, and political agendas of the revolution."

14 Neil Hopkins, Will Coster, "The Levellers, Political Literacy, and Contemporary Citizenship Education in England," *Education, Citizenship, and Social Justice* 14.1 (2019): 74. "The name 'Leveller' came from the tradition of popular rural protest that existed in England, particularly focused on resistance to changes in agricultural practice and ownership. It was used in the Midland Riots of 1607 because the rioters levelled the hedges that divided and enclosed previously common land and was probably applied to the political movement that arose towards the end of the first civil war around 1644 by its opponents, particularly the pamphleteer Marchamont Nedham. In its early stages, members of the movement, like John Lilburne, preferred to think of themselves as 'agitators'. The name was an insult

educated civilian populace via enacted laws, published in print for the express purpose of informing the public at large. Reviewing the educational dimension of the law book's history undermines the predominant historical narrative that the colony was governed by a theocratic magistracy until the end of the first Charter period (i.e., 1686). Instead, by the latter half of the seventeenth-century, administration of the law was leaving an indelible cultural imprint on what had become England's most radical colony, as it published its laws annually to the beginning of the American Revolution, and funded a public system of education that included a program of civic education to support broad education of the populace. And this portrayal of Massachusetts policies, and especially its independent stance illustrated by not only its laws, but also a colonial mint used to issue its own currency, as well as defensive posture including fortifications and militia drills, was acknowledged by Charles II himself and his ministers as they regularly referred to Massachusetts' intention of being a "free state."

The conundrum is that while the leaders of the radical factions in England, and especially the Levellers, sponsored legislative reforms that mirrored future advances in both the United States and Great Britain—e.g. written constitutions, sovereign legislatures, and government based on the "rule of law"—England's reform movement lasted only six or seven years, with its leaders imprisoned after 1653, exiled, or in hiding. Meanwhile, Massachusetts sent hundreds of men to fight in the wars against the king, and with the end of the Commonwealth it mourned the failed cause with colonial officials joining the welcome celebrations of regicides in Boston. When royal agents demanded their return, colonial leaders claimed to have no knowledge of their whereabouts, with only a few knowing that the fleeing men had already been taken to the outskirts of the colony where, unbeknownst to them or the colonials, they would spend the rest of their lives. What Massachusetts served as, in retrospect, was a timely portal for a coterie of experts in various aspects of English law who, after their emigration to the colony, were able to manage an indigenous reform program as authorized by the colonial legislature. The seventeenth-century history of Massachusetts government and law that played out via the colony's printed law books reveals how the colony passed on to its eighteenth-century counterpart a novel means to govern with the informed consent of an educated civilian populace. Understanding this colonial legal regime will

---

and recalled not only the earlier rioters but suggested that they might level society and end property ownership. It was not widely adopted by the movement until after four leaders, including Lilburne, produced a manifesto from prison in 1649. They called themselves Levellers, probably because that was the name by which they were most widely known."

require a newly sophisticated understanding of the influence and the means by which the two spheres of reformers, in England and in the colonies, were aware of each other. There is also the question of why and how the colony's legal regime could memorialize the independent stance of the seventeenth century government into the next century and challenge the (by then) established regime of parliamentary supremacy.

None of the analysis above means to imply colonial Massachusetts had a secular bent in order to portray its legal system as overshadowing this deeply religious community. Instead, since there was no constitutional dichotomy between religious and political spheres, the Puritans had started to initiate practices that forecasted future developments; such as a prohibition against congregational ministers from taking a direct role in government, like office-holding. Instead, there was stress, synergy, but ultimately a partnership between religious faith and internal reforms. David Hall's recent book cited above, *A Reforming People*, traces the earnestness of this impulse for self-improvement throughout early Massachusetts society. In her review of Hall's work, Michele Oriel explained: "Traditionally, historians have focused on the religious rather than the political dimensions of puritanism in early America, ... [but] the early Stuart monarchs inspired among the Puritans of the Massachusetts Bay Colony an intense fear of arbitrary government, and as Hall has argued, this 'fear persuaded them to limit church and state authorities in the commonwealth they established.'" This leads Oriel to point to a related research agenda: "This enticing historical parallel, which remains relatively unexplored, raises an important question about the ideological and the regional origins of the American Revolution: how did the Puritan experience of tyranny shape the opposition to British imperial authority, especially in New England?" This study of Massachusetts' enactment of the colony's 1648 law book, the *Laws and Liberties*, takes up that agenda. Moreover, Massachusetts' enactment was impacted by over a century of English legal and political reform, from the early sixteenth century through its radical culmination in the 1650's, during the Commonwealth era.[15]

15 Michelle Orihel, "All Those Truly Acquainted with those Times: John Adams and the Opposition Politics of Revolutionary England, 1640–41," *William and Mary Quarterly* 86 (Sept., 2013): 436–37. Carla Pestana, *The English Atlantic in the Age of Revolution: 1640–41* (Cambridge: Harvard Univ. Press, 2004), 10. Besides the other four books cited above by Allen, Bremer, Weimer, and Winship, the other noteworthy work dedicated to a cross-Atlantic perspective at large is Carla Pestana's monograph, "Given the importance of these years both to the history of England, Scotland, and Ireland ... and to the history of the various Atlantic plantations, it is remarkable that no book exploring these connections ... has been written heretofore." Mark Peterson, *The City State of Boston: The Rise and Fall of*

Part of this study then necessarily focuses on England's Reformation, and its Commonwealth movement, through its seventeenth-century Civil Wars and Revolution. The literature here is vast. English Early Modern studies have been a hotbed during the last half century, only returning to a simmer over the past decade or so. English "revisionist" historians endeavored from the 1970's through the 1990's to reconceive (and thereby undermine) the established Whig inspired history of an uncontested march to greater liberties and freedom under an activist Parliament. The revisionist position was that non-ideological factors—like the inability of the English crown's relatively medieval financial administration to satisfy state necessities—provided the catalysts for whatever change occurred, rather than an unending virtuous quest for greater rights and liberties. Specifically, revisionists emphasized that Parliament's very reason to exist rested on tradition, that it was convened by royal summons, and that aristocratic social norms often drove even the legislative process itself. There was also the additional stress that three kingdoms—England, Scotland, and Ireland—had on state affairs. The revisionist view was in turn countered by historians who argued, rightly, that whatever economic forces may have been in play, there was also both ideological and legislative resistance to monarchy's arbitrary power. This study follows neither camp, recognizing value in both schools.[16]

We can make the best start by keeping in mind a challenge laid down by Conrad Russell, specific to the colony of Massachusetts. Russell, the leader of the revisionist school, postulated "if there were an inherent, as distinct from contingent, revolutionary potential in the ideas developing before 1637, one would expect it to be much more visible than it appears to be in the very controlled experiment of New England"; generally, this statement reflects the accepted

---

*an Atlantic Power, 1630–1865* (Princeton: Princeton University Press, 2019). More recently, Mark Peterson has written an excellent transatlantic history of Massachusetts and England, and especially the post-1660 history concerning trade. Kevin Sharpe, *Personal Rule of Charles I* (New Haven: Yale Univ. Press, 1992), 751–57. Otherwise, European historians sometimes express frustration with English America's founding stories. For example, Professor Sharpe dismissed the "history of the puritan migration" as one of the "triumphs of myth over evidence, and of nationalist historiography over research. The textbooks, especially of American History, still tell of a mass exodus of the godly from the shores of persecution to the land of freedom."

16 See the *Huntington Library Quarterly*'s Winter 2015 issue for a retrospective on the Revisionists' School of Early Modern English History. David Cressy, "Revolutionary England 1640–1642," *Past and Present* 181 (Nov., 2003): 35–71. Most recently, David Cressy has authored the most convincing argument for a revolutionary England in the early 1640's, consistent with the dating of this work, specifically to John Pym's parliamentary speech in the Spring of 1641 as covered in Chapter 10.

view of early Massachusetts history. While Massachusetts has been portrayed as a largely traditional society, it was actually one that aggressively pursued a radical program of church and state reform as contemporarily defined. That project of reform involved mutual influences across the Atlantic, lessons of which were visible to later generations of revolutionaries. Subsequently, John Adams, who was a close student of Massachusetts and English history, drafted the Massachusetts Constitution of 1780, and both that constitutional text and process for its adoption played important roles in the successful realization of a new national government, and resulted from over a century of legislating and publishing colonial law. Perhaps the most obvious and glaring omission in comparisons between English constitutionalism and its early American offspring is that the former was perceived as the "government and its operations," not a written document, whereas the new states couldn't seem to print and publish enough constitutions and accompanying bills or declarations of rights. It is true that the Glorious Revolution's *Bill of Rights* (1689) as enacted by Parliament had a huge influence, but the most apparent explanation for such a divergence was a republican impulse to inform the people in a new era of print when the original states were founded, rather than one during the time of manuscripts centuries ago where English law was born.[17]

17 Conrad Russell, *The Causes of the English Civil War* (Oxford: Oxford Univ. Press, 1990), 9. Gordon Wood, *The Idea of America* (New York: Penguin Press, 2011), 171–87. "The first thing to emphasize is the fact that the Founders who created America's constitutional structure at the end of the eighteenth century were Englishmen with a strong sense that they were heirs of the English tradition of freedom … The most obvious difference between eighteenth-century English and American constitutionalism was the American Revolutionaries' conception of a constitution as a written document, as a fundamental law circumscribing the government. Before the American Revolution, a constitution was rarely distinguished from the government and its operations … The eighteenth-century English constitution was an unwritten mixture of laws, customs, principles, and institutions … For Americans, a constitution was something fundamental. It was a written document, possessed by every family, and carried about like the Bible to be quoted and cited article by article. Such a constitution could never be an act of the legislature; it had to be the act of the people themselves … *Massachusetts in 1780 had shown the way. It had elected a convention specially designated to form a constitution and had then placed that constitution before the people for ratification.* When the Philadelphia Convention drew up a new constitution for the nation in 1787, it knew what to do."

# PART 1

## *The English Commonwealth and the Protestant Reformation*

CHAPTER 1

# Massachusetts Capital Laws of 1642

An essay John Adams authored only a decade before the fateful year of 1775, when Massachusetts initiated armed conflict with the British Empire, shows that a colonial government featuring an educated, civic-minded public, perpetually on-guard against oligarchic interests, had already taken shape, despite the ever-encroaching tentacles of imperial power. He wrote:

> A native of America who cannot read and write is as rare … as a comet or an earthquake … It is true, there has been among us a party for some years, consisting chiefly not of the descendants of the first settlers of this country, but of high churchmen and high statesmen imported since, who affect to censure this provision for the education of our youth as a needless expense, and an imposition upon the rich in favor of the poor … And certain officers of the crown, and … other missionaries of ignorance, foppery, servility, and slavery, have been most inclined to … increase the same party. Be it remembered, however, that liberty must at all hazards be supported … [and] cannot be preserved without a general knowledge among the people, … [who] have a right, an indisputable, unalienable, indefeasible, divine right to that most dreaded and envied kind of knowledge, I mean, of the characters and conduct of their rulers. Rulers are no more than attorneys, agents, and trustees, for the people; and if the cause, the interest and trust, is insidiously betrayed, or wantonly trifled away, the people have a right to revoke the authority that they themselves have deputed, and to constitute abler and better agents, attorneys, and trustees. *And the preservation of the means of knowledge among the lowest ranks, is of more importance to the public than all the property of all the rich men in the country.*[1]

According to Emerson Baker, "so strong" was the importance Massachusetts Puritans placed on education that "by the eighteenth-century New England had one of the highest literacy rates in the history of the Western World—higher than it is today." The initial question before us then is, what motivated

1 John Adams, *A Dissertation on the Canon and Feudal Law* (1765), in *The Works of John Adams* (Boston: Little and Brown, 1851), 3: 447 @ 452, and 456–57. Luke Mayville, *John Adams and the Fear of American Oligarchy* (Princeton: Princeton Univ. Press, 2016), 7–8.

 | DOI:10.1163/9789004706347_003

the achievement of such a state of affairs as a natural precursor to the mass publication of the colony's laws in print? Surprisingly, the best way to gain insight into answering that question begins with a case of child abuse discovered and tried in the earliest years of the colony.[2]

On June 14, 1642, Daniel Fairfield, Jenken Davies, and John Hudson were arrested for sexually abusing two young girls, Dorcas and Sarah. The case convulsed Bay colonists into an "uproar" that the three men be executed. But the colony lacked laws appropriate for punishment of their offenses. Predictably, colonial regulations allowed for biblical sanction if the sentence was approved by the colony's legislature (the General Court). Upon legislators' search for the appropriate biblical punishment, however, they discovered rape was punishable as a capital penalty only if the victim was married or betrothed; the girls were ages seven and nine. Several days after the trial, the General Court passed the necessary punishments for future offenses by adding three new capital crimes to the twelve that were extant before the assaults on Dorcas and Sarah. In adding these provisions to supplement colonial regulations the General Court borrowed directly from English Common Law. Nevertheless, the presiding magistrates decided that the accused could not be executed, as no applicable capital penalties were "on the books" at the time of the crimes' commission, and just as importantly, no such laws had been "published" in the colony.[3]

Considering the reputation of Puritan Massachusetts, and its scarlet letters and witchcraft trials, why would "Godly" magistrates renowned for their righteous invocations of divine authority spare such criminals? Why not just invoke the traditional authority of English Common Law? What could have stemmed their puritanical fury? Per a journal entry of the colony's first governor, John Winthrop (1588–1649), while the "foulness of the sin, and their long continuance in it, wrought strongly with many to put them to death," no capital penalty

2 Emerson Baker, *A Storm of Witchcraft* (Oxford: Oxford Univ. Press, 2015), 46.

3 Richard Dunn, et al., eds., *The Journal of John Winthrop: 1630–1649* (Cambridge: Belknap Press, 1996), 370–74 (Oct. 1641-May 1642). Nathaniel Shurtleff, ed., *Records of the Governor and Company of the Massachusetts Bay* (Boston: 1853), 2: 12–13, 21 (June 14, 1642). Cited hereafter as *MGCR*. William Whitmore, ed., *Colonial Laws of Massachusetts. Reprinted from the Edition of 1660, with the Supplements to 1672. Containing also, The Body of Liberties of 1641* (Boston: City Council of Boston, 1889), 33 (Lib. 1), 55 (Lib. 94, §7–9). Cited hereafter as the *Body of Liberties of 1641* or the *Laws and Liberties of 1660. Deuteronomy*, 22: 13–29. Matthew Hale, *History of the Pleas of the Crown* (Philadelphia: 1847), 2: 626–32. William Blackstone, *Commentaries on the Laws of England* (Chicago: Univ. of Chicago Press, 1979), 4: 212. *Statutes of the Realm* (London: 1810–1822), 4 (Part 1): 617–18 (18 Eliz. ch. 7, §4 (1574/75)). Cited hereafter as *SR*. George Haskins, *Law and Authority in Early Massachusetts* (New York: MacMillan, 1960), 116, 150–53. J.H. Baker, *Introduction to English Legal History*, 3rd ed., (London: Butterworths, 1990), 572–73.

for these offenses had been "published in the country." After "much dispute," members of the General Court agreed that the sentences would be corporal punishment, whipping, branding, and ear cropping (i.e., removal of the prisoners' ears), but not death. According to Winthrop, the "only reason that saved their lives was … the sin was not capital by any express law of God, … nor was it made capital by any law of our own, so as we had no warrant to put them to death, and we had formerly refrained (by the advice of the elders) upon the same ground in a case of manifest adultery." In 1638, upon the convictions of several colonists for adultery, a majority of colonial ministers had advised the General Court to commute their executions. A capital punishment for adultery was on the books, but it had not been published. A sentence of execution in those earlier cases was deemed justifiable only "if the law had been sufficiently published," because colonists must be informed of what constituted a capital crime before sentencing. Winthrop noted that, since the adultery law had not been published upon its enactment in 1631, the defendants were instead whipped and banished from the colony. After those events, the adulterers' law was "confirmed and published" to the remaining colonists.[4]

Because the colony's first printing press began operations in 1639, Winthrop's reference to "publishing" in 1638 did not connote printing. Instead, publishing laws in those early years meant a proclamation read in the town square, marketplace, and church meeting, or a hand-written notice posted in public view. For instance, Dedham's town meeting ordered Eleazer Lusher, to "publish the body of Laws upon some lecture days"—or during church service—"as opportunity shall admit." This was consistent with the first of Samuel Johnson's definitions of "to publish," namely, "to discover to mankind, to make generally and openly known." Only his secondary definition stipulated to "put forth a book into the world." Johnson's *Dictionary* prioritized proclamation, even though it was published in the middle of the 18th century when printing and publishing were becoming synonymous. Colonists defined "publishing" as an announcement by whatever means were available, effective, and convenient. The first draft of the colonial law book in 1648 specified: "No man's life shall be taken

4 Richard Dunn, ed., *Journal of John Winthrop*, 249 (March 1638); 317 (December 1639); 373 (October 1641-May 1642). While congregational ministers could not hold political office, they were often called to mediate disputes. Nathaniel Shurtleff, ed., *MGCR*, 1: 82, 225. John Noble, ed., *Records of the Court of Assistants* (Boston: County of Suffolk, 1904), 2: 19. Edwin Powers, *Crime and Punishment in Early Massachusetts* (Boston: Beacon Press, 1966), 77–8. Francis Bremer, *John Winthrop* (Oxford: Oxford Univ. Press, 2003), 306, 310–312. David Hall, *The Puritans: A Transatlantic History* (Princeton: Princeton Univ. Press, 2019), 227–28. Barbara Shapiro, *Law Reform in Early Modern England* (Oxford: Hart Publishing, 2019), 123. Adultery was enacted a capital crime in 1650 under the Long Parliament during the Commonwealth era.

away, no man's person shall be arrested, restrained, banished, dismembered, nor any ways punished ... unless it be by virtue or equity of some express law of the Country ... sufficiently published."[5]

This was a strong requirement, given that even Biblical laws were deemed insufficient publication. Considering the seventh commandment's prohibition against adultery, why would Puritan ministers insist that criminal sanctions already enacted by the General Court be publicized by political authorities before enforcement? Among the English churchmen who journeyed to Massachusetts, the most renowned—John Cotton, Thomas Hooker, John Davenport, and Nathaniel Ward—had left England when religious persecution became most oppressive during the mid-1630's. After Henry VIII's supremacy over the English Church was declared via parliamentary statute in 1534, English monarchs had suppressed unorthodoxy and heresy via the High Commission and ecclesiastical courts. The most hated feature of this regime was the oath ex officio. Its memory provided a searing example of the injustice of forcing people to testify to charges of which they were unaware, and the oath was well remembered in the New World. Through the authority of their office, or "ex officio," Commissioners interrogated defendants probing for offenses against church or state without being restrained by a process of indictment. Scores of defendants entered courtrooms innocent of any crime and unaware of any guilt, only to be convicted upon their own testimony to a charge established during the interrogation; if they refused the oath defendants faced "trial" in Star Chamber. When Massachusetts magistrates invoked ex officio powers of interrogation during John Wheelwright's trial in 1637, his supporters protested they intended he "incriminate himself in the manner of the Court of High Commission." Wheelwright refused to answer the magistrates' inquiries.[6]

---

5 William Whitmore, ed., *Body of Liberties of 1641*, 33 (Lib.1). Richard Dunn, ed., *Journal of John Winthrop*, 249 (March 1638), 283 (Feb.–March 1639). Edwin Powers, *Crime and Punishment in Early Massachusetts*, 77, 578 (n. 4). Several defendants "pleaded ignorance and won an acquittal on the ground that the law in question had not been 'sufficiently published.'" Alexander Chalmers, ed., *Samuel Johnson's Dictionary of the English Language* (London: Studio Editions, 1994), 579. John Noble, ed., *Court of Assistants*, 2: 101. Don Hill, ed., *Early Records of the Town of Dedham* (Dedham: Dedham Hist. Soc., 1892), 3: 156 (1648). Hugh Amory, "Printing and Bookselling in New England," in David Hall, ed., *History of the Book in America* (Chapel Hill: Univ. of North Carolina Press, 2007), 1: 83–116. Elizabeth Eisenstein, *The Printing Press as an Agent of Change* (Cambridge: Cambridge Univ. Press, 1979), 1: 119. Chris Kyle, "Monarch and Marketplace: Proclamations as News in Early Modern England," *Huntington Library Quarterly* 78 (no. 4, 2015): 771–87.

6 Richard Dunn, ed., *Journal of John Winthrop*, 271 (Nov.-Dec., 1638). Nathaniel Shurtleff, ed., *MGCR*, 1: 189 (March 1637). William Hubbard, *A General History of New England* (Boston: Little & Brown, 1848), 281–82. Edgar McManus, *Law and Liberty in Early New England* (Amherst: Univ.

Perhaps the ministers' conviction that colonial law must be published before its enforcement in fact originated from English Common Law? That was not the case. English Common Law held that ignorance of the law was no excuse for illegal actions, per Matthew Hale, a leading seventeenth-century English jurist: "Ignorance of the municipal law of the kingdom, or of the penalty thereby inflicted upon offenders, doth not excuse any that is of the age of discretion and compos mentis [i.e., sane], from the penalty of the breach of it; because every person of the age of discretion and compos mentis is bound to know the law, and presumed so to do." His contemporary John Shepheard agreed, "it is a maxim of our own law that ignorance thereof excuseth no man, but every man is presumed to be cognizant thereof." And indeed, proclamation of statutory law had been common practice in medieval England, seemingly to support knowledge of the law and partly on account of its consistency with Canon Law. According to Thomas Aquinas, for a law to have "binding force" it must be acknowledged by those "who have to be ruled by it," and that was by making it "known to them by promulgation." Yet a 1366 case decided by the Court of Common Pleas introduced a new procedure. English justices decided that "promulgation" was unnecessary, because henceforth all of the king's subjects were required to know the enactments of Parliament. This sweeping decision belied the fact that the vast majority of Englishmen had neither access to statutory law in print, nor universal public education until the nineteenth century. No matter, from the fourteenth century onwards ignorance of the law could not be used to mitigate the severity of a criminal sentence, whether

of Mass. Press, 1993), 106–7. Christopher Hill, *Liberty Against the Law* (London: Allen Lane, 1996), 194–97. "Excommunication was a powerful weapon of the ecclesiastical courts. It could be imposed for heresy, schism, simony, perjury, usury, incest, adultery, 'or other grave crimes.'" James Stephens, *A History of the Criminal Law of England* (London: MacMillan & Co., 1883), 1: 338–40; 2: 412–17. Leonard Levy, *The Origins of the Fifth Amendment*, 2nd ed., (New York: MacMillan Co., 1986), 43–82, 173–283. Michael Braddick, *The Common Freedom of the People: John Lilburne and the English Revolution* (Oxford: Oxford Univ. Press, 2018), 14–26. David Cressy, *England on Edge: Crisis and Revolution, 1640–1642* (Oxford: Oxford Univ. Press, 2006), 282. *Rex v. Lilburn and Wharton* (1637), in T.B. Howell, ed., et. al., *State Trials* (London: T.C. Hansard, 1816), 3: 1315–1370 (#148). Lilburne was paraded through London and whipped several hundred lashes with a knotted cord for trafficking in seditious pamphlets and rebuking Laud. John Lilburne, *A Worke of the Beast*, (London: 1638), in William Haller, ed., *Tracts on Liberty* (New York: Columbia Univ. Press, 1934), 2: 3–34. John Rees, *The Leveller Revolution* (London: Verso, 2016), 41–2. Wallace Notestein, ed., *The Journal of Sir Simonds D'Ewes* (New Haven: Yale Univ. Press, 1923), 18–19. Bernard Bailyn, *The Barbarous Years* (New York: Vintage Books, 2013), 381–96. "While still only Bishop of London, from 1628 to 1633, Laud became the dominant force in both of the most powerful coercive courts, the church's High Commission and the Privy Council's Court of Star Chamber."

a capital punishment or otherwise, regardless of whether the law had been promulgated. The Massachusetts policy introduced a new standard, parting ways from the practice in England.[7]

And the British practices had their domestic critics too, particularly with regard to the frequency of capital punishment. In *Utopia*, Thomas More critiques the application of capital laws by noting the lack of any corresponding effort to inform the public of their enforcement. As Jennifer Bishop has explained, its publication in 1551 represented a "combination of humanist theory and political practice typical of the civic culture of the Edwardian Reformation, … and was part of a wider movement that encompassed both practical efforts at reform as well as theoretical discussions as to the best form that these might take." In the work itself, a lawyer lectures Raphael Hythloday on the "rigid execution of justice then being practiced on thieves," proclaiming triumphantly, they were "being executed everywhere!" But he remained perplexed by the ever-increasing numbers of these pesky offenders, even as so "few … escaped hanging." Raphael objected that such practices went "beyond the call of justice," because nothing could restrain men from "robbery when they have no other way to eat." More himself concluded, "not only you in England, but a good part of the world seems to imitate bad schoolmasters, who would rather whip their students than teach them." During the height of English law reform activists sought to ameliorate this injustice by petitioning Parliament to reduce the number of capital crimes; since the early fourteenth century thirty-five capital statutes had been enacted, with approximately fifty capital offenses in force by mid-seventeenth century. The Leveller Samuel Chidley

7 Matthew Hale, *Pleas of the Crown*, 1: 41–2 (Ch. VI, "Concerning Ignorance, and How Far it Prevails, to Excuse in Capital Crimes"). John Shepheard, *Certain proposals for regulating the law* (1651/2), 1; *Wing* S3102, Reel 1450: 10. Norman Doe, *Fundamental Authority in Late Medieval English Law* (Cambridge: Cambridge Univ. Press, 1990), 38–9. *Summa Theologica* (*First Part of the Second, Question 90—Whether Promulgation is Essential to a Law?, Art. 4*), in Anton Pegis, ed., *Introduction to Saint Thomas Aquinas* (New York: Modern Library, 1948), 614–15. Gilbert Bailey, "The Promulgation of Law," *American Political Science Review* 35 (1941): 1059–84. W.S. Holdsworth, *Sources and Literature of English Law* (Oxford: Clarendon Press, 1925), 55. Percy Winfield, *Chief Sources of English Legal History* (Cambridge: Harvard Univ. Press, 1925), 78. The *ignorance* precedent originated from a bishop's plea in 1366, claiming that because he was ignorant of a law's enactment he should be exempt from its enforcement. The royal justices rejected the bishop's attempt to void the King's law, whatever his awareness. David Harvey, *The Law Emprynted: The Printing Press as an Agent of Change* (Oxford: Hart Publishing, 2017), 118–19. "It appears from the legal texts of the time that one of the purposes of printing the law was to reduce ignorance of the law … John Rastell addressed ignorance of the law as a reason for publishing his legal dictionary. Ignorance could not offer an excuse, except where the sovereign willfully frustrated the subject's acquisition of such knowledge."

scolded members of the Rump Parliament that they had violated the "statute-laws of God" by executing thieves in such a manner, because their lives were worth more than the "trifles" they stole. Based upon a biblical punishment requiring the return or reimbursement of stolen goods, Chidley demanded a more equitable punishment "proportional to the offenses." But men were "so ignorant, cruel," and "hard-hearted" they took "the lives of the petty thieves in revenge." Some scholars have seen low enforcement rates after the Glorious Revolution, but "[a]t times of economic dearth and political repression, such as the 1620s and 1630s, the felony laws were more strictly enforced; in the wake of the enclosure riots of 1629–31, for example, the number of felony convictions is estimated to have increased by 250%." These severe measures caused Oliver Cromwell to term the statutory threshold of one shilling for felony theft to be "wicked," to "hang a man for ... thirteen pence," or a "trifle."[8]

The status of capital laws in the penal system was an important consideration for members of the General Court, and ultimately prompted the initial printing of laws undertaken by the colony. Immediately after the trial of Fairfield, Davies, and Hudson for the abuse of the two young girls, the General Court enacted New England's first education law. The *Education Act of 1642* required parents to teach their children to read the "principles of religion and the capital laws of the country." The colony's capital laws had already been

8 Thomas More, *Utopia* (1516), George Logan and Robert Adams eds., (Cambridge: Cambridge Univ. Press, 1989), 15–16, 84–5. Jennifer Bishop, "Utopia and Civil Politics in mid-Sixteenth Century England," *Historical Journal* 54 (Dec., 2011): 933–38, 950–51. Samuel Chidley, *A Cry Against a Crying Sin* (London, 1652), in *Harleian Miscellany* (London: Robert Dutton, 1810), 6: 272–82. *Exodus*, 22: 4. John Rees, *The Leveller Revolution*, 36–41, 141. Thomas Carlyle, ed., *Letters and Speeches of Oliver Cromwell* (London: Methuen & Co., 1904), 2: 541. Robert Zaller, "The Debate on Capital Punishment during the English Revolution," *American Journal of Legal History* 31 (April 1987): 126–44 @ 127. Lizzie Seal, "A Brief History of Capital Punishment in Britain," *History Today* (March 2018); (https://www.historyextra.com/period/modern/a-brief-history-of-capital-punishment-in-britain/). "Britain's 'Bloody Code' was the name given to the legal system between the late-17th and early-19th century which made more than 200 offences—many of them petty—punishable by death. Statutes introduced between 1688 and 1815 covered primarily property offences, such as pickpocketing, cutting down trees and shoplifting. Nevertheless, despite the 'mushrooming' of capital crimes, fewer people were actually executed in the 18th century than during the preceding two centuries." Bradley Chapin, *Criminal Justice in Colonial America: 1606–1660* (Athens: Univ. of Georgia Press, 1983), 8–12. Edgar McManus, *Law and Liberty in Early New England*, 30–1, 201. Richard Dunn, ed., *The Laws and Liberties of Massachusetts: Reprinted from the Unique Copy of the 1648 Edition in the Henry E. Huntington Library* (San Marino: Huntington Library, 1998), 4–5 (title *Burglary and Theft*). Cited hereafter as the *Laws and Liberties of 1648*. In 1647, the colony enacted a capital punishment for thieves on third offense after a spate of burglaries, "notwithstanding all care and means to prevent and punish the same."

incorporated into the *Body of Liberties of 1641*, a manuscript draft of one hundred laws that the General Court used to compile an official lawbook in print. But the *Body of Liberties*' section on capital laws omitted the just enacted three laws addressing the recent assaults. By mandating parents teach their children Massachusetts' now augmented list of capital punishments, members of the General Court had created a dilemma. Parents could not be expected to teach children the colony's capital penalties, under civil penalty for non-compliance, if a current text was not available. So, the General Court ordered on the same day of the education act's enactment, "such laws as make any offense to be capital shall forthwith be imprinted & published, of which laws the Secretary is to send a copy to the printer, when it hath been examined by the Governor [Winthrop], or [Magistrate Richard] Bellingham with himself, & the Treasurer to pay for the printing of them." The capital laws would be published in a standalone or broadsheet format. A reference to the colony's capital punishments, as they were amended throughout the rest of the century, was included as a provision to all future education ordinances passed during the first charter period (1629–1686).[9]

While Colonial Massachusetts' initiative in public education is well known, its partnership with printed law has gone unnoticed. The role of civic education is discounted for an era presumed to be less enlightened, and inconsistent with the early evolution of American legal history which awaited the professional practice of law; for example, the very first sentence of Lawrence Friedman's *History of American Law* declares, "The colonial period is, for most lawyers and laymen, the dark ages of American Law." While publication of the law and its consequences seems appropriate, the *ignorance of the law* doctrine is so deeply embedded in our culture we fail to see its substantive impact. But in response to an ever-growing number of English capital laws, infused with a Puritan impulse to teach godly behavior through Bible study, Massachusetts required civic education in the colony's capital penalties. By such an approach minors would be less exploitable by adults. Moreover, dissemination of the colony's punishments gave both adults and minors the agency to

9 Nathaniel Shurtleff, ed., *MGCR*, 2: 8–9 (June 14, 1642), 2: 22 (June 14, 1642). S.E. Morison, *The Puritan Pronaos* (New York: New York Univ. Press, 1936), 63, 68–73, 96–99, 101–3. Ian Green, *The Christian's ABC* (Oxford: Clarendon Press, 1996), 15. *Capitall Lawes of New-England* (London, 1643), §§ 9–11; *Thomason Tracts* 669f6 (99), Reel 245. *The Capitall Lawes of New-England, as they stand now in force in the Commonwealth. By the Court, in the years 1641. 1642 … Printed first in New-England, and reprinted in London (1643)*; (Library of Congress, (https://www.loc.gov/resource/rbpe.03300200/)). "Printing the Capital Laws in 1642," in *Publications of the Colonial Society of Massachusetts: Transactions (1927–1930)* (Boston: 1932), 27: 112–15.

avoid capital proceedings by an informed choice before entering a courtroom. Several towns had initiated such efforts before it became a matter of colonial policy. In 1639, for example, Salem had chosen "young Mr. Norris ... to teach school" before any education law had been enacted in the colony, and Boston's famous Latin School was founded in 1635. But in the years after 1642, we can see the impact of the new policy. In 1643, Cambridge dispatched John Bridge, Sergeant Winshepe, John Russell, and George Cook to ensure compliance with a law "made the last General Court for the townsmen to see to the educating [of] children." When Watertown collected £20 to build a schoolhouse, it purchased fifteen copies of the recently published "Capital Laws." The town soon hired a teacher, Richard Norcrosse, "according to an order of Court."[10]

The General Court's next education law enacted in 1647, commonly known as the *Old Deluder Act* (*or School Act*), illustrates this Protestant reform-minded heritage. With about forty percent of Massachusetts men and seventy percent of women illiterate, resulting in the inability of most parents to teach children to read, towns were required to establish schools:

> It is ... ordered, that every township in this jurisdiction, after the Lord hath increased them to the number of 50 householders, shall then forthwith appoint one within their town to teach all such children as shall resort to him to write and read ... [I]t is further ordered, that where any town shall increase to the number of 100 families or householders, they shall set up a grammar school, the master thereof being able to instruct youth so far as they may be fitted for the university, provided, that if any town neglect the performance hereof, above one year, that every such town shall pay £5 to the next school till they shall perform this order.[11]

---

10 Lawrence Friedman, *History of American Law*, 3rd ed., (New York: Simon & Schuster, 2005), 3. Lawrence Stone, "The Educational Revolution in England: 1560–1640," *Past and Present* 28 (1964): 42–3, 72. Edwin Surrency, "The Beginnings of American Legal Literature," *American Journal of Legal History* 31 (no. 3, 1987): 207–20. *Town Records of Salem: 1634–1659* (Salem: Essex Institute Press, 1868), 1 (Part 1): 97. *Records of the Town of Cambridge* (Cambridge: Cambridge City Council, 1901), 2: 47. *Watertown Records* (Watertown: Historical Society, 1894), 1: 9, 18, 21, 25.

11 Nathaniel Shurtleff, ed., *MGCR*, 2: 203 (Nov. 11, 1647). Kenneth Lockridge, *Literacy in Colonial New England* (New York: W.W. Norton, 1974), 13, 38. Carla Pestana, "The City upon a Hill under Siege," *New England Quarterly* 56 (Sept., 1983): 332–36. David Hall, "Readers and Writers in Early New England," in Hugh Armory, ed., *The Colonial Book in the Atlantic World* (Chapel Hill: Univ. of North Carolina Press, 2007), 117–51. Jennifer Monaghan, "Literacy Instruction and Gender in Colonial New England," 40 *American Quarterly* (March 1988): 27–28. Colonies that enacted education laws include: Connecticut in 1650, New Haven in 1655, New York in 1655, Plymouth in 1671, and Pennsylvania in 1683.

Fleshing out the historical allusions in the *School Act's* introductory paragraph illustrates its debt to an ongoing Protestant Reformation. The preamble reads: "It being one chief project of the old deluder, Satan, to keep men from the knowledge of the Scriptures, as in former times by keeping them in an unknown tongue, so in these latter times by persuading from the use of tongues, that so at least the true sense and meaning of the original might be clouded by false glosses of saint seeming deceivers, that learning may not be buried in the grave our fathers in the church and commonwealth, the Lord assisting our endeavors." Former times were prior to 1526 and William Tyndale's translation of the *New Testament* into English. Tyndale, "both a religious and social radical," followed Erasmus's call for a renewed spirituality via scriptural education. Erasmus had lamented that, "people who don't want the holy scriptures to be read in translation by the unlearned" believe that "Christ taught such complex doctrine that hardly anyone outside a handful of theologians could understand" its principles, as if the "chief strength of the Christian religion lay in people's ignorance of it." A century later a pamphleteer still credited the "pains of Tyndall" for achieving one of the most important steps of Reformation, the "translation of the Bible into the English Tongue … permitting all sorts of people to peruse the same." Upon provoking Henry VIII's wrath for criticizing the royal divorce, Tyndale fled to Antwerp where, after his arrest by agents of Holy Roman Emperor Charles V, he was executed for heresy by strangulation. Soon thereafter, in 1536, Henry VIII ordered a vernacular Bible placed in every English church; previously only St. Jerome's Latin version, the *Vulgate*, was sanctioned by the Roman Church. New translations of the Testaments were soon published, including the first official English vernacular edition *The Great Bible* (1539) based on Tyndale's work, the *Geneva Bible* (1560) favorite of Protestant radicals, and ultimately the *King James Bible* (1611) collated, edited, and certified by the Hampton Court Conference convened by James I.[12]

---

12 Nathaniel Shurtleff, ed., *MGCR*, 2: 203 (Nov. 11, 1647). Robert Adams, ed., *Desiderius Erasmus, The Praise of Folly and Other Writings* (New York: W.W. Norton, 1989), 117–23. *Parliaments Power, in Lawes for Religion* (August 25, 1645), 5–10; *Thomason Tracts* E298 (9), Reel 49. David Daniell, *William Tyndale: A Biography* (New Haven: Yale Univ. Press, 1994), 1, 361–84. Tyndale was responsible for ninety-percent of the New Testament in the *King James Bible*, and the first half of its Old Testament translation. Christopher Hill, *The English Bible and the Seventeenth-Century Revolution* (London: Penguin Books, 1993), 10–11. "The availability of the Bible in English was a great stimulus to learning to read; and this in its turn assisted the development of cheap printing and the distribution of books." Christopher Hill, *The Intellectual Origins of the English Revolution*, 2nd ed., (Oxford: Oxford Univ. Press, 1997), 312–17. "Tyndale was not only a religious but also a social radical, as the title of his *Parable of the Wicked Mammon* suggests. 'The rich (as James saith) persecute the true believers. The rich will never stand forth openly for the Word of God'." David Coast, "Speaking for

While the very essence of Protestantism required each believer to examine the Bible, as Christianity's spiritual source, made possible by translations into a vernacular, Protestants also believed that the true apostolic meaning of scripture could be revealed by studied examinations of the earliest transcripts of the Old and New Testaments. The resulting translations would edify all believers to Christianity's beginnings and the proper means of worship. Literal textual interpretation and instruction was a staple of being a Puritan, as well as the foundation of Christian Humanism. Humanists attacked medieval theologians for imposing theological systems on the holy book, and even for the provision of explanatory texts (or glosses) in the margins, because those interpretations obscured how the earliest Christians lived and worshipped. Richard Mather explained the complexities of translating the sacred text in the first book printed in Boston, the *Bay Psalm Book* (*1640*):

> [N]ow no Protestant doubteth but that all the books of the scripture should by God's ordinance be extant in the mother tongue of each nation, that they may be understood of all, hence the psalms are to be translated into our English tongue ... Neither let any think that we have taken liberty or poetical license to depart from the true and proper sense of David's words in the Hebrew verses, no, it hath been a special part of our religious care and faithful endeavor, to keep close to the original text.[13]

One anonymous pamphleteer complained, the ability to make such translations required years of study, "Erasmus concludeth that grammar itself is enough to make a man spend his whole life in tortures." To aggravate matters elementary education in the English language was not a public responsibility of the English Realm, as a schoolmaster thought it was unreasonable to expect

---

the People of England," *Past and Present* 244 (Aug., 2019): 74–77. A.G. Dickens, *The English Reformation*, 2nd ed., (London: BT Batsford Ltd., 1989), 213.

13 George Winship, *The Cambridge Press* (Philadelphia: Univ. of Pennsylvania Press, 1945), 26–7. S.E. Morison, *The Puritan Pronaos*, 83–109. A.G. Dickens, *The English Reformation*, 2nd ed., 87–91. Louis Wright, *Middle Class Culture in Elizabethan England* (Chapel Hill: Univ. of North Carolina Press, 1935), 339–72. Charles Webster, *The Great Instauration* (New York: Holmes & Meir, 1975), 15, 102–106, 133, 202–3. Su Fang Ng, "Translation, Interpretation, and Heresy: The Wycliffite Bible, Tyndale's Bible, and the Contested Origin," *Studies in Philology* 98 (no. 3, 2001): 316–18. Patrick Collinson, *The Reformation* (New York: Modern Library, 2004), 138. "Godly Protestantism also had much to do with the growth of educational provision and the creation of a system of social welfare (the Elizabethan Poor Law), ... among the more notable achievements of the age." *The Bay Psalm Book* (Cambridge: 1640), preface; Library of Congress, (https://www.loc.gov/exhibits/bay-psalm-book-and-american-printing/online-exhibition.html).

schools to "be troubled with teaching ABC." English parents of means taught their children to read and write, if able, or sent them to professional tutors in preparation of the study of classical languages, and especially to read Latin, so they could attend the universities. Obviously, parents at the level of subsistence farming could not afford the luxury of sending their children away from the fields, much less pay for private tutors over a period of years. In the absence of a system of universal education, literacy was a preserve of the elite and simply a required step in gaining a classical education. It was not a public responsibility of the kingdom during the Early Modern era, but instead supported by denominational or individual benefactors.[14]

Nevertheless, by the 1530's Erasmian scholarship—and its greater ambitions for literacy—was being introduced into English government by itinerant scholars like Thomas Starkey. After university study at Oxford, Avignon, and Padua, and over a decade of service to Cardinal Reginal Pole, he entered the service of Henry VIII's chief minister Thomas Cromwell in 1534 as a royal chaplain. In the years immediately prior to his appointment Starkey authored *A Dialogue Between Cardinal Pole & Thomas Lupset* (his unfinished manuscript was first published in 1871), in which he provided a "sustained case for aristocratic reform," with a heavy dose of *conciliarism*. Starkey employed two of his real-world mentors—Professor Thomas Lupset (a colleague of Erasmus) and Cardinal Reginald Pole (a supporter of limited church reform, Papal Legate to England in the 1550's, and ultimately Archbishop of Canterbury under Queen Mary)—to probe the merits of reform in church and state in dialogue form. The Pole character posited that if the Mass was to edify worshippers, as in the days of Christ's last supper, it must be delivered in vernacular or "our own tongue"; the Catholic mass would not be conducted in a vernacular until the edicts of the Second Vatican Council (1962–1965) took effect. Still, Pole thought reliance on Latin by the Pre-Tridentine Mass was a denial of God's promise of "everlasting life and perpetual joy" for English commoners, terming the practice "plain madness and folly." While English Common Law pleadings should

14 *A Discourse in Derision of the Teaching in Free Schools* (London, 1647), 2; *Thomason Tracts* E53 (7), Reel 9. S.E. Morison, *The Puritan Pronaos*, 59. David Cressy, *Literacy and the Social Order* (Cambridge: Cambridge Univ. Press, 1980), 6, 34, 186–87. David Cressy, ed., *Education in Tudor and Stuart England* (New York: St. Martin's Press, 1975), 44–45, 73, 83–4, 132–35. Lawrence Stone, "The Educational Revolution in England," 45. R.M. Fisher, "Thomas Cromwell, Humanism and Educational Reform: 1530–40," *Bulletin of the Institute of Historical Research* 50 (1977): 151–59. A.G. Dickens, *The English Reformation*, 2nd ed., 235–36. Lawrence Stone, "Literacy and Education in England: 1640–1900," *Past and Present* 42 (1969): 83–7.

be conducted in English rather than Law French, "of the Gospel surely it is much more necessary and ... expedient."[15]

Expedient? To what end? Judging from the passage the goals were both mundane and divine. Starkey explained that in this life secular law provided "civil concord," while the teachings of Christ were a guide to "everlasting life" and "perpetual joy." Only by the "observation" of scripture and service, and not the "breaking and transgression of the same," could believers be saved from "perpetual damnation." But how could this spirituality be taught? Under the model of an educated believer, it would be impossible to gain salvation with scripture "closed in a strange tongue," as if "the people were not ... bound thereto, nor to them written." Commoners might learn Latin, an impossible goal for most of the population, or the sacred book must be cast in a vernacular in order to provide accessibility. After all, the ancient Romans had conducted mass in Latin, their own native language, just as the Normans initially administered English law in French to govern their newly won Saxon kingdom. By the seventeenth century John Lilburne (the leader of the Levellers during the English Revolution) wanted to argue for full accessibility. He wrote, "seeing Parliament hath taken care that the Bible shall be in English," must not "all the binding laws in England be in English ... so every free-man may read it as well as lawyers (seeing their lives, liberties and estates as well as the other)"?[16]

---

15 Thomas Starkey, *A Dialogue Between Cardinal Pole and Thomas Lupset*, Kathleen Burton ed., (London: Chatto and Windus, 1948), 117–29. T.F. Mayer, "Thomas Starkey's Aristocratic Reform Programme," *History of Political Thought* 7 (No. 3, 1986): 439–61. Geoffrey Elton, "Reform by Statute: Thomas Starkey's Dialogue and Thomas Cromwell's Policy," *Proceedings of the British Academy* 54 (1968): 165–88. Thomas Mayer, *Thomas Starkey and the Commonweal* (Cambridge: Cambridge Univ. Press, 1989), 139–68. Antonio Forcellino, *Michelangelo*, Allan Cameron trans., (Cambridge: Polity Press, 2009), 199–207, 253–54, 275–76. S.E. Morison, *The Founding of Harvard College* (Cambridge: Harvard Univ. Press, 1935), 3–107. Christopher Hill, *The Intellectual Origins of the English Revolution*, 2nd ed., 228–31, 268–81, 293–307. *Conciliarism* was a late medieval movement within the Catholic Church that held a council of bishops, once convened, had greater authority than the Pope.

16 Thomas Starkey, *A Dialogue Between Cardinal Pole and Thomas Lupset*, 117–29. John Lilburne, *England's Birthright Justified* (1645); in *Tracts on Liberty*, William Haller ed., (New York: Columbia Univ. Press, 1934), 3: 266. Christopher Hill, *The Intellectual Origins of the English Revolution*, 2nd ed., 318–26. Andrew Sharp, ed., *The English Levellers* (Cambridge: Cambridge Univ. Press, 1998), vii–xxii. Leonard Levy, *Ranters Run Amok* (Chicago: Ivan R. Dee, 2000), 16–18. Michael Braddick, *The Common Freedom of the People: John Lilburne and the English Revolution* (Oxford: Oxford Univ. Press, 2018). Derek Hirst, "Petitions and the English Republic," *Journal of British Studies* 45 (Jan., 2006), 39. "The Levellers' discovery of the sovereignty of the people impelled them to make particular use of the mass, and therefore printed, petition." Neil Hopkins, Will Coster, "The

Pamphleteers condemned English law as a "Tower of Babel." Lawyers pled Law French in English courts, while parliamentary statutes, court records, warrants, and writs were recorded in Latin. The Diggers' leader, Gerrard Winstanley, blamed such practices for causing "much ignorance among the people" and "many sons of contention." When a "difference falls out between man and man ... neither of them know which offends the other," and if people were ignorant of the law there may as well be "no laws at all." To remedy such injustices parents should teach their children "civil" behavior, or send them to school to "read the laws of the commonwealth," so that they could "govern themselves like rational men." Lilburne claimed it was by the design of tyrants that English law was not in the "peoples' mother tongue," similar to how the Normans conducted legal administration in their native French, so that those who were "governed by them might never come to understand them." Commoners kept ignorant of their own affairs were at the mercy of the "wills of those who ride and tyrannize over them." Since God had given "his laws and the proceedings therein to his people, in their own mother tongue," how could Parliament refuse the scores of "honest and just petitions" calling for the compilation of English law into one "short, plain, and easy to be understood method in the English tongue?" After Starkey's Christian humanist goal of translating scripture into English was accomplished by mid-seventeenth century the emphasis shifted to translating secular law into the vernacular. Protestantism legitimized the idea that no matter the majesty of English law, its inaccessibility inappropriately made its operation a mystery to most, just as scripture's inaccessibility had caused earlier generations to be ignorant of God's word. The means to civic harmony were not only unknown to most commoners, from Lilburne's perspective, the kingdom's aristocracy was using the law to oppress Englishmen by depriving them access, thereby preserving their own social standing and considerable influence they had on the daily life of the kingdom.[17]

---

Levellers, Political Literacy, and Contemporary Citizenship Education in England," *Education, Citizenship, and Social Justice* 14.1 (2019): 74.

17 John Shepheard, *Certain Proposals for Regulating the Law* (1652), 1; *Wing* S3102, Reel 1450: 10. Theobald Mathew, "Law-French," *Law Quarterly Review* 54 (1938): 358–69. John Lilburne, *The Peoples Prerogative* (Feb. 17, 1648), introduction; *Thomason Tracts* E427 (4), Reel 67. *Deuteronomy*, 4: 1–14; 6: 1, 7; 16: 18–19; 27: 1–4, 8; 31: 9–13, 24–26. J.H. Baker, *Manual of Law French* (Amersham: Avebury Publishing, 1979), 9–14. Christopher Hill, ed., *Winstanley: The Law of Freedom* (Harmondsworth: Penguin Books, 1973), 345, 361, 377–78. Michael Rogers, "Gerrard Winstanley on Crime and Punishment," *Sixteenth Century Journal* 27 (Autumn 1996): 735–47. Rachel Foxley, "John Lilburne and the Citizenship of 'Free-Born Englishmen'," *Historical Journal* 47 (Dec., 2004): 851–854. "The collocation of 'free-born Englishman' is not common before Lilburne ... The inclusive force of Lilburne's

In this spirit Lilburne attacked English lawyers for putting "false glosses upon the law (merely) for their own ends," equating their practices with "our state clergy … in the days of old before the scripture was tolerated to be in English." In those earlier days university theologians, or scholars, caused "poor people [to] believe the Pope's unwritten verities were as binding as scripture rules, which the lawyers have given the Commons just cause to fear in their present practice with law cases; many of which are besides the rule of the statute law, and also justice." Lilburne's essays on law reform echoed Thomas More's *Utopia*, and the other Commonwealth reformers of the previous century:

> They have very few laws, and their training is such that they need no more. The chief fault they find with other nations is that, even with infinite volumes of laws and interpretations they cannot manage their affairs properly. They think it completely unjust to bind men by a set of laws that are too many to be read, or too obscure for anyone to understand … As they see things, all laws are promulgated for the single purpose of advising every man of his duty. Subtle interpretations admonish very few, since hardly anybody can understand them, whereas the more simple, and apparent, the sense of the law is opens it to everyone. If laws are not clear, they are useless; for simple-minded men … there might as well be no laws at all as laws which can be interpreted only … after endless disputes. The common man cannot understand this legal chicanery, and couldn't even if he devoted his whole life to studying it, since he has to earn a living in the meantime.[18]

As Barbara Shapiro has recently explained, More's "scathing attack" on English criminal law and administration echoed "proposals of radical reformers of the mid-17th century" ranging from the "abolition of the legal profession" to "reform of the punishment for theft." These "Commonwealthmen, humanist scholars devoted to public policy and the improvement of society, concerned

---

insistence on calling 'free-born' and 'free-men' is clear. The assumption that Englishmen were free and not bond was not controversial. What was controversial was the assertion that the free status of Englishmen gave them, as individuals, political status."

18 John Lilburne, *England's Birthright Justified* (1645), 3: 266. Thomas More, *Utopia*, George Logan and Robert Adams eds., 15–16, 84–5. Daniel Mandell, *The Lost Tradition of Economic Equality in America: 1600–1870* (Baltimore: Johns Hopkins Univ. Press, 2020), 10. "In England, … [a] classical republican ideal became part of the simmering conflict between renters, gentry, and aristocrats: an expanding field of civil rights derived from the *Magna Charta*; communitarian traditions of land use rights; and an increasingly powerful commonwealth ethos that the state should serve the common good."

themselves with remedying the defects of English law. Uncertainty of the law was a common theme."[19]

Did Massachusetts' impetus to print its laws result from a common Protestant mantra, or utopian impulse? Massachusetts' education laws illustrate that Protestantism was a crucial factor. As Henry Robinson reasoned, "knowledge of the laws where a man enjoys his life, liberty, and estate ... is not of less absolute necessity as to the things of this world than the knowledge of those religious, eternal, fundamental principles of faith and love." A sermon delivered to Parliament in 1645 by John Dury, however, illustrates how thoroughly religious fervor and utopian impulse were interwoven during this era. While the sermon's title, *Israel's Call to March out of Babylon Unto Jerusalem*, proclaimed a common appeal to the *Book of Revelations* (i.e., the destruction of Babylon, the second coming of Christ, and the end of the corporeal world), Dury compared an idyllic, though unreachable Jerusalem to a worldly Babylon that "God is not only working our deliverance," but to "make us instrumental towards others to help free them from ... bondage." After kings and magistrates had used their "absolute power" to treat "subjects like beasts," they "rideth upon the beast," people were kept in a state of ignorance to keep them obedient, "even as a horse turneth this way or that, only because he that rideth on him draw the bridle to the right or left hand." In the City of God, however, the treatment of people was not "arbitrary, it is altogether legal; there is but one lawgiver, Jesus Christ, and under him government is to be administered." Christ sought to "enlighten their understanding" to prevent any official from doing "what he pleaseth in an arbitrary way, whether he be high or low." In order to realize the reform of the worldly Babylon one must "look to the house of God to settle it in good order, and then look to the further settlement of the civil state." Universities must ban the "gibberish of scholastic divinity" from their lecture halls, and "inferior schools of all sorts of children and youths should be taken into serious consideration, and men of parts encouraged to have the inspections and oversight of them." This oversight was necessary as "corruption of all states and qualities of people doth arise from neglect of these schools, wherein ... all habits of dissoluteness are begotten in the souls of children." If such situations were not addressed, these children would become "useless, if not hurtful

19 Barbara Shapiro, *Law Reform in Early Modern England* (Oxford: Hart Publishing, 2019), 13, 31–2. Richard Morison suggested "unwritten" laws be recorded and "gathered together and made certain." He was "confident that codification would do much to end the confusion, delay, and expense of legal proceedings."

to the commonwealth." Utopianism was an essential element in the push for education among the English reformers.[20]

The other side of the spectrum—a focus on the more pragmatic benefits of literacy—can be seen in the work of Samuel Hartlib, a devout Protestant and reformer extraordinaire. Having established residence in London after travels across Europe, Hartlib pursued many interests and studies, but his unifying and overarching interest was in technological advances spurred on by education. In a 1641 pamphlet intended for parliamentary members he wrote, "I have read over St. Thomas More's *Utopia* and my Lord Bacon's *New Atlantis*, ... but none of them give me satisfaction how the kingdom of England may be happy." Instead, he recommended Parliament adopt a "book of Husbandry ... whereby the kingdom may maintain double the number of people, and in more plenty and prosperity than now they enjoy." If Hartlib himself was a "Parliament man," he "would labor to have this book dispatched, ... for withal my seven Liberal Arts I cannot discover how any business can be of more weight than this, wherein the public good is so greatly furthered." Hartlib proclaimed such a "Reformation shall come before the day of judgment," as there now existed "natural causes" to bring it to pass. These causes included the "art of printing," which would "so spread knowledge" that the "common people," having been made aware of "their own rights and liberties," would ultimately throw off their "oppression."[21]

---

20 Henry Robinson, *Certaine Proposals in Order to a New Modelling of the Lawes* (London: 1653), 2; *Google Books* (https://play.google.com/books/reader?id=OcJjAAAAcAAJ&pg=GBS.RA1-PA2&hl=en). John Dury, *Israels Call to March Out of Babylon unto Jerusalem* (London: 1646), 1–48; *Thomason Tracts* E310 (3), Reel 51. Alister McGrath, *Reformation Thought*, 2nd ed., (Oxford: Blackwell, 1993), 219–20. Charles Webster, *The Great Instauration*, 49, 62, 68–70. Leonard Levy, *Ranters Run Amok*, 3–51. Jonathan Scott, "What were Commonwealth Principles?," *Historical Journal* 47 (Sept., 2004): 594–95. William Tindall, *John Bunyan: Mechanick Preacher* (New York: Columbia Univ. Press, 1934; reprint, Russell & Russell, 1964), 91–5. "Levellers and Diggers grew out of the religious ferment, [and] employed religious terminology in their earlier and even in their later tracts ... Revelation had dictated a social plan to Winstanley, who called Jesus Christ the head Leveller, and who expressed his quarrel with society first in the imagery of the Scriptures, and only later ... directly in social and economic terms."

21 Samuel Hartlib, *A Description of the Famous Kingdom of Macaria* (London: Oct. 25, 1641), intro., 9–14; *Thomason Tracts*, E173 (28), Reel #30. Charles Webster, "The Authorship and Significance of Macaria," *Past and Present* 56 (1972): 34–48. Thomas Leng, "A Potent Plantation Well Armed and Policed: Huguenots, the Hartlib Circle, and British Colonization in the 1640s," *William and Mary Quarterly* 66 (Jan., 2009): 173–194. Hartlib also supported English colonization. Rob Iliffe, "Hartlib's World," in Matthew Davies and James Galloway, eds., *London and Beyond: Essays in Honour of Derek Keen* (London: Univ. of London, 2012), 103–22.

Despite the arguments of reformers like Hartlib, England did not achieve universal male literacy in this period. Neither did colonies like Pennsylvania and Virginia both of which still had male literacy rates around 60% by 1750. Kenneth Lockridge concluded that class-bias in both Pennsylvania and Virginia caused literacy rates to stagnate at levels very similar to those in England. But he also saw another ingredient at work. Although both had established "charity school movements, laws compelling education of apprentices, and itinerant schoolmasters," their male literacy did not rise appreciably during the 1700's because those colonies lacked a vital ingredient present in New England: "intense Protestantism and consequent school laws." Lockridge concluded, a "uniformly and intensely Protestant society and, above all, the systematic state action which emerges from such a society, were essential to moving male literacy the last large step to universality." In contrast to England, Pennsylvania, and Virginia, Massachusetts had achieved near universality in male literacy by 1750. The graduated establishment of elementary and grammar schools in the *1647 School Act* played a pivotal role. As illustrated by town records, greater emphasis was placed on learning English in Massachusetts than in England. As Latin schooling was often a burdensome requirement, the structure of the 1647 law ensured that a priority was placed on English literacy by the directive that elementary schools be first established in towns with fifty families and Latin became a secondary requirement only when one hundred families was reached. Consequently, while a free school in every English shire remained an ideal hope, there was "by law enjoined a school to be kept and maintained in every town" of the Massachusetts Bay colony.[22]

---

22 Kenneth Lockridge, *Literacy in Colonial New England* (New York: W.W. Norton & Co., 1974), 77–87. Jeremy Schmidt, "Charity and the Government of the Poor in the English Charity-School Movement, circa. 1700–1730," *Journal of British Studies* 49 (Oct., 2010): 774–800. The charity-school movement was in large part intended for poor relief, and donors provided support for both maintenance and discipline of the poor. But education for its own sake does not seem to have been at the forefront of the movement. Faramerz Dabhoiwala, "Summary Justice in Early Modern London," *English Historical Review* 121 (June 2006): 803–4. "The 'new Corporation of the Poor' was closely linked to Whig and dissenting interests in [London], and opposed by many prominent Tories." By the mid-1700s the Corporation had "stopped taking in poor parish children to be educated in trades, which had been its main philanthropic function. A few years later the keeper's side of the workhouse was closed down and turned into a prison for debtors. All that remained by the 1760s was an institution for employing vagrant children." Edmund Morgan, *American Slavery, American Freedom*, 187, 370–75. Nathaniel Shurtleff, ed., *MGCR*, 4 (Part 2): 190–1, 198–9 (May 1665). The quote on schools being in every Massachusetts town is excerpted from General Court's reply to questions posed by a royal commission inspecting the colony in the mid-1660's.

Clearly, the colony also established an education system as a means of social control. The *Laws and Liberties of 1648* directed, for instance, that "if any of the select men after admonition by them given to such masters of families shall find them still negligent of their duty" the adopting parents would "force them to submit to government according to the rules of this order," including the *1642 Education law's* requirement that parents teach their children to read, a catechism, and the *Capital Laws*. Massachusetts sought filial obedience just like English reformers. An illustrative example occurred when Michael Towsley and his wife appeared before Magistrate John Pynchon in 1685. Joseph Segar charged the pair with theft and assault, Michael "with his fist and she with [a] stick." Several years later the Towsleys appeared before Pynchon again, this time for stealing neighbors' livestock. Upon more damning testimony Towsley was sentenced to fifteen lashes, payment of court costs and damages, and ten lashes for his wife. As for their daughter Mary, she acknowledged she could "do no better or reform while she continues with her parents or father." Although Pynchon's sentence of indentured service acknowledged her parents were unfit, he still included a punishment of eight lashes for Mary, and that she be delivered to foster parents "with whom she may be well educated."[23]

By the 1660's a proper education had become an urgent concern as many colonists believed Massachusetts had entered a period of precipitous moral decline known as "declension." As more and more of the younger generation failed to join their parents' congregations, God would soon abandon their entire community. Of course, the original fervor of the first settlers would not be recaptured no matter how many jeremiads were preached, inspections made, or laws passed. Nevertheless, on their own initiative, Watertown's selectmen addressed a perception of a rising tide of ungodliness by more vigorous compliance with the colony's education laws. After acquiring the first copies of the *Capital Laws* in 1642, its next mention in the town record occurred in 1665, when selectmen agreed to "go through the town to examine how children are taught to read and instructed in the grounds of religion and the Capital laws." By 1668 "sad experience" had witnessed that "sin and profaneness" were

23 Richard Dunn, ed., *Laws and Liberties of 1648*, 11, title *Children*, §1. Nathaniel Shurtleff, ed., *MGCR*, 2: 8–9 (June 1642). Joseph Smith, ed., *Colonial Justice in Western Massachusetts, 1639–1702* (Cambridge: Harvard Univ. Press, 1961), 300–1, 308, 326–27. S.E. Morison, ed., *Records of the Suffolk County Court*, 30: 599 (1675). When William Scant objected to "disposing of his children ... for their good education" by "putting ... them forth to service as the law directs," the Suffolk County court ruled for the town. David Thompson, *Divided We Stand*, 119–25. E.J. Monaghan, "Literacy Instruction and Gender in Colonial New England," 27–30.

on the increase, "ensnaring ... many children and servants." The General Court ordered town constables to enforce the law on "page 16, title, *Children and Youth*," in the *Laws and Liberties of 1660*. The selectmen should keep a "vigilant eye over their brethren and neighbors" and ensure children know the "English tongue," the "capital laws," and their religious catechism. If parents neglected this order "whereby children and servants become, rude, stubborn and unruly," they were to be placed with guardians who would "force them to submit unto government." The General Court ordered copies of the law sent to town constables, and if selectmen neglected their duty they would be fined "according to the intent of the law."[24]

In 1670, Watertown's selectmen redoubled their efforts by going "through the town in their several quarters to make trial whether children and servants be educated in learning to read the English tongue, and in the knowledge of the *Capital Laws* according to the law of the country." Several years later this striking passage appears in the town record, "Thomas Fleg, John Whitny, and Joseph Bemus should go about the town to see that children were taught to read the English tongue, ... taught some orthodox catechism, and to see that each man has in his house a copy of the *Capital Laws*." The selectmen directed "copies [be] procured by Captain Mason at the printers, and they to be paid for out of the town rate" for delivery to "such of the inhabitants as have none." Town officials made their rounds of inspection with an armful of the *Capital Laws*.[25]

---

24 Nathaniel Shurtleff, ed., *MGCR*, 4 (Part 2): 395–96 (Oct. 14, 1668), 451. David Hall, *Worlds of Wonder, Days of Judgment* (Cambridge: Harvard Univ. Press, 1989), 134–42. *Watertown Records*, 1: 89. William Whitmore, ed., *Laws and Liberties of 1660*, 16, title *Children and Youth*, §1. Michael Winship, *Hot Protestants: A History of Puritanism in England and America* (New Haven: Yale Univ. 2018), 186–89. Emerson Baker, *A Storm of Witchcraft: The Salem Trials and the American Experience* (Oxford: Oxford Univ. Press, 2015), 48–49. "The degree to which Puritan declension was real is a matter of scholarly debate. Although the proportion of colonists who were full church members did decrease throughout the second half of the seventeenth century, many historians note that the Puritan commitment remained strong."

25 *Watertown Records*, 1: 9, 86, 104, 121, 124, 144. Upon the General Court's establishment of a town "tithingman" office to ensure godly deportment a few years later, Watertown "voted that the select men at the town charge are to procure two hundred copies of those several laws ... for the several inhabitants' use." The first tithingman law was passed in 1677 by the General Court, and later amended and expanded in 1679. Nathaniel Shurtleff, ed., *MGCR*, 5: 133 (May 24, 1677), 240–41 (Oct. 15, 1679). David Allen, *In English Ways* (Chapel Hill: Univ. of North Carolina Press, 1981), 219–20. David Hall, "Readers and Writers in Early New England," 117–51. E. Jennifer Monaghan, "Literacy Instruction and Gender in Colonial New England," 27. Derek Hirst, "The Failure of Godly Rule in the English Republic," *Past and Present* 132 (Aug., 1991): 33–66. The establishment of the tithingman office is commonly

But even with the focus on the civic purpose of education, the religious goals of broad education never disappeared from view. Watertown, for instance, was following common English practice with regard to religious edification, as Puritan ministers authored manuals for godly living routinely. One of the most successful, John Dod's *A Plain and Familiar Exposition of the Ten Commandments*, earned the author the nickname "Decalogue Dod" by enjoying eighteen editions over a thirty-year period. A flood of educational printed matter was issued as catechisms, primers, and ABC books. The most popular textbook was *The ABC with the Catechism*, which included biblical texts, including the Lord's Prayer and *Ten Commandments*. As students endured the drudgery of their ABC's, they were to be imbued with Christian beliefs. The enduring popularity of these textbooks in Massachusetts is illustrated by a Boston bookshop's inventory of over seven hundred spellers and primers at century's end.[26]

In sum, in the period in England when reformers were embracing aspirations for the education of ordinary people, the legislators and people of Massachusetts Bay Colony were actually implementing such a system. Their motivations fused Protestantism, and the need for access to theological texts, with utopianism; a conviction that education of ordinary people would serve improvement in the social order.

---

portrayed as another puritanical impulse of the Bay colony, but usually ignored are similar efforts undertaken during the Commonwealth and Protectorate eras in England. Bernard Capp, *England's Culture Wars: Puritan Reformation and its Enemies in the Interregnum, 1649–1660* (Oxford: Oxford Univ. Press, 2012).

26 William Haller, *The Rise of Puritanism*, 61, 116–20. Charles Webster, *The Great Instauration*, 35. When John Cotton and Thomas Hooker considered migration to Massachusetts, they sought Dod's counsel. Louis Wright, *Middle-Class Culture in Elizabethan England*, 121–296. Ian Green, *The Christian's ABC* (Oxford: Clarendon Press, 1996). Charles Butterworth, *The English Primers (1529–1545)* (Philadelphia: Univ. of Pennsylvania Press, 1953). H. Anders, "The Elizabethan ABC with the Catechism," *The Library* 41 (1936): 32–48. David Cressy, ed., *Education in Tudor and Stuart England*, 73. S.E. Morison, *The Puritan Pronaos*, 69. E. Jennifer Monaghan, "Literacy Instruction and Gender in Colonial New England," 19–22.

CHAPTER 2

# Education and Radical Religiosity

As the sixteenth century progressed into the next, a commingling of secular ideas and religious beliefs evolved chaotically with unpredictable consequences for communities across Western Europe and the English and Scottish kingdoms. While England's Commonwealth law reform movement was impacted by utopian and religious ideals, once the virulence of Reformation became clear, even a humanist champion like Thomas More shrunk from previous goals of lay access to the Bible, or popular education. And while English Protestants stressed the importance of the vernacular in church service and biblical translation, their greatest support of institutionalized education was Latin instruction and classical literature. Instruction in English literacy existed infrequently, and Parliament did not mandate universal education until the nineteenth century. Still, Samuel Harmar's 1642 petition to Parliament proclaimed universality a "work no good Christian can deny," as it "much tendeth to the worship of God and the good of the Common-wealth." He urged MP's to place "school-masters in every parish" to instruct "young children both in godliness and manners, for the good of the land." Currently, a shortage of teachers to "educate and instruct all the children … as well the poor as the rich" frustrated these goals. Although some complained, "who shall pay for children's schooling," Harmar urged enactment of property taxes to prevent "idleness among children" that too often led to "beggary and thievery," and so serve the "public good." If the kingdom's laws could be "read in every school twice a week," a "very great reformation" would occur as children would then have the "*law in their hearts*."[1]

1 Eamon Duffy, *Reformation Divided* (London: Bloomsbury, 2017), 19–49. Samuel Harmar, *Vox Populi* (London, 1642), no pagination; *Thomason Tracts* E146 (2), Reel 26. Charles Webster, *The Great Instauration* (New York: Holmes & Meier, 1975), 207–45. "Apart from rudimentary literacy, attained in a haphazard manner, the lower classes were not educated systematically … Agitation for schools found spontaneous expression in petitions from widely different sources, and eventually the Levellers' social program included a demand for sufficient free schools to ensure universal liberty." Lawrence Stone, "Literacy and Education in England: 1640–1900," *Past and Present* 42 (1969): 76, 90–7. David Cressy, *England on Edge: Crisis and Revolution, 1640–1642(Oxford: Oxford Univ. Press, 2006)*, 292. "The explosion of print in the opening years of the Long Parliament [1640–1641] was one of the most revolutionary features of the English Revolution. The quantity, character, and impact of these publications constituted an unprecedented media storm. From just six or seven hundred

 | DOI:10.1163/9789004706347_004

A debate had been engaged between those who thought that social good would come from the accessibility of legal and religious texts and those who instead worried that widespread literacy, when it intersected with radical religiosity, might prove socially destabilizing. That debate unfolded in Massachusetts too, but with a twist. Since Massachusetts moved rapidly to expand access to education, the questions about potential social destabilization were immediate and pronounced. As we saw in the last chapter, both elementary schools for English instruction and secondary grammar schools for Latin were transported to Massachusetts. But there was a significant difference between schools in the motherland and in the colony; for instance, old Dorchester's free school established in 1567, and its namesake in New England, as David Underdown has pointed out. By century's end the Dorchester Free School in England had a "solid reputation for the classical education it provided for the sons of the wealthiest parents to prepare them to serve church and commonwealth." Soon after their arrival residents of Dorchester, Massachusetts, "established a school for the training up of the children in religion, learning, and civility." While both schools were founded on a Puritan impulse, the new Dorchester school was "really was free, open to all children."[2]

In Massachusetts, when parents were unable to provide for their children's education and towns discovered that poverty was the cause, as was fairly common, during the seventeenth century the towns had to address these situations themselves. For example, when Watertown's town leaders, known as selectmen, reviewed compliance with the *1642 Education Act*, they discovered many "poor families … must be in the first place relieved." Only with such support could education of all the town's children be assured. During another round of inspection, the town's selectmen concluded that Edward Sanderson was unable to care for his children because of his abject poverty. They were stymied, however, "not knowing how to supply them with provision." The town was willing to provide the family sustenance, but his assistance "would not tend to the good of the children for their good education and bringing up, so as they may be useful in the common weal or themselves." Sanderson was such an unfit parent that monetary support alone would not improve his children's plight. So, the selectmen decided to "put out two of his children into some honest families where they may be educated and brought up in the knowledge of God." Since no system of poor relief yet existed in Massachusetts, similar to England's, it was up to the towns to do what they could. As Jonathan Dealy

known items a year in the 1630s, the numbers of known publications rose dramatically to almost nine hundred in 1640, over two thousand in 1641, and over four thousand in 1642."

2 David Underdown, *Fire from Heaven* (New Haven: Yale Univ. Press, 1992), 19–20, 137–8.

has recounted, "the English Old Poor law was unique in early modern history, in that it was a national system of poor relief, funded by systematic taxation … established over the course of the 17th century to a point it was probably transferring around £400,000 by the 1690s, … enough to feed about 5% of the population."[3]

In 1642, by "unanimous consent" Dedham's town meeting set aside land for the "publique use" of the town to build a church and school house. Originally, when Dedham enacted its town "covenant" to create a governing framework in 1636, it had included a requirement that all male children and servants of families from four to fourteen years old attend school. And if the appropriated funds for this purpose were exhausted, the town "rate," or tax, would make up the difference. In 1644, again by unanimous consent, the town pledged that upon the "great necessity" of educating children the required work to promote its "free school" would be maintained by an annual appropriation of £20. In the same year Salem ordered a "note be published on the next lecture day," or during weekly church service, that parents with "children to be kept at school would bring in their names and what they will give for one whole year." And "if any poor body hath children or a child to be put to school and not able to pay for their schooling … the town will pay it by a rate," or town tax. By the 1670s the town's school house was cross-purposed to serve as the constable's watch-house, to be built from the timbres of the soon to be torn down original meeting house. Although later in its history (1687), Hingham also depended on town taxes when student fees fell short.[4]

Towns that did not provide the schooling required by colonial law, as enacted by the General Court, were subject to suit in the county courts. In

3 *Watertown Records (Historical. Society, 1894)*, 1: 71 (1660), 105 (1671). Shurtleff, ed., MGCR, 4 (Part 1): 365. Roger Thompson, *Divided We Stand*, 107–15. Douglas Jones, "The Transformation of the Law of Poverty in Eighteenth-Century Massachusetts," *Publications of the Colonial Society of Massachusetts* 62 (1984): 153–90. Jonathan Dealy, "Coping with Risk in the Seventeenth Century: The First Age of the English Old Poor Law," in Masayuki Tanimoto, and R. Bin Wong, eds. *Public Goods Provision in the Early Modern Economy* (Berkeley: Univ. of California Press, 2019), 100–17.

4 Don Hill, ed., *Dedham Town Records* (Historical Society, 1886–1889), 3: 16 (#38—*The Covenant*), 92 (1642—*land for school*), 105 (1644), 135 (1651—*£20 annual sum extended for 7 years*), 149, 157–8, 191 (#2), 202 (1652). *Town Records of Salem (Essex Institute, 1864)*, 1: 132 (1644); 2: 163 (1673). Underdown, *Fire from Heaven*, 113–15. John Martin, *Profits in the Wilderness* (Chapel Hill: Univ. of North Carolina Press, 1991), 163–64. S.E. Morison, *Puritan Pronaos: Studies in the Intellectual Life of New England in the Seventeenth Century.* (New York: NYU Press, 1936), 62 (n. 16). Morison noted that in Dedham's 1651 tax rate parents were assessed only 5 shillings per student, which fell short of satisfying the £20 annual salary for the school teacher. *History of the Town of Hingham, Massachusetts* (Cambridge: Univ. Press, 1893), 1 (pt. II): 83–5.

1658, Newbury was presented at a session of the Essex County court for not providing a Latin schoolmaster. The town was ordered to remit £5 to the nearby Ipswich Latin school for not having its own grammar school, with the proviso that the fine would be returned if "by the next court they provide a Latin school master according to law." The colony's first law book, the *Laws and Liberties of 1648*, stipulated that a town with over one hundred families must provide a grammar school or pay a £5 fine. Ipswich did not appreciate its neighbors taking advantage of its costly endeavor. But Newbury had not wholly neglected ensuring town children were properly educated, as it had employed an elementary school teacher since 1639, and built its own schoolhouse in 1652; as S.E. Morison reminded us, one should consider the significant expense of these initiatives for small farming communities. Finally, in 1675, Newbury hired Harry Short to teach Latin grammar because the "law requires that our town should maintain a grammar school and a school master to teach to recite and read." When Andover was charged with the absence of mandated schooling its teacher testified, "Understanding that our town was presented for want of a schoolmaster, I thought it my duty to signify that for these thirty and two years I have taught any scholars that they sent to me to learn to write, and some in their grammar, and if God lengthen out my time I shall be willing to do it." Haverhill responded to the same charge, "We have made choice of Robert Ford … to teach all those to write and also arithmetic that shall come to him for that end."[5]

Not surprisingly, a class hierarchy of literacy resulted from England's education system. In his investigation of English literacy rates in early modern England David Cressy determined that by the mid-1500's male literacy was approximately 20%, and female literacy at 5%. By the 1640's the male figure had risen to 30%, and the females' to about 10%. Within these numbers Cressy

5 George Dow, ed., *Records and Files of the Quarterly Courts of Essex County* (Salem: Essex Institute, 1911–1921), 2: 70 (n. *), 8: 96–7, 100–1. Cited hereafter as *Essex County Court Record.* S.E. Morison, ed., *Records of the Suffolk County Court*, vol. 29, *Publications of the Colonial Society of Massachusetts* (1933): 182, 228. John Currier, *History of Newbury, Massachusetts* (Boston: Damrell & Upham, 1902), 124, 395–6. Richard Dunn, ed., *Laws and Liberties of 1648*, 47, title *Schools*, §2. David Cressy, *Literacy and the Social Order: Reading and Writing in Tudor and Stuart England* (Cambridge: Cambridge University Press, 1980), 29–34. S.E. Morison, *Puritan Pronaos*, 70. "The Massachusetts and Connecticut school laws certainly placed too heavy a burden on small farming communities; it is surprising that we do not find more evidence of dissatisfaction with the system, or resentment at school taxes." Edward and Elaine Gordon, *Literacy in America* (London: Praeger, 2003), 7. By 1642, "21 towns existed [in Massachusetts] … with a combined population of about 9,000. Most of them had a church and a university educated minister."

identified three "clusters" of social rank. First was the landed elite, clergy, and professionals with an average literacy in the 80th percentile; they had the means to send children to private tutors. Next were yeomen farmers and tradesmen. From 1580 to 1700 their literacy ranged from a high of 72% in London (which had the highest rates in England) to 63% in the surrounding county of Middlesex, and 27% in rural areas. The third group, comprised of subsistence farmers and wage laborers, ranged from 25% to 10%. Not surprisingly, these statistics demonstrate an "overwhelming correspondence ... between social and occupational status, and, the ability to sign one's name." Children sired by parents of the nobility and landed elite were not only afforded an education, they pursued one in order to fulfill a role consistent with their parents' *rank* in society.[6]

These statistical trends did not hold true in the case of gender. From 1560 to 1640 female literacy ranged from 5% to 10%, respectively, and Cressy concludes that, unlike male rates, female percentages did not fluctuate with social or economic rank. This is in complete divergence to the male rates' "overwhelming correspondence between social and occupational status." The explanation is that whether school-aged girls or adult women, their accepted roles were universally domestic in nature and did not require a formal education. As one schoolmaster complained, "bringing up of young maids in any kind of learning is but an accessory by the way" because they were the "pillars in the upholding of households." Although reading was "very needful for religion," ladies should never learn for learning's sake. After all he did not "meddle with needles ... nor with housewifery," but dealt "only with such things as be incident to ... learning." Young gentlemen, on the other hand, pursued a classical education because the "male is more worthy," and would be "politically ... employed." Still, most males did not enjoy a social rank sufficient for church or state service, or one that merited a university education.[7]

---

6 David Cressy, *Literacy and the Social Order*, 124–27, 137, 176. Cressy's and Lockridge's studies on a population's literacy were calculated upon the ability to sign one's name. Mary Beth Norton, *Founding Mothers and Fathers* (New York: Alfred A. Knopf, 1996), 18. Norton has explained that the "only contemporary term used to describe the elements of England's all-encompassing social and political hierarchy was '*rank*' ... Other roughly comparable words, like 'status' or 'class,' came into use later, primarily in the eighteenth and nineteenth centuries."

7 David Cressy, *Literacy and the Social Order*, 118–28, 176. R. Mulcaster, *Positions wherein those Primitive Circumstances be Examined which are Necessary for the Training up of Children* (1581); quoted in David Cressy, *Education in Tudor and Stuart England* (New York: St. Martin's Press, 1975), 109–11. John Comenius, *The Great Didactic* (1657); Cressy, Ibid., 101, 111. E. Jennifer Monaghan, "Literacy Instruction and Gender in Colonial New England," 40 *American Quarterly* (March 1988): 27–31. Massachusetts first required teaching girls to read

As we have seen, Massachusetts, in contrast, had reached a universal male literacy rate by the mid-1700s. Other British North American colonies failed to duplicate its achievement, but this was considered valuable as a hedge against radicalism and social instability. Virginia Governor William Berkeley's answer to a question on his colony's education "system" succinctly explains why:

> The same course that is taken in England out of towns, every man according to his ability instructing his children. We have forty-eight parishes, and our ministers are well paid, and ... [could] be better if they would pray oftener and preach less. But of all other commodities, so of this, the worst are sent to us, and we had few that we could boast of, since the persecution in Cromwell's tyranny drove divers worthy men hither. But I thank God, there are no free schools nor printing, and I hope we shall not have these hundred years; for learning has brought disobedience, and heresy, and sects into the world, and printing has divulged them, and libels against the best government. God keep us from both![8]

The governor's historical narrative remains generally accurate. Vernacular literacy and Bible reading had a long partnership with English radicalism and rebellion, proving to be socially combustible when joined with print and the availability of books and pamphlets. To understand these dynamics as they played out in Massachusetts, linking literacy to heterodoxy, it is useful to return to English practices.

---

in 1703, and to write in 1771; "children" in seventeenth-century colonial school laws meant male children. Charles Webster, *The Great Instauration*, 108–14, 211, 220. J.G.A. Pocock, *The Machiavellian Moment* (Princeton: Princeton Univ. Press, 1975), 338–41. Patrick Wallis, Cliff Webb, "Education and Training of Gentry Sons in Early Modern England," *Social History* 36 (Feb., 2011): 36–53.

8 William Hening, ed., *The Statutes at Large: Being a Collection of all the Laws of Virginia* (New York: R.W.G. Bartow, 1823), 2: 517 (#23). Robert Vejnar, "The State of Education in Colonial Virginia," *International Social Science Review* 77 (No. 1/2, 2002): 16. "What exactly constituted a proper education depended upon who did the defining. A number of colonial Virginians regarded a child's education as adequate if he learned some sort of trade, the rudiments of the Anglican faith, and perhaps how to write his name. Parents addressed the trade issue by instructing their children themselves, or apprenticing the youngster to a master craftsman. Religion had a role in education as well, and often a child acquired that religious component through attending Sunday services at Anglican Church ... Those colonial Virginians who had the financial means could seek a more traditional English education for their children, one that included instruction in reading, Greek, and Latin." Alan Taylor, *American Colonies* (New York: Penguin Books, 2001), 179. "Almost every New England town sustained a public grammar school, and most women and almost all men could read—which was not the case in the mother country or in any other colonial region."

In 1539, only several years after Henry VIII ordered vernacular Bibles placed in English churches, for example, King and Parliament enacted *An Act Abolishing Diversity of Opinions*, reinforcing heresy laws with earlier Roman church practices. The Act explained its necessity in the wake of "manifold ... dangers and inconveniences which have heretofore in many places and regions grown, sprung, and arisen of the diversity of minds and opinions especially [in] matters of [the] Christian religion." The rise in dissent followed the spread of literacy to the point that Henry saw it as a threat to his throne.[9]

This wasn't altogether new. Previously Lollards, and then Familists were feared and persecuted by English government for practicing a heretical Christian worship, featuring vernacular Bible reading along with other unlicensed religious texts judged subversive of England's church and state. From the Peasants Revolt in 1381, when rebels knew enough to foment "widespread destruction of manorial records from Norfolk to Kent" to erase the written evidence of their serfdom, through Jake Cade's Lollard inspired rebellion in 1450, to increasing religious radicalism building throughout the sixteenth century, literacy served as an oxidizing agent, especially when aggravated by economic displacement and deprivation. The medieval Mass itself put the opulence of the Roman Church on full display, one laden with ornate vestments and gold chalices, enhanced by the burning of incense and performed in magnificent cathedrals behind sheer silk drapes that produced a celestial effect for the congregation. Once a vernacular Bible was available, such rituals reeked of a corrupted priesthood to these radical religious groups, whose astonishment to read that Jesus and his disciples lived threadbare rather than opulent existences, similar to their own, shattered traditional norms. England's "lower" social ranks' experience of scripture as a spiritual epiphany is difficult to fully imagine today, but it must have been empowering beyond anything they could have otherwise experienced. Direct condemnation and punishment by church or state elites was initially complicated since the Bible was being used as the

9 *SR*, 3 (Part 2): 714 (31 Hen. VIII ch. XIV, §l (1539)). M.E. Ashton, "Lollardy and Sedition, 1381–1431," *Past and Present* 17 (Apr., 1960): 4–5, 12, 32. Parliamentary statute regulating and restricting itinerant preachers dated to at least 1382: "Lay preaching had already achieved popularity during Wycliffe's lifetime [1330–1384] ... The heretics literature is full of near-theological arguments justifying their frequent evasion of the law on this matter ... Itinerant preachers, who in 1382 had been made liable to immediate arrest and imprisonment in secular prisons, now [in 1388] came under further lay supervision: ... commissions were given the task of hunting out not only Wycliffite works, but also those teaching or studying them; at the same time local officials (sheriffs, mayors, bailiffs, etc.) were made generally responsible for assisting such enquiries. And offenders were subject to forfeiture as well as imprisonment."

authority to protest, but populist eruptions would nevertheless provoke violent suppression.[10]

In the late 1530's Henry VIII issued proclamations ordering the apprehension and interrogation of Anabaptists; a group that was reviled throughout Europe for riotous challenges to civil authority based only upon their objections to infant baptism. He also commanded seizure of their religious texts, while another proclamation restricted Bible reading to university graduates. In 1543 Parliament passed *An Act for the Advancement of True Religion and the Abolishment of the Contrary*, forbidding the sale or reading of prohibited texts (including "untrue" translations of Tyndale's work); per T. Wilson Hayes

10 Susan Brigden, *London and the Reformation* (Oxford: Clarendon Press, 1989), 408–9. "Contention over the freedom to read the Bible in English exposed, so they said, a rift between the social orders: 'the great part of these inordinate, rich, stiff-necked citizens will not have in their houses that lively Word of our souls, nor suffer their servants to have it' ... The Reformation was not only a religious revolution: it was also a social one, perhaps created by one. The religious transformation came at a time of profound social and economic instability, and in such a crisis the poor must have suffered most acutely." Rodney Hilton, *Medieval Peasant Movements and the English Rising of 1381* (London: Routledge, 1973), 226–27. Steven Justice, *Writing and Rebellion: England in 1381* (Berkeley: Univ. of California Press, 1994). Buchanan Sharp, *In Contempt of All Authority: Rural Artisans and Riot in the West of England, 1586–1660* (Berkeley: Univ. of California Press, 1980). J.W. Martin, "Elizabethan Familists and English Separatism," *Journal of British Studies* 20 (Autumn, 1980): 55–59. Familists' "effective use of the printing press ... was likewise a factor in raising government fears." Eamon Duffy, *The Stripping of the Altars: Traditional Religion in England, c.1400—c.1580* (New Haven: Yale University Press, 1992), 485. Christopher Hill, *The English Bible and the Seventeenth Century Revolution*, 178–203. "Popular interpretations of the New Testament could overrule the conventionally accepted status and subordination of a hierarchical society. This was indeed revolutionary ... Thomas Edwards ... noted in 1646 that 'instead of legal rights and the laws and customs of this nation, the sectaries talk and plead for natural rights and liberties such as men have from their birth.' That was a decisive break from the past, made with the help of the Bible. When we come to consider antinomianism, freedom from laws, we must recall that for some this meant freedom from social and political laws as well as moral laws. The Ranters Clarkson and Coppe claimed freedom from both." Leonard Levy, *Ranters Run Amuck* (Chicago: Ivan R. Dee, 2000), 7–9. After his service as Army Chaplain for parliamentary forces during the civil war, the "most notorious of the Ranters," Abiezer Coppe, "preached his antinomian version of the free spirit: Christ's death liberated mankind from sin, God dwells with everyone, and all shall be saved, all except perhaps the prosperous and powerful. Coppe's theology was saturated with a hatred of the rich. He assaulted 'men and women of the greater rank' in the city streets, ranting and gnashing his teeth at them, while proclaiming that the day of the Lord, the 'great Leveller,' had come ... The gospel, according to Coppe, was 'I overturn, overturn, overturn ... Behold, I the eternal God ... who am that mighty Leveller, am coming ... to Level in good earnest ... putting down the mighty from their seats, and exalting them in low degree'."

it specifically prohibited "women, artificers, journeymen, serving men of the rank of yeoman and under, husbandmen, and laborers" from reading the Bible, while "noblemen and gentlewomen could read it to themselves ... but not to others." Upon first offense, punishment would be thirty days imprisonment and a fine up to £10 sterling, and for a second forfeiture of "all his goods" and commitment to "perpetual prison." After provision of the "great liberty of ... placing in their hands the New and Old Testament," Henry VIII had felt compelled to take such action after "many seditious people" had not only "taken upon them[selves] to preach, teach, declare and set forth the same by word, sermons, disputations, and arguments, but also by printed books, printed ballads, plays, rhymes, songs and other fantasies." They "subtly and craftily" deceived "his Highness' people, and especially the youth of this realm," how the "scripture ought or should be taught," whereupon subsequently a "diversity of opinions, arguments, tumults, and schisms have been sprung and arisen among his said subjects." As Hayes observed, to no surprise there was a venerable "link between literacy and heresy in England."[11]

11 *SR*, 3 (Part 2): 894–95 (34 & 35 Hen. VIII ch. 1, §§1–2 (1542/3)). T. Wilson Hayes, "The Peaceful Apocalypse: Familism and Literacy in Sixteenth-Century England," *Sixteenth Century Journal* 17 (Summer, 1986): 131–43. G.W. Bernard, "The Making of Religious Policy, 1533–1546: Henry VIII and the Search for the Middle Way," *Historical Journal* 41 (June 1998): 321–49. After Henry VIII had made editorial changes, a 1539 draft proclamation condemning Anabaptists read, "taking and gathering divers Holy Scriptures to contrary senses and understanding, do wrest and interpret and so untruly allege the same to subvert and overturn as well the sacraments of Holy Church as the power and authority of princes and magistrates, and in effect generally, all laws and common justice, and the good and laudable ordinances and ceremonies necessary and convenient to be used and continued in this realm." Karl Gunther and Ethan Shagan, "Protestant Radicalism and Political thought in the Reign of Henry VIII," *Past and Present* 194 (Feb., 2007): 48. "In England, of course, where the threat of Lollardy had made vernacular Bibles illegal, the whole thrust of the early Reformation was the 'liberation' of the gospel. Hence there were very rarely circumstances in which it seemed appropriate to diminish the Bible's importance in favor of direct revelation. Yet that does not mean that lay people were always satisfied with, or even fully understood, the notion that they were supposed to read the Bible but not interpret it." Shannon McSheffrey, "Heresy, Orthodoxy and English Vernacular Religion 1480–1525," *Past and Present* 186 (Feb., 2005): 49. "A number of historians, drawing from evidence that even knowledge of the Lord's Prayer could be regarded as heresy in the decades around 1500, have assumed that the use of the vernacular in religion was an unequivocal marker of heresy in pre-Reformation England. While it is undeniable that both Lollards and their opponents made strong associations between heresy and the use of the English language in religion, we must also consider the flood of vernacular books coming from the early English presses, published by printers with apparently fully orthodox intentions, yet which included, among other things, versions of supposedly forbidden prayers."

Governor Berkeley, of Virginia, worshiped in the Anglican Church of England, one that was increasingly derivative of its Roman counterpart, while being a devout royalist with deep allegiance to Charles I. He welcomed political and religious refugees from Cromwell's England after returning from his own brief sojourn there in the early 1640's, during which he had joined the King on military campaign. With Charles I's execution, Berkeley fired off a condemnatory letter to Parliament pledging the colony's allegiance to his heir, Prince Charles. In 1650, the parliamentary Committee of Admiralty issued an order "interdicting" English trade with Virginia, and a navigation law followed the year after. Berkeley led Virginia's General Assembly in condemning these actions, sending a joint resolution to such effect to Europe for printing and publication. Ultimately, he provoked the dispatch of a parliamentary force to Virginia compelling his surrender in 1652, but not before his own deployment of a colonial militia force of 1,000 men to threaten armed conflict upon its arrival. Berkeley rejected the Cromwellian program in toto, whether law reform or anything to do with the regicides who had killed his king. Given the commitments of this powerful 17th century governor, it is little surprise that Virginia did not print its laws until the early 1800's. Even then, it did so only after a search of official records by Thomas Jefferson revealed their decrepit state. It so mortified him, that he urged the remnant's preservation in print. This resulted in the collection known popularly today as Hening's *Statutes at Large*.[12]

But how did Massachusetts handle the interaction between advancing literacy and heresy? As is well known, heresy was not in short supply in Massachusetts. Shortly after the Court of Election in 1636, Governor Henry Vane, John Wheelwright, and Anne Hutchinson had challenged the colony's nascent Congregational system. All three belonged to Boston's congregation and allied themselves with Minister John Cotton against the rest of the colony's congregations. Soon after the outset, this theological struggle evolved into

12 Carla Pestana, *The English Atlantic in an Age of Revolution* (Cambridge: Harvard Univ. Press, 2004), 92–117. Warren Billings, *A Little Parliament: The Virginia General Assembly in the Seventeenth Century* (Richmond: Library of Virginia, 2004), 28–31, 132–38, 173–212. Samuel Fullerton, "New England in the Royalist Imagination," *English Historical Review* 137 (Oct., 2022): 1346–76. Edmund Morgan, *American Slavery, American Freedom* (New York: W.W. Norton & Co., 1975), 250–275. Elizabeth Eisenstein, *The Printing Press as an Agent of Change (Cambridge: Univ. Press, 1979)*, 1: 113–18. Michael Hattem, *Past and Prologue: Politics and Memory in the American Revolution* (New Haven: Yale Univ. Press, 2020), 102–103. "During the imperial crisis, Cromwell appeared in New England literature as a popular counterpoint to Anglicans' commemoration of the Stuarts and to the moderate approach of most colonial elites." William Hening, ed., *The Statutes at Large*, 11 vols., (New York: R.W.G. Bartow, 1823).

a contest for civil authority as the General Court was ultimately responsible for regulating the Congregational system. With Sir Henry Vane's[13] election as governor in the last election, the Antinomians had gained a powerful ally. Although Vane was a member of the English aristocracy and son of a Privy Councilor, he was a young man in his early twenties, and a precocious one at that. After his election, an intense ecclesiastical dispute erupted over the admission of new congregants. The debate's terminology was intricately complex. Generally stated, the controversy brought into question the standards of congregational membership, and especially an applicant's examination process that, if successful, provided admission to a congregation's covenant. To dilute the process would destroy the Congregational system, because without it there could be no select congregation; and since plenary colonial citizenship (including the right to vote and hold office in colonial government) depended upon church membership, a successful challenge to the Congregational order would undermine its civil government counterpart, perhaps fatally.[14]

---

13 Edward Hyde, *History of the Rebellion* (Oxford: Clarendon Press, 1826), 1: 326–7 (Bk. III, 1640). Vane had a "very ready, sharp, and weighty expression ... [that] made men think there was something in him extraordinary ... Within a very short time after ... his studies in Magdalen college, ... he lived not with great exactness, he spent some time in France, and more in Geneva. [A]fter his return into England, [he] contracted a full prejudice and bitterness against the [English] church, both against the form of government, and the liturgy ... In this giddiness, which then much displeased ... his father, who still appeared highly conformable, and exceedingly sharp against those who were not, he transported himself into New England, a colony within a few years before planted by a mixture of all religions ... He was no sooner landed there, ... being the son of a privy-counsellor, ... he was chosen their governor [and soon had] ill fortune, ... infusing a thousand scruples of conscience, which they had not brought over with them, or heard of before, that he unsatisfied ... transported himself [back] into England."

14 David Hall *The Puritans: A Transatlantic History* (Princeton: Princeton Univ. Press, 2019), 300–27. Michael Winship, *The Times and Trials of Anne Hutchinson* (Lawrence: Univ. Press of Kansas, 2005). Perry Miller, *The New England Mind* (New York: MacMillan Co., 1939), 57–59, 375–96. James Cooper, *Tenacious of their Liberties* (Oxford: Oxford Univ. Press, 1999), 46–67. Christopher Hill, *Liberty Against the Law* (London: Allen Lane 1996), 179–92, 214–226. Edmund Morgan, *The Puritan Dilemma*, 2nd ed., (Boston, Toronto: Little Brown, and Co., 1999), 119–37. Wes Harrison, "The Role of Women in Anabaptist Thought and Practice," *Sixteenth Century Journal* 23 (Spring, 1992): 49–56. Hutchinson's treatment was consistent with practices of radical sects on the continent in denying official roles of a congregation to women. If a woman testified to her faith, it was usually compelled testimony for some perceived transgression. Women were not supposed to take a leadership role in religious matters. Patrick Campbell, "The Concept of Representation in American Political Development: Lessons of the Massachusetts Bay Puritans," *Polity* 47 (Jan., 2015): 43–44. "The use of covenants underscores the Puritans' reliance on consent. As with religious covenants, consent was the necessary first element of a political covenant. Without consent, there is no way to establish the mutual obligations necessary

During the course of the year and a half long struggle Winthrop wrote, whenever "heresies or errors of any church members" became "manifest and dangerous to the state" the General Court would intervene, and not wait for a congregation to discipline its membership. Magistrates and deputies judged both John Wheelwright and Anne Hutchinson to be a "manifest" danger to the colony, as Governor Winthrop noted in his journal, "two so opposite parties could not contain in the same body without apparent hazard of ruin to the whole." Hutchinson claimed personal knowledge of God's intent and believed fervently that the divine will did not exclude anyone from congregational membership, or restrict the exploration of one's personal conscience. Essentially, neither the ministry nor the state could articulate God's will more accurately than her own "inner light," or conscience. During interrogation by colonial ministers Hutchinson famously damned the colony thus, "for this you go about to do to me God will ruin you and your posterity, and this whole state." She not only violated her station as a woman, by challenging the freemen's congregational authority she threatened the colony's government. After her brother-in-law, Minister John Wheelwright, had delivered a sermon repudiating the Congregational order, he was convicted of "contempt and sedition." Wheelwright threatened to appeal to English justice, "if he had committed sedition … he ought to be put to death, and if we did mean to proceed against him, he meant to appeal to the King." In 1635, Attorney General Sir John Banks had filed suit to revoke the colony's charter via a writ of quo warranto. Rumors foretold the arrival of a new royal governor at any moment. Undaunted, the General Court denied Wheelwright's appeal.[15]

---

to political order … Respect for consent was long established in English thought." *The Church Covenant, Publications of the Colonial Society of Massachusetts* (Boston: CSM 1960), (https://archive.org/details/colonialsocietyo39colo/page/4).

15 Richard Dunn, et al., eds., *Journal of John Winthrop: 1630–1649* (Cambridge: Belknap Press, 1996), 193–97 (Oct., 1636), 214–220 (May 1637), 228–35 (August 1637), 239–44 (Nov. 1637). Shurtleff, ed., *MGCR*, 1: 195 (May 1637); 205–13 (Nov., 1637). John Winthrop, *A Short Story of the Rise, reign, and ruine of the Antinomians, Familists and Libertines, that infected the Churches of New England* (London: Feb. 19, 1644), 23–39; *Thomason Tracts* E33 (16), Reel 6. Edward Johnson, *Wonder Working Providence of Sion's Saviour* (London: 1654; reprint; Andover: Warren Draper, 1867), 106. William Hubbard, *A General History of New England* (Boston: Little & Brown, 1848), 283–85. "After a long agitation with her, she was pressed to declare her mind in the manner of God's dealing with her … [S]he expressed herself in a way of immediate revelation: … that the Lord spoke … to her, with a strong hand." Michael Winship, *The Times and Trials of Anne Hutchinson*, 106–14. Winship recounts Hutchinson's spirited defense gave Winthrop, Dudley, and the other magistrates all they could handle. Malcolm Gaskill, *Between Two Worlds: How the English Became Americans*, 144–46. "Hutchinson's story is only part American, for her beliefs were formed in England. Puritanism did not fragment in the wilderness; it was already fractured and defined by

Ultimately, in May 1637, Henry Vane lost the governorship to Winthrop in an election marred by riotous behavior, signaling the end of the crisis as far as leadership of the government was concerned. Wheelwright was banished along with Hutchinson and Boston's General Court deputies, William Aspinwall and John Coggeshall, the latter two having already been dismissed from the Court. Once deputies and magistrates had ordered the assorted banishments in November 1637, they enacted legislation illustrative of the historic enmity between Antinomians and Protestants:

> Whereas the opinions and revelations of Mr. Wheelwright and Mrs. Hutchinson have seduced and led into dangerous errors many of the people here in New England, in so much as there is just cause of suspicion that they, *as others in Germany in former times may*, upon some revelation, make some sudden eruption upon those that differ from them in judgment. [F]or prevention whereof, it is ordered, that all those whose names are underwritten shall (upon warning given or left at their dwelling houses) before the 30th day of this month of November, deliver in at Mr. Cane's house at Boston all such guns, pistols, swords, powder, shot, and match as they shall be owners of, or have in their custody, upon pain of ten pounds for every default to be made.

Subsequently, the Court ordered approximately sixty men to be disarmed.[16]

---

stress. Godly congregations believed in autonomy, but they never agreed on the balance between personal self-regulation … and external moderation." *The Quo Warranto of 1635*, in *New England Historical and Genealogical Register* (Boston: 1884), 48: 209–16.

16 Richard Dunn, ed., *Journal of John Winthrop*, 239–51 (Nov. 1637-March 1638). Nathaniel Shurtleff, ed., *MGCR*, 1: 205 (*Aspinwall, Coggeshall dismissed from General Court*, (Nov., 1637)), 1: 207 (*Hutchinson, Wheelwright, Aspinwall, and Coggeshall banished from the colony* (Nov., 1637)), 1: 211 (Nov. 20, 1637). Bernard Bailyn, *The Barbarous Years*, 451–56. Philip Gura, *A Glimpse of Sion's Glory: Puritan Radicalism in New England, 1620–1660* (Middletown, [CT]: Wesleyan Univ. Press, 1984), 49–92, 77–8. "One of the most unexplored aspects of radical Puritan ideology in New England is … the relationship of church and state, for implicit in his arguments, as it was in the spiritism of Hutchinson, [Roger] Williams, and the Baptists, was the priority of the Spirit over the demands and restrictions of human law. Moderate Puritans rightly believed this notion would open the way to civil as well as ecclesiastical anarchy. There has been little recognition among historians apart from a few remarks on the disarming of the Hutchinsonians, of the effect of radical spiritist ideas upon political ideology in New England, shown not only in criticisms of the civil magistrate's interference in religious matters, but also in a radically egalitarian view of society rooted in the belief that the indwelling of Christ obliterates all artificial distinctions among men. Considering the upheaval in England over the demands of the Levellers and Diggers, we should be more alert."

Whereas in England, reading itself was made the target of control, this did not occur in Massachusetts. Instead, the colonists sought to suppress heretical views by stripping those who held them of residence in the colony, or political rights and weapons. Massachusetts government based its response to the Antinomian's near insurrection on the radical faith's often referenced sixteenth-century history. The allusions to "others in Germany" and "sudden eruptions" referred to the sect's riotous uprisings on the Continent, and especially the one that occurred in the city of Münster. Massachusetts Antinomians were suspected to be in league with European Anabaptists, infamous for their violent radicalism in opposition to the mainstream Protestant practice of infant baptism. The Anabaptist revolt in Münster that occurred in 1535 ultimately became an infamous harbinger of the creed's murderous intentions. Before violence had broken out, the city was undergoing a reform program via civil ordinance typical of Protestant cities in Germany. But Anabaptists viewed a state's involvement in religion as "satanic," based on their belief that true faith could not be coerced. In turn, the English theologian Richard Hooker charged that in placing Christ in "dominion over all," with "all crowns and scepters … thrown down at his feet," the sect's true aim was to undermine authority by overturning the seats of "magistracy." Essentially, antinomianism was equated with insurrectionism and libertinism.[17]

Initially, Münster's Anabaptists threw the city's Lutheran reform movement into chaos by challenging the mainstream Protestant practice of baptizing infants, and its administration of the communion sacrament. Generally, during these earliest decades of the Protestant Reformation, the faithful were certain there was one true faith and scriptural interpretation of the Bible. Therefore, even a suggestion of divergent practices could quickly evolve into a seditious indictment of civil authority. After the Anabaptist leadership had gained a majority on the municipal council in early 1534, non-conformists were either expelled from the city or killed. Itinerant preachers helped swell the city's population by promoting a millenarian event, drawing thousands, but promising ten times that number. Jan Matthijs, the first Baptist leader, was killed (and his

17 Edward Johnson, *Wonder Working Providence*, 99. Richard Hooker, *Of the Laws of Ecclesiastical Polity*, Arthur McGrade ed., 43–4. Michael Winship, *Making Heretics: Militant Protestantism and Free Grace in Massachusetts, 1636–1641* (Princeton: Princeton Univ. Press, 2002), 166–87. Stephen Foster, "New England and the Challenge of Heresy, 1630 to 1660: The Puritan Crisis in Transatlantic Perspective," *William and Mary Quarterly* 38 (1981): 631, 643–47. Philip Gura, *A Glimpse of Sion's Glory*, 54–5, 93–5, 103, 115–16. William McLoughlin, *Soul Liberty* (Hanover: Brown Univ. Press, 1991), 4–21. Francis Bremer, *John Winthrop*, 338–40.

body mutilated) when twelve of his disciples accompanied him through the city gates to challenge the besieging forces, apparently in hopes of a messianic miracle, but simply a telling act of their desperate situation. Subsequently, Jon Beukelsz, a tailor from a nearby city known to history as John of Leyden, who had left his trade to open a "bawdy" tavern in Münster, became the uprising's popular leader. During "King John's" sixteen-month reign "Catholic icons were destroyed, and pictures, books, documents, and musical instruments were burned in the marketplace," while "valuable metals" were seized. The Bible would be the "guide for the community," and ordinances were enacted abolishing private property and legalizing polygamy. The Anabaptists remained in control of the city for a little over a year until troops of the Holy Roman Empire overwhelmed the city's defenses and slaughtered most of its remaining inhabitants.[18]

Even by the next century the Münster rebellion was memorialized as a libertine violation of every moral norm, religious and secular, of the western world. A 1644 English pamphlet detailed the city's overthrow by Anabaptists who thought it "lawful for the people to depose their magistrates." After whipping up a frenzy over infant baptism, they seized neighbors' possessions with "violent hands," took a "choice of wives," and "violated the laws as well human as divine." Ultimately, John of Leyden crowned himself king of a "New Jerusalem," married ten or more self-appointed queens, confiscated goods in the name of the citizenry, and declared his fulfillment of the second coming. To mainstream Protestants these events manifested sectarianism's inevitable

18 John Calvin, *The Institutes of the Christian Religion* (Geneva, 1559; reprint, Henry Beveridge trans., Grand Rapids [MI]: WM. B. Erdmann's Co., 1989), 2: 554 (Bk. IV, Ch. XVI, §32). Calvin believed, "No sound man … can now doubt how rashly the Church is disturbed by those who excite quarrels … because of paedobaptism." Patrick Collinson, *The Reformation* (New York: Modern Library, 2004), 65–83. With the end of the siege, "King Jan and other leaders were tortured with red-hot tongs, and executed, and their bodies were hung in cages suspended from the church tower." Friedrich Reck-Malleczewen, *A History of the Münster Anabaptists*, George B. von der Lippe trans., (New York: MacMillan, 2008), xxii–xxiv, 7–31, 39–43. "The Anabaptist movements were by no means restricted to Münster but found adherents and prophets in all German lands. Some were more radical than others, some were more militant than others. All of them, however, thought they were the chosen few and all of them were more or less brutally persecuted." Gary Waite, "The Anabaptist Movement in Amsterdam and the Netherlands, 1531–1535," *Sixteenth Century Journal* 18 (Summer, 1987): 249–65. Amsterdam had become a refugee center for separatists, including America's Pilgrims. After the Münster uprising, Amsterdam Anabaptists planned a similar event spurred on by refugees from the failed rebellion there (but it did not ultimately happen). Well over 60% of the movement were artisans whom Waite portrays as mostly economically displaced. Michael Winship, *Making Heretics: Militant Protestantism and Free Grace in Massachusetts, 1636–1641*, 22–27, 179–91.

outcome to be a libertine induced anarchy. In Massachusetts, Edward Johnson acknowledged the "opinion of many in these days of Reformation that all sorts of sectaries ... should be tolerated by civil government." But the Antinomian furor had convinced Massachusetts freemen to "practice otherwise," as "*every man will most favor his own way of profession and labor tooth and nail to maintain it.*" Under title, *Anabaptists*, Massachusetts' first law book issued in 1648 memorialized the lesson: "experience hath plentifully and often proved that since the first arising of Anabaptists about a hundred years past they have been the incendiaries of Commonwealths and the infectors of persons in the main matters of religion ... [D]iverse of this kind have since our coming into New-England appeared amongst ourselves ... whereof as others before them have denied the Ordinance of Magistracy."[19]

While Protestants rebelled from what Johnson termed the "deceivable doctrines" of the Roman Church, undisciplined interpretation of scripture, fired by the era's intense religious fervor, continued to threaten civil peace. In order to avoid anarchy, the state must regulate religion. Upon Anne Hutchinson's arrival in Rhode Island her activities soon shocked Bay colonists anew when, according to Winthrop, Anne presided over her own congregation, her sister became "infected with Anabaptism," Roger Williams had himself re-baptized, and the group "would have no magistrates." Winthrop warned, "By these examples we may see how dangerous it is to slight the censure of the church; for it was apparent that God had given them up to strange delusions." Or as Minister William Hubbard foretold, Hutchinson "walked by such a rule as cannot stand with the peace of any State or Church, ... upon such a foundation were built the tragedies of Münster and other places, and might also be in America, if ... they who are above reason and Scripture will be subject to no control."[20]

---

19 *Mock-Majesty: Or, The Siege of Münster* (London: Feb. 24, 1644), 4–15; *Thomason Tracts* E270 (50), Reel 145. Richard Dunn, ed., *Laws and Liberties of 1648*, 1–2, title *Anabaptists.* Nathaniel Shurtleff, ed., *MGCR*, 1: 211 (Nov., 1637). Edward Johnson, *Wonder Working Providence*, 11. Carla Pestana, "The City upon a Hill under Siege," *New England Quarterly* 56 (Sept. 1983): 335–39. Christopher Hill, *The Century of Revolution* (Edinburgh: Thomas Nelson, 1961), 143 (n. 1). Michael Winship, *The Times and Trials of Anne Hutchinson*, 36–38, 112–13. Alister McGrath, *Reformation Thought*, 2nd ed., (Oxford: Blackwell, 1993), 203–205. Of the two main Protestant reform movements, one was a conservative "magisterial" reformation pursuing reform via civil ordinance, while the other was a radical movement that "regarded the swearing of oaths, the use of coercive force, and the authority of the magistrate as satanic." Phillip Gura, *A Glimpse of Sion's Glory: Puritan Radicalism in New England, 1620–1660*, 93–95.

20 Edward Johnson, *Wonder Working Providence*, 91. Richard Dunn, ed., *Journal of John Winthrop*, 286–87 (March-April 1639). William Hubbard, *A General History of New*

Although the consistency of Congregational theology is often emphasized in scholarship, the synod of colonial ministers' deliberations upon John Cotton's ministry in the wake of the crisis included the review of eighty-two theological "errors" at large in the colony. Ever more radical religious beliefs were being imported via new immigrants, in addition to religious tracts from England. After the disestablishment of the Anglican Episcopacy in the 1640's, and repeal of religious uniformity, radical religiosity erupted across England for the rest of the decade. If the political echelon of freemen ever ceased to exist in Massachusetts, each town congregation would be independent of civil oversight. Without civil control colonists could adopt whatever religious beliefs each membership chose, and congregations might embrace separatism, causing potentially even greater anarchy than had occurred during the Antinomian Crisis, endangering the colony's very existence. Michael Winship has cautioned that the Court's condemnation of Hutchinson's and Wheelwright's allies as poised to "reenact the bloody apocalyptic reign of King John of Münster" may seem "paranoid," but "it should not be underestimated how culturally normative fear of Münster was."[21]

One of the central figures of the crisis was a leading congregational minister, John Cotton, who had recently left England as one of its most famous churchmen. Despite his initial willingness to be allied with Wheelwright and Hutchinson in their struggle for the legitimacy of personal conscience, paradoxically he emerged as the magistrates' most consistent defender. As a member of the second law committee appointed by the General Court, to "make a

*England*, 285. Hubbard's history of Massachusetts was written in the latter half of the 1600's. Stephen Foster, "New England and the Challenge of Heresy, 1630 to 1660," 641.

21 Edmund Morgan, *The Puritan Dilemma*, 2nd ed., 152. Richard Dunn, ed., *Journal of John Winthrop*, 232 (August 1637). *Questions of the Elders*, *MHS Proceedings* (1912/13), 46: 275–76. John Winthrop, *A Short Story of the Rise, Reign, and Ruine of the Antinomians, Familists and Libertines* (London: Feb. 19, 1644), 1–17; *Thomason Tracts* E33 (16), Reel 6. Michael Winship, *Making Heretics: Militant Protestantism and Free Grace in Massachusetts, 1636–1641* (Princeton: Princeton Univ. Press, 2002), 1–11, 83–165. Darren Staloff, *The Making of an American Thinking Class* (Oxford: Oxford Univ. Press, 1998), 40–142. Philip Gura, *A Glimpse of Sion's Glory Puritan Radicalism in New England, 1620–1660*, 20–21, 49–77. James Cooper, *Tenacious of Their Liberties* (Oxford: Oxford Univ. Press, 1999), 46–67, 88–114. Leonard Levy, *Ranters Run Amok*, 33–51. Michael Winship, *The Times and Trials of Anne Hutchinson*, 119–20. "Deputy Governor Dudley, while in England, once shared a bed in an inn with a man who started talking about his revelations. Dudley's thoughts turned to Münster, and, dreading being murdered in his sleep, he moved to another room." William Hubbard, *General History of New England*, 553. Dudley's epitaph read, "I was no libertine." Bernard Bailyn, *The Barbarous Years*, 429–31. Bernard Bailyn added, "To mention Germany, or Münster, … and possible revelations from God was to conjure up scenes of social turmoil, ultimately carnage."

draught of laws agreeable to the word of God which may be the fundamentals of this commonwealth," Cotton's committee presented a draft proposal in the midst of the crisis. The result, *Moses His Judicials*, has been used as the definitive example of a Bible Commonwealth that historians have employed to describe colonial Massachusetts (and with some reason). But this does not shed much light on the *Judicials* itself. It was far more sophisticated than simply a verbatim copy of Mosaic law. Such interpretations oversimplify not only the *Judicials*, but also principles guiding the application of biblical authority to positive law during this era.[22]

In 1643, Cotton authored a short treatise on biblical law as it applied in the colony. He reflected the era's traditional belief that scripture provided insight into natural law, which in turn indicated needful regulations for all human societies. Some biblical laws of Israel were "temporary, and only bound them during the time of the Old Testament," like laws having "special respect ... to the land of Canaan." Although this type of biblical law from ancient Israel was not suitable for contemporary times, others such as the *Ten Commandments* continued to operate "for-ever." Protestant interpretations of natural law had sixteenth-century origins, and came to be referred to as "Christian liberty" which, as Nicholas Tyacke has explained, was a "half-way house between the tyranny of the Roman Catholics and the 'licentious liberty' of the Anabaptists." This moderated faith was further refined by the application of natural law as informed by the commandments and the teachings of Christ. As Tyacke concluded, "Hence the validity of all human laws depended on their demonstrable biblical underpinning, and it followed that true Christians were morally obliged actively to resist injustice in every form." Thus, Massachusetts responded to

22 *Moses His Judicialls*, in *Hutchinson Papers*, ed. William Whitmore, (Albany: Prince Society, 1865), 1: 183–205. The titles of its ten chapters are: 1. *Of Magistrates* 2. *Of free burgesses* [*i.e., freemen*] *and free Inhabitants*; 3. *Of the Protection and Provision of the Country*; 4. *Of the Right of Inheritance*; 5. *Of Commerce*; 6. *Of Trespasses*; 7. *Of Crimes*; 8. *Of Other Crimes Less Heinous*; 9. *Of the Trial of Causes, Civil or Criminal*; and 10. *Of causes Criminal Between Our People and Foreign Nations*. Nathaniel Shurtleff, ed., *MGCR*, 1: 174 (May 25, 1636). Richard J. Ross, "Distinguishing Eternal from Transient Law: Natural Law and the Judicial Law of Moses," *Past and Present* 217 (November 2012): 79–115 @ 85. "Mosaic legalists divided the judicial laws into two groups as the first step towards figuring out which rules still applied. Ordinances of 'particular equity' prescribed 'justice according to the particular estate and condition of the Jews Commonwealth' ... By contrast, precepts of 'common' or 'general' equity continue to bind in the present day because they were made 'according to the law or instinct of nature common to all men'" and confirmed "any of the ten precepts of the Decalogue." Edmund Morgan, *The Puritan Dilemma*, 2nd ed., 129–31, 146–49. George Haskins, *Law and Authority in Early Massachusetts*, 123–26. David Hall, *A Reforming People*, 29–34, 99, 148. Bernard Bailyn, *The Barbarous Years*, 438–43.

heterodoxy through doctrine, not restrictions on reading. The doctrinal battles in Massachusetts presaged those that would then later unfold in England, as more colonists would return home from 1640 to 1660 than new immigrants settled in the colony, including key figures like Nathaniel Ward, Israel Stoughton, and Richard Saltonstall, Jr.[23]

After his expulsion from the House of Deputies for supporting Anne Hutchinson during the Antinomian crisis, and a brief sojourn in in Rhode Island, William Aspinwall ultimately returned to England and became a leading pamphleteer of the Fifth Monarchists. Based on the monarchists' literal reading of passages from the *Book of Daniel,* they believed in the imminent return of Christ, and a violent one if necessary:

> Within a few months of his arrival … he published *A Brief Description of the Fifth Monarchy*, in which he argued that the only laws binding the saints were those legislated by God and recorded in the Bible. He urged earthly rulers—who were to be chosen by all the people from those who were full church members—not to administer laws that mixed earthly expediency with divine wisdom but simply to institute and enforce the divine standards available in Scripture … In the … pamphlet [*Thunder from Heaven* (1657)] he paid a debt to [John Cotton] by chastising [Massachusetts] colonists for not having adopted *Moses His Judicials*, which Aspinwall had gotten republished.[24]

---

23 John Cotton, *How Far Moses His Judicialls Bind Mass[achusetts]* (1643), *MHS Proceedings* (Second Series/1902), 16: 280–84. Nicholas Tyacke, "The Puritan Paradigm of English Politics," *Historical Journal* 53 (no. 3, 2010): 529–31. Howard Schweber, "Ordering Principles: The Adjudication of Criminal Cases in Puritan Massachusetts, 1629–1650," *Law and Society Review* 32 (no.2, 1998): 370–71. William Sachse, "The Migration of New Englanders to England, 1640–1660," *American Historical Review* 53 (Jan., 1948): 251–78.

24 Philip Gura, *A Glimpse of Sion's Glory*, 138–140. Perez Zagorin, *A History of Political Thought in the English Revolution* (1954; reprint, New York: Humanities Press, 1966), 96–105. The Fifth Monarchists practiced "a millenarian Utopianism, developed after 1649 … [as] the last wave of a burning social protest which the Revolution set in motion. The evils they would sweep away—tithes, the oppression of the rich, corrupt lawyers—were those denounced by the left wing," but they remained "unsecularized." J.F. Maclear, "New England and the Fifth Monarchy: The Quest for the Millennium in Early American Puritanism," *William and Mary Quarterly* 32 (Apr., 1975): 238–58. *An Abstract of the Laws of New England*, in William Whitmore, ed., *Hutchinson Papers*, ed. William Whitmore, (Albany: Prince Society, 1865), 1: 183–205, 183 (n. 119). This is the draft of the *Judicials* taken to England by Aspinwall.

In January 1661, Venner's Rising signaled the Fifth Monarchists' final gambit, when fewer than one hundred men-at-arms rampaged through London's streets and alleyways for several days in an attempt to overthrow Charles II (1660–1685) in the name of "King Jesus." The King's leading minister, the 1st Earl of Clarendon, described its leader, Thomas Venner, as "a zealot returned from New England."[25]

While Massachusetts' struggle with radical sectarians was soon replicated in England on a national scale, erupting in the late 1640's and persisting throughout the 1650's, doing great damage to Parliament's and Cromwell's attempts to govern, its own Antinomian crisis greatly enhanced the standing of the conservative faction of colonial leadership. Governor Winthrop emerged as Congregationalism's most vigilant defender, and he regained much of the support he had lost during earlier struggles over taxation. Moreover, he now had an example of the divine vengeance that would fall upon any challenge to the magistracy, justifying their right to, after election, govern the colony as they saw fit. Concomitantly, New England's novel system of worship became a potential model in London for a new church system, but soon fell out of favor amongst those known as "independents" who supported no set system beyond freedom of conscience; the Levellers would emerge from this faction later in the decade. Winthrop himself did not hesitate to seize upon the potent example of the consequences of undermining the magistracy during future controversies.[26]

---

25 T.H. Lister, *Life and Administration of Edward, Earl of Clarendon* (London: Longman, 1838), 2: 61–65.

26 Nathaniel Shurtleff, ed., *MGCR*, 1: 207 (Nov. 2, 1637). Carla Pestana, *The English Atlantic in the Age of Revolution: 1640–41* (Cambridge: Harvard Univ. Press, 2004), 59–80. Edmund Morgan, *The Puritan Dilemma*, 2nd ed., 122–31, 141–44. David Hall, *The Puritans*, 237. The "'Antinomian Controversy' anticipated the confusion that overtook the Puritan movement in 1640s England." Michael Winship, *The Times and Trials of Anne Hutchinson*, 119–20. Bernard Bailyn, *The Barbarous Years*, 429–31. "[T]hey were haunted by the common memory of the devastation of Münster a century earlier, when tens of thousands of Anabaptist zealots, led by a Dutch tailor who claimed authority directly from God, had instituted rule by the saints, abolished property, and sanctioned polygamy—only to be slaughtered en masse by enraged armies encouraged by Luther himself." John Winthrop, *A Short Story of the Rise, Reign, and Ruine of the Antinomians, Familists and Libertines, that Infected the Churches of New England* (London, 1644), 42. The General "Court did clearly discern, where the fountain was of all our distempers, and the Tragedy of Munster (to such as had read it) gave just occasion to fear the danger we were in, seeing (by the judgment of Luther writing of those troublous times) we had not to do with so simple a Devil, as managed that business, … to use his utmost cunning to undermine the Kingdom of Christ here (as the same Luther foretold)." Robert Wall, "The Membership of the General Court," 350–52. Francis Bremer, *John Winthrop*, 351.

Finally, the nexus between reading and radicalism raised political, as well as sectarian, problems. As we have seen, while Massachusetts' dissemination of printed law was very much in the spirit of Protestantism, it did not reflect official English practice. Although in England initiatives were made from the early 1500's to disseminate English law beyond the King's courts, royal officers, and the Inns of Court, an official statutory edition authorized by Parliament was not realized until the nineteenth century, and only in the latter half of that century did the state provide statutory law publications to public libraries. Until then, access to reading the law was privileged by social and political rank, and the cost of grammar school and university education, to include residence at the Inns of Court.

Here, too, as in the case of religious sectarianism, a notable difference opens up in terms of how radicalism was handled in the two legal contexts. In England, Common Law operated within the kingdom, but its administration was largely an oral regime of pleadings exclusively before its courts and justices that existed alongside the crown's prerogative courts (e.g., Star Chamber), with proclamations, warrants and other methods of governance available to the monarch to deal with all sorts of exigencies. Social control was achieved through a structure of deputies from the King. Consider this 1551 proclamation issued by Edward VI (1547–1553):

> I would wish ... the superfluous and tedious statutes were brought into one sum together and made more plain and short, to the intent that men might the better understand them, which I think shall much help to advance the profit of the commonwealth. Nevertheless, when all these laws be made, established, and enacted, they serve to no purpose except they be fully and duly executed. By whom? By those that have authority to execute [them]. That is to say, the noblemen and justices of peace. Wherefore I would wish that after this Parliament were ended, the noblemen, except a few that should be with me, went to their counties and there should see the statutes fully and duly executed.[27]

27 W.K. Jordan, ed., *The Chronicle and Political Papers of King Edward VI* (Ithaca: Cornell Univ. Press, 1966), 166–67. Anthony Fletcher, *Reform in the Provinces* (New Haven: Yale Univ. Press, 1986). Cynthia Herrup, "Law and Morality in Seventeenth-Century England," *Past and Present* 106 (1985): 102–23. J.S. Cockburn, *A History of English Assizes: 1558–1714* (Cambridge: Cambridge Univ. Press, 1972). Wilfrid Prest, "Legal Education of the Gentry at the Inns of Court, 1560–1640," *Past and Present* 38 (1967): 20–39.

While the intent of the proclamation sounds benign, even benevolent, it was issued in the wake of uprisings that had erupted in 1549 concentrated in the county of Norfolk, in East Anglia, where the vast majority of Massachusetts' first settlers originated, commanding the enforcement arm of the King's law, the landed gentry, to police their own counties. Beginning in Norfolk, demonstrations against avaricious governance had led to scattered riots protesting the enclosure of fields and high rents, and the rebels eventually appealed to Edward VI's Protector, the Duke of Somerset, hoping for a fair review of their grievances. However, the very members of the gentry they hoped the crown would intercede with on their behalf were the same men who enforced the law on behalf of the crown:

> We pray that your grace to give license and authority by your gracious commission under your great seal to such commissioners as your poor commons hath chosen, or to as many of them as your majesty and your council shall appoint and think meet, for to redress and reform all such good laws, statutes, proclamations, and all other your proceedings, which hath been hidden by your justices of your peace, sheriffs, escheators, and other your officers from your poor commons, since the 1st year of the reign of your noble grandfather King Henry VII. [28]

By the time Edward's Proclamation issued in 1551, the rebellions had been suppressed by the Earl of Warwick, who, after succeeding Somerset on the Privy Council, had led the avenging army (with a significant mercenary contingent) to restore order. His annihilation of the rebel forces entailed a bloody aftermath of thousands of casualties, including approximately 300 executions, with some of the local gentry demanding more! The rebellion's namesake, Robert Kett (a member of the lesser gentry himself, selected leader by happenstance), was convicted of high treason and hung "in chains from Norwich castle," while his brother William shared a similar fate from the tower of a nearby abbey. Both were gruesome warnings to the county's remaining inhabitants made by a leadership fearful of any large scale rising that might march on London.[29]

28 *The Demands of the Rebels Led by Ket* (1549), in A.E. Bland, P.A. Brown, and R.H. Tawney, eds., *English Economic History: Select Documents* (New York: MacMillan Co., 1919), 247 @ 250 (#8). Andy Wood, *The 1549 Rebellions and the Making of Early Modern England* (Cambridge: Cambridge Univ. Press, 2007), 55–82.

29 Jane Whittle, "Lords and Tenants in Kett's Rebellion 1549," *Past and Present* 207 (2010): 3–52. Ethan Shagan, "Protector Somerset and the 1549 Rebellions," *English Historical Review* 114 (1999): 34–63. Andy Wood, *The 1549 Rebellions and the Making of Early Modern England*, 55–82. Alan Taylor, *American Colonies* (New York: Penguin Books, 2001), 160–70.

Colonial Massachusetts' first governor, John Winthrop, was representative of England's gentry class whose duty was to "keep the King's peace" in the local shires and counties through offices like the Justice of the Peace. Winthrop has enjoyed an historical reputation as a fair man and effective governor, as his steady leadership held the colony's government (and people) together through its first tumultuous years. As a justice of the peace (JP), judge on the Court of Wards, and lord of Groton manor, Winthrop would oppose commoners' active participation in government, consistent with his experience and English tradition. Recently Daniel Mandell has described his role in law enforcement, "Winthrop, like most Englishmen, assumed that his country's prosperity depended on the stability of this hierarchy, and those with power and property enforced that presumption."[30]

To some, the colony's commitment to the spread of literacy seemed antithetical to the traditional strategy for maintaining order. Nathaniel Ward, who had traveled the continent and studied English law before being condemned for non-conformity and sailing to Massachusetts, worried that publication of the laws would undermine them. Upon the General Court's order to distribute drafts of proposed liberties to the colony's towns, Ward warned Winthrop of a rising populist tide:

> I have [an] ... earnest request, ... [t]hat you would advise ... the [standing] council whether it will not be of ill consequence to send the [General] Court business to the common consideration of the freemen. I fear it will too much *exauctorate* the power of that Court to prostrate matters in that manner. I suspect both Commonwealth and Churches have descended too low already. I see the spirits of the people run high, and what they get they hold. They may not be denied their proper and lawful liberties, but I question whether it be of God to interest the inferior sort in that which should be reserved *inter optimates penes quos est sancire*.[31]

---

A.G. Dickens, *The English Reformation*, 2nd ed., 221. "Kett's revolt in Norfolk, significantly from the first in the hands of laymen, produced a strongly anticlerical manifesto and, though essentially a revolt against enclosures, had a Protestant flavor in so far as it took notice of religious issues ... In short, this was not a revolt against the Protestant government, the policies of which it approved, but against the Norfolk gentry. It did not march on London but concentrated upon rectifying the regional situation."

30 Daniel Mandell, *The Lost Tradition of Economic Equality in America: 1600–1870*, 7–10.

31 *Nathaniel Ward to John Winthrop* (Dec. 22, 1639), in Adam Winthrop, Fitz-John Winthrop, and Waitstill Winthrop, eds., *Winthrop Papers* (Boston: MHS, 1924–1945), 4: 162–3. Cited hereafter as *Winthrop Papers*. Nathaniel Shurtleff, ed., *MGCR*, 1: 279, 292, 340, 344. Francis Bremer, *John Winthrop*, 67–123. S.E. Morison, *Builders of the Bay Colony* (New York: Houghton Mifflin, 1930), 51–54, 221–25. Roger Thompson, *Divided We Stand*,

On one hand, Ward feared the distribution of draft legislation to colonists would marginalize the authority of the General Court, and on the other he expressed his belief (memorialized in Latin) that law-making should be reserved to the "best people whose job it is to establish the laws." Generally, Ward recognized a growing radicalism amongst Bay colonists who, as represented by deputies in the legislature's lower house, did not cross a great ocean to be at the mercy of Old-World traditions of rule by religious or secular elites. In the spirit of Protestants' rejection of scholastic interpretation of scripture, this yeoman class of "freemen" would challenge the authority of Massachusetts' famed "godly" magistrates, demanding their participation in colonial government's enactment, interpretation, and administration of the law. Winthrop saw the dangers. As Stephen Foster recounted, similar circumstances must have weighed on Winthrop as he planned the voyage to Massachusetts prompting his famous remark, "'this land grows weary of her inhabitants,' as well as his less well-known warning of social war in England as bitter and as violent as the Peasants' War had been in Germany." The Peasants' War (1524–1525) had erupted across the Holy Roman Empire, in the geographical area of today's Germany, which was still very much a feudal territory divided into various states, cities, and principalities, secular and religious. The professional militaries of the various polities made short work of the peasantry, and although hard to know with certainty, it appears that at least 100,000 peasants were killed during the war and a similar number perished of starvation or sickness in its aftermath. From such perspectives, for a traditional member of the English gentry to make such a comparison must alert the historical observer of the seriousness of the transformations English speaking peoples were undergoing during this era. And indeed, as the celebrated historian of the Reformation A.G. Dickens related, "Taking their cue from the quasi-Lutheran article of the German peasant-rebels of 1524–5, the Norfolk leaders [of Kett's] propounded their famous demand, 'We pray that all bondmen [i.e., serfs] may be made free, for God made all free with his precious blood-shedding.'"[32]

---

23. Alexander Chalmers, ed., *Samuel Johnson's Dictionary of the English Language*, 252. *Exauctorate*: "to dismiss from service."

32 Daniel Mandell, *The Lost Tradition of Economic Equality in America: 1600–1870*, 11–12. The "most important challenges were driven by the Reformation's rejection of Catholic hierarchy and power." Stephen Foster, *The Long Argument: English Puritanism and the Shaping of New England Culture (1570–1700)* (Chapel Hill: Univ. of North Carolina Press, 1991), 108–113. A.G. Dickens, *The English Reformation*, 2nd ed., 221. *The Demands of the Rebels Led by Ket* (1549), in Bland, et. al., eds., *English Economic History: Select Documents*, 249. "We pray that all bond men may be made free, for God made all free with his precious blood-shedding."

Considering the multiple crises of the 1630's, Winthrop made a wise decision in not trying to oppose the town freemen's review and consideration of the colony's new laws that would eventually become the *Body of Liberties of 1641*. Since 1635, the General Court had passed resolutions memorializing an intent to publish a body of colonial law, and for the magistrates to have reneged on their commitment at this point would have created another major crisis. Ultimately, Nathaniel Ward would become a leading supporter of publishing laws periodically, but even though he was the primary draftsmen of the *Body of Liberties*, at this point he feared the freemen's aggressive stance more than the magistrates' exercise of their own tradition-based authority.

# PART 2

## *Creating a Legal Authority in the "New World"*

CHAPTER 3

# No Taxation without Representation

Before any legal code could be promulgated to colonists, the nature of legal authority itself, and its operations, had to be established. None of these things were a given when the colony came into existence in 1630 except the very general and duplicative instructions in *Massachusetts Charter of 1629*; it included two forms of government (a council for the company's affairs and an initial group of governors and assistants who would oversee the selection of "freemen" to pass laws within the colony itself). Consequently, the story of the creation of *Laws and Liberties* is also a story about how legislative and judicial authorities within an institutional structure developed beyond the *Charter*. While English influences were many, it is also the case that the colonists undertook what was essentially a constituting project with significant independence and isolation. They functioned as another source of jurisprudential innovation during the remarkably fertile 17th century. This chapter, as well as the next several, will cover the key aspects of the conceptualization of legal authority that they developed. Notably, their work, as in other contexts, started from a need to determine questions about the authority to tax.[1]

As affairs stood in Massachusetts' new colonial government in 1631, by "show of hands" the freemen had agreed to meet every May to elect assistants, who would in turn elect the governor and the deputy governor, and the latter group of officials would administer colonial affairs. However, the assistants soon set off controversy in February 1632 upon authorizing a £60 tax to build a fort at Cambridge. According to Governor Winthrop, Pastor George Phillips and Elder Richard Brown led the resistance to its collection in Watertown, and upon assembling the people, they "delivered their opinions that it was not safe to pay monies after that sort, for fear of bringing themselves and posterity into *bondage*." As recounted in the governor's *Journal*, after being summoned to Boston and "much debate," Phillips and Brown withdrew their objections:

> The ground of their error was … that they took this government to be no other but as of a mayor and aldermen, who have not power to make laws or raise taxations without the people; but understanding that this government was rather in the nature of a Parliament, and that no assistant

1 Nathaniel Shurtleff, ed., *MGCR*, 1: 3–20 (March 1628/1629).

 | DOI:10.1163/9789004706347_005

> could be chosen but by the freemen, who had power likewise to remove the assistants and put in others, and therefore at every General Court (which was to be held once every year) they had free liberty to consider and propound anything concerning the same, and to declare their grievances … they were fully satisfied.[2]

David Hall has observed, because the "principle of consent on which every Parliament of the 1620s had insisted" was at the "heart" of the Watertown complaint, its "rhetoric … echoed … parliamentarians protesting the extraordinary levies of Charles I." Hall's interpretation of this colonial tax dust-up does not address why the Watertown protestors withdrew their objections on Winthrop's citation of English borough precedents. If taxation should only be levied by the consent of representatives in Parliament, and Watertown was objecting to not being included in the approval of the taxation, we must ask why the citation of parliamentary precedent resolved the incident. Especially considering that opposition to borough taxation was a common enough event in English locales. Why then would Phillips and Brown be silenced by the rhetoric of parliamentary dissent?[3]

Focusing on the "bondage" rhetoric included in the Watertown complaint will help us unravel the meaning of this exchange, and a deeper investigation of the event will help us uncover the genesis of the Massachusetts endeavor itself. Theophilius Clinton, Earl of Lincoln, employed similar rhetoric in his opposition to Charles I's attempts to tax without parliamentary consent.

---

2 Richard Dunn, ed., *Journal of John Winthrop: 1630–1649* (*Cambridge: Belknap Press, 1996*), 63, n. 69 (Jan.-Feb. 1632). Nathaniel Shurtleff, ed., *MGCR*, 1: 93 (Feb. 3, 1632). John Noble, ed., *Records of the Court of Assistants* (Boston: County of Suffolk, 1904), 2: 20. Edmund Morgan, *The Puritan Dilemma*, 2nd ed., (Toronto: Little, Brown, and Co., 1998), 86–97. Francis Bremer, *John Winthrop* (Oxford: Oxford Univ. Press, 2003), 211–12. James Cooper, Jr., *Tenacious of their Liberties* (Oxford: Oxford Univ. Press, 1998), 23–33. Roger Thompson, *Divided We Stand: Watertown Massachusetts, 1630–1680* (Amherst: Univ. of Massachusetts Press, 2001), 38–40. Robert Wall, *Massachusetts Bay: The Crucial Decade* (New Haven: Yale Univ. Press, 1972), 6–7. George Haskins, *Law and Authority in Early Massachusetts* (New York: Macmillan, 1960), 29–30. Charles Hilkey, *Legal Development in Colonial Massachusetts* (New York: Columbia Univ. Press, 1910), 15.

3 Richard Dunn, ed., *Journal of John Winthrop*, 63, n. 69 (Jan.-Feb. 1632). David Hall, *A Reforming People* (New York: Alfred A. Knopf, 2011), 26. Francis Bremer, *John Winthrop*, 141–50, 211–12. Roger Thompson, *Divided We Stand: Watertown Massachusetts, 1630–1680*, 20–42. Mark Kishlansky, *Parliamentary Selection* (Cambridge Univ. Press, 1986), 31–2. Edmund Morgan, *Puritan Dilemma*, 2nd ed., 95–97. J.P. Sommerville, "Ideology, Property, and the Constitution," in Richard Cust, Anne Hughes eds., *Conflict in Early Stuart England* (London: Longman, 1989), 47–61. James Savage, ed., *The History of New England*, 1: 14 (n. 1), 58 (n. 2). Philip Gura, *A Glimpse of Sion's Glory* (Middletown: Wesleyan Univ. Press, 1984), 31–37, 159.

Richard Cust has described Lincoln as a devout Puritan who represented "part of the peerage who saw the 'service of the commonwealth,' or 'country,' as their calling … and obligation to provide virtuous service to the state as a whole by striving to protect 'publick liberties' and the laws of the land." Lincoln, like a number of other peers, opposed the "Forced Loan" that Charles I's ministers tried to collect in the late 1620's, and he was ultimately imprisoned in the Tower of London, without trial, for his refusal to remit payment; the term itself was supposed to lessen opposition by implying it was a one-time "loan," rather than a new permanent tax. The Earl also distributed, and was the probable author of a pamphlet published in 1627 condemning the crown's collection of the loan:

> Beware and consider what you do concerning these subsidies and loans which are now demanded of you lest you give away not only your money, but your liberty and property in your own goods … If this course be not withstood, but take effect, we shall be ourselves the instruments of our own slavery and the loss of the privilege we have hitherto enjoyed, that our goods cannot be taken from us without consent of Parliament.[4]

Based on Lincoln's personal relationships with future leaders of Massachusetts, as well as the written correspondence of Thomas Dudley to the Countess of Lincoln (the Earl's wife, and daughter of Viscount Saye and Sele), Michael Winship has convincingly argued that the "Bay Company itself emerged out of agitation against the Forced Loan in Lincolnshire." Dudley had written the countess a detailed account of the colony itself as well as the effort to secure a charter from the crown for its settlement. There are several notable examples of Lincoln's associations with future colonial leaders: for example, Lincoln protected John Cotton when he ran afoul of the episcopacy before leaving for the New World (at the time Cotton was one of the most famous Puritan churchmen in England); another one of Lincoln's clients was Richard Bellingham, a future colonial governor and Member of the 1628 Parliament; and finally,

4 Earl of Lincoln, *To all English Freeholders from a Well-Wisher of Theirs* (Jan. 24, 1627), in Graham Seel, and David Smith, eds., *The Early Stuart Kings: 1603–1642* (London: Routledge, 2001), 63 (source 1). Richard Cust, *The Forced Loan and English Politics* (Oxford: Clarendon Press, 1987), 170–72. Richard Cust, *Charles I and the Aristocracy* (Cambridge: Cambridge Univ. Press, 2013), 51. Austin Woolrych, *Britain in Revolution, 1625–1660* (Oxford: Oxford Univ. Press, 2002), 53, 55. "The Tudor monarchs had quite often demanded forced loans from corporations and wealthy individuals, but in 1626 … [t]o the public at large it was indistinguishable from a large parliamentary grant, except Parliament had not granted it."

his estate steward, Thomas Dudley, would become the colony's first deputy governor, and longtime colonial magistrate. Upon his patron's arrest, Dudley took his place in organizing county resistance to the collection of the extra-parliamentary tax.[5]

Lincoln's seemingly overly dramatic invocation of slavery did not refer to the enslavement of African Americans, or to South or Central American native peoples then under Spanish subjugation. Instead, he was referring to an earlier period in English history when serfs or "villains" labored on the Lord's manor. Parliamentary resistance to taxation by Charles I was long remembered in Massachusetts. In his opinion of *Giddings v. Brown* (1657), Magistrate Samuel Symonds recalled that "in England it cannot be denied but that men's estates were sometimes unduly taken from them ... by force" and "by fraud," and sometimes even by the "law itself" during the days of "shipmoney," or Charles I's attempts to raise taxation without parliamentary consent. His policies had deprived Englishmen of their "greatest outward right or liberty," because though "Parliament may tax," taxation without its consent threatened the estates of "every man." In England, only "one sort of men" could "be deprived of their goods" in such a way. They were known as "slaves," or "villeynes to the lord of the manor." A pejorative linkage of slavery and serfdom had existed for centuries. At the beginning of the fourteenth century Andrew Horne described villeinage, or serfdom, as beyond the "memory of man." By the "law of nature all creatures ought to be free," but in reality, Englishmen had been "enslaved" like "birds in cages." By the eighteenth century, Samuel Johnson defined a slave

5 Michael Winship, *Godly Republicanism* (Cambridge: Harvard Univ. Press, 2012), 188–93, 309 (n. 19). "Thomas Dudley to Bridget, Countess of Lincoln" (March 12/28, 1631), in Everett Emerson, ed., *Letters from New England* (Amherst: Univ. of Mass. Press, 1976), 70–1. "Touching the Plantation which we here have begun, it fell out thus:-About the year 1627, some friends being together in Lincolnshire fell into some discourse on New England, and planting the gospel there, and after some deliberation we imparted our reasons by letters and messages to some in London and the West Country, where it was likewise deliberately thought upon, and at length with often negotiation so ripened that in the year 1628 we procured a patent from his majesty for our planting between the Matachusets Bay and the Charles River on the south and the river Merimack, ... also for the government of those who ... should inhabit" there. Francis Bremer, *John Winthrop*, 153–54, 243, 273, 312–15. Bernard Bailyn, *The Barbarous Years* (New York: Vintage Books, 2013), 389–93. Francis Bremer, *First Founders* (Durham: Univ. of New Hampshire Press, 2012), 64–70. "In June 1629 the Earl of Lincoln hosted a meeting ... where various groups ... gathered to lay the plans of the Massachusetts Bay Company." Michael Winship, *Hot Protestants* (New Haven: Yale Univ. Press, 2018), 75–77. S.E. Morison, *Builders of the Bay Colony* (Boston: Houghton Mifflin Company, 1930), 65–68.

as someone who was "mancipated," or enslaved, by a master. Such a person was a "dependent," not a "freeman."[6]

John Locke's *Second Treatise of Government* provides a valuable perspective on the evolution of this rhetoric by describing the "natural liberty of man … to be free from any superior power on earth," and the "liberty of man in society" could only be ensured by "no other legislative power but that established" by the consent of the commonwealth. Then people would not be "under the dominion of any will, or restraint of any law, but what the legislative shall enact." J.P. Sommerville has traced the origins of Locke's formulation to early seventeenth-century England: because personal liberty "depended on property in the literal sense, … to deprive a man of property in his goods was to reduce him to villeinage." The principal way to avoid such a calamity was to deputize representatives to ensure government did not tax a people beyond its means. If a monarch was able to tax at will, a yeoman's property would be devoured by government revenue's insatiable appetite; and at some point, it could not produce enough income for heirs, a dowry, the eligibility to vote, or even to ensure survival itself. Inevitably, yeomen overly taxed would be consigned to a virtual state of slavery. As Francis Bremer concluded, "clearly, English concerns about arbitrary taxation such as the so-called Forced Loan had been carried to the New World."[7]

6 *Giddings v. Brown* (1657), in *Hutchinson Papers*, ed. William Whitmore, (Albany: Prince Society, 1865), 2: 4–6. Michael Hattem, *Past and Prologue: Politics and Memory in the American Revolution* (New Haven: Yale Univ. Press, 2020), 98–99. David Konig, *Law and Society in Puritan Massachusetts* (Chapel Hill: Univ. of North Carolina Press, 1979), 93–5. Andrew Horne, *Mirrour of Justices* (Washington, D.C.: John Byrne & Co., 1903), 123 (Ch. 2, §28). Lorenzo Sabbadini, *Property, Liberty, and Self-Ownership in Seventeenth-Century England* (McGill-Queen's Univ. Press, 2020), 5–13. The "republican concept of liberty … is predicated on a dichotomy, originating in Roman law, between the free-man and the slave," and freedom is a "condition of non-subjection to arbitrary power." Johann P. Sommerville, "English and Roman Liberty in the Monarchical Republic of Early Stuart England," in John McDiarmid, ed., *The Monarchical Republic of Early Modern England* (London: Routledge, 2007), 212–214. "In English legal theory … villeins were bondmen. They were not personally free. Speaking in the Parliament of 1628, the lawyer John Selden asserted that the key 'difference in their persons' between 'villeins and freemen' was that freemen 'cannot be imprisoned at pleasure' while villeins can."

7 Peter Laslett, ed., *John Locke, Two Treatises of Government* (Cambridge: Cambridge Univ. Press, 1988), 283–84 (*Second Treatise*, Bk. 4 (Of Slavery), §22). J.P. Sommerville, *Politics and Ideology in England: 1603–1640* (London: Longman, 1986), 148–49. Glenn Burgess, *British Political Thought, 1500–1660* (New York: Palgrave Macmillan, 2009), 170–73, 326. "Some Independents and Levellers seem to have been reaching during the 1640's towards the conclusion that monarchy was incompatible with the liberty of free-born Englishmen, whom it inevitably reduced to slavery" if not "based on consent" of the governed. Tim Harris, *Rebellion: Britain's First Stuart Kings* (Oxford: Oxford Univ. Press, 2014), 25. "One had to own 40 shillings worth

So, to the original question, why did Winthrop's allusion to parliamentary representation overcome Watertown's objections to arbitrary government in the Court of Assistants' enactment of the £60 tax? After its resident magistrate Sir Richard Saltonstall returned to England in 1631, no other assistant lived in Watertown throughout most of the 1600's. When this factor is equated with contemporary English definitions of parliamentary representation, the rationale behind Winthrop's parliamentary model for settlement of the controversy becomes clear. According to Sir Thomas Smith, Parliament "representeth … the whole realm both the head and the body," because "every Englishmen is intended to be there present, either in person or by procuration of attorneys" or representatives. Therefore, "consent of the Parliament is taken to be every man's consent." Sir Edward Coke concurred, even "though he be chosen for one particular county or borough, yet when he … sit[s] in parliaments he serveth for the whole realm." Because king, lords, and commons represented the entire kingdom, Winthrop's reference allayed the fears of Watertown's freemen. Within the parliamentary model townsmen were still represented, even if an assistant did not reside within their town's precincts, as each assistant represented the entire colony. Nevertheless, as new towns were created by the General Court, and the Court of Assistants' membership continued to decline, freemen from the other towns realized Watertown's dilemma was becoming their own. Edward Rossitor died shortly after the Winthrop fleet landed. When Saltonstall, Sr., left the colony for England, assistants Thomas Sharpe and William Vassall joined him. Reverend Isaac Johnson, brother-in-law of the Earl of Lincoln and another original stockholder, succumbed to disease soon after landing. Edward Johnson (no relation) lamented the "death of that worthy personage" as the loss of a "chief pillar to support this new erected building." Afterwards, "many weeping eyes" and "fainting hearts" feared the "fall of the present work."[8]

---

of freehold land to vote in county elections." As a "result of inflation during the sixteenth century … perhaps as many as 27–40 per cent of adult males had the right to vote by 1640." Francis Bremer, *John Winthrop*, 180–81, 206–12.

8 Susan Moore, *Abandoning America* (Woodbridge: Boydell Press, 2013), 347 (Sir Richard Saltonstall, (1586–1658)). *MHS Collections: Third Series* (Boston: 1846), 9: 119–122. An original signee of the Massachusetts *Charter*, Saltonstall, Sr., left the colony upon experiencing his first winter. After his return to England, he continued to be a stalwart supporter of the colony, but later criticized congregationalism's membership criteria and supported the Quakers. Ultimately, he gained high office in the English Commonwealth. Thomas Smith, *De Republica Anglorum*, ed. Mary Dewar, (Cambridge: Cambridge Univ. Press, 1982), 79. Richard Dunn, ed., *Journal of John Winthrop*, 63–4. Shurtleff, ed., *MGCR*, 1: 16 (March 1629). John Noble, ed., *Records of the Court of Assistants*, 2: 12. Francis Bremer, *John Winthrop*, 193–95. Roger Thompson, *Divided We Stand*, 14, 40–41, 56–7. Edmund Morgan, *Puritan Dilemma*, 2nd ed., 54, 91–97.

Besides the well-known motivation of religious oppression that propelled colonists across the Atlantic, the latter 1620's was a time of historic political turbulence in England that saw the King's first minister, the Duke of Buckingham, assassinated in August 1628, and his murderer John Felton celebrated as an heroic foil to the rule of an unjust monarch. For several years Charles I had tried to cajole Parliament into providing new taxes, and even though additional revenue measures were enacted, more always seemed to be needed. From the mid-1620's it became a state-driven necessity based on military action James I (1603–1625) had initiated amidst the clamor of the more fervent Protestants in his kingdom; English Puritans had long demanded that he join the Protestant alliance fighting a powerful group of Catholic nations in the Thirty Years War (1618–1648). However, once engaged, Charles I and his first minister the Duke of Buckingham badly mis-managed a series of military campaigns to the level of criminal incompetence, resulting in a series of catastrophic defeats. Although Puritans viewed the war with Spain (1625–1630), soon to be followed by one with France (1627–1629), as existential struggles against Rome and its evil Papists, after Charles I's royal decree for the assembly of Parliament in 1626, its members refused to provide funds sufficient to support English land and sea forces without redress of the kingdom's domestic grievances. Summoned again for the same purpose in 1628, Parliament repeated its insistence that these national grievances be addressed first, especially in the wake of Charles I's authorization of extra-parliamentary taxation via a "Forced Loan." Members demanded in a *Petition of Right* that Englishmen not be "compelled to contribute to any tax ... not set by common consent in Parliament." While this historic document ultimately enshrined the principle that taxation is only legitimately authorized via the enactment of laws by a popularly elected body, its genesis derived from Charles I's summary imprisonment of subjects who refused to

---

Robert Wall, "The Membership of the Massachusetts General Court," (Ph.D. Diss., Yale Univ., 1965), 184, 258, 338, 454, 622–23. James Savage, ed., *History of New England* (Boston: Felps and Farnam, 1825), 1: 28 (n. 3). Richard Cust, "Politics and the Electorate in the 1620s," in R. Cust, and A. Hughes eds., *Conflict in Early Stuart England* (New York, London: Longman, 1989), 140–1. Edward Johnson, *Wonder Working Providence* (London, 1654; reprint, Andover: Warren Draper, 1867), 38. Richard Cust, *The Forced Loan and English Politics*, 172. Mark Kishlansky, *Parliamentary Selection*, 13–18. *Records of the Company of the Massachusetts Bay, Collections of the American Antiquarian Society* (1865), 3: lxvii–lxix. Johnson's burial plot became part of Boston's King's Chapel Burying Ground—with John Hampden named as one of the executors to his will. Hampden was an early supporter of colonization. Johnson's wife, daughter of the 3rd Earl of Lincoln, Theophilius Clinton, had died the month before.

pay taxes he thought necessary to defend his kingdom, but not approved by Parliament.[9]

The legality of the crown's "loan" was complicated by the foreign wars that Charles I thought compelled him to authorize it, rather than initially conceived solely to circumvent parliamentary authority. The King's letter of instructions for its collection began by repeating his summons of Parliament in 1626, which addressed both the "weighty affairs concerning the Church of England, and the defense and safety of the Kingdom." He had hoped Parliament would provide him supply, or tax revenue, "not for our own private use, but for the common safety of us our people." While Parliament's 1626 session had provided him some revenue to support the war effort, although withholding a traditional lifetime grant of import/export duties (i.e., tunnage and poundage), the funds authorized were so meager that Charles complained Parliament had failed to secure the "public defense of the Kingdom, for which they were specially called." Upon his dismissal of Parliament, Charles decreed that since his "people cannot be defended and maintained but is in imminent and apparent danger ... by a vigilant and powerful enemy," the loan had become an "*unavoidable necessity*" to defend his kingdom and wage war on Spain.[10]

---

9 *Petition of Right* (May 1628), in Robert Johnson, et.al., eds., *Commons Debates of 1628* (New Haven: Yale Univ. Press, 1977), 3: 339–41. Tim Harris, *Rebellion: Britain's First Stuart Kings*, 186–222, 252–78. Nicholas Tyacke, "Revolutionary Puritanism in Anglo-American Perspective," *Huntington Library Quarterly* 78 (Winter 2015): 753–56. Richard Cust, *The Forced Loan and English Politics*, 319. "War was mainly responsible for the financial pressures which so preoccupied Charles and his advisers and which had led to the adoption of the loan in the first place." George Johnson, ed., *The Fairfax Correspondence: Memoirs of the Reign of Charles I* (London: Richard Bentley, 1848), 1: 80–6. Kevin Sharpe, *Personal Rule of Charles I* (New Haven: Yale Univ. Press, 1992), 49. "John Felton ... claimed the Parliamentary Remonstrance [to redress grievances] as his inspiration and authority; leading Parliamentarians were connected with Felton and thinly veiled their support for his act." Richard Cust, *Charles I and the Aristocracy: 1625–1642*, 46–55. Conrad Russell, *The Causes of the English Civil War* (Oxford: Oxford Univ. Press, 1990), 183–92. L.J. Reeve, "The Legal Status of the Petition of Right," *Historical Journal* 29 (June 1986): 257–58. The *Petition* "anticipated the attitudes of those in the Long Parliament who came to oppose the Caroline regime."

10 *The King's Letter and Instructions for the Collection of a Free Gift* (July 7, 1626), in Samuel Gardiner, ed., *Constitutional Documents of the Puritan Revolution: 1625–1660* (London: Longman, Green & Co., 1911), 46–49. Kevin Sharpe, *Personal Rule of Charles I*, 15–23. "The dissolution of the 1626 Parliament in June without a grant of subsidies necessitated some extraordinary source of revenue for the war." Austin Woolrych, *Britain in Revolution, 1625–1660*, 17. "Parliament rarely resorted to withholding subsidies as a lever for exacting concessions or the redress of grievances; it happened only four times before the Civil War." Johann Sommerville, *Royalists and Patriots: Politics and Ideology in England: 1603–1640*, 2nd ed., (New York: Longman, 1999), 151. Charles I in part justified the Loan "by appealing to necessity—and thus effectively claiming extra-legal emergency

At the end of the 1628 session of Parliament, which also failed to provide sufficient revenue for the crown, its members were again dismissed by Charles I after it became clear that the *Petition of Right* would not end their tax protest. One of the *Petition's* grievances condemned the treatment of subjects who had challenged their imprisonment after refusing to pay the loan. Upon suing for the issuance of a writ of habeas corpus in what became known as the *Five Knight's Case*, the attorney general produced a royal order of arrest and imprisonment by his "Majesty's special command." This had led Parliament to challenge the process of collecting the loan during its 1628 session, as the crown's treatment of the appellants appeared to violate *article thirty-nine* of *Magna Charta* and its guarantee that no man should be deprived of his property or imprisoned without due process of law. As the King and his Privy Council witnessed the damaging effects of the loan's collection upon their subjects' loyalty, exacerbated by several tracts authored by Anglian ministers (Sibthorpe and Manwaring) defending the King's divine right to tax without Parliament, it was decided emergency powers of state would be invoked to avoid public trial. Future parliamentary leader John Pym warned, "If Parliaments be taken away, mischiefs and disorders must needs abound, without any possibility of good laws to reform them; grievances will daily increase, without opportunities or means to redress them; and what readier way can there be to distractions betwixt the King and People, to tumults and distempers in state, than this?"[11]

Still, many precedents for summary arrest and imprisonment by royal warrant in matters of state existed, as acknowledged by the foremost champion of English Common Law, and now parliamentary member, Sir Edward Coke. During Coke's service as Elizabeth I's Attorney General, an office whose duty his successor Francis Bacon described as guarding the prerogative, he routinely

powers—and yet assured his subjects that he 'ever intended' them to enjoy 'property of goods.'" Mark Kishlansky, *A Monarchy Transformed: Britain 1603–1714* (New York: Penguin Books, 1996), 109. The Loan was "a fiscal success [but] a political catastrophe. The King had to imprison his subjects, dismiss his chief justice, and replace Lord Lieutenants and JPs to enforce compliance."

11 *Five Knights Case* (1627), in T.B. Howell, ed., *State Trials* (London: T.C. Hansard, 1816), 3: 1–234 (#127). Robert Johnson, et al., eds., *Commons Debates of 1628* (New Haven: Yale Univ. Press, 1977), 2: 100 (March 25, 1628); 2: 103 (Wandesford); 2: 106. *Mr. Pym's Speech at the Delivery of the Charges against Dr. Manwaring (1628)*, in *Historical Collections* (London: 1659), 1: 595 @ 600. Tim Harris, *Rebellion: The First Stuart Kings*, 253–62. David Cressy, *Charles I and the People of England* (Oxford: Oxford Univ. Press, 2015), 96–103. Glenn Burgess, *British Political Thought: 1500–1660*, 174–5. *Article 39*: "No free man is to be arrested, or imprisoned, or disseised, or outlawed, or exiled, or in any other way ruined, nor will we go against him or send against him, except by the lawful judgment of his peers or by the law of the land."

executed royal warrants for summary arrest and torture. After challenging James I's prerogative with the preeminence of Common Law, which no judge had dared heretofore, Coke was removed as Chief Justice of King's Bench. Yet at the beginning of Parliament's 1628 session Members pledged their loyalty to the prerogative, including Coke: "I shall ever be as ready to maintain the King's prerogative as any man" in light of an earlier parliamentary position in 1606, that his "prerogative is the supreme part of the laws of the realm." But his fellow Member Christopher Wandesford recognized their dilemma, "Moderation is the best way to wind us out of this dark labyrinth. No question deserves more the wisdom of this House than those where the King's prerogative and the subject's liberty jostle together." After the leader of the House of Commons, Sir John Eliot, was taken to the Tower of London on orders of Charles I, he described the issue as "a point so tender it will hardly bear a mention," to the extent that "even our thoughts are dangerous." During his imprisonment he assisted John Winthrop in drawing up plans for colonization with future parliamentary leader John Hampden as intermediary.[12]

Through the end of the reign of Elizabeth I (1558–1603) no common law judge had challenged a royal warrant. Members of the House of Commons who did so from the 1620's through the early 1640's, joined by Chief Justice of King's Bench Randolph Crew dismissed by Charles I for not issuing an advisory opinion in the *Five Knights Case* (1627), along with a minority of common law justices on the bench during the 1630's, asserted that common law precedent bound the monarch unless a national emergency was manifest. Just before

---

12 Catherine Drinker Bowen, *The Lion and the Throne: The Life and Times of Sir Edward Coke* (Boston: Little, Brown and Company, 1956), 76–81, 139–59, 190–217, 291–92. Harold Berman, *Law and Revolution: The Impact of the Protestant Reformations on the Western Legal Tradition* (Cambridge: Belknap Press, 2003), 2: 214–15. Linda Popofsky, "Habeas Corpus and 'Liberty of the Subject': Legal Arguments for the Petition of Right in the Parliament of 1628," *The Historian* 41 (Feb., 1979): 260–74. Charles I proceeded to get his advisory opinion "by secretly polling the King's Bench Judges on May 28, 1628." *Rex v. Elliot, Hollis and Valentine* (1629), in T.B. Howell, ed., *State Trials* (London: T.C. Hansard, 1816), 3: 294–335 (#130). Richard Cust, *The Forced Loan and English Politics*, 331. "[I]n the Parliament of 1628 … the [forced] loan [itself] … attracted little discussion—largely because the [Privy] Council conceded at an early stage that it was indefensible—the main focus of debate became the issue of imprisonment without showing cause, which had surfaced because of the stand taken by loan resisters." Sir John Eliot quoted in William White, "Sir John Eliot's the Monarchie of Man and Early Stuart Political Thought," *Historical Journal* 62 (no. 3, 2019): 644–48. Plans for Massachusetts colonization were found in Eliot's papers in his own hand. Francis Bremer, *John Winthrop: America's Forgotten Founding Father*, 206. Sir John Eliot, *The Grounds for Settling a Planation in New England*, in MHS *Proceedings (1864–1865)* (Boston: MHS, 1865), 8: 413–30; (https://archive.org/details/proceedingsmasso6socigoog/page/n439).

Parliament sent him the *Petition of Right*, Charles I tried to calm the tumult via correspondence to the House of Lords, whose members shared it with the Commons. Charles complained, "Yet we find it still insisted upon that in no case whatsoever (though they … concern matters of state and government) we, or our Privy Council, have power to commit any without cause," even in instances where, if the "cause be shown, the service itself could thereby be destroyed and defeated." While he pledged "neither we nor our Privy Council shall or will at any time here commit or command to prison" in any case which did not "concern the state, the public good and safety of us and our people," he refused to surrender his power of summary arrest after "so many ages within this kingdom practiced," or it "would soon dissolve the very foundation and frame of our monarchy."[13]

While those opposed to the King's tax policies in the House of Commons, and the country, anticipated a reckoning in the *Five Knights Case* between the law and the crown, the substantive issues of the loan's legality were never addressed. After citations of myriads of precedents arguing the prisoners' rights under *Magna Charta's* article thirty-nine, as well as multiple attacks on the process of arrest, Chief Justice Nicholas Hyde stated the essential matter of the court's decision. Because the royal warrant had many precedents in matters of state security, and its issuance by the "special command of the king" was proven beyond doubt, the prisoners could not be released unless Charles I himself authorized it; only the monarch could overturn his own order of summary arrest. Sir Thomas Wentworth, future first minister under Charles as the Earl of Strafford, warned the Commons, "I hope it shall never be stirred here whether the King be above the law or the law be above the King," because his prerogative authority was beyond the scrutiny of his subjects. When the king's attorney, Sir Francis Nethersole, argued the necessity of emergency powers in instances when the monarch required absolute authority to protect his

13 Robert Johnson, et al., eds., *Commons Debates of 1628*, 3: 372 (May 12, 1628). Catherine Drinker Bowen, *The Lion and the Throne: The Life and Times of Sir Edward Coke*, 92. "It was true that in England torture was not used as penalty after conviction but only before trial, to induce confession; true also that warrants came never from common law judges but from the Queen or Privy Council—in short from that mystic authority known as the prerogative, where all blame could rest." After his service ended as Attorney General, "Coke said repeatedly that in England the prerogative was limited by common law. (Under two Stuart kings, he was to risk his life to prove it). *Yet in Elizabeth's day, no common law judge seems to have questioned the royal warrant.*" Paul Halliday, G. Edward White, "The Suspension Clause," *Virginia Law Review* 94 (no. 3, 2008): 604–623. After 1689, once Parliament controlled suspension of habeas corpus it consistently provided summary powers of arrest in matters of state.

kingdom, he justified its use by an ancient maxim, *salus populi suprema lex esto* (i.e., the people's welfare is the highest law). John Selden, a member of the Commons and one of the country's most brilliant legal minds, served as the prisoners' counsel. The following year during floor debate Selden rejoindered Nerthersole's argument, "*Salus Populi suprema lex, et libertas popula summa volus populi*"; or, "the welfare of the people is the supreme law, and the liberty of the people is the supreme welfare of the people."[14]

Unrestrained by the prerogative's responsibilities to protect the state, even when juxtaposed with property rights of the subject, upon its reassembly in 1629 the House of Commons challenged the King on matters of state, taxation, and religion. Indeed, on review of the debates from 1628 to 1629 it is apparent that Members were spoiling for a fight. Upon Charles I's order of Parliament's dissolution and dismissal, a riot ensued in the Commons' chamber on March 2, 1629. With the Speaker of the House physically restrained, Sir John Eliot proclaimed that taxation without parliamentary consent was a betrayal of the "liberties of England," and any supporter of such policy was an "enemy" of the kingdom. This incendiary malaise, infused with religious oppression by England's bishops, caused many Puritans to sail for New England. As Mark Kishlansky summarized events: "In little more than a decade 16,000 men and women abandoned England on this errand into the wilderness. Some fled actual persecution, though most fled the threat of it, believing that something was seriously wrong—a fear that increased under the pressures of what they believed was arbitrary government." Ultimately, according to the most recent scholarship, this migration "firmly embedded New England in anti-puritan theories of international godly intrigue. It would remain central to these formulations for decades to follow."[15]

---

14 *Five Knights Case* (1627), in ed., T.B. Howell, *State Trials*, 3: 51–59 (CJ White's opinion). Robert Johnson, et al., eds., *Commons Debates of 1628*, 2: 183 (March 28, 1628; 2: 183 (n.109)); 3: 98 (April 26, 1628). Paul Christianson, "Arguments on Billeting and Martial Law in the Parliament of 1628," *Historical Journal* 37 (Sept., 1994): 539–67. Kevin Sharpe, *The Personal Rule of Charles I*, 17–19, 59–60. "During the period 1626 to 1629 we hear increasingly a new language ... of necessity, and of the public safety contrasted with private interests ... Whilst his subjects pursued, as Charles saw it, their private interests [in Parliament], they unkinged the monarch upon whom God had placed the responsibility for protection of his people." J.A. Guy, "The Origins of the Petition of Right Reconsidered," *Historical Journal*, 25 (June 1982): 289–312. Mark Kishlansky, "Tyranny Denied: Charles I, Attorney General Heath, and the *Five Knights' Case*," *Historical Journal* 42 (Mar., 1999): 53–83. Richard Tuck, *Philosophy and Government: 1572–1651* (Cambridge: Cambridge Univ. Press, 1993), 205–212.

15 Mark Kishlansky, *A Monarchy Transformed*, 108–118. Michael Winship, *Godly Republicans: Puritans, Pilgrims, and a City on a Hill*, 188–94. David Hall, *A Reforming People*,

Just before the next General Court for election of officials in the Spring of 1632, the government began to unravel upon Deputy Governor Dudley's resignation for the ostensible sake of "public peace." Governor Winthrop and the remaining assistants refused his pleas to leave government. With the precipitous decline of assistants, the remaining magistrates could not spare him, and might afford the spectacle of such divisions even less. The only extant record of this dispute is provided by the governor's *Journal*, with its portrayal of Dudley as being a "contrary" man with little talent for leadership. Because Winthrop's *Journal* is the only source for this dispute, it must be relied upon, but with some care, since the governor was one of the main disputants. Dudley was undoubtedly a contentious man, but this does not mark him eccentric in early Massachusetts church or state affairs. Although Winthrop was still held in the highest regard, he was human after all, and his account is biased in favor of his own position. At this formative stage of governing the confusion amongst the assistants concerning their authority in relation to the governor's is of little surprise.[16]

---

22–38. Francis Bremer, *John Winthrop*, 148–51, 207–212, 327–29. S.E. Morison, *Builders of the Bay Colony*, 54–64. Samuel Fullerton, "New England in the Royalist Imagination," *English Historical Review* 137 (Oct., 2022): 1350. Adrian C. Weimer, *Constitutional Culture* (Philadelphia: Univ. of Pennsylvania Press, 2023), 11–15. The royalist criticisms of New England as a Puritan enclave of non-conformists and rebels was only reinforced by the King's execution in 1649. Edmund Morgan, *The Puritan Dilemma*, 2nd ed., 15–28, 158–62. Stephen Foster, *The Long Argument* (Chapel Hill: Univ. of North Carolina Press, 1991), 137. "As [John] Pym, [Sir Walter] Earle, and Sir Nathaniel Rich took advantage of the growing desperation of MPs, they secured a major share of the parliamentary leadership and ensured that the Puritan program became inseparable from the demand for limitations on the arbitrary power of the crown." Bailyn, *The Barbarous Years*, 178. "With Charles I's dissolution of Parliament, after having struggled with it since his accession, having imprisoned its most forceful leaders, and having continued to tax without consent, the nation's public life was in turmoil and the danger of monarchical autocracy was palpable; ... total convulsion of religious life was less predictable, but threatening signs were multiplying."

16 Richard Dunn, ed., *Journal of John Winthrop*, 64–8, xxvii–xxx. Even when Dudley was informed that his resignation was "not allowed," he refused to submit. James Savage, ed., *History of New England*, 1: 73 (n. 1). Savage noted that the subsequent May 1st meeting between the magistrates and Dudley was "undoubtedly a private meeting, for notice of it is not found in the *Records*." Edmund Morgan, *Puritan Dilemma*, 2nd ed., 76–7, 91–94. Benjamin Carp, "Edmund S. Morgan and the Urgency of Good Leadership," *Reviews in American History* 44 (March 2016): 1–18. Morgan's seemingly excessive praise of Winthrop was a feature of his scholarship that saw political leadership hierarchies as essential for a state's survival. Francis Bremer, *John Winthrop*, 212–17. Francis Bremer, *First Founders*, 64–70. Dudley had both considerable military leadership and legal experience. Robert Wall, *Massachusetts Bay: The Crucial Decade*, 8. Mark Cahn, "Punishment, Discretion, and

In August 1632, the two men confronted each other in front of the rest of the magistrates and expressed their respective grievances with considerable "bitterness." At some point Dudley demanded that Governor Winthrop express his understanding of the "ground and limits of his authority," as authorized by the *Charter*. Dudley argued that Winthrop had "no more authority than every assistant," except his right to "call courts." Winthrop predictably disagreed. Initially, he emphasized that as governor he had no "greater authority than he might by the patent," or charter, but even if all his powers as governor were not expressly enumerated in the *Charter*, its very provision of his office provided "whatsoever power belonged to a governor by common law of the statutes" of England. Dudley was clearly frustrated by such an expansive description of the governor's powers. Beginning his rebuttal "somewhat apprehensively," he quickly whipped himself into a "passion, telling the governor that if he were so round, he would be round too." Then, "both fell into much bitterness." The era's pejorative definition for "round" criticized circular or convoluted reasoning. Dudley had a point. After asking Winthrop to describe his powers, and if they were authorized by the *Charter*, Winthrop retorted that the governor's office included a centuries-long list of common law and statutory powers of English magistrates. Accordingly, Winthrop maintained that he had not violated any charter provisions, and while admitting "some slips," he could state with justification that he had never intentionally "taken advantage of his authority to oppress … any man, or to benefit himself." Nevertheless, Dudley held firm, accusing Winthrop of a secret intent to "make himself popular," in order to "gain absolute power and bring all the assistants under his power."[17]

Today we reflexively interpret political popularity as an implicit good, but that has not always been the case. As David Underdown explained, during this era a man of similar rank who accused a fellow magistrate of seeking popularity implied a strident criticism, because seeking favor from commoners undermined authority by appealing to a "popular sovereignty." Despite Dudley's representation of the Earl of Lincoln in obstructing the collection of Charles I's forced loan, he was not acting upon a Whig ideology in support

---

the Codification of Prescribed Penalties in Colonial Massachusetts," *American Journal of Legal History* 33 (1989): 120–21.

17 Richard Dunn, ed., *Journal of John Winthrop*, 72–7 (July-August 1632). "Capt. Tho. Wiggin to Sec. Coke" (Nov. 19, 1632), *CSP, Colonial Series (1574–1660)*, ed. W. Noel Sainsbury, (London: Longman, 1860), 1: 156–57 (#68). "He [John Winthrop] is a discrete and sober man, wearing plain apparel, assisting in any ordinary labor, and ruling with much mildness and justice." Edmund Morgan, *Puritan Dilemma*, 2nd ed., 92–4. Alexander Chalmers, ed., *Samuel Johnson's Dictionary of the English Language* (London: Studio Editions, 1994), 626.

of representative institutions depending on popular input and support. To posit whiggish principles in Dudley is anachronistic and swings too far to the other end of the interpretive spectrum. As Underdown warned, in or "out of Parliament early Stuart gentlemen repeatedly insisted that a popular government was not what they wanted." Instead, Dudley simply wanted a list of powers Winthrop thought the governorship provided, and one that all assistants could agree upon. Although Dudley's attacks on Winthrop have appeared petty in retrospect, as he sought to force Winthrop to deal more harshly with colonists, his insistence on a transparent decision-making process in a new body politic was reasonable.[18]

Dudley's unease proved contagious. In May 1632, soon after his resignation, the freemen petitioned for greater political participation; his antagonism towards Winthrop, joined with Watertown's earlier protest, precipitated events. During the Court of Assistants held a week before the General Court for colonial elections, when the freemen would gather, Winthrop warned his fellow assistants that the "people intended … the governor might be chosen by the whole Court, and not by the assistants only." Magistrate Roger Ludlow reacted passionately to the news, "then we should have no government … wherein every man might do what he pleased"; Winthrop and Dudley were not the only assistants jealous of their authority, and to some, electoral politics still signified a process of endorsement rather than a liberty of choice. Despite Ludlow's objection, the freemen secured greater electoral power in the 1632 session with the assistants' agreement that they could participate in elections for the deputy governor and the governor, so long as the latter two officials

18 Francis Bremer, *First Founders*, 64–70. David Underdown, *A Freeborn People* (Oxford: Clarendon Press, 1996), 25. Richard Cust, *Charles I and the Aristocracy, 1625–1642*, 54. A "fear of popularity," common in political discourse since the sixteenth century, was a "notion that there was a conspiracy of factious and self-interested trouble-makers, seeking to play on the irrational and destructive impulses of the 'multitude' to advance their own ends." This fear applied especially to property-less men thought to be easily manipulated. *At the Meeting of the Officers* [*at Putney*] (Oct. 29, 1647), in ed., C.H. Firth, ed., *The Clarke Papers* (UK: Camden Society, 1891), 1: 280 @ 342. A soldier, Mr. Pettis, commented during debate over the franchise, "I conceive the reason why we would exclude apprentices, or servants [is] … they depend upon the will of other men and should be afraid to displease [them]." David Como, "Making 'the Heads of the Proposals': The King, the Army, the Levellers, and the Roads to Putney," *English Historical Review* 135 (Feb., 2021): 1407–12. "Lilburne argued … 'every free man of England, as well poor as rich, whose life estate &c. is to be taken away by the law, may have a vote in choosing those that are to make the law, it being a maxim in nature, that no man justly can be bound without his own consent'. This ostensibly placed the franchise in all 'free' men, no matter how poor (leaving conveniently ambiguous the status of servants, apprentices and other 'unfree' adults)."

were elected exclusively from the assistants' rank. The assistants also conceded that two freemen from every town could "confer" with them on any future tax measures. But the freemen's delegates would not participate directly in appropriating taxation or enacting legislation. Instead, they would "advise with the governor and assistants about the raising of a public stock [or tax], so as what they should agree upon should bind all." The unofficial status of the freemen's delegates is confirmed by their omission in the roster of participants listed for assistants' meetings over the next several years.[19]

Instead of utilizing the new process for taxation in the next General Court of Election in May 1633, when the freemen gathered to vote, the magistrates waited several months before summoning their delegates the following October when only magistrates were present. Only then did Dudley, Winthrop, and the rest of the magistrates order the collection of a new tax, a hefty sum of £400 for colonial defense. After notice was given the following Spring for the general court of election in May 1634, however, instead of waiting for the governor to summon their representatives, the freemen dispatched delegates peremptorily before it convened. At which point, these proxy representatives demanded to read the colonial charter, and concluded, "thereby, that all their laws should be made at the general court" instead of the Court of Assistants.[20]

These new representatives proceeded to object that the freemen were being taxed without their consent, and demanded to know why "all their laws" were not "made at the general court?" Governor Winthrop responded that when the *Charter* was granted the "number of freemen was supposed to be (as in like corporations) so few … as they might well join in making laws; but now they were grown to so great a body, as it was not possible for them to make or execute laws, but they must choose others for that purpose." Even if the freemen chose representatives for "that work," however, "they were not furnished with sufficient number of men qualified for such a business, neither could the commonwealth bear the loss of time of so many as must intend it." Several years before Winthrop had told many of these same men that the assistants

19 Edmund Morgan, *The Puritan Dilemma*, 2nd ed., 91–99. Robert Wall, *Massachusetts Bay: The Crucial Decade*, 7. Richard Dunn, ed., *Journal of John Winthrop*, 63–8. Francis Bremer, *John Winthrop*, 214–15, 243. David Hall, *The Faithful Shepherd* (Cambridge: Harvard Univ. Press, 2006), 137–39. Nathaniel Shurtleff, ed., *MGCR*, 1: 95 (May 9, 1632). Winthrop's description of the deputies' powers at this point is consistent with the General Court *Record*.

20 Nathaniel Shurtleff, ed., *MGCR*, 1: 95 (May 9, 1632), 106 (July 2, 1633), 110 (Oct. 4, 1633), 119 (May 14, 1634). Richard Dunn, ed., *Journal of John Winthrop*, 113–14, 113 (n. 68). Edmund Morgan, *Puritan Dilemma*, 2nd ed., 98–101. Robert Wall, *Massachusetts Bay: The Crucial Decade*, 8–12.

represented them on a parliamentary model to quell their tax protests. Now, he used the corporate model to persuade them that they were too many of them to participate directly in government, and added they were not qualified for that service anyway. Winthrop conceded, in the future the General Court could "make an order that once in the year a certain number should be appointed (upon summons from the governor) to *revise all laws*," and "reform what they found amiss" in existing laws, but the freemen would not be allowed to "make any new laws." Instead, they must "prefer their grievances to the Court of Assistants," and the magistrates pledged to pass no new taxation "without the consent of such a committee"; they would also be consulted on the distribution of new land. As Samuel Eliot Morison quipped, the freemen would not be "put off with such chaff." Instead, they proceeded to realize an historically significant partnership with the magistrates in governing the colony.[21]

The very first order of business in the general court session of May 1634 was to amend the freemen's oath that had been established in 1629. Both similarly acknowledged the legitimacy of the extant government, that the oath-taker follow its laws and ordinances and make timely notification to its officials of any seditious activities. A salient difference between the two was the addition of the following language to the amended 1634 oath: "when I shall be called to give my voice touching any such matter of this state, wherein freemen are to deal, I will give my vote and suffrage as I shall judge in my own conscience may best conduce and tend to the public welfare of the body, without respect of person, or favor of any man." What did conscience and suffrage mean in this era? William Haller's description of conscience is accurate, and concise, "preachers told the people that they must obey conscience, thinking that they could hold the conscience of the saints in their own keeping. But when they said one thing to the saints and conscience said another, the reformers were destined to find their authority as fragile as ... pope and prelate." The importance of conscience

21 Richard Dunn, ed., *Journal of John Winthrop*, 113–14, 113 (n. 68). Edmund Morgan, *The Puritan Dilemma*, 2nd ed., 82, 89, 95–101, 140–41. S.E. Morison, *Builders of the Bay Colony*, 83–90. Charles Hilkey, *Legal Development in Colonial Massachusetts*, 16–17. After reviewing the same entries in the General Court record, Hilkey quipped, how well Governor Winthrop's suggested course of action was followed "is shown by what took place during the next few weeks." Francis Bremer, *John Winthrop*, 217–18. More recently, Francis Bremer termed Winthrop's proposals to the freemen and their deputies as "clearly insufficient." Michael Winship, *Godly Republicanism*, 194. Winship interpreted the 1634 session's inclusion of the freemen's deputies as making it consistent with provisions of the *Charter*, and Republican in form. David Hall, "Review: Heads Must Roll—The Dynamics of Radical Puritanism in Stuart England and Early New England," *Reviews in American History* 42 (June 2014): 219–226.

in Protestantism cannot be overstated, and its volatile manifestations produced spontaneous agitation against church and state institutions, not only in England's North American colonies, but in both England and Scotland, as well as across Europe. As for "suffrage," a secular definition meant electing either local borough officials or members of Parliament. Essentially, the freemen intended to actively participate in government, instead of approving passively. They were prepared to contest candidates or proposed laws "without respect of person, or favor of any man," rather than defer to their "betters" for the sake of communal harmony.[22]

Moreover, the freemen's united appearance convinced the magistrates that a new definition of the General Court as the supreme legislative body in the colony, in place of the court of assistants, was appropriate: "none but the General Court hath power to make and establish laws, nor to elect and appoint officers, as governor, deputy governor, assistants, treasurer, secretary, captain, … or any of like moment, or to remove such upon misdemeanor, as also to set out the duties and powers of the said officers." The electoral part of the order was the provision that Magistrate Ludlow had railed at two years before. It also included lower government officials under the assistants and governors, like militia officers. During the General Court of Elections in May 1632, Winthrop reported a "proposition … that every company of trained men might choose their own captain and officers; but the governor [Winthrop himself] giving them reasons to the contrary, they were satisfied." By 1634, the freemen were no longer content to allow the magistrates to designate military appointments.[23]

Most importantly, in its future sessions the General Court would "make and establish laws." Winthrop's attempts to reconcile the freemen to a passive role in government had not only failed, it served as a provocation to their aspirations that, from hindsight, spurred on their challenge to the magistrates' authority. The issue of taxation was also settled in the freemen's favor unconditionally, with enactment of a law that "none but the General Court hath power to raise monies and taxes and to dispose of lands," or to "give and confirm properties." Taxation must be approved by the magistrates and the freemen's representatives. Also, the vast expanse of land at the colony's disposal, and the enormous influence it conferred upon those who controlled its distribution, would be

---

22 *Oath of a Freeman*, in Nathaniel Shurtleff, ed., *MGCR*, 1: 117 (May 14, 1634). William Haller, *The Rise of Puritanism* (New York: Columbia Univ. Press, 1938), 172. Alexander Chalmers, ed., *Samuel Johnson's Dictionary of the English Language*, 715. Walter Skeat, ed., *Dictionary of English Etymology* (1884; reprint, Hertfordshire: Wordsworth, 1993), 480.

23 Nathaniel Shurtleff, ed., *MGCR*, 1: 117 (May 14, 1634). Richard Dunn, ed., *Journal of John Winthrop*, 68.

shared by the freemen, not by grant of superior authority, but as a legislative right. Essentially, the court of assistants would no longer enact taxation or regulate the freemen's property without their consent. Finally, the freemen were to elect two or three representatives from each town to "deal on their behalf in the public affairs of the commonwealth." Their representatives would be known as deputies, and enjoy the "full power and voices of all the said freemen, derived to them for the making and establishing of laws, granting of lands, etc., and to deal in all other affairs of the *commonwealth*."[24]

How was such a sweeping agenda achieved? The freemen's preemptive choice and delegation of representatives to meet with Governor Winthrop just before the General Court of Elections was key. Weeks earlier Winthrop had addressed their ad hoc delegates as, at best, unofficial proxies, which they were. But the arrival of all the freemen for the elections of colonial office held during General Court session of May 1634 dwarfed the handful of assistants and won the day. What could the magistrates do in the face of the united appearance of the freemen, or "good men" of the colony? Deputy Israel Stoughton left us a version of these events from the freemen's perspective:

> [T]he government was solely in the hands of the assistants. The people chose them magistrates, and then they made laws, disposed lands, raised monies, punished offenders … at their discretion. Neither did the people know the patent [the charter] nor what prerogative and liberty they had by the same. But there being some monies raised and a speech of more, it made some inquisitive into matters and particularly after the patent. [A]bout which time Mr. Winthrop, governor, having the patent did give way to the country upon their motion to see it, and all the magistrates (as in charity I must say) were willing to admit the people to join with themselves in the governance of the state, by 3 deputies for each town. So, in May, last year [1634], there was a General Court, wherein things were so agitated.

For the first time the freemen's representatives or deputies, including Stoughton, were listed individually in the official record with the attending magistrates.[25]

---

24 Nathaniel Shurtleff, ed., *MGCR*, 1: 117–19 (May 14, 1634).

25 Israel Stoughton, *A Relation Concerning New England*, *MHS Proceedings (1860–1862)*, 5: 136–38. Robert Wall, "The Membership of the Massachusetts General Court," 350–51. Nathaniel Shurtleff, ed., *MGCR*, 1: 116–7. The deputies listed were: "Mr. Goodwin, Mr. Spencer, Mr. Talcott, Mr. Feakes, Mr. Browne, Mr. Oldham, Mr. Beecher, Mr. Palmer, Roberte Moulton, Capt. Turner, Mr. Willis, Mr. Edw. Tomlins, Mr. Holgrave, Mr. Coxeall,

Several other entries for the May session leave no doubt of its significance. First, assistants and deputies agreed that "no trial shall pass upon any for life or banishment, but by a jury so summoned or by the General Court." There had been complaints of the magistrates' arbitrary treatment of some colonists, ones that Winthrop had warned his fellow magistrates from repeating. For example, soon after the Winthrop fleet's arrival Sir Richard Saltonstall was fined £5 by his fellow assistants for whipping colonists. Another incident saw Henry Lyn whipped and banished from the colony for "writing into England falsely and maliciously against the government and execution of justice here." Thomas Knower was "put in bilbowes"—shackles attached to the feet fastened to an iron bar—"for threatening the Court that if he should be punished, he would have it tried in England." Thomas Dexter was "disenfranchised"—or stripped of his freemanship—and fined £50 "for speaking reproachful and seditious words against the government here established." The assistants condemned him for "saying this captious government will bring all to naught." John Endecott admitted "striking" Dexter but confided that the "manner of his carriage … would have provoked a very patient man." The court of assistants had also stripped Robert Coles of his freemanship for drunkenness and ordered him to "wear about his neck, and so to hang upon his outward garment, a D made of red cloth … for a year." The sentence of the scarlet letter was remitted, and only a handful were ever recorded as sanctioned during the colony's earliest years. Finally, the General Court fined Magistrate William Pynchon for violating a law prohibiting the provision of firearms to Indians; he had done so while he was trapping and trading furs with Native American guides. Certainly, from his contemporaries' perspectives this could be seen as a risky provision. Yet, the deputies' chief objection was that other colonists had been punished for the very same practice under a law passed by the assistants, but not enforced in the case of Magistrate Pynchon. The deputies rightly censured both the assistants and Pynchon for this gross injustice, concomitantly declaring the General Court supreme in colonial government.[26]

Edmond Quinsey, Capt. John Underhill, John Johnson, William Heath, Mr. Alcocke, Mr. Israel Stoughton, William Felpes, George Hull, Mr. Conant, Frauncis Weston."

26 Nathaniel Shurtleff, ed., *MGCR*, 1: 76 (Sept., 1630), 112, 118 (May 1634). John Noble, ed., *Records of the Court of Assistants*, 2: 9, 19, 21, 27, 30–1. In 1632, the Court of Assistants exceeded its own punishment of fine and imprisonment, ordering "Richard Hopkins … be severely whipped and branded with a hot iron on one of his cheeks for selling pieces, powder, and shot to the Indians." Hopkins had sold two guns and some powder to one Native American, James Sagamore. Richard Dunn, ed., *Journal of John Winthrop*, 79 (n. 23), 111 (n. 57), 116. *Hutchinson Papers*, ed. William Whitmore, (Albany: Prince Society, 1865), 1: 52. Francis Bremer, *John Winthrop*, 209–11. Edmund Morgan, *Puritan Dilemma*,

Upon entering the events of the May session in his *Journal* Winthrop made the best of the magistrates' comeuppance. He conceded that several "good orders were made this court," while acknowledging that the "assistants were questioned by the freemen for some errors in their government." There had been "fines imposed," but they were "remitted again before the court brake up." Not before Winthrop had lost the election for the governorship to Thomas Dudley.[27]

The freemen's peaceful victory should not be seen as a defeat for John Winthrop, and his vision of a godly commonwealth. Instead, the freemen's participation in passing legislation initiated several noteworthy traditions in Massachusetts: of a sitting legislature that enacted a spectrum of laws for the colony, including authorization of set levels of taxation, as well as annual elections for the governor, assistants, and deputies. This process of self-government would endure, except between the late 1680's and early 1690's, until the British Empire tried to impose its will on North American colonial matters beginning in the 1760's via the imposition of parliamentary revenue enactments.

During the 1630's about half of the other English colonies, whether formally designated as a charter or dominion colony, or currently still unrecognized like Rhode Island and New Haven, had insisted upon, and ultimately secured representation by a legislative body. Those colonies that did not enjoy representation were mostly run by powerful English nobles, known as proprietors, who tried to extract rents and fees from colonists without granting outright property ownership. As Carla Pestana explained, "the New England colonies were exceptional in escaping from direct intervention by a proprietor or distant charter company, but their goals were shared by leading colonists everywhere who strove for these benefits." By September of 1634, Massachusetts assistants, most commonly referred to as magistrates, and the freemen's deputies commenced their own legislative deliberations. But even with additional General Court sessions the deputies' participation would amount to only a month or so of the entire year. Meanwhile, the magistrates continued to sit in judgment in

2nd ed., 76–7. Bernard Bailyn, *The New England Merchants in the Seventeenth Century*, 2nd ed., (Cambridge: Harvard Univ. Press, 1979), 27–9. Charles Hilkey, *Legal Development in Colonial Massachusetts*, 18.

27 Richard Dunn, ed., *Journal of John Winthrop*, 113–14, 116 (n. 82). David Hall, *A Reforming People*, 27–28. Hall termed Winthrop's journal entry on these events as a "toneless description of what followed," signifying his unhappiness with the results of the General Court of May 1634. Shurtleff, ed., *MGCR*, 1: 10–12, 16–18 (March 1629); *MGCR*, 117 (May 14, 1634). *Winthrop Papers* (Boston: MHS, 1924–45), 4: 380–82. William Hening, ed., *Virginia Statutes at Large* (New York: R.W.G. Bartow, 1823), 1: 89–90, 103 (§8), 110–112. Edmund Morgan, *Puritan Dilemma*, 2nd ed., 75–89, 98–101, 140.

the court of assistants with much greater frequency. So, after inclusion in the General Court, the deputies still had to establish their role within the judicial process, and even the legislative process had procedural gaps. To this point the parties had agreed that the General Court would raise taxes, enact laws, and review the judicial decisions of the court of assistants in capital cases. But a bicameral legislature, as we understand it, had not been created. Instead, deputies and magistrates continued to deliberate as one group until the mid-1640's. So, questions like, "What will the procedure of the two groups voting in one assembly be?," and, "How will our new laws be ratified?," arose as a matter of course. As George Haskins described the colony's nascent politics, these "conflicts were all aspects of the same source of difference between the deputies and the magistrates, namely the problem of the basis of political power and of the allocation of spheres of authority within the colony." Until the legislative process itself was agreed upon no controversial law, much less a book of colonial law, could be enacted.[28]

28 George Haskins, *Law and Authority in Early Massachusetts*, 39. Carla Pestana, *The English Atlantic in an Age of Revolution: 1640–1661* (Cambridge: Harvard Univ. Press, 2004), 14–18. Charles Hilkey, *Legal Development in Colonial Massachusetts*, 141.

CHAPTER 4

# The Negative Voice

At this point in Massachusetts' brief history, the General Court was both the colony's supreme legislature and judicial court. Its jurisdiction reflected the late Medieval/Early Modern period when legislation was closely joined to judicial authority, while modern concepts of executive power only began to emerge at mid-century. Matthew Hale, successor to Edward Coke and John Selden as the preeminent Common Law jurist, described Parliament as the "highest court of this kingdom," as illustrated by capital cases still tried there, such as impeachments. But he omitted Parliament from his chapter on jurisdictions as it was unlike "other ordinary courts," perhaps because some of his contemporaries were championing its role as a supreme council. Meanwhile, Justices of the Peace (JP) administered matters later centuries would designate as more appropriate for municipal councils. Although Bay colonists regularly cited the Massachusetts *Charter of 1629* as fundamental authority, like a modern constitution, especially during political or theological crises, its directives were duplicative, sometimes contradictory, and could not be amended. In order to understand Massachusetts' executive and legislative powers, we must temporarily leave aside modern understandings of constitutions and separation of powers, and instead focus on the colony's veto power, or "negative voice." The struggle to establish a veto power in the new government was crucial to the stabilization of legal authority.[1]

1 Charles McIlwain, *The High Court of Parliament and Its Supremacy* (New Haven: Yale Univ. Press, 1910), 291. "It is absolutely necessary to rid ourselves of the modern idea of the law-making and law-interpreting bodies as mutually exclusive, and external to each other, … [as] suggested by the more modern doctrine of legislative sovereignty." Matthew Hale, *The History of the Pleas of the Crown* (Philadelphia: Robert Small, 1847), 2: 1–2. Edmund Morgan, *The Puritan Dilemma*, 2nd ed., (New York: Longman, 1999), 140–42. Francis Bremer, *John Winthrop* (Oxford: Oxford Univ. Press, 2003), 105–23. Sir Robert Filmer, *The Anarchy of a Limited or Mixed Monarchy* (1648), in J.P. Sommerville, ed., *Patriarcha and Other Writings* (Cambridge: Cambridge Univ. Press, 1991), 132–36. "There never was … any people governed without a power of making laws … [I]n a monarchy the legislative power must be in one, according to the rule of Aristotle, who said that 'government was in one, or in a few, or in many' … [I]f restrained by some law, is not the power of that law, and of them that made that law, above his supreme power? … *When the law must rule and govern the monarch, and not the monarch the law, he hath at the most but a gubernative or executive power*." Michael Mendle, "The Great Council of Parliament and the First Ordinances: The Constitutional Theory of the Civil War," *Journal of British Studies* 31 (Apr., 1992): 133–162. Mendle reviewed a "virtually

 | DOI:10.1163/9789004706347_006

In 1631, the magistrates had ordered that "for time to come no man shall be admitted to the freedom of this body politic, but such as are members of some of the churches," so that its membership "may be preserved of honest and good men." The requirement of congregational membership for freemanship also applied to voting in colony level elections. In May 1634, those same good men had secured the right to be represented in the General Court, and by that Fall deputies and magistrates were enacting legislation to safeguard their godly community. Governor Winthrop noted in his journal, while the Court proceeded to pass "many laws," including regulations of tobacco, "immodest fashions," and "costly apparel," its primary focus was the "removal of Newtown." A group of townspeople from Newtown intent on founding a new colony in Connecticut requested the General Court provide its official approval to proceed under the leadership of Minister Thomas Hooker.[2]

After debate on the matter the issue was put to a vote, with fifteen deputies supporting the group's departure, and ten opposed; on the assistants' side, Governor Dudley and two other magistrates were in favor of the move, while Deputy Governor Roger Ludlow and three assistants disapproved of Newtown's request. The combined tally had Dudley's minority of magistrates (3) joined with a majority of deputies (15) sanctioning the Hooker group's departure, while Ludlow and three other magistrates (4) joined a minority of deputies (10) in opposition. A slim majority of magistrates had voted against a course of action advocated by a majority of deputies. Winthrop reported, "upon this grew a great difference between the governor and the assistants, and the deputies." Since the deputies and the magistrates met together with no process to resolve a divided vote, a dispute arose upon the deputies' refusal to "yield the assistants a negative voice," or veto power. If the magistrates voted with the deputies without distinction they could be outvoted if the deputies remained united. Winthrop noted the magistrates' opposition to such an outcome,

---

uninvestigated strand of parliamentary conceptualization": that its "two houses ... constituted the king's great council."

2 Nathaniel Shurtleff, ed., *MGCR*, 1: 87 (May 8, 1631), 126 (Sept. 3, 1634). Richard Dunn, ed., *Journal of John Winthrop* (Cambridge: Belknap Press, 1996), 79 (n. 19), 95, 101 (Aug.-Nov. 1633), 125–28 (Sept. 1634). Francis Bremer, *John Winthrop*, 253–59. Derek Hirst, "The Failure of Godly Rule in the English Republic," *Past and Present* 132 (Aug., 1991): 49–50. "English soil was certainly prepared for the rooting of discipline. The abiding characteristic of the seventeenth-century moral laws ... was their expedited procedures. Successive acts against swearing and cursing, against drunkenness and against the profanation of the sabbath, required the testimony of merely a single witness for proof ... Additionally, the position of Justices of the Peace was strengthened during the Interregnum." Karen Kupperman, *Providence Island, 1630–1641* (Cambridge: Cambridge Univ. Press, 1993), 249–52, 326–34.

"considering how dangerous it might be to the commonwealth if they should not keep that strength to balance the greater number of the deputies."[3]

In England, the negative voice was the monarch's veto power, but unlike the modern veto it could not be overridden. Moreover, it existed within a model of governance that functioned very differently than the modern sovereign state. In the late 1500's a leading theologian of the Anglican Church, Richard Hooker, described the monarch's "supremacy of power" in legislative matters as "principally in the strength of a negative voice," both to preserve the tradition-bound English Common Law as well as to manage an ever-increasing number of statutes churned out by Parliament. Ebenezer Davies' twentieth-century reaction to Hooker's description illustrates the differing medieval and modern assumptions surrounding a veto power, "Such a definition of sovereignty is disappointing and unusual," as it was properly "defined in more positive terms, generally as the power of legislation." The medieval principality bedevils modern understanding because its authority did not flow directly from a unified sovereign power as in a constitutional state; Daniel Lee has recently described the era as "constitutionalism without states." Official authority did, as Walter Ullmann described it, reach its "apogee in the monarch from whom it descended in a graded manner to lower personnel," as "the monarch possessed [a] plentitude of power which he distributed—allegorically speaking—downward." While it was a common saying that the king was the "fountain" of justice and law, and although an aristocratic nobility partnered with the episcopacy of the Roman Church ruled in this era, their joint operation did not manifest a unified sovereign public entity. Instead, the medieval principality was a quilted patchwork of feudal authorities joined by sworn allegiance based on reciprocal needs. As secular authority descended from the monarch, it flowed into the horizontal gullies of adjunct jurisdictions; these tributaries scarred the hillside of a kingdom that, internally, took the form of an anthill rather than a pyramidal bureaucratic organization. At its very top privy councilors, great lords, judges, and prelates presided. The hillside itself was marked by various authorities, from the greater to the lesser nobility, royal and church courts, with chartered entities like boroughs and guilds intermixed. Natural law, informed by divine nature and accessible by human reason, was the supreme fundamental law

3 Richard Dunn, ed., *Journal of John Winthrop*, 127–28 (Sept., 1634). Edmund Morgan, *The Puritan Dilemma*, 2nd ed., 138–42. S.E. Morison, *Builders of the Bay Colony* (New York: Houghton Mifflin Co., 1930), 91–93. Francis Bremer, *John Winthrop*, 243–55. George Haskins, *Law and Authority in Early Massachusetts* (New York: MacMillan Co., 1960), 38. Robert Wall, *Massachusetts Bay: The Crucial Decade* (New Haven: Yale Univ. Press, 1972), 50. Bernard Bailyn, *The Barbarous Years* (New York: Vintage Books, 2013), 408–9.

that ungirded its hodgepodge of jurisdictions, but as one descended, relations were regulated by human laws that were meant to conform to "morality."[4]

Today "jurisdiction" refers primarily to judicial authority, joined to its law enforcement counterparts operating within a set geographical territory. But as Brian Tierny explained, the term retained its medieval definition—when it "commonly meant the power of ruling in general"—well into the seventeenth century. A jurisdictional authority possessed a "right to govern," and was infused by a spectrum of "rights and powers." In the English scheme, the greatest jurisdiction was undoubtedly the monarch's, whose exclusive authority reached its zenith in her prerogative powers of church and state. But as Mark Howe described the sixteenth-century "jurisdiction," it "referred to many courts, some the Queen's, some not, … and many laws, some derived from royal prerogative, and others rooted in tradition." Before sovereignty was conceived as one unified entity, it was perfectly natural to view it as a spectrum of distributive jurisdictions, from the largest portion of royal authority to all types of lesser magistrates, secular and spiritual. During a meeting of Parliament, and a gathering of its great mound of jurisdictions, even Elizabeth I (1558–1603) struggled to control its mass. Although she consistently defended her rights of prerogative (or absolute authority) in matters such as royal marriage and succession, foreign affairs, governing the church, internal state security, and royal administration, her negative voice was a vital means to control the nobility, the episcopacy, and the gentry. In such a throng of competing jurisdictions separated by only law and custom, most importantly, law classified what the monarch and tradition allowed. In this spirit, the negative voice provided the monarch a vital means to limit parliamentary initiative and preserve the status quo. Or as Minister Richard Hooker described it, "Be it in states of regiment popular,

4 Ebenezer Davies, *The Political Ideas of Richard Hooker* (London: SPCK, 1946), 74. Richard Hooker, *Of the Laws of Ecclesiastical Polity*, Arthur McGrade ed., (Cambridge: Cambridge Univ. Press, 1989), 194 (Bk. 8, Ch. 6, §11). Hooker published most of the *Laws of Ecclesiastical Polity* between 1593 and 1597. Walter Ullmann, *The Relevance of Medieval Ecclesiastical History* (Cambridge: Cambridge Univ. Press, 1966), 17–18. Daniel Lee, *Popular Sovereignty in Early Modern Constitutional Thought* (Oxford: Oxford Univ. Press, 2016), 5–10, 98–120. "[T]he question of constituting public authority in the absence of the state was the major question of constitutional theory before the seventeenth century, disagreement over which yielded … a steady stream of constitutional and political thought … Without a notion of the state as the uncontested center of public authority carving out a space for politics, … concepts of authority were commingled together with private right." Norman Doe, *Fundamental Authority in Late Medieval English Law* (Cambridge: Cambridge Univ. Press, 1990), 60–69. R.W. and A.J. Carlyle, *A History of Medieval Political Theory in the West*, 3rd ed., (Edinburgh: William Blackwood and Sons, 1916), 3: 41, 184. J.H. Baker, *An Introduction to English Legal History*, 3rd ed., (London: Butterworths, 1990), 14–43.

aristocratic, or regal, principality resteth in that person or those persons unto whom is given the right of excluding any kind of law, whatsoever it be, before establishment." By the 1640's Sir John Spelman still claimed the prerogative right of "negative voice" for Charles I, without whom Parliament "may not make any laws."[5]

Obviously, the magistrates' claim to the negative voice during this era was of far greater import than a simple refusal to allow Hooker's congregation the right to migrate to Connecticut. Instead, the deputies realized the assistants' goal was to maintain control of the General Court's legislative process, one to which they had just gained access. When John Cotton delivered a sermon describing the negative voice as a power to be shared between the magistrates, the body of freemen, and the ministry, Winthrop rejected any commensurate power to the magistracy, "although all were not satisfied about the negative voice to be left to the magistrates ... no man moved" against it. David Hall identified an important influence of English politics in these exchanges: "that a negative voice was so provocative owed a great deal to the fact that Charles I was claiming the very same privilege. That so many people listened impatiently when Winthrop declared the magistrates were like 'gods' (as the Old Testament and Calvinist tradition warranted him saying) had something to do with the fact that James I had used exactly the same language in addressing Parliament

5 Brian Tierny, *Religion, Law, and the Growth of Constitutional Thought: 1150–1650* (Cambridge: Cambridge Univ. Press, 1982), 30–1. Mark Howe, "The Sources and Nature of Law in Colonial Massachusetts," in *Selected Essays*, George Billias ed., (Barre [MA]: Barre Publishers, 1965), 3–5. E.W. Ives, *The Common Lawyers of Pre-Reformation England* (Cambridge: Cambridge Univ. Press, 1983), 9–10, 244. Charles McIlwain, *The High Court of Parliament*, 129–34. Sir Thomas Smith, *De Republica Anglorum*, ed. Mary Dewar, (Cambridge: Cambridge Univ. Press, 1982), 78, 85–8, 103. Smith posited the "most high and absolute power of the realm of England ... in Parliament," while believing this was consistent with monarchy's "absolute power" in certain cases. When all ranks of nobility and commonality were summoned by royal warrant to sit in Parliament, the sum of their authority when joined with royal prerogative constituted an "absolute power" in all cases. Geoffrey Elton, *The Parliament of England* (Cambridge: Cambridge Univ. Press, 1986), 123–26. Conrad Russell, *The Crisis of Parliaments* (London: Oxford Univ. Press, 1971), 220–21. Richard Hooker, *Of the Laws of Ecclesiastical Polity*, ed. Arthur McGrade, 194 (Bk. 8, Ch. 6, §11). Sir John Spelman, *A View of a Printed Book Entitled Observations Upon His Majesties Late Answers and Expresses* (Oxford: University Printer, 1643), 20–23 (unpaginated); *Thomason Tracts* E245 (22), Reel 42. Michael Mendle, *Henry Parker and the English Civil War* (Cambridge: Cambridge Univ. Press, 1995), 104–5. J.P. Sommerville, *Royalists and Patriots: Politics and Ideology in England (1603–1640)*, 2nd ed., (London: Longman, 1999), 37–54. By the early seventeenth century, even common law justices maintained that while the English monarch had "agreed to abide by established laws in ordinary cases," they had "reserved an absolute power to act as they saw fit in extraordinary circumstances—and they defined what counted as an extraordinary circumstance."

in 1610." Conrad Russell went a step further in describing the governor's articulation of his own authority, "Winthrop did much to meet the Puritan ideal of the 'godly prince,' while at the same time developing a doctrine of his prerogative almost as high-flown as that of James I."[6]

In 1598, James VI of Scotland (1567–1625) equated the "proper office of a king towards his subjects" with a person's head and the rest of his body, because "from the head, being the seat of judgment, proceedeth the care and foresight of guiding … the body." This care and guidance included employing each man of the kingdom "in their own office, as long as they are able for it." But if any were "affected with any infirmity," the king, as head of state, must "provide for their remedy, in case it be curable, and if otherwise … cut them off for fear of infecting the rest." By 1610, approaching a decade on the English throne, James I (1603–1625) based his claims of divine right on scriptural authority, "kings are not only God's lieutenants upon earth and sit upon God's throne, but even by God himself they are called Gods." Despite the exclusivity of James's claims, many political authorities in Early Stuart England derived legitimacy from God's sovereignty, or natural law, such as the "godly magistrate." The most renowned Puritan theologian of the Elizabethan era, William Perkins, described society as "distinguished by order," as "God hath appointed that in every society one person should be above another; not making all equal, as though the body should be all head and nothing else"; hierarchy, not equality, was the era's accepted norm. To enforce the law equitably, one must embody Christian principles "in executing the office of a magistrate in bearing the sword" of civil justice. As Samuel Ward (brother of Massachusetts minister

6 Richard Dunn, ed., *Journal of John Winthrop*, 128 (Sept., 1634). David Hall, *A Reforming People* (New York: Alfred A. Knopf, 2011), 29–30, 205–6 (n. 12). Winthrop certainly did alarm the freemen with his claim of divine authority, even if it was not based on monarchical divine right absolutism; as Professor Hall explained, Winthrop's use of a godly magistrate's authority derived from sixteenth century Protestant origins and specifically Theodore Beza's *Rights of Magistrates*. Ernst Kantorowicz, "Mysteries of State: An Absolutist Concept and its Late Medieval Origins." *Harvard Theological Review* 48 (1955): 65–91. Edmund Morgan, *The Puritan Dilemma*, 2nd ed., 138–42. Conrad Russell, *The Origins of the English Civil War* (London: Macmillan Press, 1973), 22. T.H. Breen, *The Character of a Good Ruler* (New Haven: Yale Univ. Press, 1970), 59. "A battle over the character of magisterial authority began as soon as the settlers attempted to define the rulers' powers with precision. One group of Puritans claimed that their civil leaders held broad discretionary powers and, within obvious scriptural limits, were free to govern the commonwealth as they alone saw fit. The opposition responded that the citizens themselves had delegated prerogatives to their magistrates. This faction expected rulers to stay within any constitutional boundaries which the freemen might set."

Nathaniel Ward) proclaimed, magistrates thus "qualified and chosen" were fit to "judge the people."[7]

Deputy Israel Stoughton left a very different account of colonial affairs than Winthrop's as they stood at this point. He agreed that Cotton's proposal for compromise extended a "power of suspension" to assistants and deputies "in cases where they agree not, until the mind of the whole body of the country may conveniently be known." In his opinion, however, the issue should then be settled by majority vote without distinction between deputies and assistants. This was "proposed and approved by ministers and country, but not by [the] magistrates." A "to doo … about a negative voice for the magistrates" had resulted, with Winthrop and like-minded magistrates insisting that the General Court could pass no law or issue a judicial ruling without their majority vote. Even if the entire colony and "3 of 7 of the magistrates like and desire it," identical to the magistrates' vote on the Hooker group's request, Winthrop and the magistrates maintained that the General Court could not issue a ruling. Stoughton

7 James VI, *The Trew Law of Free Monarchies* (1598; reprint, 1616), ed. Johann Sommerville, *King James VI and I: Political Writings* (Cambridge: Cambridge Univ. Press, 1994), 76–7. James I, *A Speech to the Lords and Commons of the Parliament at White-Hall* (1610), in Ibid., 181. Harold Berman, *Law and Revolution: The Impact of the Protestant Reformations on the Western Legal Tradition* (Cambridge: Belknap Press, 2003), 2: 213. In response to challenges to the prerogative by the House of Commons and common law courts, James felt compelled to "expound systematically—and eventually to publish in book form—a theory of absolute monarchy which his predecessors had wisely left largely implicit and ambiguous." Ian Williams, "James VI and I, *rex and judex*: One King as Judge in Two Kingdoms," in eds. William Eves, et. al., *Common Law, Civil Law, and Colonial Law: Essays in Comparative English Legal History from the Twelfth to the Twentieth Centuries* (Cambridge: Cambridge Univ. Press, 2021), 98–99. William Perkins, *Treatise of the Vocations or Callings of Men*, in Edmund Morgan, ed., *Puritan Political Ideas: 1558–1794* (Indianapolis: Bobbs-Merrill Co., 1965), 50–6. Tim Harris, *Rebellion: Britain's First Stuart Kings*, (Oxford: Oxford Univ. Press, 2013), 11–41. Godfrey Davies, *The Early Stuarts* (Oxford: Clarendon Press, 1949), 31–44. Glenn Burgess, *British Political Thought: 1500–1660* (New York: Palgrave MacMillan, 2009), 143–52. John Eusden, *Puritans, Lawyers, and Politics in Early Seventeenth-Century England* (New Haven: Yale Univ. Press, 1958; reprint, Archon Books, 1965), 56. "By the time of James' accession, the theory [of divine right of kings] had the following main points: (1) a king has an individual right, derived from God, to his throne; (2) this right is hereditary; (3) a king is responsible to God alone; (4) a king's prerogative—or right to rule is of a higher order than the ordinary law of the land … What James started, Charles was to continue." J.P. Sommerville, *Politics and Ideology in England* (London, New York: Longman, 1986), 12. Royal absolutists "held that whatever the form of government—monarchy, aristocracy or democracy—the powers of the governor were derived from God alone." Samuel Ward, *Jethro's Justice of Peace: At a Sermon Preached at a General Assize Held at Bury St. Edmonds*, intro. and epilogue by Nathaniel Ward, (London: Griffin & John Marriot 1618), 5; *Google Books* (https://books.google.com/books/about/Jethro_s_Justice_of_Peace_A_sermon_on_Ex.html?id=A7FoAAAAcAAJ).

responded that no explicit grant of the voice was made in any part of the colony's *Charter*, "I know none that have read the patent (excepting magistrates) that esteem it their due."[8]

Because Stoughton was the incipient leader of the protest his fellow deputies persuaded him to publish his position, and he complied reluctantly, penning a dozen reasons for his opposition to the measure. Stoughton's list eventually came into Winthrop's possession, who then shared it with the rest of the magistrates. At the next General Court, the assistants were united in charging Stoughton, in "bitter terms," for "denying them to be magistrates," and carried the day. In March 1635 the Court ordered Stoughton's list "be burnt, as being weak and offensive," and barred him from holding "public office in the commonwealth within this jurisdiction for the space of three years for affirming the assistants were no magistrates." Winthrop also condemned him for "affirming that the power of the governor was but ministerial." Stoughton acknowledged that Winthrop denounced him as a "troubler of Israel," and an "underminer of the State," but he "utterly denied" these charges. Instead, Stoughton claimed to have "freed the State" and was baffled by the tempest his tract had created, because in his opinion it represented the "judgment of every man in the land." Israel wrote his brother in England when the furor had subsided, the "main accusation which they stuck too was that I denied the assistants to be magistrates and made them but ministers of justice." A "charge I denied." According to the era's most popular JP manual, *The Countrey Justice*, a Justice's authority was sometimes "ministerial, or regular and limited," while in other cases "judicial or absolute" like the power of a judge. A ministerial power operated by virtue of a "higher authority," and could "proceed no further" than the commission of the peace or statute authorizing its activity. On other occasions, however, when "circumstances can neither be comprehended in the commission, nor foreseen at the time of the making of the statutes," JP's took on the role of a judge or magistrate. Essentially, a ministerial jurisdiction was limited by some superior authority, while its magisterial counterpart exercised a broad judicial discretion.[9]

---

8 Israel Stoughton, *A Relation Concerning New England*, MHS *Proceedings (1860–1862)*, 5: 136. S.E. Morison, *Builders of the Bay Colony*, 91. Francis Bremer, *John Winthrop*, 244–46. Robert Wall, *Massachusetts Bay: The Crucial Decade*, 12.

9 Israel Stoughton, *A Relation Concerning New England*, 5: 136–39. Michael Dalton, *Countrey Justice*, (1618); (reprint, Norwood [NJ]: Walter J. Johnson Inc., 1975), 17–18. Nathaniel Shurtleff, ed., *MGCR*, 1: 135–36 (March 4, 1635). "Mr. Israel Stoughton hath written a certain book which hath occasioned much trouble & offense to the Court." Richard Dunn, ed., *Journal of John Winthrop*, 142 (March 1635). David Hall, *A Reforming People*, 28–30. Robert Wall, "Membership of the Massachusetts General Court," (Ph.D. Diss., Yale University, 1965), 350–51.

Stoughton interpreted the colonial *Charter* as providing the assistants "power ministerial according to the greater vote of the General Court's," but "not magisterial according to their own discretion." Instead, magisterial authority must operate via the sanction of a majority vote in the General Court, without distinction between assistant and deputy. In Stoughton's own words, whatever "I intended and meant" about "their power, call it ministerial, or magisterial, … [it] was not so great that they could do … or hinder" anything "according to their own wills." Instead, the assistants "must hear and respect" the decisions of the General Court as rendered by the "whole company of freemen." The magistrates counterattacked, insisting that Stoughton be stripped of his freemanship, and the deputies went along; the Levellers' own attack on the King's negative voice the following decade illustrates the radicalism of Stoughton's position. As the Leveller William Walwyn wrote in 1646 concerning the monarchy's negative voice, "in this way of voting in all affairs of the commonwealth, being not chose thereunto by the people, they are therein masters and lords of the people—which necessarily implies the people to be their servants and vassals." Similarly, Stoughton maintained his opposition to the magistrates was based on their claim to a "power … over our persons, goods, and lives, without any law of ours." Nevertheless, Roger Ludlow and John Winthrop persisted, accusing Stoughton of confessing an intent to undermine the magistracy in a private meeting. Fortunately, for Stoughton's sake, a fourth person surreptitiously overheard the conversation, and Magistrate Ludlow's congregation ultimately decided he had misrepresented Stoughton's position. Soon, Stoughton was cleared of all charges, prompting many of the colony's leading men—including Richard Bellingham, John Cotton, Thomas Hooker, and Nathaniel Ward—to recoil from the "dealings" of his opponents.[10]

10 Israel Stoughton, *A Relation Concerning New England*, 5: 139–40. Nathaniel Shurtleff, ed., *MGCR*, 1: 135–36 (March 4, 1635). David Hall, *A Reforming People*, 205–6 (n.12). According to Hall, Stoughton's distinction between "magisterial" and "ministerial" authority had origins as far back as the medieval University of Paris, and made familiar to Massachusetts ministers by its use in the Netherlands; we will see the distinction was also made in Leveller pamphlets in Revolutionary England. The radical nature of Stoughton's position is further illustrated by, first Parliament's, and then the Levellers' opposition to the negative voice. Conrad Russell, *The Causes of the English Civil War*, 142. "By the summer of 1642 the key point Parliamentarians were trying to establish was that the King had no negative voice: they invoked 'the obligation that lieth upon the kings of this realm, to pass such bills as are offered to them by both Houses of Parliament, in the name and for the good of the whole kingdom.'" Rachel Foxley, *The Levellers: Radical Political Thought in the English Revolution* (Manchester: Manchester Univ. Press, 2013), 35. "[T]he denial of the veto power … was to become a hallmark of Leveller thought." Richard Overton, William

This turn of events manifested itself at the very next session of the General Court. In May 1635, John Haynes (a member of Thomas Hooker's congregation and later governor of Connecticut) defeated Roger Ludlow for the Massachusetts governorship at the annual election, and Richard Bellingham defeated Ludlow, Winthrop, and Dudley for the deputy governorship. Stoughton reported that "Mr. Winthrop had very many hands against him for being either governor ... or assistant." Ludlow was not even reelected as magistrate. Ironically, after initially voting against the group's request to leave Massachusetts, he would migrate to Connecticut and become one of the early leaders of the new settlement. Only a few months before, Winthrop thought that the magistrates had prevailed in both securing the negative voice, and, in preventing the settlement of a new colony by Massachusetts colonists it could little afford to lose. Now he railed at Ludlow's humiliation, by removing him from the magistracy the people were determined to "*exercise their absolute power*." Just a week before the election Stoughton thought it "almost past question" that Ludlow would be chosen governor. Ludlow's misreport had undone him. Stoughton was restored to the rank of freemen in May 1636, and he again represented Dorchester in the General Court as a deputy. In 1637, he was elected assistant owing to his opposition to the Antinomians as well as his military service against the Pequot tribe, during which the colony exacted a terrible revenge for a handful of fatal attacks on colonists.[11]

Surprisingly, considering the intensity of the dispute, Stoughton did not harbor resentment towards Winthrop for long, even though at one point he complained that they "defame me as if I had held some anabaptistical opinion about magistrates." Nevertheless, after the crisis had receded, he reasoned that while Winthrop was "indeed a man of men," he was still "but a man," and subject to human frailties. While many "had idolized him," most "do now confess their error." Still, he believed Winthrop to be a "godly man and a worthy magistrate, notwithstanding some few passages." In closing, he urged his brother to keep his letter private and not aggravate reports portraying the colony as "strangely

---

Walwyn, *A Remonstrance of Many Thousand Citizens* (London: 1646); in Andrew Sharp ed., *The English Levellers* (Cambridge: Cambridge Univ. Press, 1998), 38.

11 Israel Stoughton, *A Relation Concerning New England*, 5: 141. Nathaniel Shurtleff, ed., *MGCR*, 1: 145 (May 6, 1635), 175 (May 25, 1636), 185 (Dec. 7, 1636), 195 (May 17, 1637). Richard Dunn, ed., *Journal of John Winthrop*, 142 (n. 86–87), 144 (May 1635), 158 (n. 57). Francis Bremer, *John Winthrop*, 243. Robert Wall, "Membership of the Massachusetts General Court," 338, 350–51, 542. Bernard Bailyn, *The Barbarous Years*, 101–16, 443–49, 500–1. Peter Mancall, *The Trials of Thomas Morton* (New Haven: Yale Univ. Press, 2019), 154–64. Malcom Gaskill, *Between Two Worlds: How the English Became Americans* (New York: Basic Books, 2014), 140–43.

troubled." Israel admitted "we have weaknesses and wants," and "differences arise, who questions this?" But "how can it be otherwise?" To assure him the matter was settled, Israel relayed that Winthrop had "confessed ... publicly this last Court" he had "over shot himself." Winthrop noted in his journal only that several differences between the magistrates and the deputies had been "cleared with full satisfaction to all parties." To his credit, Winthrop acknowledged that the deputies perceived a "great danger to our state, in regard that our magistrates for want of positive laws in many cases might proceed according to their discretions." So, the magistrates had agreed that "some men should be appointed to frame a body of grounds of laws in resemblance to a *Magna Charta"* which, after adoption, would "be received for the fundamental laws."[12]

Thomas Aquinas used positive law to describe the laws that men enacted to "govern the commonwealths they set up."[13] Winthrop's use of the term was more specific. He employed it to describe the deputies' fear of the magistrates' discretion, and that the freemen thought positive law would protect them from "arbitrary" government. Samuel Johnson's *Dictionary* cites Milton's definition of positive, as "absolute, particular, direct, not implied." "Direct" and "not implied" fits the case because in the deputies' judgment the danger lay in the magistrates' ability to proceed "according to their discretions." On this point both Winthrop and Stoughton agreed. In May 1635, when Winthrop entered the deputies' demand for positive law in his journal, that same month the General Court ordered Governor Haynes, Deputy Governor Bellingham, Thomas Dudley and Winthrop to draft "laws as they shall judge needful for the well ordering of this plantation, and to present the same to the next Court." Consequently, the deputies believed that if the colony's laws were recorded

---

12 Israel Stoughton, *A Relation Concerning New England*, 5: 140–43. Richard Dunn, ed., *Journal of John Winthrop*, 146 (May 1635). S.E. Morison, *Builders of the Bay Colony*, 91–2. Edmund Morgan, *The Puritan Dilemma*, 2nd ed., 142–44.

13 R.C. Van Caenegem, *An Historical Introduction to Private Law* (Cambridge: Cambridge Univ. Press, 1992), 115–44. F.J. Shirley, *Richard Hooker and Contemporary Political Ideas* (London: SPCK, 1949), 71–92. Ebenezer Davies, *The Political Ideas of Richard Hooker*, 27–61. Richard Hooker, *Of the Laws of Ecclesiastical Polity*, ed. Arthur McGrade, 117 (Bk. 1, Ch. 15, §1). George Haskins, *Law and Authority in Early Massachusetts*, 118–19. The medieval "ius positivum" (positive law) was used by Thomas Aquinas in contrast to "ius naturale," or natural law. Subsequently, Aquinas's definition was adopted by Richard Hooker near the end of the sixteenth century, and his three examples of positive law included "civil constitutions peculiar unto each particular commonweal," and "all the judicials which God gave unto the people of Israel to observe."

in writing, and in some detail, the magistrates could no longer issue arbitrary decisions at their discretion.[14]

A General Court order that Winthrop cited regularly in future years seems to contradict the deputies' demands for enactment of written laws, as it appears to identify Massachusetts as a theocracy ruled by "godly" magistrates who used the Bible as its fundamental legal text. In 1636, a unified General Court had authorized the magistrates to "hear and determine all causes according to the laws now established, and where there is no law, then as near the law of God as they can." Why would the deputies have agreed to such a law, allowing the magistrates to decide cases on the "law of God," only a year after objecting to their arbitrary jurisdiction in the absence of written law? Contradiction disappears upon the reinsertion of the excerpt into the original act:

> The Governor, Deputy Governor, Thomas Dudley, John Haynes, Richard Bellingham, Esq., Mr. Cotton, Mr. Peters, and Mr. Shepard are entreated to make a draught of laws agreeable to the word of God, which may be the fundamentals of this commonwealth, and to present the same to the next General Court. And it is ordered that *in the meantime* the magistrates and associates shall proceed in the courts to hear and determine all causes according to the laws now established, and where there is no law, then as near the law of God as they can.

According to Norman Doe it was "entirely orthodox" to discover principles of positive law via scripture, because medieval notions of natural law held it "superior to human law." Anticipating adoption of new legislation, the deputies conceded that, in the "meantime," standard procedure would suffice.[15]

---

14 Nathaniel Shurtleff, ed., *MGCR*, 1: 147 (May 6, 1635). Richard Dunn, ed., *Journal of John Winthrop*, 146 (n.1). George Haskins, *Law and Authority in Early Massachusetts*, 30–37, 118–25. Edmund Morgan, *The Puritan Dilemma*, 2nd ed., 138–155. S.E. Morison, *Builders of the Bay Colony*, 225–30. Peter Hoffer, *Law and People in Colonial America* (Baltimore: Johns Hopkins Univ. Press, 1989), 16–24. Mark Cahn, "Punishment, Discretion, and the Codification of Prescribed Penalties in Colonial Massachusetts," *American Journal of Legal History* 33 (1989): 107–36. Charles Hilkey, *Legal Development in Colonial Massachusetts: 1630–1686* (New York: Columbia Univ. Press, 1910), 65–69.

15 Nathaniel Shurtleff, ed., *MGCR*, 1: 174–75 (May 25, 1636). Norman Doe, *Fundamental Authority in Late Medieval English Law*, 83. William Nelson, "The Utopian Legal Order of the Massachusetts Bay Colony, 1630–1686," *American Journal of Legal History* 47 (Apr., 2005), 192–93. Richard Ross, "The Career of Puritan Jurisprudence," *Law and History Review* 26 (2008): 227–58.

During the one-year interim between the appointments of the two committees—the first being appointed in May 1635—a compromise on the inflammatory issue of the negative voice was reached that would last until the middle of the 1640's. Stoughton had predicted that a "power of suspension" must reside in both parties "in cases where they agree not." While he remained convinced that magistrates and deputies should vote together without distinction, his prediction of a potential compromise was enacted into law in March 1636:

> [W]hereas it may fall out that in some of these General Courts, to be held by the magistrates and deputies, there may arise some difference of judgment in doubtful cases, it is therefore ordered that no law, order, or sentence shall pass as an act of Court without the consent of the greater part of the magistrates on one part, and the greater number of the deputies on the other part; and for want of such accord, the cause or order shall be suspended, and if either part think it so material, there shall be forthwith a committee chosen, the one half by the magistrates, and the other half by the deputies, and the committee so chosen [is] to elect an umpire, who together shall have power to hear and determine the cause in question.[16]

The law proceeded to create four new "inferior quarterly courts" in Boston, Salem, Cambridge, and Ipswich to hear "civil causes whereof the debt of damage shall not exceed £10, and all criminal cases not concerning life, member, or banishment"; such exceptional cases would remain under the jurisdiction of the court of assistants or the General Court. These new courts would be presided over by magistrates joined by "persons of worth as shall from time to time be appointed by the General Court" after their nomination by the towns; the newly created associate judges were also authorized to base their judgements upon a standard of the "law of God." Delegating such minor cases to these inferior courts relieved the General Court of most of its judicial business, and it would subsequently meet biannually, rather than quarterly sessions as originally agreed to in 1634. One session would convene in May for annual elections and other affairs, with the second held in the Fall "for making laws and other public occasions of the commonwealth." With the compromise on

16 Shurtleff, ed., *MGCR*, 1: 170 (March 3, 1636). Israel Stoughton, "*A Relation Concerning New England*," 5: 136.

the negative voice, neither a law, nor a judgment, could pass without majority votes of both magistrates and deputies.[17]

A law passed during the same session demonstrates the freemen's expanding jurisdiction in the colony. On March 3, 1636, the General Court adopted the *Town Act*, establishing formal authority for Massachusetts town government that remains famous to this day:

> Whereas particular towns have many things which concern only themselves, and the ordering of their own affairs, and disposing of businesses in their own town, it is therefore ordered that the freemen of every town, or the major part of them, shall only have power to dispose of their own lands and woods, with all the privileges and appurtenances of the said towns, to grant lots, and make such orders as may concern the well ordering of their own towns, not repugnant to the laws and orders here established by the General Court; as also to lay fines and penalties for the breach of these orders.

The magnitude of this grant is evident in conjunction with an order made the previous September, "none but [the] freemen shall have any vote in any town."[18]

As the magistrates' jurisdiction was being reigned-in, the freemen were amassing considerable power at the expense of the colony's "inhabitants," or those who were non-congregants. Magistrates like Dudley, Winthrop, and Ludlow were obviously jealous of their own authority, but as the deputies passed laws empowering the freemen it was increasingly clear that they also coveted political power. From a modern perspective, shouldn't the freemen have established a more equitable polity by granting greater access to the political system? Indeed, according to an ideology of natural rights this should have been their goal, but that idea became popular in the next century, and then only as applied to white propertied males. Hierarchy was seventeenth-century Massachusetts' reality in both church and state. As David Ramsey explained in his history of the American Revolution published in 1789, after praising Bay

17 Nathaniel Shurtleff, ed., *MGCR*, 1: 169–70 (March 3, 1636). Richard Dunn, ed., *Journal of John Winthrop*, 174 (March 1636). Francis Bremer, *John Winthrop*, 244–45. George Haskins, *Law and Authority in Early Massachusetts*, 32–37.

18 Nathaniel Shurtleff, ed., *MGCR*, 1: 172 (March 3, 1636), 1: 161 (Sept. 3, 1635). Mark Peterson, *The City State of Boston* (Princeton: Princeton Univ. Press, 2019), 143. Massachusetts "created an attractive structure for land distribution. Its incorporated towns gave colonists freehold title to their lands, free of any rents or obligations due to the crown or landlords."

colonists for rebelling against the Anglican church in pursuit of "liberty" for their own beliefs, only to then pursue uniformity in church government and turn "persecutors," "[n]o better apology can be made for this inconsistent conduct, than that the true grounds of liberty of conscience were then neither understood, nor practiced by any sect of Christians."[19]

While Stoughton and the deputies appeared to be triumphant in the negative voice controversy, it signaled only a lull in the struggle. The voice remained controversial throughout the first charter period (1629–1686), because in addition to a veto power, it delineated legislative and judicial authorities between magistrates and deputies before a modern separation of powers was conceived; the General Court enacted legislation as well as decided judicial cases like capital trials and impeachments. Stoughton left the colony in the early 1640's to fight in England under Oliver Cromwell's command in Colonel Thomas Rainsborough's regiment (Thomas was John Winthrop's brother-in-law by virtue of his son Stephen's marriage to Judith Rainsborough, and famous for his participation in the Putney Debates). The Rainsborough family had settled in the colony in 1636, including Thomas's brother, William, who also returned to England with members of the Massachusetts Artillery Company; after Thomas's assassination by royalists, William adopted a standard for his cavalry troop featuring an "image of the king's decapitated head ... with the motto *Salus Populi Suprema Lex*." Governor Winthrop's son, Colonel Stephen Winthrop, commanded his own cavalry regiment under Cromwell and never returned to Massachusetts, dying in England in the late 1650's. Stoughton died of disease during the war's earliest years, but his position on the voice remained definitive for decades.[20]

---

19 Gordon Wood, *The Radicalism of the American Revolution* (New York: Vintage Books, 1993), 229–32. "The revolutionaries aimed at nothing less than a reconstitution of American society. They hoped to destroy the bonds holding together the older monarchical society—kinship, patriarchy, and patronage ... Nothing contributed more to this explosion of energy than did the idea of equality. Equality was in fact the most radical and most powerful ideological force let loose in the Revolution." David Ramsay, *The History of the American Revolution* (Philadelphia: R. Aitken & Son, 1789), 1: 8–9. Ramsay's two volume history of the American Revolution was in John Adams' library, and provides an interesting perspective on the revolutionary generation's view of the founding of Massachusetts.

20 Nicholas Tyack, "Revolutionary Puritanism in Anglo-American Perspective," *Huntington Library Quarterly* 78 (Winter 2015): 763–64. Leslie Stephen, and Sidney Lee, eds., *The Dictionary of National Biography* (London: Oxford University Press, 1917), 18: 1325–26. "During the Putney Debates in 1647, both Thomas and William Rainsborough [spoke] in favor of extending the franchise. New England [also] contributed at least fifteen parliamentary army chaplains" including Hugh Peters. Charles Firth, Godfrey Davies, *The Regimental History of Cromwell's Army* (Oxford: Clarendon Press, 1940), 1: 175–92, 235, 417–23. Firth termed it "remarkable" that "three, if not more," of Thomas Rainsborough's

Renewed controversy over the voice erupted in the Summer of 1642, even though the General Court's process of enacting legislation and issuing judicial decisions seemed well established. But, strangely enough, the seed of this latest controversy arose when a wealthy Boston merchant, Robert Keayne, found a stray pig in 1636. He kept it for several years, giving public notice that it was in his possession so the owner might claim the sow. While "many came and saw her," no one ever claimed it, at least according to Keayne, and he had the pig slaughtered. Soon thereafter Goody Sherman charged that he had "killed her sow," filing formal complaint before his congregation in Boston, where he was cleared. At about the same time Keayne was accused of price gouging, and censured by his congregation for "selling his wares at excessive rates to the dishonor of God's name, the offense of the General Court, and [to] the public scandal of the country"; he was an easy target for populist rage as the colony experienced a devastating period of economic depression triggered by the collapse of immigration upon rumors of Parliament's recall in the late 1630's. Stung by Sherman's accusations, Keayne informed Governor Winthrop that Sherman had a male lodger, London merchant George Story, while her husband was abroad. As a result, the pair was now living "under suspicion." Sherman lost her suit against Keayne and £3 in court costs, as well as his countersuit for slander and a judgment of £20.[21]

---

regiment of foot's "officers were emigrants to New England." Susan Moore, *Abandoning America: Life-Stories from Early New England* (Woodbridge: Boydell Press, 2013), 58–61 (*Nehemiah Bourne* (1611–1691)); 260–61 (*William Rainsborough* (1617–1673)); 286–87 (*Israel Stoughton* (1602/3–1644)); 327–28 (*Stephen Winthrop* (1619–1658)). Winthrop, Jr., had risen from captain to colonel by 1654 in the New Model Army. Nehemiah Bourne served as solider, merchant, ship captain, and ultimately rear-admiral. Adrian Tinniswood, *The Rainborowes* (New York: Basic Books, 2013), 58–9, 72–3, 289. After his brother Thomas' assassination, William Rainsborough troop's colors featured an "image of the king's decapitated head ... with the motto *Salus Populi Suprema Lex*." Steven Archibald, *English Civil War Flags: Cavalry Cornets* (Hertfordshire: Redcrest Publishing, 2021), 37, 66. After his dismissal from service by Cromwell and House of Commons' sanctions for religious radicalism, William Rainsborough returned to Massachusetts. Mark Kishlansky, "The Army and the Levellers: The Roads to Putney," *Historical Journal* 22 (Dec., 1979): 759–824. Malcolm Gaskill, *Between Two Worlds*, 151–56, 178. Francis Bremer, *First Founders* (Durham: Univ. of New Hampshire Press, 2012), 113–29, 131–46. John Rees, *The Leveller Revolution* (London: Versa 2016), 49–50, 296–99.

21 *John Winthrop's Summary of the Case Between Richard Sherman and Robert Keayne* (1642), in *Winthrop Papers*, 4: 349–52. *MHS* (http://www.masshist.org/publications/winthrop/index.php/view/PWF04d321). Richard Dunn, ed., *Journal of John Winthrop*, 305–309 (Nov., 1639), 395–98 (June 1642), 451–58 (Oct. 1642-Sept., 1643). George Dow, ed., *Essex County Court Record* (Salem: Essex Institute, 1911), 1: 27. Thomas Lechford, *Notebook*, ed. Edward E. Hale, Jr., (Boston, 1885; reprint, Camden: Picton Press, 1988), 430–31. Bernard Bailyn, "The Apologia of Robert Keayne," *William and Mary Quarterly* 7 (1950): 572–75. S.E.

Ultimately, the case came before the General Court where its members were again divided in judgment, and this changed the nature of *Sherman v. Keayne* from a communal spat to a colony level crisis. After witness testimony, and follow-on debate, the issue was put to a vote, with 2 magistrates and 15 deputies for Sherman, 7 magistrates and 8 deputies for Keayne, and 7 deputies undecided. Once more a majority of deputies and minority of magistrates had voted against a minority of deputies and majority group of magistrates. Winthrop explained, Story's appeal was thereby moot, because "no sentence could by law pass without the greater number of both." In his eighteenth-century history of the Bay colony, Thomas Hutchinson concluded that Sherman's litigation prompted the deputies to challenge the magistrates' negative voice so bitterly that they demanded to meet separately from the magistrates, and prompted the establishment of the first bicameral legislature in Massachusetts. But Winthrop disagreed with this interpretation a century before: the case was not "dismissed ... by occasion of a negative vote of the magistrates (as is misreported), but by a fundamental and just law ... made upon serious consideration and advice with all the elders." He interpreted the law to operate so that "no sentence could by law pass without" the consent of the "greater part" of the magistrates and the deputies.[22]

Winthrop was citing the law, as enacted in 1636, that established the negative vote as part of General Court procedure in the wake of the Stoughton controversy.[23] Its final resolution—according to Stoughton's prediction—granted both magistrates and deputies a veto, so that neither group could approve a

---

Morison, *Builders of the Bay Colony*, 162. Francis Bremer, *John Winthrop*, 315–17, 352–54. Bernard Bailyn, *The New England Merchants*, 2nd ed., 41–44. Darrett Rutman, *Winthrop's Boston* (New York: W.W. Norton & Co., 1965), 234–47. Perry Miller, *The New England Mind: From Colony to Province* (New York: MacMillan Co., 1939), 37. Bernard Bailyn, *Barbarous Years*, 406–7, 465–68.

22 Nathaniel Shurtleff, ed., *MGCR*, 2: 12 (June 1642). Richard Dunn, ed., *Journal of John Winthrop*, 395–98 (June 1642). *Winthrop Papers*, 4: 350–52. Thomas Hutchinson, *The History of the Colony and Province of Massachusetts-Bay*, 2nd ed. (London: 1765), 1: 142–43. Francis Bremer, *John Winthrop*, 351–57. William Whitmore, ed., *Body of Liberties of 1641*, 41 (Lib. 36). *Sherman v. Keayne* came before the General Court under *Liberty 36*, "every man shall have liberty to complain to the General Court of any injustice done him in any court of assistants."

23 Nathaniel Shurtleff, ed., *MGCR*, 1: 170 (March 3, 1636): "And whereas it may fall out that in some of these General Courts to be held by the magistrates and deputies, there may arise some difference of judgment in doubtful cases, it is therefore ordered that no law, order, or sentence shall pass as an act of Court without the consent of the greater part of the magistrates on one part, and the greater number of the deputies on the other part; and for want of such accord the cause or order shall be suspended, and if either part think it so material there shall be forthwith a committee chosen, the one half by the magistrates

law or verdict without the other's concurrence. Winthrop's point was that the magistrates had not exercised a veto as an implied power of their office, as the King did in Parliament. Instead, deputies and magistrates each exercised a veto in the Court's legislative process by majority vote of their respective groups. Because the English monarch's negative voice signified royal authority over any parliamentary enactment, this prompted Stoughton's challenge to its acquisition by the magistrates. But now, with both majorities of magistrates and deputies necessary to pass an ordinance, Winthrop argued that no legislative predominance of one group over the other was possible. It had only become an issue when a divided vote worked in favor of the unpopular Keayne. Despite his best efforts, Winthrop noted Story's punishment had caused "many to speak unreverently" of the General Court, "especially of the magistrates, and the report went that their negative voice had hindered the course of justice." Public discontent became so heated that demands were made that "these magistrates must be put out" of their offices, so that the "power of the negative voice might be taken away."[24]

Even by the following year Winthrop noted the "sow business" was not "yet digested in the country," and colonial ministers were asked to mediate between magistrates and deputies by conducting their own investigation. After hearing conflicting testimony, the ministers concluded no basis existed for the General Court to "proceed to judgment in the case." Every magistrate agreed with this finding except Richard Bellingham, "who still maintained his former opinion, and would have the magistrates lay down their negative voice." One of the two magistrates who had voted with the majority of deputies in *Sherman v. Keayne* was Bellingham, and the other was most likely Richard Saltonstall, Jr., who had written a tract critical of the standing council. While Saltonstall, Jr., eventually withdrew his criticism, Bellingham "stood divided from the rest" of the magistrates. Several attempts to reconcile Bellingham and Winthrop failed to overcome an enduring personal animosity evident in a case heard by the General Court in December 1639. When then Governor Winthrop attempted to stop Bellingham from badgering a defendant in a lawsuit brought by his brother-in-law, the latter retorted, "Sir, I speak not to you." Upon Winthrop's ruling that his oft repeated question "was already answered," Bellingham rose and proclaimed, if he did not have "liberty to speak he would no longer sit there." Winthrop protested that "it was his place to manage the proceedings of the court," but let the matter drop. The counterpoint came in 1643 with the

---

and the other half by the deputies, and the committee so chosen to elect an umpire, who together shall have power to hear and determine the cause in question."

24 Richard Dunn, ed., *Journal of John Winthrop*, 398 (n. 89), 456–58.

enactment of a law that forbid magistrates from hearing cases involving a relative, "by birth or by marriage," avoiding such conflicts of interest in the future.[25]

In an essay entitled *Defense of the Negative Vote,* written in the Spring of 1643, Winthrop predictably dismissed the idea that Massachusetts should ever become a "mere Democracy," employing Athens as an historical reference to demonstrate that democratic governments were short-lived and ended catastrophically. Still, he readily acknowledged that the deputies were the "representatives of the people," constituting the "democratical" part of colonial government, which Winthrop termed a "mixed aristocracy"; these were Aristotelean references to monarchy, aristocracy, and democracy, forerunners to modern concepts of separate branches of government. Winthrop's primary disagreement with two of his fellow magistrates who steadfastly supported the deputies, Richard Bellingham and Richard Saltonstall, Jr., was over their support for allowing the deputies to exercise judicial and executive authorities, which he opposed unconditionally. Even then, however, Winthrop conceded that the deputies and magistrates exercised "all the power legislative and the chief power judicial of this body politic," and without each other they had "no power"; both observations are entirely consistent with applicable laws passed by the General Court to this point. Finally, and most remarkably, Winthrop ostensibly agreed with Bellingham's conception that "*the greatest power is in the people; therefore, it should be in their deputies.*" Considering that in this era of English politics popular sovereignty is attributed to the Levellers, a group that did not congeal until the later 1640's, Winthrop's response is remarkable even if it simply intended to appease the deputies. Because it confirms the deputies' pursuit of a popular sovereignty on behalf of the majority of colonial

---

25 Susan Moore, *Abandoning America: Life-Stories from Early New England* (Woodbridge: Boydell Press, 2013), 268–70; *Richard Saltonstall* (1610–1694). After these controversies Saltonstall, Jr., returned to England and joined his father as a member of the High Court of Justice under the Commonwealth, ultimately securing the post of customs commissioner for England. He continued to travel back and forth to the colony, remaining its benefactor, as well as of Harvard College, to include a £50 donation to the regicides Whalley and Goffe; he was one of the few who knew where they were hiding (in Hadley, MA). After being jailed for not swearing allegiance to Charles II, and upon his return to Massachusetts sometime after 1663, he was elected an assistant. After one of his numerous voyages back to England Richard took ill and died at his son-in-law's (Sir Edward Moseley) home in Lancashire. Nathaniel Shurtleff, ed., *MGCR*, 2: 39 (May 10, 1643). Richard Dunn, ed., *Journal of John Winthrop,* 312–13 (Dec., 1639), 451–58 (Oct. 1642-Sept. 1643), 456 (n. 63). Francis Bremer, *John Winthrop,* 310, 351. Edmund Morgan, *The Puritan Dilemma,* 2nd ed., 144–45. S.E. Morison, *Builders of the Bay Colony,* 93.

freemen, as does their fight to secure a share of legislative and judicial power via the negative voice.[26]

26 *John Winthrop's Defense of the Negative Vote,* (June 1643) in *Winthrop Papers,* 4: 380–84, 88–90. Winthrop also clarified his distinction between the judicial role of magistrates and deputies as related to popular sovereignty: "Answ: originally and virtually it is [in the people], but when they have chosen them judges etc.: their judiciary power is actually in those to whom they have committed it and those are their magistrates in such order as before is declared," referencing his earlier citations of laws passed by the General Court. Richard Dunn, ed., *John Winthrop's Journal,* 456–8 (notes 61–63) (Oct. 1642-Sept. 1643). Trever Saunders, ed., *Aristotle: The Politics,* T.A. Sinclair trans., (London: Penguin Books, 1992), 160–61 (Bk. II, Ch. xii, 1273b27), 190 (Bk. III, Ch. vii, 1279a32). Francis Bremer, *John Winthrop,* 350–52. Samuel Glover, "The Putney Debates: Popular versus Élitist Republicanism," *Past and Present* 164 (Aug., 1999): 75–6. "In the 1640s 'democracy' was still held in suspicion, understood by the definitions provided by Aristotle, Thucydides, Polybius and Machiavelli. Aristotle had defined democracy as the rule by the propertyless over the propertied, leading to inevitable redistribution or abolition of private property. The histories of Thucydides and Polybius illustrated this definition by demonstrating that democracy inevitably degenerated into civil war, 'anarchy' and mob rule. Commenting upon Roman and Florentine history, Machiavelli also characterized mass participatory politics as a constant state of turmoil and class conflict, which led inevitably to the Caesarization of Rome and, in Florence the rise of the Medici." Richard Ashcraft, *Revolutionary Politics and Locke's Two Treatises of Government* (Princeton: Princeton Univ. Press, 1986), 145–64. "Even with the English property requirement the male electorate was greater from the 1620's than one might suppose, and even amongst the Levellers (by far the most radical group on a universal male electorate based on natural rights) there was still much debate on which male economic based groups would not be included."

CHAPTER 5

# The Standing Council

A final conundrum concerning the relation between executive and legislative power had to be resolved before legal authority and the legal system were stable enough for codification and printed promulgation. Another controversy which arose from the General Court's creation of a "standing" council several years earlier in 1636, soon distracted its proceedings on its most recent legislative initiatives. The council represented the closest institutional manifestation of an executive cabinet within Massachusetts during the seventeenth century. It had become necessary to supplement the General Court's now biannual meetings as a result of the creation of the quarterly courts. The standing council would convene when the General Court was not in session, primarily concerning matters involving colonial defense, with its meetings kept secret. By that time, the primary external threat to the colony stemmed from the Privy Council's creation of Committee for New England in 1633, headed by Archbishop Laud. In 1634, upon receiving notice of ships sailing for New England, Laud complained, "If suffered to go in such swarms, it will be a decrease of the king's people here, an increase of the adversaries of the episcopal state, and will also be an overthrow of trade." Winthrop's journal entries make repeated reference to the Committee's efforts to recall the Massachusetts *Charter*, whereby the colony's territory and right to form a government was originally granted by Charles I in 1629. Now, the king's preeminent bishop had stated his intent to dispatch a royal governor to take over the colony's government.[1]

1 Nathaniel Shurtleff, ed., *MGCR*, 1: 125 (Sept., 1634), 138–39 (March 1635), 146–47 (May 1635), 167 (March 3, 1636). Richard Dunn, ed., *Journal of John Winthrop* (Cambridge: Belknap Press, 1996), 120–23 (July-August 1634). "[T]he Archbishop & others of the Council … sent out warrant to stay the ships, & to call in our patent"; Ibid., 128–29 (July-Sept., 1634), 221 (June 1637), 258–59 (June 1638). *Acts of the Privy Council: Colonial Series (1613–1680)* (Hereford: HMSO, 1908): 1: 187 (May 1633). A "Committee for New England" was created in May 1633, headed by Archbishop Laud; Ibid., 1: 199 (Feb. 1634). In February 1634, Laud ordered a stay on all ships bound for New England, because of the "great number of his majesty's subjects" leaving for New England "known to be ill affected and discontented with [England's] Civil as [well as] Ecclesiastical Government." Everett Emerson, *Letters from New England* (Amherst: Univ. of Mass. Press, 1975), 120. Frederick Poole, ed., *Wonder Working Providence of Sions Saviour* (Andover: Warren Draper, 1867), lviii (introduction). *Anonymous to John Winthrop, Winthrop Papers*, 3: 397–403 (May 1637). The letter urged colonists to stop sending incendiary letters about English church and state authorities, one predicting "wars with England" in a few years. Such threats caused the "whole kingdom to … be full of prejudice against you." Carla Pestana,

 | DOI:10.1163/9789004706347_007

Winthrop also noted that several members of the Privy Council who thought favorably of the colony might be amendable to moving there under certain conditions, and so the colony naturally pursued an alliance with these powerful nobles. In the Summer of 1634 two of these men, William Fiennes (Viscount Saye and Sele) and Robert Greville (Baron Brooke), sent a list of requirements for their residence in Massachusetts. Several years later John Cotton responded on behalf of the colony when the need for such alliances had become most acute. He acknowledged their demands that two "ranks of men" (gentlemen and freeholders) be established in the colony, citizenship must not be linked to church membership, and the governor would be chosen from a rank of "gentlemen." Cotton assured the pair that the governor was chosen from a discrete group of magistrates, and a council recently created needed gentlemen like themselves. Indeed, the freemen had only chosen two magistrates (Winthrop and Dudley), "not willing to choose more until they see what further better choice the Lord will send over." Citing Jean Bodin, author of *Six Books of the Republic* (1576), advocating the necessity of a unified sovereignty of government, Cotton tried to entice their lordships by acknowledging that although the colony's government was popularly elected, since the magistracy was composed of a small, elite group, it was aristocratic rather than popular in form. Ultimately, however, Cotton had to answer their inquiry directly, without nuance, concerning the arrangement of church and state: "none are admitted freemen of this commonwealth but such as are first admitted members of some church." Neither Brooke nor Saye and Sele ultimately chose to reside in Massachusetts for reasons still contested by historians, but the colony's Congregational system appears to have been determinate.[2]

---

*The English Atlantic in the Age of Revolution: 1640–41* (Cambridge: Harvard Univ. Press, 2004), 59–60. "For a euphoric period in the first years of the Long Parliament, New England stood near the center of the movement to reform the English church."

2 Richard Dunn, ed., *Journal of John Winthrop*, 258–59 (June 1638), 298 (June 1639). Sargent Bush, Jr., ed., *Correspondence of John Cotton*, 243–49 (1636), 519–23 (1634). Nathaniel Shurtleff, ed., *MGCR*, 1: 167 (March 3, 1636). Francis Bremer, *John Winthrop* (Oxford: Oxford Univ. Press, 2003), 238–40, 255–56, 302–309, 332. J.S. Maloy, "Bodin's Puritan Readers and Radical Democracy in Early New England," *History of Ideas* 78 (Jan., 2017): 1–5. William Hubbard, *A General History of New England* (Boston: Little & Brown, 1848), 234–35, 243–44, 262. Winthrop, Dudley, and Governor Henry Vane were elected to the standing council to serve for "a term of life." After Vane left the colony, the deputies demanded that any future candidate must have resided in the colony for at least a year. Karen Kupperman, "Definitions of Liberty on the Eve of Civil War: Lord Saye and Sele, Lord Brooke, and the American Puritan Colonies," *Historical Journal* 32 (Mar., 1989): 20–21, 27–32. Phillip Gura, *A Glimpse of Sion's Glory* (Middletown, [CT]: Wesleyan University Press, 1984), 79. In 1640, Saye and Sele had informed Governor Winthrop of his support of the Providence colony, in part because he sensed a "movement toward more democratic government in Massachusetts, a change brought on by a rapidly

In 1635, the crown initiated an official action to revoke the Massachusetts *Charter* in the form of a writ of quo warranto. Archbishop Laud was militantly opposed to the colony and its Puritan inhabitants, while Ferdinando Gorges termed the colony's founding illegitimate, as he claimed charter ownership of the same territory. According to Nicholas Tyack, their opposition to the current government persuaded Charles I to establish a new colonial oversight body:

> In April 1634, upon testimonials on the independent form of church government and that English worshippers were being excluded, a royal commission was created "for making laws and orders for government of English colonies planted in foreign parts." Headed by Archbishop Laud, this twelve-man body was empowered not only to make laws, but also to fine and imprison, to appoint "judges and magistrates," to institute courts "as well ecclesiastical as civil," and if necessary, to remove "the governors or rulers" on complaint. They were also given authority "over all the charters and letters patents," along with the right to revoke them. Clearly, Massachusetts was a principal target and the intention, as it emerged, was to send a governor general who would take matters in hand.[3]

---

intensifying labor shortage and the consequent benefit to the lower classes, who began to press for more power in the House of Deputies. 'No wise man,' Lord Saye and Sele wrote the Governor, 'should be so foolish to live where every man is master, and masters must not correct their servants'." Bernard Bailyn, *The Barbarous Years* (New York; Vintage Books, 2012), 167–71, 369–71. Robert Ashton, *The English Civil War: Conservatism and Revolution, 1603–1649*, 2nd ed., (London: Weidenfeld & Nicholson, 1989), 332–35. Ultimately, Saye and Sele abandoned his alliance with Parliament's Independent party, which favored religious toleration, and joined the Presbyterian party when the danger to Charles I became most acute in 1647, "the threat to stability and the social order, which they deemed to be an inescapable consequence of the radical solutions canvassed in the army and by the more extreme parliamentary Independents, dictated a significant shift to the right."

3 *Quo Warranto of 1635*, in *New England Historical and Genealogical Register, 1884* (Boston: the Society, 1884), 48: 209–16. Richard Dunn, ed., *Journal of John Winthrop*, 274–75 (Dec., 1638), 290–96 (May 1639). *Commission to Archbishop Laud, and Others, to Govern New England* (April 28, 1634), *The New England Historical and Genealogical Register, 1860* (Boston: 1860), 14: 343–45. Nicholas Tyack, "Revolutionary Puritanism in Anglo-American Perspective," *Huntington Library Quarterly* 78 (Dec. 2015): 758–59. Peter Mancall, *The Trials of Thomas Morton* (New Haven: Yale Univ. Press, 2019), 121–30. Karen Kupperman, *Providence Island, 1630–1641*, (Cambridge: Cambridge Univ. Press, 1993), 327. Mark Peterson, *The City State of Boston* (Princeton: Princeton Univ. Press, 2019), 141–44. "Gorges and Mason retained restrictive control on the land grants they issued to settlers in their territories, acting more like feudal proprietors who expect annual fees or quitrents from their subjects, and they also expected to retain a strong hand in governing their colonies from afar," similar to Viscount Saye and Sele's sponsorship of the Providence Island settlement.

Although the creation of this new governing commission appeared to supersede all claims to New England, the crown thought it prudent to pursue revocation of the *Charter of 1629* before proceeding with the takeover of colonial government. However, a charter had to be physically returned to the court in order to proceed to its revocation. With the colony's refusal to dispatch agents to England the crown's endeavors were temporarily stymied. Ultimately, however, the Massachusetts *Charter* was revoked in 1637 along with other English corporations, in effect for non-appearance. Somewhat quixotically, Winthrop denied the common law court of King's Bench the authority to issue its judgment, even though he noted the arrival of two English ships in the Spring of 1637 carrying "a copy of a commission, from the commissioners for New England, to divers of the magistrates here." The crown notified the magistracy that "there was no lawful authority in force here," and new leadership would soon be dispatched to the colony.[4]

Initially, in July 1634, the magistrates had received a letter from Matthew Craddock (governor of the Massachusetts Bay Company before the migration) alerting them to the imminent issuance of a quo warranto, and they convened to discuss the threat to the *Charter* and whether to send a colonial delegation to England. They decided that despite the "strict charge to deliver in the Patent," they would answer "Craddock's letter, but not to return any answer or excuse to the [Privy] Council at this time." By September 1634, the General Court had created committees for "military affairs" and "fortifications," with the former to take command "in case of any war that may befall us, and also that

4 Richard Dunn, ed., *Journal of John Winthrop*, 221 (n. 99) (June 3, 1637); 365 (Sept. 1641). Peter Mancall, *The Trials of Thomas Morton*, 121–30. Robert Toppan, *Edward Randolph: His Letters and Official Papers* (Boston: Prince Society, 1898), 1: 13–21. "Although the commission to the Archbishop of Canterbury would seem, from its comprehensive terms, to override the charter of Massachusetts, it was determined to vacate the patent legally, and accordingly a writ of quo warranto was issued in 1635, the principal instigators, besides the Archbishop, being Sir Ferdinando Gorges and Captain Mason, who were already known to be the declared enemies of the Puritan colony. They were the leading spirits in the Council for New England, and had devised a scheme to divide the entire northern part of the continent into twelve provinces, with a general governor over the whole, dependent upon the authority of the King." *Quo Warranto of 1635*, in *New England Historical and Genealogical Register, 1884* (Boston: The Society, 1884), 48: 216. "Whereupon Judgment was given for the King that the Liberties and Franchises of the said Corporator should be seized into the King's hands and the said Mathew Cradock his Body to be taken into the King's hands for usurping the said liberty." Francis Bremer, *John Winthrop*, 240. "Order of the Privy Council, requiring the Attorney General to call in the patent granted to the Governor of New England, and to present it to the Board, or to the Committee of Foreign Plantations" (May 3, 1637), CSP, *Colonial Series (1574–1660)*, ed. W. Noel Sainsbury, (London: Longman, 1860), 1: 251 (#49); "Minutes of Proceedings in King's Bench," Ibid., (#50).

the commissioners, or the major part of them, shall have power to imprison or confine any that they shall judge to be enemies to the commonwealth." The Court proceeded to pass "orders to improve the forts in Boston harbor and elsewhere, strengthen the militia, and gave Winthrop and three other assistants powers of commanders-in-chief in 'any war that may befall us for the space of a year.'" During this same period the assistants ordered the collection of the £400 tax for the fort at Cambridge (formerly Newtown), the construction of other batteries and fortifications around Boston harbor, and the militia increased its training as the colony prepared its defenses. Upon a rumor of several "large" ships offshore, a contemporary account reported "there was an alarm presently given" early one Sunday and "all the train bands [of militia] in Boston, and towns adjacent were in arms in the streets." The "public report was that it was to oppose the landing of an enemy, a governor sent from England"; and indeed, a warship had been dispatched but was forced to turn around as it was deemed "unseaworthy" (at this very time Charles I was attempting to collect a "Ship Money" tax for refitting his fleet). As Michael Winship reported, by 1634 colonial loyalty oaths had omitted any "mention of the King," and the following year the General Court ordered a beacon placed "on the sentry hill in Boston, which came to be known as Beacon Hill, to give notice of any danger to the colony."[5]

By 1638 the General Court had finally replied to the Lord Commissioners of Plantations to address their threats against the colony, expressing regret that they perceived its government to be seditious, while acknowledging their demand for a colonial deputation to return the *Charter* to England. If the crown carried through with its threats, "many thousand souls will be exposed to ruin, being laid open to the injuries of all men ... and then will this whole country fall into the hands of the French or Dutch." And if, ultimately, the *Charter* "was taken away from us ... the common people here will conceive his Majesty has cast them off, and that, hereby, they are freed from their allegiance and subjection, and ... will be ready to confederate themselves under a

5 Richard Dunn, ed., *Journal of John Winthrop*, 120–21 (July 1634). Shurtleff, ed., *MGCR*, 1: 113 (*Authorization of new fort* (March 1634)); *MGCR*, 1: 123, 125 (*Fortifications and Military Affairs Committees created* (Sept. 1634)); *MGCR*, 1: 137–38 (*Beacon on sentry hill; Committee for Military Affairs* reauthorized (March 1635)). Michael Winship, *Godly Republicanism* (Cambridge: Cambridge Univ. Press, 2012), 201–203. Samuel Maverick, *A Brief Description of New England and the Several Townes Therein* (London: 1660; reprint, Boston: MHS, 1885), 18. The contemporary account is Maverick's, and is consistent with military preparations within the colony. Adrian C. Weimer, *Constitutional Culture* (Philadelphia: Univ. of Pennsylvania Press, 2023), 15. Robert Toppan, *Edward Randolph: His Letters and Official Papers*, 1: 13–21. Bremer, *John Winthrop*, 239–40.

new government, for their necessary safety and subsistence." A year later Bay colonists were delivered from this most radical of solutions upon the intercept of Privy Council correspondence to an ardent enemy of the colony, Reverend George Burdett, revealing the crown's near-term intentions. Burdett served as an agent to Archbishop Laud, reporting that Bay colonists were "using all diligence to fortify themselves," and were resolved to "resist any authority that should come out of England." But rather than "church discipline," they were more focused on the colony's "sovereignty … [as] it was accounted perjury and treason in our general courts to speak of appeals to the King." He interpreted the colony's recent correspondence as seeming "to menace revolt and the erection of a new government." The Archbishop could only reply that King and Council were presently occupied with matters of state and must defer on the Massachusetts situation. Scotland was in rebellion, enraged by Laud's disastrous policy of trying to impose England's *Book of Common Prayer* on its Protestant church, the Kirk.[6]

Amid these developments, John Cotton proposed to the General Court that in order to facilitate residence of English nobles who were friends of the colony the term of "governor ought to be for his life." According to Winthrop, this provided yet "another occasion of increasing the people's jealousy of their magistrates." To aggravate matters, most of Cotton's fellow ministers criticized his sermon "with much zeal." Consequently, "notice was taken of it by the people, not as a matter of dispute, but as if there had been some plot to put it in practice" by the magistrates to take over the government. The deputies demanded that the standing council be abolished, mainly because its councilors enjoyed a life tenure. Specifically, they objected that if a magistrate was not chosen to

6 *General Court to Lord Commissioners of Plantations*, (Sept. 6, 1638), in Thomas Hutchinson, *The History of the Massachusetts Bay*, 2nd ed., (London: 1765), 1: 507–9 (Appendix v). Richard Dunn, ed., *Journal of John Winthrop*, 292–96 (May 1639). "Geo. Burdett to Archbishop Laud" (Nov. 29, 1638), *CSP, Colonial Series (1574–1660)*, ed. W. Noel Sainsbury, (London: Longman, 1860), 1: 283–84 (#129). William Hubbard, A *General History of New England*, 263–73. Although the effort to replace the Massachusetts chartered government started in the early 1630's, and proceeded through 1638, no *final attempt* to take over the government was made by the King's ministers. If the Scottish rising and Parliament's recall had not intervened, all evidence indicates the colony would have resorted to armed resistance to any English governor who tried to take control of the government. S.E. Morison, *Builders of the Bay Colony* (Boston: Houghton Mifflin Company, 1930), 228–29. Francis Bremer, *John Winthrop*, 229–40, 327, 332–34. "Charles was determined to impose conformity to the religious system crafted by William Laud throughout his domains, in Scotland and Ireland as well as England. As a step toward achieving this he imposed a new Prayer Book on Scotland in 1637. This precipitated riots in Glasgow and Edinburgh. A general Assembly in Scotland overthrew the royal supremacy, abolished bishops, and restored a full Presbyterian system."

serve again as an assistant, via a subsequent appointment to the newly created council he could serve without election. Before events in Scotland had distracted Archbishop Laud, and the Privy Council, the freemen's deputies had voted for the creation of an executive council to entice powerful nobles to settle in Massachusetts and enhance the colony's survivability. But with the Scottish revolt such threats had melted away. Winthrop accused the freemen of hypocrisy, observing "how strictly the people would seem to stick to their patent [or charter] where they think it makes for their advantage, but are content to decline it where it will not warrant such liberties as they have taken up without warrant from thence." On the other hand, based on their English experience, yeomen had good cause to fear the establishment of a life tenure for colonial leadership. Winthrop admitted his opponents enjoyed significant popular support "even in open court, and much partaking in the country."[7]

Perhaps, responding to this pressure, Governor Winthrop soon reported an agreement to appoint a new committee to "compile a body of fundamental laws" with the full participation of the town's freemen. The General Court enacted the following resolution in March 1638:

> For the well ordering of these plantations now in the beginning thereof, it having been found by the little time of experience we have here had, that the want of written laws have put the Court into many doubts and much trouble in many particular cases, this Court hath therefore ordered that *the freemen of every town (or some part thereof chosen by the rest) within this jurisdiction shall assemble together in their several towns*, and collect the heads of such necessary and fundamental laws as may be suitable to the times and places where God by his providence hath cast us, and the heads of such laws to deliver in writing to the Governor for the time being before the 5th day of the … month called June, next.

The Court instructed the committee members to draft a "compendious abridgment" of colonial law, and "reduce them into as few heads [or titles] as they may." Once this work was accomplished the draft would be presented to the General Court "for approbation or refusal … in autumn next."[8]

---

7 Nathaniel Shurtleff, ed., *MGCR*, 1: 167 (March 3, 1636), 264 (June 6, 1639). Richard Dunn, ed., *Journal of John Winthrop*, 292–96 (May 1639), 352, 358–59 (June-Oct., 1641), 367 (Sept. 1641-June 1642), 377 (Dec., 1641), 452 (Oct. 1642-May 1643). Mark Kishlansky, *A Monarchy Transformed: Britain 1603–1714* (London: Penguin Books, 1997), 138–42.

8 Nathaniel Shurtleff, ed., *MGCR*, 1: 222 (March 12, 1638), 262 (June 6, 1639). The committee stipulated two deadlines for the work's completion. The first being the following June when it was to send a list of "the heads of such laws … in writing" to Governor Winthrop, which

By the end of 1639, law committees previously chosen had presented their drafts for review. The General Court directed Winthrop, Dudley, Bellingham, and Stoughton and six deputies to review the work and compile it into one draft, and then make copies so that they could be distributed to the towns for the freemen's review. Winthrop admitted:

> The people had long desired a body of laws and thought their condition very unsafe while so much power rested in the discretion of magistrates. Diverse attempts had been made at former courts, and the matter referred to some of the magistrates and some of the elders, but still it came to no effect. For, being committed to the care of many, whatsoever was done by some was still disliked or neglected by others. At last, it was referred to Mr. Cotton and Mr. Nathaniel Ward, and each of them framed a model [and] presented to this General Court.[9]

Nathaniel Ward's substantial common law experience explains his appointment to lead a law reform committee. After the award of a Master of Arts by Emmanuel College in 1603, he had studied at the Inns of Court and practiced law for a short period, availing himself the opportunity to "read almost all the Common Law of England and some statutes." But, ultimately he decided to follow a theological calling in the English church. After being ejected from his ministry in 1633, and enduring two years of court proceedings charging him with forty-three offenses of non-conformity, he sailed to Massachusetts. In 1638, Ward received his first appointment to a law committee, and a year later he was appointed to chair the committee that submitted a draft of liberties to the Court. As its completion neared Ward warned Winthrop about sending it to the towns, since the "spirits of the people run high," and those liberties "they get, they hold."[10]

---

was noted delivered in the Court record, with the second coming the following Fall 1639 when the General Court would make a "compendious abridgment" of colonial law. Richard Dunn, ed., *Journal of John Winthrop*, 258–59 (June 1638). Francis Bremer, *John Winthrop*, 229–37, 304–305. Mark Kishlansky, *A Monarchy Transformed: Britain 1603–1714*, 138–42. Nicholas Tyack, "Revolutionary Puritanism in Anglo-American Perspective," 760–61.

9 Richard Dunn, ed., *Journal of John Winthrop*, 314–15 (Dec., 1639). Shurtleff, ed., *MGCR*, 1: 279 (Nov. 5, 1639). Robert Wall, "Membership of the Massachusetts General Court," 256, 351, 376, 564. Patrick Campbell, "Concept of Representation in American Political Development: Lessons of the Massachusetts Bay Puritans," *Polity* 47 (Jan., 2015): 51–54.

10 Nathaniel Shurtleff, ed., *MGCR*, 1: 222 (March 12, 1638). Richard Dunn, ed., *Journal of John Winthrop*, 380 (Dec., 1641). William Whitmore, ed., *Colonial Laws of Massachusetts. Reprinted from the Edition of 1660* (Boston: 1889), 18–19. Edmund Morgan, *Puritan Dilemma*, 2nd ed., 151–55. John Dean, *A Memoir of the Rev. Nathaniel Ward* (Albany: J. Munsell,

Ward needn't have bothered, as Winthrop opposed the deputies' demands to be included in colonial government. Winthrop believed the magistrates should articulate colonial law as tradition dictated via a process known as "*pro re nata.*" As customs were being imported into the colony by ever increasing numbers of new colonists, it would take time to collate a new set of uniform laws based on these disparate traditions. Nevertheless, he feared enactment of new laws by the General Court, would provide the colony's enemies in England the necessary justification to revoke its *Charter*. But "to raise up laws by practice and custom" would constitute "no transgression" of the *Charter*, because "to bring it to a custom by practice for the magistrates to perform, it is no law made repugnant" to English law.[11]

Considering Archbishop Laud's actions already taken to undermine the colony, Winthrop's fear of transgressing the *Charter* was more than justified and would prove prescient. In the absence of an authoritative process to determine when colonial law became "repugnant to the law of England," Winthrop sought to establish new laws suitable to the colony's unique environment via traditional English common law process. According to Thomas Littleton's fifteenth-century treatise, "no custom is allowable, but only such custom as ... the memory of man runneth not to the contrary." If a custom's use was "time out of mind," or of immemorial usage, English judges should incorporate it into the Common Law. Sir Edward Coke, the most famous English jurist of the era, had called such venerable law the Ancient Constitution of England. Since Winthrop was schooled in this Common Law tradition, he was confident that via such judicial processes the colony could adopt suitable laws while avoiding unwanted intervention by English authorities.[12]

---

1868), 20–29. Leslie Stephen, and Sidney Lee eds., *Dictionary of National Biography* (New York: MacMillan Co., 1908), 20: 785. *Nathaniel Ward to John Winthrop*, in *Winthrop Papers*, 4: 162–63 (Dec., 1639). Robert Wall, *Massachusetts Bay: The Crucial Decade* (New Haven: Yale Univ. Press, 1972), 14–16. George Haskins, *Law and Authority in Early Massachusetts* (New York: Macmillan, 1960), 36, 120. Bernard Bailyn, *The Barbarous Years*, 384. Nathaniel Ward was "singled out as an 'absolute inconformitarian,' ... [and] subject to court proceedings for two years ... [on] forty-three articles, including a charge that he had denounced ritualistic prayers as something 'a parrot might be taught'."

11 Richard Dunn, ed., *Journal of John Winthrop*, 314–15 (Dec., 1639). S.E. Morison, *Builders of the Bay Colony*, 97. Morgan, *The Puritan Dilemma*, 2nd ed., 149–51. Haskins, *Law and Authority in Early Massachusetts*, 120–28. Bremer, *John Winthrop*, 105–23, 208, 305–306. *Black's Law Dictionary*, 4th ed., (St. Paul: West Publishing Co., 1968), 1364. *Pro Re Nata*: "For the occasion as it may arise; adapted to meet the particular occasion."

12 Thomas Littleton, *Lyttleton, His Treatise of Tenures* (1481–1482), T.E. Tomlins ed., (New York: Russell & Russell, 1970), 200 (Bk. II, Ch. 10, §§169–170). John Fraser, ed., *The Reports of Sir Edward Coke* (London: Butterworth, 1826), 4: iii–iv. William Blackstone, *Commentaries on the Laws of England* (Chicago: Univ. of Chicago Press, 1979), 1: 68–9, 86,

Winthrop's attendance at the Inns of Court and tenure as a Justice of the Peace had prepared him to apply customary experience. So, his advocacy for law to develop pro re nata, or as circumstance dictated via judicial ruling, was logical to him. While the unique circumstances of Bay colonists partly supported such a process, from the deputies' perspective this approach would grant the magistrates absolute control of the law's evolution; while seated as chief magistrates of the colony's courts, and deciding which customs would be adopted or discarded after arising from the daily practices within the colony, magistrates would ipso facto articulate the law. The deputies feared Winthrop's idea of judge-made law because it would provide the magistracy too much discretion in governing Massachusetts. To limit this power, they demanded a comprehensive edition of law, drafted and adopted under the authority of the General Court. As George Haskins realized, the magistrates opposed a "written code [that] would put a bridle upon their own power and discretionary authority, which they regarded as necessary for the accomplishment of their tasks." The synergy between Massachusetts and English law reform was most pronounced in demands that new laws favorable to the public good be enacted, printed, and widely distributed. Ignorance of the law was seen as government's responsibility, and its publication intended to promote a fairer and more harmonious society in one true Commonwealth.[13]

Within the colony itself, however, a deepening conflict between the magistrates and deputies over control of its government's executive power stemmed from the eventful year of 1643 when Charles de La Tour, the French governor of Acadia, arrived unannounced in Boston harbor with 150 troops, virtually on John Winthrop's doorstep, seeking the colony's assistance in his ongoing warfare with another claimant to the governorship of the French colony, Charles d'Aulnay. Winthrop and the standing council permitted Boston merchants to

---

156. J.H. Baker, *An Introduction to English Legal History*, 3rd ed., (London: Butterworths, 1990), 173. "There is an obvious conflict between the letter of … statutes and the spirit of the common law; but, so far, it is Coke's common law which has prevailed. The legislation cannot itself be set aside; but much can be done by way of interpretation, using the presumption in favor of procedural fairness. Coke had insisted that discretion, even absolute discretion, was a science controlled by law and not an arbitrary power." Barbara Shapiro, *Law Reform in Early Modern England* (Oxford: Hart Publishing, 2019), 58. John Adamson, *The Noble Revolt: The Overthrow of Charles I* (London: Weidenfeld & Nicholson, 2007), 415. "Antiquarian scholarship, far from being a quaint by-way of legal knowledge, had the potential to unlock hidden authorities: long-forgotten conventions, sanctioned by the authority of the past, which could be replicated in the here-and-now so as to redefine the relative powers of nobles and kings."

13 George Haskins, *Law and Authority in Early Massachusetts*, 35–36.

sell La Tour provisions in order to stimulate Boston's deeply depressed economy, including the provision of two sailing ships for his return voyage to Acadia (i.e., present-day Nova Scotia/Northern Maine). About seventy colonists joined La Tour's flotilla as mercenaries. What could be wrong with a policy that might sew discord between enemies of the colony, with Boston merchants profiting from French fratricide?[14]

On the very day that the Boston men, ships, and supplies sailed out of the town's harbor, however, Essex County's magistrates and ministers issued a petition in protest of the council's assistance of La Tour's force; as Massachusetts' northernmost county its residents would bear the brunt of any French counterattack. In a devastating critique, the petition charged Winthrop and the other magistrates on the standing council of endangering the colony's common welfare. Magistrate Richard Saltonstall, Jr., renewed his criticism of the council, accusing its members of ignoring the "advice" of the General Court "in a representative course." Winthrop countered that the council must act when "sudden affairs of state" did not allow time for the Court's reassembly. But no force had attacked, or even threatened the colony. La Tour had simply requested assistance. Winthrop confided the complicating factor in his journal, "if the Court had been assembled, we knew they would not have given him aid without consent of the commissioners of the other colonies, and for a bare permission, we might do it without the Court." Just months before La Tour's arrival, *Articles of Confederation* had been signed on May 10, 1643, by representatives of Massachusetts, Connecticut, New Haven, and Plymouth, creating a defensive confederacy: the United Colonies. Section five of the treaty stipulated each member must aid a fellow colony in a defensive war, but if the colony in need had initiated the conflict it was bound to satisfy damages suffered by *all* combatants on each side. Any interference with French affairs threatened such a calamity.[15]

---

14 Richard Dunn, ed., *Journal of John Winthrop*, 441–51, 466–67 (June-July 1643). Francis Bremer, *John Winthrop*, 323–24, 343–47. Mark Peterson, *The City State of Boston*, 75–79.

15 *Richard Saltonstall and others to the Governor, Deputy Governor, Assistants, and Elders*, (July 14, 1643), in *Winthrop Papers*, 4: 397–401. The letter was signed by Richard Saltonstall, Jr., Simon Bradstreet, Samuel Symonds, Nathaniel Ward, Ezechial Rogers, Nathaniel Rogers, and John Norton. Nathaniel Shurtleff, ed., *MGCR*, 2: 33 (May 10, 1643). Winthrop had been elected governor at the last Court of Elections in 1643, with John Endecott chosen as deputy governor. Richard Dunn, ed., *Journal of John Winthrop*, 446–47 (June-July 1643). Nathaniel Shurtleff, ed., *MGCR*, 2: 35 (May 10, 1635). Massachusetts commissioners were appointed in the spring session of 1643. "The Articles of Confederation," in *Journal of John Winthrop*, ed. Richard Dunn, ed., et al., 435–36 (§5): "It is further agreed, that if any of these jurisdictions, or any plantation under or in combination with them, be invaded by any enemy whatsoever, upon notice and request of any three magistrates of

Still, Winthrop took exception to Essex County's "great offense at these proceedings." He denied the standing council had declared war, "as if we had permitted our ships … to fight with D'Aulnay, whereas we only permitted them to be hired by La Tour to conduct him home." The Essex men had already objected, "Not to forbid, when there is notice and power, is to bid … To permit volunteers to issue out in aid of a friend is never done without an act of state, where any state is." As for Winthrop's claim the council only provided La Tour with an armed escort back to Acadia, upon the convoy's arrival La Tour's forces (including the Boston mercenaries) attacked D'Aulnay's fort, killing three of his men. On the sailing of the fleet the month before the Essex petitioners warned Winthrop of these very consequences: "If D'Aulnay or France shall hereafter demand any of them [i.e., the volunteers] from us as enemies, or murderers … will our Court protect them?; 2. If any of the parents or wives shall require their lives at our hands who shall answer them?; 3. If any of their widows or children shall require sustenance, or any maimed soldier in this expedition call for maintenance, who shall give it to them?" Winthrop condemned the petitioners' "zealous care of the public safety" for questioning the council's decision. His principal defense now rested on the council's Christian duty to care for a neighbor's welfare (La Tour's) before its own. The colony's economic depression that now threatened its existence had undermined the council's judgment.[16]

---

that jurisdiction so invaded, the rest of the confederates, without any further notice or expostulation, shall forthwith send aid to the confederate in danger … But in any such case of sending men for present aid, whether before or after such order or alteration, it is agreed that at the meeting of the commissioners for this confederation, the cause of such war or invasion be duly considered, and if it appear that the fault lay in the party invaded, that then that jurisdiction or plantation make just satisfaction both to the invaders whom they have injured, and bear all the charge of the war themselves without requiring any allowance from the rest of the confederates." James Savage, ed., *History of New England* (Boston: Felps and Farnam, 1825), 2: 381–83. Saltonstall, Jr., and Hathorne wrote a letter, dated August 16, 1645, to the other commissioners of the United Colonies admitting the circumstances as described above. Edmund Morgan, *The Puritan Dilemma*, 2nd ed., 171–74. S.E. Morison, *Builders of the Bay Colony*, 235–37. Robert Wall, *Massachusetts Bay: The Crucial Decade*, 42–4, 50, 68. Francis Bremer, *John Winthrop*, 326–27, 345–47. Neal Dugre, "Repairing the Breach: Puritan Expansion, Commonwealth Formation, and the Origins of the United Colonies of New England," *New England Quarterly* 91 (Sept., 2018): 414–18.

16 *Richard Saltonstall and others to the Governor, Deputy Governor, Assistants, and Elders*, (July 14, 1643), in *Winthrop Papers*, 4: 399–400. *John Winthrop to Richard Saltonstall and Others*, (July 21, 1643), in *Winthrop Papers*, 4: 402–10. Richard Dunn, ed., *Journal of John Winthrop*, 448–49 (June-July 1643), 464 (July 1643), 467–68 (July 1643), 473–74 (Sept.-August 1643). Francis Bremer, *John Winthrop*, 346–47.

Future events highlighted not only the council's rash provocation of the French but reignited the entire controversy over the magistrates' arbitrary power. By July 1644, La Tour had notified Winthrop of his divestment of Acadia's governorship upon D'Aulnay's royal certification by Louis XIV's ministers. Winthrop and his fellow councilors were forced to grapple with the reality that D'Aulnay would soon return as the governor of Acadia. Faced with this scenario the council agreed denial was their only option. Upon D'Aulnay's arrival in Boston to protest the "wrong done" by the Massachusetts flotilla, and presenting his royal credentials, the council informed him that the "ships and most of the men were strangers to us and had no commission from us, nor any permission to use any hostility." When D'Aulnay proposed a confederation between Massachusetts and Acadia, Winthrop and the other magistrates replied, audaciously, "we could not conclude any league with him without the advice of the commissioners of the United Colonies." Ultimately, the General Court was forced to appoint a commission to negotiate compensation for the attack on D'Aulnay's fort. To add insult to injury, in September 1644 the United Colonies amended the *Articles of Confederation* to the effect that signatories could not deploy militia into hostilities without its explicit approval.[17]

Winthrop and his fellow council members had committed a gross blunder by providing military assistance to La Tour hastily, without considering the possibility of his dismissal as Acadia's governor, and what that might portend; since there were two men vying for the governor's office, and the standing council was obviously aware of this fact, there seems little excuse for such a provocative and potentially costly action. The council had also come very close to a manifest betrayal of neighboring colonies only a month after a treaty of defensive alliance was signed, even if Massachusetts was by far its most senior (and powerful) member. To aggravate matters, the most determined opponent to the standing council, Richard Saltonstall, Jr., had signed a petition warning Governor Winthrop of these dangers at the outset. The other Essex County

---

17 Richard Dunn, ed., *Journal of John Winthrop*, 518, 523–24 (July 1644), 539–40 (Sept., 1644), 544–47 (Sept.-Oct., 1644), 570–72 (April 1645), 178–82, 201–4. Nathaniel Shurtleff, ed., *MGCR*, 2: 157–59 (May 22, 1646); 3: 16 (June 16, 1645). Harry Ward, *The United Colonies of New England: 1643–1690* (New York: Vantage Press, 1961), 91–6. In the aftermath, Winthrop lost both the governorship and his seat on the council of the United Colonies. "When the authorities of the Bay realized how serious the consequences might be … [a] committee headed by Richard Saltonstall found that the 'grounds of war ought to be just,' and for 'the justice of this war … we conceive that all the light and information New England hath … cannot be sufficient for us to determine it positively.' The matter of the La Tour-d'Aulnay rivalry was thus brought before the next meeting of the Commissioners of the United Colonies."

signatories illustrate a tide of changing alliances, one of whom was Nathaniel Ward. Several years earlier he had urged Winthrop to reconsider a planned distribution of manuscript drafts of the *Body of Liberties* to the towns based on his distrust of the freemen. Minister John Norton, another signatory of the Essex petition, had authored a "Small Treatise" in defense of the magistrate's negative vote in the summer of 1643.[18]

Winthrop complained, bitterly, "such protestations are public and judicial acts and therefore must be warranted by some authority," a power he believed the Essex magistrates and ministers did not possess. His journal entries brooded that the council's decision to help La Tour caused "aspersions" to be heaped upon the magistrates, "as if they intended to bring in an arbitrary government." Although the *Laws and Liberties of 1648* reauthorized the standing council to deal with "the weighty and sudden occasions which may be then in hand," and continue its service as a council of state to provide for the colony's defense as matters required, the same section stipulated that the General Court should convene "when ... time and opportunity will safely admit."[19]

Immediately after the controversial election in 1644, when the deputies tried to unseat Winthrop from his governorship, in large part for his complicity in the French fiasco, the deputies proposed that the standing council should be reauthorized via a *commission*, or grant of authority, from the General Court. Moreover, several magistrates then sitting on the council should be replaced by several deputies and Nathanial Ward. In order to justify the proposal, the deputies repeated Israel Stoughton's position that the "governor and assistants had no power out of court but what was given them by the General Court." The question of whether the assistants' power was of a ministerial nature, like a delegated power, or a magisterial one with inherent privileges and duties, had been reopened. Stoughton's main contention was that the assistants' power did not extend to governing "according to their own wills." Instead, the magistrates "must hear and respect" the decisions of the General Court. Neither the compromise on the negative voice in 1636, nor its apparent resolution via the

18 S.E. Morison, *Builders of the Bay Colony*, 235–36. *Richard Saltonstall and Others to the Governor* (July 14, 1643), in *Winthrop Papers*, 4: 401. John Norton, *A Small Treatise on the Negative Vote*, 46: 279–85. *Nathaniel Ward to John Winthrop*, (Dec. 22, 1639), in *Winthrop Papers*, 4: 162–63.

19 *John Winthrop to Richard Saltonstall and Others*, (July 21, 1643), 4: 402–3. Richard Dunn, ed., *Journal of John Winthrop*, 510–15 (May-June 1644). Richard Dunn, ed., *Laws and Liberties of 1648*, 14, title *Councill*. Nathaniel Shurtleff, ed., *MGCR*, 3: 16 (June 16, 1645). The La Tour affair was still a matter of controversy in the Summer of 1645.

creation of a bicameral legislature in March 1644, would resolve this fundamental issue.[20]

Winthrop identified Nathaniel Ward as one of the leaders of the Essex coalition, noting his support of the General Court's issuance of a commission to "order all affairs of the government"; Ward had also signed the Essex petition that condemned the standing council's support of La Tour. His concept of a commission was like Stoughton's, in so far as both men believed that the authority of government officials derived from a superior power that would oversee their actions. In the matter of the council's power, however, Ward proposed that the magistrates must adhere to a rule established by the General Court, only "accountable commissions must have power to consult and execute against" unpredictable dangers that might threaten the colony. Even emergencies must not be addressed "by one or a few men's discretion," but only as "sanctioned by supreme councils." Ward's concept of a commission represented the deputies' position because it held the General Court as the supreme authority in colonial government. In a similar spirit, upon the deputies' challenge of the proper limits of the United Colonies' conciliar power upon its dispatch of a military force against the Narragansett tribe, William Bradford, governor of Plymouth colony, noted that the "deputies of the Massachusetts Court ... made a question whether it was legally done without their commission." Bradford responded, according to the *Articles of Confederation* the council of the United Colonies (U.C.) had properly dispatched the troops in its executive role. If the U.C. council had to wait for the Massachusetts General Court to assemble and reach a decision, the troops could not have had "due effect." Since the council had the power to order the deployment, and "it was a case of such present and urgent necessity as could not stay [until] the calling of the Court," troops had been deployed. In the wake of the La Tour controversy in the summer of 1643, the General Court ordered the greater part of the magistrates, as well as deputies from Boston, Charleston, Cambridge (formerly Newtown), Roxbury, and Dorchester, to form a committee to oversee the arrest of Samuel Gorton and his followers' expulsion from Narragansett land, as well as to monitor the actions of the U.C. to ensure "they are not to enter into any war against the

---

20 Richard Dunn, ed., *Journal of John Winthrop*, 511–13 (May-June 1644). Robert Wall, *Massachusetts Bay: The Crucial Decade*, 75–78. Israel Stoughton, *A Relation Concerning New England*, *MHS Proceedings* (1860–1862): 5: 139. Francis Bremer, *John Winthrop*, 357–58. *Black's Law Dictionary*, 4th ed., (St. Paul: West Publishing Co., 1968), 339. *Commission*: "A warrant or authority or letters patent, issuing from the government, or one of its departments, or a court, empowering a person or persons named to do certain acts, or to exercise jurisdiction, or to perform the duties and exercise the authority of an office."

Indians (except defensive) before this court be again assembled." During the Court's next session it ordered the imprisonment of Gorton, a religious radical expelled from practically every New England colony for his "abominable heresies."[21]

Despite the General Court's, and more importantly a majority of magistrates' deferral to the demands of deputies and freemen that they be included in oversight of U.C. military matters, Winthrop continued to oppose the deputies' proposed commission for several reasons. First, it would "overthrow the foundation of our government" by removing the distinction between magistrates and deputies, a distinction that he had vigorously defended for many years. Second, it would undermine the freemen's liberty because they had elected the magistrates to the council, and any replacements would violate their electoral rights; the magistrates' authority was secured by a process of election stipulated by the *Charter*, so the General Court could not dismiss any members of the standing council without cause. Upon the deputies' objection that the standing council itself was not authorized by the *Charter*, but existed by virtue of a law passed in the General Court, Winthrop thundered, the "governor and assistants had power of government before we had any written laws or had kept any courts; and to make a man a governor over a people, gives him, by necessary consequence, power to govern that people, otherwise there were no power in any commonwealth to order, dispose, or punish in any case where ... no positive law declared in." Although the General Court had the authority to "order and direct" the magistrates for the common welfare of the colony,

---

21 Nathaniel Shurtleff, ed., *MGCR*, 2: 46 (Sept., 1643); 2: 52 (Oct., 1643). Richard Dunn, ed., *Journal of John Winthrop*, 511 (May-June 1644). Nathaniel Ward, *The Simple Cobbler of Aggawam in America* (London: Jan. 29, 1647), 49–50; *Thomason Tracts*, E 372 (21), Reel 59. S.E. Morison, *Builders of the Bay Colony*, 237–42. William Bradford, *Of Plymouth Plantation: 1620–1647*, S.E. Morison ed., (New York: Alfred Knopf, 1953), 342–43. Neal Dugre, "Repairing the Breach: Puritan Expansion, Commonwealth Formation, and the Origins of the United Colonies of New England," *New England Quarterly* 91 (Sept., 2018), 404–10. "The smaller plantations, convinced of the legitimacy of the threat, were eager to head off Miantonomi and his allies with a preemptive strike. Yet the Massachusetts Council doubted the rumors and concluded that hasty action was unwarranted." Alden Vaughan, *New England Frontier: Puritans and Indians, 1620–1675*, 3rd ed., (Norman: Univ. of Oklahoma Press, 1995), 155–61. The deputies' objection to the dispatch of troops was a matter of self-interest, "Massachusetts had no desire to commit its men in a war against tribes which had done its own citizens no harm." Harry Ward, *The United Colonies of New England*, 37–43, 49–58, 77, 136–39. The year before Massachusetts had taken the side of two Narragansett chiefs against Samuel Gorton and his community, and Bay Colony forces ejected his group from Pawtuxet; the motive for this allegiance was maneuvering by Winthrop and other magistrates to procure that same territory for the colony.

when they sat on the standing council their authority extended to "all affairs thereof without any commission" or oversight by the General Court.[22]

Ward was unpersuaded, rejecting Winthrop's broad conception of the magistrates' authority. Despite it being established at the outset of the colony's settlement, that original bestowal of authority, on its own, did not make it supreme. Because, Ward argued, even if authority derived from "time out of mind of man before Adam was made," it was not ipso facto just or wise. Justice had existed "before time, and will be after it," so tradition did not certify wisdom; time had "neither politics nor ethics, good nor evil in it; it is an empty thing, as empty as a New-English purse, and emptier it cannot be." Moreover, if authority emanated only from tradition, a citizenry could never form a government based on its own principles and ideas in a conscious design to address exigent circumstances. A marked change had occurred from the man who advised Winthrop a few years earlier that only the "best people" should make the law. Ultimately, Ward rejected the customary authority of kings and magistrates, insisting that men use their own innate faculties to establish government as they saw fit. Politics was tabula rasa, or the empty thing of time on which man sketched his own design. It followed that if a people could establish a political state suitable to its own needs and requirements, then the "rule and reason will be found all one."[23]

The deputies followed Ward's lead and rejected the magistrates' claim to divine authority, or absolute omnipotence in matters of state when the General Court was not in session. As Francis Bremer laid out the two respective positions, "While Winthrop had been forced over the years to yield to the freemen and their deputies' greater powers than he thought desirable, … he had consistently maintained not only a broad interpretation of magisterial authority, but also the need for those magistrates to derive their authority from the direct vote of the freemen." On the deputies' side, William Hathorne "maintained that 'the

22 Richard Dunn, ed., *Journal of John Winthrop*, 512–13 (June 1644). Robert Wall, *Massachusetts Bay*, 75–78.

23 Richard Dunn, ed., *Journal of John Winthrop*, 512 (June 1644). Nathaniel Ward, *The Simple Cobbler of Aggawam in America* (Jan. 29, 1647); *Thomason Tracts* E 372 (21), Reel 59, 50–1. S.E. Morison, *Builders of the Bay Colony*, 235–43. Bernard Bailyn, *The Barbarous Years*, 471. "Nathaniel Ward, who had been expelled from his ministry in 1632 and for twelve years thereafter had preached in Ipswich, Massachusetts, explained in his rollicking, satirical *Simple Cobler of Aggawam* (1647), with appropriate reference to Hebrews 11:9, that while 'no man ought to forsake his own country [except] upon extraordinary cause … when that cause ceases, he is bound in conscience to return if he can.' Ward could and did. He ended his notable career in England, as rector of a church some four miles from his original parish."

governor and assistants had no power' between sessions of the court other than granted them specifically by the court. This clearly flew in the face of the colony's brief history, but the deputies appeared adamant." After the deputies proposed several variations to supersede the standing council by commission, with the magistrates rejecting each one, it was agreed the Court should adjourn. The magistrates informed the deputies that during the recess "if occasion required, they must act according to the power and trust committed to them." If, for example, a commensurate threat arose the standing council was prepared to deploy troops. Hathorne replied ominously, "You will not be obeyed."[24]

The magistrates prepared a *Declaration* of their position, with intent to publish it in the colony, maintaining the standing council's authority derived from both the *Charter* and the freemen's election of the magistrates. The council-members acknowledged they were bound "to govern by law, both fundamental and positive, and not contrary thereunto, and that the General Court only hath power to make and establish such wholesome laws, orders, and ordinances." They maintained that the magistrates' authority was ordained "by God … to study and endeavor the welfare of this commonwealth, and consequently to further the establishing and declaring of all necessary and wholesome laws with certain penalties." The deputies' initiative to impose a commission on the standing council's authority was part of a broader campaign to incorporate specific penalties in colonial legislation. The magistrates' resistance aimed at retention of their discretionary powers, and to remain free of legislative restraints that might interfere with actions necessary to safeguard the common welfare against all threats. While the deputies might offer advice, the power of judicial interpretation and executive decision remained the magistracy's exclusive jurisdiction. At this point, the deputies requested the creation of a committee to determine the following question (one whose premise the deputies opposed and the magistrates supported): did the standing council, when the General Court was not in session, have power to "act in all cases subject to government, according to the said patent and the laws of this jurisdiction; and when necessary occasions call for action from authority, in cases where there is no particular express law provided, there to be guided by the word of God,

24 Richard Dunn, ed., *Journal of John Winthrop*, 512–13 (June 1644). Francis Bremer, *John Winthrop*, 356–58. S.E. Morison, *Builders of the Bay Colony*, 237. "The object of this standing committee, of course, was to check the power of the Assistants, and to prevent them from committing more costly mistakes in foreign policy. It was a sort of democratic counter-proposal to John Cotton's life counsel of three … The negative voice enabled the Assistants to defeat the Essex proposition, and, despite Hathorne's prophecy, they were obeyed."

'til the General Court give particular rules in such cases?" This passage, and the context within which it was drafted, illustrates the colonists' conflation of "judicial" sentences (as we understand them) with foreign policy decisions, fusing both into a "power to act in all cases." Considering that, to colonists, "cases" encompassed everything from the trial of a petty theft to a council decision to commit troops in an undeclared war, the freemen's trepidation in the face of such sweeping state authority is certainly understandable.[25]

Upon his return to England Nathaniel Ward was invited to address Parliament on June 30, 1647, as the New Model Army and Presbyterians in Parliament vied for control of the nation. Only a little over a month later the Army ended the argument by occupying London, striking an alliance with the Levellers and Independent church government supporters. Cumulatively, these actions ignited mass public protests and petitioning of Parliament in one of England's most revolutionary moments. Ward warned his fellow Englishmen against undermining national government in this political cauldron, since kingdoms were established "by order"; if "popular bodies are confused they are for that time impolitized," and when "political rule fails, then the strength of a state fails." Ultimately, when "authority fails, justice fails." States infected with such infirmities became "bodies out of joint, full of divisions, discontent, and rulers had little or no power to rule them whom they have misruled." Charles I, prisoner of one faction or another since his defeat, was now "weakened and unfitted to rule," but his impotence only highlighted the necessity of a supreme executive, "if a common-wealth be headless, the people will be brainless." And nothing justified the Army's menacing posture toward its own sovereign, Parliament, "let us lament that such honorable and serviceable troops should have ... mounted upon ... saddles of John á Leyden's make."[26]

25 *Declaration of the Governor, Deputy Governor, and Assistants of Massachusetts* (June 28, 1644), in *Winthrop Papers*, 4: 467. Richard Dunn, ed., *Journal of John Winthrop*, 513–15 (June 1644).

26 Nathaniel Ward, *A Sermon Preached Before the Honorable House of Commons: at their late monethly fast, being on Wednesday, June 30. 1647* (London: 1647), 9–22; *Wing* W785, Reel 904: 51. S.E. Morison, *Builders of the Bay Colony*, 237–42. Robert Ashton, *Counter-Revolution* (New Haven: Yale Univ. Press, 1994). Mark Kishlansky, *A Monarchy Transformed*, 170–77. Professor Kishlansky termed the New Model Army's occupation of London in August 1647 as its own attack on "Parliamentary tyranny." Robert Ashton, *Counter Revolution: The Second Civil War and its Origins, 1646–8* (New Haven: Yale Univ. Press, 1996), 178–96. The march of the New Model Army into London was viewed by contemporaries as quite orderly, considering Parliament was then dominated by the Presbyterian party which refused to satisfy the soldiers' considerable back-pay, and whose intention was to disband the army. *Declaration of the Army* (June 1647), in J.P. Kenyon, ed., *The Stuart Constitution*, 2nd ed., (Cambridge: Cambridge Univ. Press, 1986), 263–68.

# PART 3

## *Publishing Massachusetts Laws and Liberties*

CHAPTER 6

# The Body of Liberties of 1641

Now that we have reviewed how the major issues of government were resolved to facilitate a law book's production, we can proceed to the story of the publication of the *Laws and Liberties* itself. Preparation of drafts for a new colonial law book had continued despite the ongoing acrimony between magistrates and deputies. Near the end of 1639 Winthrop noted in his journal, "to satisfy the people … two models were digested with diverse alterations and additions … and sent to every town to be considered … by the magistrates and elders, and then to be published by the constables *to all the people*." Dispatch of the legislative proposals to the towns would provide opportunity for amendment, not just the freemen's examination, if "any man should think … that anything therein ought to be altered, he might acquaint some of the deputies … the next court." Both *Moses His Judicials* and the *Body of Liberties*, usually attributed to the authorship of John Cotton and Nathanial Ward, respectively, would be the subjects of this review. The *Body of Liberties*' enactment at the end of 1641 marked the mid-point in drafting proposals for a printed law book, officially authorized and published by the General Court seven years later. While it has enjoyed greater historical attention than the law books, the reason for which will be explained at the end of the next chapter, the *Liberties*' regulation of matters of church and state has not been fully appreciated. Because several of its regulations would impact controversies soon to engulf the General Court and the colony, and those addressing the structure of churches illustrate how Congregationalism was supposed to operate, special attention will be given to their review.[1]

---

1 Richard Dunn, ed., *Journal of John Winthrop: 1630–1649* (Cambridge: Belknap Press, 1996), 314–15 (Dec., 1639). Winthrop identified the two proposals as those of "Mr. Cotton and Mr. Nathaniel Ward, … each of them framed a model." Francis Gray, "Remarks on the Early Laws of Massachusetts Bay; with the Code adopted in 1641, and called THE BODY OF LIBERTIES," *MHS Collections* (*Third Series/1838*), 7: 191–237. The extant copies of *Moses His Judicials* derive from those editions printed in London as part of Hutchinson's history of the colony cited below, and the *Body of Liberties* survives by virtue of another copy made at the dawn of the American Revolution by Governor Hutchinson while in exile. *"Moses His Judicialls"* (1637), in *Hutchinson Papers*, ed. William Whitmore, (Albany: Prince Society, 1865), 1: 183–205. George Haskins, *Law and Authority in Early Massachusetts* (New York: MacMillan Co., 1960), 123–40. David Hall, *A Reforming People* (New York: Alfred A. Knopf, 2011), 147–154.

 DOI:10.1163/9789004706347_008

To recapitulate, in 1636 the General Court had chosen Governor Vane, Deputy Governor Winthrop, Thomas Dudley, John Haynes, Richard Bellingham, John Cotton, Hugh Peters, and Thomas Shepard to draft laws that "may be the fundamentals of this commonwealth." The law committee appointed after the Antinomian Crisis two years later included many of the same men: Winthrop, Dudley, Bellingham, Peters, Shepard, Peter Buckley, George Phillips, Nathaniel Ward, William Spencer, and William Hathorne. Cotton and Ward were not members of both committees. Cotton had been appointed to the 1636 committee that drafted *Moses His Judicials*. Ward was appointed to the 1638 committee with instructions to solicit suggestions from the town freemen of "necessary and fundamental laws as may be suitable to the times," in order to compile a "compendious abridgment" of Massachusetts law. Winthrop reported these efforts had been largely in vain, because "whatsoever was done by some was still disliked or neglected by others." Nevertheless, magistrates and deputies had been directed to review several drafts of laws Winthrop attributed to "Mr. Cotton and Mr. Nathaniel Ward." Another committee was then created, composed of Winthrop, Dudley, Bellingham, and Stoughton, to compile a final draft for review by the Court. After the "elders of the churches and other freemen of this commonwealth" had examined the completed draft, the General Court record notes delivery of a "breviate of laws" in its Spring session of 1640 for review, and Thomas Lechford—an attorney from England—was employed to prepare manuscript copies for the towns.[2]

Individual town records are sketchy on the deliberations on the *Liberties*, as most information was memorialized in records of the colonial government. Based upon the General Court's record we know that any additions or modifications made by the town freemen were at the discretion of the deputies to adopt, which makes perfect sense because the deputies represented them. Minimally, the freemen's examination of the proposals garnered additional support and avoided unnecessary contention in the General Court. While Nathaniel Ward feared the *Liberties*' distribution, by then Winthrop realized

2 Nathaniel Shurtleff, ed., *MGCR*, 1: 174–75 (May 25, 1636), 222 (March 12, 1638), 279 (Nov. 5, 1639), 292–93 (May 13, 1640). Richard Dunn, ed., *Journal of John Winthrop*, 314–15 (Dec., 1639). Edmund Morgan, *The Puritan Dilemma*, 2nd ed., (New York: Longman, 1999), 130–31, 148–55. Thomas Lechford, *Notebook: Kept by Thomas Lechford* (Boston: 1885; reprint, Edward Hale, Jr., et al. eds., Camden [Maine]: Picton Press, 1988), 237–38. Among the several different proposals Lechford copied included a "breviate of the body of Lawes for the Country" which was delivered to the constable of Dorchester. Angela Fernandez, "Record-Keeping and Other Troublemaking: Thomas Lechford and Law Reform in Colonial Massachusetts," *Law and History Review* 23 (2005): 235–77. *Questions of the Elders*, *MHS Proceedings* (1912/13), 46: 275–76.

some new edition of colonial law was inevitable; participating in the process to shape the *Liberties* form and content would lead to a better outcome than the magistrates' earlier obstructionism. To oppose the process forthrightly would result in enactment of laws that undermined the magistracy's authority, while arousing the freemen's suspicion of arbitrary power.

In October 1641, a year and a half after the breviate was received by the General Court, its members ordered Governor Richard Bellingham (1592–1672) and Deputy William Hathorne to ask Nathanial Ward for the final draft of the "liberties and of the capital laws to be transcribed and sent to the several towns." Upon Bellingham's election to the governorship in June 1641, the General Court had appointed him to "peruse all the laws and take notice what may be fit to be repealed, what to be certified, and what to stand, and to make return to the next General Court." His considerable experience explains why he was a member of every law committee created to this point. As Recorder of "Old" Boston from 1625 to 1633 he served as the town's attorney, and he was also a Member of Parliament (MP) during the volatile sessions of 1628 and 1629. So, Bellingham was eminently qualified to draft the final copy of the *Body of Liberties*. In December 1641, the General Court ratified the *Liberties* as colonial law, "the body of laws formerly sent forth among the freemen ... was voted to stand in force," and Winthrop confirmed the December "session continued three weeks, and established 100 laws which were called the Body of Liberties." It was "composed by Mr. Nathaniel Ward ... and had been revised and altered by the court, and sent forth into every town to be further considered of, and now again in this court, they were revised, amended, and presented, and so established for three years, by that experience to have them fully amended and established to be perpetual." Deputy Governor Endecott, Emmanuel Downing, and William Hathorne were ordered to have "19 copies of the laws, liberties, and the forms of oaths transcribed," and to "be paid for by the constable of each town." There is no entry in the Court record, or the records kept for the Cambridge press, that the *Liberties* was ever printed. Instead, it was "transcribed"—or copied by hand—and distributed to the towns for review.[3]

3 Nathaniel Shurtleff, ed., *MGCR*, 1: 147, 174–75, 222, 279, 319, 340, 344. Edmund Morgan, *The Puritan Dilemma*, 2nd ed., 148–55. Robert Wall, "Membership of the Massachusetts General Court, 1634–1686," (Ph.D. diss., Yale University, 1965), 265–67. Leslie Stephen, and Sidney Lee, eds., *Dictionary of National Biography* (New York: Macmillan, 1908), 2: 194. Dumas Malone, and Allen Johnson, eds., *Dictionary of American Biography* (New York: Charles Scribner's Sons, 1929), 2: 166–67. As explained in Chapter 1, by June 1642 the *Capital Laws* had been printed as a broadsheet primarily to educate the colony's children, but for adults as well. William Whitmore, ed., *The Colonial Laws of Massachusetts. Reprinted from the Edition of 1660*, viii–xvi, 9. Richard Dunn, ed., *Journal of John Winthrop*, 359–60 (June 1641), 380 (Dec.,

Scholars have termed the *Liberties* a code, a bill of rights, and even a "modern state constitution." While Peter Hoffer applied the common description a "written code of law" to the *Liberties*, he realized that it also resembled the hallmark of English Common Law, the *Magna Charta* (1215). Of the four possible models, apart from the Army's and Levellers' draft constitutions known as the *Agreement of the People* several years off (1647–1649), only *Magna Charta* was available to colonists because the first modern codes, constitutions, and bills of rights were achieved half a century or well after 1641. Why note this prochronism? Because available models for the *Body of Liberties*, or eventually the *Laws and Liberties*, should focus on formats that were available to Nathaniel Ward and his colleagues. While a focus on the "origins" of the US *Constitution* and the *Bill of Rights* was common in Legal History's formative years, their use as models to investigate formats for Massachusetts' editions of the *Liberties*, or the follow-on law books, can obscure the actual precedents for both publications.[4]

Similarly, for analytical purposes, describing the *Body of Liberties* as a code, or an example of codification, obscures the essential question of what existing formats influenced the colonists. Before the adoption of the *Code Civil des Français* of 1804, in England a "code" meant a book of law. In the 1760's William Blackstone described it by reference to Roman law, "By the civil law, absolutely taken, is generally understood the civil or municipal law of the Roman empire, as comprised in the *Institutes*, the *Code*, and the *Digest* of the emperor Justinian." After his review of Emperor Justinian's initiative to condense Roman law into a "code," or a book, Blackstone concluded that the overwhelming mass of Roman law had made it unmanageable and prompted the compilation known as the *Corpus Juris Civilis*, not translated into English

---

1641). "Bellingham, Richard II (1592–1672) of Manton and Boston," *History of Parliament*; (https://www.historyofparliamentonline.org/volume/1604-1629/member/bellingham-richard-ii-1592-1672).

4 David Hall, *A Reforming People*, 31–2. Hall described the *Liberties*' introduction as "language informed by the Petition of Right and evocations of consent in English political debate … The seventh point in the Body of Liberties brought this point to bear on the Standing Council … by specifying this court could not act on its own but only with 'consent of a Court general, or by authority derived from the same'." Ian Gentles, "The Agreements of the People and their Political Context," in Michael Mendle, ed., *The Putney Debates of 1647* (Cambridge: Cambridge Univ. Press, 2010), 148–174. "The document for which the Leveller movement is best known is the *Agreement of the People*. Between October 1647 and May 1649, the London Levellers and their allies in the New Model Army published three versions of this projected constitution for England." David Konig, *Law and Society in Puritan Massachusetts: Essex County: 1629–1692* (Chapel Hill: Univ. of North Carolina Press, 1979), 35, 104, 108. George Haskins, "Codification of the Law in Colonial Massachusetts," *Indiana Law Journal* 30 (1954): 8. Edmund Morgan, *The Puritan Dilemma*, 2nd ed., 152.

until mid-eighteenth century. "Codification" was coined by Jeremy Bentham (1748–1832) after the first volume of Blackstone's *Commentaries* was published in 1765. Previously, a "code" had distinct meaning—as a book of laws—before the process of codification as a sovereign act certifying a corpus of uniform laws to encompass a national jurisdiction. Modern French codification both compiled and edited the existing laws of the kingdom, while adding new laws demanded by the exigencies of Revolution. Only then did a new body of French law supersede all existing ordinances, customs, and jurisdictions as a legislative act. Instead of a gradual centuries-long erosion of feudal jurisdictions as in England, one comprehensive edition of a national code demolished the vestiges of the Ancien Regimé residing in its jurisdictions and customary law (coutumes). Because Massachusetts printed its law books a century and a half earlier, "code" or "codification" is unhelpful as either an available format or legislative precedent.[5]

What formats were available to Massachusetts legislators and draftsmen in the 1640's? The primary one was *Magna Charta*. As originally negotiated by King John and his nobility in 1215, the great charter of English liberties begins with an introductory section in which its authority under the titles of King John, the nobility, and the church is announced, followed by sixty-three individual sections. The *Body of Liberties of 1641* also begins with an introduction, followed by ninety-eight numbered sections with a concluding paragraph of instructions for its future administration; its ninety-eight sections plus the introductory and concluding remarks add up to Winthrop's count of the *Liberties*' authorization

5 *Body of Liberties* (1641), in William Whitmore, ed. *The Colonial Laws of Massachusetts. Reprinted from the Edition of 1660, with the Supplements to 1672. Containing also, The Body of Liberties of 1641.* (Boston: 1889), 29–68. David Hall, *A Reforming People*, 147–54, 235 (n. 51). Professor Hall cites Haskins' *Law and Authority in Early Massachusetts* to describe the *Laws and Liberties* "as the first printed code of laws in the Western world." Haskins actually traced the origin of the law book's format to medieval precedents. R.C. Van Caenegem, *An Historical Introduction to Private Law*, 1–15, 91–93, 115–46. John Merryman, *The Civil Law Tradition*, 2nd ed., (Stanford: Stanford University Press, 1985), 26–33. Łukasz Jan Korporowicz, "George Harris and the Comparative Legal Background of the First English Translation of Justinian's Institutes," in William Eves, et. al., eds., *Common Law, Civil Law, and Colonial Law: Essays in Comparative English Legal History from the Twelfth to the Twentieth Centuries* (Cambridge: Cambridge Univ. Press, 2021), 120–39. François Furet, *Revolutionary France*, trans. Antonia Nevill, (Oxford: Blackwell Publishers, 1992), 218–235. William Blackstone, *Commentaries on the Laws of England* (Chicago: Univ. of Chicago, 1979), 1: 80–1. J.H. Baker, *An Introduction to English Legal History*, 3rd ed., (London: Butterworths, 1990), 249 (n. 108). Alexander Chalmers, ed., *Samuel Johnson's Dictionary of the English Language* (London: Studio Editions, 1993), 24. Daniel Coquillette, "Radical Lawmakers in Colonial Massachusetts," *New England Quarterly* 67 (1994): 191.

of "100 Laws." While Edgar McManus thought it "resembled a bill of rights," he recognized *Liberty 1* expanded upon *Magna Charta*'s famous *thirty-ninth article* that became the essential authority guaranteeing due process:

> No man's life shall be taken away, no man's honor or good name shall be stained, no man's person shall be arrested, restrained, banished, dismembered, nor any ways punished, no man shall be deprived of his wife or children, no man's goods or estate shall be taken away from him, nor any way in damaged under color of law or countenance of authority, unless it be by virtue or equity of some express law of the Country warranting the same, established by a General Court and sufficiently published, or in case of the defect of law in any particular case by the word of God. And in capital cases, or in cases concerning dismembering or banishment, according to that word to be judged by the General Court.[6]

The influence of *Magna Charta* on Massachusetts legislators is further illustrated by official correspondence that the General Court sent to Parliament a few years after the adoption of the *Liberties*. Upon Massachusetts inhabitants' (i.e., non-congregants) petition to Parliament charging the colony had violated its charter by passing laws "repugnant to the laws of England," the General Court responded by comparing colonial law with English law to illustrate that whatever differences existed "between such an ancient, populous, wealthy kingdom" as England, and "so poor an infant thin colony" as Massachusetts,

6 *Magna Charta*, (1215), Art. 39: "No free man shall be captured or imprisoned or disseised, or outlawed, or exiled, or in any way destroyed, nor will we go against him or send against him, except by the lawful judgment of his peers or by the law of the land." William Whitmore, ed., *Body of Liberties of 1641*, 33 (*Liberty 1*). George Haskins, *Law and Authority in Early Massachusetts*, 129. Rodney Mott, *Due Process of Law* (Indianapolis: Bobbs-Merrill, 1926), 31, 93. J.H. Baker, *An Introduction to English Legal History*, 3rd ed., 537–38. Nathaniel Shurtleff, ed., *MGCR*, 1: 118 (May 14, 1634): "It … is agreed, that no trial shall pass upon any, for life or banishment, but by a jury so summoned, or by the General Court." The principle of trial by jury was already affirmed in Massachusetts by the mid-1630's. *Hutchinson Papers* (Albany: Prince Society, 1865), 1: 202 (Ch. 9, §§2–3). *Moses his Judicials* directed that "[t]rial by jurors shall not be denied … partly to preserve the liberty of the people, and partly to prevent suspicion of partiality of any magistrates in the court." William Whitmore, ed., *Body of Liberties of 1641*, 39. *Liberty 29* granted "all persons in criminal cases" the choice "whether they will be tried by the bench or by a jury, unless … the law upon just reason hath otherwise determined." *Liberty 30* guaranteed "every delinquent (to be judged by a jury)" the option to "challenge any of the jurors." Edgar McManus, *Law and Liberty in Early New England* (Amherst: Univ. of Massachusetts Press, 1993), 9, 99. McManus explained, while "Massachusetts provided for jury trial in all felony prosecutions," by 1634 other "minor offenses were tried … upon the governing statute."

were to be expected. In one column the committee listed the "fundamental and common laws and customs of England, beginning with *Magna Charta*." The clearest indication of the degree of influence that it had on early legislation occurred at the very beginning of the effort in 1635, when the General Court ordered a draft of laws "for the well ordering of this plantation" Winthrop had expressed his hope that its members would enact "laws in resemblance to a *Magna Charta*."[7]

Within this format the Massachusetts *Body of Liberties of 1641* described the relationship between freemen and inhabitants (or non-church members), the towns and the colony, and the colony and its congregations. *Liberties 62 and 67*, for example, repeated the prohibition that only freemen could participate in colony level elections, and *Liberty 70* recertified the vital privilege that they had won during the 1634 Court of Elections, "All freemen called to give any advice, vote, verdict, or sentence in any court, counsel, or civil assembly, shall have full freedom to do it according to their true judgments and consciences." In both colony and town, citizenship remained the domain of male congregational members as "freemen," as only they could vote in colony level elections. While *Liberty 12* expanded participation in town meetings to include non-congregational members ("Every man, whether inhabitant or foreigner, free or not free, shall have liberty to come to any public court, counsel, or town meeting, and either by speech or writing to move any lawful, seasonable, and material question ... so it be done in convenient time, due order, and respective manner"), *Liberty 56* ensured that the freemen would have oversight of the inhabitants' participation: "If any man shall behave himself offensively at any town meeting, the rest of the freemen then present shall have power

---

7 *A Declaration of the General Court concerning a Remonstrance and Petition Exhibited at last Session of this Court by Doctor Child* (1646), in *Hutchinson Papers* (Albany: Prince Society, 1865), 1: 227–31. Nathaniel Shurtleff, ed., *MGCR*, 1: 147 (May 6, 1635). Richard Dunn, ed., *Journal of John Winthrop*, 146 (May 1635). Richard Morris, "Massachusetts and the Common Law: The Declaration of 1646," in David Flaherty, ed., *Essays in the History of Early American Law* (Chapel Hill: Univ. of North Carolina Press, 1969), 135–46. The *Declaration's* first nine sections listed the colony's laws and liberties beside the corresponding sections of *Magna Charta*. *Liberty 1* was in the same column as articles 39 and 40 of the *Great Charter* as best as colonists could recollect: "No man shall be condemned but by lawful trial; Justice shall not be sold, deferred nor denied to any man. All men's liberties and free customs shall be reserved." Austin Poole, *From Domesday Book to Magna Carta: 1087–1216* (Oxford: Clarendon Press, 1951), 475. Article 40 of *Magna Charta* stated: "To no one will we sell, to no one will we deny or delay right or justice." The joining of articles 39 and 40 was a traditional one. William Whitmore, ed., *The Colonial Laws of Massachusetts. Reprinted from the Edition of 1660*, 14–18. Rodney Mott, *Due Process of Law*, 95 (n. 35). Richard Morris, *Studies in the History of American Law* (New York: Columbia Univ. Press, 1930), 30.

to sentence him for his offense." And *Liberty 66* reiterated the *1636 Town Act*, reserving control of town affairs to the freemen once they had taken an oath of allegiance. According to Richard Hooker, Massachusetts law was thereby repugnant to English law, because membership in church and state was synonymous in England: "there is not any man of the Church of England but the same man is a member of the commonwealth, nor a member of the commonwealth which is not also a member of the Church of England."[8]

*Liberty 66* also forged a vital link between town and colonial governments, "freemen of every township shall have power to make such bylaws and constitutions as may concern the welfare of their town, provided they be not criminal, but only of a prudential nature." But those bylaws could not be "repugnant to the public laws and order of the Country" as enacted by the General Court. Just as the colonial charter prohibited the colony passing laws repugnant to English law, Massachusetts towns were enjoined from passing local ordinances, known as "prudentials," that contravened laws enacted by the General Court. Massachusetts towns were not virtually autonomous as they have often been portrayed. Since the deputies voted to adopt the *Body of Liberties* after its review by the freemen in the towns which had elected them, the idea that the towns were somehow detached from the General Court's authority is not supported by the historical record. Instead, the colony's education acts demonstrate a partnership between the General Court and the towns. As we have already reviewed, when town selectmen did not follow the colony's school regulations enacted by the Court they were routinely brought to account in the colony's county courts. The General Court and town governments were coordinate powers, not adversarial jurisdictions, with the Court's authority both adjudicative and supreme. By century's end the towns did contest centralization of power in Boston, but by that time the governor was appointed by the crown under the second Massachusetts charter. It is premature to place such a proto-imperial struggle in the middle of the seventeenth century when town freemen, represented by their elected magistrates and deputies, governed the colony through the General Court; even during times of struggle, they were joined by the rank of freeman, one based upon Congregational membership. Within this model the *Liberties* prescribed the ecclesiastical role of the freeman. With no Episcopal or Presbyterian hierarchy, or even a shared theology

8 William Whitmore, ed., *Body of Liberties of 1641*, 35 (*Lib. 12*), 45 (*Lib. 56*), 47 (*Lib. 66*), 49 (*Libs. 69 & 70*). Nathaniel Shurtleff, ed., *MGCR*, 1: 172 (March 3, 1636). Richard Hooker, *Of the Laws of Ecclesiastical Polity*, ed. Arthur McGrade, (Cambridge: Cambridge Univ. Press, 1989), 130 (Bk. 8, Ch. 1, §2). Kenneth Lockridge, Alan Kreider, "Evolution of Massachusetts Town Government: 1640–1740," *William and Mary Quarterly* 23 (1966): 550–62.

besides the contents of the Bible to unify town congregations, the freemen were the mortar that bonded "our Churches and Civil State" together. In this sense, Edmund Morgan deftly described the draft laws as a "blueprint of the whole Puritan experiment." During future controversies, colonial government would face both civil and religious challenges, in which the celestial and civil realms inevitably became more intertwined.[9]

Many of the *Body of Liberties of 1641* most important provisions focus on the relationship between congregation and colony. Regulations under the title, *Liberties more peculiarly concerning the freemen*, attempted to delineate civil and religious institutional jurisdictions. *Liberty 58* decreed, "Civil Authority has power and liberty to see the peace and ordinances and rules of Christ observed in every church according to his word, so it be done in a civil and not in an ecclesiastical way." Essentially, the General Court was authorized to regulate worship, not to clarify theological disputes or unnecessarily settle intricacies thereof; instead, the Court would ensure a general conformity. Congregational members were provided ecclesiastical freedom by the limitation of the General Court's regulatory powers to "civil" matters, while *Liberty 59* ensured church membership could not provide immunity from colonial law, "Civil Authority hath power and liberty to deal with any Church member in a way of civil justice, notwithstanding any church relation, office, or interest." *Liberty 60* made the colony's civil officers immune to church discipline that aimed to undermine their official duties, "No church censure shall degrade or depose any man from any civil dignity, office or authority he shall have in the commonwealth"; this regulation soon made itself felt when a congregation objected to a town militia appointment. Thomas Lechford, no friend of congregationalism, or the colony for that matter, admitted "magistrates and church-leaders labor for a just and equal correspondence in jurisdictions, not to entrench one on the other, neither the civil magistrates to be exempt from ecclesiastical censure, nor the ministers from civil … power," at least in a seventeenth-century sense.[10]

9 William Whitmore, ed., *Body of Liberties of 1641*, 35 (Lib. 12), 45 (Lib. 56), 47 (Lib. 66). David Allen, *In English Ways* (Chapel Hill: Univ. of North Carolina Press, 1981), 5. David Allen, "Notes and Documents: The Zuckerman Thesis and the Process of Legal Rationalization in Provincial Massachusetts," *William and Mary Quarterly* 29 (1972): 456. Professor Allen dated the integration of different levels of colonial government to the 1700's. Bushman, *King and People in Provincial Massachusetts*, 2nd ed., (Chapel Hill: Univ. of North Carolina Press, 1985), 99–111. Elmer Russell, *Review of American Colonial Legislation by the King in Council* (New York: Octagon Books, 1976), 15–36. Morgan, *The Puritan Dilemma*, 2nd ed., 152.

10 William Whitmore, ed., *Body of Liberties of 1641*, 47. After its first seventeen sections, liberties 18–57 were listed under the title *Rites, Rules, and Liberties concerning Judicial proceedings*; 58–78 under *Liberties more peculiarly concerning the free men*; 79–80 under *Liberties of Women*; 81–84 under *Liberties of Children*; 85–88 under *Liberties of Servants*;

To counterbalance these provisions of civil power over religion, *Liberty 95* provided for the "freedom" of congregations. First, biblical authority's supremacy was proclaimed, "Every Church hath full liberty to exercise all the ordinances of God, according to the rules of scripture." Next, a congregation's right to elect its own officials was reaffirmed, "Every Church hath free liberty of election and ordination of all their officers from time to time, provided they be able, pious and orthodox." If ministers were not sufficiently orthodox, the General Court could and did intervene; with no association with the Anglican church, or enforcement powers granted to Massachusetts ministers as a collective entity, only the General Court could rule in such matters. While each congregation would determine its own membership, "Every Church hath free liberty of admission, recommendation, dismissal, and expulsion," only the magistracy and colonial courts could try and punish those who broke the law: "All Churches have liberty to deal with any of their members in a church way that are in the hand of justice. So, it be not to retard or hinder the course" of civil authorities. Instead of a doctrinal uniformity, the General Court directed the ministry to deliberate on the proper form of Christian worship, similar to Puritan practices in the sixteenth century before the crown and the Anglican episcopacy suppressed such meetings: "once in every month of the year … it shall be lawful for the ministers and elders … to assemble … in public Christian Conference," so that "nothing be … imposed by way of authority from one or more churches upon another, but only by way of brotherly conference … to the satisfying of every man's conscience."[11]

89–91 under *Liberties of Foreigners and Strangers*; 92–93 under *Of the Bruit Creature* (or *Liberties of Animals*); *Liberty 94* contained the twelve sections of the *Capitall Laws*; *Liberty 95 A Declaration of the Liberties the Lord Jesus hath given to the Churches*; with its final sections addressing its own future administration and operation. This system of conceptual titles was not utilized again after the *Liberties*. Thomas Lechford, *Plaine Dealing: Or, Newes from New-England* (London, 1642); MHS *Collections (3rd Series/1833)*, 3: 74. Thomas Lechford, *Notebook*, ed. Edward Hale, 274–78. Michael Winship, *Godly Republicanism* (Cambridge: Harvard Univ. Press, 2012), 217. "In the Massachusetts constitutional project, church and state were conceived of roughly as two separate spheres. Church elders could not serve in public offices; the churches could not give secular punishments such as fines and imprisonment; and while the state was supposed to protect the churches, it was not supposed to interfere spiritually with them. This cooperative but clear separation of church and state had always been a goal for radical Puritans, and the oppressively 'theocratic' nature of Massachusetts' church-state establishment can be greatly exaggerated by historians." David Hall, *The Puritans: A Transatlantic History* (Princeton: Princeton Univ. Press, 2019), 225–32.

11 William Whitmore, ed., *Body of Liberties of 1641*, 57–59 (Lib. 95). S.E. Morison, *Builders of the Bay Colony* (New York: Houghton Mifflin Co., 1930), 229–34. Francis Bremer, *John*

These regulations expressed salient touchstones of the Protestant Reformation. Reliance on biblical authorities would be *the* guide for proper worship, in which conscience would play an essential role. But civil authority must safeguard congregations against wayward members, or those who might destroy the whole via sectarianism. Still, each congregation could choose its own minister, as long as he was sufficiently orthodox, and regulate their own membership. In sum, each congregation would be guided by scripture if it did not wander into unorthodoxy. But as Thomas Lechford warned, in a system that eschewed a uniform theology, regulation of worship must be a contingent endeavor, "if all churches are so free ... are they not in danger to become so many fractions, sects, [and] divisions." While political and religious membership was synonymous in the English church, Massachusetts Congregationalism aimed to safeguard spiritual freedom to the greatest extent possible via an independent church government. Uniformity amongst these congregations would be enforced by the General Court, and a grant of secular citizenship being contingent upon church membership was the price of this novel system. Such paradoxes of faith consequent to the Henrician Reformation ultimately produced not only a legacy of statutory regulation of worship, but also its legitimacy. In part, the First Amendment's guarantee of religious freedom from state interference is, at bottom, a civil ordinance. It was a natural outcome of a centuries-long English experience of Parliament's regulation of its national church.[12]

---

*Winthrop* (Oxford: Oxford Univ. Press, 2003), 47–48, 53–56, 141, 219–20, 234–35. Michael Winship, *Hot Protestants* (New Have: Yale Univ. Press, 2018), 31–36, 42–49.

12 Thomas Lechford, *Notebook*, ed., Edward Hale, 274–78. Robert Wall, *Massachusetts Bay: The Crucial Decade* (New Haven: Yale Univ. Press, 1972), 33. Christopher Hill, *Liberty Against the Law* (London: Allen Lane, 1996), 179–92. William Haller, *The Rise of Puritanism* (Columbia Univ. Press, 1938), 173–81. Patrick Collinson, *The Reformation* (New York: Modern Library, 2004), 126. "The key to what happened was the common law of England, which determined that what the royal government ordered by way of religious change was for the most part carried out, however unpopular it might have been." Glenn Burgess, *British Political Thought: 1500–1660* (New York: MacMillan Palgrave, 2009), 31–6, 44–8. "Henry VIII and Thomas Cromwell, willy-nilly, established the ideas of parliamentary omnicompetence and parliamentary sovereignty, which became obviously triumphant by the reign of Elizabeth ... That Parliament could legislate on all matters by the 1530s cannot be doubted." *Attainder of Archbishop* [*Laud*] *of Canterbury* (Jan. 4, 1645), CSP, *Domestic Series* (*1644–1645*), ed. William Douglas, (London: HMSO, 1890), 20: 228–29 (#3). Archbishop Laud was executed, in part, for "endeavoring to subvert the laws and government of the Kingdom of England, and instead thereof to introduce an arbitrary and tyrannical government against law, and to alter God's true religion by law established in the realm."

The authority of the *Body of Liberties* as law was dependent on its certification by the General Court. Concomitantly, Massachusetts government could not have functioned if the corpus of its laws was repealed upon the *Liberties*' enactment, because the latter was not a comprehensive statement of colonial law. For example, no mention was made of the 1636 order on the negative voice, and the Court could not function without it. While the *Liberties* was adopted by the General Court, its members did not concomitantly repeal all other existing laws. Instead, the *Body of Liberties* was intended to be a supplement to colonial law, and its distribution in manuscript form illustrates it was an intermediary step to a final book of law in print. Its concluding section stipulated that over the following three years it was to be reviewed and amended: "if any General Court … shall fail or forget to read and present at such Courts shall forfeit 20 shillings a man, and every deputy 10 shillings a man for each neglect, which shall be paid out of their proper estate, and not by the country or towns which choose them." According to Winthrop, "by that experience" the *Liberties* would be "established to be perpetual."[13]

One would expect that with the enactment of the *Body of Liberties* in 1641, magistrates and deputies had finally transcended their mutual animosity. But it did not even signify a lull in the struggle. Immediately after its passage Deputy William Hathorne made a motion that several of the oldest magistrates should be forced to retire because "they were grown poor." Hathorne could not have expected his ploy to succeed. Instead, the deputies were determined that "some certain penalty" must be enacted for lying and swearing, and not left

13 William Whitmore, ed., *Body of Liberties of 1641*, 33 (*intro.*), 45 (*Lib. 51*), 61 (*Libs. 96 & 97*). *Liberty 96* stated the authority of the *Liberties:* "Howsoever these above specified rites, freedoms, immunities, authorities, and privileges … are expressed only under the name and title of liberties, and not in the exact form of laws or statutes, yet we do with one consent fully authorize, and earnestly entreat all that are and shall be in authority to consider them as laws, and not to fail to inflict condign punishment upon every man impartially, that shall infringe or violate any of them." The *Liberties*' introduction announced the General Court's duty, as its members "further establish[ed] this Government, to collect and express all such freedoms as for present we foresee may concern us, and our posterity after us. And to ratify them with our solemn consent. We do therefore this day religiously and unanimously decree and confirm these following rites, liberties, and privileges concerning our Churches, and Civil State to be respectively, impartially, and inviolably enjoyed and observed throughout our jurisdiction for-ever." Nathaniel Shurtleff, ed., *MGCR*, 1: 344 (Dec. 4, 1641). Winthrop noted the Court's enactment of the *Body of Liberties* under December 10, even though it was passed on December 4. Richard Dunn, ed., *Journal of John Winthrop*, 380 (Dec., 1641). Winthrop also noted the enactment in his *Journal.* George Haskins, *Law and Authority in Early Massachusetts,* 131–32. Lawrence Friedman, *A History of American Law*, 3rd ed., (New York: Simon & Schuster, 2005), 50–53.

to the discretion of the magistrates. Deputy Governor John Endecott rose in opposition to the proposal, arguing that it was improper to pass such laws, not because he was opposed to criminalizing such offenses, but "in respect of the certain punishment." The magistrates insisted that only they could render specific punishments based on the law, while the deputies contended punishments should be stipulated in laws enacted by the General Court. Ultimately, Deputy Hathorne charged that Endecott intended to "have the government arbitrary," whereupon the "matter grew to some heat, for the deputy [governor] was a wise and a stout gentleman." Except for its capital punishments, the *Liberties* did not include specific criminal penalties. This essential matter had been left unresolved.[14]

The magistrates opposed specific penalties in legislation, or any enactment that might restrict their judicial discretion based on biblical authority and its referral of such matters "to the judges." Such restrictions were unjust in their eyes because an equitable judgment must take into consideration either the aggravating or mitigating circumstances of any potential criminal act, and inform a sentence in being more lenient or severe. Every case had to be judged before a sentence was handed down as each one comprised a unique set of facts, and address aggravating or mitigating circumstances, ones that a legislative body could not be aware of upon enactment, "God gave a certain law where he left the punishment arbitrary, so as we have a clear rule to guide the law where the punishment might be uncertain." The deputies countered, if such arguments were accepted "we might as well leave all laws arbitrary, at the discretion of the judge."[15]

The modern pejorative definition of arbitrary power was just emerging in the mid-1600s. In his justice of the peace manual *Eirenarcha*, William Lambarde described "arbitrary judgments" as those "referred to discretion." This reflected the etymological origins of arbitrary: arbitration, or arbitrament, "the power

---

14 Richard Dunn, ed., *Journal of John Winthrop*, 380–381 (Dec., 1641). James Savage, ed., *The History of New England* (Boston: Felps and Farnam, 1825), 2: 52–4 (n. 2). Robert Wall, "The Membership of the Massachusetts General Court," 259, 378, 498. Nathaniel Shurtleff, ed., *MGCR*, 1: 319 (June 2, 1641), 2: 67 (May, 29 1644). Governor Bellingham and Deputy Governor Endecott were elected in June 1641. George Haskins, *Law and Authority in Early Massachusetts*, 131–37. Edmund Morgan, *The Puritan Dilemma*, 2nd ed., 149–53, 156–58. S.E. Morison, *Builders of the Bay Colony*, 62. Francis Bremer, *John Winthrop*, 305–306, 359. "There were at least forty crimes for which no sentence was mandated," and "Winthrop believed that this was as it should be."

15 Richard Dunn, ed., *Journal of John Winthrop*, 381–83 (Dec. 1641-Jan. 1642). Mark Cahn, "Punishment, Discretion, and the Codification of Prescribed Penalties in Colonial Massachusetts," *American Journal of Legal History* 33 (1989): 124 (n. 100).

to decide for others; absolute authority." By the early 1660's a leading political theorist of the English Commonwealth defined three types of arbitrary power in "reference to laws." In *A System of Politics* James Harrington explained, "there must in every judicatory"—or system of distributing justice—"be some arbitrary power." The first belonged to the "sovereign" power of making and interpreting the law; the second was "applying laws to cases which are never one like the other"; and the third was "in reconciling the laws" amongst each other. A legislature could never enact enough laws to cover every case that came before a court, because there was an infinite number of scenarios. Nevertheless, while judicial discretion was indispensable, Harrington believed that the "law which leaves the least arbitrary power to the judge or judicatory is the most perfect law." This description of arbitrary power illustrates that no clear division between legislative and judicial jurisdictions existed at this point in history. Monarchy's most resolute defender, Robert Filmer, formulated this state of affairs in a maxim and a question: while the "chief mark of supremacy" was to "judge in the highest causes and last appeals," the "main question in these our days is where this power legislative remains or is placed?" Everyone agreed that arbitrary power encompassed law-making and interpretative powers, the issue at hand was who possessed such an absolute sovereign power? William Prynne articulated the following as an "infallible maxim of the ... Common, Civil, and Canon Law": the "Court or person to whom the last appeal is to be made is the Supreme Power."[16]

John Milton articulated an early modern rationale for rule by law, as guided by passages from Cicero, that limited arbitrary power via legislation enacted by

16 William Lambarde, *Eirenarcha: or the Office of the Justice of the Peace* (London: 1619), 569 (Bk. 4, Ch. 15); *Google Books*: (https://www.google.com/books/edition/_/o-A1AQAAMAAJ?hl=en&gbpv=0). "The judgments then of the Justices of the Peace are in some cases arbitrarie (or referred to discretion) and in other some cases prescribed or limited." Leslie Brown, ed., *The New Shorter Oxford English Dictionary* (Oxford: Clarendon Press, 1961), 1: 107. "Arbitrary 1. Dependent on will or pleasure; *Law* (now *Hist.*) dependent on the decision of a legally recognized authority; discretionary." Ibid., "Arbitrament 1. The right or capacity to decide for oneself; free will ... 2. The power to decide for others; absolute authority." C.T. Lewis, ed., *An Elementary Latin Dictionary* (Oxford: Oxford Univ. Press, 1891), 69. "Arbitrium—In law, a judgment, decision of an arbitrator." James Harrington, *A System of Politics*, in J.G.A. Pocock, ed., *The Commonwealth of Oceana and A System of Politics* (Cambridge Univ. Press, 1992), 288–89. Robert Filmer, *The Free-Holders Grand Inquest* (1648), in J.P. Sommerville, ed., *Patriarcha and Other Writings* (Cambridge: Cambridge Univ. Press, 1991), 100, 113. William Prynne, *The Soveraigne Powers of Parliaments and Kingdomes* (London: by Order of Parliament, August 2, 1643), 93 (*1st Part*); *Google Books*: (https://www.google.com/books/edition/The_Soveraigne_Power_of_Parliaments_and/Lpg-AQAAMAAJ?hl=en&gbpv=0).

a republican form of government. He began with the premise, since "all men were naturally born free" they could establish government for the common welfare. While a "power of self-defense" had inhered in every man in ancient times, eventually kings and magistrates were selected to keep the peace. Not as perpetual "lord and masters," however, but only as "deputies and commissioners to execute, by virtue of their entrusted power, that justice which else every man by the bond of nature and of covenant must have executed for himself." Originally, kings and magistrates ruled according to "their own arbitrement," or judgment; but once the "temptation of such a power [was] left absolute in their hands, [it] perverted them at length to injustice and partiality." These experiences made Englishmen realize that "committing arbitrary power to any" was inherently dangerous, so they enacted "laws, either framed or consented to by all," to "confine and limit the authority of whom they chose to govern them." While these laws required the magistrate to be "set above the people, … so the law was set above the magistrate" to ensure the "power of kings and magistrates is nothing else but what is only derivative, transferred, and committed to them *in trust* from the people to the common good of them all, in whom the power yet remains fundamentally, and cannot be taken away." Winthrop denied that an arbitrary discretion exercised by the magistrates marked Massachusetts' legal system as unjust. As God's representatives on Earth, it was the magistrates' duty to administer justice in the colony, as only their divinely endowed wisdom could administer the law equitably. How could the deputies determine a just punishment via legislation before a crime had even occurred? How would they know if extenuating circumstances existed in a case? Recalling Israel Stoughton's charge that the magistrates claimed "power simply by their places over our persons, goods, and lives without any law of ours," the critical issue is obvious.[17]

The magistrates were not completely unified on Winthrop's conception of their authority. Richard Bellingham and Richard Saltonstall, Jr., supported

17 John Milton, *Tenure of Kings and Magistrates* (London: 1649), in *John Milton: Complete Poems and Major Prose*, Merritt Hughes ed., (New York: Odyssey Press, 1954), 754. Quentin Skinner, "Classical Liberty and the Coming of the English Civil War," in *Republicanism: A Shared European Heritage*, vol. 2, *The Values of Republicanism in Early Modern Europe* (Cambridge: Cambridge Univ. Press, 2002), 12–14. Milton borrowed from Cicero in enunciating a "golden rule" of government: "'When giving laws to free peoples,' [Cicero] reminds us once again, we must first ensure that they are never dominated by the wills of their magistrates. We must ensure that they are entirely ruled by laws, so that 'just as the magistrates govern the people, so the laws govern the magistrates.'" Dunn, ed., *Journal of John Winthrop*, 381–83 (Dec. 1641). Israel Stoughton, "A Relation Concerning New England," *MHS Proceedings (1860–1862)*, 5: 139–40.

the deputies' attempts to gain greater governmental power unconditionally. Saltonstall, Jr., authored a tract attacking the standing council in the early 1640's; both men opposed the magistracy's judicial power as supported by the negative voice, as well as their claim of executive authority on the standing council. While Saltonstall's tract has not survived, Winthrop wrote several letters and journal entries on the matter, followed by a treatise on the negative vote itself. Francis Bremer has described the outcome, after examining the essay over the summer, including a review by the congregational ministers, the General Court found its argument to be untenable, as a "council to make decisions between meetings of the court was in fact essential for the security of the commonwealth." Meanwhile, Winthrop informed the deputies and freemen, "this council as counsellors, have no power of judicature"; his aim must have been to reassure the people that the standing council would not become a prerogative court like Star Chamber or High Commission, empowered to render criminal judgments against colonists. In his treatise on the negative vote written a short time later, he speculated on the likely consequences for any unjust decision reached by the magistrates in council: "either the shame of it would make them change their judgment, or they should be manifest to all the Country … and then they would be soon removed, and called to account."[18]

After magistrates and deputies had returned to their respective towns to deliberate on the controversy during the summer of 1643, they achieved compromise via legislation once again:

> Forasmuch as, after long experience, we find divers inconveniences in the manner of proceeding in courts by magistrates and deputies sitting together, and accounting it wisdom to follow the laudable practice of other states who have laid groundworks for government and order in the issuing of business of greatest and highest consequence,–It is therefore ordered, first, that the magistrates may sit and act business by themselves, by drawing up bills and orders which they shall see good in their wisdom, which having agreed upon, they may present them to the deputies … and accordingly to give their assent or dissent, the deputies in like manner sitting apart by themselves, and consulting such orders and laws as they in their discretion and experience shall find meet for common good, which agreed upon by them, they may present to the magistrates, who … may consent unto them or disallow them; and when any orders have passed

18 Richard Dunn, ed., *Journal of John Winthrop*, 390–91 (May 1642); 418–20 (Oct., 1642). *Winthrop Papers*, 4: 347–48 (May 1642); 4: 390 #4 (June 1643). Nathaniel Shurtleff, ed., *MGCR*, 2: 5 (May 1642), 2: 20–21 (June 1642). Francis Bremer, *John Winthrop*, 350–52. Robert Wall, *Massachusetts Bay: The Crucial Decade*, 41–92.

> the approbation of both magistrates and deputies, then such orders to be engrossed [i.e., drafted as a final bill], and in the last day of the Court to be read deliberately, and full assent to be given; provided, also, that all matters of judicature which this Court shall take cognizance of shall be issued in a like manner.[19]

While *Sherman v. Keayne* and its divided vote between magistrates and deputies had precipitated the immediate crisis leading to this enactment, the establishment of a bicameral legislature stemmed from the initial controversy on the negative voice, opposition to which was led by Israel Stoughton.[20]

The establishment of a bicameral legislature sealed the breech for now. Although, procedurally speaking, the compromise appeared to be a complete victory for the magistrates, as they retained their veto power in judicial cases as well as legislation. Winthrop had lectured them that to discredit one law, "all the acts of that court should be void also." Since a majority of deputies had agreed to the 1636 law that provided both parties a negative voice, to disavow that agreement at this point would undermine the jurisdiction of the General Court in legislative matters achieved only two years before. Nevertheless, the deputies had won important procedural rights of their own, such as to deliberate separate from the magistrates and keep their own official record of proceedings. During earlier controversies, when deputies and magistrates had voted differently, fundamental crises had erupted. Now, sitting apart from the magistrates in their own deliberations would allow the deputies to form policies before matters were reconciled between the houses. One of the first entries in the House of Deputy's record noted the election of the combative William Hathorne as "Speaker for this Court, by the House."[21]

19 Nathaniel Shurtleff, ed., *MGCR*, 2: 40 (May 10, 1643); 2: 58–9 (March 7, 1644).

20 Richard Dunn, ed., *Journal of John Winthrop*, 503 (March 1644). S.E. Morison, *Builders of the Bay Colony*, 93. John Norton, "A Small Treatise on the Negative Vote," *MHS Proceedings* (*1912–1913*); 46: 283. In 1643, the deputies still repeated Israel Stoughton's argument in opposition to the magistrates' veto power, "The number of the deputies exceeding the number of the magistrates, therefore no reason why votes of unequal numbers should be equal."

21 *John Winthrop's Defense of the Negative Vote*, in *Winthrop Papers* 4: 385–89. Nathaniel Shurtleff, ed., *MGCR*, 3: 2–3 (May 29, 1644), v–vi. "The third volume of the Massachusetts Colony *Records* contains the proceedings of the House of Deputies, commencing with those of the General Court of Election held in May 1644, and ending with those of the May Court in 1657," after which the General Court reverted to one record for both houses. Richard Dunn, ed., *Journal of John Winthrop*, 379 (n. 30), 380 (n. 33), 503 (n. 9). Francis Bremer, *John Winthrop*, 352–57. "Hathorne was a deputy representing Salem and assumed a leadership role among his fellow representatives, seeking to enlarge their authority and often irritating the magistrates in the process." He was also a relative of Nathaniel

Concomitant with these events, in the wake of the La Tour controversy (as covered in Chapter 5) the freemen were more determined than ever to rein in the magistrate's discretion, especially the townsmen from Essex County. Recently, the General Court had divided the colony into four counties: Suffolk, Middlesex, Essex, and Norfolk. While the "county" had played a significant role in England in centuries past, to this point in the colony's history its government had consisted of the General Court, the standing council, the court of assistants, the quarterly courts, and town meetings. Upon the creation of Essex County its freemen formed a coalition to challenge the control of the standing council by the magistrates from Suffolk and Middlesex counties; because council meetings were held in Boston, the magistrates who attended most regularly were from those latter two counties. The standing council's decision to support La Tour had been made without representatives from Essex County and prompted the petition condemning the council. In a series of meetings held to determine a strategy for the upcoming General Court of Election in the Spring of 1644, Essex freemen decided to concentrate their votes for the governorship on a candidate residing in their county, but they did not constitute enough of a majority to accomplish this goal. According to Winthrop, what began as an Essex coalition became "so strong a party among the deputies of the smaller towns (being most of them mean men, and such as had small understanding in affairs of state), as they easily carried all these among the deputies."[22]

On May 29, 1644, the goal of the Essex coalition was realized with the election of Salem resident, Magistrate John Endecott. While he had allied himself with Winthrop to retain the negative vote, Endecott vigorously opposed the standing council's decision to aid La Tour. After the French governor's first visit he warned Winthrop, the "country hereabouts is much troubled that they are so entertained and have their liberty ... to bring their soldiers ashore." Endecott could see no benefit in "having anything to do with these idolatrous French." But just a month later he reassured Winthrop of his continued friendship and allegiance, despite the council's decision. Although Governor Endecott remained an opponent to any provision of assistance to the French, the deputies realized he would not join their initiative as a long-time ally of Winthrop

---

Hawthorne. George Haskins, *Law and Authority in Early Massachusetts*, 38–42. T.H. Breen, *The Character of a Good Ruler* (New Haven: Yale Univ. Press, 1970), 84.

22 Richard Dunn, ed., *Journal of John Winthrop*, 510–11 (May-June 1644). Nathaniel Shurtleff, ed., *MGCR*, 2: 38 (May 10, 1643). Robert Wall, *Massachusetts Bay: The Crucial Decade, 1640–1650*, 14–15, 42, 69–75. S.E. Morison, *Builders of the Bay Colony*, 235–38. Francis Bremer, *John Winthrop*, 357. Robert Palmer, *The County Courts of Medieval England: 1150–1350* (Princeton: Princeton Univ. Press, 1982).

in the magistracy, including his opposition to specific penalties in legislation. The freemen ultimately achieved unseating John Winthrop as governor, but his election as deputy governor demonstrated a majority of the electorate's continued support.[23]

Shortly before his return to England, Ward authored a plan for a non-arbitrary process for ruler and ruled in *The Simple Cobbler of Aggawam in America*. He had long thought it "possible in a time of peace and in some king's reign for … statesmen to cut an exquisite thread between, and quite through, kings' prerogatives and subjects' liberties." Years earlier, in the early 1620's, he expressed initial interest in "the redress of many abuses crept into offices and officers." After "having spent so much time in the study of law and execution of some offices," he was "weary of the errors I saw." This caused him to "heartily wish the reformation of them." By the 1640's, Ward realized that while "authority must have power to make and keep people honest, … states [sh]ould let people know so much before-hand by some safe woven manifesto." Like Winthrop, he agreed that "royal prerogatives" and "popular liberties" were "not of man's making, but God's." But Ward had reached a conclusion at odds with the common opinion that held divinely inspired judgments as supreme: while man should "measure them out by God's rule," where his "wisdom cannot reach," human "experience must mend." In his final analysis, the "best standard to measure prerogatives is the plough staff," whose interest the former must serve, and "to measure liberties, the scepter," because the latter ultimately guaranteed their enjoyment. If these "terms were a little altered into loyal prerogatives and royal liberties, then we should be sure to have royal kings and loyal subjects." Ward had diagnosed the resolution of the magistrate/deputy struggle via the colony's first printed law book, the *Laws and Liberties of 1648*:

> Subjects their King, the King his Subjects greet,
> Once the Scepter and the Plough-staff meet.[24]

---

23 Nathaniel Shurtleff, ed., *MGCR*, 2: 66 (May 29, 1644). *Copy of a Letter from Mr. Endecott to Governor Winthrop, about La Tour* (June 19, 1643), in *Hutchinson Papers* (Albany: Prince Society, 1865), 1: 127. *Copy of a Letter from Mr. Endecott to Governor Winthrop, about the French* (July 26, 1643), in *Hutchinson Papers*, 1: 134–35. Edmund Morgan, *The Puritan Dilemma*, 2nd ed., 171–74. Harry Ward, *The United Colonies of New England* (New York: Vantage Press, 1961), 92. On his initial visit to Boston, La Tour had "posed as a Huguenot" in an attempt to avoid agitating Bay colonists.

24 Nathaniel Ward, *The Simple Cobbler of Aggawam in America* (London: Jan. 29, 1647), 49–51; *Thomason Tracts*, E 372 (21), Reel 59. Alexander Chalmers, ed., *Samuel Johnson's Dictionary of the English Language*, 819. I substituted "once" for "whlome," in the last line of verse based on Johnson's definition. Samuel Ward, *Jethro's Justice of Peace*. (London: Edward Griffin & John Marriot, 1618), 71–2; *Google Books* (https://www.google.com/books/edition/_/A7FoAAAAcAAJ?hl=en).

CHAPTER 7

# Divine Magistracy vs. a Rule of Law

In the wake of the La Tour controversy, the deputies sought to rein-in the magistracy via laws with specific regulations and penalties to check the growth of what they perceived as an emerging despotism. Amidst these controversies, Governor Endecott bewailed the "great differences" between the magistrates and the deputies. As in earlier disputes two of the magistrates' own, Richard Bellingham and Richard Saltonstall, Jr., continued to lead the deputies' resistance to the Winthrop led group of magistrates. During a meeting of the standing council Endecott condemned the deputies' attempts to limit the magistrates' authority when convened as the council by regulating it via a commission approved by the General Court. In order to resolve this and other issues, he asked the elders to mediate a "thorough reconciliation," a service they had performed several times before, so the "place and power of magistrates and deputies might be known."[1]

Before the elders answered the questions presented to them by the magistrates and deputies during the General Court session in November 1644, they addressed the inquiry posed by the Court during its previous session.[2] The ministry's position was that the "magistrates are, by patent [or colonial charter] and election of the people, the standing council of the commonwealth in the vacancy of the General Court, and accordingly may act in all cases pertaining to government according to the patent, and laws made by the said General Court." They concluded, however, "We do not find that by the patent they are expressly directed to proceed by the word of God; but we understand that by a law or liberty of the country they may act in cases

1 Richard Dunn, ed., *Journal of John Winthrop* (Cambridge: Belknap Press, 1996), 530–31 (August 1644). *Declaration of the Governor, Deputy Governor, and Assistants of Massachusetts*, in *Winthrop Papers*, 4: 467. Edmund Morgan, *The Puritan Dilemma*, 2nd ed., (Boston: Little, Brown, and Co., 1999), 144–45. Roger Thompson, *Watertown Massachusetts: 1630–1680* (Amherst: Univ. of Massachusetts Press, 2001), 14–57.

2 Nathaniel Shurtleff, ed., *MGCR*, 2: 90–1 (Nov. 13, 1644). "Whether the magistrates are, by patent and elections of the people, the standing council of this commonwealth in the vacancy of the General Court, and have power accordingly to act in all cases subject to government, according to the said patent, and the laws of this jurisdiction; and when any necessary occasions call for action from authority, in cases where there is no particular express law provided, there to be guided by the word of God until the General Court give particular rules in such cases. July 2, 1644." Richard Dunn, ed., *Journal of John Winthrop*, 554 (n. 18) (Oct., 1644).

 | DOI:10.1163/9789004706347_009

wherein as yet there is no express law, so that in such acts they proceed according to the word of God." The ministers were referring to the law enacted in 1636 that appointed John Cotton to the committee that drafted *Moses His Judicials*, "in the meantime the magistrates … shall proceed in the courts to hear and determine all causes according to the laws now established, and where there is no law, then as near the law of God as they can." In sum, while the ministers accepted the council's legitimacy, they still maintained that the magistrates' authority to make decisions per the "the law of God" derived from the 1636 law enacted by the General Court. It was not an implied power of their office. In rejecting the magistrates' claim to a divinely endowed discretionary power, the Congregational ministry certainly made a strange beginning from our modern perspective. One would have supposed, even if they were challenging the magistrates' right to interpret biblical law, perhaps to secure that right for themselves, it wouldn't be based on the authority of human or positive law. But as Edmund Morgan confirmed, the ministers' support of the deputies' initiative for more "specific legislation" was manifest.[3]

The ministers proceeded to field the remaining questions posed by the deputies and the magistrates. The deputies began by asking whether the *Charter* provided the magistrates the power to "dispense justice in the vacancy of the General Court, without some law or order?" The ministers believed the magistrates must govern according to "some law or order" as the "rule of their administration"; therefore, in the future all necessary laws should be enacted by the General Court for "regulating of all particulars, as far as may be." If such regulations were impractical in some situations, then the magistrates must govern according to "general rules," or their discretion. The deputies proceeded, asking whether the General Court possessed a "power in particular cases to choose any commissioners, either assistants or freemen?"; this addressed their earlier attempt to regulate the standing council. They qualified their inquiry by disavowing any intention of taking "away the peoples' liberties in elections." The ministers were unpersuaded. If the deputies intended that such a commission might deal with "all cases of constant judicature and counsel," as in the court

3 Nathaniel Shurtleff, ed., *MGCR*, 1: 174–75 (May 25, 1636); 2: 90–91 (Nov. 13, 1644). Richard Dunn, ed., *Journal of John Winthrop*, 554–55 (Oct., 1644), 554 (n. 18). Edmund Morgan, *The Puritan Dilemma*, 2nd ed., 146. "Though the clergy had no political authority of any kind, they did enjoy a very powerful indirect influence … When a difficult decision had to be made, the magistrates frequently consulted the ministers, who were learned men and wise in the laws of God. In this way, a back door was left open through which they could influence state policy … Although for the most part they supported the magistrates, they agreed with the deputies on the need for specific legislation to reduce discretionary authority."

of assistants or county courts, "we answer negatively." But in the most important issues the magistrates were "limited by the General Court as the supreme council." The following year Nathaniel Ward wrote, a "supreme council" must "sanction" the determination of such "essentials."[4]

Now it was the magistrates' turn. Predictably their first question was if the *Charter* authorized the deputies to exercise judicial and executive power. The ministers replied, "if we speak of the constant and usual administration thereof, we do not find it is granted to the freemen or deputies ... by any law of the country." Under the general directives of the *Charter*, as defined by colonial law, the magistrates were the judges in the colony's lower courts and sat on the standing council. But there were several scenarios in which the General Court was provided the jurisdiction to hear judicial cases. The first occurred by the "law of the country" granting the General Court an appellate jurisdiction; *Liberty 1* did so in "capital cases, or in cases concerning dismembering or banishment." The second occurred in the "case of defect or delinquency of a magistrate"; *Liberty 67* enabled the freemen to discharge any government official upon a proven offense, as decided and judged by the General Court. In their roles of judicial and executive administration of the government the magistrates were supreme. If not, the General Court would be making decisions on everything from military matters to criminal and civil cases. The colony's government could not function under such a scenario.[5]

Finally, the magistrates asked "whether a judge be bound to pronounce such sentence as a positive [i.e., colonial law] prescribes," even if it was too severe or did not provide sufficient punishment for a heinous offense. The ministers realized that judicial sentences should reflect the circumstances surrounding a crime that either aggravated or mitigated its commission, but cautioned the magistrates to take care in sentencing offenders. If defendants "whose sins be alike circumstantiated with another" were punished more severely, they would think they were "unequally dealt with." But in cases where a "crime deserveth a greater punishment" than the law allowed, "no power" justified the magistracy to "go higher" until, "by conference with the lawgivers," permission was

4 Nathaniel Shurtleff, ed., *MGCR*, 2: 91–2 (Nov. 13, 1644). Richard Dunn, ed., *Journal of John Winthrop* 558–60 (Oct., 1644).

5 Nathaniel Shurtleff, ed., *MGCR*, 2: 92–93 (Nov. 13, 1644). The elders elaborated, when "we speak of the power of freemen by patent the same may be said of the deputies, so far ... as the power of the freemen is delegated to them by order of law." Richard Dunn, ed., *Journal of John Winthrop*, 555–56 (Oct., 1644). William Whitmore, ed., *Body of Liberties of 1641*, 33, 47. *Liberty 67* was incorporated in the *Laws and Liberties of 1648*. Richard Dunn, ed., *Laws and Liberties of 1648*, 21, title *Elections*, §4.

given to exceed the prescribed punishment. The ministers had already urged the General Court to regulate all such "particular" circumstances, but only in the absence of legislative direction could the magistrates refer to scripture. The deputies' last question addressed the fundamental issue of this most recent dispute: "whether the General Court, consisting of magistrates and deputies, be not the chief civil power of the commonwealth, … to describe the power of magistracy, and prescribe laws to all, and do all other acts which belong to such a power?" The ministers concurred, the Court was the "chief civil power of the commonwealth, so as to describe the power of the magistracy, and to prescribe (in a civil way) laws unto all not repugnant to the laws of God." This clearly undermined Winthrop's position, and like-minded assistants, that only they could interpret colonial law via insight into human nature by virtue of a divinely endowed authority.[6]

The ministers' mediation reflected the office that the magistrates had modeled their own judicial powers on: England's Justice of the Peace (JP). By 1603, three hundred and nine parliamentary statutes regulated this officialdom. Michael Dalton's justification for authoring his JP manual, *The Countrey Justice*, was an ever-increasing "multiplicity of Statutes," as "every Parliament" saw fit to pass new laws or amend older ones. Consequently, it had become a "work very hard and laborious for gentlemen not conversant in the study of laws (although otherwise very industrious) to proceed as by the Commission they ought and are prescribed." Upon such "considerations, and for their ease principally, I have published this work." Obviously, statute law was part and parcel of the everyday life of a JP, an office secured by royal appointment via a Commission of the Peace. Upon the magistrates' refusal to incorporate penalties into new laws after the enactment of the *Body of Liberties*, the deputies had objected that the "statutes in England set down a certain penalty for most offenses." But the magistrates persisted in denying the deputies a greater role in government by dismissing parliamentary precedent, "We are not bound to make such examples ourselves."[7]

6 Shurtleff, ed., *MGCR*, 2: 91–5 (Nov. 13, 1644). Dunn, ed., *Journal of John Winthrop*, 555–58 (Oct., 1644). Robert Wall, *Massachusetts Bay: The Crucial Decade* (New Haven: Yale Univ. Press, 1972), 90–92. David Hall, *A Reforming People* (New York: Alfred A. Knopf, 2011), 34–35. "Near the end of their deliberations, the ministers arrived at the heart of the matter … Yes, the General Court was 'the chief power' … with judicial authority resting mainly with the magistrates."

7 Michael Dalton, *Countrey Justice (1618)* (Norwood: Walter Johnson, 1975), *The Epistle*. Richard Dunn, ed., *Journal of John Winthrop*, 383 (Dec., 1641). William Lambarde, *Eirenarcha: or the Office of the Justice of the Peace* (London: 1619), 57–8 (Bk. 1, Ch. 2); *Google Books*: (https://www.google.com/books/edition/_/o-A1AQAAMAAJ?hl=en&gbpv=0). The predecessor to Dalton's JP manual, Lambarde's *Eirenarcha* advised, even with authority to reconcile conflicting laws,

Instead of utilizing the ministers' mediation to achieve a compromise with the deputies, Winthrop led the magistrates in their resistance to any qualification of their powers via new legislation. As S.E. Morison explained, they considered themselves "exclusive partners with God in the divine covenant to rule the Bay." Indeed, in the eyes of the "magistrates the right of the matter was that law, in a Bible Commonwealth, must be God's law as revealed in scripture." The magistrate was "God's own justice, appointed during good behavior, with complete discretion as to the particular law of God that he should apply, and the punishments he should mete out." Although the ministry clearly supported an enlarged political role for the deputies, the magistrates' negative vote prevented the enactment of any legislation that circumscribed their existing authority without their approval. Owing to their dual role as assistants in the upper house of the General Court, the magistrates perpetuated their hold on the "preponderance of political power" with their judicial authority to "declare law in all civil and criminal cases, and to fix the penalty."[8]

Winthrop's opposition to the deputies' claim of judicial authority, especially of setting "penalties in laws" in cases of "variable degrees of guilt," led the freemen to "suspect that he and some others of the magistrates did affect an arbitrary government." So, he authored a "small treatise about these points, showing what arbitrary government was, and that our government (in the state it now stood) was not arbitrary, neither in the ground and foundation of it, nor in the exercise and administration thereof." He defined an arbitrary government as one without a rule for its administration, and, that did not hold elections. In a state where the "people have liberty to admit, or reject their governors," on the other hand, and had a "rule by which they shall be governed and judged, this is not an arbitrary government." While Massachusetts had organized its government by "disposing a certain number of persons into a body

JPs should not "arrogate unto themselves authority to use their discretion, and to play (as it were) the Chancellor in every case that commeth before them." Instead, a JP must "contain himself within the limits of law, and (being soberly wise) do not use his own discretion, but only where the law permits, and the present case requireth it." Francis Bremer, *John Winthrop* (Oxford: Oxford Univ. Press, 2003), 106–109. Approximately seventy-five JPs comprised Suffolk County's Commission of the Peace during John Winthrop's tenure after his appointment as a JP in 1615. Anthony Fletcher, *Reform in the Provinces: The Government of Stuart England* (New Haven: Yale Univ. Press, 1986), 3–4. "The scope of the JP's work had been much extended by the Tudors. Their duties sprang from two sources: statutes, and the commission of the peace which appointed them. By 1603, no fewer than 309 statutes imposed restrictions or duties upon JPs; 176 of which had been passed since 1485." John Bellamy, *Crime and the Courts in England: 1660–1800* (Princeton: Princeton Univ. Press, 1986), 5–6.

8 S.E. Morison, *Builders of the Bay Colony*, 225–26. Robert Wall, *Massachusetts Bay: The Crucial Decade*, 89.

politic" under the *Charter*, Winthrop claimed it was composed of two distinct political memberships. The magistrates were preeminent, possessing authority to govern the colony "not as a person, but as a *state*." The town freemen were an adjunct constituency, who had only the "power of liberty" of electing the town selectmen and deputies in the General Court; they did not govern. Consent to new legislation or taxation was guaranteed, but the exercise of political authority inhered in the governor, deputy governor, and assistants as a "distinct member" from the freemen's liberty of counsel: "*otherwise our state should be a mere Democracy*."[9]

In Winthrop's essay, *Defense of the Negative Vote*, written a year earlier, he had identified "several branches" of government in the *Charter*. Having discovered "both those branches," he concluded they must be "intended to be for some use." A year later in the midst of a political controversy he defined those clauses as follows. One branch was supposed to provide a government for the "inhabitants within the plantation." He recalled, prior to the *Massachusetts Charter of 1629*, charters of Virginia, Bermuda, and the West Indies required their "chief government" to remain in the "hands of the company residing in England." Winthrop claimed he had a similar proviso struck from the Massachusetts *Charter*, and replaced by the following clause:

> It shall and may be lawful, to and for the governor, etc., and such of the freemen of the said Company for the time being, as shall be assembled in any of their General Courts aforesaid, or in any other courts to be specially summoned and assembled for that purpose, or the greater part of them, where of the Governor or Deputy Governor and 6 of the assistants, to be always 7, from time to time, to make, ordain, and establish all manner of wholesome and reasonable orders, laws, statutes, and ordinances, directions and instructions, not contrary to the laws of this our realm of

9 *The Returnes of the Committee of the house of Dep. concerning the Book about Arbitrary Government*, in *Winthrop Papers*, 4: 483–84. Richard Dunn, ed., *Journal of John Winthrop*, 561–63 (Oct., 1644). Francis Bremer, *John Winthrop*, 354–60. William Nelson, "The Utopian Legal Order of the Massachusetts Bay Colony, 1630–1686," *American Journal of Legal History* 47 (2005): 183–230. Richard Ross, "The Career of Puritan Jurisprudence," *Law and History Review* 26 (2008): 227–58. John Winthrop, *Discourse on Arbitrary Government* (July 1644), in *Winthrop Papers*, 4: 468–69; MHS (https://www.masshist.org/publications/winthrop/index.php/view/PWF04d410).

> England: as well for settling of the forms and ceremonies of government and magistracy, fit and necessary for the said plantation.[10]

His recollection of events is not accurate since the decision to transfer the government was reached during the Company's meeting in Cambridge, England, on August 29, 1629, soon after he joined the company, but before his election as governor the following October. By majority vote the government was transferred "legally" by virtue of existing provisions in the *Charter* granted *the previous March.* In other words, because the clause Winthrop cited (above) was in the original *Charter* granted in March of 1629, it could not have been "inserted" the following August. It was already in the *Charter*. Despite this documented chain of events, Winthrop claimed his group negotiated these changes in the draft charter and proceeded to utilize his interpretation to secure the magistracy's position.[11]

Did Winthrop purposefully reverse the sequence of events in order to serve his own purposes? Upon his initial examination of the two branches of government in 1643 he admitted his confusion, they must be "be intended … for

10 John Winthrop, *Discourse on Arbitrary Government* (1644), *Winthrop Papers*, 4: 469–71. Winthrop, *Defense of the Negative Vote* (1643), Ibid., 4: 381; *MHS* (https://www.masshist.org/publications/winthrop/index.php/view/PWF04d350).

11 Carl Bridenbaugh, *Vexed and Troubled Englishmen: 1590–1642* (New York: Oxford Univ. Press, 1968), 436–440. William Hubbard, *A General History of New England* (Boston: Mass. Hist. Society, 1848), 120–24. Nathaniel Shurtleff, ed., *MGCR*, 1: 50 (Aug. 29, 1629). "[T]he committees … appointed to … consider … the government of the Company's plantation in New England … debated their arguments and reasons on both sides … [A]fter a long debate, Mr. deputy [governor] put it to the question, as followeth: As many of you as desire to have the patent and the government of the plantation to be transferred to New England, so as it may be done legally, hold up your hands. So many as will not hold up your hands. Where, by erection of hands, it appeared by the general consent of the Company, that the government and patent should be settled in New England, accordingly an order to be drawn." *Massachusetts Charter of 1629*, in Nathaniel Shurtleff, ed., *MGCR*, 1: 16–17 (March 4, 1629). "[I]t shall be lawful to and for the Governor or Deputy Governor and such of the Assistants and freemen of the said Company for the time being as shall be assembled in any of their General Courts aforesaid, or in any other courts to be specially summoned and assembled for that purpose … (whereof the Governor or Deputy Governor and six of the Assistants, to be always seven,) from time to time to make ordain, and establish all manner of wholesome and reasonable orders, laws, statutes, and ordinances, directions, and instructions not contrary to the laws of this our realm England, as well for settling of the forms and ceremonies of government and magistracy fit and necessary for the said plantation and the inhabitants there, and for naming and styling all sorts of officers, both superior and inferior, which they shall find needful for that government and plantation, and the distinguishing and settling forth of the several duties, powers, and limits of every such office and place."

some use." It is possible that his memory of events fifteen years past was not completely reliable. And yet, his subsequent application of his discovery that two forms of government were in the *Charter*—call them "branches," "clauses," or what you will—was fortuitous for the case at hand. His discovery of the two branches now formed the "foundation" of the magistrates' authority, with the freemen exercising only rights of election and counsel. To aggravate matters, Winthrop had used Charles Herle's English pamphlet, "newly come over," in an earlier essay to establish the *Charter* as the colony's fundamental law. If the *Charter's* provisions were immutable, and Winthrop's interpretation became established, the deputies would be relegated to an inferior status in Massachusetts government in perpetuity.[12]

Concomitantly, Winthrop tried to reassure the deputies and the freemen that the magistrates' authority was regulated by colonial law. In 1634, the General Court had won the right to admit freemen, enact legislation, choose the chief officers of the government, consent to taxation, appoint military officers, and regulate the distribution of the colony's territory. The freemen had also secured representation in the General Court, and by colonial law they could remove any government official as long as the cause was "alleged and proved."[13] As far as the deputies' demand that the standing council be controlled by the General Court's commission, the government already operated on a general rule for the "practice of public administration." The rule that regulated magisterial authority was of the deputies' own making. It had been enacted in 1636 to appoint Cotton's law committee, "until a body of fundamental laws ... was established, all causes should be heard and determined, according to the laws already in force, and where no law is, there, as near the law of God as may be." According to Winthrop, this power was controlled by the *Body of Liberties*' guarantee of due process cited in the last chapter, based on *Magna Charta*'s

12 John Winthrop, *Discourse on Arbitrary Government* (July, 1644), in *Winthrop Papers*, 4: 468–71. *John Winthrop's Defense of the Negative Vote* (June 5, 1643), in *Winthrop Papers*, 4: 380–82, 390–91. William Haller, ed., *Tracts on Liberty in the Puritan Revolution* (New York: Columbia Univ. Press, 1934), 1: 27 (n. 16). Charles Herle, *A Fuller Answer to a Treatise Written by Dr. Ferne* (London, Dec. 29, 1642), 8; *Thomason Tracts* E244 (27), Reel 42. Winthrop copied Herle's pamphlet practically verbatim on this point. Herle was a presbyterian minister, and his pamphlet probably came to Winthrop's attention because of his other writings that criticized Massachusetts' Independent church structure, provoking the following pamphlet response. Richard Mather, *A modest and brotherly answer to Mr. Charles Herle his book, against the Independency of Churches* (London: Overton, 1644); *Early English Books*: (http://name.umdl.umich.edu/A88947.0001.001). David Como, "Print, Censorship, and Ideological Escalation in the English Civil War," *Journal of British Studies* 51 (Oct., 2012): 820–57.

13 John Winthrop, *Discourse on Arbitrary Government* (July 1644), in *Winthrop Papers*, 4: 471.

article 39. The interaction of these two laws provided the "officers of this body politic ... a rule to walk by in all their administrations, which ... is the Word of God." Since the magistrates' administration had been consistent with these authorities, Winthrop claimed the government had no "semblance of arbitrariness." Besides, it was "not possible in the infancy of a plantation, subject to so many and variable occurrences, to hold so exactly to rules, as when a state is once settled." Otherwise, the colony already had all the laws it required.[14]

Winthrop's description of the godly magistrate was supported by both tradition and scripture. In his own words, "Judges are Gods upon earth, therefore, in their administrations they are to hold forth the wisdom and mercy of God ... as well as his justice, as occasion shall require." In support, he cited God's "sure promise of divine assistance" to his judges in the *Book of Deuteronomy*, "Judges and officers ... the Lord thy God giveth thee ... and they shall judge the people with just judgment." The Protestant theologian John Calvin's articulation of magistracy was even more potent, "When those who bear the office of magistrate are called Gods, let no one suppose that there is little weight in that appellation," because they possess a "commission from God" that invested them with "divine authority." It was the magistrate who represented the "person of God, as whose substitutes they in a manner act." Winthrop also drew upon a model of magisterial authority authored by one of the most respected Puritan divines of the Elizabethan era. In *Christian Equity*, William Perkins repeated the common assumption that a magistrate "possessed broad discretionary power in interpreting the law." Even in Perkins' day a "godly justice of the peace was a magistrate, a ruler, like England's chief magistrate," whose most important duty was "the same as the monarch's: to promote God's glory and enforce obedience to his law." By the 1640's, parliamentarians' challenge of Charles I's prerogative, in the name of "King and Parliament," required a rationale to support their claim of understanding state matters better than the king himself. As John Goodwin counseled his fellow Englishmen, when a godly magistrate acted in the defense of their laws, liberties, and property against a superior official, the people were "bound to obey the inferior" magistrate.[15]

---

14 John Winthrop, *Discourse on Arbitrary Government* (1644), in *Winthrop Papers*, 4: 471–78. Nathaniel Shurtleff, ed., *MGCR*, 1: 174–75 (May 25, 1636). Robert Wall, *Massachusetts Bay*, 86–8. Mark Cahn, "Punishment, Discretion, and the Codification of Prescribed Penalties," *American Journal of Legal History* 33 (1989): 120–26.

15 Winthrop, *Discourse on Arbitrary Government* (1644), in *Winthrop Papers*, 4: 475–76. *Deuteronomy*, 16: 18. John Calvin, *The Institutes of the Christian Religion*, Henry Beveridge ed., and trans., (Geneva, 1559; reprint, Grand Rapids [MI]: WM.B. Erdmann's Co., 1989), 2: 653–4 (Bk. IV, Ch. XX, §4). J.P. Sommerville, *Politics and Ideology in England* (New York: Longman, 1986), 1–21. Francis Bremer, *John Winthrop*, 107–112. Timothy

Elidad Blackwell's sermon for the Lord Mayor of London illustrates the growing potency of the godly magistrate in England during a revolutionary era. Using the common metaphor of the human body as the political state, Blackwell noted that the English body politic suffered "offenders and offenses" like "noxious humors and diseases." To remedy such maladies judges and magistrates were appointed for the "healing and curing of those diseases." But would a physician prescribe a cure before examining a patient, and diagnosing the disease? Of course, a good physician did no such thing, and so magistrates with human frailties should never attempt to determine a just sentence in every possible circumstance depending only upon their own capabilities. Only God's infinite wisdom foresaw events, as "he is omniscient, knows all things, and therefore needs no ... trial to inform his knowledge." Although magistracy was charged with serving "every ones' good, yet it is not every one's work," and therefore God had "appointed judges in the land ... to judge, to rule, to govern." In the same year Winthrop wrote, the "determination of law belongs properly to God, he is the only lawgiver, but he hath given power and gifts to men to interpret his laws, and this belongs principally to the highest authority in a commonwealth, and subordinately to other magistrates and judges."[16]

Quoting "extensively" from Thomas Aquinas's *Summa Theologica*, Winthrop also utilized sources for his *Discourse* that were anathema to his fellow

Breen, *Character of a Good Ruler* (New Haven: Yale Univ. Press, 1970), 13. William Perkins, *Epieikeia: Or a Treatise of Christian Equity and Moderation*, in Ian Breward, ed., *The Work of William Perkins* (Appleford [UK]: The Sutton Courtenay Press, 1970), 26, 484–85. John Goodwin, *Anti-Cavalierisme* (London: 1642), in William Haller, ed., *Tracts on Liberty* (New York: Columbia Univ. Press, 1934), 2: 244–45. Theodore Beza, *Rights of Magistrates* (1574), in Julian Franklin, ed., *Constitutionalism and Resistance in the Sixteenth Century* (New York: Pegasus Press, 1969), 100–135. Michael Winship, *Hot Protestants: A History of Puritanism in England and America* (New Have: Yale Univ. Press, 2018), 30. John Witte, Jr., "Right, Resistance and Revolution in the Western Tradition: Early Protestant Foundations," *Law and History Review* 26 (2008): 556–57. Beza's emphasis on the necessity of election of lower magistrates in order to oppose unlawful superior magistrates partly explains Winthrop's position, "For Beza, the people's right to vote for or consent to their rulers was essential to the legitimacy of the political regime. Throughout history ... he argued, magistrates are put into their offices by the election or consent of the people."

16 Elidad Blackwell, *A Caveat for Magistrates* (June 30, 1645), 1, 8; *Thomason Tracts*, E 290 (120), Reel 48. John Winthrop, *Discourse on Arbitrary Government* (July 1644), in *Winthrop Papers*, 4: 480. Hugh Peters, *A Good Work for a Good Magistrate* (June 17, 1651), 32, 36; *Thomason Tracts*, E1364 (2), Reel 179. Richard Tuck, "Power and Authority in Seventeenth-Century England," *Historical Journal* 17 (March, 1974): 47. "In all theories except radical Calvinism, the pronouncements of a superior were morally charged—such to consider how to avoid following them, even without offending the magistrate, was to consider committing a sin."

Puritans; when one of his descendants collated his personal papers, he discovered an excerpt from the *Summa Theologica* copied in the governor's handwriting attached to the original manuscript copy of the *Discourse*. Winthrop was borrowing a medieval concept of European Civil Law whose origin derived from nearly two millennia before, one that was well known to English judges and attorneys. As explained in earlier chapters, Natural Law was fundamental to Medieval legal regimes, because positive or human law had to be consistent with its principles, or risk illegitimacy; divine reason was the key to revealing whether human judgment and law was consistent with this superior law, and thereby, just. Medieval legal scholars were thoroughly familiar with Aquinas's passage, based on Aristotelian principle, that it was impossible to enact a law to cover every case, as there were an infinite number of scenarios for human behavior. While Winthrop's treatise on arbitrary government was clothed in seventeenth-century spirituality, his position that legislation must be applied by judicial interpretation was grounded upon ancient authority, and, a European Civil Law tradition. Even when multiple laws apply to a case, there is no guarantee that one will provide a ready-made solution; it is more probable that the greater the number of laws that apply, the greater chance they will conflict with one another and require interpretation. Winthrop's concept of discretion as an indispensable component of jurisprudence was accurate, as was the deputies' objection that insufficient detail in legislation would provide too much judicial discretion and threaten tyranny. In the end, a measure of balance was most required.[17]

17 *Extract from St. Thomas Aquinas*, in *Winthrop Papers*, 4: 482–3, 468 (n. 1), 482 (n. 1); *MHS* (https://www.masshist.org/publications/winthrop/index.php/view/PWF04d411). "In the arrangement of the … the original manuscript … the extract from St. Thomas Aquinas is placed immediately following the *Discourse*." Hugh Tredennick, ed., *The Ethics of Aristotle*, J.A. Thompson trans., (Harmondsworth: Penguin Books, 1976), 198–200 (Bk. V, 1137a17-1130b24, "A digression on equity, which corrects the deficiencies of legal justice"). "[J]ustice and equity coincide, and although both are good, equity is superior," as "all law is universal, and there are some things about which it is not possible to pronounce rightly in general terms; therefore in cases where it is necessary to make a general pronouncement, but impossible to do so rightly, the law takes account of the majority of cases … [W]hen law states a general rule, and a case arises … that is exceptional, then it is right, where the legislator owing to the generality of his language has erred in not covering the case, to correct the omission by a ruling such as the legislator himself would have given if he had been … aware of the circumstance." J. Budziszewski, *Commentary on Thomas Aquinas's Virtue Ethics* (Cambridge: Cambridge Univ. Press, 2017), 214–227 (Part II, ii, Q. 60, A. 5). S.E. Morison, *Builders of the Bay Colony*, 128 (n. 1). "In the inventories in the first volume of *Salem Probate Records*, I find one copy of Aquinas's *Summa*, and only one of Calvin's *Institutes*. John Harvard had more volumes by the 'angelic doctor' in his library than he had volumes of Calvin." Francis Bremer, *John Winthrop*, 359–60. "Winthrop used

No matter how well supported by scholarly authorities, past or present, Winthrop's essay was inherently threatening to the deputies as it contained no legislative regulation of judicial power; the magistrates would make judgments based on their own discretionary interpretations of scripture that were, in turn, dispositive of natural law principles in individual cases. Moreover, the deputies were disqualified from questioning the magistrates' judgments because they were not of a sufficiently divine status. During the General Court session of November 1644, when the elders performed their mediation, the deputies had deliberated upon a "dangerous libel of some unknown author," and "a committee was presently appointed to examine it." The "libel" was none other than Winthrop's *Discourse on Arbitrary Government*. Although it had been authored anonymously, the deputies were well-aware of the author's identity, and Winthrop in turn knew that the deputies' sanction was in retribution for his earlier positions; the atmosphere surrounding the ministry's mediation had been poisoned from the start. The House of Deputies issued a report on the *Book about Arbitrary Government*, rejecting its delineation between the magistrates' authority and the freemen's liberty. By giving "liberty to the freemen, to advise and counsel, instead of power and authority," would extinguish their "power and privileges." Concerning the "rule" for government administration, the deputies listed "these dangerous positions": that "general Rules are sufficient to clear a state from arbitrary government," and "judges ought to have liberty to vary from such general rules when they see cause." Finally, the deputies condemned the essay's "bitter" censure of human legislation as its most "dangerous passages." Winthrop was unimpressed, "no … promise of divine assistance is made to them that may be produced."[18]

scriptural grounds for his arguments (and also turned to the writings of Thomas Aquinas, though not explicitly referring to that Catholic theologian)." A. Wijffels, "Law Books at Cambridge, 1500–1640," in Peter Birks, ed., *The Life of the Law* (London: Hambledon Press, 1993), 61–68. Canon and Civil law treatises were available to Winthrop when he attended Cambridge University. *Dr. Bonham's Case* (1610), 77 *English Reports* 638 @ 652. Ibid., (n. c). Roy Stone, "Bacon as Lawyer and Jurist," *ARSP* 54 (no. 4, 1968): 455–59, 464–69. William Lambarde, *Eirenarcha: the Office of the Justice of the Peace* (London: 1619), 57–8. *Google Books*: (https://www.google.com/books/edition/_/o-A1AQAAMAAJ?hl=en&gbpv=0). "Howbeit our … Laws of Parliament, although they also do endeavor (for the most part) to hold the same course; yet forasmuch as every considerable circumstance cannot be foreseen at the time of the making of the laws, they are many times left to be supplied (by the discretion of the Execution of the Law) that thing which was not conveniently comprehended before-hand, by the wisdom of the Author of the Law."

18 *The Returns of the Committee of the house of Dep. concerning the Book about Arbitrary Government*, in *Winthrop Papers*, 4: 483–85; *MHS* (https://www.masshist.org/publications/winthrop/index.php/view/PWF04d412). Richard Dunn, ed., *Journal of John Winthrop*, 561–63 (Oct., 1644). Mark Cahn, "Punishment, Discretion, and the Codification

With the positions of both magistrates and deputies clearly tendered, further conflict was inevitable. Once again, a local controversy provided the deputies ammunition to challenge the magistrates' position in government. Or, in Winthrop's own words, "then fell out the Hingham case." It was a dispute that the deputies "eagerly laid hold on and pursued to the utmost, for they doubted not but they could now make it appear either that the magistrates had abused their authority, or else that their authority was too great to consist with the people's liberty, and therefore ought to be reduced within narrower bounds." Grounds for the controversy were laid when the Hingham town militia was raised to company size. Upon the election for the new post of captain created by this increase in the command under colonial law, the troop held an election and selected the current commander, Lieutenant Anthony Eames, with the results dispatched to Boston for the council to certify. However, the Hingham militia proceeded to hold another election and chose Deputy Bozoan Allen as their captain, instead of Eames; the troop defended its second selection on the basis that the first election remained uncertified.[19]

The four magistrates on the standing council who heard the dispute, including Deputy Governor Winthrop, thought differently. Winthrop believed that Eames, after his long service in the town's militia, deserved the captaincy and did not merit the withdrawal of his name after election. Moreover, as Eames's assistant, Allen had learned his military skills under his leadership. Ultimately, Winthrop and the other magistrates sitting in council deferred upon the election itself, ordering both officers to retain their prior rank until the General Court could meet and decide the issue. While this seems to have been the correct course, Winthrop's involvement calls into question the council's ability to deal fairly with Bozoan Allen. His journal entries describe Allen as "one of the delinquents in the common cause" who had delivered several "false and reproachful speeches concerning the deputy governor, and the book he wrote about arbitrary government." Allen, in turn, condemned Winthrop's *Discourse* as "worse than Gorton's letters." Samuel Gorton had been banished from Massachusetts in 1644 for heresy after earlier ejections from practically every other New England colony; Malcom Gaskill sarcastically described him as an "eccentric clothier who disrespected everyone except Christ." The Gortonists claimed first-hand knowledge of divine will like Anne Hutchinson before them, with

of Prescribed Penalties in Colonial Massachusetts," 129–30. Robert Wall, *Massachusetts Bay, The Crucial Decade*, 87–88. John Bellamy, *Criminal Law and Society in Late Medieval and Tudor England* (New York: St. Martin's Press, 1984), 90–114.

19 Richard Dunn, ed., *Journal of John Winthrop*, 575–95 (Spring 1645). Robert Wall, *Massachusetts Bay: Crucial Decade*, 94–5.

the same air of infallibility. Deputy Allen seized upon Gorton's example: the treatise should have cost the author "his ears if not his head," for claiming a similar intimate knowledge of the divine will.[20]

Upon the news that the standing council had refused to confirm Allen's selection, Hingham's militiamen took matters into their own hands. When Eames ordered the men to reassemble for exercises, a majority mutinied. Even upon delivery of a written order from the standing council, the militiamen rebuked Eames and told him he should go home and resign his commission "honorably," as advised by the proper authority. Previous divisions amongst the magistrates were now being felt. Bellingham had talked to Eames before he left Boston to reassume command. With no apparent authority to do so, as Bellingham was one-half of a distinct minority of two magistrates, he had instructed the lieutenant to "honorably lay down his place." The militiamen mocked Eames's command granted by the standing council, what did the "magistrates to do with them?" Even if all the magistrates had reappointed Eames it would signify "nothing." When the Hingham militia took a final vote two-thirds voted for Allen, with the rest remaining loyal to Eames and the council.[21]

Although the Hingham Militia's mutiny began as a local affair, it grew into a colony-level crisis when the town's most powerful family, the Hobarts, threw their support behind Allen. When Minister Peter Hobart tried to excommunicate Eames from the town's congregational assembly, a dozen of his supporters

---

20 Richard Dunn, ed., *Journal of John Winthrop*, 575–76, 593 (May-July 1645). Nathaniel Shurtleff, ed., *MGCR*, 2: 51–2 (Oct., 1643). Robert Wall, *Massachusetts Bay: The Crucial Decade*, 94–5. George Willison, *Saints and Strangers* (New York: Reynal & Hitchcock, 1945), 352–54. Francis Bremer, *John Winthrop*, 340–43. Adelos Gorton, *The Life and Times of Samuel Gorton* (Philadelphia: Historical Society of Pennsylvania, 1908), 51. Michelle Burnham, "Samuel Gorton's Leveller Aesthetics and the Economics of Colonial Dissent," *William and Mary Quarterly* 67 (July 2010): 435–40. Burnham identified some of Gorton's writings as similar to "English radical writings of the 1640's." Bernard Bailyn, *The Barbarous Years* (New York: Vintage Books, 2012), 435–37. After his banishment and return to England in 1644, "Gorton immersed himself in London's perfervid sectarian underground, preaching universal salvation to the General Baptists in the Bell Alley conventicle of Leveller Thomas Lamb, and sharing the pulpit with inspired enthusiasts, male and female." John Ree, *The Leveller Revolution* (London: Verso, 2016), 61–65. "Lamb was an important figure in the Leveller movement. He provided a vital link between the political mobilizations of the Levellers and the Baptist congregations." Malcom Gaskill, *Between Two Worlds: How the English Became Americans* (New York: Basic Books, 2014), 157–59. Gorton "antagonized" Winthrop by his "singular recognition" of the crown's "authority" to govern the colonies in "all civil respects."

21 Richard Dunn, ed., *Journal of John Winthrop*, 575 (n. 2), 575–76 (May 1645). Robert Wall, *Massachusetts Bay: The Crucial Decade*, 94–7. Nathaniel Shurtleff, ed., *MGCR*, 3: 22 (no. 2, *Return of the Committee*).

left the service with him. Now, the town's militia and its congregation were divided. Before the General Court could act, however, magistrates on the standing council (Winthrop, Endecott, Increase Nowell, and William Hibbins) summoned the leaders of the revolt (three of whom were the Hobart brothers, including Deputy Joshua Hobart) to Boston. Subsequently, these same magistrates ordered another group of men to appear for obstructing Eames's command. These events prompted eighty-one Hingham townsmen, under the leadership of Minister Hobart, to petition the House of Deputies to hear their case, instead of the court of assistants. While the petition claimed that Allen's election was supported by colonial law, the General Court had enacted several laws on the topic; a 1636 law ordered the election of captains and lieutenants to be certified by the standing council, but a law passed two years earlier granted the General Court final approval of military officers. The Hingham militia's flouting of standing council orders, aggravated by mocking its authority, provoked the magistrates' intervention. But the council's sullied reputation from the La Tour/D'Aulnay affair guaranteed more controversy would follow.[22]

The petitioners objected that their fellow townsmen had been compelled to appear before the standing council, after the contested militia election, and forced to post bail to ensure their appearance before the court of assistants. When some of the Hingham freemen had refused bail, they were arrested and jailed, where they remained. The petitioners condemned the magistrates for their presumptuous challenge to the "liberty and power of the General Court, and our own liberty granted to us by the said Court, and the country in general" to elect a militia leader. Ultimately, the "Liberty of an English free-born member" of the colony was at stake. According to English procedure, however, a JP had the power to "suppress, and bind to the peace, or good behavior, all affrayors, and all persons unlawfully and riotously assembled." To restore order,

22 *The Petition of the greater part of the Inhabitants of Hingham*, in MHS *Collections* (*Second Series/1846*): 4: 108. Richard Dunn, ed., *Journal of John Winthrop*, 576–79 (May 1645), 594–95 (May 1645). Nathaniel Shurtleff, ed., *MGCR*, 1: 117 (March 14, 1634). "[N]one but the General Court hath power to make … and appoint officers, as governor, deputy governor, assistants, treasurer, secretary, captain, lieutenants, ensigns, or any of like moment." *MGCR*, 1: 187 (Dec. 13, 1636). "[F]or the captains and lieutenants to the several companies the several towns shall make choice of some principal man, or two, or three, in each town, and present them to the [standing] counsel, who shall appoint one of them to the said office in each company." *MGCR*, 3: 22 (June 16, 1645). The magistrates referred the deputies to the 1636 law. Robert Wall, *Massachusetts Bay*, 98–9. Robert Wall, "The Membership of the Massachusetts General Court," (Ph.D. diss., Yale University, 1965), 358, 363–66. *History of the Town of Hingham, Massachusetts* (Cambridge: University Press, 1893), 2: 335. Minister Peter Hobart led the town's church for 44 years until his death in 1675; he was a graduate of Cambridge Univ. (B.A./M.A.).

JP's required bonds of recognizance to ensure that the accused appeared at trial. In lieu of bond, imprisonment resulted; one should be reminded that a JP's powers had been granted to the assistants in 1631.[23]

The Hingham petitioners also objected that the standing council's interference in the militia election caused a "schism in our church, and trouble to some of our members for witnessing against a delinquent," namely Lieutenant Eames. Essentially, the "Ordinances of Jesus Christ in his Church is slighted, and the free passage thereof stopped, to the endangering of the liberty of the churches amongst us." Under the *Body of Liberties of 1641* congregations were granted "free liberty of ... expulsion," and could "deal with any of their members in a church way that are in the hand of justice," but only if did not "hinder the course" of civil justice or "degrade or depose any man from any civil dignity, office, or authority he shall have in the commonwealth." In other words, congregations could punish members as long as it did not interfere with their performance of civil duties; Hingham's congregation certainly intended to "degrade" Eames's command and "depose" him from his captaincy in casting him out.[24]

If not for the circumstances surrounding the summons of the Hingham townsmen and the attempted excommunication of Eames, this matter would have been deadlocked in such a thicket of church/state regulations. The summons of the second group of townsmen was on the charge of deceiving the Hingham militia, to the effect that neither Governor Dudley nor Deputy Governor Winthrop had authorized Eames to resume command. These men had gone to Winthrop's home, when no other magistrate was present, to demand why they had been summoned and the identity of their accusers. After the meeting Winthrop maintained that he told them as much about the case as he could remember, but refused to identify the witnesses against them. A magistrate was not "bound to let a criminal offender know his accusers before the day of trial, but only in his own discretion, lest the accuser might be taken off or perverted." In England, after an affray or public disorder had been

23 *The Petition of the greater part of the Inhabitants of Hingham*, 4: 108. Richard Dunn, ed., *Journal of John Winthrop*, 576–78 (May 1645). Nathaniel Shurtleff, ed., *MGCR*, 1: 89 (July 5, 1631). Michael Dalton, *Countrey Justice, 1618*, 16, 69. Joel Samaha, "The Recognizance in Elizabethan Law Enforcement," *American Journal of Legal History* 25 (1981): 189–204. Cynthia Herrup, *The Common Peace: Participation and Criminal Law in Seventeenth Century England* (Cambridge: Cambridge Univ. Press, 1989), 85–92.

24 *The Petition of the greater part of the Inhabitants of Hingham*, 4: 108–9. Richard Dunn, ed., *Journal of John Winthrop*, 594–95 (May 1645). William Whitmore, ed., *Body of Liberties of 1641*, 57 (*Lib. 95*, §§3–4, §8), 47 (*Lib. 60*). Francis Bremer, *John Winthrop*, 340–43. Robert Wall, *Massachusetts Bay: The Crucial Decade*, 99–105.

suppressed, at least two JPs were required to make a record of testimony from witnesses and note their own impressions. As Dalton explained in his JP manual, because the "record of the justices and sheriff is a sufficient conviction in itself against the offenders," it had to be "formal and certain." Parliamentary statute established these processes during an era in which criminal defendants could not testify under oath, were not afforded defense counsel, and no discovery process of evidence before trial was required. Process must have been small consolation to the Hingham men, however, as they would face trial upon the record made by the standing council at the next court of assistants where only magistrates presided.[25]

Predictably, the Hingham freemen petitioned the General Court for relief, "We humbly sue to this honored Court to be pleased to grant us an honorable and free hearing." After appointing a committee to examine the petition the House of Deputies agreed to hear their case of "false imprisonment," leaving Winthrop and most of the other magistrates to marvel at their grant. Undeterred, in May 1645 the deputies inaugurated an impeachment process under the authority of *Liberty 67*; in his essay on arbitrary government Winthrop himself had referred to the freemen's ability to remove any senior official if justification for such action could be "alleged and proved." After its recent rediscovery of the medieval precedent of impeachment, Parliament had unleashed it on some of the king's leading ministers, including Francis Bacon, the Duke of Buckingham, and just recently the Earl of Strafford (1641), presaging a struggle for control of England's militia between the King and Parliament. No requirement for criminal charges to be established by a process of indictment before trial had been included in the "new" process. Winthrop's prosecutors would be Deputy Joshua Hobart and Deputy Allen, the latter being the very man denied the captaincy by the standing council. When the deputies requested that the magistrates agree to this examination, they replied that such a procedure was "prejudicial to authority and the honor of the court," as it required a magistrate

25 Richard Dunn, ed., *Journal of John Winthrop*, 577–78 (May 1645), 591–92 (July 1645). Robert Wall, *Massachusetts Bay: The Crucial Decade*, 93–100. Michael Dalton, *The Countrey Justice, 1618*, 69, 84–96. William Blackstone, *Commentaries on the Laws of England* (Chicago: Univ. of Chicago Press, 1979), 4: 146–47. John Bellamy, *Criminal Law and Society in Late Medieval and Tudor England*, 90–114. Barbara Shapiro, *Beyond Reasonable Doubt and Probable Cause: Historical Perspectives on the Anglo-American Law of Evidence* (Berkeley: Univ. of California Press, 1991), 148–64. Nathaniel Shurtleff, ed., *MGCR*, 2: 279–80 (May 1649). In 1649, the General Court passed a law forbidding colonists from asking a magistrate for an advisory opinion in a case they would be party to because it placed magistrates in an untenable situation.

to "answer criminally in a cause, wherein nothing of that nature could be laid to his charge." Nevertheless, the deputies insisted on Winthrop's prosecution.[26]

Although, in part, the *Hingham Petition* charged Winthrop and his fellow councilors with an abuse of power in summoning and imprisoning those who refused to post bond, for the above stated reasons those allegations were untenable. Winthrop knew that as a JP he could suppress any such "mutinous practice" in "open disturbance of the peace and slighting of authority." The men in question had been summoned "by warrant to the constable to bring them," and ordered to appear at the next court of assistants. Those who refused to post bond were incarcerated. Some of the three hundred plus statutory provisions that regulated and empowered JPs also utilized methods of summary justice, including "arbitration, adjudication, or punishment, without a formal trial." According to Faramerz Dabhoiwala, by the seventeenth century "many

26 *The Petition of the greater part of the Inhabitants of Hingham*, 4: 109. Nathaniel Shurtleff, ed., *MGCR*, 3: 12, 15, 17–18, 26 (May-July 1645). Richard Dunn, ed., *Journal of John Winthrop*, 578–79. Robert Wall, *Massachusetts Bay: The Crucial Decade*, 105–6. Robert Wall, "Membership of the Massachusetts General Court," 356, 358, 366. William Whitmore, ed., *Body of Liberties of 1641*, 47 (Lib. #67). "It is the constant liberty of the free men of this plantation to choose yearly at the Court of Election out of the freemen all the General officers of this Jurisdiction. If they *please to discharge them* the day of Election by way of vote, they may do it *without showing cause. But if at any other general Court, we hold it due justice, that the reasons thereof be alleged and proved.*" The Court of Election was held annually in the Spring. John Winthrop, *Discourse on Arbitrary Government* (July, 1644), in *Winthrop Papers*, 4: 471. Francis Bremer, *John Winthrop*, 340–43. John Adamson, *The Noble Revolt: The Overthrow of Charles I* (London: Weidenfeld & Nicholson, 2007), 220. "[I]mpeachment in 1641 was a relatively novel and unfamiliar procedure. Although often used in the Middle Ages, it had fallen into desuetude in the mid-fifteenth century, and not revived until 1621, the best part of two centuries later. For precedents, lawyers were forced to go back to the days of the Wars of the Roses, and ever since the revival of formal impeachments … aspects of its procedures had remained in a state of flux." John Eusden, *Puritans, Lawyers, and Politics in Early Seventeenth-Century England* (New Haven: Yale Univ. Press, 1958; reprint, Archon Books, 1965), 150–53. "A refusal to respect persons simply because they possessed de facto power was a hallmark of parliamentary activity in the early seventeenth century … The parliamentary opposition also sought to limit the crown's ministers and representatives." J.P. Sommerville, *Politics and Ideology in England: 1603–1640*, 2nd ed., (London: Longman, 1999), 237–38. Christopher Hill, *The Century of Revolution: 1603–1714* (Edinburgh: Thomas Nelson & Sons, 1961), 60–2, 111. As Hill saw it, "The years 1604 to 1629 have been described as those in which the House of Commons 'won the initiative' … It is important to be clear about what winning the initiative meant. Constitutional historians sometimes write as though members of Parliament valued their 'liberties and privileges' as things in themselves, as though they revived extinct procedures like impeachment out of pure antiquarianism … [A]ll these procedural devices, old and new, were means to an end: to imposing the will of the Commons on the government."

more men and women were subjected to various forms of summary justice at this time than were ever sent to trial by jury." Because this jurisdictional expansion had occurred before the Bay colonists had migrated, the petitioners' resistance to a judgment by the magistrates is even more understandable.[27]

Upon the commencement of Winthrop's impeachment, he rose from his seat on the magistrate's bench and calmly walked to the defendant's table. Upon his fellow magistrates' objections, he explained that "being criminally accused he might not sit as a judge in that cause, and if he were upon the bench, it would be a great disadvantage to him, for he could not take that liberty to plead the cause." Winthrop defended his conduct in this matter as well within his authority, and carried out "according to the equity of [our] laws ... and the custom and laws of England, and our constant practice here these fifteen years." Allen and Hobart proceeded with their examination. What had occurred during his meeting with the group of Hingham men at his home? Winthrop asked the Court whether the testimony of such "delinquents may be received as competent witnesses against a magistrate in such a case," but since he had taken the seat of the accused such an objection was superfluous. Winthrop presented a spirited defense, "magistrates could try some criminal causes without a jury," and he "knew no law of God *or* man which required a judge to make known to the party his accusers (or rather witnesses) before the cause came to hearing." Instead, when two JP's recorded an indictment of a public riot it became, in effect, a trial record determinative of innocence or guilt; upon court certification as genuine and properly executed it constituted a guilty verdict. Considering the ultimate effect of the magistrates' record as ensuring convictions of the Hingham militiamen, one can certainly understand their insistence that they receive some form of trial. But once again, the law lacked clarity on their right to jury trial in this particular case. *Liberty 29*

27 Richard Dunn, ed., *Journal of John Winthrop*, 2: 579–80 (May 1645). Robert Wall, *Massachusetts Bay: The Crucial Decade*, 107–8. Faramerz Dabhoiwala, "Summary Justice in Early Modern London," *English Historical Review* 121 (June 2006), 796–97. "The simplest type of law in this period, but one of the least studied, was summary justice. Under statute and common law, justices of the peace acting alone or in concert had the authority to deal with a wide variety of administrative, civil and criminal matters, settling them by arbitration, adjudication or punishment, without a formal trial. Many of these powers had been introduced under the Tudors. The same was true of houses of correction, which were from the later sixteenth century onwards founded across the country to incarcerate petty offenders who had been summarily convicted. But the real expansion of summary jurisdiction occurred during the seventeenth and eighteenth centuries, when the procedure came to be used very extensively. It seems entirely possible that many more men and women were subjected to various forms of summary justice at this time than were ever sent to trial by jury."

provided that criminal defendants could "choose whether they will be tried by the bench or by a jury, unless it be where the law upon just reason has otherwise determined." The earliest draft of colonial law, *Moses His Judicials*, provided an interesting counterpoint for the necessity of trial by jury, one that was omitted in the *Body of Liberties*: "Trial by jurors shall not be denied, ... partly to preserve the liberty of the people, and partly to prevent suspicion of partiality of any magistrates in the court."[28]

Finally, Allen and Hobart proceeded to the accusation that went to the heart of the magistrate-deputy dispute. Allegedly, during the meeting at his home, Winthrop invoked *his* interpretation of divine authority to justify his refusal to identify the witnesses who would testify against the Hingham men. This was the last item with which the deputies had any hope of discrediting him, and it symbolized their chief grievance about his *Discourse on Arbitrary Government*: its defense of the magistracy's divine sanction to judge the essential matters of the colony. Winthrop admitted that two of the men, John Foulsham and John Towers, "charged him to have said that it was against the law of God *and* man" to identify the witnesses. He denied joining both natural *and* positive law in such a way since he knew of no divine prohibition concerning witnesses, but even "if he had been mistaken," should a magistrate be questioned as a criminal when he had not acted with "wickedness or willfulness?" In Winthrop's journal account of these events, after his exoneration the Hingham petitioners, along with his prosecutors (deputies Hobart and Allen), and Elder Peter Hobart (who tried to excommunicate Lieutenant Eames from the town congregation) were fined for their contempt of authority. But the record of the House of Deputies tells a very different story. After weeks of intense negotiations with the magistrates a slim majority of the deputies remained defiant. They maintained that the standing council did not have the authority to appoint Eames to command, Magistrate Bellingham had lawfully advised him to resign his commission, by refusing his order Eames had thereby caused "this disturbance," and Winthrop "did offend in saying that it was contrary to the law of God *and* man to know their accusers before the time of trial." Ultimately, a majority of magistrates conceded that "if the words 'did offend' be meant criminally, we dissent, but if they mean ... he did err and speak amiss in so saying, we assent." After all, Winthrop had given "full satisfaction when publicly he confessed that if he so said it was a mistake," even if "he owned it not being contrary to his judgment." Based on Winthrop's own *Discourse on Arbitrary Government*, such ideas were

---

28 Richard Dunn, ed., *Journal of John Winthrop*, 579–81 (May 1645), 591–93 (July 1645). William Whitmore, ed., *Body of Liberties of 1641*, 39. *Moses His Judicials*, in *Hutchinson Papers* (Albany: Prince Society, 1865), 1: 183 @ 202 (Ch. 9, §11).

entirely consistent with his judgment and political philosophy that he had expressed these past fifteen years! Nevertheless, his fellow magistrates had distanced themselves from Winthrop's unyielding conception of the godly magistrate by implying, to the deputies no less, that in the future he should keep his opinions of God's intent in legal matters to himself![29]

Both Winthrop's *Journal* and the record of the House of Assistants omitted his fellow magistrates' responses to the deputies. According to Winthrop's version of events, upon his exoneration he had retaken his seat on the magistrates' dais and proceeded to lecture a packed courthouse on the divine station of the magistracy and its duty to govern the colony:

> It may be of some good use to inform and rectify the judgments of some of the people, and may prevent such distempers as have arisen amongst us. *The great questions that have troubled the country are about the authority of the magistrates and the liberty of the people.* It is yourselves who have called us to this office, and being called by you, we have our authority from God, in way of an ordinance, such as hath the image of God eminently stamped upon it, the contempt and violation whereof hath been vindicated with examples of divine vengeance.[30]

Obviously, the intended impression for his readers was, that was that, with the General Court proceeding to other business with the magistrates firmly at the helm. Subsequently, Winthrop's representation of his victory over the deputies as absolute, and settling the long running dispute, has been followed verbatim for nearly four centuries, practically without question. His detailed record of events provided in his *Journal*, until his death in 1649, has perpetuated his historiographical legerdemain ever since. It remains an invaluable source to study this period of history; one cannot do without it.

The outstanding (and most influential) example is Perry Miller's adoption of Winthrop's interpretation of these events whole, using it to declare the godly magistrate supreme:

---

29 Richard Dunn, ed., *Journal of John Winthrop*, 580–84 (May 1645). Francis Bremer, *John Winthrop*, 361–64. Nathaniel Shurtleff, ed., *MGCR*, 3: 21–2 (June 16, 1645). Robert Wall, *Massachusetts Bay: The Crucial Decade*, 99.

30 Richard Dunn, ed., *Journal of John Winthrop*, 581–95 (May-July 1645). Nathaniel Shurtleff, ed., *MGCR*, 3: 19–26; 2: 113–14. S.E. Morison, *Builders of the Bay Colony*, 101–103, 225–26. Perry Miller, *The New England Mind: The Seventeenth Century* (New York: Macmillan Co., 1939), 422–29. Robert Wall, *Massachusetts Bay: The Crucial Decade*, 107–19. Timothy Breen, *Character of a Good Ruler*, xii, 59, 77, 82–83. Francis Bremer, *John Winthrop*, 349, 364–65.

> For fifteen years he was spokesman for the magistrates in a tense struggle with the lower house of the General Court, with the deputies who were, according to him, actuated by a "democratical spirit." From the very first, the freemen strove to confine the magistrates within explicit limitations, and from Winthrop's point of view were ready to sacrifice the Bible commonwealth for a *mere* constitutional republic … by insisting that the magistrates be drastically pinioned to definite rules, … demanding strict observance of the charter, … forcing the publication of a written code of laws, … endeavoring to fix specific penalties for all offenses … to leave magistrates no discretion to vary any punishment to fit the crime, and at last by trying to deprive the magistrates of their power to negate acts of the lower house. At each crisis in the struggle Winthrop set forth the arguments by which the leaders finally won their case.[31]

Miller thereby assisted Winthrop in establishing his conception of early Massachusetts history as a deferral on a "mere constitutional republic" in favor of rule by the godly magistrate.

In the meantime, the adoption of the Massachusetts law book in 1647, and its publication in 1648, has faded into historical oblivion to the point that its very existence rarely merits more than a mention in histories of the period, if that; Morris Cohen has described the Laws and Liberties citation, before a handful of more recent works cited in this work's introduction, as a standalone oddity. But if a law book was adopted in 1648 in the aftermath of the Hingham case and Winthrop's trial—one that contained specific penalties, which it did—then the deputies had not only limited the godly magistrates' arbitrary discretion, they had established a definitive precedent of legislative power in North America signifying the importance of limiting executive and judicial discretion. Indeed, Winthrop had acknowledged that the deputies' foremost goal after the commission dispute was to adopt a "body of laws, with prescript penalties in all cases, as nothing might be left to the discretion of the magistrates." In the aftermath of Winthrop's trial, in fact, the General Court proceeded to adopt a law book that was distributed within the colony, and the record of the House of Deputies is first to note these developments. An entry made on the same day of Winthrop's acquittal states, "several persons out of each county shall be chosen to draw up a body of laws and present them to the consideration of the General Court, at the next sitting." Almost two months before, when the deputies originally received the Hingham petition, they

31 Perry Miller, *The New England Mind: The Seventeenth Century*, 422.

appointed a committee to "draw certain bills for positive laws, as against lying, Sabbath breaking, swearing, drunkenness, etc., & present what they shall doe therein to this house." By the date of Winthrop's trial, the deputies had already announced their intention to draft and enact additional laws to complete the law book.[32]

The next chapter will trace the editorial preparation, enactment, and publication in print of the *Laws and Liberties of 1648* by the General Court. Two more editions would be published in 1660 and 1672 before the colony's charter was revoked. Who led the effort to draft and adopt the *Laws and Liberties of 1648*? Because of his determined resistance to his fellow magistrates in support of the deputies and town freemen, Richard Bellingham was chosen to provide the resolve and expertise necessary to realize the long sought-after endeavor of an official colonial law book. As Deputy Edward Johnson memorialized the event, Magistrate Bellingham also possessed the requisite leadership to see the initiative through to fruition:

> Richardus now arise must thou, Christ see hath thee to plead;
> His people's cause, with equal Laws, in wilderness them lead.
> Though slow of speech, thy counsel reach, shall each occasion well,
> Sure thy stern look, it cannot brook, those wickedly rebel.

32 Nathaniel Shurtleff, ed., *MGCR*, 3: 11–27 (May 14-July 1, 1645); 2: 109, 113 (May 14, 1645). The magistrates *Record* notes the same county committees with identical memberships, and lists them and the fines of the petitioners under the date May 14, 1645, the first day of the General Court session in which the *Hingham Petition* was presented. But the fines were negotiated over much of the following month. The magistrates' record thereby implies that nothing of any of significance had occurred except the punishment of the Hingham petitioners. Winthrop's *Journal* confirms the deputies' account of intricate negotiations between magistrates and deputies, while omitting much of its substance and ultimate ruling. Richard Dunn, ed., *Journal of John Winthrop*, 589–91 (July 1645), 581–82 (May-June 1645). "[T]he deputies ... spent divers days about it, and made two or three returns to the magistrates, and though they found the [Hingham] petition false and scandalous, and so voted it, yet they would not agree to any censure. The magistrates, on the other side, were resolved for censure, and for the deputy's [i.e., Winthrop's] full acquittal. The deputies ... growing weary of the court, for it began (3) 14 [i.e., May, 14] and brake not up (save one week) till (5) 5 [i.e., July, 5], were content they [i.e., the petitioners] should pay the charges of the court." Morris Cohen, "Legal Literature in Colonial Massachusetts," *Publications of the Colonial Society of Massachusetts*, 62: 243–72 (https://www.colonialsociety.org/node/917). David Hall, *A Reforming People: Puritanism and the Transformation of Public Life in New England* (New York: Alfred A. Knopf, 2011), 147–154. Hall believes the *Laws and Liberties* are an historic precedent in the history of codification, with additional commentary in his more recent work. David Hall, *The Puritans: A Transatlantic History* (Princeton: Princeton Univ. Press, 2019), 236.

*With labor's might, thy pen indite, doth Laws for peoples' learning;*
*That judge with skill, and not with will, unarbitrate discerning.*[33]

---

33 Edward Johnson, *Wonder-Working Providence of Sions Saviour*, 67–8. Francis Bremer, *John Winthrop*, 305. S.E. Morison, *Builders of the Bay Colony*, 263. Robert Wall, "The Membership of the Massachusetts General Court," 591. Initially, Johnson was elected a deputy of Woburn in 1643, serving until 1671. Subsequently, he became "one of the most important members of the lower house."

CHAPTER 8

# The Laws and Liberties of 1648

Having completed the narrative journey to the threshold of the adoption of the *Laws and Liberties*, it's time to examine its compilation and survey a sample of its contents as compared to contemporary English reforms. Upon John Winthrop's exoneration the General Court created new law committees to complete a draft of the colonial law book. During the following session more members were appointed and ordered to "return to this Court a result of their thoughts," in order to satisfy the "expectation of the country in establishing a body of laws." The committees delivered their work during the next session in May 1646, per resolution of both houses:

> This Court thankfully accepts … the labors returned by the several committees of the several shires, and being very unwilling such precious labors should fall to the ground without that good success, as is generally hoped for, … desire Richard Bellingham, Esq., Mr. Symonds, Lieutenant Duncan, Lieutenant Johnson, and Mr. Ward do cause each committees return about a body of laws to be transcribed, so as each committee may have the … abbreviation of the laws in force, which Mr. Bellingham took great store of pains, and to good purpose, in and upon the whole, and make return to the next session of this Court, at which time the Court intends, by the favor and blessing of God, to proceed to the establishing of so many of them as shall be thought most fit for a body of laws.

According to Winthrop himself, with the submission of "many laws" to the General Court members had "much difficulty" reaching a consensus. So, a new committee was appointed to "extract out of the whole such as should be thought fit to be established, and so to reduce them into one volume."[1]

The Court was soon forced to defer further work on the book, however, as "much other business" occupied its members. During the same spring session of 1646, Dr. Robert Child and his supporters petitioned for fundamental changes to Massachusetts government. Child's interests were not primarily political or religious. Instead, after his first visit to the colony in the late 1630's

1 Nathaniel Shurtleff, ed., *MGCR*, 2:128 (Oct. 1, 1645), 157 (May 22, 1646); 3:26–7 (Oct. 2, 1645), 74 (May 6, 1646). Richard Dunn, ed., *Journal of John Winthrop* (Cambridge: Belknap Press, 1996), 622 (May 1646).

 | DOI:10.1163/9789004706347_010

he invested in several business ventures, including an iron foundry. Winthrop reported that the "business was well approved by the Court as a thing much conducing to the good of the country," as the colony could not afford to undertake these projects and was desperate to encourage manufacturing to revive its depressed economy. Initially, the General Court authorized the founding of two towns (with congregations) near the foundry to house workmen. But the relationship between the investors and the Court soured when the production of enough ore to realize a profit failed to materialize. Since a chronic shortage of laborers had hampered the operation from the start, Child pressed for severing the colony's linkage of citizenship and church membership to encourage more settlers to come to the colony; as Carla Pestana has reported, "the association of New England congregationalism with religious persecution had a profound impact on the discussion of church reformation" in England. Ultimately, to stave off financial ruin, Child sponsored a petition that challenged the practice of excluding non-church members from voting and holding office.[2]

One of the co-signers of the petition, William Vassall, and its scope, ensured the freemen's opposition. Although Vassall was one of the original assistants who sailed with Winthrop's fleet, he soon came to oppose Congregationalism as a violation of conscience. He and his family had promptly boarded ship back to England, only to return to Plymouth colony in 1635, where he again denounced its church government. Ultimately, he joined with the non-members of each colony's congregation threatening the general courts of Massachusetts and Plymouth that if they resisted admittance of all colonists to full church membership, he would alert Parliament and its Presbyterian majority. It was not an idle threat since his brother, John Vassall, sat on the Commission for Foreign Plantations that provided colonial oversight for the king. In the Spring of 1646, the General Court received a petition signed by Vassall, Child, and several others demanding to know why non-congregants were being excluded

2 Nathaniel Shurtleff, ed., *MGCR*, 2: 155–56 (May 22, 1646). Richard Dunn, ed., *Journal of John Winthrop*, 567–78 (April 1645), 622 (May 1646), 608–9 (Sept., 1645). In 1645, Winthrop attested that there were many "books coming out of England, some in defense of Anabaptism and other errors, and for liberty of conscience as a shelter for their toleration," while others supported "Presbyterial government ... against the congregational way." Margaret Newell, "Robert Child and the Entrepreneurial Vision," *New England Quarterly* 68 (1995): 239–46. William Whitmore, ed., *The Colonial Laws of Massachusetts. Reprinted from the Edition of 1660* (Boston: City Council of Boston, 1889), 74. Bernard Bailyn, *The Barbarous Years* (New York: Vintage Books, 2012), 479–89. Robert Wall, *Massachusetts Bay* (New Haven: Yale Univ. Press, 1970), 164–71, 235–38. Edmund Morgan, *The Puritan Dilemma*, 2nd ed., (New York: Longman, 1999), 179–82. Carla Pestana, *The English Atlantic in the Age of Revolution: 1640–41* (Cambridge: Harvard Univ. Press, 2004), 70–80.

from citizenship, especially since the colony operated under a charter granted by Charles I which forbid it from making any law "repugnant to the laws of England." Such a policy was obviously not "according to the laws of England, which may seem strange to our countrymen, yea to the whole world, considering we are all English." Without legitimate "laws or liberties, or any body of laws here so established," the Bay colony's government had violated the petitioners' "natural rights as freeborn subjects of the English nation," even though they were "known friends to the honorable and victorious Houses of Parliament." Based only upon their fidelity to England's Anglican church, they had been denied church membership, electoral rights, eligibility for service in colonial government, as well as taxed without representation. The House of Deputies acknowledged the petitioners' charge that "those now in authority ... exercise an unwarranted dominion and an arbitrary government, ... thereby to make them slaves."[3]

But the deputies, like the magistrates, had founded the Congregational system to purify the practices of the English Church. With the abolition of the requirement that plenary citizenship depended on congregational membership, the General Court would lose control of the colony's congregations. When it became known that Child's petition was dispatched to Parliament, magistrates and deputies reacted aggressively to the threat, following it with their own *Declaration of the General Court*. They denied the assertion that the "liberties and privileges in our charter belong to all freeborn English men,

3 Nathaniel Shurtleff, ed., *MGCR*, 3: 90–4 (Nov. 4, 1646); 3: 90 (no. 4) (Nov. 4, 1646); 2: 162–75 (Oct. 7-Nov. 4, 1646). *A Remonstrance and Petition of Robert Child,* in *Hutchinson Papers* (Albany: Prince Society, 1865), 2: 214–21. James Savage, ed., *History of New England* (Boston: 1825), 2: 260–62 (n. 2). John Child, *New Englands Jonas Cast Up at London,* (London: 1647), *MHS Collections (Second Series/1846)*, 4: 115. Margaret Newell, "Robert Child and the Entrepreneurial Vision," 224 (n. 2), 255. Robert Wall, *Massachusetts Bay: The Crucial Decade*, 164. Philip Gura, *A Glimpse of Sion's Glory* (Middletown: Wesleyan Univ. Press, 1984), 198–203. Francis Bremer, *John Winthrop* (Oxford: Oxford Univ. Press, 2003), 362–69. Leslie Stephen and Sidney Lee, eds., *Dictionary of National Biography* (New York: Macmillan, 1908), 20: 156–8. Bernard Bailyn, *The New England Merchants*, 2nd ed., (Cambridge: Harvard Univ. Press, 1979), 107. Susan Moore, *Abandoning America: Life-Stories from Early New England* (Woodbridge: Boydell Press, 2013), 299–300; (*William Vassall* (1592–1655)). William and his brother Samuel were both assistants in the Company when its *Charter* was granted in 1629, and amongst its earliest supporters. Ultimately, William made his home in Barbados and died there. John Coffey, "Puritanism and Liberty Revisited," *Historical Journal* 41 (no. 4, 1998): 962–71. Edmund Morgan, *Visible Saints: The History of a Puritan Idea* (New York: New York Univ. Press, 1963), 12–13, 110–12. The petitioners threatened to notify the ascendant Presbyterian party in Parliament which, while not as hierarchical as the English episcopacy, was anathema to Massachusetts Congregationalists and English Independents who opposed any rigid religious uniformity.

inhabitants here," because the *Charter* stipulated that the colony could admit its own members. Within the colony itself, the General Court condemned the petitioners' claim that it was an "arbitrary government" of "intolerable bondage," depriving colonists a guarantee of "their lives and liberties." Owing to the chaotic nature of English politics at this time Massachusetts escaped intervention once more. Child was imprisoned and fined £50, with the other petitioners fined from £10 to £40. The divisive relationship between the magistrates and the deputies had been mitigated by the threat of parliamentary intervention. In the meantime, the colony had lost an important promoter of an industry it desperately needed, but the political and religious costs were simply too high to bear.[4]

One can reasonably think that the *Child Petition* should have had greater resonance by reminding colonists of their English origins, and the authority of English law. These two identities course through colonial history all the way to the American Revolution, when colonists fought for their "English Liberties." Moreover, since Parliament had triumphed over Charles I, whose bishops had persecuted the colony's faithful, forcing them to leave England, surely now Massachusetts could rejoin the mother country. However, by the Fall of 1646, Parliament officially abolished the Episcopacy after enacting a "toothless version of voluntary religion" earlier in the year with no independent authority or significant enforcement muscle. As the head of church and state, Charles I, was "guest" (or prisoner) of several factions during the next several years, Massachusetts would keep any new state religion sponsored by Parliament at arm's length.[5]

4 *A Declaration of the General Court holden at Boston 4 (9) 1646, concerning a Remonstrance and Petition exhibited at last Session of this Court by Doctor Child,* in *Hutchinson Papers* (Albany: Prince Society, 1865), 1: 223–47. Nathaniel Shurtleff, ed., *MGCR*, 3: 90–1, 94, 162, 175. William Bradford, *Of Plymouth Plantation*, S.E. Morison ed., (New York: Alfred A. Knopf, 1953), 346–47. John Child, *New Englands Jonas Cast Up at London*, (London: 1647), 4: 107–21. Edward Winslow, *New-Englands Salamander* (London: 1647), *MHS Collections (Third Series/ 1830)*, 2: 110–45. Richard Morris, "Massachusetts and the Common Law: The Declaration of 1646," in ed. David Flaherty, *Essays in the History of American Law* (Chapel Hill: Univ. of North Carolina Press, 1969), 135–46. Francis Bremer, *John Winthrop*, 365–69. Robert Wall, *Massachusetts Bay: The Crucial Decade*, 173–4. Philip Gura, *A Glimpse of Sion's Glory*, 195–203. Bernard Bailyn, *The Barbarous Years*, 486–88. After "furious lobbying by both sides" Parliament confirmed the Massachusetts *Charter's* authority.

5 Richard Dunn, ed. *Journal of John Winthrop*, 341 (Feb., 1641), 432 (May 1643). David Hall, *The Puritans: A Transatlantic History* (Princeton: Princeton Univ. Press, 2019), 267–74. The English "state church that limped into being in 1646 was a toothless version of voluntary religion. No national assembly was ever authorized, synods rarely met, protecting the Sunday Sabbath faltered despite various attempts to preserve it, and mandatory attendance" was rarely enforced as a plethora of new sects and modes of worship sprang forth during the 1650's.

Concomitantly, England's political and religious upheavals were creating an environment ripe for legal reform, and topics for parliamentary debate and pamphleteers. As the King's authority wasted away, the royal foundation of English law crumbled. So, consequent to the Child petition's complaint of the absence of a body of laws and liberties in Massachusetts, the freemen had a ready-made solution. The unity created by the petition overcame earlier differences, and the General Court passed this resolution late in 1646:

> The Court, being deeply sensible of the earnest expectation of the country in general for this Court's completing of a body of laws for the better and more orderly wielding all the affairs of this commonwealth, willing also to their utmost to answer their honest and hearty desires therein, unexpectedly prevented by multitude of other pressing occasions, think fit and necessary that this Court make choice of two or three of our honored magistrates, with as many of the deputies, to peruse, examine, compare, transcribe, correct, and compose in good order all the liberties, laws, and orders extant with us, and further to peruse and perfect all such others as are drawn up, and to present such of them as they find necessary for us, as also to suggest what they deem needful to be added, as also to consider and contrive some good method and order, titles and tables for compiling the whole, so as we may have ready recourse to any of them upon all occasions, *whereby we may manifest our utter disaffection to arbitrary government*, and so all relations be safely and sweetly directed and perfected in all their just rights and privileges, desiring thereby to make way for printing of laws for more public and profitable use of us and our successors.[6]

Governor Winthrop, Richard Bellingham, William Hibbins, Joseph Hill, and Nathaniel Duncan were appointed to the new committee.[7]

William Hibbins, Richard Bellingham's brother-in-law, had arrived in the colony in 1634. He was elected to several colonial offices after the political carnage of the Antinomian crisis, including town selectman in 1639, and deputy in 1641. He was elected assistant in 1643, after which he served on several law committees. Of the five-man committee appointed by the General Court in

6 Nathaniel Shurtleff, ed., *MGCR*, 2: 168–69 (Nov. 4, 1646). Donald Veall, *The Popular Movement for Law Reform: 1640–1660* (Oxford: Clarendon Press, 1970), 74. In 1646, England's law reform movement was in its infancy, but whatever was ultimately achieved did not survive the restoration of Charles II in 1660.

7 Nathaniel Shurtleff, ed., *MGCR*, 2: 168–69 (Nov. 4, 1646).

1646, three were magistrates including Governor Winthrop. Nathaniel Duncan had been a member of the original Dorchester Company, the predecessor to the Massachusetts Bay Company. He had served as a selectman, town clerk, and deputy of Dorchester until moving to Boston in 1645. He was elected the colony's auditor general in October of that year, charged with keeping a "copy of the records and orders of Court." Duncan also served on several law committees. Joseph Hills was elected a Malden selectman in 1644, town deputy in 1646 (followed by his first appointment to a law committee), and the very next year he was elected speaker of the House of Deputies. There's no apparent cause for his meteoric political rise except for his background as a merchant, and related expertise in English law as evidenced by his ownership of Pulton's abridgement of English statutes, the finest book of its kind. Subsequently, he became a leading draftsman of the Massachusetts law books into the 1660's.[8]

Soon the General Court began to enact legislation that would fill the book of colonial law. George Haskins termed it "an outburst of unprecedented legislative activity" that continued until the adoption of *The Book of the General Laws and Liberties of 1648*, with one-third of its contents from laws passed since 1646, and a quarter of its provisions enacted before 1640. Approximately ninety of the *Body of Liberties*' one-hundred sections were also included. One provision provided non-congregants a vote in town elections, and to approve regulations, but the General Court stipulated freemen must still constitute a majority in town meetings. Nevertheless, the *Child petition* had put the colony on notice that it must make the government more inclusive, if only incrementally.[9]

8 William Whitmore, *Colonial Laws of Massachusetts. Reprinted from the Edition of 1660*, 80–2. George Winship, *The Cambridge Press* (Philadelphia: Univ. of Penn. Press, 1945), 106–7. Nathaniel Shurtleff, ed., *MGCR*, 2: 61, 109, 128, 196, 217, 230, 239, 246, 262, 286; 3: 54; 4 (Part 1): 35, 138, 180, 182, 271; 5: 377 (Oct. 11, 1682). Over the years Hill petitioned the General Court for support for his service composing and transcribing "all laws of publique concernment, coppie-wise … in reference to [the] publique good," which he claimed ultimately led to his blindness. Robert Wall, "The Membership of the Massachusetts General Court," (Ph.D. diss., Yale University, 1965), 276–77, 343–44, 586. George Haskins, *Law and Authority in Early Massachusetts* (New York: Macmillan Co., 1960), 133–34. Stephen Lee, ed., *Dictionary of National Biography*, 2: 194; 21: 697–702. Deloraine Corey, *History of Malden, Mass.: 1633–1785* (Malden: 1899), 165–184 (Ch. VI).

9 Nathaniel Shurtleff, ed., *MGCR*, 2: 167–81, 191, 194–97, 203–5, 208–12, 216–20, 230–31, 239, 246, 259–63; 3: 84–103, 109–11, 114, 125, 130, 136, 141–44, 157, 162. Laws were enacted punishing blasphemy, heretics, absence from church worship, swearing, theft, and any child over sixteen years who struck their parent could be put to death; bakers were required to mark their bread, several laws were passed under title *Judicial Proceedings*; support was provided to poor scholars so they would not go to England; a law forbid "man-stealing"; and under title *Prudential Laws* town selectmen could charge malefactors and "idle" children before county courts amongst other enactments. Hall, *The Puritans*, 236. Wall, *Massachusetts Bay: The Crucial Decade*, 174. Haskins, *Law and Authority in Early Massachusetts*, 113–40.

Even with this progress members of the General Court were impatient that a law book was not yet achieved, and added another committee member, Edward Johnson, to assist in the work. The following session in November witnessed the enactment of even more legislation, including the *1647 School Act*, town courts were established to hear disputes less than 40 shillings, and a system of weights and measures was established. To prevent "long, tedious and confused pleadings in civil actions," plaintiffs were ordered to present written statements before trial. And the deputies achieved their long-standing demand that penalties be attached to offenses and not left to the magistrates' discretion. The following titles in the *Laws and Liberties of 1648* included specific punishments enacted after the *Body of Liberties of 1641*, with all but one passed since 1646: *Burglarie and Theft*, *Forgerie*, *Gaming*, *Drunkenness*, *Lying*, *Profane Swearing*, and *Tobacco*. Meanwhile, law committees were given "liberty to make some changes of form" in the laws, to "put in apt words as occasion shall require" to ensure the printed laws were "conveniently penned," as long as the "meaning in any law … be not changed." To assist their endeavors, the General Court ordered law books by "*Sir Edward Cook Upon Littleton*, two of the *Book of Entries*, two of *Sir Edward Coke upon Magna Charta*, two of the *New Terms of the Law*, two of Dalton's *Justice of the Peace* manuals, and two of Sir Edward Coke's *Reports*."[10]

In its November 1647 session the General Court issued directions for the law book's publication. Committees would submit their respective list of laws with necessary amendments to be included in the new law book, a new committee would prepare the laws for printing, and yet another committee was to inspect the finished draft. By March 1648 Edward Rawson, secretary of the upper House of Assistants, was ordered to join Joseph Hill in collecting all the "amendments of the books of laws passed and make them as one." Speaker Hill would return the original to the General Court, while Secretary Rawson kept the other "sealed up, till the next Court." The following May a "copy of the laws in the 2 rolls … were (by order of Court) sealed up, with intent that if hereafter any question should arise about the copy now at the press, it might be examined by this, whereby the faithfulness of the committee might be tried." The following October, as six-hundred copies of the *Laws and Liberties of 1648* were

Whitmore, ed., *Body of Liberties of 1641*, 47 (Lib. 66). Timothy Breen, "Who Governs: The Town Franchise in Seventeenth Century Massachusetts," *William and Mary Quarterly* 27 (1970): 461. Adrian Weimer, *A Constitutional Culture* (Philadelphia: Univ. of Pennsylvania Press, 2023), 130–53.

10 Nathaniel Shurtleff, ed., *MGCR*, 2: 203, 208–12, 219 (Nov. 11, 1647). Richard Dunn, ed., *Laws and Liberties of 1648*, 4–5, 23–24, 30, 35–36, 45, 50.

being printed, the Court ordered that "books of laws now at the press" be sold "at three shillings."[11]

Deputy Edward Johnson memorialized the colony's accomplishment, after the General Court's enactment of the *Laws and Liberties* in 1647, it "committed them to the press, and in the year 1648 they were printed." In the future, "all who intend to transport themselves hither may know this is no place of licentious liberty, nor will this people suffer any to trample down this Vineyard of the Lord." While the law book's purpose was to "promote the Ordinances of Christ," by enacting these "laws, liberties, and privileges" the freemen hoped to silence objections that "caused many to malign their civil government." Now the laws could be examined by "all men, to the end that none may plead ignorance." As Daniel Coquillette explained, the law book's alphabetical format provided ready access; to find regulations for bakers one had only to flip a few pages to the "B" section of the book. Since learning one's ABC's comprised the most rudimentary education, even those with limited schooling could intuitively understand the book's indexing. Finally, the Court ordered the books sold at a specific price for public sale. Upon the printing of the *Laws and Liberties of 1660*, the Court directed the treasurer to "disburse ... what shall be necessary tending towards the printing of the laws unto Samuel Green."[12]

Starting in 1485, English printers had begun to compile their own editions of statutory collections for profit, at first by an alphabetized indexing, and later by regnal year. While the *Laws and Liberties of 1648* emulated English statute books and JP manuals, those were not official publications sponsored by King or Commonwealth. The origins of printing English law in the abridgment format dates from early sixteenth-century England. In the 1520's Johannes Rastell first edited and printed statutes organized by alphabetical titles, under

11 Nathaniel Shurtleff, ed., *MGCR*, 2: 217, 230, 239, 262. Robert Wall, "Membership of the Massachusetts General Court," 300. William Whitmore, ed., *Colonial Laws of Massachusetts. Reprinted from the Edition of 1660*, 76–7. *Massachusetts Laws and Liberties of 1648*: (https://www.colonialsociety.org/sites/default/files/csm-volume62/csm-volume62-p252.jpg).

12 Edward Johnson, *Wonder Working Providence of Sion's Saviour* (London: 1654; reprint, Andover: Warren Draper, 1867), 205–6 ("Chap. V. Of the great pains and care taken by those in Authority, for the compiling of Laws for this little Commonwealth."). The General Court "passed an Act of confirmation upon them, and so committed them to the Press ... in 1648." Daniel Coquillette, "Radical Lawmakers in Colonial Massachusetts," *New England Quarterly* 67 (June, 1994): 200–1. H. Anders, "The Elizabethan ABC with the Catechism," *The Library* 41 (1936): 32–48. Theobold Mathew, "Law-French," *Law Quarterly Review* 54 (1938): 358–69. J.H. Baker, *Manual of Law French* (Amersham: Avebury Publishing, 1979), 9–14. E. Jennifer Monaghan, "Literacy Instruction and Gender in Colonial New England," *American Quarterly* 40 (March 1988): 22.

which he provided a translation of older laws in Latin or French into English. He included numbered sub-sections under his titles, with cross references to other helpful entries at the end of each section, just like the *Laws and Liberties*. Johannes Rastell was Thomas More's brother-in-law, and joined his initiative to reform the English Commonwealth and its laws before Henry VIII made his fateful decision to break with Rome. Barbara Shapiro has described Rastell as a "humanist lawyer" who, being a supporter of a "'good reasonable common law' in English," sent Henry VIII's chief minister Thomas Cromwell "proposals … for improving the common law and Chancery," including a "reduction of fees in all courts." Editorial rights of his collection of statutes passed on to Rastell's son William, and ultimately to Ferdinando Pulton. Although Pulton eventually listed statutes by the year of the monarch's reign in which they were adopted (i.e., the regnal year), Michael Dalton's *Countrey Justice* featured alphabetized titles beginning with its first printing in 1618, a year after which the most popular Justice of the Peace manual, *Eirenarcha* by William Lambarde, went out of print. Colonists' familiarity with the *Countrey Justice* is evident per the General Court's order of several copies as it neared completion of the final drafts of the law book. Its contents served as both a reference to English law as well as a format for the *Laws and Liberties*.[13]

13 Nathaniel Shurtleff, ed., *MGCR*, 1: 222 (March 12, 1638), 277 (Nov. 5, 1639); 4 (Part 1): 50, 306, 391. The printer complained that he could not sell all of the 600 copies of the 1648 law book because of amendments made after its enactment. The General Court granted the press £20 recompense. In 1657, when the press's operator petitioned that "he hath suffered much damage by erecting the printing press at Cambridge," the Court granted him 300 acres of land. *In 1639, the Court defined a "public rate" as "only such rates as assessed by order of the public Court for the country's occasions, and no other."* David Harvey, *The Law Emprynted: The Printing Press as an Agent of Change* (Oxford: Hart Publishing, 2017), 107–60, 281–82. Richard Ross, "The Commoning of the Common Law: The Renaissance Debate over Printing English Law, 1520–1640," *University of Pennsylvania Law Review* 146 (no. 2, 1998): 324–57. H.J. Byrom, "Richard Tottell," *The Library* 8 (1927–28): 224–30. Howard Graham, "The Rastells and the Printed English Law Book of the Renaissance," *Law Library Journal* 47 (1954): 6–25. John Cowley, "The Abridgement of the Statutes," *The Library* 12 (1931): 128–31. Geoffrey Elton, *Reform and Renewal* (Cambridge: Cambridge Univ. Press, 1973), 138–51. Daniel Coquillette, "Radical Lawmakers in Colonial Massachusetts," 200–201. Wilfrid Prest, "William Lambarde, Elizabethan Law Reform, and Early Stuart Politics," *Journal of British Studies* 34 (Oct., 1995): 464–80. Barbara Shapiro, *Law Reform in Early Modern England* (Oxford: Hart Publishing, 2019), 32–33, 55–61. Johannes Rastell, *An Abridgment of the Statutes* (1527); *STC* 9518, Reel 6. Johannes Rastell, *The Great Abridgement of the Statutes* (1531); *STC* 9521, Reel 6. William Rastell, *Collection of all the Statutes* (1557); *STC* 9306, Reel 1686. Ferdinando Pulton, *Collection of Sundrie Statutes Frequent in Use* (1618); *STC* 9328, Reel 1515.

In 1652, on the other side of the Atlantic, John Shepheard demanded English law must be "evident to the meanest capacity" to order to inform people of their "duty and the penalty of transgressing," because "it is a miserable slavery where the law is uncertain or unknown." Richard Overton pleaded, the "Laws of the Land (locked up from common capacities in the Latin and French tongues)" must be printed in English so a commoner who could read "may fully understand his own proceedings in law." Or, as the Levellers demanded of Parliament in the *Large Petition* (1647):

> [Y]ou will settle a just, speedy, plain and unburdensome way for deciding of controversies, and suits in law, and reduce all laws, to the nearest agreement with Christianity, and publish them in the English tongue, and that all process and proceedings therein may be ... also in English, ... that each one who can read, may the better understand their own affairs, and that the duties of all judges, officers, and practicers in the Law, and of all magistrates and officers in the common-wealth, may be prescribed, their fees limited under strict penalties, and published in print, to the knowledge and view of all men, *by which just and equitable means this Nation shall be for ever freed of an oppression, more burdensome and troublesome then all the oppressions hitherto by this Parliament removed.*[14]

Several centuries earlier a 1362 parliamentary statute lamented the "great mischiefs" of laws "pleaded, showed, and judged in the French Tongue, which is

14 John Shepheard, *Certain Proposals for Regulating the Law* (1652), 1–2; *Wing* S3102, Reel 1450: 10. Richard Overton, *Appeale from the Degenerate Representative Body* (July 1647), in G.E. Aylmer, ed., *The Levellers in the English Revolution* (Ithaca: Cornell Univ. Press, 1975), 85. *To the Right Honourable and Supreme Authority of this Nation* (1647) [i.e., *The Large Petition*], in G.E. Aylmer, ed., *The Levellers and the English Revolution*, 79–80 (no. 7). John Eusden, *Puritans, Lawyers, and Politics in Early Seventeenth-Century England* (New Haven: Yale Univ. Press, 1958; reprint, Archon Books, 1965), 47. "The Levellers and their fellow Republicans were among the first in England to propose explicitly a written constitution which would then become fundamental law." John Rees, *The Leveller Revolution* (London: Versa, 2016), 69–72. "Both Parliament and the king urged on repeated attempts to stem the tide of unlicensed pamphlets ... This created a running battle between the Stationers' Company and other authorities and the secret presses ... Leveller works were among those burnt by authorities and ... between 1640 and 1660 Lilburne had more of his works consigned to the flames than any other author." Barbara Shapiro, *Law Reform in Early Modern England*, 104. "Parliament continued to exert control over the press ... Ordinances designed to regulate printing and to prevent publication of scandalous pamphlets were passed in 1643 and 1647. Parliament was determined to establish control over the press." David Como, "Secret Printing and the Crisis of 1640," *Past and Present* 196 (Aug., 2007): 38–39, 54.

much unknown in the said Realm." The statute of Edward III noted that the use of foreign languages to record English law had created an absurd situation in the royal courts, as litigants had "no knowledge, nor understanding of that which is said for them or against them." In 1648, John Lilburne cited Andrew Horne's *Mirror of Justices*, written at the turn of the 13th and 14th centuries, in support of his own attacks on English law. Horne, a successful merchant, had written a half a century before the 1362 statute's enactment, "It is an abuse that the laws, and the customs of the realm ... are not put into writing, whereby ... they might be known by all men." Lilburne scoffed, only "jugglers, deceivers, deluders, and tyrants wish to have their laws not in peoples' mother tongue; but will have them put into Latin or French ... [so] the people that are governed by them may never come to understand them, ... [and] shall be fettered with this bondage." In 1650, the House of Commons passed an *Act for turning the books of the law, and all process and proceedings in courts of justice into English*, but upon Charles II's restoration Parliament rescinded the 1650 Act, employing the ancient languages once more. In 1731, with familiar refrain that "many and great mischiefs do frequently happen ... from the proceedings in courts of justice being in an unknown language," Parliament finally "Englished" the Common Law for good. A Yorkshire petition complained, "obliging grand jury men ... to make their presentments in a language which few of them understand ... are great occasions of the delay of justice, and give room to the most dangerous frauds." An onlooker thought it "strange that this was not enacted before."[15]

To aggravate matters, the storage of the official collection of statutes in the Tower of London made access to the corpus of English law virtually impossible. Even with the "sessional" printing of English statutes by royal and for-profit printers, an official collection was not achieved until the early nineteenth century (and then only with laws enacted to 1714). Previously, for-profit printers

15 *SR*, 1: 375–76 (36 Edw. III, 1, ch. 15); *SR*, 5: 180 (12 Car. II, ch. 3, §4). John Lilburne, *The Peoples Prerogative* (Feb. 1648), intro.; *Thomason Tracts* E427 (4), Reel 67. Andrew Horne, *Mirrour of Justices*, William Robinson trans., (Washington, D.C.: John Byrne & Co., 1903), xi–xix, 232 (Ch. V, §1, #3). Frederick Maitland, intro., *Mirror of Justices* (London: Seldon Society, 1895), xlvii. Presupposing the book's authorship "in 1289, the talk of 'false judges,' the hints that the chancery and the exchequer are full of perjurers and thieves, are not without point and truth. It was a time of great scandal." C.H. Firth, and R.S. Rait, eds., *Acts and Ordinances of the Interregnum: 1642–1660* (London: HMSO, 1911), 2: 455–56. *The Statutes: Revised Edition* (London: 1871), 2: 370–71 (4 Geo. II, ch. 26). The Yorkshire petition is cited in Wilfrid Prest, "Law Reform in Eighteenth-Century England," in ed. Peter Birks, *The Life of the Law* (London: Hambledon Press, 1993), 114. T. Mathew, "Law French," *Law Quarterly Review* 54 (July 1938): 358–69.

secured ownership of the laws by royal patent, or agreement, to print sundry classifications of official business. This included everything from bibles to ABC books, and statutory law. Once patents were granted, however, English government had little to do with its legal publications. Besides the sessional statutes, and the process by which a statute was included, and thereby made "public," the clerks of Parliament forwarded laws to the various print shops that ultimately decided which laws to include in their own *Statutes at Large* compilations. These collections not only lacked official certification, but they were also incomplete and erroneous. As Daniel Harvey has recently explained, "Prior to printing, the copying of statutes was laborious and expensive—each copy having to be made individually—no two ever going to be exactly the same … *Judges themselves did not have a current set of statutes available for reference,*" resulting in misquotations, and leading to their sporadic citation. Even by the early 1640's, MP Sir Simonds D'Ewes complained that "many of the statutes were false printed," and urged printers to compare their proofs with parliamentary "records" before publishing final copies. Francis Bacon had sponsored a consolidation of English law in 1616, *A Proposition to his Majesty touching the Compiling and Amending the Laws of England,* before becoming Chancellor, and his subsequent impeachment for corruption. As Attorney General, Bacon noted the great volume of statutes, coupled with notoriously slow trial process, required such publications. Lastly, Elizabeth Eisenstein has reminded us of a vitally important perspective historians should remember that is beyond print: "Historians are trained to discriminate between manuscript sources and printed texts; but they are not trained to think with equal care about how manuscripts appeared when this sort of discrimination was inconceivable—when everything was 'off the record' … [except] that … read to those who were within earshot."[16]

16 J.H. Baker, *An Introduction to English Legal History*, 3rd ed., (Boston: Butterworths, 1990), 236–37, 249–50. "The medieval courts had no authentic texts available to them, and argument in court rarely turned on the precise wording of a statute. In the absence of official records, the public and their legal advisors relied on private collections of statutes; hundreds of examples survive, hardly any two of them the same. These manuscripts were never wholly complete … It was these private statute-books rather than the public records which formed the basis of the series of printed statutes which began to appear in 1481, and were frequently re-edited in successive centuries as 'statutes at large'. Not until 1810–1822 was an official edition of the old statutes (down to 1713) published; but even the impressive elephant-folio volumes of the *Statutes of the Realm* were acknowledged to be incomplete and to contain apocrypha. In the case of medieval legislation, then, sovereign authority was in practice considerably modified by the vagaries of tradition." Austin Woolrych, *Commonwealth to Protectorate* (Oxford: Clarendon Press, 1982), 269–73. David Harvey, *The Law Emprynted: The Printing Press as an Agent of Change*, 107–60, 196–97, 281–82. Richard

A handful of Massachusetts magistrates had practiced law in England, including Richard Bellingham and John Winthrop, but only one person was a professional lawyer in the earliest decades of the colony. During his residence in the colony during the early 1640's Thomas Lechford complained that colonists disdained both English lawyers and common law precedents, "I fear it is not a little degree of pride and dangerous improvidence to slight all former laws of the Church or State, cases of experience and precedents, to go hammer out new … upon the Word of God." He warned colonists not to "despise" legal knowledge or lawyers "lest you repent too late." Despite his efforts, "parties in all causes speak themselves for the most part, and some of the magistrates where they think cause requireth, do the part of advocates without fee or reward." Because Lechford drafted copies of the *Body of Liberties of 1641*, he was well aware of *Liberty 26*, "Every man that findeth himself unfit to plead his own cause in any Court shall have liberty to employ any man against whom the court doth not except to help him, provided he give him no fee or reward for his pains." *Liberty 25* provided non-lawyers the opportunity to plead their own cases in the colony's courts, "No summons, pleading, judgment, or any kind of proceeding in court or course of justice shall be abated, arrested or reversed upon any kind of circumstantial errors or mistakes, if the person and cause be rightly understood by the court." Although *Liberty 25* was incorporated in future editions of the *Laws and Liberties, Liberty 26* was omitted from the 1648 edition. Lawyering for a fee was not officially encouraged, but it was no longer illegal. From that date county court proceedings occasionally featured colonists representing clients, yet they hardly constituted a professional group

---

Ross, "The Commoning of the Common Law: The Renaissance Debate over Printing English Law, 1520–1640," 324–57. Geoffrey Elton, "The Sessional Printing of Statutes, 1484–1547," in E.W. Ives, et al., eds., *Wealth and Power in Tudor England* (London: Athlone Press, 1978), 68–86. Geoffrey Elton, *The Parliament of England: 1559–1581* (Cambridge: Cambridge Univ. Press, 1986), 44–45. "If an act was left out of the statute at the end of the session it was, irrespective of its import, private by the one criterion that really mattered: in litigation, it could not be pleaded generally but had to be produced in an exemplification under the great seal or a copy formally certified by the clerk of the Parliament if the court was to take notice of it … The acts left unprinted [were] … therefore left private." George Grossman, *Legal Research* (Oxford: Oxford Univ. Press, 1994), 102–28. Wallace Notestein, ed., *The Journal of Sir Simonds D'Ewes* (New Haven: Yale Univ. Press, 1923), 157 (n. 17). Basil Montagu, ed., *Works of Francis Bacon* (Philadelphia: Carey & Hart, 1841), 2: 229–233. Barbara Shapiro, "Sir Francis Bacon and the Mid-Seventeenth Century Movement for Law Reform," *American Journal of Legal History* 24 (October 1980): 331–362. Daniel Coquillette, "Past the Pillars of Hercules: Francis Bacon and the Science of Rulemaking," *University of Michigan Journal of Law Reform* 46 (no. 2, 2013): 567–73. Elizabeth Eisenstein, *The Printing Press as an Agent of Change* (Cambridge: Cambridge Univ. Press, 1979), 1: 10, 103.

since innkeepers sometimes represented defendants. Not until the publication of the 1673 annual law pamphlet could attorneys represent clients for a fee.[17]

The first *Book of the General Laws and Liberties* was printed at the end of 1648. By 1685, the General Court received notification that the *Charter of 1629* had been revoked. With the dissolution of the Colony's "foundation," the colony's law books also lost their authority. Nevertheless, during the period of their existence a revolution occurred in legislative procedure. While historical analyses of the first Massachusetts law book (the *Laws and Liberties of 1648*) are available, hardly any attention has been given to the succeeding law books published in 1660 and 1672, much less the sessional pamphlets issued during the interim periods between those major editions, or the Court's initiatives

17 William Whitmore, ed., *Body of Liberties of 1641*, 39. Richard Dunn, ed., *Laws and Liberties of 1648*, 49, title *Summons*, §1. Whitmore, ed., *Lawes and Liberties of 1660*, 4, title *Attachments-Summons*, §2. William Whitmore, ed., *The Colonial Law of Massachusetts. Reprinted from the Edition of 1672* (Boston: City Council, 1887), 7, title *Attachments-Summons*, §2; 211 (Oct. 15, 1673). Cited hereafter as the *Laws and Liberties of 1672*. George Dow, ed., *Essex County Court Record* (Salem: Essex Institute, 1911–21), 3: 58, 84; 4: 178, 185–86; 6: 224, 432; 8: 93. Nathaniel Shurtleff, ed., *MGCR*, 2: 279–80 (May 2, 1649); 4 (Part 2): 563 (Oct. 15, 1673). Charles Hilkey, *Legal Development in Colonial Massachusetts: 1630–1686* (New York: Columbia Univ. Press, 1910), 60–5. Thomas Lechford, *Notebook*, Edward Hale ed., (Boston, 1885; reprint, Camden: Picton Press, 1988), 44–50, 87–90, 182–83, 440–41. Thomas Lechford, *Plain Dealing* (London: 1642); in *MHS Collections (1833)*: 3: 55–128 @ 3: 85–86. William Whitmore, ed., *Hutchinson Papers* (Albany: Prince Society, 1865), 2: 8. According to Massachusetts Magistrate Samuel Symonds' decision of *Giddings v. Brown* (1657), printed law successfully limited magisterial discretion just as the deputies intended, as he commented it was improper to "interpret general sentences in positive or court laws." A century later Thomas Hutchinson noted in the marginalia, "this is quite contrary to the rules following for interpretation of laws." William Blackstone, *Commentaries on the Laws of England*, 1: 68–9, 86, 156. Blackstone acknowledged that the "omnipotence of Parliament" was manifest, because "what they do no authority upon earth can undo." But "as to customs, or the common law," that remained the "law by which proceedings and determinations in the King's ordinary courts of justice are guided." How were "customs or maxims to be known, and by whom is their validity to be determined?" Of course, "by the judges in the several courts of justice" who were the "depository of the laws, the living oracles, who must decide in all cases." J.H. Baker, *Introduction to English Legal History*, 3rd ed., 173. "There is an obvious conflict between the letter of … statutes and the spirit of the common law; but, so far, it is Coke's common law which has prevailed. The legislation cannot itself be set aside; but much can be done by way of interpretation, using the presumption in favor of procedural fairness. Coke had insisted that discretion, even absolute discretion, was a science controlled by law and not an arbitrary power." David Lieberman, "Blackstone's Science of Legislation," *Journal of British Studies* 27 (1988): 117–149. Barbara Shapiro, *Law Reform in Early Modern England*, 56–7, 178. Angela Fernandez, "Record-Keeping and Other Troublemaking: Thomas Lechford and Law Reform in Colonial Massachusetts," *Law and History Review* 23 (2005): 235–77.

to draft and compile collections on topics such as trade, official conduct, and martial law.[18]

Just a year after the issuance of the *Laws and Liberties of 1648*, the General Court testified to the good-affect the law book was having on colonial life. In the fall of 1649 both houses agreed that the experience of the past year had demonstrated the "great benefit" of "putting the laws in print." Magistrates and deputies thought it "very requisite that those laws that have passed the consent of the General Court, since the book of laws was printed, should be forthwith committed to the press." The Court appointed a new committee chaired by Richard Bellingham to prepare the supplementary edition. So began a regular process of printing pamphlets during the interims between the major editions of 1648, 1660, and 1672, to update colonists on recent legislation. Those pamphlets were initially printed in 1650, 1654, 1657, and became annual publications after 1663 through 1686.[19]

While the *Laws and Liberties of 1648* was at the press, the General Court turned its attention to its own record keeping:

> For … the end that the records … either amongst the magistrates or deputies, may hereafter be more exactly recorded, *and kept for public use*—It is

18 William Whitmore entitled his 1660 and 1672 editions "The Colonial Laws of Massachusetts." But the original 1660 edition followed its 1648 predecessor verbatim, entitled "The Book of the General Laws and Liberties." The 1672 edition was changed to *The General Laws and Liberties*. Each new edition of the colonial law book was issued every twelve years. John Cushing, ed., *A Bibliography of the Laws and Resolves of the Massachusetts Bay: 1642–1780* (Wilmington: MHS, 1984), 2 (no. 3), 4 (no. 12), 10 (no. 28). Hugh Amory, *First Impressions: Printing in Cambridge, 1639–1989* (Cambridge: Harvard Univ., 1989), 57. Nathaniel Shurtleff, ed., *MGCR*, 5: 465 (Jan. 28, 1685), 479 (May 27, 1685), 484 (June 4, 1685). Morris Cohen, "Legal Literature in Colonial Massachusetts," *Publications of the Colonial Society of Massachusetts* (1984), 62: 243–72. "First Among Many: The Bay Psalm Book and Early Moments in American Printing," *Library of Congress*, (https://www.loc.gov/exhibits/bay-psalm-book-and-american-printing/online-exhibition.html). Shurtleff, ed., *MGCR*, 2: 286; 3: 193, 252, 308, 317–18, 342–43, 429; 4 (Part 1): 35, 119, 138, 149, 180, 195, 271, 324, 337, 350, 356, 391, 422, 441–42; 4 (Part 2): 4, 136, 330, 345, 388, 409, 418, 449, 453, 463, 467–69, 511, 559, 562, 575; 5: 49–50, 236, 268, 294, 301, 337, 464, 476, 479, 484. William Whitmore, ed., *Colonial Laws of Massachusetts. Reprinted from the Edition of 1660*, 79–117.

19 Nathaniel Shurtleff, ed., *MGCR*, 3: 173. John Cushing, ed., *A Bibliography of the Laws and Resolves of the Massachusetts Bay*, 6–29. The 1650's supplements are not extant, but Whitmore provided citations from the General Court *Record* that testify to their existence. William Whitmore, ed., *The Colonial Laws of Massachusetts. Reprinted From the Edition of 1660, with the Supplements to 1672*, 78–97. Morris Cohen, "Legal Literature in Colonial Massachusetts," 62: 250–4.

> hereby ordered, that as there is a secretary amongst the magistrates, (who is the general officer of the common wealth for the keeping the public records of the same), so there shall be a clerk amongst the deputies to be chosen by them from time to time; that … there be provided, by the auditor, four large paper books in folio, bound up with velum and pasteboard, two whereof to be delivered to the secretary, and two to the clerk of the house of deputies, one to be a journal to each of them, the other for the fair entry of all laws, acts, and orders, etc., that shall pass the magistrates and deputies, that of the secretaries to be the public record.

Furthermore, the Court directed that all previous "laws, orders, and acts of Court contained in the old books that are of force, and not ordered to be printed, be transcribed in some alphabetical or methodical way by direction of some committee that this Court shall please to appoint, and delivered to the secretary to record in … the said book of records."[20]

How did the General Court determine which laws should be transferred from the new book of *Records*, or the record of all of its laws and orders, to the *Book of the General Laws and Liberties* that was for the "public use" of colonists themselves? The introduction of the *Laws and Liberties of 1648* explained, for "such laws and orders as are not of general concernment we have not put them into this book, but they remain still in force and are to be seen in the book of the Records of the Court, but all general laws not here inserted nor mentioned to be still of force are to be accounted repealed." General laws applied to the people of the colony at large, or some broad category thereof. Non-general laws or orders in the official *Record* included General Court deliberations on private petitions to its resolution of intra-town disputes on issues such as contested boundary lines. Thereby, the introduction of the *Laws and Liberties of 1648* had made vital delineations between the responsibilities of the government, its processes and framework, regulations concerning church, market and home, and colonists' personal liberties. Other business concerning General Court decisions on issues brought by individual entities, whether it concerned counties, towns, congregations, or persons, remained in the *Record* because such information was not essential to "public" life. Moreover, access to the Court's official business was guaranteed by the 1648 law book under title, *Records*:

---

20 Nathaniel Shurtleff, ed., *MGCR*, 2: 259–60 (Oct. 18, 1648). To this order we owe the existence of Nathaniel Shurtleff's irreplaceable edition of the *Records of the Governor and Company of the Massachusetts Bay. True Copie of the Court Booke of the Governor and Society of the Massachusetts Bay in New England, 1640–1646, Digital Commonwealth*; (https://ark.digitalcommonwealth.org/ark:/50959/ms35v6054).

> [E]very man shall have liberty to record in the public rolls of any court, any testimony given upon oath in the same court, or before two assistants; or any deed or evidence legally confirmed, there to remain in perpetuam rei memoriam [i.e., in perpetual memory of the matter]. And that every inhabitant of the Country shall have free liberty to search and view any rolls, records, or registers of any court or office, except the council. And to have a transcript or exemplification thereof written, examined and signed by the hand of the officer of the office, paying the appointed fees thereof.[21]

And in 1654 the General Court of Massachusetts ordered:

> [H]enceforth, the secretary shall within ten days after this present sessions, and so from time to time, deliver a copy of all laws that are to be published unto the … printer, who shall forthwith make an impression thereof, to the number of five, six, or seven hundred, as the Court shall order; … the Treasurer shall … pay for … [and] distribute the books, to every magistrate—one, to every Court—one, to the secretary—one, to each town where no magistrate dwells—one, and the rest amongst the towns that bear public charge with[in] the jurisdiction, according to the number of freemen in each town.[22]

In Massachusetts, publishing the colony's law for public awareness caused the process of legislation as it was practiced in this era to be stood upon its head. Instead of a legislature enacting laws whose meaning was eventually interpreted by judges after controversies had arisen, if a law appeared to operate contrary to the community's wishes, colonists simply reported problems to their local deputies. This enabled magistrates and deputies to craft laws harmonious with the environment in which they operated, rather than passing law upon law to remedy disruptions caused by earlier laws. This process is verifiable because such revisions were made with reference to the law books,

---

21 Richard Dunn, ed., *Laws and Liberties of 1648*, intro., 46–7, title *Records*, §5. The proceedings of the standing council were exempt because its members decided matters of war and peace, or ones that we describe as matters concerning "national security." Nathaniel Shurtleff, ed., *MGCR*, 217–19 (Nov. 11, 1647); 4 (Part 1): 299 (May 6, 1657); 4 (Part 2): 144 (May 3, 1665). Ultimately, the General Court defined "rolls, records, or register of any Court or office" as those that "concern particular persons in matters of justice, license grant, or approbation, or of such laws as are of public concernment."

22 Nathaniel Shurtleff, ed., *MGCR*, 4 (Part 1): 182 (May 3, 1654), 422 (May 31, 1660). J.H. Baker, *Introduction to English Legal History*, 3rd ed., 234–37.

their titles, and by referencing section and page number. Soon after the distribution of the *Laws and Liberties of 1648*, for example, an objection was lodged about one of its provisions on page 7, directing that in order to sue for damaged fencing by wayward livestock a plaintiff had to certify that such damage had occurred by an inspection of two men from the nearest town. The Court directed that the plaintiff could initiate his action before such an inspection was conducted. A more comedic complaint addressed title, *Prophane Swearing*. An overworked constable wondered if he had to take a convict to the stocks for each spoken profanity, even if the offender had uttered "twenty or forty profane oaths," requiring that many trips even if he lived "two or three miles from the place of execution." The General Court deferred to the "discretion of the magistrate whom it concerns ... with respect to the season of the year."[23]

One of the most extensive revisions to the 1648 law book occurred in 1651 under title, *Leather*. The *Leather Act of 1642*, as incorporated in the *Laws and Liberties of 1648*, authorized the appointment of leather inspectors to search "any house, shop or warehouse, or any other place where they conceive leather illegally delivered is like to be found, whether wrought into shoes, boots or otherwise." The processes of curing and tanning leather were both complicated and time consuming. Because tanners regularly worked with limited resources, there was great temptation to expedite the nine months to two-year process of curing hides, with shoddy product the result. Parliament had enacted multiple statutes regulating tanners. Similarly, the General Court's original *1642 Leather Act* resulted from "deceits and abuses which in other places have been and are commonly practiced by the tanners, curriers, and workers of leather, [and] ... which accrue to the several members of this commonwealth by leather not sufficiently tanned." The 1651 revision specified "tanned and dried" meant the "whole hide, or other piece or pieces of leather," so that "one-sixteenth part insufficiently" tanned would be a violation. Such exacting regulations ensured a vital raw material for personal items like shoes, as well as saddles, harnesses, farming tools, and industrial equipment like belts, was of serviceable material.[24]

23 Nathaniel Shurtleff, ed., *MGCR*, 3: 186–87 (May 23, 1650), 3: 204–205 (June 19, 1650). Richard Dunn, ed., *Laws and Liberties of 1648*, 6–7, title, *Cattel. Cornfields. Fences.*, §3; 5, title *Profane Swearing*. William Whitmore, *Colonial Laws of Massachusetts of 1660*, 86–92.

24 Nathaniel Shurtleff, ed., *MGCR*, 2: 18–20 (June 14, 1642); 3: 225 (May 22, 1651). Richard Dunn, ed., *Laws and Liberties of 1648*, 32–34, title *Leather*. *Suffolk County Court Record*, ed. S.E. Morison, (Boston: Colonial Society of Massachusetts, 1933), 29: 117, 413. Thomas Lechford, *Notebook*, Edward Hales ed., 408. L.A. Clarkson, "Organization of the English Leather Industry in the Late Sixteenth and Seventeenth Centuries," *Economic History Review* 13

In 1652, the General Court turned its attention to title, *Bakers*. On market day, merchants, craftsmen, and farmers brought their wares for sale. Complaints had been lodged against bakers for trying to cheat colonists at market by selling them underweight goods:

> Whereas it appears to this Court that there is much deceit used by some bakers and others, who, when the clerks of the markets comes to weigh their bread pretend they have none but for their own use, and yet afterwards put their bread to sale which, upon trial, hath been found too light; for prevention of such abuses for time to come, it is ordered by this Court and the authority thereof, that all persons within this jurisdiction who shall usually sell bread, within doors or without, shall at all times hereafter have all their bread that they either put to sale, or spend in their families, made of assizes marked and yielded to trial of the aforesaid clerks, as is directed for bread, by order of this Court, in the printed book, page 3, title *Bakers*, and under the penalties therein expressed.

Bakers came to markets carting their own product, and only upon arrival were their goods weighed and certified by market officials. The General Court's amendment directed that every baker should put his mark on each loaf of bread for sale, with a table of weights and prices provided in the legislation. Like its leather regulations, the law book directed officials to "weigh the said bread as oft as they see cause, and to seize all such as they find defective." The 1652 amendment authorized seizure of goods and penalty of forfeiture just as English penal statutes had done for centuries, except in Massachusetts the provision of regulatory information protected market participants against official corruption.[25]

Owing to these revisions the General Court compensated the Cambridge Press for unsold copies of the *Laws and Liberties of 1648*. New law books and sessional pamphlets were continually issued to revise and update those laws which had either expired, or were modified in due course. On the other side of

---

(1960/61): 245–49. D.M. Dean, "Public or Private? London, Leather and Legislation in Elizabethan England," *Historical Journal* 31 (1988): 525–48.

25 Richard Dunn, ed., *Laws and Liberties of 1648*, 3, title *Bakers*. Nathaniel Shurtleff, ed., *MGCR*, 3: 266 (May 27, 1652). Daniel Coquillette, "Radical Lawmakers in Colonial Massachusetts," 200–1. H. Anders, "The Elizabethan ABC with the Catechism," 32–48. Hugh Amory, *First Impressions*, 38. David Cressy, *Literacy and the Social Order* (Cambridge: Cambridge Univ. Press, 1980), 7, 11, 20–1. Elizabeth Eisenstein, *The Printing Press as an Agent of Change*, 1: 78, 88–9, 100–5, 247. James Davis, "Baking for the Common Good: A Reassessment of the Assize of Bread in Medieval England," *Economic History Review* 57 (Aug., 2004): 465–502.

the Atlantic the "prolific radical pamphleteer," John Warr, condemned England's legal system as the "badge of our oppression," because "so many" were the statutes, opinions, and regulations that you might as well give up rather than "seek relief." The nation had become "lost in the law." Gerrard Winstanley, leader of the Diggers, believed much "misery" was caused when the "mind of the law, the judgment of the Parliament, and the government of the land is resolved into the breast of the judges." If only judges knew the law how could English commoners possibly follow its direction? Law was not primarily for the courtroom, it was supposed to regulate and inform the community. But what did Englishmen get instead, "good laws made by an industrious Parliament are like good eggs laid by a silly goose, and as soon as she hath laid them, she goes her way and lets others take them, and never looks after them more, so that if you lay a stone in her nest, she will sit upon it as if it were an egg."[26]

Increasing reliance on law books in Massachusetts was evident upon the issuance of the *Laws and Liberties of 1660*. The General Court sensed, "it being a matter of some concernment to the country ... to understand when this last impression of the laws is to be in force," magistrates and deputies ordered that the new law book would take effect in a month. Its earliest amendment concerned the despised influx of a radical sect known as Quakers, as a new capital law condemned any of its members who returned to the colony already under a sentence of banishment. A continuing problem of a lack of specie was evident by the repeal of a section in the new 1660 law book on page 78. Previously, "satisfaction of debts and payments" in wampum (or Indian beads) were accepted, but their use had caused creditors extreme "inconvenience." The General Court had to look elsewhere for an acceptable medium of exchange to combat a shortage of currency within the colony, one that wreaked a destructive deflationary cycle and played havoc with colonial merchants and farmers. In 1669, the Court amended the *Laws and Liberties of 1660*, page 62, sec. 2, to curtail the exportation of money. Officials could stop anyone from leaving the colony with more than "necessary expenses."[27]

---

26 Nathaniel Shurtleff, ed., *MGCR*, 3: 160, 183–84, 187, 203. Magistrates and deputies acknowledged that "the Court's alteration of some things in those books ... made them unvendable." John Warr, *The Corruption and Deficiency of the laws of England Soberly Discovered* (London: 1649), in T. Park ed., *The Harleian Miscellany* (London, 1808–13), 6: 214, 220. Barbara Shapiro, *Law Reform in Early Modern England*, 127. Gerrard Winstanley, *The Law of Freedom* (1652), ed. Christopher Hill, (Harmondsworth: Penguin Books, 1973), 336. Michael Rogers, "Gerrard Winstanley on Crime and Punishment," *Sixteenth Century Journal* 27 (1996): 735–47.

27 Shurtleff, ed., *MGCR*, 3: 261–62 (May 27, 1652), 283 (Oct. 19, 1652); 4 (Part 1): 432–33 (Oct. 16, 1660); 4 (Part 2): 4 (May 22, 1661), 42 (May 7, 1662), 420–21 (May 19, 1669). Whitmore,

In 1670, after being unable to sell some of the 1648 law books, the General Court's order for a new edition that would issue as the *Laws and Liberties of 1672* seems, by then, routine:

> Whereas there is a great want of law books for the use of several Courts and inhabitants in this jurisdiction at present, and very few of them that are extant or complete, containing all laws now in force amongst us, it is therefore ordered by this Court that Major Eliazer Lusher [assistant], Capt. Thomas Clark [deputy, Boston], Capt. Edward Johnson [deputy, Wooburne], Capt. Hopestill Foster [deputy, Dorchester], Capt. George Corwin [deputy, Salem], and Capt. Joshua Hubbard [deputy, Hingham], or any four of them, whereof Major Lusher shall be one, shall and hereby are appointed to be a committee to peruse all our laws now in force, to collect and draw up any literal errors, or misplacing words or sentences therein, or any liberties infringed, and to make a convenient table for the ready finding of all things therein, that so they may be fitted for the press, and the same to present to the next session of this Court.[28]

In the penultimate stage before the albeit short lived English Commonwealth, reformers issued multiple tracts demanding publication of the law. *The Lawyers Bane* urged Parliament to summarize and publish the mass of statutory law, because men should "understand those laws and ordinances by which their rights, privileges, interests, and estates are secured." It was unjust "to punish any man for ... doing contrary to that which he neither knows, nor can know." If law was made accessible, and "any men should plead ignorance, ... it could be no other than willful and affected." To achieve a new law book a "competent number of impartial, indifferent, and unbiased men ... may be chosen by the consent of the King and Parliament, being the representative body of the whole kingdom, to consult and take into serious consideration the whole body of the present laws." They should compile "new, good, equal, just, and necessary laws, plain, easy, and free from all dilemmas and ambiguities," with the "old names and distinctions as of Common, Civil, and Statute Laws ... repealed

ed., *Lawes and Liberties of 1660*, 31, title *Ferryes*, §2; 36, title *Heresie of Quakers*, §9; 62, title *Money*, §2; 78, title *Wampampeag*; 14, title *Charges Publick*, §3. Jonathan Barth, "'A Peculiar Stampe of Our Own': The Massachusetts Mint and the Battle over Sovereignty, 1652–1691," *William and Mary Quarterly* 87 (Sept., 2014): 490–525. Mark Peterson, *The City State of Boston* (Princeton: Princeton Univ. Press, 2019), 43–54.

28 Shurtleff, ed., *MGCR*, 4 (Part 2): 453 (May 1670), 467–69 (Oct., 1670), 514 (May 1672), 559 (May 1673).

and taken away for ever." Finally, "if public schools were in every parish erected for teaching to read and write the English tongue," the law could be accessed even by the "vulgar."[29]

The Leveller pamphleteer and close confidant of John Lilburne, Richard Overton, demanded "all Laws of the Land (locked up from common capacities in the Latin or French tongues)" be "translated into the English tongue." This included "all records, orders, processes, writs, and other proceedings," which should be "issued forth in the English tongue ... without all or any Latin or French Phrases or Terms." Then, the "meanest English commoner that can but read written hand in his own tongue may fully understand his own proceedings in the Law." To support such reforms Overton suggested that every English town "destitute of free-schools (for the due nurture and education of children)" be provided a "competent number of such schools founded, erected, and endowed at the public charges." This would ensure that "few or none of the *free men of England* may, for the future, be ignorant of reading and writing." Albertus Warren warned fellow lawyers not to object that "ordinary men will not be much wiser" by the law's translation into English. At least "they will be better satisfied, if not with the reason of the law (because perhaps they cannot reach it)," by the refreshment of their "spirits" when "it shall lie in their own powers to be their own counselors." Warren rejected the era's motto that "ignorance is the nurse of civil devotion." Instead, he believed that until every Englishman could "read his duty in English and look into that which must regulate his deportment and interest civil" would the "reason of law be cleared." Or, as the Leveller William Walwyn warned, the "*greatest safety* will be found in open and universal justice, who relieth on any other will be deceived."[30]

---

29 Benjamin Nicholson, *The Lawyers Bane* (1647); *Thomason Tracts* E401 (36), Reel 63, 1–3, 6–7; *Early English Books Online* (http://name.umdl.umich.edu/A89678.0001.001). Austin Woolrych, *From Commonwealth to Protectorate*, 273. Donald Veall, *The Popular Movement for Law Reform*, 74. "Whilst the outcome of the Civil War was in doubt, the law pamphlets were mainly confined to complaints about the ecclesiastical courts and imprisonment for debt, but after the decisive defeat of the Royalist forces at Naseby in June 1645, the whole field of law began to be questioned. The most active periods for law reform pamphlets were 1646–1649, the time of Leveller ascendancy," and "1653, the year of the Barebones Parliament." John Rees, *The Leveller Revolution*, 76. "A core of Leveller activists remained engaged in writing, printing and distributing material throughout the 1640s. Lilburne, Overton, Walwyn, Larner, Prince, the Chidleys ... sustained the production of revolutionary publications in illegal conditions for a decade. They were hunted, prosecuted, and imprisoned throughout. They printed everything from single-sheet petitions and leaflets to substantial books and ... newspapers."

30 Richard Overton, *Appeale from the Degenerate Representative Body* (1647), 85–6. Albertus Warren, *The Royalist Reformed: Or Considerations of Advice to Gentlemen, Divines, Lawyers* (1650), 35, 39–41; *Thomason Tracts* E582 (4), Reel 89. William Walwyn, *England's*

*An Experimental Essay* observed, since the "Common Law in England consisteth of many ancient customs … to rectify inconveniences in those customs, as grievances have arisen, statutes have been made from time to time in Parliaments, which hath caused a multiplying of laws … to the puzzling of all people who are not lawyers." To remedy this state of affairs it was necessary to establish the law "one way alike throughout the kingdom," so "every understanding man would be as well able to judge of right, as any judge of the law now is, or can be." For example, "if there were a law made, that whosoever did hurt another by word or deed, should make recompense to the party hurt, according to the quality of offense, people would be more careful." Now, on the other hand, "none know now how to have recompense but a lawyer, and that with more expense of money and time than most injuries are worth." Without a "compass of the laws" people "care not what they do." If Parliament enacted a "very brief" corpus of laws, the "whole sum of the law would all be rendered useless by the former ordering of matters," and to replace the "vast body of the law, a few plain brief laws like a new Magna Charta might be made." Based on the maxim "*Salus Populi and Suprema Lex*"—the public good is the supreme law—the "brief contents of all the laws might be printed in a table or little book, for every one that can read to make use of." According to David Underdown, "Salus Populi … is repeatedly echoed in Army and Leveller propaganda in the autumn of 1648," in part, to "justify a thorough-going program of constitutional reform." A year earlier, at Putney, the Army's draft of a written constitution, *An Agreement of the People*, was introduced in meetings between officers and Leveller agitators led by Colonel Thomas Rainsborough, whose extended family resided in Boston in the 1630's.[31]

Now, comparatively, let's consider a handful of the Bay colony's achievements to this same point in time. School legislation required both town schoolhouses and parental instruction of the *Capital Laws*. A system of county

*Lamentable Slavery* (1645), in William Haller ed., *Tracts on Liberty* (New York: Columbia Univ. Press, 1934), 3: 318. Perez Zagorin, *A History of Political Thought in the English Revolution* (New York: Humanities Press, 1966), 19–29. Barbara Shapiro, *Law Reform in Early Modern England*, 106–11, 124. Henry Parker (a lawyer himself) opposed the Leveller law reform program. David Como, "Secret Printing and the Crisis of 1640," 82. "The Levellers did not just publish books, they were masters of the art of print propaganda" and operated "underground presses and distribution networks."

31 *An Experimental Essay touching the Reformation of the Laws of England* (August 17, 1648), 1–5; *Thomason Tracts* E459 (20), Reel 73. David Underdown, *Pride's Purge* (London: George Allen & Unwin, 1971), 123. Gary De Krey, "Amon Wilbee and Leveller Beginnings, 1647–8," *English Historical Review* 137 (April 2022): 444. Adrian Tinniswood, *The Rainborowes* (New York: Basic Books, 2013), 58–9, 72–3.

courts meeting in quarterly sessions provided access to debt collection and other processes. A system of debtor attachment was expediting seizures of real and personal property, in which a debtor's imprisonment was the last resort. Publication of colonial law was clarifying economic regulations by informing buyer and seller on the legal means to execute market transactions, including the provision of weights and measures. Printed laws in books, interim pamphlets, and single sheets were readily available, many at public charge. Finally, owing to the laws' dissemination, and periodic reissuance, colonists need not fear state-sponsored market bounty-hunters. Most importantly, the introduction to the *Laws and Liberties of 1660*'s explained how publication of the laws would reinforce the legitimacy of the Massachusetts commonwealth:

> When laws may be read in men's lives, they appear more beautiful than in the fairest print, and promise a longer duration than engraved in marble. Weaker fences will secure against gentle creatures, though walls of brass be insufficient against forcible intruders. *If breach of order doth argue violence of men, more than weakness of the law, it will be every man's prudence to defend the authority of the laws, to avoid the censure of* [*the*] *impetuous, and to cover rather than make gaps, whereat the most innocent may enter and destroy that provision which was made for their preservation.*[32]

32 William Whitmore, ed., *Lawes and Liberties of 1660*, 120. *For the More Equal Distribution of the Law Books when they shall be Printed*, in Nathaniel Shurtleff, ed., *MGCR*, 4 (Part 1): 422 (May 31, 1660). David Hall, *A Reforming People: Puritanism and the Transformation of Public Life in New England*, 147–54. Michael Winship, *Hot Protestants: A History of Puritanism in England and America* (New Haven: Yale Univ. Press, 2018), 166–67. Christopher Tomlins, *Freedom Bound: Law, Labor, and Civic Identity in Colonizing English America, 1580–1865* (Cambridge: Cambridge Univ. Press, 2010), 246–58. "The relationship between the colony's settler inhabitants and law throughout the first generation of settlement is best represented in language that appears in the *Lawes and Libertyes of 1648*, as the product of a struggle over the 'Countenance of Authority.' The phrase signifies acceptance of the legitimacy of governmental rule over the lives, liberties, and properties of inhabitants, but simultaneously conveys two fundamental principles: that rule should have a definite basis or expression rather than be discretionary and mysterious; and hence, that it should be knowable."

# PART 4

## *Transatlantic Legal Reform and Popular Sovereignty*

CHAPTER 9

# Penal Laws, Debt, and Early Modern Markets

In the first chapter we saw a partnership between Christian and civic humanism, under the common banner of a Commonwealth reform movement, that ultimately helped produce Massachusetts *Laws and Liberties* in 1648. And as initially mentioned in the introduction, an important aspect of the remaining part of this story will be the Levellers, a still relatively mysterious group of reformers who emerged in the latter half of the 1640's and preferred to be called "agitators." One can usefully think of the group as the first modern political activists with a special talent for using the era's media (the printing press facilitating quick publication of everything from single broadsheets to books) intended to shape public opinion. There has been much valuable recent work on their activities, but the challenge in judging their historic significance remains. The Levellers represent a rare occurrence in history before our modern era, when "ordinary" people took "center stage" in the historical drama spurred on by unprecedented events that saw London under almost constant upheaval, featuring violent riots alongside massive peaceful demonstrations, and constant public petitioning of Parliament by hundreds to thousands of Londoners. Concomitantly, the city printing presses exploded with thousands of pamphlets and broadsides of every political persuasion. With the defeat of Charles I in the latter half of the 1640's, Parliament's victorious armies became a political force comprised mostly of propertyless men. This has, in part, led to accusations that the Leveller movement itself was a proto-Marxian or communist ideology, even though its leadership disavowed any intention to redistribute property or anything of the sort. What has been overlooked are the consequences of well-intended regulations' (and some not so well intentioned) destructive impact on English markets, aggravated by obsolete methods of exchange in a pre-contract economy. Essentially, commoners, yeomen, and workmen of all types who had to "make a living" ultimately fought some of England's bloodiest battles and suffered terribly during the wartime years. Once their sacrifices had been made in blood they endeavored to better their condition, and those of their families, very similar to the impulse that caused Massachusetts freemen to cross a vast ocean on a slim hope that they might make a better world for themselves in what they considered to be a wilderness.[1]

1 Neil Hopkins, Will Coster, "The Levellers, Political Literacy, and Contemporary Citizenship Education in England," *Education, Citizenship, and Social Justice* 14.1 (2019): 74. "The name

 | DOI:10.1163/9789004706347_011

While Law French and statutory law illustrate the inaccessibility of English law, the reasons behind the English people's need to access the law in their daily economic lives are amongst the more challenging aspects to unravel. First, as David Wooton has reminded us, during this era there was no "freedom to buy and sell: quite apart from government granted monopolies … selling could take place only under carefully controlled conditions" like state-sanctioned market-days. Second, yeoman, tradesmen, and merchants supported reform because their daily survival required navigation of a labyrinth of English law (statutory and common law). A leading factor in the law's complexity and avaricious operation in markets was caused by parliamentary "penal laws"—more commonly known as means for religious persecution in the latter seventeenth century—that allowed "informers" to seize illicit goods and reap one-half of any fine levied, with the remainder going to the crown. In the absence of a public uniformed enforcement, a series of parliamentary statutes authorized private agents to enforce statutory market regulations on a fee basis that became a means to raise state revenue. Predictably, once bounties were proffered matters soon got out of hand.[2]

---

'Leveller' came from the tradition of popular rural protest that existed in England, particularly focused on resistance to changes in agricultural practice and ownership. It was used in the Midland Riots of 1607 because the rioters levelled the hedges that divided and enclosed previously common land … In its early stages, members of the movement, like John Lilburne, preferred to think of themselves as 'agitators'." Rachel Foxley, *The Levellers* (Manchester: Manchester Univ. Press, 2013). John Rees, *The Leveller Revolution* (London: Versa, 2016). Michael Braddick, *The Common Freedom of the People: John Lilburne and the English Revolution* (Oxford: Oxford Univ. Press, 2018). William Ball, *The Rule of a Freeborne People* (June 18, 1646), 15; in *Thomason Tracts* E341(1) Reel 55. "[W]hat can be of more dangerous consequence" than when "opinion[s] … take root in the minds of the common people? And what can sooner cause them to take root then that they find and read a printed book?"

2 David Wooton, ed., *Divine Right and Democracy* (New York: Penguin Books, 1986), 25. Also, "[g]uilds exercised a monopoly control over many trades." M.W. Beresford, "The Common Informer, Penal Statutes, and Economic Regulation," *Economic History Review* 10 (1957): 221–37. After examining Exchequer records for Michaelmas term Beresford discovered that in one year, 1615, 185 penal suits claimed "£555,000 in fines for wool illegally sold." Geoffrey Elton, "Informing for Profit: A Sidelight of Tudor Methods of Law-Enforcement," *Cambridge Historical Journal* 11 (1953): 149–67. G.R. Elton, "Reform by Statute: Thomas Starkey's Dialogue and Thomas Cromwell's Policy," *Proceedings of the British Academy* 54 (1968): 165–88. "Notes: The History and Development of Qui Tam," *Washington University Law Quarterly* (1972): 81–115. W.H. Bryson, *The Equity Side of the Exchequer* (Cambridge: Cambridge Univ. Press, 1975), 9–33, 93–105. Whitney Jones, *The Tudor Commonwealth: 1529–1559* (London: Athalone Press, 1970), 13, 30, 167, 206. Margaret Davies, *The Enforcement of English Apprenticeship: 1563–1642* (Cambridge: Harvard Univ. Press, 1956), 21–30, 65–66. William Harrison, *The Description of England*, ed. Georges Edelen, (Washington: Folger Shakespeare Library, 1968; reprint, 1994), 175–76, 246–47, 434–45. Francis Bremer, *John Winthrop* (Oxford: Oxford Univ. Press, 2003), 15.

To aggravate this situation, the crown sold franchises to enforce penal laws which included an exclusive monopoly right to bring suits on certain regulations. Eventually, these grants featured subsidiary rights saleable to informers who would actually file the suits. Powerful syndicates soon formed to reap great profit, wielding considerable influence in court and Parliament. Ultimately, informers employed tactics such as threatening suits against market participants to elicit bribes to withdraw their action; costs of traveling to London and legal representation made this a very effective means of coercion. Edward Coke bewailed the subversion of penal laws' original intent to benefit the common welfare, "under the reverend mantle of law and justice instituted for protection of the innocent, and the good of the commonwealth," informers "vex and depauperize the subject and commonly the poorer sort, for malice or private ends, and never the love of justice." Coke's "favorite example" of abuse was a 1364 statutory penalty regulating poultry prices; since its threshold price to incur a penalty had remained the same while inflation increased prices by about 500%, every poultryman left in the kingdom was in violation of this statute and subject to a suit. Conrad Russell termed the sum of these practices "perilously close to blackmail."[3]

"The England in which these men had been born was undergoing vast economic changes that had forced reconsideration of traditional economic practices." Stephen Foster, *The Long Argument* (Chapel Hill: Univ. of North Carolina Press, 1991), 110–14. "The years 1629 and 1630 were certainly bleak: a pervasive crisis in employment in the textile industries was followed hard by a particularly poor harvest ... The problem was not ... depression per se, any more than it was Catholic military successes. Rather, the real provoking evil could be found in the ... the intertwined vices of ... outright cruelty and dishonesty ... Winthrop attributed the danger of social conflict ... more to the shortsighted selfishness of the rich as to the desperation of the poor."

3 Edward Coke, *The Third Part of the Institutes* (London: E.&R. Brooke, 1797), 191–94 (Ch. 88, *Against Vexatious Relators, Informers, and Promoters upon Penal Statutes*). Stephen White, *Sir Edward Coke and "The Grievances of the Commonwealth"* (Chapel Hill: Univ. of North Carolina Press, 1981), 27–85. M.W. Beresford, "The Common Informer," 236. Conrad Russell, *Causes of the English Civil War* (Oxford: Clarendon Press, 1990), 176–82. *An Act concerning Informers*, SR, 1: 378–79 (37 Ed. III ch. 3 (1364)); SR, 4 (Part 2): 801–2 (31 Eliz. I, ch. 5 (1588)); "For that divers of the Queen Majesties' Subjects be daily, unjustly vexed and disquieted by divers common Informers upon Penal Statutes, notwithstanding any former Statute that hath been heretofore made against these disorders." Christopher Hill, *Intellectual Origins of the English Revolution*, 2nd ed., (Oxford: Clarendon Press, 1997), 228. Coke "systematized English law, and ... continued the process of liberalizing it [by] adapting it to the needs of a commercial society. In so doing he had to challenge ... monopolies and gilded privileges, arbitrary taxation and arbitrary arrest, [and] paternal control over the economic life of the country. This brought the common law into conflict with the prerogative and its courts." Wilfred Prest, "Judicial Corruption in Early Modern England," *Past and Present* 133 (1991): 67–95. Jessica Warner, et. al., "A Predatory Social Structure: Informers in Westminster, 1737–1741," *Journal*

One of the earliest informers who attempted to collect fines under the penal laws' regulation of trade during the first half of the sixteenth century, George Whelplay, entered a plea of "qui tam"—or "as much for the king as for myself"—before the Exchequer of Pleas. This was an extension of Exchequer's jurisdiction (normally restricted to cases of crown revenue), allowing informers to bring suits upon a statutory fine enacted to the crown's benefit. The plea reflected a penal statute's standard proviso that the informer would collect one-half the fine or value of confiscated materials, with the other half going to the crown. After Whelplay had entered his plea before Exchequer, the Barons decided which law was applicable in the present case, and then sent it back to a county court to be heard and decided before a local jury. He regularly lost his suits despite overwhelming evidence, and even with pressure on jurors from Star Chamber to convict.[4]

Operating penal statutes included regulations of enclosures, price gouging, and usury. In the case of enclosures, for example, seven statutes had been enacted from 1485 to 1559 to prevent or reverse the process. Because the nobility and gentry constituted local law enforcement for parliamentary statute and royal proclamation in their roles as justices of the peace, however, they were uniquely placed to frustrate enforcement of penal regulations that ran counter to their own personal economic interests. This situation, and its inherent contradictions, was aptly described by Thomas Starkey, "Princes and lords seldom look to the good order and wealth of their subjects; only, they look to the receiving of their rents and revenues of their lands." If Parliament relied on county-level enforcement, or precisely those jurisdictions controlled by the very men penal laws sought to regulate, any hope for reform was doomed. These circumstances had been one of the primary causes of Kett's Rebellion (as covered at the end of Chapter 2), explaining earlier efforts of Henry VIII's secretary and leading advisor, Thomas Cromwell, attempted new reforms. Similarly, Hugh Latimer urged Edward VI and his councilors to authorize "promoters" or informers to bring suits against those who flouted the King's laws, "There lacketh one thing in this realm that it hath need of, for God's sake make some promoters, such as were in King Henry the Seventh's days, … men to promote

*of Interdisciplinary History* 30 (2000): 617–34. William Holdsworth, *A History of English Law* (Boston: Little, Brown, and Co., 1924), 4: 343–61.

4 Geoffrey Elton, "Informing for Profit: A Sidelight of Tudor Methods of Law-Enforcement," *Cambridge Historical Journal* 11 (1953): 149–67. "Notes: The History and Development of Qui Tam," *Washington University Law Quarterly* (1972): 81–115. W. H. Bryson, *The Equity Side of the Exchequer* (Cambridge: Cambridge Univ. Press, 1975), 9–33, 93–105.

... transgressors" such as "rent-raisers, oppressors of the poor, extortioners, bribers, usurers."[5]

While the young King and his council were aware of the need for some measure of reform, they were far more alarmed at Kett's rising in Norfolk that threatened his reign, and they promptly dispatched military forces to suppress it. Edward VI died in 1553 before any substantive reform was realized, but adjustments were soon achieved under Queen Mary (1553–1558). A 1558 statute provided, any informer who was frustrated pursuing qui tam on a penal statute in local tribunals could appeal to the central courts at Westminster. There a new jury could be chosen and the case would be heard anew, usually before the Barons of Exchequer.[6] The next adjustment came under Queen Elizabeth (1558–1603) in a meeting of all the common law judges in a forum known as Exchequer Chamber. Chief Justice of the Court of Common Pleas, James Dyer (1512–1582), reported that the justices convened in November of 1563 "by command of the Queen to devise how ... penal statutes ... would be best put in[to] execution." The issue before the court was whether informers, by the crown's command, had standing to file suits of qui tam at the central courts at Westminster without first appearing in local courts? Nine of the twelve judges thought it within the power of the Queen's "prerogative" to stipulate which jurisdiction could hear such suits. Just two years later, however, the Queen issued a proclamation to protect informers after reports of "great disorders" saw them "abused" and "beaten" around Westminster Hall.[7]

---

5 Thomas Starkey, *A Dialogue Between Reginald Pole and Thomas Lupset*, ed. Kathleen Burton (London: Chatto and Windus, 1948), 86–7, 111–14. G.R. Elton, "Reform by Statute: Thomas Starkey's Dialogue and Thomas Cromwell's Policy," 165–88. Whitney Jones, *The Tudor Commonwealth*, 30, 167. T.F.T. Plucknett, "Some Proposed Legislation of Henry VIII," *RHS Transactions* 19 (1936): 119–44.

6 *SR*, 4 (Part 1): 328 (4–5 Phil. & Mary, ch. 7). Margaret Davies, *The Enforcement of English Apprenticeship: A Study in Applied Mercantilism, 1563–1642* (Cambridge: Harvard University Press, 1956), 30. Davies reported that "the calendar of informations on penal statutes in the Exchequer grows heavier ... from 1557, with a sharper acceleration in the 1560's." M.W. Beresford, "The Common Informer," 222–32. D.L. Thomas, and N.E. Evans, "John Shakespeare in the Exchequer," *Shakespeare Quarterly* 35 (1984): 315–318.

7 James Dyer, *Reports of Cases in the Reigns of Hen. VIII, Ed. VI, Q. Mary, and Q. Eliz.*, trans. John Vaillant, 3 vols., (London: J. Butterworth, 1794), 2: 236.a. Margaret Davies, *The Enforcement of English Apprenticeship*, 26, 65. *Journals of the House of Commons: 1547–1629* (London, 1802), 1: 73. In October 1566, Elizabeth's minister Sir Nicholas Throckmorton put forward a "Bill touching Informations upon Penal Statutes, with Costs for Defendants." The parliamentary session ended before it was considered. Robert Steele, ed., *A Bibliography of Royal Proclamations of the Tudor and Stuart Sovereigns* (Oxford: Clarendon Press, 1910), 1: 66 (#620).

Rioters undoubtedly resented the new regime's operation, in so far as it removed the regulation and prosecution of market offenses from local jurisdictions to the national level. Another irritant was that the force policing English markets did not consist of a regulated officialdom. Instead, private individuals, similar to bounty hunters, were pursuing statutory penalties for personal profit regardless of the public good or general economic health. William Harrison provided a firsthand description: many "poor men are daily abused and utterly undone by sundry varlets that go about the country as promoters, or brokers between the pettifoggers of the law and the common people, only to kindle and espy coals of contention whereby the one side may reap commodity."[8]

Edward Coke led parliamentary reform in 1621 and 1624; the former session was prorogued on account of Francis Bacon's impeachment before any reforms were realized. Coke acknowledged, "many penal laws obsolete, and in time grown impossible, or inconvenient to be performed, remained as snares [to] … vex and entangle the subject." Although Coke and Francis Bacon were life-long enemies, they agreed on the need for wide ranging statutory reform. In 1593 a young Bacon sponsored the creation of a commission to "lessen the volume of laws being so many in number that neither common people can practice them, nor the lawyer sufficiently understand them." A bill to create a "special commission to examine penal laws" was introduced in 1614, but James I prorogued (the Addled) Parliament before it could be considered. Despite these initiatives to reduce the number of penal laws, Parliament's singular achievement came in 1624 with the repeal of sixty statutes, of which fifty were economic regulations. A member of the repealing committee, William Hakewill, thought two hundred and fifty laws were "fit to be repealed, which remain only as so many snares to entrap men." Charles I appointed itinerant royal commissions to police penal law abuses. But follow-on commissions were soon dispatched to mitigate their predecessors' corrupt behavior. G.E. Aylmer noted that many of these reforming commissions eventually gained scandalous reputations, as many members sat on the initial "less reputable ones," sometimes simultaneously.[9]

---

8 William Harrison, *The Description of England* (London, 1577–87), ed. George Edelen, 175–6.

9 Wilfrid Prest, *The Rise of the Barristers: A Social History of the English Bar (1590–1640)* (Oxford: Clarendon Press, 1991), 296–98. "Private law and litigation now play such a relatively insignificant part in the life of most western societies that a major effort of imagination is required to grasp their central prominence in early modern times. The late sixteenth and early seventeenth centuries constituted possibly the most litigious era in English history, as well as a time when legal forms and institutions impinged upon almost every aspect of daily life. The explosion of litigation which so alarmed contemporaries was facilitated by the low initial cost of going to law, and the fact that attorneys commonly allowed their clients to sue on credit … [T]he players were not drawn solely from the landed elite,

English Common Law's regulation of real property holdings, especially as related to creditor/debtor relations, exacerbated the chaos that penal statutes wreaked in English markets. Perhaps the greatest triumph of modern law has been its decriminalization of creditor/debtor relations. During the 17th and 18th centuries British and colonial debtors were routinely imprisoned until they satisfied their creditors in an era devoid of credit agencies, instant credit checks, or fine print on bills of sales. Debts had to be litigated one at a time, as necessary. As a result of these historical circumstances, G.B. Warden recognized that the "most pervasive object" of English "reformers arose out of problems of indebtedness and property." Only in the modern era has contract law, or regulations of buying and selling, become a matter subsumed to the point its operation goes largely unnoticed. After Massachusetts colonists sailed for the New World, it took several centuries to settle the law of contract, mainly via the plea trespass-on-the-case. Jumping ahead several centuries to illustrate that era's means of economic transactions, since the early 1800's US contract law's guiding principle has been *caveat emptor*, or that a contract's written provisions are dispositive unless fraud is alleged and proven. Although contractual agreements and obligations came to be actionable via writs of trespass-on-the-case over several centuries, one still had to appear in court where outcomes were uncertain. Modern contract law has successfully mitigated such suits, so that successive generations have become accustomed to everyday economic transactions without much thought of a lawsuit. Before the modern era of contract each transaction raised such a possibility, and the fear of one.[10]

---

but also included peasants, artisans, craftsmen, and merchants ... For most litigants of all classes, going to law, far from being a game, was rather, a deadly serious enterprise, hazardous of outcome and proverbially expensive in 'both charge and travail'." Edward Coke, *The Third Part of the Institutes* (London: 1797), 191. Stephen White, *Sir Edward Coke and "The Grievances of the Commonwealth,"* 27–85. Barbara Shapiro, *Law Reform in Early Modern England* (Oxford: Hart Publishing, 2019), 64–78. James I also supported law reform, and specifically penal statutes. M.W. Beresford, "The Common Informer, Penal Statutes, and Economic Regulation," 228–36. Margaret Davies, *Enforcement of English Apprenticeship*, 20–28, 71–2. *SR*, vol. 4 (Part 2): 1214–15 (21 Jac. I, ch. 4); 1235–40 (21 Jac. I, ch. 28). Wallace Notestein, ed., *Commons Debates: 1621* (New Haven: Yale Univ. Press, 1935), 2: 72. *Winthrop Papers*, 1: 309. Maija Jansson, ed., *Proceedings in Parliament 1614 (House of Commons)* (Philadelphia: American Philosophical Society, 1988), 49 (n.7). G.E. Aylmer, "Attempts at Administrative Reform, 1625–40," *English Historical Review* 72 (1957): 230–32. John Kenyon, ed., *The Stuart Constitution*, 2nd ed., (Cambridge: Cambridge Univ. Press, 1986), 104–6. Linda Peck, *Court Patronage and Corruption in Early Stuart England* (London: Routledge, 1993), 134–60.

10 G.B. Warden, "Law Reform in New England and England," *William and Mary Quarterly* 35 (1978): 681. Hugh Peters, *A Word for the Army and Two Words to the Kingdom* (1647) in *Harleian Miscellany* (London: 1810), 6: 72. "[I]f I might not offend court and gentry, I would

In the preceding Medieval manor regime, a comparatively small number of managers (or stewards) had administered the creditor/debtor relations of the entire kingdom. Manorial lords held their own courts to enable tenants to transact business, and so a local economy was conducted with the lord's steward in attendance. Instead of specie, labor and crops were exchanged between the tenants themselves, and in homage to their lord. The manorial steward also litigated in the King's courts for his lordship, when royal fees were at issue, or after a dispute with an entity or person outside the manor was joined. After a period of relative prosperity for England's peasant class in the wake of the Black Death, with the decline of the manorial system, and enclosure of lands for agricultural usage (mainly livestock grazing), the creditor/debtor regime in localities was gradually supplanted by suits brought to the central courts in London at Westminster Hall. In the period between 1580 to 1640 suits brought to the royal courts of King's Bench, Common Pleas, Exchequer, Chancery, and Requests averaged 60,000 actions annually, in tandem with 400,000 cases heard in the kingdom's municipal courts, with rural courts adding 500,000 cases. This volume of cases reflected an increase in market transactions, making debtor law evermore integral to market activity.[11]

say the wrapping up of so many of them in gowns, and scuffling at Westminster, is rather a mark of their meanness and jejuneness, and our slavery and folly ... that, to this day, we can neither buy nor sell, convey nor make testaments, without great and questionable parchments." Harold Berman, *Law and Revolution* (Cambridge: Belknap Press, 2003), 2: 337–41 ("Contract"). Daniel Hulsebosch, "The Ancient Constitution and the Expanding Empire: Sir Edward Coke's British Jurisprudence," *Law and History Review* 21 (Autumn 2003): 453–54.

11 C.W. Brooks, *Pettyfoggers and Vipers of the Commonwealth* (Cambridge: Cambridge Univ. Press, 1986), 70–9, 93–5. From 1560–1640, rising economic activity in England drove an increase of litigation in the royal courts. By the latter date actions of debt accounted for 88% of all Common Pleas business, compared with 67% in 1560. J.H. Baker, "The English Legal Profession, 1450–1550," in Wilfrid Prest, ed., *Lawyers in Early Modern Europe and America* (New York: Holmes & Meier Publishers, 1981), 16–41. Alan Kulikoff, *From British Peasants to Colonial American Farmers* (Chapel Hill: Univ. of North Carolina Press, 2000), 7–22. A.W.B. Simpson, *Introduction to the History of the Land Law* (Oxford: Oxford Univ. Press, 1961), 1–76. Austin Woolrych, *Britain in Revolution, 1625–1660* (Oxford: Oxford Univ. Press, 2002), 14. "The greatest strains upon English society had been the relentless rise in prices, already almost sixfold, and a doubling of the population from about 2.3 million to almost 4.6 million in 1625. Wage-earners were a minority in this pre-industrial society, but there was a surplus of labor, and the real value of wages fell by half. Small landholders, mostly customary tenants with a plot that they could regard as their own and hope to pass to their heirs, were more numerous than wage-laborers." William Holdsworth, *A History of English Law* (Boston: Little, Brown, and Co., 1924), 4: 364. "The Agrarian Revolution: ... This revolution involved the abolition of the system of common field cultivation, and the substitution for it of individual ownership or occupation of continuous tracts of land,

Although enclosure [i.e., fencing-off] of English farmland would begin to fill the ranks of an industrial workforce in the eighteenth century, until then the kingdom's population was dispersed, as industry had yet to concentrate in the largest cities, with London's population of half a million inhabitants by 1700 being the exception. As the sixteenth century wound down, and the seventeenth century progressed, increasing numbers of laborers, farmers, tradesmen, and craftsmen found themselves on their own without recourse to the manor lord or common fields. In turn, these men, along with a rising merchant class, filled Westminster Hall's court dockets as litigants in creditor/debtor actions. Craig Muldrew confirmed the "great increase in the number of disputes was the result of economic growth, … [as] most litigation throughout the country involved debts and contracts," totaling 80% to 90% of cases before common law courts. Contemporaries noted swarms of litigants overwhelming the courts, "how can the judges at Westminster confine and contract all the Law of England in and to Westminster, and into 4 terms yearly, to be only determined by them?"[12]

The era's process of debt collection greatly aggravated these matters, because it was a complex maze of processes with gatekeepers posted at every turn. An expensive document from the Chancery was required to initiate a suit, and

which could be devoted either to pasture or to arable farms. Consequently, the old cultivating community was broken up, many of the smaller owners were evicted from the land, and rights of common either in the open fields or in the waste disappeared."

12 Craig Muldrew, "The Culture of Reconciliation: Community and the Settlement of Economic Disputes in Early Modern England," *Historical Journal* 39 (Dec., 1996): 915–22. C.W. Brooks, *Pettyfoggers and Vipers of the Commonwealth*, 94–6. John Jones, *Lawyers UnMask'd or, A Discovery of their Matchless Villanies* (1653), 17; *Wing* J971A, Reel 1507: 3. Edward Coke, *The Third Part of the Institutes* (London: 1797), 192. "Informers, and many times the king's attorney, drew all informations for any offense, in any place with the realm of England against any penal law, to some of the king's courts at Westminster, to the intolerable charge, vexation, and trouble of the subject." *An Act for the Punishment of Vagabonds, and Relief of the Poor and Impotent*, in SR, vol. 4 (Part 2/B): 590–98 (14 Eliz. ch. 5 (1572)),—"I. Where all the parts of this Realm of England and Wales be presently with Rogues, Vagabonds, and Sturdy Beggars exceedingly pestered, by means whereof daily happeneth in the same Realm horrible Murders, Theft, and other great outrage … & to the great annoyance of the Common Weale." Whitney Jones, *The Tudor Commonwealth*, 117. "The allusion to beggary points to that aspect of poverty which probably aroused most concern in Tudor England: the wandering beggars … The great increase in numbers which made them appear a social menace probably took place from about 1520." Alan Kulikoff, *From British Peasants to Colonial American Farmers*, 23–27. Malcom Gaskill, *Between Two Worlds* (New York: Basic Books, 2014), 6. "Smallholdings were consolidated, arable land converted to pasture and orchards. Tenants, already hit by lower wages and higher prices, were squeezed out, swelling the ranks of the laboring poor."

additional actions followed upon a defendant's nonappearance; once he did appear it took several terms of court to try a debtor's case. Even then he could enter a plea to "wage his law," whereby common law tradition allowed him to summon oath-takers who, by reciting a precise form of testimony, could clear him from the debt by swearing to his honest dealings in the community; these "compurgators" were often for hire. To make matters worse, as Craig Muldrew discovered, "[w]itnesses seem to have been the most important form of security of debts and other agreements through all levels of society." Obviously, in an economy in which ever greater numbers of transactions were being made breakdowns were inevitable. To relieve the resulting backlogs of cases, English judges created summary processes to expedite seizures, including making debtors liable to arrest and imprisonment contingent only upon the sworn testament of his creditor. John Cooke, one of the era's leading reformers who ultimately took on the infamous role of lead prosecutor of Charles I as the Commonwealth's Solicitor General, noted that creditors were also victims of the current creditor/debtor regime owing to the immense difficulties involved in collecting bills and wages. From experience, Cooke knew many litigants who had "just debts owing them" but could not afford to "pay officers fees to recover them"; a "poor man cannot sue for his wages … for a matter of 20 shillings," because it "will cost him forty in the getting of it."[13]

13 John Cooke, *Vindication of the Professors and Profession of the Law* (1646), 7; in *Thomason Tracts* E320 (17), Reel 52. Marjorie Blatcher, *The Court of King's Bench: 1450–1550* (London: Athlone Press, 1978), 105–66. Geoffrey Robertson, *The Tyrannicide Brief: The Story of the Man who Sent Charles I to the Scaffold* (New York: Pantheon Books, 2005), 10–14. John Cooke's law reform tracts were "visionary," advocating "abolition of the death sentence other than for murder and treason; the end of imprisonment for debt; the abolition of Latin in the courts and many other reforms that did not come about for centuries. He was the first to claim that poverty was a major cause of crime (so offenders who acted from hunger and desperation should be put on probation)." Craig Muldrew, "The Culture of Reconciliation: Community and the Settlement of Economic Disputes in Early Modern England," 926–27. "A large part of the population was still illiterate, and for those who could manage some reading, or perhaps writing, the complexity of legal forms must have been daunting, or simply too expensive, as Leveller criticism of the legal system during the civil war era indicates." J.H. Baker, *An Introduction to English Legal History*, 3rd ed., (London: Butterworths, 1990), 367. C.W. Brooks, *Pettyfoggers and Vipers of the Commonwealth*, 70–95. Mark Kishlansky, *A Monarchy Transformed: Britain 1603–1714* (New York: Penguin Books, 1996), 6–33. Barbara Shapiro, *Law Reform in Early Modern England*, 55. "Lawyers and non-lawyers complained of the confusing and disorderly state of the common law, conflicting judicial opinions, and confusion to what statutes were actually in force." Ian Williams, "Perjury, Wager of Law, and Debt in the Elizabethan Star Chamber," *Legal History Miscellany* (Oct. 15, 2019): (https://legalhistorymiscellany.com/2019/10/15/perjury-wager-of-law-and-debt-in-the-elizabethan-star-chamber/).

Ironically, these new processes meant to ameliorate earlier abuses created new injustices, including the "vindictive arrest of enemies, the incarceration of debtors, and their exposure to predatory warders and court officials." Since every institution in the process (from courts to jails) was fee-based, rather than salaried, abuses inevitably arose by manufactured and solicited suits. In 1624, John Winthrop drafted a parliamentary petition objecting to the *Great Delays in Suits of Law*, so great that a "plaintiff or defendant often dieth before the suit be ended." He had personally witnessed many "subjects of this kingdom ... oppressed by chargeable suits and their bodies arrested and imprisoned for every small debt and trespass, to the undoing of many poor families and to the great damage of the Commonwealth." Winthrop's distress was certainly heartfelt, but inherently contradictory; while condemning lawyers for manufacturing suits, which in turn created an insurmountable backlog of cases, he also lamented the interminable and costly proceedings that resulted. Clearly, from a historical perspective, the lack of appropriate regulations in a rapidly expanding economy had undermined both markets and legal process. To the present-day, creditor/debtor regulations are controversial, as what one side advocates as reform is inevitably experienced as injury by the other.[14]

As markets were subject to increasingly corrupt influences present in England during this era, they instilled fear in participants, depressed market activity, encouraged illegal behavior, and even provided some with an impulse to emigrate to foreign shores. In 1628, Reverend John White of Dorchester, England, as advised and assisted by John Winthrop and Reverend Francis Higginson, included the following point in their generic plan for colonial

14 *Common Grievances Groaning for Reformation* (1624), in *Winthrop Papers*, (Boston: MHS, 1929), 1: 295–310. Francis Bremer, *John Winthrop*, 140–41. During this period Winthrop helped draft a statement entitled, "'Common Grievances Groaning for Reformation,' a catalogue of complaints that the godly ... had about the tendencies of their times ... Pauperism and vagrancy were increasing, charity was strained, and theft and crimes of violence were on the rise." Robert Winthrop, ed., *Life and Letters of John Winthrop: 1588–1630* (Boston: MHS, 1863), 1: 220–23. "We find among his papers no less than three original drafts of bills which either were, or were intended to be, introduced into Parliament. They are wholly in his own handwriting, on large paper, with ample margins, and prepared as if for the consideration of a Legislative Committee. One of them is entitled, ... 'An Act for the preventing of the multitude of causeless suits, and of the great vexation of the inferior sort of people thereby', ... A reference to the *Journals of Parliament*, and to the *English Statutes at Large*, proves that the subject-matter of these bills underwent much consideration and much legislation in the years 1626 and 1628. The bills ... never became law." Craig Muldrew, "The Culture of Reconciliation: Community and the Settlement of Disputes in Early Modern England," 929–42. Ian Duffy, "English Bankrupts, 1571–1861," *American Journal of Legal History* 24 (1980): 283–305.

settlement: "[In England] trades are carried on so deceitfully & unrighteously as it is almost impossible for a good upright man to maintain his charge & to live comfortably in his profession." What had been a series of domestic crises during the first decades of the seventeenth century became a national crisis upon the outbreak of military conflict, spanning more than a decade starting from the end of the 1630's; seeing English, Scottish, and Irish armies exploit any civilian population they encountered when they were on the march. There were complaints from the very beginning of the Scottish campaigns, and a few years later contemporaries were lamenting the suffering of the "poor handicraftsmen [who] are already driven to miserable want in all counties, and especially in London." After years of civil war, economic matters reached a crisis point according to the anonymous 1648 pamphlet, *The mournfull Cryes of many thousand Poore Tradesmen, who are ready to famish through decay of Trade*. The tract blamed much of the suffering on high taxes and parliamentary corruption, and only observance of the nation's "common rights and freedoms" could remedy their ills. Otherwise, "let us be governed by plain written laws in our own tongue, and pay your ministers of justice out of a common treasury, that every one may have justice freely and impartially."[15]

The consequences of the flawed regime of 17th century English creditor/debtor regulations operating in a wartime environment provoked repeated petitioning of Parliament (only a handful of examples can be shared in this work). *A Declaration and Appeal* demanded, "being a freeborn people, and no villeins and slaves," Englishmen must not be imprisoned for debt. *Magna Charta* had forbidden freemen from being "outlawed" without "lawful judgment of his peers or by the law of the land." Moreover, their incarceration "tendeth to none other end then to the enrichment of lawyers, attorneys,

15 *General Observations for the plantation of New England* (1628), in Winthrop Papers (Boston: MHS, 1931), 2: 111–12. Wallace Notestein, ed., *The Journal of Sir Simonds D'Ewes* (New Haven: Yale Univ. Press, 1923), 22–23. *The Mournfull Cryes of Many Thousand Poore Tradesmen, who are Ready to Famish through Decay of Trade* (London: 1648); *EEBO* (http://quod.lib.umich.edu/e/eebo2/A89397.0001.001). David Cressy, *England on Edge* (Oxford: Oxford Univ. Press, 2006), 56. "By 1642 the political and economic crises were almost inseparable. Sir Simonds D'Ewes remarked in January 1642, 'all men are put into such a general distraction and fear by present jealousies between his majesty and the parliament there is neither buying nor selling nor almost any commerce or trade' ... Writing in February 1642, Henry Oxinden remarked on the economic impact of the 'great distractions' of the realm. 'The poor handi-craftsmen are already driven to miserable want in all counties and especially in [London]; ... There were petitioning women of a great number last Tuesday at the parliament, and so far as I could learn their great and old grievance was want of trading.'" Ellen McArthur, "Women Petitioners and the Long Parliament," *English Historical Review* 24 (Oct., 1909): 698–709.

solicitors and jailers, and to the utter ruin of thousands of us your oppressed brethren, and of our wives and children." *The Humble Remonstrance* lamented that imprisoned debtors might as well be "persons condemned to the slavery of the gallies" of the "Turks." *A Pitiful Remonstrance* craved "deliverance from this unjust, inhumane slavery of imprisonment for debt, illegally fastened as on us, so, on this whole Nation and their posterity, contrary to the Law of God, and the fundamental great *Charter* of England's Liberty." *The Womens Petition* decried the "Norman Yoke of bondage and oppression ... still continued upon this Nation, by the impious, oppressive, dilatory, and most chargeable practice of the Law, and destructive imprisonment of men and women for debt, in the several prisons ... and dungeons of cruelty in this Land."[16] John Jones condemned the heinous conditions resulting from jailors charging prisoners for food, clothing, and private rooms:

> Further, the sickness of the minds and souls imprisoned is aggravated with the consideration of the wants, and miseries which their wives, children, and families (that were wont to be sustained by their liberties to care and provide for them) must endure by their captivity, ... more sensible of their hunger and thrift, cold, and nakedness when they have sold even their apparel, as well for night as day, to pay their jailers' and their masters' extortions; and prolong their own miseries so far as their abilities last. And the cruelty of their jailers (when they fail to bribe them) in crowding them in dungeons where they must infect one another with a necessitated contagion, caused by their jailers' covetousness, to gain by hiring all the rooms and liberties of the prison, ordained by law to lawful prisoners, to cheaters, voluntary prisoners ... by which they live

16 *The Humble Remonstrance and Complaint of Many Thousands of Poor Distressed Prisoners* (Feb. 3, 1643), 3–8; *Thomason Tracts* E88 (8), Reel 15. *The Humble Petition of the Poor Distressed Prisoners in Ludgate* (Dec. 20, 1644); *Thomason Tracts* E21 (33), Reel 4. *A Declaration and Appeal* (Nov. 1645); *Thomason Tracts* 669 f10 (40), Reel 246. *A Pittiful Remonstrance, or just Complaint* (July 7, 1648): *Thomason Tracts* 669 f17 (68), Reel 246. *Abuses Discovered, whereby ... the Poor Debter and their Families Tyrannically Destroyed* (June 15, 1649); *Thomason Tracts* 669 f14 (41), Reel 246. *The Womens Petition* (Oct. 30, 1651); *Thomason Tracts* 669 f16 (26), Reel 246. William Blackstone, *Commentaries on the Laws of England* (Chicago: Univ. of Chicago Press, 1979), 3: 153–59; 4: 416–17. Craig Muldrew, "The Culture of Reconciliation: Community and the Settlement of Economic Disputes in Early Modern England," 926–27. Norval Morris, and David Rothman, eds., *The Oxford History of the Prison* (Oxford: Oxford Univ. Press, 1995), 80–89, 302–11. Blair Worden, *The Rump Parliament* (Cambridge: Cambridge Univ. Press, 1973), 108–18. Marjorie Blatcher, *The Court of King's Bench*, 162–3. T.F.T. Plucknett, *A Concise History of the Common Law*, 5th ed., (Boston: Little, Brown, and Company, 1956), 22–3.

> riotously upon their creditors charge, and their creditors perish for want of their own.[17]

This economic oppression cried out for reform. On September 4, 1649, Parliament passed its initial reform of creditor/debtor relations, popularly known as the *Five Pound Act*. Prisoners were to be discharged upon an oath that their total possessions did not exceed £5, an amount not including "necessary wearing apparel and bedding for himself, his wife, and children, and tools necessary for his trade or occupation." His creditor was provided thirty-day notification to appear in court to prove a prisoner's oath false. If no action was taken, the prisoner would be released. But this was no bankruptcy action in the modern sense. While the court would provide the prisoner with the tools of his trade, if any, and the means of bare subsistence, the previous debt would stand until he satisfied his creditors. Nevertheless, the act was progressive in recognizing that while incarcerated, or deprived of his tools, a prisoner could neither repay his creditors, nor support his family. Subsequently, several acts authorized a writ of habeas corpus to facilitate a prisoner's access to the oath procedure.[18]

The most fundamental reforms were enacted on October 5, 1653, during the Nominate (or Barebones) Parliament, via legislation entitled, *An Act for the*

---

17 John Jones, *Every Mans Case or, Lawyers Routed* (July 5, 1652), 21–2; *Thomason Tracts* E1406 (2), Reel 181. James Frese, *Every Man's Right* (June 15, 1646), 6–7; *Thomason Tracts* E340 (2), Reel 55. *A Brief Dialogue Between Creditor and Prisoner* (Sept. 5, 1653), 3–8; *Thomason Tracts* E713 (5), Reel 110. W.J. Sheehan, "Finding Solace in Eighteenth-Century Newgate," in J.S. Cockburne, ed., *Crime in England: 1550–1800* (London: Methuen & Co., 1977), 229–45. Donald Veall, *The Popular Movement for Law Reform* (Oxford: Clarendon Press, 1970), 39–63, 112. C.W. Brooks, *Pettyfoggers and Vipers of the Commonwealth*, 143. A.W.B. Simpson, *An Introduction to the History of the Land Law*, 163–94. G.B. Warden, "Law Reform in England and New England," 681. Michael Braddick, *The Common Freedom of the People: John Lilburne and the English Revolution*, 26–27. Seventeenth-century English prisons were "privately run," and those who could afford better accommodations did so and paid for their food as "those working in the prisons often depended on tips and fees." Inmates "able to make financial arrangements could live in some comfort." Those who could not pay faced starvation.

18 C.H. Firth and R.S. Rait, eds., *Acts and Ordinances of the Interregnum: 1642–1660* (London: HMSO, 1911), 2: 240–1, 321–4, 378–79. If the prisoner refused the oath he was to be imprisoned. The Act of April 6, 1650 provided for the temporary release. *A further Additional Act for Relief of Poor Prisoners*, in Ibid., 2: 582 (April 27, 1652). The 1652 act reauthorized the earlier laws. Donald Veall, *The Popular Movement for Law Reform*, 145–50, 148 (n. 2). Blair Worden, *The Rump Parliament*, 107–110. W.J. Jones, "The Foundations of English Bankruptcy: Statutes and Commissions in the Early Modern Period," *Transactions of the American Philosophical Society* 69 (no. 3, 1979): 1–63.

*relief of Creditors and Poor Prisoners*, that accomplished several long sought-after goals. First, county courts were established to hear creditor/debtor litigation, and judges would enjoy commensurate powers within their respective jurisdictions as their brethren on the national level; the necessity of county courts, or accessible justice, was one of the most common demands of reformers. By creating more legal venues for litigation of creditor/debtor disputes, Parliament acknowledged that an expansion of economic activity was overwhelming the national courts at Westminster. The ordinance also authorized judges to expedite auditing the estates of imprisoned debtors, and most importantly, real estate was liable to seizure for repayment of debts. Previously, only merchants could be declared bankrupts and subject to confiscation of their "lands and tenements." Finally, prisoners were to be incarcerated only if they refused restitution. Justice Edward Atkins, who had resigned from the bench after Charles I's execution, and Baron Thorpe issued a report to Parliament on its new legislation. By ordering a review of debt cases already decided, they accused the body of overreaching its authority. The examination of debtors' estates, and follow-on restitutions, would undo property transfers already executed and violate the "fundamental laws of this nation" under which real property was sacrosanct.[19]

On the other side of the Atlantic, Massachusetts not only mirrored the demands of English reformers, it anticipated those reforms, and corrected the stubborn problems that remained. In 1641, the *Body of Liberties* had forbidden the arrest of any colonist for debt if the "law can find competent means of

---

19 Firth and Rait, eds., *Acts and Ordinances of the Interregnum*, 2: 753–64, 860, 888–89, 911–15. Mary Cotterell, "Interregnum Law Reform: The Hale Commission of 1652," *English Historical Review* 83 (1968): 690, 697, 701. Stuart Prall, *The Agitation for Law Reform during the Puritan Revolution: 1640–1660* (The Hague: Martinus Nijhoff, 1966), 60–1, 95–7. "*Relief of Creditors and Poor Prisoners* authorized the appointment of seventeen commissioners to investigate the justifications for debtors' incarceration, and they were to operate free of any 'principles of the common law.' Parliament itself would provide oversight … They were to examine in minute detail the financial conditions of each prisoner for debt, judge his financial soundness and then either declare him bankrupt and confiscate his entire estate, or force the sale of enough property to cover the debts incurred … The corrupt practices of the jailers and of charities for the relief of prisoners were also to be investigated." Donald Veall, *Popular Movement for Law Reform*, 145–51. William Sheppard, *England's Balme* (London: 1657), 56–8; *Thomason Tracts* E1675 (2), Reel 209. Nancy Matthews, *William Sheppard: Cromwell's Law Reformer* (Cambridge: Cambridge Univ. Press, 1984), 7, 34, 104. *Reasons for the Continuance of the Process of Arrest* (June 10, 1659); *Thomason Tracts* 669 f21 (48), Reel 247. G.B. Nourse, "Law Reform Under the Commonwealth and Protectorate," *Law Quarterly Review* 75 (1959): 512–16. *An Ordinance for relief of Creditors and Poor Prisoners* (April 29, 1654), in CSP, *Domestic Series (1654)*, ed. Mary Green, (London: Longman & Co., 1880), 7: 134–35 (#94a.).

satisfaction otherwise from his estate," if not then an arrest should be made. In 1647, the colony forbid marshals from seizing "any man's necessary bedding, apparel tools, or arms, other implements of household which are for the necessary upholding of his life," as Parliament did two years later in its own *Five Pound Act.* In Massachusetts, if a debtor's personal property did not satisfy creditor liens a marshal could seize his "land or person" six years before similar parliamentary enactments. How did a new colony anticipate such reforms? Colonists had experienced the same market inequities and inefficient practices in England, and once the magistrates' resistance was overcome market regulations could be enacted and printed. As for English reforms that resembled already enacted Massachusetts laws, as Nancy Matthews acknowledged, "by the 1650s there was enough information available in England so that any interested observer could acquaint himself with [how the colony's] government and court system … were intended to work, either by studying the printed laws, sermons and pamphlets, or by seeking information from any one of the hundreds of New Englanders who had returned to the mother country since the beginning of the civil war."[20]

Reeling from economic depression, and possessing an abundance of territory, the General Court had little choice but to make real property a fungible asset within its exchange economy. Debtors must not be allowed to shield real property from creditors if its economy was to survive. While lack of specie plagued colonial Massachusetts throughout the Revolution and beyond, land was plentiful until later in the century, in part because no colonial aristocracy dominated land ownership in the colony, as the towns controlled its distribution. Upon Charles II's restoration, with Interregnum ordinances stricken from the rolls, Parliament was compelled to enact new statutes regulating creditor/debtor process in 1661, 1671, and 1678. Although the Privy Council ordered the Bay colony to reestablish debtor imprisonment in the early 1700's, the colony

20 William Whitmore, ed., *Body of Liberties of 1641*, 41 (Lib. 33). Nathaniel Shurtleff, ed., *MGCR*, 1: 304, 307 (Oct. 7, 1641), 2: 204 (Nov. 11, 1647); 4 (Part 2): 42 (May 7, 1662). Ultimately, Massachusetts adopted the specific £5 threshold. Richard Dunn, ed., *Journal of John Winthrop: 1630–1649* (Cambridge: Belknap Press, 1996), 328 (June 1640). Thomas Hutchinson, *History of the Colony and Province of Massachusetts-Bay*, 2nd ed., (London: M. Richardson, 1765), 1: 93–4. Bernard Bailyn, *The New England Merchants*, 2nd ed., (Cambridge: Harvard Univ. Press, 1979), 46–9. George Haskins, *Law and Authority in Early Massachusetts* (New York: Macmillan, 1960), 215–21. G.B. Warden, "Law Reform in England and New England," 682–83. Nancy Matthews, *William Sheppard: Cromwell's Law Reformer*, 31–41, 172–74.

continued to capitalize real property. Meanwhile, Parliament did not abolish imprisonment for debt until 1869.[21]

In Massachusetts, by 1644 the General Court had established a process for claimants in civil suits to initiate an action against a defendant's personal or real property: for "attachments of goods and chattels, or of lands and hereditaments, legal notice shall be given to ye party or left in writing at his house or place of usual abode, otherwise ye suit shall not proceed." Under title, *Arrests*, the *Laws and Liberties of 1648* repeated an earlier guarantee that "no man's person shall be kept in prison for debt but when there appears some estate which he will not produce." Title, *Attachments*, stipulated a defendant be notified by warrant of any suit, and if he did not appear, judgment would be entered against him. Thereafter, an execution for the defendant's property, real or personal, would issue to a marshal or constable as long as the plaintiff posted bond in case his opponent renewed his suit during the following term. With the printing of the *Laws and Liberties of 1660* many of the reforms and innovations made in its predecessor of 1648, the *Body of Liberties of 1641*, and other sundry laws were under title, *Attachments/Summons*, creating a streamlined process for debt collection. Its introductory section provided, "it shall be the liberty of every plaintiff to take out either summons or attachment against any defendant," allowing a plaintiff to either demand a debtor's presence in court or place a lien on his property. Legal notice of the attachment had to be presented to the defendant "in writing at his house," or the "suit shall not proceed." The next section forbid the abatement of any "summons, pleading, judgment, or any kind of proceeding in courts" resulting from "circumstantial errors or mistakes, if the person and cause be rightly understood." Under title, *Barratry*, the 1660 law book censured "any man" if a "common barrater, vexing others

21 John Brooke, *The Heart of the Commonwealth* (Amherst: Univ. of Massachusetts Press, 1989), 41–65, 101–108. David Konig, *Law and Society in Puritan Massachusetts* (Chapel Hill: Univ. of North Carolina Press, 1979), 38–40. William Nelson, *Americanization of the Common Law* (Cambridge: Harvard Univ. Press, 1975), 41–44. Robert Freer, "Imprisonment for Debt in Massachusetts before 1800," *Mississippi Valley Historical Review* 48 (1961): 252–69. W. Cunningham, *The Growth of English Industry in Modern Times* (Cambridge: Univ. Press, 1892), 208–10. Barbara Shapiro, *Law Reform in Early Modern England*, 26–27, 50. After 1543, "subsequent parliaments would continue to wrestle with the problems of both poor and wealthy imprisoned debtors." *An Act for Prevention of Vexations and Oppressions by Delays and Arrests in Suits of Law*, in SR, 5: 323–34 (13 Car. II st. 2, ch. 3 (1661)). *An Act for the Releife and Release of Poore Distressed Prisoners for Debt* in SR, 5: 734 (22/23 Car. II, ch. 20 (1670/1)); SR, 5: 887 (30 Car. II, ch. 4 (1678)). *The London Gazette*, No. 23524 (Aug. 10, 1869), pg. 4441; (https://www.thegazette.co.uk/London/issue/23524/data.pdf). *The Debtors Act, 1869* (32 & 33 Vict. c. 62); (https://www.legislation.gov.uk/ukpga/Vict/32-33/62/enacted).

with unjust, frequent, and endless suits." Title, *Actions*, sanctioned a plaintiff for claiming "debts to vex his adversary," liable to fines of "treble damages to the party grieved," and "forty shillings to the common Treasury."[22]

English reformers had demanded many of the same processes. For example, Hugh Peters proposed that "summons may be left at men's houses" to eliminate the "nest of bailiffs maintained" by English courts to arrest debtors. John Shepheard agreed, "a sufficient summons might serve turn well enough, and so in default of not answering the plaintiff upon proof and evidence given might proceed to judgment and execution." William Leach thought a "process of summons or attachment by goods," or personal property, would suffice in place of arrest and incarceration. If a defendant did not appear after such notification, then the "plaintiff in such action may proceed to judgment." On the topic of England's technically laden process of pleading, John Cooke proposed that "if a case be pleaded sufficiently for matter and substance," and the "right is most conspicuous and evident to the judgment of the court," even if some administrative misstep or legal technicality arose the "party shall have the fruit and benefit of the suit." As John March objected, a "client sues not at law ... to make cases or questions, or to occasion scruples about nice formalities, but to have justice done."[23]

---

22 Nathaniel Shurtleff, ed., *MGCR*, 2: 80 (Nov. 12, 1644). Richard Dunn, ed., *Laws and Liberties of 1648*, 2–3. George Haskins, *Law and Authority in Early Massachusetts*, 215–20. William Whitmore, ed., *Lawes and Liberties of 1660*, 1–2, 4–5. William Whitmore, ed., *Body of Liberties of 1641*, 39. F. Emmison, *Elizabethan Life* (Chelmsford: ECC, 1970), 1: 139–47. Thorp Wolford, "Lawes and Liberties of 1648," in David Flaherty, ed. *Essays in the History of Early American Law* (Chapel Hill: Univ. of North Carolina Press, 1969), 159. *Atkinson v. Williams* (1672), in John Cronin, ed., *Court of Assistants* (Boston: Suffolk County, 1928), 3: 215–16. *Hutchinson, Savage v. Armitage* (1674), in George Dow, ed., *Essex County Court Record* (Salem: Essex Institute, 1914), 5: 376. David Hall, *A Reforming People* (New York: Knopf, 2011), 148–49. "The *Lawes and Liberties* was the fruit of prolonged agitation in England about the excessive costs of doing legal business, the length of time it took to resolve civil disputes, the remoteness of most courts from where people actually lived, the obscurity of the law, the corruption of justice, the harsh treatment of thieves and debtors, and the privileges granted the aristocratic class." Bernard Bailyn, *The Barbarous Years*, (New York: Vintage Books, 2013), 477–78. "The economic situation after 1640 was desperate. Lacking the cash and credit supplied by incoming heads of families, colonists' purchases of necessary goods could not be funded. Their credit in England dried up, the price of cattle collapsed, the markets for agriculture products became gutted, debts could not be discharged, and grain ceased to have monetary value. Friends in England warned that 'if there not be some course taken for better payments of our creditors our trade will utterly cease.'"

23 Hugh Peters, *Good Work for a Good Magistrate* (1651), 34 (no. 9); *Thomason Tracts*, E1364 (2), Reel 179. John Shepheard, *Certain Proposals for Regulating the Law* (1652), 7. John Cooke, *The Vindication of the Professors and Profession of the Law* (1646), 23. John March,

The *Laws and Liberties of 1648* also authorized a bankruptcy type process in which a colonial court or appointed commissioners administered "an oath to the party, or any others, suspected … in concealing his estate." Originally, in 1542, Parliament began enacting a series of statutes establishing a new class of debtor known as "bankrupts," to be judged by commissioners empowered to examine debtors under oath. But this was no modern bankruptcy protection, since only indebted merchants could be charged with a "fraudulent act of bankruptcy." Subsequently, English statutory law was pointedly aimed at "mercantile misconduct" (or the growing merchant class), seeking to streamline creditors' confiscation of a merchant's real and personal property, but not to forgive debts. During this same era English Common Law protected real property from attachment for debts. While the statutory definition of bankruptcy remained convoluted for centuries, it ultimately classified debtors as either merchants, tradesmen, and yeomen, or landowners (i.e., the landed gentry and titled aristocracy). Blackstone hectored merchants unmercifully for their "fraudulent" bankruptcies, comparing them to counterfeiters of the coin of the realm, and noting that "atrocious species of crime" was rightly a felony offense. By exempting the gentry from the statutory definition of bankruptcy, however, landed estates were exempt from execution for debts until the nineteenth century, as only half of any real estate was available to creditors by common law process. Even when landowners signed over their estates as collateral, arrangements strictly enforceable at common law, courts of equity provided the means for evasion and relief from these agreements. If merchants and craftsmen had been allowed to trade without confiscatory market penalties, and attach real property for debts in collecting their bills, England's landed aristocracy would have been terminally undermined.[24]

---

*Amicus Republicae* (1651), 77; *Thomason Tracts* E1360 (1), Reel 179. William Leach, *Bills Proposed for Acts* (1651), 52–3; *Thomason Tracts* E632 (2), Reel 97.

24 Richard Dunn, ed., *Laws and Liberties of 1648*, 2–3, title *Arrests*. Firth and Rait, eds., *Acts and Ordinances*, 2: 321–24. *The Laws Discovery* (1653), in *Harleian Miscellany*, T. Park ed., (London: 1808–1813), 6: 323 (no. XVIII). John Shepheard, *Certain Proposals for Regulating the Law* (1652), 7. W.J. Jones, "The Foundations of English Bankruptcy: Statutes and Commissions in the Early Modern Period," *Transactions of the American Philosophical Society* 69 (no. 3, 1979): 1–63. *An Act for the further Description of a Bankrupt*, SR, 3: 889–901 (34 & 35 Henry VIII ch. 4 (1542–43)). John Warr, *The Corruption and Deficiency of the laws of England* (London: 1649), in *Harleian Miscellany*, T. Park ed., (London: 1808–1813), 6: 220, 222–23. William Blackstone, *Commentaries on the Laws of England*, 4: 156 (Ch. 12, §3, *Offences Against the Public Trade*); 2: 479–82. Per Blackstone, the "acts of bankruptcy … being so numerous, and the whole law of bankrupts being an innovation on the common law, our courts of justice have been tender of extending … acts of bankruptcy by any construction." *However, "a man's removing his goods privately, to prevent their being*

While English Common Law had evolved to protect real property from confiscation by the crown, or oppressive regulations of its usage that would unduly undermine its value or utility, John Shepheard still lamented the advantage held by the landed gentry and nobility in economic matters: the "Law seems … too mild and remiss against the estates of debtors, and against their persons … much too rigid and severe." He thought "every man, as well as tradesmen, might be brought within the statute of Bankrupts." William Bagwell put the merchant's disability to verse:

> A Merchant when he once begins to fail,
> Is like a ship at sea without a sail.
> Which floats upon the waters and is tossed,
> And tumbled up and down until she's lost.
> In thy declining time thou knew not whither to go,
> So that the Sergeants brought thee hither.
> Now thy trading and thy credit too is lost,
> And here thou knows not what to do.[25]

By imprisoning debtors and exempting real property from debt repayment, market transactions were, in effect, criminalized, prompting merchants like Gerrard Winstanley (leader of the radical Digger movement featuring squatters who claimed a natural right to occupy land) to curse English markets. Stuart Prall concluded, the governing classes' "fear of anarchy which

*seized in execution, was no act of bankruptcy."* Blackstone admitted, "everything is in favor of the creditors, … the laws seem … rigid and severe against the bankrupt," and referred to bankrupts as those "unfortunate traders." Claire Priest, *Credit Nation: Property Laws and Institutions in Early America* (Princeton: Princeton Univ. Press, 2021), 59–73. English property law was "defined by stark distinctions in the treatment of … real … and personal property … With regard to the claims of creditors, the law maintained the cohesion of English estates and protected land from involuntary seizure" by protecting "title ownership of land from the claims of all unsecured creditors," while the Court of Chancery established "procedural hurdles to foreclosure on land to satisfy secured debts." J.H. Baker, *An Introduction to English Legal History*, 3rd ed., 78–9. Ian Duffy, "English Bankrupts," 283–97. As statutory language evolved over several centuries the definition of fraudulent bankruptcy focused on those who were engaged in "buying and selling," and ultimately covered some classes of tradesmen and craftsmen. Steve Pincus, "Rethinking Mercantilism: Political Economy, the British Empire, and the Atlantic World in the Seventeenth and Eighteenth Centuries," *William and Mary Quarterly* 69 (Jan., 2012): 14–23.

25 John Shepheard, *Certain Proposals for Regulating the Law* (1652), 7. William Bagwell, *The Distressed Merchant* (August 25, 1645), 60; *Thomason Tracts* E265 (1), Reel 44. Noga Morag-Levine, "The Case of Proclamations (1610), Aldred's Case (1610), and the Origins of the Sic Utere/Salus Populi Antithesis," *Law and History Review* 40 (no. 3, 2022): 385–87.

the demands of reformers instilled in the hearts and minds of 'men of substance' was undoubtedly genuine, for they were in fact challenging the very substance of organized English society": the inviolability of real property.[26]

In colonial Massachusetts, on the other hand, market participants and their goods (real or personal) were subject to a legal process akin to English bankruptcy, but without the criminal sanctions. Land registration was essential to this accomplishment, and integral to the colony's economic regulations. With its persistent shortage of currency, and the absence of modern contract law, property was the primary means to secure credit. Massachusetts forbid the transfer of real estate if it intended to "defeat any man from due debts or legacies," and debtors could not hide assets by conveying them surreptitiously to a third party. Real property was only conveyable after it was "certified unto the recorder or secretary for the General Court within six months," to ensure ownership of the land was clear of liens or attachments. English reformers pursued similar reforms. William Leach, a "prolific pamphleteer," believed a registration system would prevent men from "fraudulently and secretly" conveying their "estates to their allies" to avoid creditors. John Shepheard believed that if real estate transactions were recorded, then "creditors should be sure of their debts." Henry Robinson, scion of a prosperous merchant family, proposed a "county register of conveyances … together with another register of bonds and bills of debt," to prevent unnecessary lawsuits and "facilitate and enlarge trade and navigation." Meanwhile, Massachusetts' registration of property was far easier after only a decade of existence, as one English landowner complained,

---

26 Stuart Prall, *The Agitation for Law Reform during the Puritan Revolution: 1640–1660*, 47–48, 102. "[T]he gentry, the group which in the early 1640's was fighting to uphold the common and fundamental laws of the realm against an arbitrary monarch, became the new villain and had to continue the struggle for the law against the new revolutionary forces: the Levellers, the Sects, the Diggers, and other anti-common law doctrinaires … A significant part of the hard core of the reformers was to be found among the smaller tradesmen who hoped for a loosening of the bounds that the common law placed upon commerce." J.D. Alsop, "Ethics in the Marketplace: Gerrard Winstanley's London Bankruptcy, 1643," *Journal of British Studies* 28 (1989): 97–119. Winstanley's future radicalism as a Digger stemmed from his own bankruptcy's disastrous impact on his life. He railed, "For matter of buying and selling, the earth stinks with such unrighteousness, that for my part, though I was bred a tradesman, yet it is so hard a thing to pick out a poor living that a man shall sooner be cheated of his bread, than get bread by trading among men, if by plain dealing he put trust in any." Christopher Hill, *Liberty Against the Law* (London: Allen Lane, 1996), 274. "Winstanley was no vagabond … The son of a Lancashire merchant, Winstanley had been apprenticed to a London clothier … Ruined by the interruption of trade between Lancashire and the capital during the civil war, Winstanley withdrew to his wife's county of Surrey. Even there, 'by the burden of taxes and much free-quarter' he 'found the burden heavier than I could bear.'"

if "people must register all their deeds for the time past, then many thousands will be ... undoing themselves" by the consequent discovery of "flaws" in the "title of their estates." Upon Parliament's review of the Hale Commission's proposals in the early 1650's to establish county land registers to facilitate the attachment of real property for debt, however, a committee composed mainly of lawyers (outnumbering the radicals' contingent) failed to define an "incumbrance," or a claim or lien, over three months. A permanent solution for integrating real property went unaddressed during the brief period of parliamentary law reform from the late 1640's through the mid-1650's.[27]

Demands for a new compilation of English law in print came to a head in the Nominate (or Barebones) Parliament of 1653 which was divided into "two fierce parties, the one consisting of the adherents of Cromwell, the other of Levellers, Anabaptists, and Fifth-Monarchy men." The radicals insisted that the "laws ought to be easy, plain, and short, so as they were to be subject to them" can "know and understand them." Now law books were so expensive and "voluminous, ... intricate, and uncertain," few were able to gain "knowledge of them." Pulton's fourteen-hundred-page statute book's introduction noted its readership was comprised of lawyers at the Inns of Court, merchants, the gentry, and other "discreet men" who "desired that the statutes which be now

---

27 Richard Dunn, ed., *Lawes and Liberties of 1648*, 13–14, title *Conveyances fraudulent.* Shurtleff, ed., *MGCR*, 1: 306–7 (Oct. 7, 1640); 3: 172–73 (Oct. 18, 1649). Whitmore, ed., *Laws and Liberties of 1660*, 20, title *Conveyances*, §3. Donald Veall, *The Popular Movement for Law Reform*, 219. Barbara Shapiro, *Law Reform in Early Modern England*, 22–23, 121–53. As early as 1529, a bill entitled, *Enrollment of Bargains and Contracts of Lands and Tenements*, was introduced in Parliament. William Leach, *Propositions: For Recording and Registering of Deeds and Conveyances* (June 20, 1651), 2–10; *Thomason Tracts* E632 (5), Reel 97. John Shepheard, *Proposals for regulating the law*, 4. Henry Robinson, *Certain Considerations in Order to a More Speedy, Cheap, and Equal Distribution of Justice throughout the Nation* (1651), ii (intro.); *Wing* R1668, Reel 577: 1. Thorp Wolford, "The Lawes and Liberties of 1648," 175 (n. 133). *Reasons Against the Bill Entitled: An Act for County Registers* (August 1653), *Thomason Tracts* E708 (15), Reel 109. Mary Cotterell, "Interregnum Law Reform: The Hale Commission of 1652," 696–97. Blair Worden, *The Rump Parliament*, 113–15. Austin Woolrych, *Britain in Revolution, 1625–1660*, 454, 517–18. Austin Woolrych, *Commonwealth to Protectorate* (Oxford: Clarendon Press, 1982), 266–68. David Konig, "Community Custom and the Common Law: Social Change and Land Law in Seventeenth Century Massachusetts," *American Journal of Legal History* 18 (April 1974): 137–77. Mark Howe, "The Recording of Deeds," *Boston University Law Review* 28 (1948): 1–6. James Sullivan, *The History of Land Titles in Massachusetts* (Boston: Thomas & Andrews, 1801; reprint, Buffalo: William S. Hein, 1981), 381 (Appendix). Sullivan cited the *Laws and Liberties*' 1658 supplement as the initiation of a system of deeds in the colony (Title *Conveyances Deeds and Writings*). A copy of the 1650's sessional publications of the Laws and Liberties has not survived.

in life, force, and general use, might be selected and set forth in one book." Its editors had searched the "original records ... in the Tower of London," so that "knowledge of our laws, customs and statutes" could "direct every subject, the better to govern himself." But a gentleman most required such knowledge to "defend his heritage and possessions in tranquility." On the reformers' side, as recounted by Christopher Hill, an itemized list of demands included: "pick-pockets and horse thieves should not be executed for the first offense; that burning should cease to be the death penalty for women; that accused persons refusing to plead should no longer be pressed to death; that genuine bankrupts should be released, while the goods of fraudulent debtors should be seized and sold."[28]

---

28 *An Exact Relation of the Proceedings and Transactions of the late Parliament* (1654), in *Somers Tracts* (London: 1811), 6: 267–68, 276–78. *Several Draughts of Acts heretofore prepared by Persons appointed to consider of the Inconveniences, Delay, Charge, and Irregularity in the Proceedings of the Law. Printed by an Order of Parliament of the 12th of July, 1653*, in *Somers Tracts* (London: 1811), 6: 177–245. Marchmont Nedham, *A True State of the Case of the Commonwealth of England* (Feb. 8, 1654), 16–25; *Thomason Tracts* E728 (5), Reel 112. Ferdinando Pulton, *A Collection of Sundrie Statutes* (London: Fletcher, Haviland, & Young. Assignors of I. More Esq., 1632), intro.; STC 9329, Reel 1516. Mary Cotterell, "Interregnum Law Reform: The Hale Commission of 1652," 689–704. John Cowley, *A Bibliography of Abridgments, Digests, Dictionaries, and Indexes of English Law to the Year 1800* (London: Selden Society, 1932), xxxiv–xxxv, 48–9, 51–6. Austin Woolrych, *From Commonwealth to Protectorate*, 270–73, 392. "If it is an error to regard the Commonwealth as originally begotten by a principled belief in the superiority of republican government, it is equally so to see Barebone's Parliament as primarily an attempt to erect a rule of the saints in preparation for the millennium. Neither error is total, of course, for just as there had been some convinced republicans in both parliament and army in December 1648, so in the spring and summer of 1653 there were, both in the Council of Officers and among its nominees to the supreme authority, millenarians of the kind who believed that they had a divine call to erect Christ's kingdom there and then. But they were nothing like a majority in either body, and Cromwell was not one of them." Austin Woolrych, *Britain in Revolution, 1625–1660*, 454, 517–18, 548–50. "There were three broad schools of thought" in parliamentary law reform: "The first, which Cromwell and the moderate majority adhered, wanted to preserve ... the common law ... in its essentials but to improve and expedite its procedures"; the second was the "more radical Levellers who aimed to scrap [the legal system] altogether. They wanted to replace it with a simple written code that would be easily comprehensible by the laity and could be competently administered by popularly elected magistrates, holding court at frequent intervals in every county, without need for professional advocates. The third school of reformers consisted of the Fifth Monarchists and other extreme sectaries, who believed that the Kingdom of Christ was in process of being established and that the only laws fit to be observed in it were those contained in the scriptures, whether in the Mosaic Code or the teachings of Christ." Andrew Sharp, *The English Levellers* (Cambridge, Cambridge Univ. Press, 1998), xiii. The Leveller law reform program included putting the law in English, "no imprisonment for

Upon the opening of the Nominate Parliament in 1653, after its summons by the Army Council under Cromwell's authority, the appointment of a committee to reform English law immediately provoked controversy. Initially, the radical faction stated an intention to compare the kingdom's law to Mosaic law, in order to "reduce" the "great volumes of law … into the bigness of a pocket books, *as it is proportionable in New England.*" However, upon its proposal that a new "body" of law was to be compiled, rather than the previously agreed to description, "model," the latter meaning an intent only to edit and streamline the laws rather than re-write English law in its entirety, Cromwell's moderate wing pounced. Its members accused the radicals of conspiring "to rule the nation by virtue of a supposed right of saint-ship in themselves," and form a government in which "men could have had no other right but what they must have derived for them, and their party." If these "saints" wanted a small book of laws, why were "so many laws … ordained the last Parliament," which in "a few years more would have mounted the statute-book above the reach of a student's purse." According to Shapiro, "Cromwell took a more moderate approach to law reform" and rejected the radicals' proposals in favor of social stability. Nevertheless, his legal advisor, William Sheppard, continued to lobby for "one plain, complete, and methodical treatise or abridgment of the whole Common and Statute Law," and make those "things that are now obscure and uncertain, clear and certain."[29]

debt; the prison system should be more humane; punishments should fit crimes; capital punishment should be reserved for murder and treason"; procedure should be simplified; juries should sit in all cases; and legal fees should be "restrained." Christopher Hill, *God's Englishmen: Oliver Cromwell and the English Revolution* (London: Weidenfeld & Nicholson, 1970), 140–41.

29 Marchmont Nedham, *A True State of the Case of the Commonwealth of England* (1654), 16–25. *An Exact Relation of the Proceedings and Transactions of the late Parliament* (1654), 6: 266–67, 276–78. Christopher Hill, *God's Englishmen: Oliver Cromwell and the English Revolution*, 140–41. "The reformers proposed to codify the law, as had recently been done successfully in Massachusetts. That is the meaning of the oft-quoted phrase about reducing the great volumes of the law 'into the bigness of a pocket book, as it is proportionable in New England and elsewhere.'" William Sheppard, *Englands Balme* (1657), 6, 41–2. Nancy Matthews, *William Sheppard: Cromwell's Law Reformer*, 31–41, 172–74. Cromwell had appointed Sheppard to be his "legal adviser" and "serve as a personal consultant on matters 'tending to the regulation of the law' and, second, to frame a comprehensive program of law reform." Sheppard's "judicial and legal reforms … bore a striking resemblance to the system established a quarter of a century earlier by the founding magistrates of the Massachusetts Bay Colony." Barbara Shapiro, *Law reform in Early Modern England*, 138–41, 158–59. While Sheppard "placed himself in the moderate camp, several provisions [in *England's Balme*] had more in common with the radical agenda." Carla Pestana, *The English Atlantic in an Age of Revolution*, 132–37.

While other New England colonies drafted civil codes they occurred after 1648, with the exception of Plymouth colony that enacted one in 1636, but it was not printed until 1671. Significantly the latter included the rights of freemen to enact laws and trial-by-jury; Plymouth was integrated into Massachusetts as a county in 1691. Ultimately, select provisions of the *Laws and Liberties* were adopted throughout the New England and Northeastern colonies, as well as their mid-Atlantic neighbors.[30]

---

30 George Haskins and Samuel Ewing, "The Spread of Massachusetts Law in the Seventeenth Century," *University of Pennsylvania Law Review* 106 (1958): 413–18. *Library of Congress;* (https://www.loc.gov/item/today-in-history/october-04/).

CHAPTER 10

# Ship Money, *Rex v. Hampden*, and Reason of State

Although the Levellers played a leading role in English law reform during this era, their history is brief. They formed at the end of the 1640's as it became more and more obvious that the English state was undergoing fundamental change. Only several years later Cromwell purged its radical elements from the New Model Army, the law reform movement peaked in 1653 with the Barebones Parliament, several years after which John Lilburne and other leading Levellers were either imprisoned, exiled, or on the run. So, the question has always been, no matter how enlightened or revolutionary, what real impact did they ultimately have, in England or elsewhere? We have seen that in addition to their support of the *Laws and Liberties* during the Barebones Parliament, and their release of several editions of their own version of a written constitutions at the end of the 1640's, the Levellers, with Lilburne in the lead when not imprisoned, supported publication of English law in the vernacular and in prose laypeople could readily understand. As Barbara Shapiro recognized, and as covered in Chapter 9, Massachusetts was often in the lead in enacting reform. Even though colonists had shared similar English experiences that motivated them to pursue such enactments, they had not had to overcome the titanic forces then in play in England, especially as represented by the entrenched landed nobility and gentry, neither of whom would tolerate the Levellers' critiques.[1]

In the following passage John Winthrop, faithful governor but long-time opponent of the freemen's attempts to carve out an active role in colonial government, listed their attempts to wrestle power from the magistracy, with "salus populi" as their "transcendent rule to walk by":

1 Tim Harris, "The Leveller Legacy: From the Restoration to the Exclusion Crisis," in Michael Mendle, ed., *The Putney Debates* (Cambridge: Cambridge Univ. Press, 2001), 219–23. Barbara Shapiro, *Law Reform in Early Modern England: 1540–1700* (Oxford: Hart Publishing, 2019), 116–18. "Little attention has been given to the similarities between English mid-century radical reformers and the emerging law of the New England colonies … Brief law codes, demanded by Levellers and religious radicals, were a common feature of the New England colonies. New England codes, some of them introduced before the rise of English radical movements, tended to be short, easy to understand and written in the English language … We should not simply assume that New England colonies consciously shaped their law and legal institutions according to … English reformers … Many colonial developments were already being put in place before the deluge of radical pamphlets."

 | DOI:10.1163/9789004706347_012

> Some of the deputies had seriously conceived that the magistrates affected an arbitrary government, and that they had (or sought to have) an unlimited power to do what they pleased without control … For prevention whereof they judged it not unlawful to use even extreme remedies, as if *salus populi had been now the transcendent rule to walk by*, and that magistracy must be no other, in effect, than a ministerial office, and all authority, both legislative, consultative, and judicial must be exercised by the people in their body representative. Hereupon they labored, equis et velis [i.e., might and main], to take away the negative vote. Failing of that, they pleaded that the magistrates had no power out of the General Court, but what must be derived from the General Court; and so, they would have put upon them commissions for what was to be done in the vacancy of the General Court, and some of themselves to be joined with the magistrates, and some of the magistrates left out … *This project not prevailing, the next is for such a body of laws with prescript penalties in all cases, as nothing might be left to the discretion of the magistrates.*

Fortunately, the governor identified the source from which the freemen drew salus populi, "Parliament had taught us that salus populi suprema lex."[2] The maxim had played a key role in some of the most consequential events in both English politics and law since the early 1600's, right until political matters came to a head in the early 1640s, at which point parliamentary leadership coopted it to incite a revolutionary populist movement.

In December 1640, Winthrop noted receiving "news of the Scots entering into England, and the calling of a Parliament, and the hope of a thorough reformation, etc., whereupon some among us began to think of returning back to England." The Scots had successfully defended their national church during several seasons of military campaigns, known as the Bishops' Wars (1639–40). After the armies had reached an initial stalemate, Charles I summoned the Short Parliament in this interim between campaigns, as it convened for only several weeks in the Spring of 1640 before ending acrimoniously over new taxation. After Charles's decisive defeat later in the year, seeing his forces offer only a desultory defense, he summoned the "Long Parliament" that remained in session until 1649. John Tinker warned Winthrop to expect only "a small quantity of passengers" travelling to the colony, as compared to earlier years,

2 Richard Dunn, et al., eds., *Journal of John Winthrop: 1630–1649* (Cambridge: Belknap Press, 1996), 589–91 (July 3, 1645); 526, no. 1 (August 1644). David Hall, *A Reforming People* (New York: Alfred A. Knopf, 2011), 31–38. Francis Bremer, *John Winthrop: America's Forgotten Founding Father* (Oxford: Oxford Univ. Press, 2003), 337–38.

because great anticipation was building for a "reformation in England, by the intended Parliament." But Tinker doubted England's ills were remediable, seeing only "troublesome times approaching." Lawrence Wright reported the selection of new parliamentary members, while the "King *upon his own charge*" mobilized thirty thousand infantrymen and about seven thousand cavalry, "we say against the Scots; but we know not." John Harrison described the great procession led by the King and his nobility, followed by its Members, at the opening of the Short Parliament, "from Whitehall in great magnificence to Westminster," noting Charles I's "long speech." Only a month later Brampton Gurdon lamented the great upheaval in the wake of the Short Parliament's dismissal, but he drew comfort from its refusal "to give a penny to the K[ing] in his intended war against the Scots." Subsequently, Charles I went to great lengths to prevent the House of Commons "from protesting against … ship money, … which grew burdensome all the kingdom over."[3]

"Ship money" referred to the collection of taxation during Charles I's "personal" rule without Parliament during the 1630's which, like the Forced Loan of the previous decade, was justified by his emergency powers to defend the kingdom. Parliamentary sessions during the late 1620's acknowledged the need to substantially enlarge the English navy, with at least twenty-five ships required to safeguard England's commercial vessels in the Channel and ensure them access to international trade routes. The chief foreign threats to England's commercial fleet were the Spanish, the French, and the Dutch, with piracy also taking a toll. While, to many, Charles I seemed to use the tax to undermine parliamentary authority, a ship money tax had been collected in port cities for national defense for centuries, and its collection did enable new English ships to sail in the 1630's. Nevertheless, as Kevin Sharpe admitted, "Though ship money was paid, there is evidence of resistance from the beginning."[4]

---

3 Richard Dunn, ed., *Winthrop's Journal*, 341 (Oct.-Dec., 1640). *John Tinker to John Winthrop*, (Feb. 26, 1640), in *Winthrop Papers*, 4: 205–206. *Lawrence Wright to John Winthrop*, (March 26, 1640), in Ibid., 4: 220. *John Harrison, Jr., to John Winthrop*, (April 15, 1640), in Ibid., 4: 226–27. *Brampton Gurden to John Winthrop*, (May 13, 1640), in Ibid., 4: 243–44. Edmund Ludlow, *Memoirs of Edmund Ludlow* (London: 1751), 4. "The king by his agents earnestly pressed them to grant him present supplies for use of his army; but they, sensible of former usage, after they had gratified him in that particular, and of the insupportable burdens they lay under, refused to grant any subsidies until their grievances should be redressed." David Hall, *The Puritans: A Transatlantic History* (Princeton: Princeton Univ. Press, 2019), 287–93.

4 Kevin Sharpe, *Personal Rule of Charles I* (New Haven: Yale Univ. Press, 1992), 545–52, 717–21. In 1635, ship money was extended from port cities to the entire kingdom which appeared to violate precedent. Adrian Tinniswood, *The Rainborowes: One Family's Quest to Build a New England* (New York: Basic Books, 2013), 3–54. Several fleets that sailed by virtue of the tax ultimately tilted the struggle over the sea-lanes into England's favor by 1640. Henrik

The first writs for collection of the tax issued on October 20, 1634, with London's writ proclaiming Charles I's duty to "provide for the defense of the kingdom, safeguard of the sea, security of our subjects, safe conduct of ships and merchandise to our kingdom of England coming, and from the same kingdom to foreign parts passing." While the tax was initially resisted via technical objections to its collection, such as challenges to the apportionment of the amounts collected, there was no fundamental challenge to the crown's prerogative in this regard until the late 1630's. As the decade progressed without Parliament being called into session, and a royal gambit for an extended personal rule appearing ever more likely, local resistance predictably increased. In 1637, Robert Ryece recounted to Winthrop that the King had become "exceeding[ly] angry" upon his visit to Shropshire "for his bad entertainment," with only a dozen townsmen accompanying the county sheriff to greet his royal party, and no "gentleman" to be found among the lot. According to Ryece, "Shipmony" had caused "every man's general absence," leaving "none at home but the wife." Levies for additional streams of royal income aggravated collection of the tax, such as monopolies sold for manufacture to include enforcement powers. Upon Parliament's reassembly in November 1640, amidst guffaws from fellow Members, Sir Simonds D'Ewes urged repeal of the most troublesome penal laws, like the one concerning the sale of soap, as such means to raise revenue were destructive of "those things that are so necessary that we cannot spare." Linda Peck noted the crown had already rescinded "most of its grants of monopoly because of parliamentary opposition or the fear of it."[5]

Langelüddecke, "'I finde all men and my officers all soe unwilling': The Collection of Ship Money, 1635–1640," *Journal of British Studies*, 46 (July 2007): 509–542. "Ship Money was raised year after year and seemed to turn into a permanent national tax that lacked any parliamentary approval."

5 *First Writ of Ship-Money* (Oct. 20, 1634), in Samuel Gardiner, ed., *Constitutional Documents of the Puritan Revolution: 1625–1660* (Oxford: Clarendon Press, 1906), 105–108. *Robert Ryece to John Winthrop* (March 2, 1637), in *Winthrop Papers*, 3: 355–63. Kevin Sharpe, *The Personal Rule of Charles I*, 552–620, 665–82. Mark Kishlansky, *Monarchy Transformed* (London: Penguin Books, 1997), 98–99, 121–22. Ship money was a "traditional assessment, justified by the king's emergency power to provide for the safety of the realm, and thus it avoided the prohibition on non-parliamentary taxation expressed in the *Petition of Right*." J.P. Sommerville, *Royalists and Patriots*, 2nd ed., (New York: Longman, 1999), 140, 144–45. "The first two Stuart kings levied a number of taxes without the consent of Parliament. Particular taxes attracted opposition for many reasons, of which some had little to do with constitutional principle ... But it would be mistaken to suppose that principled antagonism towards the crown's financial policies were merely a negligible afterthought, developed at a late date to provide a specious excuse for opposition. From the very beginning of James I's reign two separate accounts of the relationship between royal power and the subject's property were current in England. Absolute royal power faced absolute property. The result was conflict." Wallace Notestein,

While other notable men sought to challenge the Ship-Money tax, John Hampden's refusal of payment without the "consent of Parliament" became the controlling case. To guard against such challenges, Charles I had already tasked his royal justices on the Common Pleas, King's Bench, and Exchequer to issue several advisory opinions on the following query:

> When the good and safety of the realm of the kingdom is concerned, and the whole kingdom is in danger; Whether may not the king … command all the subjects of this kingdom, *at their charge*, to provide and furnish such number of ships, with men, victuals and munition, and for such time as he shall think fit, for the defense and safeguard of the kingdom from such danger and peril; and by law compel the doing thereof, in case of refusal or refractoriness? *And whether, in such a case, is not the king sole judge, both of the danger, and when and how the same is to be prevented and avoided.*

Subsequently, the twelve common law justices concurred with the King's interpretation of his emergency powers, and its most potent feature, "your majesty is the sole judge, both in the danger, and when and how the same is to be prevented and avoided."[6]

Upon John Hampden's refusal to pay the tax the issue was joined in *Rex v. Hampden* (1637–1638). Hampden had become a member of Parliament during its later 1620's sessions, and was mentored by its principal leader, Sir John Eliot,

ed., *The Journal of Sir Simonds D'Ewes* (New Haven: Yale Univ. Press, 1923), 54 (n. 3). Linda Peck, *Court Patronage and Corruption in Early Stuart England* (London: Routledge, 1993), 134–60. *The Grant of a Monopoly for the Manufacture of Soap* (1623), in A.E. Bland, et al., eds., *English Economic History: Select Documents* (New York: Macmillan Co., 1919), 461–65 (#18). Henry Hallam, *Constitutional History of England*, 6th ed., (London: John Murray, 1850), 1: 429–30. In 1639, Charles I "annulled … a number of commissions that had been issued in order to obtain money by compounding with offenders against penal statutes." John Kenyon, ed., *The Stuart Constitution*, 2nd ed., (Cambridge: Cambridge Univ. Press, 1986), 104–106. "The most important single cause of Star Chamber's unpopularity was the role it was called upon to play in the enforcement of the King's social and economic policies."

6 Wallace Notestein, ed., *The Journal of Sir Simonds D'Ewes*, 3–4. *Rex v. Hampden* (1637), in T.B. Howell, ed., *State Trials* (London: T.C. Hansard, 1816), 3: 826–1254 (#147). *The King's Letter to the Judges*, (Feb. 2, 1836) in *State Trials*, 3: 842–44. Kevin Sharpe, *The Personal Rule of Charles I*, 59, 659–65, 719–21. "During the period 1626 to 1629 we hear increasingly a new language: the language of necessity and of public safety contrasted with private interests." *The Judges' Answer* (1637), in *State Trials*, 3: 844–46. Michael Mendle, "The Ship Money Case, the Case of Shipmony, and the Development of Henry Parker's Absolutism," *Historical Journal* 32 (1989): 517–18. Richard Noble, "Lions or Jackals: The Independence of the Judges in *Rex. v. Hampden*," *Stanford Law Review* 14 (July 1962): 715–17.

with whom he remained a close friend and confidant until Eliot's death in the Tower for his role in the mutinous end to Parliament's 1629 session. Hampden also shared committee memberships with John Pym, Sir Edward Coke, and John Selden, and ultimately became an early supporter of colonizing New England. He was a leader of Parliament upon its reassembly in 1640, and its opposition to Charles I leading to civil warfare. His prosecution features hundreds of pages of arguments, but since modern case precedent did not emerge until the next century (in part because reliable case records did not exist, and those that did were mostly not in print), attorneys cited a myriad of jumbled authorities, including cases and statutes ancient and recent, as supported by natural law or biblical principles, intermingled with European civil law maxims.[7]

Because the same judges presiding in *Rex v. Hampden* had already provided Charles I several unanimous advisory opinions in his favor, Hampden's prospects were not promising. Moreover, the fundamental issues underlying the case were the same in principle as the *Five Knights Case* (1627), except that the current issues were not able to be pled in the earlier case once the King's royal warrant was introduced to supersede the issuance of a writ of habeas corpus. But the royal prerogative's inviolability was the same, in so far as the King's subjects could not challenge his judgment or actions in state matters. The argument that remained available to Hampden's counsel was the defense counsel's attack on the prerogative in 1627, made by John Selden, maintaining rights of due process were violated upon his arrest and incarceration without trial for refusing payment of the tax. Even as Hampden's counsel Oliver St. John (future parliamentary leader and chief justice of the Common Pleas) made a supporting argument on these privileges of property, however, he acknowledged the royal prerogative was inviolable in this matter, "by the law the safety of the realm is to be provided for; *salus populi suprema lex*." The maxim was irresistible no matter "the persons who are to bear the charge of it, or of the persons whom the law hath entrusted with the care and power of this common

7 Richard Noble, "Lions or Jackals: The Independence of the Judges in *Rex. v. Hampden*," 717–34. D. Alan Orr, "A Prospectus of a 'New' Constitutional History of Early Modern England," *Albion* 36 (no. 3, 2004): 430–50. Stephen Leslie, and Sidney Lee, eds. *Dictionary of National Biography* (New York: Macmillan, 1908), 8: 1138–39. Barbara Shapiro, *Law Reform in Early Modern England* (Oxford: Hart Publishing, 2019), 35, 55–57. Coke's "12 volumes of *Reports* ... were designed to reform the state of law reporting." Ian Williams, "Learning the 'New Law of the Star Chamber': Legal Education and Legal Literature in Early-Stuart England," *The Journal of Legal History* 43 (no.3, 2022): 243–61. Daniel Hulsebosch, "The Ancient Constitution and the Expanding Empire: Sir Edward Coke's British Jurisprudence," *Law and History Review* 21 (Autumn 2003): 451–70. David Smith, *Sir Edward Coke and the Reformation of the Laws* (Cambridge: Cambridge Univ. Press, 2014), 40–56.

defense." Sir Edward Littleton, the king's solicitor general, supported the crown's case with opposing counsel's own admission, the "fundamental reason is the exact rule of the law … cited by that learned gentleman, Mr. St. John, '*salus populi suprema lex*.' All other laws positive are subordinate to this law, and are to be regulated by it. We are not to talk of positive laws, until we have a kingdom to use them … Nay, positive laws are abrogated by reason, when the safety of the kingdom and people are in danger." St. John's corollary argument—the emergency nature justifying the tax wasn't sufficiently expressed in the ship money writ—could not overcome the monarch's prerogative in exigent matters of war and peace to safeguard his kingdom. Richard Tuck thought that amongst all the instances of the crown's invocations of "salus populi" during the later stages of Charles I's rule, its use in this case was the "most spectacular," although the maxim's subsequent deployment during Parliament's impeachment of the Earl of Strafford several years later was equally momentous.[8]

The great surprise of *Rex v. Hampden* was its slim seven to five majority decision in Charles I's favor, which certainly upended his original goal of settling the matter via unanimous advisory opinions. In the end, as Kevin Sharpe summarized the Justices' opinions, "their general view was that for ordinary

8 Kevin Sharpe, *The Personal Rule of Charles I*, 721–23. *Rex v. Hampden*, *State Trials*, 3: 859, 906, 926, 971–72. St. John's co-counsel, Robert Holborne, also deferred to the king's emergency powers: "by the policy of the kingdom the king cannot charge the subject, yet the king may, without the advice in parliament, in cases extraordinary, where in his judgment the safety of the kingdom is in instant danger, and that the business will not admit the calling of a parliament … [I]n such cases property must yield, for 'salus populi suprema lex'." Richard Noble, "Lions or Jackals: The Independence of the Judges in *Rex. v. Hampden*," 733, 734–59. Noble had sympathy for the majority, "At the margin, the law was unclear and they can be excused for giving the benefit of the doubt to the king." *Five Knights Case* (1627) in T.B. Howell, ed., *State Trials* (London: T.C. Hansard, 1816), 3: 1 @ 35 (#127). Attorney General Heath had argued, since the king was the "fountain of justice … shall we … not submit to his command, but make inquiries whether they be lawful, and say that the King doth not this or that in the course of justice?" Michael Mendle, "The Ship Money Case, the Case of Shipmony, and the Development of Henry Parker's Absolutism," 517–20. Lorenzo Sabbadini, *Property, Liberty, and Self-Ownership in Seventeenth-Century England* (McGill-Queen's Univ. Press, 2020), 39–43. William Palmer, "Oliver St. John and the Legal Language of Revolution in England: 1640–1642," *The Historian* 51 (Feb., 1989): 263–82. David Wooton, ed., *Divine Right and Democracy* (New York: Penguin Books, 1986), 35. The Petition of Right was "intended to end absolutism by introducing a new contract between king and people: it failed … because it placed no constraint upon the extra-legal prerogative of the king and provided no definition of the circumstances under which he could have recourse to such prerogative." Daniel Lee, *Popular Sovereignty in Early Modern England* (Oxford: Oxford Univ. Press, 2016), 278–80. Richard Tuck, *Philosophy and Government: 1572–1651* (Cambridge: Cambridge Univ. Press, 1993), 223–24.

defense the King must expend his own revenues or go to Parliament; in the case of emergency most agreed he was sole judge of the danger and bound to take measures to avert it." But Justice Sir Richard Hutton dissented on whether there was, in fact, an emergency in the present case. While acknowledging his earlier advisory opinion for the King, he would be of that "same opinion … yet this writ [of ship money] doth not pursue the direction thereof; for though we agreed, that the King might charge in case of a general danger, yet this was, and is intended, not a danger of pirates, but an imminent necessity, and apparent danger." In other words, the crown had used an apparent danger of pirates at sea as pretext to achieve the imminent necessity of revenue for the King, because the public welfare was never under imminent threat. Essentially, as Justice Hutton concluded, "For I do agree in the time of war, when there is an enemy in the field, the King may take goods from the subject; such a danger, and such a necessity, ought to be in this case, as in case of a fire like to consume all without speedy help, such a danger as tends to overthrow the kingdom." Charles I's advisor, Edward Hyde, feared the decision's effect on an already heated public opinion, as a temporary tax in times of public danger was now made permanent as a matter of law. Many were determined to resist such a precedent.[9]

While English common lawyers claimed salus populi suprema lex as their own, it originally derived from ancient sources of Roman law. Francis Bacon thought the maxim originated from Roman Law's earliest text, the "*Twelve Tables*, salus populi suprema lex." Quentin Skinner has traced its origins to Roman literature's classical ideas of liberty and republicanism, ones that were familiar to "anyone in late-sixteenth- or early-seventeenth-century England who had received a university education" featuring the ever more popular principles of humanism. Jean Bodin's *Six Books of the Commonwealth*, first published in 1576 (and in English in 1606), cited the maxim as the chief means of "policing of a country," or what is today termed national security: "I agree that such necessity is prior to all rules … One must always bear in mind

9 *Rex v. Hampden*, *State Trials*, 3: 1198, 1252–54. Michael Mendle, "The Ship Money Case, the Case of Shipmony, and the Development of Henry Parker's Absolutism," 520–21. Conrad Russell, *The Crisis of Parliaments* (London: Oxford Univ. Press, 1971), 320–22. Edward Hyde (1st Earl of Clarendon), *History of the Rebellion and Civil Wars* (Oxford: Clarendon Press, 1826), 1: 122–25. The "damage … cannot be expressed, that the crown and state sustained by the deserved reproach and infamy that attended the judges, by being made use of in this and like acts of power; there being no possibility to preserve the dignity, reverence, and estimation of the laws themselves, but by the integrity … of the judges." There was "no question" the "next parliament proceedeth principally from their contempt" and "scandal of that judgment." J.P. Sommerville, *Royalists and Patriots*, 151.

the principle to which there is no exception, salus populi suprema lex esto." Similar to crown counsel, Sir Edward Littleton's use of the maxim as an a priori law of state, superior to positive or man-made laws, Bodin posited salus populi as "prior to all rules about legislation." The reason was simple, a sovereign national jurisdiction rested upon a state's viability; as Littleton had put it, "We are not to talk of positive laws, until we have a kingdom to use them."[10]

J.P. Sommerville's version of how salus populi emerged in English politics also features Jean Bodin's *Six Books of the Commonwealth*. Bodin's concept of sovereignty, tailored to meet the needs of France's sixteenth-century monarchy and government, "included final control over legislation, as well as the right to choose magistrates and ministers." But Professor Sommerville took the extra step of contextualizing the maxim's use within the arena of English politics during the struggle between King and Parliament in the 1620's:

> In the early Stuart parliaments people often argued that in England the King could not tax or legislate without parliamentary consent, and claimed that he was not empowered to violate rights of property or of personal freedom. Supporters of the crown responded that the King ought ordinarily to respect English liberties, *but that in a case of necessity, or for reason of state, or salus populi*, the King could infringe them, and that it was the king alone who was authorized to decide whether or not

10 Quentin Skinner, "Classical Liberty and the Coming of the English Civil War," in *Republicanism: A Shared European Heritage*, vol. 2, *The Values of Republicanism in Early Modern Europe* (Cambridge: Cambridge Univ. Press, 2002), 9–23. Jean Bodin, *Six Books of the Commonwealth*, M.J. Tooley ed. and trans., (Oxford: Alden Press, 1955), 127 (Bk. IV, Ch. 3). Daniel Lee, *Popular Sovereignty in Early Modern Constitutional Thought* (Oxford: Oxford Univ. Press, 2016), 273. By the early 1600's Bodin had become the "champion" of an "emerging English theory of royal absolutism." Brian Vickers, ed., *Francis Bacon* (Oxford: Oxford Univ. Press, 1996), 448. Francis Bacon, *The Essays or Counsels Civill and Morall of Sir Francis Bacon* (*Baron of Verulam, Viscount St. Alban*), (1597), Christopher Morley intro., (reprint; New York: Heritage Press, 1944), 178–79 ("Of Judicature"). Bacon's 1597 essay demonstrates that his understanding of the relationship between the King and "his" judges was anachronistic by 1641. "Fourthly, for that which may concern the Sovereign and Estate. Judges ought *above all* to remember the conclusion of the *Roman Twelve Tables*; *Salus Populi suprema Lex*; and to know that laws, except that be in order to that end, are but things captious, and oracles not well inspired. Therefore, it is a happy thing in a state when kings and states do often consult with judges; and again, when judges do often consult with the king and state: the one, when there is matter of law intervenient in business of state; when there is some consideration of state intervenient in matter of law … Let judges also remember that Solomon's throne was supported by lions on both sides; let them be lions, but yet lions under the throne; being circumspect that they do not check or oppose any points of sovereignty."

> an emergency existed. Such reasoning was employed to justify the Forced Loan of 1626–27, and the imprisonment without cause shown of people who refused it. Earlier, the King's right to imprison in emergencies without showing cause had been widely recognized, but in 1628 the House of Commons decided that the King had never in fact possessed any such right, and some argued that the King had no discretionary powers at all to rule outside the law in emergencies. The law of the land ... provided sufficiently for all possible emergencies, so no extra-legal powers were needed. In part, *this position was developed as a response to Charles I's use of emergency powers in what seemed to many to be no emergencies.*[11]

From the perspective of the 1640's, when the titanic struggle between King and Parliament was rejoined after a decade of Charles I's personal rule, MPs' challenge to the royal prerogative necessarily focused on its use to justify a public emergency, in large part, to avoid another dismissal from government. Again, according to Richard Tuck, since the late 1620's the "use of the language of necessity by the crown and its supporters ... alarmed many MPs, and there was a great deal of opposition to it, and the measures that seemed to be justified by it." Once reconvened, new parliamentary leaders emerged with experience from the 1620's sessions, including John Pym and John Hampden. In 1626, Pym had claimed an extra-legal authority for Parliament similar to the crown's prerogative during impeachment proceedings against the Duke of Buckingham for corruption: the "Court of Parliament" should be the judge of the essential interests of the nation, because its "proceedings are not limited by the Civil or Common Laws, but matters are adjudged according as they stand in opposition to, or conformity with, that which is *suprema lex, salus populi.*"[12]

11 J.P. Sommerville, "English and Roman Liberty in the Monarchical Republic of Early Stuart England," in ed., John F. McDiarmid, *The Monarchical Republic of Early Modern England* (London: Routledge, 2007), 214. J.P. Sommerville, *Royalists and Patriots*, 143, 148–9, 157. Richard Bourke, "Review: Revising the Cambridge School: Republicanism Revisited," *Political Theory* 46 (June 2018): 469–74. Richard Tuck, *The Sleeping Sovereign: The Invention of Modern Democracy* (Cambridge: Cambridge Univ. Press, 2016), 1–61.

12 Richard Tuck, *Philosophy and Government: 1572–1651*, 118–19. Perez Zagorin, "The Political Beliefs of John Pym to 1629," *English Historical Review* 109 (Sept., 1994): 879–80. According to Perez Zagorin, "Although the meaning of this statement is perhaps not wholly clear, it appears to suggest that Pym looked on Parliament, when acting in its judicial capacity, as not restricted by positive law and entitled to base its decisions on the principle that the safety of the people and state is the supreme law." *The Commons Declaration and Impeachment against the Duke of Buckingham* (May 1626), in John Rushworth, ed., *Historical Collections* (London: 1721), 1: 302 @ 335. John Pym, *A Declaration of the Grievances*

Not long after its popularization made possible by Bodin's works, the maxim's use by the English crown began with its deployment in a case concerning impositions, or taxation of foreign trade, known as *Bates' Case* (1606). A leading cause of Elizabeth I's Exchequer operating in deficit resulted from her deference to the nobility in financial matters, a means to help an aging queen secure her throne from ever-younger and more vigorous potential successors. Despite a five-fold inflationary increase during the sixteenth century, their taxes had been cut in half by its end, with sizeable arrears in fees for crown grants. To plug the resulting budgetary gaps, beginning in the 1580s the crown supplemented monopoly grants already being made to encourage manufacture of various goods with grants to "inexperienced courtiers in return for rents." In her final parliamentary appearance, Elizabeth regretted "that my grants should be made grievances to my people, … I could give no rest to my thoughts until I reformed it." While she died before fulfilling her promise, according to Wallace McCaffrey, by projecting her reign as focused on the English people's welfare, and not just her own "ruling house" and nobility, she had fostered an "embryonic notion that the monarch's … conduct of the public business should be shaped," at least in part, "by the interests of the nation." Nevertheless, her failure to modernize the Exchequer's ability to raise sufficient wartime revenue forced the crown to depend on "ad hoc improvisations," leaving its officials dependent on "the civil magistracies of the shires at home and a ramshackle framework of make-do arrangements abroad."[13]

---

*of the Kingdom* (1641), in *Somers Tracts* (London: 1810), 4: 392; (http://name.umdl.umich.edu/A56322.0001.001). Pym described the "three great faculties and functions of parliament" as composed of "legislative, judiciary, and conciliary power." Margaret Judson, *Crisis of the Constitution: An Essay in Constitutional and Political Thought in England, 1603–1645* (1949; reprint, New York: Octagon Books, 1980). 299–305. Blair Worden, "Cromwell and the Protectorate," in *God's Instruments* (Oxford: Oxford Univ. Press, 2012), 239–43. "Recent advances in the study of seventeenth-century parliaments are indebted to the challenge levelled by Conrad Russell and other historians at 'Whig' interpretations. Yet something has been lost by Russell's insistence that parliament was 'an event' rather than 'an institution'. It was both. The event mattered because the institution mattered. The politically inspired exploration of medieval history by 17th century lawyers … involved the recovery … of a vision of parliament as the great council of the realm, where ultimate authority and … emergency powers lay … How else can we explain the confidence of the Long Parliament in 1642, when it claimed to control the militia; bypassed the royal veto; asserted that, as a repository of the community's will, it was entitled to place necessity above the law; and took over the executive?" Conrad Russell, *Causes of the English Civil War* (Oxford: Clarendon Press, 1990), 142–53.

13 Wallace McCaffery, *Elizabeth I: War and Politics, 1588–1603* (Princeton: Princeton Univ. Press, 1992), 59–69. Christopher Haigh, *Elizabeth I* (London: Longman, 1988), 61–64, 108–10. *Copy of the Golden Speech*, in Leah Marcus, et al., eds., *Elizabeth I: Collected Works*

To aggravate matters, upon James I's ascension to the English throne he inherited two wars, one against the Irish, the Nine Years War (1594–1603), and the enduring Anglo-Spanish War (1585–1604) of Armada fame. These conflicts had exhausted England's people and resources, and the new king brought with him existing debts from his own Scottish household as well. He had little choice but to accept a peace initiative by the new Spanish king, Phillip III, even though anti-Spanish public ferment would hound him the rest of his reign. When he called Parliament into session in 1604, Members granted him customs duties (i.e., tonnage and poundage) for the length of his reign, per tradition, but refused additional subsidies for the time being, no matter the manifest need to provide the crown with more dependable sources of revenue. In order to realize greater state revenues, the crown embraced a new governing mantra, "reason of state" (sometimes termed *policy* in early English works), first introduced to the courts of Europe by Giovanni Botero in the late 1500's. It described the need to administer governance with greater care and specialization that was necessary to reinvigorate the prerogative for a more dynamic age. This mantra was reinforced by Bodin's concept of salus populi, or the principle that monarchs could supersede enacted law in cases of national emergency (Botero did not include the maxim in his own work). Tuck identified reason of state as a component of a new wave of absolutism sweeping across Europe at the end of the sixteenth century, in tandem with a more pessimistic "new humanism" that succeeded the earlier Ciceronian version which had animated England's Commonwealth reform movement. Tuck terms the new version as both "anti-constitutional" and "often anti-ethical." Upon the Court of

---

(Chicago: Univ. of Chicago Press, 2000), 341. John Cramsie, *Kingship and Crown Policy under James VI and James I* (Woodbridge: RHS, 2002), 1–5. "The [tax] system was obsolete, corrupt and administratively inefficient, and its manifold failings included decayed rents from crown lands, undervalued parliamentary subsidy ratings, and imperfect customs administration." Michael Braddick, "The Early Modern English State and the Question of Differentiation, from 1550 to 1700," *Comparative Studies in Society and History* 38 (Jan., 1996): 92–111. State formation occurred in the absence of a central bureaucracy of revenue collection, as it was administered locally. Conrad Russell, *The Crisis of Parliaments*, 218–222, 244–51, 257, 266–82. Harold Berman, *Law and Revolution: The Impact of the Protestant Reformations on the Western Legal Tradition*, 2: 201–5. During this era "financial cost of warfare rose dramatically as feudal levies were replaced by mercenaries and armies increased in size and military campaigns increased in frequency and length. In order to raise money to wage war, monarchs mortgaged crown lands and forfeited them when they lost. With the diminution of crown lands, taxes imposed on large landholders and merchants became more onerous," with "resentment" growing "accordingly." Ellen Paterson, "The Politics of Starch: Guilds, Monopolies, and Petitioning in Late Elizabethan and Early Stuart London," *The London Journal* (2022): 2–6; (https://www.tandfonline.com/doi/full/10.1080/03058034.2022.2038461).

Exchequer's endorsement of James' royal decree for new taxes on foreign trade (known as impositions) as a permanent grant, thereby breaking with tradition, resistance soon followed.[14]

While James I was familiar with English politics, he was a novice at managing England's Parliament, and especially inartful in hiding his short temper and ultimate contempt for the body. His new subjects became, in turn, increasingly suspicious of any initiative that undermined its traditions, and especially its established right to consent to new taxation. As Sir Edwin Sandys reported out of the Committee for Impositions in 1614, "Although the impositions are immediately on the merchants, yet is sensible to the whole body of the kingdom," as the "King cannot impose but by act of Parliament." While English monarchs had ordered the collection of impositions in the past (import duties being known as "imposts"), all had been rescinded upon parliamentary "complaint," with none ever made permanent by statute. Still, England's ever-growing foreign

14 Peter Burke, "Reason of State," in J.H. Burns, ed., *Cambridge History of Political Thought: 1450–1700* (Cambridge: Cambridge Univ. Press, 1991), 479–84. The "Italian phrase *ragione degli stati* had been employed around the year 1547," but it was in the "1580s or thereabouts that the new coinage passed into general currency. By the time Giovanni Botero published *Ragion di Stato* (1589) [the term] … was 'a constant subject of discussion in some courts' … Botero was quickly translated into German, French, Spanish, and Latin and so contributed to the new term; *razón de estado, ratio status, raison d'état.* The Germans tended to use the Latin phrase, while the English, until the 1620s at least, to use the Italian, or to replace it by '*policy*'." The concept was central to political thought for about a century. Amongst its differing interpretations Scipione Ammirato advised, "A prince should not be described as acting from reason of state if it can be shown that this was done through ordinary legal channels." Instead, "*reason of state*" referred properly to "cases when the law is broken, or more exactly overridden, by the ruler for the public good." Richard Tuck, *Philosophy and Government: 1572–1651* (Cambridge: Cambridge Univ. Press, 1993), xii–xiv, 65–119. Geoff Baldwin, "Reason of State and English Parliaments, 1610–1642," *History of Political Thought* 25 (Winter 2004): 620–41 @ 623–625. *Reason of state* "has been neglected in discussions of British political theory because it does not fit with either a Whig or a revisionist account of the early seventeenth century." The theory itself was "based on necessary action, which has its origins in the republican Cicero's accounts of politics [i.e., salus populi] … Here the substantive ends become important in any discussion of justice, especially if such ends can be discussed under the notion of *necessitas*, necessity." Robert Bireley, ed., *Botero: The Reason of State* (Cambridge: Cambridge Univ. Press, 2017). Jamie Trace, "The Only Early English Translation of Giovanni Botero's Della Ragion di Stato: Richard Etherington and Sloane MS. 1065," *Electronic British Library Journal* Art. #4 (2016): 1–27; (https://bl.iro.bl.uk/concern/articles/03d8040c-72c7-45d5-8c56-9b8456922439?locale=pt-BR). Trace concludes, "'policy' and politics were now clearly more firmly associated with reason of state … [and] more obviously tied to commerce and colonies. Ultimately, Etherington's manuscript gives us an insight into how Botero's *Della Ragion di Stato* was being read and understood in early 17th century England … as a treatise worthy of politicians' attention."

trade was an increasingly legitimate candidate for new revenue to facilitate the crown's execution of its state responsibilities. As Parliament constantly agitated for action against the Catholic powers, its membership was exceedingly coy about fully funding such campaigns.[15]

Meanwhile, as merchants were squeezed ever tighter for revenue, James I had come to covet the profits of the burgeoning international trade. But as they subsequently faced ruin and bankruptcy, many joined Parliament in common cause against impositions. John Bates, soon to be convicted a fraudulent bankrupt, and already paying rates of tonnage and poundage, barred the crown's revenue agents from boarding his vessel, thereby refusing payment of the £896 impost he owed the Exchequer. Upon the common law court of Exchequer's hearing of his case in 1606, Chief Baron Fleming authored *Bates'* historic opinion that cast a decades-long shadow:

> [T]he King's power is double, ordinary and absolute, and they are several laws and ends, that of the ordinary is for the profit of particular subjects, for the execution of civil justice, … and this exercised by equity and justice in ordinary Courts, and with us Common Law, and these Laws cannot be changed, without Parliament … [T]he absolute power of the King is not that which is converted or executed to *private* use, to the benefit of any particular person, but is only that which is applied to the general benefit of the people, and is *Salus populi*; as the people is the body, and the King the head and this power is guided by the rules … most properly named *policy and Government*, and as the constitution, of this body varieth with the time, … *the matter in question is a material matter of state, and ought to be ruled by the rules of policy*, and if it be so, the King hath done well to execute his extraordinary power.[16]

15 Pauline Croft, "Fresh Light on Bate's Case," *Historical Journal* 30 (no. 3, 1987): 523–26. Glenn Burgess, *British Political Thought: 1500–1660* (New York: Palgrave Macmillan, 2009), 152–70. Ernest Thomas, *Leading Cases in Constitutional Law* (London: 1876), 18–20. Maija Jansson, ed., *Proceedings in Parliament 1614 (House of Commons)* (Philadelphia: APS, 1988), 221–222 (May 12, 1614). S.R. Gardiner, *The Puritan Revolution: 1603–1660* (London: Longman, 1911), 17–20.

16 Pauline Croft, "Fresh Light on Bate's Case," 523–26, 532–39. Lee Esturlid, "Where Everything is Weighed in the Scales of Material Interest: Anglo-Turkish Trade, Piracy and Diplomacy during the Jacobean Period," *European Economic History* 22 (1993): 613–25. Tim Harris, *Rebellion: Britain's First Stuart Kings* (Oxford: Oxford Univ. Press, 2014), 117–35. Margaret Judson, *The Crisis of the Constitution* (1949; reprint, New York: Octagon Books, 1980), 107–29. *Bates' Case* (1606), in *Lane's Exchequer Reports* (London: Henry Sweet, 1884), 33 @ 44–45; [2 *State Trials* 371]. Conrad Russell, *Crisis of Parliaments*, 273–75. David Wooton, ed.,

This passage represents a momentous royal claim of exclusive jurisdiction over a public sphere of policy-making that might eclipse even statutory law, at a crucial point in a centuries long evolution of state formation, based only upon the authority of a common law court whose judges were appointed by the king.

A petition issued by Parliament in 1610 challenging impositions illustrates the perceived novelty of the royal claim made in *Bates*':

> Howbeit, *seeing it hath pleased your Majesty to insist upon that Judgment in the Exchequer*, as being direction sufficient for us, without further examination; upon great desire of leaving your Majesty unsatisfied in no one point of our intents and proceedings, we profess, touching that judgment, that we neither do, nor will, take upon us to reverse it; *but our desire is, to know the reasons whereupon the same was grounded*; and the rather, for that a general conceit is had, that the reasons of that judgment may be extended much farther, even to the utter ruin of the ancient liberty of this kingdom, and of your subjects' right of *propriety* of their lands and goods.

In the same session a bill *Against Taxes and Impositions* was introduced, proclaiming that "no tax, imposition, or charge" be collected "but such as by common consent in Parliament hath been … allowed of and ordained." A follow-on petition several months later objected, "The policy and constitution of this your kingdom appropriates unto the kings of this realm, with the assent of the Parliament, as well as the sovereign power of making laws, as that of taxing or imposing upon the subject's goods or merchandizes, wherein they have justly such a *propriety*, as may not without their consent be altered or changed." The key word in these documents, per its seventeenth-century definition provided by Thomas Hobbes in *Leviathan*, is *propriety*: as "annexed to the Soveraigntie, the whole power of prescribing the rules, whereby every man may know, what Goods he may enjoy, and what Actions he may do, without being molested by any of his fellow subjects: And this is it men call Propriety." In her study of the 1614 "Addled" Parliament that foundered over impositions, Maija Jansson realized "the argument … was not about the petty sums extracted from merchants, but about who had the right to impose those taxes—the King or the

*Divine Right and Democracy*, 23–4. Exchequer's decision in *Bates'* gave the "Crown the right to set customs duties as it chose." Ian Williams, "James VI and I, *rex and judex*: One King as Judge in Two Kingdoms," in William Eves, et. al., eds., *Common Law, Civil Law, and Colonial Law: Essays in Comparative English Legal History from the Twelfth to the Twentieth Centuries* (Cambridge: Cambridge Univ. Press, 2021), 99. James I had a copy of Bodin's work by 1577, only a year after its initial publication.

Parliament—and the concomitant question, in whose power was it to define that right—the courts of law or the high court of Parliament?" In other words, was the "opinion in *Bates' case* ipso facto law?"[17]

Resistance remained heated even by the summer of 1628, as Charles I continued to enjoy revenues by virtue of his father's perpetual grant of levying impositions which he refused to relinquish. Initially, Parliament had provided him a single annual grant of tonnage and poundage, traditionally approved for the entire reign of a monarch, in an attempt to regulate the crown's income; by parliamentary count, from the first imposition in 1608 until 1614, over 1,300 had been levied. Nevertheless, the 1625 grant lapsed without any renewal, and even *after* Charles I had received the *Petition of Right* (1628), Members demanded in a follow-on *Remonstrance* that impositions could not continue without their express approval. Upon his refusal of the *Remonstrance*, Charles dissolved the session, chastising his Lords that only "under" his kingship did they interpret law that he as king did exclusively "make" and "declare." No wonder, even thirty-five years after *Bates'*, John Pym condemned "this single, distracted, and divided judgment" for precipitating a "breach" with the King ever since. According to Conrad Russell, once the Long Parliament had reversed both the *Ship Money* and *Bates'* decisions its leadership was determined to realize a "share in executive power." But first its Members insisted on the enactment of a statute, certified by Charles I, forbidding any tax or imposition without Parliament's consent.[18]

---

17 *Petition to the King respecting Impositions* (May 23, 1610); *Journals of the House of Commons* (London: 1803), 1: 431–2; (http://www.british-history.ac.uk/commons-jrnl/vol1/pp431-432). *Petition to the King on Impositions upon Merchandise* (July 7, 1610); E.R. Foster, ed., *Proceedings in Parliament: The House of Commons* (New Haven: Yale Univ. Press, 1966), 2: 110–18 (May 22–25, 1610), 266–67 (July 7, 1610). *Bill Against Impositions*, in Samuel Gardiner, ed., *Parliamentary Debates in 1610* (London: Camden Society, 1862), 162–63, 123–24 (n. *a*). *House of Lords Journal* (London: HMSO, 1767–1830), 2: 653. The Lords received the following bill from the Commons on July 20, 1610: "An Act against the Taxes and Impositions upon Merchants and other Subjects of this Realm, or Upon their Wares, Goods, and Chattels." John Cramsie, *Kingship and Crown Policy under James VI and James I*, 18–19. Richard Tuck, ed., *Hobbes: Leviathan* (Cambridge: Cambridge Univ. Press, 2017), 125. Maija Jansson, ed., *Proceedings in Parliament 1614* (*House of Commons*), xxi–xxii.

18 Linda Popofsky, "The Crisis over Tonnage and Poundage in Parliament in 1629," *Past and Present* 126 (1990): 45–75. Perez Zagorin, *Rebels and Rulers: 1500–1660* (Cambridge: Cambridge Univ. Press, 1982), 2: 134–37. Maija Jansson, ed., *Proceedings in Parliament 1614* (*House of Commons*), 221–22. *The Remonstrance against Tonnage and Poundage* (June 25, 1628), in Robert Johnson, et al., eds., *Commons Debates of 1628* (New Haven: Yale Univ. Press, 1977), 4: 470–71. *Cobbett's Parliamentary History of England* (London: 1807), 2: 434 (June 28, 1628). Barbara Shapiro, *Law Reform in Early Modern England*, 79–80. The Lords' medieval

Upon Parliament's reassembly in December 1640 to deal with the crown's deficit finances in the wake of the Scottish incursion, the decision of *Rex v. Hampden* was vacated, the justices who supported it impeached, their advisory opinions in favor of the crown condemned as "extrajudicial" and "against the laws and statutes of this realm," and henceforth the *Petition of Right* was to be "firmly and strictly holden and observed." Parliament then proceeded to impeach the King's leading minister, the Earl of Strafford, with Hampden's former counsel, Oliver St. John, leading the prosecution.[19]

---

jurisdiction was briefly revived in the 1620's through the 1660's largely via the impeachment process, and receiving petitions on an array of issues. John Pym, *A Declaration of the Grievances of the Kingdom* (1641), in *Somers Tracts* (London: 1810), 4: 396–97; (http://name.umdl.umich.edu/A56322.0001.001). Conrad Russell, *The Crisis of Parliaments*, 274–5, 317, 329–30. *A Subsidy granted to the King of Tunnage Poundage*, in SR, 5: 104 (16 Car. I ch. VIII (1640)). "No subsidy, custom, impost or other charge whatsoever ought or may be laid ... without common consent in Parliament."

19 William Palmer, "Oliver St. John and the Legal Language of Revolution in England: 1640–1642," 263–82. J.H. Baker, *An Introduction to English Legal History*, 3rd ed., 191. "James I and Charles I removed several more judges [after Coke] who refused to behave as the government wished, and judicial office became less secure than it had ever been. The judges who stayed in office were often associated in popular perception with the government of the day, and within a few decades the awesome judiciary which the people had revered at the beginning of the century came to be regarded, rightly or wrongly, as an instrument of prerogative rule. The decision of a majority of the judges in favor of the imposition of ship-money in 1638 brought their reputation to its lowest ebb, and in 1641 several of the ship-money judges were impeached." John Adamson, *The Noble Revolt* (London: Weidenfeld & Nicholson, 2007), 152–58. In general, St. John advocated for a "reformed commonwealth," which entailed the "king's public acceptance of the principle that the royal prerogative was bounded by the common law and that it was his High Court of Parliament that was its ultimate interpreter ... That, in turn, required the king to renounce a central axiom of the last half century of monarchical theory ... [that his] monarchical powers, being immediately from God, stood above, and therefore unconstrained by, the common law." *An Act for declaring unlawful and void the late proceedings touching Ship money and for the vacating of all Records and Process concerning the same* (Aug. 7, 1641; Gardiner's dating); in SR, 5: 116–17 (16 Car. I ch. XIV (1640)). *Accusation and Impeachment of John Lord Finch* (Printed, 1640), in *Somers Tracts* (London: 1810), 4: 129–32. *Proceedings in Parliament against John Lord Finch, Baron of Fordwich, Lord Keeper, for High Treason* (1640), in T.B. Howell, ed., *State Trials* (London: T.C. Hansard, 1816), 4: 1–22 (#151). Austin Woolrych, *Britain in Revolution, 1625–1660* (Oxford: Oxford Univ. Press, 2002), 168, 184. Chief Justice Finch fled the country, while the six other justices of the majority's opinion were "never brought to trial"; Finch was the Speaker of the Commons in 1629 when Eliot had made his fiery speech. Star Chamber and High Commission were abolished by statute enacted on July 5, 1641. Harold Berman, *Law and Revolution: The Impact of the Protestant Reformations on the Western Legal Tradition*, 2: 207. "Before 1640, judges served at the will of the monarch," after "1689, they were given independence of the crown and life tenure."

Strafford testified that upon his return from Ireland he proposed a compromise whereby the crown would give-up the Ship Money tax in exchange for traditional supply and a redress of grievances. Upon Parliament's refusal of his initiative, he advised Charles in such a "case of absolute and unavoidable necessity," under "salus populi suprema lex" in defense of "Himself and Kingdom," the monarch was "absolved from ordinary rules." This was not a reflexive rationale or ad hoc defense, as Strafford had previously written to Justice Richard Hutton, whose opinion in *Rex v. Hampden* (1637) cast doubt on the extremity of the threat, restating the crown's justification for Charles's position in *Rex v. Hampden*. In "business of so mighty importance" he saluted Chief Justice Finch's unequivocal support of the King, as the "power of levies of forces at sea and land for the very, *not feigned*, relief and safety of the public, is such a property of sovereignty, as were the crown willing, yet can it not divest itself thereof: *Salus Populi suprema Lex*; nay, in cases of extremity, *even above Acts of Parliament*." In times of "public danger and necessity such a levy" as Ship-Money justified itself for preservation of the realm, with the King as "the sole judge." Strafford's gambit to gain Hutton's support failed, however, as the Justice had died the previous February before receiving his correspondence on the matter.[20]

20 *Answers to 28 Special Articles*, in, *Rushworth Collections: Tryal of Thomas Earl of Strafford* (London: 1721), 8: 22 @ 29–30. *The Lord Deputy to Mr. Justice Hutton* (Sept. 13, 1639), in *The Earl of Strafforde's Letters and Dispatches* (London: William Boyer, 1739), 2: 388–89. Sidney Lee, ed., *Dictionary of National Biography*, 10: 359–60. Despite the wide disparity in the dates, and that Justice Hutton did have a namesake son who succeeded him, Sir Richard Hutton, Jr., judging from the letter's introductory remarks there is no doubt that Strafford was writing to Hutton, Sr., because it referred to the charge of treason levied against him by Rev. Thomas Harrison for his decision in *Rex v. Hampden*; ultimately Hutton, Sr., countersued and as Strafford notes, "it did very well deserve punishment, and yourself to be preserved and justified"—Hutton winning his countersuit with an award of £10,000 in damages. William Palmer, "Oliver St. John and the Legal Language of Revolution in England: 1640–1642," 263–282. Barbara Shapiro, *Law Reform in Early Modern England*, 99–103. "When it turned out to be difficult to prove the charge of treason, it was argued that, though individually Stafford's acts did not constitute treason, together they constituted 'cumulative treason,' a previously unknown concept. Finding it impossible to convict Strafford of a known crime, Parliament revived the act of attainder to realize his execution. Attainder was a legislative act declaring the accused guilty without the need for a standard of proof." Oliver St. John, *An Argument of Law Concerning the Bill of Attainder of High-treason of Thomas, Earle of Strafford: At a Conference in a Committee of both Houses of Parliament* (London: 1641), 42–3; *Google Books* (https://www.google.com/books/edition/_/-dhCAQAAMAAJ?hl=en&gbpv=0). "Parliament is the great body politic, it comprehends all from the King to the beggar: ... it hath power over itself, and every one of the members for the preservation of the whole: It's both physician and the patient: if the

On April 12, 1641, parliamentary floor-spokesman for impeachment, John Pym, countered Strafford's claim by proclaiming that as the "universal" and "supreme" law salus populi was the preeminent end of English government, not to serve the prerogative, but to guarantee the people's welfare. Indeed, Pym described this supreme law to be the "boundary" and "measure" between the "King's prerogative and the people's liberty." Englishmen's lives, liberties, and "estates are all in the keeping of the law." He condemned Charles I's tax measures enforced without parliamentary consent as "contrary to the laws and liberties of this Kingdom." While acknowledging the King might properly employ his "sovereign power … for the public good," with "many glorious effects," Pym denied his prerogative extended to authorizing "any tax or imposition upon his people without their consent in Parliament." Reflecting on taxation's burgeoning use for "emergencies," Lord Brooke quipped, "If a prince hath power to command the persons and estates of his subjects in case of necessity, and the same prince be sole judge of necessity, it will be no wonder to me if that people be ever necessitous." A decade later, Massachusetts Magistrate Samuel Symonds condemned the "late" Earl of Strafford's "treacherous and perfidious attempt to alter the frame of [England's] polity."[21]

body be distempered, it hath power to open the vein to let out the corrupt blood; … if one member be … gangrened, it hath power to cut if off for the preservation of the rest."

21 John Pym, *The Declaration of John Pym Esquire, Upon the Whole Matter of the charge of High Treason against Thomas Earle of Strafford, April 12, 1641* (London, 1641), 5–14; *Wing* P4260, Reel 1512: 17; *Early English Books Online*: (http://name.umdl.umich.edu/A70881.0001.001). *The Speech or Declaration of John Pym Esquire* (April 12, 1641), in *Rushworth Collections: Tryal of Thomas Earl of Strafford* (London: 1721), 8: 661–70. *Somers Tracts* (London: 1810), 4: 209. First two articles of Strafford's impeachment: "I. That he hath designed to subvert the fundamental laws of England and Ireland, and to introduce an arbitrary and tyrannical form of government, and to advise the king to establish it by violence and arms … II. That he traitorously usurped in both the said realms, regal power over the lives, estates and privileges of the subjects." *Journals of the House of Commons* (London: 1803), 2: 118–20 (April 12, 1641); 2: 131 (April 30, 1641). On April 12, 1641, Parliament deliberated on trial charges against Strafford until both houses conceded, and a bill of attainder was read a second time. On April 30, the Commons ordered Pym to submit transcripts of his speeches given at the beginning and end of Strafford's trial. John Adamson, *The Noble Revolt: The Overthrow of Charles I*, 3–20, 226–37. Pym's April 12th speech, subsequently printed, is the one given at the end of Strafford's trial, whose prosecution collapsed on April 10, 1641, leading to the final passage of the bill of attainder. Sheila Lambert, "The Opening of the Long Parliament," *Historical Journal* 27 (June 1984): 275–80. J.A.W. Gunn, *Politics and the Public Interest in the Seventeenth Century* (Toronto: Univ. of Toronto Press, 1969), 1–35. Lord Brooke, *A Discourse Opening the Nature of that Episcopacy which is Exercised in England* (1642), in William Haller, ed., *Tracts on Liberty* (New York: Columbia Univ. Press, 1934), 2: 55. *Case of George Giddings and Others of Ipswich*, (Samuel Symonds' decision, 1657), in *Hutchinson Papers* (Albany: Prince Society, 1865), 2: 1, @ 11–12. Austin

January of 1642 would see Charles I fail in his bid to arrest five MPs, including John Hampden and John Pym, after ordering his supporters to storm the chamber. As he gathered allies and assembled his armies over the coming months, royalists and parliamentarians exchanged broadsides in a war of print that anticipated armed hostilities. The King described his government as a mixture of "absolute monarch, aristocracy, and democracy." Consequently, "laws are jointly made by a king, by a house of peers, and by a house of commons chosen by the people, all having free votes and particular privileges." To monarchy was entrusted a "power of treaties of war and peace, of making peers, of choosing officers and councilors of state, judges for law, commanders for forts and castles, giving commissions for raising men, to make war abroad or to prevent or provide against invasions or insurrections at home." As for Parliament, it was no more than an adjunct member of government that assembled only upon the King's command. After eleven years of Charles's personal rule, Parliament passed the *Triennial Act* in February 1641, requiring its reassembly every three years; since Edward VI's reign, Parliament had been in session every three and a half years on average, with grants of subsidiary revenue to the monarch listed at the end of enacted statutes, redress of grievances by the monarch being a procedural reality. The following May, the *Continuance Act* forbid its dismissal without enactment of a statute to such effect; John Collins has described this Act as "one of the most radical transformations of the legal system in English history." In this evolving parliamentary supremacy, the pamphlet *Maxims of Mixt Monarchy* termed the king a mere "third estate," as "legislative power" could not be exercised "out of Parliament." According to John Winthrop, Bay colonists believed the King had no "absolute power without the Parliament." Robert Filmer (1588–1653), England's preeminent divine right polemicist, termed such claims nonsense, the "liberties and privileges of both houses have

---

Woolrych, *Britain in Revolution, 1625–1660*, 173–207. Strafford's "bill of attainder ... passed its third reading on 21 April [1641] by 204 votes to 59." Ibid., 199. "[T]he catholic Earl of Atrim, ... by his own later account, received orders from Charles I in late summer of 1641 to reassemble all he could of Strafford's disbanded troops," and "if occasion should offer, for use against ... Parliament." Richard Cust, *Charles I and the Aristocracy, 1625–1642* (Cambridge: Cambridge Univ. Press, 2013), 215–16, 233–34. In November 1640, Charles I and Strafford planned to "overawe" Parliament with the Tower of London garrison, and several months later the "Army Plot" would have the King's northern army free Strafford from the Tower. It launched in the Spring of 1641 and failed disastrously. The King did not deny knowledge of either plot, and an attempt to seize Portsmouth to facilitate the King and Queen's escape was foiled. Michael Mendle, *Henry Parker and the English Civil War* (Cambridge: Cambridge Univ. Press, 1995), 5, 18, 32–50.

but one and the self-same foundation, which is nothing else but the mere and sole grace of kings."[22]

Henry Parker's *Observations Upon Some of his Majesties Late Answers and Expresses* was published in July 1642, a work Robert Zaller described as having "extraordinary impact" in transforming "the landscape of political debate … as clearly as any gunshot could the onset of civil war." Faced with centuries of monarchic rule, Parker conceived of a popular sovereignty based on the "transcendent" origin of all political states with which he created a powerful ideology at an historic moment: "Power is originally inherent in the people, and it is nothing else but that might and vigor which such or such a society of men contains in itself." Its guiding principle undergirded all body politics, and this "Paramount Law" supported "all human laws": "salus populi" or the public welfare. Because kingship was founded to "preserve" the people, the royal prerogative must serve the people's welfare or become an illegitimate authority, as it portended only a descent into tyranny. G.P. Gooch entitled his chapter on these events in his *History of Democratic Ideas in the Seventeenth Century* (1898), "The Birth of Republicanism."[23]

---

22 *The King's Answer to the Nineteen Propositions*, (June 18, 1642), in J.P. Kenyon, ed., *The Stuart Constitution* (Cambridge: Cambridge Univ. Press, 1986), 18–19. *An Act for the Preventing of Inconveniences Happening by the Long Intermissions of Parliament* [i.e., The Triennial Act], SR, 5: 54–57 (16 Car. I ch. 1 (Feb. 15, 1641)); *An Act for the Preventing of Inconveniences which may happen by the Untimely Adjourning, Proroguing or Dissolving of this Present Parliament*, SR, 5: 103–4 (17 Car. I ch. 7 (May 10, 1641)). Harold Berman, *Law and Revolution*, 2: 216–17. John M. Collins, "The Long Parliament and the Law of Necessity in Seventeenth Century England," *Past and Present* 247 (May 2020): 23–24. "Worried that Charles might attempt to dissolve it before the execution of Strafford could take place … MPs … passed the [Continuance] act simultaneously with the Earl's attainder. The act declared that owing to the 'imminent danger' this Kingdom is in … the king could not dissolve Parliament … Through the Continuance Act the Long Parliament fundamentally reshaped the legal order." *Maxims of Mixt Monarchy* (Feb. 6, 1643), 4–5; *Thomason Tracts* E88 (15), Reel 15. Michael Mendle, *Dangerous Positions* (Tuscaloosa: Univ. of Alabama Press, 1985). Robert Filmer, *The Free-Holders Grand Inquest Touching Our Soveraigne Lord the King and His Parliament* (1648), in J.P. Sommerville, ed., *Patriarcha and Other Writings* (Cambridge: Cambridge Univ. Press, 1991), 99. Richard Dunn, ed., *Journal of John Winthrop*, 528 (August 1644). Glenn Burgess, *British Political Thought*, 176–80.

23 Henry Parker, *Observations Upon Some of his Majesties Late Answers* (1642), in William Haller, ed., *Tracts on Liberty* (New York: Columbia Univ. Press, 1934), 2: 167–69; 1: 23–28. William Haller, *The Rise of Puritanism* (Columbia Univ. Press, 1938), 365–70. "Parker's *Observations*, clear and plausible, was a singularly effective pamphlet and takes a striking place in the literature of revolution." Robert Zaller, "Henry Parker and the Regiment of True Government," *Proceedings of the American Philosophical Society* 135 (June 1991): 264–85. Margaret Judson, *The Crisis of the Constitution*, 411–19. G.P. Gooch, *The History of English Democratic Ideas in the Seventeenth Century* (Cambridge: Univ. Press, 1898), 103–10 (Ch. 3,

Parker was professionally and ideologically committed to an ongoing political struggle between King and Parliament. To understand his use of salus populi suprema lex, and grasp why Massachusetts freemen made it their own, a summary of events leading to its composition is requisite. Parker's ostensible target was a pamphlet published under the king's name, *Upon Some of his Majesties Late Answers and Expresses*, which sought to counter Parliament's own *Nineteen Propositions* issued in June 1642 that would strip Charles I of his prerogative. Its first three sections demanded that Privy Councilors be replaced by new members approved by both houses of Parliament; second, all "matters as concern the public" be conducted within the confines of the "High Court of Parliament," and not by the "advice of private men, or ... unknown or unsworn councilors"; and third, even senior officials of English government must be approved by Parliament. Although Charles initially agreed to a nomination process, *Eikōn Basilikē*—reputed to be his autobiography—recounted his final response, "They sit in Parliament as my subjects, not my superiors: called to be my councilors, not dictators: their summons extends to recommend their advice, not command my duty."[24]

---

*The Birth of Republicanism*). "Monarchy has lost all sanctity and romance for the writer [i.e., Parker]. God is no more the author of one form of government than of another. All power is originally in the People, and God only confirms that form which is selected by common consent. Since the office of King was instituted to preserve the commonalty, it is absurd to imagine any nation would give itself absolutely into the hands of an individual. The Charter of Nature entitles the subjects of all countries to safety, and the community, by virtue of its paramount interest, may justly seize power and use it for its own preservation. It may judge of public necessity without the king, who has 'no negative voice,' ... The justification of this is to be found in the fact that whereas the sting of monarchy is the danger of bondage, no age furnishes a story of a Parliament freely elected exercising any tyranny. The full bearing of this remarkable pamphlet and of the position which was now reached was at once recognized by the royalists." Vimala Pasupathi, "Mars Rising: Army Pamphlets and London Culture post 1642," *Yearbook of English Studies* 44 (2014): 244–245. "In 1642, Parliament launched a major propaganda campaign to ... provide proof that the Houses had the authority to raise an army."

24 *His Maiesties Answer to the XIX Propositions of Both Houses of Parliament* (Oxford: 1642); *Google Books* (https://books.google.com/books?vid=BL:A0022003739). *The Nineteen Propositions* (June 1, 1642) in J.P. Kenyon, ed., *The Stuart Constitution*, 222–26. *Eikōn Basilikē: The Pourtraicture of His Sacred Majestie in His Solitudes and Sufferings* (Feb., 1649), 79; *Google Books* (https://books.google.com/books?id=Pi1QAQAAIAAJ&source=gbs_similarbooks). Charles's authorship is contested. David Wooton, ed., *Divine Right and Democracy*, 36. The *Propositions* tried "to make absolute monarchy impossible: the king was to abandon control of the armed forces, to resign his right to choose his own counsellors and to dismiss judges who displeased him, to give up sole control of religion, foreign policy, and the education and marriage of the heir to the throne. Such terms were unacceptable to Charles." John Adamson, *The Noble Revolt: The Overthrow of Charles I*,

The *Propositions* represented the last attempt by King and Parliament to reach a compromise since Charles's attempt to arrest five Members of the House of Commons the previous January. According to MP Edmund Ludlow: "The King … went in person to the House of Commons, attended not only with his ordinary guard of pensioners, but also with those desperadoes that for some time he had entertained at Whitehall, to the number of three or four hundred, armed with partizans [i.e., pikes], sword and pistol." With thousands of Londoners rioting in the city's streets and alleyways, David Cressy described Charles I's last sojourn through the city before departing his capital to raise an army:

> The missing members had found refuge in the city, and the rest of the Commons adjourned there to Guildhall. Citizens were determined to welcome and protect them. When the King entered the city on 5 January, John Dillingham reports, he "had the worst day in London … that ever he had." It was a chilling and threatening reception—some might say treasonous … The normally respectful crowd shouted "privilege of parliament" and "prayed god to turn the heart of the king," shutting up all their shops and standing at their doors with swords and halberds. At the King's meeting with the Lord Mayor and Alderman, some of the common councilmen chanted, "parliament, privileges of parliament," while a smaller group cried "God bless the king."[25]

---

415–20. *Sir Patrick Wemyss to Earle of Ormonde* (Sept. 25, 1641), in *A Collection of Original Letters and Papers, 1641–1660 (Found among the Duke of Ormond's Papers)* (London: 1739), 1: 1–5. "The King has been earnest to have the nomination of the officers of state and counsellors, … and at last it was agreed Saturday last, that the King should make choice of them with consent and approbation of Parliament." David Como, "Making 'the Heads of the Proposals': The King, the Army, the Levellers, and the Roads to Putney," *English Historical Review* 135 (Feb., 2021): 1383. The Army's *Heads of the Proposals* (June 1647) reiterated the need to "give parliament the right in perpetuity to nominate the great officers of state, with the king choosing from among three parliamentary nominees." Corinne Weston, "The Theory of Mixed Monarchy Under Charles I and After," *English Historical Review* 75 (1960): 426–43. J.G.A. Pocock, *The Machiavellian Moment* (Princeton: Princeton Univ. Press, 1975), 361–66. *Cobbett's Parliamentary History of England* (London: 1807), 2: 1324, 1389.

25 Edmund Ludlow, *Memoirs of Edmund Ludlow, Esq.; Lieutenant-General of Horse, Commander in Chief of the Forces in Ireland, one of the Council of State, Member of Parliament which began on Nov. 3, 1640* (London: 1751), 5–17. Robert Zaller, "Henry Parker and the Regiment of True Government," 864–72. *Cobbett's Parliamentary History of England*, 2: 1008–18. David Cressy, *England on Edge* (Oxford: Oxford Univ. Press, 2006), 393.

As the King traveled north, under John Pym's leadership the House of Commons solicited support from the House of Lords to seize control of the nation's militia. Traditionally, a county's militia was commanded by a royally appointed Lord Lieutenant. According to Sir Thomas Smith's sixteenth-century treatise, command of the kingdom's armed forces was the most basic prerogative power, as in "war and peace" a king's "word is a law … without process of law or form of judgment." His "martial law" could interdict "sudden insurrections and rebellions" only if it was an absolute authority, as military "necessity requireth speedy execution." Despite centuries of the monarch's command of the militia, however, Parliament enacted the *Militia Ordinance* unilaterally in March 1642. Not only did such an appointment power defy precedent, the law was an "ordinance," rather than a statute, as the latter took effect only upon royal approval of a bill previously passed by both Houses. As a pamphleteer explained, "Statutes of the Realm are the … absolute judgments of the Parliament established by the King, with the common consent of the three estates, who do represent the whole and entire Body of the Realm of England." After Charles attempted to enter Hull the following April to secure its royal armory, only to be rebuffed, MPs charged "the King, as seduced by wicked counsel, intends to make war upon his Parliament." Those remaining Lords who had not joined Charles I at York instructed the Hull garrison to be on alert "in case there be a necessity for raising the forces of the country."[26]

Charles I was well aware of his prerogative rights as monarch, including his authority as supreme military commander of the realm. In a proclamation

26 Sir Thomas Smith, *De Republica Anglorum*, ed. Mary Dewar, (Cambridge: Cambridge Univ. Press, 1982), 81–6 (Bk. II, Chaps. 2–3). Geoffrey Elton, *The Parliament of England: 1559–1581* (New York: Cambridge Univ. Press, 1986), 91–130. Michael Mendle, "The Great Council of Parliament and the First Ordinances," *Journal of British Studies* 31 (Apr., 1992): 143–160. Parliamentarians ultimately claimed they constituted the "supreme judicature, … declaring the law even as they executed it." John Eusden, *Puritans, Lawyers, and Politics in Early Seventeenth-Century England* (New Haven: Yale Univ. Press, 1958), 161. "Pym and his colleagues made a pretense of searching for precedents to their acts, even when they were in the novel process of doing away with the High Commission and other aspects of kingly rule. But in reality, the members of the Long Parliament passed legislation which was neither based on old laws nor promulgated according to the customary procedure." *Brief Collections out of Magna Charta* (1643), 4; *Thomason Tracts* E38 (12), Reel 7. *The Militia Ordinance*, in *Acts and Ordinances of the Interregnum, 1642–1660*, C.H. Firth and R.S. Rait eds., (London: HMSO, 1911), 1: 1–5 (March 5, 1642). David Como, "Making 'the Heads of the Proposals': The King, the Army, the Levellers, and the Roads to Putney," 1393–94. "Hard-line parliamentarians" saw the "veto" as "one of the most central issues at stake in England's civil wars, and from 1643 onwards" they ensured Parliament could "pass legislation without hindrance." *Journals of the House of Commons*, 2: 588–90 (May 27, 1642). *Journals of the House of Lords* (London: HMSO, 1767–1830) 5: 85–88 (May 27, 1642).

condemning the *Militia Ordinance*, he jabbed at his parliamentary enemies, "hereunto all subjects are bound to aid the King as their sovereign lord, at all seasons when need shall be." Now, however, "under color and pretense of an Ordinance of Parliament, without our consent, or any commission or warrant from us, … the trained bands of militia of this kingdom … are intended to be in arms and drawn into companies in a warlike manner." He charged "malignant persons" with ulterior motives of seducing "our good subjects from their due obedience to us and the laws of this our kingdom, … and under a specious pretense of putting our trained bands into a posture, draw and engage our good subjects in a warlike posture against us." He warned his subjects that such behavior constituted "treason." Meanwhile, as Richard Tuck has reminded us, Charles I was limited in being able to raise forces under his feudal rights or the more "normal process of hiring professionals."[27]

Eventually, Parliament relented and acknowledged English law *supported* the royal proclamation forbidding militias from rallying to the parliamentary standard. Nevertheless, MPs felt compelled to seize command of the militia because Charles had refused to "discharge that duty and trust … to provide for the safety of the Parliament and peace of the kingdom, for which the Ordinance concerning the militia was made." Pym repeated his earlier concept of Parliament's conciliar authority, first articulated during Buckingham's impeachment in the 1620's, to justify its emergency actions: the "High Court of Parliament is not only a court of judicature, enabled by the laws to adjudge and determine the rights and liberties of the kingdom, … it is likewise a council, to provide for the necessities, prevent the imminent dangers, and preserve the public peace and safety of the kingdom." Upon the foundation of this "constitution and policy," Parliament declared the royal proclamation's attempt to outlaw compliance with its own *Militia Ordinance* "void in law, and of none effect." As the king "cannot declare the law contrary to the judgment and resolution of any of the inferior courts of justice, much less against the High Court of Parliament," he could not disavow the *Militia Ordinance* by proclamation. Otherwise, his edicts would "become laws," and subvert "the law of the land, and the rights and liberties of the subjects." On the other hand, Charles I refused to deal with Members who sought "all power … vested in the House of Commons," inciting the "common people" to indulge "all their wild humors" in the name of "parity" and "liberty," with "all rights," "proprieties," and "distinctions of families and merit" destroyed. He especially condemned his royal

27 *The King's Proclamation Condemning the Militia Ordinance* (May 27, 1642), in Samuel Gardiner, ed., *Constitutional Documents of the Puritan Revolution*, 248–49. Richard Tuck, *Philosophy and Government: 1572–1651*, 224–25.

justices' imprisonment for "executing the law," lamenting "our negative voice (our greatest and most sovereign privilege) is boldly denied."[28] On the other side of the Atlantic, Nathaniel Ward reported in the mid-1640's, "we hear that Majestas Imperi [i.e., the royal prerogative] hath challenged Salus Populi into the field, the one fighting for prerogatives, the other defending liberties."[29]

---

28 *An Ordinance of the Lords and Commons in Parliament, for the Safety and Defence of the Kingdom of England, and Dominion of Wales* ['The *Militia Ordinance*'], in *Acts and Ordinances of the Interregnum, 1642–1660*, Firth and Rait eds., 1: 1–5 (March 5, 1642). *The Nineteen Propositions* (1 June 1642), in J.P. Kenyon, ed., *The Stuart Constitution*, 2nd ed., 222–26. *Declaration of the Houses in Defence of the Militia Ordinance* (June 6, 1642), in Samuel Gardiner, ed., *Constitutional Documents of the Puritan Revolution*, 254–58. *The King's Answer to the Nineteen Propositions* (18 June 1642), in J.P. Kenyon, ed., *The Stuart Constitution*, 2nd ed., 18–20. *By the King. A Proclamation warning all His Majesties Good Subjects no longer to be Misled by the Votes, Orders, and Pretended Ordinances, of one, or both Houses by reason the Members do not Enjoy the Freedome and Liberty of Parliament* (June 20, 1643), (Oxford: Univ. Printer, 1643); *Early English Books Online* (http://name.umdl.umich.edu/A79038.0001.001). *To the Right honorable, the Commons of England in Parliament Assembled* [i.e., The Humble Petition] (Sept. 11, 1648), in Andrew Sharp, ed., *The English Levellers* (Cambridge: Cambridge Univ. Press, 1998), 131–32. Michael Mendle, "The Ship Money Case, the Case of Shipmony, and the Development of Henry Parker's Absolutism," 531–32. "The full notion of bicameral parliamentary absolutism emerged in the spring and early summer of 1642 ... The [militia] ordinance was a response to an emergency; there was no claim that what was done was ordinarily legal." Richard Tuck, *Philosophy and Government: 1572–1651*, 221–31. "The issue upon which constitutionalism gave way in England was the creation of a new military organization," as it became "clear to most participants in the debates inside and outside of Westminster during 1642 that the English Parliament was making a novel claim" concerning its control of the militia.

29 Nathaniel Ward, *Simple Cobbler of Agawam* (London: 1647), 44; *Thomason Tracts* E372 (21), Reel 59.

CHAPTER 11

# Popular Sovereignty: Salus Populi Suprema Lex

As Margaret Judson noted in her pioneering scholarship on Henry Parker, during this era there was a pronounced dissonance between the desperate conflict of King and Parliament and the great pride with which the country had previously held its government, "The greatest obstacle writers faced when they spoke out on behalf of the Commonwealth government was the deeply held conviction that monarchy was not only indispensable in the English polity, but indeed 'the perfectest state of government,' as John Pym ... pronounced in 1621." England had largely avoided the religious strife that overtook the continent during the last century, with Elizabeth I successfully issuing a national creed in the form of the *Book of Common Prayer* with parliamentary approval, which in the name of a newly established national church facilitated her endeavor to avoid "making windows into men's souls." Despite many near misses on being drawn into European conflicts, and an attempted Spanish invasion towards the end of the century, England emerged relatively unscathed. But as covered in the last chapter, modernity had entered the national fray early in the following century with *Bates' Case*, and the necessity of providing an antiquated kingdom a more decisive means of administering government through making "policy," which remains the general purpose of modern governance today. As King and Parliament struggled over controlling this new policy-making power, however, it soon became clear that such a unified sovereign authority had despotic tendences, no matter who was in charge.[1]

Henry Parker's (1604–1652) *Observations Upon Some of his Majesties Late Answers and Expresses* was published only months before the first of two civil wars between Charles I and Parliament began in the Fall of 1642; a work Richard Tuck has termed "the most influential and informative defense" of the idea that "Parliament was entitled to do anything for the public safety." At the time, Parker was secretary to the Earl of Essex, general of one of Parliament's armies,

1 Margaret Judson, *From Tradition to Political Reality* (Hamden [CT]: Archon Books, 1980), 15–25. Margaret Judson, *Crisis of the Constitution: An Essay in Constitutional and Political Thought in England, 1603–1645* (1949; reprint, New York: Octagon Books, 1980), 44–170, 305. "[A]s Parliament during these years encroached upon the king, claiming more and more of his power in the name of the nation, Parliament seemed to assume without question that its voice was truly the voice of the nation ... and [it] could work out ways to enable it to be controlled ultimately by the nation."

 | DOI:10.1163/9789004706347_013

soon to be followed by his appointment as secretary to Parliament's Committee of Safety that made him a close confidant of parliamentary leader John Pym (1584–1643). In April 1641, Pym had asserted salus populi was the "element of all laws, out of which they are derived," and the "end of all laws, to which they are designed." Parker's *Observations* declared, the "safety of the people is to be valued above any right" of royal prerogative, "as much as the end is to be preferred before the means." How could Parliament judge the people's interest better than the King? In "public consultations the many eyes of so many choice gentlemen out of all parts see more than fewer," enhancing "the great interest the Parliament has in common justice and tranquility." Essentially, the "true nature" of "Parliamentary Power" was its continual exercise of "public consent" by representing the will of the people. Charles I countered, Parliament's dissolution of his prerogative had unleashed an "arbitrary unlimitable power" that its members themselves would abuse. Parker acknowledged the necessity of an arbitrary power in every polity, but only a legislature could safely exercise its fearsome power. If entrusted to a king or an aristocracy "there may be danger in it," but Parliament was "neither one nor few, it is indeed the state itself" by virtue of its "*equally and geometrically proportionable*" representation. The royalist Robert Filmer agreed on the necessity of arbitrary power, but it was the king's jurisdiction alone: "it is not possible for kings to see the laws executed, except there be a power in kings both to judge when the laws are duly executed, and when not." Still, Parker insisted that "since most countries have found out an art and peaceable order for public assemblies," by "election and representation," Parliament constituted the supreme authority.[2]

Parker would have his readers believe that representative government was the prevailing norm, when in fact parliamentary seats had been apportioned

2 Richard Tuck, *Philosophy and Government: 1572–1651* (Cambridge: Cambridge Univ. Press, 1993), 226–36. *The Speech or Declaration of John Pym Esquire* (April 12, 1641), in *Rushworth Collections: Tryal of Thomas Earl of Strafford* (London: 1721), 8: 661. J.P. Sommerville, *Politics and Ideology in England: 1603–1640* (London: Longman, 1986), 74. Henry Parker, *Observations Upon Some of his Majesties Late Answers and Expresses* (1642), in William Haller, ed., *Tracts on Liberty* (New York: Columbia Univ. Press, 1934), 2: 177–200. *The King's Answer to the Nineteen Propositions* (June 18, 1642), in J.P. Kenyon, ed., *The Stuart Constitution*, 2nd ed., (Cambridge: Cambridge Univ. Press, 1986), 18–20. Michael Mendle, *Henry Parker and the English Civil War* (Cambridge: Cambridge Univ. Press, 1995), 19, 83. Michael Mendle, "The Ship Money Case, the Case of Shipmony, and the Development of Henry Parker's Absolutism," *Historical Journal* 32 (no. 3, 1989): 517–25. Robert Filmer, *Free-Holders Grand Inquest*, in J.P. Sommerville, ed., *Patriarcha and Other Writings* (Cambridge: Cambridge Univ. Press, 1991): 99–100, 114. Robert Ashton, "From Cavalier to Roundhead Tyranny," in John Morrill, ed., *Reactions to the English Civil War: 1642–1649* (New York: St. Martin's Press, 1982), 185–207. Robert Ashton, *Counter Revolution* (New Haven: Yale Univ. Press, 1996), 81–116.

via traditional rights and privileges over centuries, not by census of population distribution. Since he had already set aside a mountain of precedent supporting the King's command of the militia, as well as Parliament's inability to enact statutory law on its own authority, why not claim a just king would not refute his model of representative government? Parker's aim was to convince readers extraordinary times required an arbitrary power only Parliament would exercise responsibly. Filmer waded through his dissemblance in *The Anarchy of a Limited or Mixed Monarchy*, challenging the "Observator ... to name but one kingdom that hath either now or heretofore found out this art or peaceable order." Englishmen did not enjoy representation in many parts of the kingdom, no matter how the "Observator ... useth the strength of his wit to overthrow absolute and arbitrary government"; and recall, heretofore parliamentary representation was based on the paradigm that each member represented the entire kingdom. While Filmer's critique of Parker's essay was accurate historically, as England's "rotten boroughs" having to await a nineteenth-century parliamentary statutory reform attest, Parker's essay had a decisive impact throughout the 1640's. An anonymous royalist initially reacted, "If the People make a King, they are more King themselves, or if they give power, they have more power: and may resume and exercise that power when they please." By 1647, a royalist under the pseudonym Theophilius Craterus lamented, just as Winthrop had several years earlier, "every man who hath arrived to one sentence in Latin is ready to beat me down with the irresistible power of axiom ... Salus Populi lex Summa," or the public good is the highest law. Craterus feared it was now "a rule of God of nature," and "uncontrollable." Indeed, a parliamentary supporter proclaimed salus populi suprema lex "the supreme and cardinal law, to which all laws are to stoop," a phrase taken directly from Parker's *The Case of Shipmoney* (1640).[3]

3 Robert Filmer, *The Anarchy of a Limited or Mixed Monarchy* (1648), in J.P. Sommerville, ed., *Patriarcha and Other Writings* (Cambridge: Cambridge Univ. Press, 1991), 132–63. *Animadversions upon those notes which the late Observator hath published* (London: 1642), 5; *Early English Books* (http://name.umdl.umich.edu/A75367.0001.001). Theophilus Craterus, *A Calm Consolatory View of the Sad Tempestuous Affairs in England* (London: April 19, 1647), 5–6; *Thomason Tracts*, E384 (13), Reel 61. Richard Tuck, ed., *Hobbes: Leviathan* (Cambridge: Cambridge Univ. Press, 2017), 125. Michael Mendle, *Henry Parker and the English Civil War*, 37–41. Michael Mendle, "The Ship Money Case," 519–20. Edmund Morgan, *Inventing the People* (New York: W.W. Norton, 1988), 13–15, 58–89. Daniel Lee, *Popular Sovereignty in Early Modern Constitutional Thought* (Oxford: Oxford Univ. Press, 2016), 3–5, 288–309. David Hall, *A Reforming People* (New York: Alfred A. Knopf, 2011), 14–15. David Cressy, *Charles I and the People of England* (Oxford: Oxford Univ. Press, 2015), 293–99. Samuel Rutherford, *Lex, Rex: The Law and the Prince. A Dispute for the Just Prerogative of King and People* (London: 1644), 218; *Thomason Tracts* E11 (5), Reel 2. Richard Tuck, *Philosophy and*

Another royal polemicist, and "early Hobbist," Dudley Digges, recoiled from Parker's equation of popular sovereignty with fundamental law. He attacked any postulation that the "essential cause of power is the people" as an "inference most weak," because it would follow that "he which hath all their power ... must needs be greater and more powerful than they." Digges mocked Parker's "proof" that as the "people be the true ... cause of power, it is a rule in nature. Strange that men upon such palpable sophistry should endeavor to cast off monarchy." John Milton countered, it was Digges himself who endangered the crown, because it was "never so secure ... when fenced in by the wisdom of Parliaments, [and] submits to their determinations; so, it is never so much in danger, as when it exalts itself above and against them, and endeavoureth an absoluteness of sovereignty." Besides, Milton wondered, "what is the sophistry the Observator stands accused of?" Digges charged that salus populi had brought many kingdoms "to ruin and confusion!" Milton countered that no specific examples of these ruined nations were cited, only illusory "phantasms or chimeras." He urged his fellow Englishmen not to be cowed by such hollow threats, but instead to "secure ourselves from apparent and visible dangers." The following year Milton proclaimed, if a king violated his coronation oath, endangering the public good, Parliament must fulfill its first responsibility to protect the people.[4]

Once salus populi suprema lex was conceived as natural law, purposed to secure the public welfare, a vital step to a revolutionary popular sovereignty had been achieved. If commoners could judge law in relation to their own

---

*Government: 1572–1651*, 227. Parker's *Case of Shipmoney* stated, "The supreme of all human laws is salus populi. To this law all laws almost stoop."

4 Richard Tuck, "Power and Authority in Seventeenth Century England," *Historical Journal* 17 (March, 1974): 43. Dudley Digges, *An Answer to a Printed Book, Intituled, Observations upon some of His Majesties Late Answers and Expresses* (Oxford: 1642), 10–20; *Early English Books Online* (http://name.umdl.umich.edu/A35993.0001.001). John Milton, *A Reply to the Answer (printed by His Majesties command at Oxford) to a printed booke intituled Observations* (London: 1642), 6–11; *Early English Books Online* (http://name.umdl.umich.edu/A50950.0001.001). John Milton, *A Soveraigne Salve to Cure the Blind, or, A Vindication of the Power and Priviledges Claim'd or Executed by the Lords and Commons in Parliament* (London: 1643), 19–25; *Early English Books Online* (http://name.umdl.umich.edu/A89494.0001.001). Christopher Hill, *Milton and the English Revolution* (New York: Penguin Books, 1979), 100. "Milton agreed with the Levellers in rejecting the communist theories which the Diggers ... preached. He agreed with Levellers (and Diggers) in their opposition to tithes, their rejection of monarchy and the House of Lords, their belief that magistrates should be elected, and that resistance to tyranny was not only a right but a duty." Alison Chapman, "Milton and Legal Reform," *Renaissance Quarterly* 69 (no. 2, 2016): 529–65. Martin Dzelzainis, "History and Ideology: Milton, the Levellers, and the Council of State in 1649," *Huntington Library Quarterly* 68 (March 2005): 269–287.

welfare, political activism was no longer an exclusive preserve of the nobility, gentry, or an episcopacy or religious ministry. As John Goodwin reasoned, "every private man should scan, examine, judge, and determine either the righteousness or unrighteousness of the King's command" without university training or divine sanction, since anyone could see if the "bow be straight, or the string bent and crooked." Another pamphleteer cautioned against being distracted by "other men's counsels"; could anyone "tell better than yourselves where your shoe pincheth you, and what is most expedient for you to do?" Why be "led like children and fools by the nose, to be made stalking horses of other men's designs whose interests are dissonant and inconsistent with yours." John Warr wondered, if the "end of just laws is the safety and freedom of a people," why were they based on lawyers' interpretations, or that "contentious way of law which the oppressed man stands in no more need of than the tender-hearted Christian of Thomas Aquinas to resolve him of his doubts." William Ball argued, because salus populi was the "chief object and end of government," Englishmen had "no judges of their common interest but themselves." Even if the public welfare was under threat, the people, via their "representatives, or trustees, ought to be judges primary, or in the first place." John Lilburne and Richard Overton agreed, "all magisterial power in England whatever are but officers of trust, and bound up with this limitation, to be executed for the good of the trusters." John Warr concluded, the "People is the true and proper interest of the Common-wealth," and as its authority was "fundamentally ... seated in the People," *the* "power of rulers is but ministerial and in order to the people's good," justified by that "known maxim, the safety of the people is the supreme law."[5]

5 John Goodwin, *Anti-Cavilierisme* (London: 1642), in William Haller, ed., *Tracts on Liberty*, 2: 236. *A New-found Stratagem* (April 4, 1647), 4–11; *Thomason Tracts* E384 (11), Reel 61. John Warr, *The Corruption and Deficiency of the Laws of England* (1649), in T. Park, ed., *Harleian Miscellany* (London: 1808–1813), 6: 215–24. William Ball, *The Power of Kings Discussed* (Jan. 30, 1649), 3; *Thomason Tracts* E540 (21), Reel 84. John Lilburne, and Richard Overton, *The Out-Cryes of Oppressed Commons* (Feb. 28, 1647), 7–18; *Thomason Tracts* E378 (13), Reel 60. John Warr, *The Privileges of the People* (Feb. 5, 1649); *Thomason Tracts* E541 (12), Reel 84. David Wooton, ed., *Divine Right and Democracy* (New York: Penguin Books, 1986), 45–56. J.A.W. Gunn, *Politics and the Public Interest in the Seventeenth Century* (Toronto: University of Toronto Press, 1969), 1–35. David Cressy, *Charles I and the People of England*, 26–51. "The king and his counsellors were adamant that only people of their own understanding and status should concern themselves with state affairs ... 'The scum of the commons, the tags and rags of the people, base mechanicks, men of little knowledge, less honesty, and no discretion at all,' had no business with public matters, preached Michael Wigmore in 1633 ... Unfortunately for the Caroline regime, too few people found this conservative ideology persuasive ... [T]he evidence is overwhelming that people of all sorts were hungry for news and information, and

Chaplain to Charles I, Henry Ferne, countered on the king's behalf, no "law of the land" justified resistance to the king despite those who "work upon your fears, that tell you of fundamental laws, and … [that] the Gospel and Liberties, and all you have, are in most imminent danger without taking up arms." This had precipitated the "power of arms being taken from the prince by setting up the *Militia*, then that power used against him by an army in the field." Ferne pleaded, "the fundamentals must needs be such as will bear a settled government of this land, such as are not contradictory to the written established laws." Despite tradition, the King's enemies who "plead for Power of resistance in the people, lay the first groundwork of their fundamentals thus: Power is originally in and from the people, and if when by election they have entrusted a Prince with the Power, he will not discharge his trust, then it falls to the people; or, as in this Kingdom to the two Houses of Parliament (the representative body of the people) to see to it; they may reassume the power." Ferne acknowledged, "this is the bottom of the fundamentals as they are now discovered to the people … [by the] Observator, and all others that plead for this power of resistance."[6]

In his rejoinder to Ferne, the leading Presbyterian constitutionalist, Charles Herle, noted "court-doctors," or the crown's Civil Law attorneys, known as "civilians," had recently opined that "safety being the end of government, and the King only by God solely entrusted with it, he is not bound by or to any human laws in managing it to that its end." Ferne similarly argued that the "sole supremacy of power was in the King's person, and … his judgment was

---

eager to share opinions of high concern." David Como, "Print, Censorship, and Ideological Escalation in the English Civil War," *Journal of British Studies* 51 (Oct., 2012): 823. In the early 1640's the "traditional system of press licensing, overseen by the episcopal authorities and the Stationers' Company, effectively crumbled … The king and his council were placed in a profoundly defensive position and had little choice but to watch as obnoxious, unlicensed publications attacking courtiers … spilled from London's presses." David Coast, "Speaking for the People of England," *Past and Present* 244 (Aug., 2019): 272–81. "The people, it was claimed, had a right to discuss state matters that would directly affect them." Pauline Maier, *From Resistance to Revolution: Colonial Radicals and the Development of American Opposition to Great Britain* (New York: Alfred A. Knopf, 1973), 37. Trenchard and Gordon's *CATO's Letters* adopted the theme of the public's ability, and right, to judge political matters.

6 Henry Ferne, *The Resolving of Conscience upon this Question whether upon such a supposition or case as is now usually made (the King will not discharge his trust, but is bent or seduced to subvert religion, laws, and liberties) subjects may take arms and resist* (York: 1642), intro., 3, 14–15, 20; *Early English Books Online* (http://name.umdl.umich.edu/A41219.0001.001). Rachel Foxley, *The Levellers* (Manchester: Manchester Univ. Press, 2013), 53. "From the start of the war, parliamentarian theories of government by consent, especially those in which political power came originally from the people themselves, were an irresistible target of royalist writers. Henry Ferne was in the vanguard of the royalist campaign."

the sole supreme rule of that power." Herle rejected the idea that there was no fundamental law of safety that restrained the King, as statutory or positive law is "superstructive and not fundamental," such laws were "repealable and alterable," while "fundamentals cannot [be]: a foundation must not be stirred while the building stands." England's fundamental laws were in *Magna Charta*, as well as "the original frame of this co-ordinate government of the 3 estates in Parliament consented to, and contrived by the People," though "much jeered at in this and other pamphlets." Rather than guaranteeing the kingdom's "absolute safety," by insisting the final "judgment is in the King," Ferne would only commit to the people's "preservation." Herle argued "this power of last resolution" must not be possessed by the King or his prerogative: "Where should the arbitrariness of this reside in the State's user, but *where it was at first in the consent and reason of the state.* Which as (we have seen) the law places in the votes of Parliament, where this arbitrariness is allayed and balanced by number, trust, [and] self-interest, it is best secured from doing hurt."[7]

Nevertheless, Ferne had reason to suspect the ultimate safety of Parker's reliance on the supremacy of the public good, since when "right and just will not defend a thing, then necessity is usually pleaded; as if, because salus populi in a good sense is suprema lex, everything must be honest which is … imagined to conduct to the proposed end." In reality, Ferne noted the "state has means of preservation such as the law has prescribed, though not such as are here pretended to in this power of resistance; which though seemingly

7 Charles Herle, *A Fuller Answer to a Treatise Written by Dr. Ferne* (London: Dec. 29, 1642), 5–6, 13, 20; *Thomason Tracts* E244 (27), Reel 42. This was the tract that John Winthrop cited in his essays to buttress his case for the magistrates having an unrestricted judicial power covered in Chapter 7. Richard Tuck, *Philosophy and Government: 1572–1651*, 234–35. "In England, although Calvinist Presbyterians in the early 1640's were part of the parliamentary coalition against the King, they too tried to hold on to [a] constitutional program. The most brilliant was Charles Herle—brilliant precisely because he managed to combine a post-Parkerian account of the public interest with a traditional Calvinist political theory." Daniel Lee, *Popular Sovereignty in Early Modern Constitutional Thought*, 275–82. "Roman Law made a considerable intellectual and social impact in England. Beginning especially in the sixteenth century Roman law attracted interest from 'English civilians.'" Hans Pawlisch, "Sir John Davies, the Ancient Constitution, and Civil Law," *Historical Journal* 23 (Sept., 1980): 689–702 @ 691. "In his treatise on impositions, Davies argued that the king's right to levy impositions had no relationship to parliamentary authority at all," as it was based upon natural law "which pertained to the crown alone." Henry Parker, *Reformation in Courts, and Cases Testamentary* (London: 1650), 3–4. *Early English Books Online* (http://name.umdl.umich.edu/A91346.0001.001). Parker had immense respect for European Civil Law unlike most common law attorneys. "There is scarce a state in Christendom whose highest councils and judicatories are not mainly swayed by the profound Professors of Civil Law: and as learned politicians are generally the ablest servants to all States."

plausible, yet true reason will conclude them dangerous, and at this day, God knows, we see it." What Ferne and his fellow Englishmen saw, no matter their allegiance, was the destruction wrought by civil war, as "we feel and groan under the evils brought upon us through this power of resistance, the law silenced, the property and liberties of the subject everywhere invaded"; during this period England lost a greater percentage of population than during both World Wars combined, taxation doubled, consecutive harvests failed, and economic activity collapsed. Ferne warned that the English people had become "discontented," as MPs had failed to "discharge the trust committed to them" while taking "power to themselves"; similar charges would be levied against every Parliament that convened through the 1650s, especially when the Rump Parliament refused new elections. Herbert Palmer, another critic of Ferne's, and within a year Master of Queens' College, Cambridge, thought salus populi was implicitly good if the people's "safety" was its only goal. Yet Palmer was uncertain of the maxim's origins, "I believe there is no written law for this but the general maxim salus populi suprema lex." In *Table Talk*, Common Law authority John Selden confirmed the maxim had no force in English law, whatsoever, only an ideological one: "[t]here is not anything in the world so much abused as this sentence, 'salus populi suprema lex esto'; for *we apply it, as if we ought to forsake the known law when it may be most for the advantage of the people*, when it means no such thing," but only "in all the laws you make, have a special eye to the good of the people."[8]

---

8 H. Ferne, *The Resolving of Conscience upon this Question whether upon such a supposition or case as is now usually made (the King will not discharge his trust, but is bent or seduced to subvert religion, laws, and liberties) subjects may take arms and resist* (York: 1642), 23–25, 28–30; *Early English Books Online* (http://name.umdl.umich.edu/A41219.0001.001). Herbert Palmer, *Scripture and Reason Pleaded for Defensive Armes: or the whole Controversie about Subjects Taking Up Armes wherein … an Answer is punctually directed to Dr. Fernes Booke, Entituled, Resolving of Conscience* (London: 1643), 42, 46; *Early English Books Online* (http://name.umdl.umich.edu/A55033.0001.001). Michael Braddick, "The Early Modern English State and the Question of Differentiation, from 1550 to 1700," *Comparative Studies in Society and History* 38 (Jan., 1996): 100. It is estimated "3.7% of the population of England and Wales died as a result of the wars (compared with 2.6% of the population of the U.K. in WWI or 0.6% in WWII)," while "wartime revenues, measured as a proportion of total national wealth, doubled during the 1640's." Samuel Reynolds, ed., *The Table Talk of John Selden* (Oxford: Clarendon Press, 1892), viiii–xi, 131 (CII, "People"). Seldon died in 1654, and his manuscript was published posthumously in 1689. Richard Tuck, *Philosophy and Government: 1572–1651*, 211–21. After Selden served as counsel in the *Five Knights' Case* during the 1620's, for which he was imprisoned in the Tower, he had receded from public life. Steve Hindle, "Dearth and the English Revolution: The Harvest Crisis of 1647–50," *Economic History Review* 61 (Aug., 2008): 64–98. Robert Ashton, *Counter Revolution: The Second Civil War and its Origins, 1646–8*, 43–69, 132–34. Blair Worden, "Cromwell and the Protectorate,"

Selden and Bacon had encountered salus populi in Marcus Tullius Cicero's *De Legibus* (or his treatise *On the Laws*) and its passage on the powers of the consuls of the Roman Republic; twin executives invested with supreme civil and military authority. Cicero had written, "There shall be two magistrates with royal powers ... In the field they shall hold the supreme military power; they shall be subject to no one; the safety of the people shall be their highest law." Unlike Selden's warning of its lack of authority, Cicero posited the maxim as *the* supreme state authority, because in Rome's case (in the first century B.C.E.) it pertained to the two offices of supreme executive power that, along with the Roman Senate, governed the Republic. Since the consuls were also the supreme military commanders in a violent western hemisphere, even if Rome's insatiable geographic ambitions caused much of the mayhem, investiture of those offices with absolute military authority pertained to state survival. Cicero's definition was thereby consistent with salus populi's use by Charles I and his attorneys in *Rex v. Hampden*, and in turn as it was deployed by John Pym. It not only facilitated both sides' claim to supreme sovereignty, but upon Pym's declaration of national emergency, as amplified by Parker's pamphlet, salus populi suprema lex became an explosive populist force. Ironically, as both entities attempted to bar the other from power, they floundered for want of a legitimate process to exercise authority, with each ultimately condemned for wielding an illegal arbitrary power in their attempts to govern the state alone.[9]

---

in *God's Instruments: Political Conduct in the England of Oliver Cromwell* (Oxford: Oxford Univ. Press, 2012), 239–43.

9 Samuel Reynolds, ed., *The Table Talk of John Selden*, 131 (CII, *People*). Francis Bacon, *The Essays or Counsels Civill and Morall*, (1597), reprint, with an Introduction by Christopher Morley, (New York: Heritage Press, 1944), 178–79 (*Of Judicature*). Clinton Keyes, ed., *Cicero: De Re Publica, De Legibus* (Cambridge: Harvard Univ. Press, 1928), 465–67 (*Laws* III. III. 8). Quentin Skinner, "Classical Liberty and the Coming of the English Civil War," in *Republicanism: A Shared European Heritage; Volume 2. The Values of Republicanism in Early Modern Europe* (Cambridge: Cambridge Univ. Press, 2002), 9–28. J.P. Sommerville, "English and Roman Liberty in the Monarchical Republic of Early Stuart England," in John McDiarmid, ed., *The Monarchical Republic of Early Modern England* (London: Routledge, 2007), 201–16. Benjamin Straumann, "Constitutional Thought in the Late Roman Republic," *History of Political Thought* 32 (no. 2, 2011): 280–92. Ian Scott-Kilvert, trans., *Polybius: The Rise of the Roman Empire* (London: Penguin Books, 1979), 312–13 (Bk. VI, no. 12). "The consuls, until such time as they are required to lead out the legions, remain in Rome and exercise supreme authority over all public affairs ... As for preparations for war and the general conduct of operations in the field, their power is almost absolute. They are entitled to make whatever demands they consider appropriate ... Thus, if anyone were to consider this element in the constitution alone, they could reasonably say it is a pure example of monarch or kingship." Alan Cromartie, "Parliamentary Sovereignty, Popular Sovereignty, and Henry Parker's Adjudicative Standpoint," in Richard Bourke, Quentin Skinner, eds.,

Even while having served both Charles I and his son, Charles II, Edward Hyde, 1st Earl of Clarendon, provided posterity an assessment of both sides of the conflict in his eight volume, *History of the Rebellion*. He recounted, initially, Charles I had deployed salus populi "beyond its bounds, to the prejudice of the just rights of the subject," an apparent reference to the Forced Loan and imprisonment without trial of those who refused payment. Next, a "supposed necessity was then thought ground enough to create a power, and a bare averment of that necessity," being the Ship Money tax, "to beget a practice to impose what tax they thought convenient upon the subject." Now, with Parliament's recall, its Members' claim of a "supposed necessity … is as confidently, and more fatally, concluded a good ground to exclude the crown from the use of power." In all these instances, the "same maxim of salus populi suprema lex, which had been used to the infringing the liberty of the one, made use of for the destroying the rights of the other." By December 1648, only weeks after Pride's Purge of parliamentary members allied with the Presbyterian party who sought compromise with the King, and only a month before his execution, a pamphlet published in the name of Parliament's supreme military commander, Lord General Thomas Fairfax, lamented: "We are not ignorant that the rule salus populi suprema lex is most apt to be misapplied, some men framing pretenses of public extremity. Therefore, … we are full of sad apprehensions of the extremity at hand." Fairfax's deep regret over the King's execution is palpable. Only the month before, upon Oliver Cromwell's review of the draft *Newport Treaty* that Parliament was negotiating with the King in order to bring about the end of hostilities, he wondered if "Salus Populi be a sound position?"[10]

---

*Popular Sovereignty in Historical Perspective* (Cambridge: Cambridge Univ. Press, 2016), 142–63. J.G.A. Pocock, *Machiavellian Moment* (Princeton: Princeton Univ. Press, 1975), 357–77.

10 Edward Hyde (1st Earl of Clarendon), *History of the Rebellion* (Oxford: Clarendon Press, 1826), 2: 444–45. Robert Ashton, "From Cavalier to Roundhead Tyranny, 1642–9," 185–86. Ashton described this as Clarendon's "most telling criticisms" the "crown itself had gone too far during the eleven years of personal government in the 1630s." *An Abridgment of the late remonstrance of the army* (London: 1648), title page, 3; *Early English Books Online* (http://name.umdl.umich.edu/A23670.0001.001). *Oliver Cromwell to Col. Robert Hammond* (Nov. 25, 1648; Letter no. LXXXV), in *Letters and Speeches of Oliver Cromwell*, ed. Thomas Carlyle, (London: Methuen Co., 1904), 1: 395–96, 399 (n. 3). Lord John Morley, *Oliver Cromwell* (New York: Century, 1902), 255–58. Cromwell understood "salus populi" would "serve just as well for Strafford or for Charles as it served for Ireton and the army," as "usurpation by troopers must be neither more nor less hard to justify in principle than usurpation by a king." Mark Kishlansky, "Mission Impossible: Charles I, Oliver Cromwell and the Regicide," *English Historical Review* 125 (Aug., 2010): 845–6. The treaty signified a final "attempt to persuade the king to accept [a] … restricted prerogative."

Thomas Hobbes' *Elements of the Law* was published in 1640 just two years before Parker's *Observations*, proclaiming the supreme law of nations and monarchy: this "law over sovereigns" was the "same thing contained in this sentence, salus populi suprema lex," encompassing "not the mere preservation of their [subjects'] lives, but generally their benefit and good." Any royal act that might "hurt … the people in general" would constitute "breaches of the law of nature and of the divine law," punishable by "pain of eternal death." This supreme duty entailed "the means of levying soldiers, and of having money, arms, ships, and fortified places in readiness for defense." Hobbes' rationale was a natural progression from *Bates' Case*, and *Rex v. Hampden*, as *Elements* was published before John Pym invoked salus populi in 1641. By 1643, William Prynne, Parliament's indefatigable defender, articulated a conception of prerogative nearly identical to Hobbes', "Salus Populi, being not only that Suprema Lex, but [the] principal end for which all royal power was instituted by God and Man." However, if monarchy became "incompatible … with the public weale or safety," Pyrnne thought it must yield, because the royal prerogative existed only to "defend the people's liberties."[11]

Charles Herle was ready to do violence to protect the people: "the state is in its unsound and rotten parts to be lanced, it may be dismembered, and who will go about such a cure, but he will first bind the patient"; echoing James I's diagnosis for derelict parts of his own realm. Herle was not alone. In November 1642, the ultimate of radical solutions appeared in *The Unlimited Prerogative of King's Subverted*: the "king who is the head of the state, if a corrupted and a festered member that may endanger the destruction of the body of the state, ought to be cut off for the preservation of the whole, for salus populi suprema lex." Sir John Spelman's royalist critique of Parker's *Observations* conceded, while salus populi may seem a "means of preservation, … the best way to preserve a kingdom or people is not to allow them … to rise against … their king" to begin with. After all, no king would willingly create himself a "tyrant," destroying his subjects' "lives and fortunes," and making them "slaves and vassals to

11 Thomas Hobbes, *De Corpore Politico, or, The Elements of Law, Moral and Politick* (London: 1640), (Pt. II, Ch. IX), in William Molesworth, ed., *The English Works of Thomas Hobbes* (London: 1840), 4: 213–20. J.G.A. Pocock, *Machiavellian Moment*, 380. *Leviathan* sought to artificially recreate "authority from a state of dereliction." Barbara Shapiro, *Law Reform in Early Modern England*, 127–28. Leviathan (1651) "attacked the clergy, the legal profession and common law, and insisted the body of law be 'short' and written 'in as proper and significant terms as may be'." William Prynne, *Soveraigne Powers of Parliaments and Kingdomes in Four Partes together with an Appendix* (1643), 40–47 (Part 1); *Google Books*: (https://www.google.com/books/edition/The_Soveraigne_Power_of_Parliaments_and/Lpg-AQAAMAAJ?hl=en&gbpv=0).

his arbitrary power." While Spelman (or any other royalist) never provided a method to interdict a monarch's descent into tyranny, he admitted, no other tract "hath so much intoxicated the vulgar, or entangled the more understanding, as these *Observations*, wherein treachery is more cunningly mixed with some show of reason." Following Pym's lead, Parker had fatally undermined the royal prerogative by denying its exclusive claim, and follow-on authority, to safeguard the state. Daniel Lee has described the results, "by attributing a collective agency to people, popular sovereignty suddenly became more than simply ... resistance of a disenfranchised class to an existing institutional order. It became, by itself, the foundation for a viable, though radically populist, constitutional norm."[12]

In 1644, with the outcome of England's civil war still being contested, the General Court had announced its unabashed support for the godly parliamentarians:

> Whereas the civil wars and dissensions in our native country, through the seditious words and carriages of many evil affected persons, cause divisions in many places of government in America, some professing themselves for the king, and others for the Parliament, not considering that the Parliament themselves profess that they stand for the king and Parliament against the malignant Papists and delinquents in that kingdom, it is therefore ordered, that what person whosoever shall, by word, writing, or action, *endeavor to disturb our peace*, directly or indirectly, by drawing a party, *under pretense that he is for the King of England*, and such as adjoin with him, against the Parliament, *shall be accounted as an offender of an high nature against this common wealth, and to be proceeded with either capitally or otherwise*, according to the quality and degree of his offense.[13]

12 Charles Herle, *A Fuller Answer to a Treatise Written by Dr. Ferne* (Dec. 29, 1642), 7; *Thomason Tracts* E244 (27), Reel 42. *The Unlimited Prerogative of Kings Subverted* (Nov. 21, 1642), 5–7; *Thomason Tracts* E127 (32), Reel 22. Sir John Spelman, *A View of a Printed Book Intituled Observations upon His Majesties late answers and expresses* (Oxford: 1642), 3, 29 (29 unpaginated); *Thomason Tracts* E245 (22), Reel 42. Daniel Lee, *Popular Sovereignty in Early Modern Constitutional Thought*, 302–9. Howard Nenner, "Loyalty and the Law," *Journal of British Studies* 48 (no. 4, 2009): 859–70. "In the configuration of divine-right kingship, the people are obliged to the king, but to whom or to what is the king to be loyal?" Cesare Cuttica, "The English Regicide and Patriarchalism," *Renaissance and Reformation* 36 (no. 2, 2013): 136. In theory "republics had no head in either state or church: each individual was authorized to judge on his own regarding political and religious matters."

13 Nathaniel Shurtleff, ed., *MGCR*, 2: 69 (May 20, 1644). Francis Bremer, "In Defense of Regicide: John Cotton on the Execution of Charles I," *William and Mary Quarterly* 37

But as Nathaniel Ward recounted, after the execution of Charles I in January 1649, parliamentary leadership (with support of the army) had ultimately realized the founding of the English Republic by forcibly ejecting Members unlikely to sign his death warrant. This left a fraction of the House of Commons to deliberate, as the pejoratively named "Rump" Parliament, or lesser half. Indeed, according to Ward's count, a little more than a third of the House's membership remained and was carefully calibrated to meet Parliament's quorum requirement. But a quorum could never represent the nation, as this ejection was "against the consent of two thirds of the people," and "by force and faction," it was no longer "the elected Parliament of the people, but the selected Parliament of a faction." Ward maintained that in the event Charles I

(1980): 105. Cotton "strove to allay any doubts his listeners might have still entertained about the purge of Parliament, the execution of the King, and the continuing progress of the English Revolution … [and] was not alone in preaching these sentiments." *John Cotton to Oliver Cromwell* (July 28, 1651), in Sargent Bush, Jr., ed., *The Correspondence of John Cotton* (Chapel Hill: Univ. of North Carolina Press, 2001), 458–64. "I am not ignorant that you suffer no small dishonor in the tongues of many, not only as a sectary, but as out of your calling, being sat on work (as is pretended) by a usurped power, and yourself (with the army) exercising a power destructive in some cases to the privileges of Parliament, and the liberty and safety of the kingdom. But 3 or 4 principles there be, upon which it seemeth to me your proceedings have been grounded and carried on, and wherein my judgment … hath been fully satisfied: 1. That the concessions of the late king never came up to such a posture as whereon to lay a firm foundation of a safe peace, either to church or commonwealth. 2. That when the Parliament was full, and assisted with the commissioners of Scotland (in the treaty of Uxbridge or Newport, or elsewhere) they agreed together that the king could not be restored to his former state upon such terms … and … when the army discerned, not only their own safeties, but the safety of religion and state, and their cause and victories in defense thereof, all of them given away in that prevarication, I know not how they could have approved their faithfulness better to the state and cause, then by purging Parliament of such corrupt humors, and presenting the king to public trial. 3. That the army, though they be inferior and subordinated to the state that giveth them commission and pay; yet neither their consciences nor services are mercenary … 4. These things are clear to mine own apprehension, that I am fully satisfied, that you have all this while fought the Lord's battles." *Oliver Cromwell to John Cotton* (Oct. 2, 1651), in Sargent Bush, Jr., ed., *Correspondence of John Cotton*, 468–70. "Worthy Sir, and my Christian Friend, I received yours a few days thence, it was welcome to me, because signed by you, whom I love and honor in the Lord, but more to see some of the same grounds of our actions in you, that do in us to quiet us to our work." Michael Winship, *Godly Republicanism (Cambridge: Cambridge Univ. Press, 2012)*, 183–85. "For Cotton, King Charles's assault on the Scottish saints was the sharply escalated but logical terminus to what had been over a half century of Protestant English monarchs taking up power against law and contesting with God's people. Cotton's endorsement of armed resistance was an equally escalated terminus to long-standing unease about their monarch's goals. Another puritan terminus was Massachusetts itself."

had arrested a similar number of Members during his storming of Parliament, its remainder would have been just as illegitimate as the Rump's. In retrospect, the English Republic was stillborn, because even though the Long Parliament was originally selected by an unreformed electorate, the failure to conduct a subsequent election delegitimized all future parliamentary sessions during this era.[14]

With the defeat of Charles I's forces, and his residence or imprisonment by various opponents over the next several years, the Levellers were eager to perform major surgery on England's body politic, only to be frustrated by Parliament and Cromwell. As the royalist Sir Edward Nicholas reported:

> The three estates under the King in the English Parliament are now resolved into a small number in the House of Commons, who manage their great affairs as a Council of State. This is generally disgusted by most men, if they durst vent their thoughts. The greatest opposers of it are a faction of their own party, whom they call Levellers; but are indeed the true Independents [i.e., of church government] according to their former principles. They are for Democracy, and rather than suffer their co-partners to lord it over them in this aristocratical way, will bustle against them, though thereby they open a gap to Monarchy again.[15]

In a petition presented to the House of Commons in September 1648 signed by 40,000 people, John Lilburne and William Walwyn recounted why they had originally taken up arms against Charles I. Their reasoning is imbued with Henry Parker's *Observations'* championing of the preeminence of the safety of the nation and its people, as well as the principle of reason of state being

---

14 Nathaniel Ward, *A Religious Demurrer, Concerning Submission to the Present Power* (London: 1649), 1–7; *Early English Books* (http://name.umdl.umich.edu/A97134.0001.001).

15 *Sir E. Nicholas to the E. of Ormond* (May 3, 1649), in Thomas Carte, ed., *A Collection of Original Letters and Papers Concerning the Affairs of England Found among the Duke of Ormond's Papers (1641–1660)* (London: 1739), 1: 270 @ 273. David Coast, "Speaking for the People of England," 84–86. "A key component of the theory of popular sovereignty developed by the Levellers was the notion that the interests of the people were different from those of their supposed representatives in Parliament ... Traditional political thought held that Parliament was the only body capable representing the kingdom and addressing the monarch on its behalf." Gary De Krey, "Amon Wilbee and Leveller Beginnings, 1647–8," *English Historical Review* 137 (April 2022): 420–21. De Krey makes the case that the Leveller's emergence represented civilian and Army political advocacy, and centered less on the argument between King and Parliament or Republicanism versus Democratic politics, but rather "a vision of responsible and accountable government."

triggered by the imminence of the threat which justified *superseding* established laws:

> When we considered the manifold oppressions brought upon the nation by the king, his Lords and bishops, and that his honorable House [of Commons] had declared their deep sense thereof, and that—for the continuance of that power which had so oppressed us—it was evident the king intended to raise forces and make war … [U]pon this, *knowing the safety of the people to be above law and that to adjudge thereof appertained to the supreme authority* [i.e., Parliament] *and not the supreme magistrate, and being satisfied in our consciences that the public safety and freedom was in imminent danger*, we concluded we had not only a just cause to maintain, but the supreme authority of the nation to justify, defend and indemnify us in time to come in what we should perform by direction thereof—*though against the known law of the land.*[16]

After publication of Parker's *Observations* in 1642, the republican Henry Marten (a confidant of John Lilburne's) had taken up the standard of the public good in Parliament. The pamphlet, *Remonstrans Redivivus,* served as its platform with Parker's maxim of supremacy of the public good as first principle, exhorting Members "to be Judges of, and providers for the safety of the Commonwealth: being limited by no customs, no precedents, nor statutes made by former parliaments." Secondly, Parliament's power derived from the "supreme

16 John Lilburne, William Walwyn, *Humble Petition of Divers Well-Affected Persons* (1648), in Andrew Sharp, ed., *The English Levellers* (Cambridge: Cambridge Univ. Press, 1998), 131–32 (n. 1). Michael Mendle, *Henry Parker and the English Civil War*, 70–71. "The locus classicus of the emergence of parliamentary absolutism was the political crisis associated with the militia in the spring and summer of 1642, when the two houses found reason to break with the letter of the law and the traditional constitution in order to preserve themselves … Like the royalist absolutism upon which it drew, parliamentary absolutism was a theory predicated upon the existence of emergencies, which were the necessary, validating preconditions of the exercise of absolute power." Perez Zagorin, *A History of Political Thought in the English Revolution* (New York: Humanities Press, 1966), 9 (n. 3). David Wooton, "From Rebellion to Revolution: The Crisis of the Winter of 1642/3 and the Origins of Civil War Radicalism," *English Historical Review* 105 (July 1990): 654–69. Rachel Foxley, *The Levellers: Radical Political Thought in the English Revolution* (Manchester: Manchester Univ. Press, 2013), 21–55. Michael Braddick, *The Common Freedom of the People: John Lilburne and the English Revolution* (Oxford: Oxford Univ. Press, 2018), 132–57, 293–98. Eliot Vernon, Philip Baker, "What was the First 'Agreement of the People'?," *Historical Journal* 53 (March 2010): 53. Lorenzo Sabbadini, "Popular Sovereignty and Representation in the English Civil War," in Richard Bourke and Quentin Skinner, eds., *Popular Sovereignty in Historical Perspective* (Cambridge: Univ. Press, 2016), 175–83.

power being in the whole people," whose duty it was to protect the people "for the preservation and well-being of the Commonwealth." Third, "all just magistracy in this kingdom" existed solely for the "execution of the laws," and was a "matter of trust only for the good of the people; … [i]t being most agreeable to reason that those who by the consent of all are entrusted with the making of laws, should direct those that are to put the same in execution." Fourth, "all Magistrates and Officers of the Kingdom are accountable to the Parliament." And fifth, "that the King (though the chief magistrate or officer of the Kingdom) doth not personally judge in any Court, nor can of right interpose his personal command or judgement against the proceedings thereof." Upon the victorious New Model Army's occupation of London in the summer of 1647, several of its members delivered the first of three editions of An Agreement of the People (1647) to Army leadership, section 5 of which stated: "That as the laws ought to be equal, so they must be good, and not evidently destructive to the safety and well-being of the people." According to Ian Gentles, "common to all the versions … was a call for a broadened franchise, electoral redistribution according to population, liberty of conscience in religious matters, the dissolution of the Long Parliament, fresh elections every one or two years, and a list of powers that were reserved by the people themselves." The proposal for a broadened franchise ultimately included all men who were aged 21 or more, while excluding "servants, beggars or Royalists." These reforms also provided for "abolition of the death penalty except for murder."[17]

17 *Remonstrans Redivivus: or An Accompt of the Remonstrance and Petition* (London: T.P. and M.S., 1643), 4–6; *Google Books* (https://www.google.com/books/edition/_/tQpcAAAAQAAJ?hl=en). *The Agreement of the People as Presented to the Council of the Army* (Oct. 28, 1647), in Samuel R. Gardiner, *The Constitutional Documents of the Puritan Revolution*, 3rd ed., (Oxford: Clarendon Press, 1906), (#73) 333 @ 335. John Rees, *The Leveller Revolution* (London: Versa, 2016), 88–91. "'Supreme power being in the whole people, Parliaments were by them constituted to manage the same for the preservation and well-being of the Commonwealth', and that the king was not necessary for Parliament to enact laws … were mainstays of future Leveller thought and, at this time, only articulated in Parliament by Henry Marten and his few supporters." Eliot Vernon, Philip Baker, "What was the First 'Agreement of the People?'," 39–45. "It is revealing that it was [Edward] Sexby who, on the first day of the Putney debates, introduced [John] Wildman, [Maxmillian] Petty, and the new agent delegates, and that [Thomas] Rainsborough was famously outspoken in support of elements of the *Agreement* … Less than a thousand words in length, the Agreement consisted of two sections of numbered clauses, together with brief introductory and concluding statements. The first section, concerning parliaments, called for the dissolution of the Long Parliament; a redistribution of seats 'according to the number of the Inhabitants'; and for biennial meetings of parliament, affirming that the power of the representative 'is inferior only to theirs who choose them'." Ian Gentles, "The Agreements of the People and their Political Context," in Michael Mendle, ed., *The Putney Debates*

The arrival of Quakers in Massachusetts in the mid-1650s had revealed other qualities of salus populi when subject to a majority's will, as empowered by statutory enactments to ensure the people's protection: a witches' brew of fatal consequences. This sect had become a final affiliation of fellowship for many members of other radical factions in England that had formed around increasingly fantastical beliefs, including personal knowledge of the will of God, an imminent millenarianism, sexual licentiousness (as defined by the mores of the era), and, most radically, the Bible was an unnecessary component for Christian worship. Quaker services, called "meetings," were conducted without a minister, featuring strange and threatening quake-like contortions by participants. A primary tenet of Quakerism ensured Massachusetts freemen would oppose its followers with all their might: their faithful not only rejected government regulation, they obstructed government leaders with peaceful, but obdurate methods in order to challenge civil magistrates' authority without apparent fear.[18]

Upon the arrival of the first two avowed Quakers (Mary Fisher and Ann Austin) in the Fall of 1656, with over a hundred books and pamphlets amongst their baggage, signaling their intent to proselytize, the General Court enacted new laws to persecute itinerant Quakers. Upon Fisher's heckling of Governor Endecott as an "oppressor" on his way to Sunday service, her jail cell windows were boarded up. Mary next attacked colonial ministers while under

---

*of 1647* (Cambridge: Cambridge Univ. Press, 2010), 148–174. Samuel Glover, "The Putney Debates: Popular versus Élitist Republicanism," *Past and Present* 164 (Aug., 1999): 48–51. "The origins of Levellers' ideas have long fascinated historians. North American scholars, particularly the disciples of William Haller, saw the Levellers as the radical democratic edge of the puritan movement." L.J. Trinterud, "William Haller, Historian of Puritanism," *Journal of British Studies* 5 (May 1966): 33–55.

18 Christopher Hill, *The World Turned Upside Down: Radical Ideas During the English Revolution* (London: Penguin Books, 1972), 148–207. Thomas Hutchinson, *History of the Colony of Massachusetts Bay*, 2nd ed., (London: M. Richardson, 1765), 1: 196–205 (1656–1660). Philip Gura, *A Glimpse of Sion's Glory* (Middletown: Wesleyan Univ. Press, 1989), 49–50, 126–52. Stephen Foster, "New England and the Challenge of Heresy, 1630 to 1660," *William and Mary Quarterly* 38 (Oct., 1981): 641–43. Eamon Duffy, *Reformation Divided* (London: Bloomsbury, 2017), 413–429, 428. "The Quaker movement distilled out of the chaos of the Revolution and the tawdry material of half-baked mysticism a form of mystical and ethical identification with Christ which turned men and women not inwards but outwards, to their fellows, to the poor and oppressed, even to their enemies, and to the rich, on whom they also had compassion." John Miller, "'A Suffering People': English Quakers and Their Neighbours c. 1650-c. 1700," *Past and Present* 188 (Aug., 2005): 75–84. Quakers were despised by English peoples on both sides of the Atlantic Ocean, and harassment included both verbal and physical abuse; state punishments included long-term imprisonment and execution.

interrogation, cursing them as "hirelings, deceivers of the people, Baal's priests, the seed of the serpent, of the brood of Ishmael and the like." In 1658, the General Court enacted a death penalty for any Quaker who returned to the colony after sentenced to banishment, while Quakers at large were regularly tried in county courts for lesser offences. William Robinson, Marmaduke Stephenson, and Mary Dyer were the first to be condemned. Robinson's and Stephenson's initial encounter with Massachusetts authorities occurred in mid-1659 upon their disruption of Boston's congregational service. Once before the court of assistants the pair identified "themselves Quakers by their words and behavior"; Stephenson claimed God had anointed him "prophet to the nations" as he plowed his field in Skipton, Yorkshire. The magistrates decided that since the pair had entered "this jurisdiction pretending their immediate call from God to bear testimony against our law for persecuting the saints," refusing to leave the colony, they would be executed under colonial law. Mary Dyer soon travelled from Rhode Island to "visit the prisoners, the Quakers," based upon her belief that the "*light within her is the rule*." Dyer, banished with her friend Anne Hutchinson decades ago, had returned in her old age to confront the magistrates. While she was reprieved upon her son's plea for mercy, initially Dyer refused to leave Stephenson and Robinson on the gallows. Shortly before their executions the pair mocked Bostonians' righteousness, "Oh ye Hypocrites! How can you sing, and keep such a noise concerning religion, when your hands are full of blood."[19]

19 Nathaniel Shurtleff, ed., *MGCR*, 3: 356 (August 22, 1654), 415–16 (Oct. 14, 1656); 4 (Part 1): 78 (May 26, 1652), 199, 204 (Oct. 18, 1654), 277–79 (May 14, 1656), 308–9 (Oct. 14, 1657), 367 (May 11, 1659), 345–47 (Oct. 19, 1658), 383 (Oct. 18, 1659). In 1652, the General Court enacted a £50 fine and "severe" whipping for those who impugned the "Holy Scriptures," and banishment or death on second offense. Thomas Hutchinson, *History of the Colony of Massachusetts Bay*, 2nd ed., 196–205 (1656–1660). "At a Meeting of the Magistrates 21st of July 1659," in John Cronin, ed., *Court of Assistants* (Boston: 1928), 3: 69–70 (June 16, 1659). *Order to Bring ye Quakers to Trial and Sentence of Death against Wm Robinson, Marmaduke Stephenson, and Mary Dyer*, in Nathaniel Shurtleff, ed., *MGCR*, 4 (Part 1): George Dow, ed., *Essex County Court Record* (Salem: Essex Institute, 1912), 2: 107, 110, 118, 161, 163, 194, 202, 219 (1658–1660). Amanda Herbert, "Companions in Preaching and Suffering," *Early American Studies* 9 (Winter 2011): 80. "Early Quaker texts, printed and circulated widely throughout America, Britain and the West Indian colonies, were part of a deliberate campaign to disseminate authoritative information about the faith." Carla Pestana, "The City upon a Hill under Siege: The Puritan Perception of the Quaker Threat to Massachusetts Bay, 1656–1661," *New England Quarterly* 56 (Sept. 1983): 323–53. Malcom Gaskill, *Between Two Worlds* (New York: Basic Books, 2014), 220–24. Ultimately, Mary Dyer returned to the colony under sentence of banishment and was executed by colonial authorities.

Massachusetts soon came under attack by the crown for its brutalization of the Quakers. After Stephenson's and Robinson's executions, the General Court issued a defense of its actions in a *Declaration* published in London in 1659. Magistrates and deputies complained that "men of perverse principles may take occasion hereby to calumniate us and render us as bloody persecutors," defending the colony's actions as "supported by the authority of this Court, the laws of the country, and the laws of God." From their perspectives radical sectarians, including Quakers, had threatened the colony with their "pernicious opinions" and "contemptuous behavior to authority." Colonists had sought only to "secure the peace and order here established against their attempts, whose design we were well assured by our own experience (as well as by the example of their predecessors, *in Munster*), was to undermine and ruin the same." Under a law "made and published ... that such persons should be banished, on pain of death," the men had been executed legally. The General Court's sponsored broadsheet concluded, because the Quakers had "violently and willfully" challenged colonial law, and ultimately the Congregational system itself, it had been forced to act in Massachusetts' "*just and necessary defense*" under the "*sovereign law, salus populi.*" Nevertheless, the colony's representative in London, John Leverett, warned the Court, "The Quakers I hear have been with the King concerning your putting to death those of their friends executed at Boston. The general vogue of people is that a governor will be sent over."[20]

---

20 *Declaration of the General Court of the Massachusetts ... October 18, 1659. Concerning the Execution of Two Quakers*, in MHS *Proceedings* (Oct. 1908-June 1909), 42: 203–4; (https://archive.org/details/proceedingsofmass2v42mass/page/n237); *Early English Books Online*; (https://quod.lib.umich.edu/e/eebo/A50066.0001.001?view=toc). *Courts Declarations to vindicate their Proceedings against Quakers*, in Nathaniel Shurtleff, ed., MGCR, 4 (Part 1): 384–90 (Oct. 19, 1659); (https://archive.org/details/recordsofgoverno41mass/page/384). *Copy of a Letter from Mr. John Leverett to Governor Endecott and the General Court* (Sept. 13, 1660), in *Hutchinson Papers* (Albany: Prince Society, 1865), 2: 40–41. Carla Pestana, "The Quaker Executions as Myth and History," *Journal of American History* 80 (Sept., 1993): 441–69. Edwin Powers, *Crime and Punishment in Early Massachusetts: 1620–1692* (Boston: Beacon Press. 1966), 334–41. Bernard Bailyn, *The Barbarous Years: Conflict of Civilization, 1660–1675* (New York: Vintage Books, 2012), 460–65. "Winthrop, Dudley, Cotton, Hooker, and even Shepard were safely dead when in 1656 the first of the itinerant Quakers—two Englishwomen from Barbados—arrived in Boston harbor to spread the word of the impending end of the world and the need for all to recognize the Inner Light that God had instilled in them. The Puritan authorities, like the Dutch, were horrified ... New England's leaders knew that in the great cacophony of factions and sects that had exploded in the upheaval of England's civil war, Quakerism had emerged as the ultimate descent from rational, Biblicist, clerical Protestantism." Christopher Hill, *The World Turned Upside Down*, 232–52. By 1656, after existing for only several years, the Quakers "rapid

The Court's *Declaration* was to no good effect in England. In the chaotic aftermath of Cromwell's death, his son Richard had been appointed Protector, and several Parliaments were summoned. But even the promise of a new Parliament produced only acrimony as, once convened, Members accused each other of divided loyalties exhibited over the duration. William Cole railed, "Ye have once more erected the words of salus populi, and declare it ought to be suprema lex, the good old cause is now cried up," but "[w]ho will now not only speak, but do us any good?" Reflective of Cole's belief that "the end of all laws and magistracy ought principally to tend to the ease, safety, and well-being of the people governed," he condemned "the gentry, … seeing the laws are so corrupt and chargeable, they … still keep the poor in such subjection, that not only their own tenants, but other poor that live near them must … obey them, … else they run the hazard of being undone." This type of "populist vision" had been championed by the Levellers since the group's inception in 1647, contrasting the "poor man of this kingdom" versus his landlord, or the "man of power" who, aided by lawyers and judges, "encumbered the law with baffling procedures that benefited the privileged." Jonathan Scott's description of the uniquely English seventeenth century conception of republican government explains the esteem law reform was held, even being venerated as a leading means of securing the people's welfare: "This was a vision, not of liberty from government, but through it," via a "practical realization" of the positive benefits of government policy and action.[21]

Richard Cromwell's regime did not last even a year. A 1659 pamphlet pleaded, with the current dissolution of England's "constitution of civil government," the "people's deputies" must convene for "their common safety and welfare, … for the exercise of all just authority over a free people ought (under God) to arise from their own consent." Upon the Restoration of Charles II to his father's throne, the General Court pledged to defend itself against "any foreign prince of potentate whatsoever," and prevent "all plots and conspiracies"

---

expansion" gave "men of property cause for alarm, making them apprehensive of 'some Levelling design'."

21 William Cole, *A Rod for the Lawyers* (1659); in *Harleian Miscellany* (London: 1810), 7: 25–34. Austin Woolrych, *Britain in Revolution: 1625–1660* (Oxford: Oxford Univ. Press, 2002), 707–79. Blair Worden, "Cromwell and the Protectorate," 252–59. "Lies, Stories, Misinformation and Collective Memory: Extracting Vipers and Unmasking Cavaliers in the 1659 Parliament," *The History of Parliament*; (https://thehistoryofparliament.wordpress.com/2022/03/17/lies-stories-misinformation-and-collective-memory-extracting-vipers-and-unmasking-cavaliers-in-the-1659-parliament/). Gary De Krey, "Amon Wilbee and Leveller Beginnings, 1647–8," 426–27. Jonathan Scott, "What were Commonwealth Principles?," *Historical Journal* 47 (Sept., 2004): 594–600.

against the new king. Once in London, the colony's agents promised the colony would pursue the "peace and prosperity of our King and nation, by a faithful discharge in the governor of this people committed to our care." It would also punish all behavior as forbidden by the *Ten Commandments* and "against the peace of our sovereign lord the King, his royal crown and dignity," while propagating the gospel by "defending and upholding the true Christian or Protestant religion according to the faith given by our Lord Jesus Christ." Unsatisfied, Charles II demanded once more, consistent with his *Declaration of Breda* (1660), that the Quakers be allowed to worship freely. Reluctantly, the General Court complied. Still, magistrates and deputies grumbled, only by "just and necessary rules of our government and condition for preservation of religion, order, and peace" required the enactment of laws to protect the colony "against Quakers, in reference to their restless intrusions and impetuous disturbance." Upon their return to London, they had filled the "royal ears of our sovereign lord the King with complaints against us," procuring "a letter from his majesty to forbear their corporal punishment or death." Colonists believed that if "his majesty were rightly informed he would be far from giving them such favor or weakening his authority here." But since the General Court had no wish to "offend his majesty," its members repealed the "laws in force against Quakers … as they respect corporal punishment or death." A day of "solemn humiliation" was then proclaimed within the colony itself, to atone for its sins precipitating this "cursed combination of Antichrist and his adherents to ruin and trample upon all the sincere servants of God."[22]

In late 1662, the King restated his decree of a general "freedom of liberty of conscience," but it omitted Quakers, "whose principles being inconsistent with any kind of government" had made "it necessary, with the advice of our Parliament, … to make a sharp law against." Indeed, the Cavalier Parliament's first enacted statute condemned the "mischiefs and dangers" caused by Quakers' refusal to "take lawful oaths." As Charles II tried to expand religious toleration by requiring an oath of loyalty early in his reign, Quakers' dogmatic refusal to take any type of civil oath provoked great resentment in both Parliament and the nation. The English people were exhausted by well

22 *The Humble Petition of divers well-affected Persons delivered the 6th day of July, 1659 to the Supreme Authority, the Parliament of the Common-Wealth of* England (London: T. Brewster, 1659) 6; *Hathi Trust* (https://catalog.hathitrust.org/Record/102258555). Nathaniel Shurtleff, ed., *MGCR*, 4 (Part 2): 25–6, 34–5 (Nov. 27, 1661). Perry Miller, *The New England Mind: From Colony to Province* (Boston: Beacon Press, 1953), 123–24. Philip Gura, *A Glimpse of Sion's Glory: Puritan Radicalism in New England, 1620–1660*, (Middletown, [CT]: Wesleyan University Press, 1984), 150.

over a decade of a spectrum of religious radicalism since the dissolution of the Anglican episcopacy in 1646, just a year after which Parliament had condemned "the perilous condition that this Kingdom is in, through the abominable blasphemies, and damnable heresies, vented and spread abroad therein, tending to the subversion of the Faith." Most notoriously, in 1656, James Naylor and a handful of followers in Bristol had reenacted Jesus of Nazareth's Palm Sunday procession, and upon interrogation he claimed to be Christ himself. Christopher Hill described the consequences: Naylor was "flogged ferociously (and died of it three years later) … Panic fear of Quakers contributed significantly to the restoration of Charles II in 1660, men of property preferring the traditional constitution and the old law to the anarchy of the inner light."[23]

23 Tim Harris, *Politics Under the Later Stuarts* (London: Longman, 1993), 40–46. Craig Horle, *The Quakers and the English Legal System: 1660–1688* (Philadelphia: Univ. of Pennsylvania Press, 1988), 65–95. *An Act for preventing the Mischiefs and Dangers that may arise by certaine Persons called Quakers and others refusing to take lawfull Oaths*, SR, 5: 350–51 (14 C. II., ch. 1). *An Ordinance concerning the growth and spreading of Errors, Heresies, and Blasphemies, and for setting apart a day of Public Humiliation* (Feb. 4, 1647), in Firth and Rait, eds., *Acts and Ordinances of the Interregnum*, 1: 913–14. *The Grand Imposter Examined*, in T.B. Howell, ed., *State Trials* (London: T.C. Hansard, 1816), 5: 827–42 (#200). *James Nailor, Quaker* (1656), *British Museum*; (https://www.britishmuseum.org/collection/object/P_1953-0411-61). Derek Hirst, "The Failure of Godly Rule in the English Republic," *Past and Present* 132 (Aug., 1991): 33–66. Michael Winship, *Godly Republicanism: Puritans, Pilgrims, and a City on a Hill*, 233–38. Christopher Hill, *The English Bible and the Seventeenth Century Revolution* (London: Allen Lane, 1993), 243–45. Robert Ashton, *Counter Revolution: The Second Civil War and its Origins, 1646–8* (New Haven: Yale Univ. Press, 1996), 241–45. Austin Woolrych, *Britain in Revolution*, 298–300, 448–49. David Wooton, ed., *Divine Right and Democracy*, 38. When "Charles II returned to the throne in 1660 as the divine-right ruler of a limited monarchy, committed (at least initially) to not imprisoning without cause shown, taxing without consent, or governing without Parliament, the traditional claim that the king must not be held accountable to his subjects was reasserted in the doctrine of non-resistance (a doctrine to which all members of corporations, clergymen, and teachers were required to declare … [under] oath)." Barbara Shapiro, *Law Reform in Early Modern England* (Oxford: Hart, 2019), 121. The Commonwealth had its own "pledge of loyalty," the "Engagement."

# PART 5

## *Imperial Ambitions*

CHAPTER 12

# An Arbitrary, Absolute, and Unlimited Power

Until quite recently, Massachusetts colonial history of the latter half of the seventeenth century was mostly unexplored. While this work has covered the colony's law books, also a largely previously overlooked topic, the first half of the seventeenth-century of the colony's history has enjoyed much more coverage and is best known. Starting with the end of the 1640's, traditional coverage of the colony's history largely ends with Winthrop's exoneration of the deputies' impeachment, and his death only a few years later in 1649; the enactment of the law books occurred between these two events. Traditionally, most histories proceed to the early 18th century concerning the colony's history, at most noting the recalcitrant behavior of Massachusetts freemen. However, the General Court and the English crown came into direct and sustained conflict beginning with the Restoration of Charles II in 1660, until the revocation of the colonial charter in 1684. Much of the conflict was over trade, and that issue inevitably cast the two parties into a fundamental and decades long disagreement over whose law was sovereign. The answer was plain to most, even in New England, as the other colonies deferred to the English monarch and Parliament. But this was not the case in Massachusetts, and projecting to the next century and the events leading to the Revolution (especially in the Bay colony) the era seems especially relevant.

The Summer of 1644 is a good starting point in this regard, as H.M.S. Mary was seized in Boston harbor under the authority of Robert Rich, Earl of Warwick, Lord High Admiral of Parliament's fleet. Because Boston merchants had cargoes onboard the prize, the General Court petitioned Parliament that no other seizures of his Majesty's ships be made in Massachusetts waters. The internal debate amongst leadership on the colony's response to the seizure occurred in a meeting at Salem attended by magistrates and ministers. Some argued it must be opposed to preserve the "people's liberties." Another group asserted that nothing could "bar us from opposing any commission or other foreign power that might indeed tend to our hurt and violate our liberty," as Parliament itself "had taught us salus populi suprema lex." Others urged caution. No one could deny "Parliament's power in this case unless we should deny the foundation of our government by our patent," or charter. For now, the colony should bide its time, and if a future Parliament exhibited a "malignant spirit, then if we have strength sufficient, we may make use of salus populi to withstand any authority from thence to our hurt." There was even a claim that

 | DOI:10.1163/9789004706347_014

as a republic in its own right Massachusetts was subject "to no other power but ourselves." But this position was deemed untenable, as Charles I had not possessed an "absolute power without Parliament," and without such an unconditional sovereignty he could not have created the colony a republic via his grant of the *Charter of 1629*. Although colonial leadership realized Parliament had utilized salus populi suprema lex as an emergency authority for self-defense, they wisely decided not to deploy it in the present case because of the potentially fatal consequences for their still fledgling body politic. Moderate counsel ultimately carried the day. But its reasoning was surprisingly irreverent, considering the potential threat was Parliament itself.[1]

Only several years after the Winthrop fleet's landing, in December 1633 John Winthrop's brother-in-law, Emmanuel Downing, wrote Secretary of State Sir John Coke to disabuse him of reports that Bay colonists would "revolt from their allegiance, and join in trade with strangers," and ultimately, upon increasing to "a great number, … shake off this State." In April 1635, upon ordering Massachusetts to return its *Charter*, the Council for New England charged Bay colonists had made "themselves a free people" by adopting "new laws and new concepts for religion," fashioning themselves as "absolute masters of the country." Upon news that Parliament was in session after more than a decade, Winthrop confided in his journal, "some of our friends wrote to us advice to … solicit" its Members for favorable treatment. But after deliberation within the colony, "we declined, … if we should put ourselves under the protection of the Parliament, we must then be subject to all such laws as they should make, or at least such as they might impose upon us." Even if "they should intend our good, … it might prove very prejudicial to us." Obviously, Winthrop believed parliamentary legislation did not apply to the colony. An example of this independent streak was the omission of a loyalty oath to the King. Its first part had posed the dilemma, "You shall bear true faith and allegiance to our sovereign Lord King Charles." Colonists thought it unseemly to take such a pledge, as

1 Richard Dunn, ed., *Journal of John Winthrop* (Cambridge: Belknap Press, 1996), 524–28 (July-August 1644). *Humble Petition of the Court of the Massachusetts*, in Shurtleff, ed., *MGCR*, 2: 121 (May 14, 1645). Francis Bremer, *John Winthrop* (Oxford: Oxford Univ. Press, 2003), 336–38. Mark Peterson, *City State of Boston* (Princeton: Princeton Univ. Press, 2019), 79–82. Bernard Bailyn, *New England Merchants in the Seventeenth Century*, 2nd ed., (Cambridge: Harvard Univ. Press, 1979), 91–93. David Lee, *Popular Sovereignty in Early Modern Constitutional Thought* (Oxford: Oxford Univ. Press, 2016), 14–15, 114–27. George Beer, *Origins of the British Colonial System* (New York: Macmillan Co., 1908), 301–2. The crown claimed "exclusive jurisdiction over the colonies," and "until the eve of the Civil War Parliament passed no act directly affecting the colonies." Carla Pestana, *English Atlantic in an Age of Revolution* (Cambridge: Harvard Univ. Press, 2004), 39.

Charles I had "violated the privileges of Parliament, and made war upon them, and thereby had lost much of his kingdom and many of his subjects."[2]

In 1651, the General Court petitioned a now victorious Parliament, objecting to its notice of dispatching a governor with a new charter to the colony under the authority of the just created *English Commonwealth*.[3] The Court saw no reason to "take a new patent," or "keep our courts" and "issue out warrants" under Commonwealth authority. After all, the colony had not conducted its legal process in the name of the "late King's," executed in January 1649. Magistrates and deputies reminded Parliament that it had faithfully supported its policies, unlike rebellious royalist colonies Virginia and Bermuda. Moreover, before colonists had consented to "so great an undertaking" of sailing for the New World, in which "not only our estates but also the lives of ourselves and our posterity" were at risk, they had secured a charter from the "late King, who then ruled all." Under that *Charter* "liberty and power was granted to us to live under the

---

2 *Emmanuel Downing to Sir John Coke* (Dec. 12, 1633), in MHS *Proceedings* (*Second Series/1892–1894*): 28: 383–84. *An Act for the Resignation of the Great Charter of New England* (April 25, 1635), in *Records of the Council for New England* (Cambridge: 1867), 75–78. Francis Bremer, *John Winthrop*, 232–33. Richard Dunn, ed., *Journal of John Winthrop*, 345–46 (Feb. 1641), 432 (May 1643). Francis Bremer, *John Winthrop*, 367–68. Mark Peterson, *The City-State of Boston*, 79–82.

3 *An Act Declaring and Constituting the People of England to be a Commonwealth and Free-State* (May 19, 1649), in Firth and Rait, eds., *Acts and Ordinances,* 2: 122. "Be it Declared and Enacted by this present Parliament and by the Authority of the same, that the People of England and all the Dominions and Territories thereunto belonging are and shall be, and are hereby Constituted, Made, Established and Confirmed to be a Commonwealth and Free-State: and shall henceforth be Governed as a Commonwealth and Free-State, by the Supreme Authority of this Nation, The Representatives of the People in Parliament, and by such as they shall appoint and constitute as Officers and Ministers under them for the good of the People, and that without any King or House of Lords." *An Act for Abolishing the Kingly Office in England and Ireland, and the Dominions thereunto belonging* (March 17, 1649), in *Acts and Ordinances*, 2: 18–20. "[I]t ... hath been found by experience, that the Office of a King in this Nation and Ireland ... is unnecessary, burthensome and dangerous to the liberty, safety and publique interest of the people, and that ... use hath been made of the Regal power and prerogative to oppress, and impoverish and enslave the Subject; and that usually any one person in such power, makes it his interest to encroach upon the just freedom and liberty of his people, and to promote setting their own will and power above the laws, that so they might enslave these Kingdoms to their own Lust." *An Act for Abolishing the House of Peers* (March 19, 1649) in *Acts and Ordinances*., 2: 24. *Settling the Government* (Jan. 4, 1649), in *Journals of the House of Commons* (London: 1803), 6: 111. "Resolved, ... That the Commons of England, in Parliament assembled, do Declare, That the People are, under God, the Original of all just power: And ... that ... the Parliament assembled, being chosen by, and representing the People, have the Supreme power in this Nation: And do also Declare, that whatsoever is enacted, or declared for Law, by ... Parliament, hath the Force of Law, ... although the consent and concurrence of King, House of Peers, be not had thereunto."

government of a governor," "magistrates of our own choosing," and by "laws of our own making (not being repugnant to the laws of England)." Although "such was the duty and love we bear our Parliament that we were ready to rise and fall with them." After dispatching agents to London, including John Leverett who had served in the New Model Army, the General Court pledged 500 volunteers to Cromwell's campaign against the Dutch colony headquartered on Manhattan Island. Leverett was to serve as co-commander, but a treaty ending the first Anglo-Dutch war (1652–1654) was signed before the campaign could begin.[4]

Upon Charles II's restoration to the English throne after the death of Oliver Cromwell, and collapse of the Commonwealth's remnants, the General Court dispatched agents to London with instructions to ensure the crown perpetuated its privileges granted in the *Charter of 1629*; its envoys' primary charge was to secure those "that we have hitherto enjoyed in church and commonwealth, without any other power imposed over us, or any other infringement of them which would be destructive to the ends of our coming hither." The Court also petitioned the crown that "no appeals … in any case, civil or criminal," would be taken to England. Considering the nature of "this poor place," and its great

4 *Copy of a Petition to the Parliament in 1651*, in Thomas Hutchinson, *History of the Colony of Massachusetts Bay*, 2nd ed., (London: M. Richardson, 1765), 516–19 (Appendix, Numb. VIII); *Copy of an Address to Oliver Cromwell, in 1654* (Aug. 24, 1654), 523–25 (Appendix, Numb. X); *Copy of an Address from the Massachusetts Colony to King Charles 2d in 1664*, 537–43 (Appendix, Numb. XVI); 195 (1655). Massachusetts enjoyed duty-free shipping until the Restoration. In 1647, Parliament extended duty-free shipping for the colonies in the Americas for three years. *An Ordinance for Encouragement of Adventurers to the several Plantations of Virginia, Bermudas, Barbados, and other places in America* (Jan. 23, 1647), in Firth, Rait, eds., *Acts and Ordinances*, 912–13. Carla Pestana, *The English Atlantic in an Age of Revolution*, 99–120. In 1650, Parliament embargoed trade with royalist led Virginia and other Caribbean colonies, recalled their colonial charters, and threatened to "reduce any … that stood against Parliament." *An Act for Prohibiting Trade with the Barbadoes, Virginia, Bermuda, and Antegos* (Oct. 3, 1650), in Firth, Rait, eds., *Acts and Ordinances of the Interregnum*, 2: 425–29. "[A]cts of Rebellion have been committed by many persons inhabiting in Barbada's, Antego, Bermudas and Virginia, whereby they have most traitorously … usurped a power of government, … have set up themselves in opposition to, and distinct from this State and Commonwealth, many of the chief actors in, and promoters of these rebellions, having been transported … to the said plantations in foreign ships, without … consent of the Parliament of England." *Instructions from Oliver Cromwell to Robert Sedgwick and John Leverett* (Feb. 8, 1653), MHS: *John Leverett Papers*; (https://www.masshist.org/database/viewer.php?item_id=1921&pid=20&from=/features/saltonstall/john-leverett&ft=Saltonstall%2520Family%2520Collections). *Journals of the House of Commons* (London: House of Commons, 1803), 6: 478 (Oct. 3, 1650). Malcom Gaskill, *Between Two Worlds: How the English Became Americans* (New York: Basic Books, 2014), 186–201.

distance that separated it from the mother country, such a process would be an "intolerable and unsupportable burden." Colonists hoped especially that their Congregational system remained undisturbed, reminding the King that the *Charter* "conferred upon this plantation by your royal father" guaranteed "our liberty to walk in the faith of the gospel" based on "pure scripture worship," providing Bay colonists with "full and absolute power and authority to correct, punish, pardon, govern, and rule all such the subjects … [who] shall adventure themselves in any voyage thither." Only because his father had vouchsafed these privileges had they journeyed "with our wives, our little ones, and our substance, from that pleasant land over the Atlantic Ocean into the vast … wilderness." Magistrates and deputies reassured Charles II they had not left England "upon any dissatisfaction as to the constitution of the civil state," and of their neutrality during the "late vicissitudes and successive over-turnings of state." Charles II was well aware of Massachusetts' parliamentary allegiance. But since the colony had never formally pledged itself to Parliament, the Commonwealth, or Lord Protector Cromwell, its attempt to remain a distant entity across a great ocean was initially successful. At the same time the colony's leadership, and Congregationalists especially, must have felt a depressing sense of isolation as Adrian Weimer has described their predicament, "When the experiment of Puritan rule failed in 1660, nonconformists on both sides of the Atlantic had to reimagine their lives in the aftermath of a crushing political defeat."[5]

During the Summer of 1661, the General Court issued two resolutions, *Concerning our Liberties*, and, *Concerning our duties of allegiance to our sovereign lord the King*. After stating the by now familiar claim that the *Charter of 1629* was the "main foundation of our civil polity here," the General Court described the colony as a "body politic in fact and name." As such, it possessed absolute authority to admit freemen to elect a "governor, deputy governor, assistants, and their select representative or deputies." These officials possessed "full power and authority both legislative and executive for the government of all the people here, whether inhabitants or strangers, both concerning

5 *To the Right Honorable the Lords and Commons now Assembled in Parliament. The Humble Petition and Address of the General Court of the Colony of Massachusetts in New England*, (Dec. 19, 1660), in Nathaniel Shurtleff, ed., *MGCR*, 4 (Part 1): 453–54; *Instructions for Our Honored Friends Capt. John Leverett, or in his absence, Richard Saltonstall and Henry Ashurst, Esqs.* (Dec. 19, 1660), in *MGCR*, 4 (Part 1): 455–56; *Order about Quakers*, (May 22, 1661), in *MGCR*, 4 (Part 2): 2–4; *General Court to Charles II* (Dec. 19, 1660), in *MGCR*, 4 (Part 1): 449–53; *Massachusetts Charter of 1629*, in *MGCR*., 1: 17–18 (March 4, 1629). Adrian C. Weimer, *Constitutional Culture* (Philadelphia: Univ. of Pennsylvania Press, 2023), 21–2.

ecclesiastics and in civils, without appeal, excepting law or laws repugnant to the laws of England." Colonists were determined to defend themselves "both by land and sea, against all such person or persons as shall at any time attempt or enterprise [its] destruction, invasion, detriment, or annoyance." Finally, magistrates and deputies were resolved that "any imposition prejudicial to the country, contrary to any just law of ours not repugnant to the laws of England," would constitute an "infringement of our right." Although Massachusetts' agents greatly tempered the official colonial position upon their arrival in London, according to crown officials "they failed to alter the King's dismal view of the New England situation."[6]

In 1662 the colony received more royal correspondence, this time in the form of a fundamental challenge to its Congregational system. First, the King granted pardons to any colonists who had taken Parliament's side in the "late troubles" (except regicides), and reauthorized the *Massachusetts Charter* granted "by our royal father of blessed memory." But he notified the General Court of his intent to review all of its "laws and ordinances," and revoke any "which are contrary or derogative to our authority and government." In the meantime, the colony must allow worship according to the *Book of Common Prayer*, the official epistle of the English Church recently reauthorized by Parliament, and ensure colonists had access to baptism in the colony's congregations. Charles II also ordered candidates for civil office be made eligible for election without the requirement of congregational membership, and "all freeholders of competent estates" who were "orthodox in religion (though of different persuasions concerning church-government)" should have a "vote in the election of all officers civil or military." Obviously, the crown was aware of the exclusion of non-congregants from participation in the colony's government; at the outset of their review of colonial ordinances the crown's ministers

---

6 Nathaniel Shurtleff, ed., *MGCR*, 4 (Part 2): 24–26 (June 10, 1661). Paul Lucas, "Colony or Commonwealth: Massachusetts Bay, 1661–1666," *William and Mary Quarterly* 24 (Jan., 1967): 90–96. Upon review of these events, Lucas described a split between a "commonwealth" party within the colony that held Massachusetts was an independent state, and a "slim majority of moderate magistrates" who, in alliance with the colony's ministers, opposed any statement of independency be carried back to England. Instead, the moderate party supported a deferential stance towards King and Parliament acknowledging their supremacy. Ultimately, the deputies refused to consider changing the original policy, and with support of the commonwealth faction's leadership, Governor Endecott and Deputy Governor Bellingham, the colony's independent stance was retained and carried to England. Michael Winship, *Hot Protestants* (New Haven: Yale Univ. Press, 2018), 189–91, 233–36. Adrian Weimer, *Constitutional Culture* (Philadelphia: Univ. of Pennsylvania, Press, 2023). Since Lucas's work, Adrian Weimer was the first to cover the latter half of seventeenth century Massachusetts history in a methodical fashion, and is a long overdue addition to the colony's historiography.

had struck at the very heart of the Congregational system. The General Court acknowledged their demand that its legal processes run in "his majesty's name"; judging by future complaints this pledge went unfulfilled for some time. More than a year before the King sent his 1662 correspondence, Captain Breedon provided the Council for Foreign Plantations the *Laws and Liberties of 1660* during his report on illicit colonial trade with foreign powers. Breedon referenced the Massachusetts law book on oath-taking, by page number, to highlight the absence of a pledge of allegiance to the king; oaths were instead sworn to the General Court and the colony. He reminded the council, "It is not unknown to you that they look upon themselves as a free state."[7]

The General Court did not respond to the King's inquiries concerning its congregational system until the following Summer of 1664, at which time it appeared to rescind previous laws that restricted participation in colony level government and elections to "members of churches," while retaining the freemen qualification for full citizenship. Admission of freemen would now be dependent on the presentation of a certificate from a local minister that the applicant was "orthodox in religion," along with a similar document from the town's selectmen that they owned a "proper estate" large enough to pay at least ten shillings in annual taxation; these qualifications would allow the applicant to vote in colonial elections and hold office in the colony's government. As the crown heard increasing complaints of arbitrary treatment by the General Court, pressure was building within the colony to defer to the King and avoid more serious consequences.[8]

7 *Copy of a Letter from Charles II to the Massachusetts* (June 14, 1662), in *Hutchinson Papers* (Albany: Prince Society, 1865), 2: 100–4. Nathaniel Shurtleff, ed., *MGCR*, 4 (Part 2): 37 (Dec. 31, 1661); 58–59 (Oct. 8, 1662); 194 (May 1665). Perry Miller, *The New England Mind: From Colony to Province* (Boston: Beacon Press, 1953), 93–104. Elmer Russell, *The Review of American Colonial Legislation by the King in Council* (New York: Colombia Univ. Press, 1915), 5–36. *Capt. Thos. Breedon to the Council for Foreign Plantations* (March 11, 1661), in *CSP, America and West Indies (1661–1668)*, 5: 15–16 (#45). Bernard Bailyn, *The New England Merchants*, 2nd ed., 114–17. Breedon allied himself with Thomas Deane to secure a claim to Nova Scotia, joining a lineage of claimants against the Massachusetts *Charter*. Breedon's copy of the Massachusetts law book left no doubt of the colony's form of church and state government. Michael Winship, *Hot Protestants*, 235. Upon Breedon's return to the Colony he was "fined and imprisoned for his disloyalty, insolence, and contempt." John Winthrop, Jr., bailed him out of prison.

8 Nathaniel Shurtleff, ed., *MGCR*, 4 (Part 1): 420 (May 31, 1660); 4 (Part 2): 74 (May 27, 1663), 117–18 (August 3, 1664). Paul Lucas, "Colony or Commonwealth: Massachusetts Bay, 1661–1666," 93–98. *Report of Robert Mason, John Exton, G. Sweet, W. Turner, and Sir Rich. Ford, Doctors of Laws, to the King. On petition of Robert Mason, proprietor of the province of* [*New*] *Hampshire, and Edward Godfrey, late Governor of the province of Maine* (Feb. 15,1662), in *CSP, America and West Indies (1661–1668)*, 5: 75 (#230). "That the ... colony of the Massachusetts have for many years past endeavored to model themselves into a free state without any

By the date of the colonial response to the royal inquiry, however, Charles II had already appointed a royal commission to inspect his New England colonies, and one of the commissioners was Samuel Maverick. As a long faithful member of the English Church Maverick had signed the *Child Petition* (1646), demanding political equality for inhabitants or non-church members. More recently, in a 1660 pamphlet Maverick complained colonists required "swearing their subjects to submit to laws made only by themselves," thereby showing "what esteem they have of the laws of England." He also charged that the colony had set up its own mint to coin money, "melting down all the English coin they can get"; a treasonous act no other English or British colony had dared attempt heretofore. Although colonists claimed they had made the journey originally to "enjoy liberty of conscience," now they "denied it to others [by] ... debarring many from sacraments, ... because they cannot join with them in church-fellowship." Once restored to the throne, Charles II reauthorized England's national church, along with its episcopacy and uniform theology, by statute, with the intent that "nothing" would assist the "settling of the peace of this nation" more than a "universal agreement in the public worship of Almighty God." The only scenario more threatening to the Massachusetts' Congregational system than the rebirth of the English national church itself, was the return of Samuel Maverick as a royal commissioner.[9]

relation to the Crown of England, issuing writs in their own names, imposing oaths to be true to themselves contrary to that of allegiance, coining money with their own stamp and signature, exercising arbitrary power, and allowing no appeals to England. Some have publicly affirmed they would oppose any Governor sent by the King, and rather than submit any appeal to England would sell their colony to the King of Spain."

9 *An Act for the Uniformity of Publique Prayers and Administration of Sacraments and other Rites and Ceremonies and for establishing the Form of making, ordaining, and consecrating Bishops, Priests, and Deacons in the Church of England*, *SR*, 5: 364–70 (14 Car. II, ch. 4). Nathniel Shurtleff, ed., *MGCR*, 4 (Part 2): 130, 192 ("9th instruction," nos. 3 & 4). Samuel Maverick, *A Briefe Discription of New England and the Several Townes therein, together with the Present Government* (London: 1660; reprint, Boston: MHS, 1885), 19. Paul Lucas, "Colony or Commonwealth: Massachusetts Bay," 95–100. Robert Wall, *Massachusetts Bay: The Crucial Decade* (New Haven: Yale Univ. Press, 1972), 237. Jonathan Barth, "'A Peculiar Stampe of Our Own': The Massachusetts Mint and the Battle over Sovereignty, 1652–1691," *William and Mary Quarterly* 87 (Sept., 2014): 490–525. "The Boston mint ... constitutes the most compelling evidence available to historians that a prominent and outspoken faction within the colony, before 1688, deemed themselves politically independent from England." Mark Peterson, *The City-State of Boston*, 85–117, 121. "One of the most important things that independent states do is to create and maintain a money supply. That is why it was so unusual for Massachusetts, ostensibly a colony of another state, to begin creating its own high-grade silver coinage in 1652; no other British colony was ever so bold." Henry Mares, "Fraud and Dishonesty in King's Bench and Star Chamber," *American Journal of*

The commissioners arrived on July 23, 1664, bearing credentials and correspondence from Charles II. Upon arrival they conveyed royal salutations to his Massachusetts subjects, jesting sardonically that the King hoped that upon its return the commission could disabuse him of the "malicious calumnies which wicked and unquiet spirits perpetually labor to infuse into the minds of men, *that our subjects in those parts do not submit to our government, but look upon themselves as independent upon us and our laws*." Although the King re-confirmed the *Charter* and expressed his satisfaction with colonial correspondence, he noted several directives in his letter of June 28, 1662, remained unresolved. He was especially perplexed by a failure to admit more colonists into government, but left such matters to his commissioners' attention, "persons of known affection to our service, and of long experience." His four representatives, Colonel Richard Nichols, Sir Robert Carr, Sir George Cartwright, and Samuel Maverick, were granted a sweeping royal jurisdiction. They were charged to inspect New England's colonies with "full power and authority to hear, receive, examine, determine all complaints and appeals in all causes and matters," both in "criminal and civil" cases, and to ensure the "peace and security of the said country, *according to their good and sound discretions*." While the flotilla's four hundred troops were forbid from disembarking in Boston harbor while under arms, Colonel Nichols soon sailed with the main body to attack the Dutch colony of New Netherland, and Sir Roger Carr led a detachment to the Delaware Bay.[10]

*Legal History* 59 (no. 2, 2019): 226. "Counterfeiting of gold or silver had been a statutory treason since medieval times," and a misdemeanor for "brass or copper coins."

10 *Several Transactions Passing Between his Majesty's Honorable Commissioners and the General Court and [Standing] Council, according to what the Court ordered to be recorded*, in Shurtleff, ed., MGCR, 4 (Part 2): 157–235. The General Court had learned of the Commissioners arrival only the month before. *Charles II to Massachusetts General Court* (April 23, 1664), MGCR, 4 (Part 2): 158–61. *The King to the Governor and Council of Massachusetts Bay* (April 23, 1664), in CSP, *America and West Indies (1661–1668)*, 5: 201 (715). Charles II alerted the colony in April 1664 of his intention to send the commissioners. Paul Lucas, "Colony or Commonwealth: Massachusetts Bay, 1661–1666," 98–103. Wim Klooster, *The Dutch Moment: War, Trade, and Settlement in the Seventeenth-Century Atlantic World* (Ithaca: Cornell Univ. Press, 2016), 96–100. William Hubbard, *A General History of New England* (Boston: Little & Brown, 1848), 718–21 (July-Oct.,1664). The Royal Commission was granted on April 25, 1664, New Amsterdam capitulated in August 1664, and English forces occupied Delaware Bay in October 1664. Alan Taylor, *American Colonies: The Settling of North America* (New York: Penguin Books, 2001), 248–62. "Taken by surprise in the undeclared war, New Netherland could not resist the arrival of three English warships bearing three hundred soldiers." Mark Peterson, *The City-State of Boston*, 72–75.

While these English forces were on campaign, magistrates and deputies dispatched correspondence to the King; the long-delayed response to his 1662 letter being used to object to his royal grant of authority to the commissioners. The General Court reminded Charles II that Massachusetts' settlement had been financed and endured by colonists at the hazard of their very lives. Now, in the presence of a royal commission, "instead of being governed by rulers of our own choosing (which is the fundamental privilege of our patent), and by laws of our own, we are like to be subjected to the arbitrary power of strangers, proceeding not by any established law, but by their own discretions!" Governor Endecott protested that "our patent gives a sufficient royal warrant & discharge to all officers and persons for executing & observing the laws here made & published." Inevitably, the General Court's power in "executing and observing the laws," as authorized by the colonial *Charter*, could "not be discharged" without endless "complaints and appeals" to the "determinations of new judges." Thereby, "our government and administrations will be made void and of none effect." After pleading the colony's poverty, Endecott warned that if the royal commissioners' policies ultimately drove "this people out of the country, ... it will be hard to find another people that will stay long or stand under any considerable burden, seeing it is not a country where men can subsist without hard labor & great frugality."[11]

On February 25, 1665, Secretary of State William Morrice responded on behalf of the King, scolding Bay colonists that Charles II was "not pleased" with their petitions concerning the commissioners, believing they resulted from the "contrivance of a few persons who have had too long authority there." Morrice accused colonists of being ungrateful of their monarch's removal of the Dutch threat, and promise to observe colonists' charter rights. When all he had expected in return was the "cheerful obedience which is due to him," only to have Bay colonists rebuff his royal commissioners. The King singled out John Endecott for this rebellious behavior as he had been in the colony's leadership during the "late revolutions," making clear his royal preference that another governor be chosen at the next election. During the colony's earliest

11 *Copy of a Letter from Charles II to the Massachusetts* (June 14, 1662), in Whitmore, ed., *Hutchinson Papers*, 2: 100–4. *General Court to the King's most Excellent Majesty* (Oct. 19, 1664), in Nathaniel Shurtleff, ed., MGCR, 4 (Part 2): 129–33. *Governor John Endecott to Charles II* (Oct. 20, 1664), in MGCR, 4 (Part 2): 168–73. Endecott died on March 15, 1665, just a little more than a month before the return of the Commissioners to Boston. *Copy of the Address of the Massachusetts Colony to King Charles the 2nd, in 1664. 'To the kings most Excellent Majesty, The Humble Supplication of the General Court of the Massachusetts Colony in New England'* (Oct. 25, 1664), in Thomas Hutchinson, *History of the Colony of Massachusetts Bay*, 2nd ed., 537–43 (Appendix, Numb. XVI).

years Endecott had cut St. George's cross out of the English flag in a famous protest of the Anglican church's popish idolatry.[12]

After the conclusion of the military campaigns and inspections of the other New England colonies, on their return to Boston in April 1665 the commissioners proceeded with their examination of Massachusetts' current law book. They also demanded, per royal instruction, that any traitors attainted (i.e., condemned by statutory enactment), or surviving regicides, be "apprehended and put on ship-board and sent hither." Anticipating Charles II's restoration, a pair of regicides, Lt. General Edward Whalley and Major General William Goffe, had sailed for New England, not to see their families again. During the trials of their fellow regicides in England, "the prosecution alleged that the King's execution was the culmination of a terrorist plot devised by Puritans in Massachusetts, who dispatched [Hugh] Peters and young Henry Vane to implement it in conspiracy with Cromwell and [John] Cooke," lead prosecutor of Charles I. Not only were Whalley and Goffe feted upon their arrival, after Governor Endecott had welcomed them personally, upon news of royal-agents in the vicinity intent on arresting the pair they were spirited out of Boston. Endecott issued warrants for their arrest and deputized several marshals, but only well after their departure; he subsequently requested assistance from fellow colonial governors upon Charles II's order. Now, four years later, the royal commissioners demanded action, emphasizing the King would "not suffer the *Act of Indemnity* to be violated," warning colonists to take far greater "care for their future behavior."[13]

---

12 *Sec. Sir Wm. Morrice's answer to the New England petition* (Feb. 25, 1665), in *CSP, America and West Indies (1661–1668)*, 5: 282 (#945). Francis Bremer, *John Winthrop*, 229, 238. In "November 1634, the English flag used by the [Salem] trained band had been mutilated. At this time the flag Englishmen commonly utilized was a white ensign with the red cross of St. George in one of its quarters. John Endecott, believing that 'the red cross was given to the King of England by the Pope, as an ensign of victory and as a superstitious thing, and a relic of Antichrist,' cut it out with his sword. Endecott was more known for his zeal than his diplomacy, and it was feared that his action 'would be taken as an act of rebellion, or of the like measure, in defacing the King's colors'." David Hall, *The Puritans* (Princeton: Princeton Univ. Press, 2019), 226–27, 327–29. David Hall pointed out, "Two years later the government eliminated the St. George's cross except in the flag at the fort which guarded the harbor," and that Roger Williams had urged on Endecott in defacing the flag when he was Salem's minister. Malcom Gaskill, *Between Two Worlds: How the English Became Americans*, 121–27.

13 *Part of the King's Instruction to Us, 10th Instruction* (May 1665), in Nathaniel Shurtleff, ed., *MGCR*, 4 (Part 2): 192–94. William Hubbard, *A General History of New England* (Boston: Little & Brown, 1848), 726–29 (April-May 1665). "[T]he [General] Court having answered several instructions, relating to Whalley and Goffe, the Act of Navigation, Thomas Dean, the Oath of Allegiance, &c, on [May] 18th the Commissioners, coming into

The commissioners proceeded to convey royal demands that colonists take oaths to the King, legal matters be certified under his name, and England's *Book of Common Prayer* be adopted. An appeal by John Porter, Jr., to the commissioners seeking relief from earlier judgments of Massachusetts courts momentarily distracted them from their royal instructions, including a review of the *Laws and Liberties*. Young Porter appeared to present an excellent opportunity to exercise their royal grant of "absolute" judicial power and undermine the General Court, as he was the son of one of the richest men of the colony, John Porter, Sr. Based on young Porter's complaints of injustices done to him by the colony's courts, and acting upon a version of the colony's history provided by Samuel Maverick, the appeal by a scion of a prestigious Bay colonist was too opportune to ignore.[14]

---

Court, declared, that they were sorry to find, by the Court's answer, that they put a greater value upon their own conceptions than upon the wisdom of his Majesty and Council, and that they would reduce all to this question, 'do you acknowledge his Majesty's Commission?'" *An Act of Free and General Pardon Indemnity and Oblivion* in, *SR*, 5: 226 (12 Car. II, ch. XI). Samuel Fullerton, "New England in the Royalist Imagination," *English Historical Review* (Oct., 2022): 1356–8. Geoffrey Robertson, *The Tyrannicide Brief: The Story of the Man who Sent Charles I to the Scaffold* (New York: Pantheon Books, 2005), 1–7. Matthew Jenkinson, *Charles I's Killers in America* (Oxford: Oxford Univ. Press, 2019), 5–75. Douglas Wilson, "Web of Secrecy: Goffe, Whalley, and the Legend of Hadley," *New England Quarterly* 60 (Dec., 1987): 515–48. The pair of high-ranking members of the New Model Army and Protectorate, Edward Whalley and William Goffe, had fled to Massachusetts soon after the death of their patron and commander, Oliver Cromwell, where they were warmly received. Upon Charles II's restoration to the throne, warrants were issued for their arrest and execution. *John Endecott (Governor of Massachusetts) to Governors of Connecticut, New Haven, and Plymouth*, (May 7, 1661), in John Brodhead, ed., *Documents Relative to the Colonial History of the State of New York; Procured in Holland, England and France* (Albany: 1853), 3: 41–2. "Having received a letter from the Kings Majesty … in case that Colonel Whalley and Colonel Goffe be come into your parts, as … [they] fled from hence … from the justice of the English Nation, … that you would be pleased to deliver them … to Boston." *Sir Robert Carr to Sec. Lord Arlington* (Dec. 14, 1665), in *CSP, America and West Indies (1661–1668)*, 5: 345 (#1103). "Colonel Whalley and Goff were entertained by the magistrates with great solemnity and feasted in every place; after, they were told they were Traitors, and ought to be apprehended. They made their abode at Cambridge until they were furnished with horses and a guide, and sent away to Newhaven for their more security … They of this Colony [i.e., Massachusetts] say that king Charles I gave them the power to make laws and execute them, & granted them a Charter as a warrant against himself & his successors, and as long as they pay the fifth part of gold and silver ore which they shall get, they are free to use their privileges granted them, & that they are not obliged to the King, but by civility."

14 Nathaniel Shurtleff, ed., *MGCR*, 4 (Part 2): 195, 217–8. Robert Wall, "Membership of the Massachusetts General Court: 1634–1686," (Ph.D. diss., Yale Univ., 1965), 520–1. Bernard Bailyn, *The New England Merchants*, 2nd ed., 119–21.

But Porter, Jr., had misrepresented himself. His troubles started on a voyage to the Caribbean as his father's business agent, whereupon he squandered the sizeable sum of £400, while making a fiasco of his father's other affairs. Although Porter, Sr., made good on his son's debts upon his return to the colony, Porter, Jr., vilified his parents, cursing his father a thief, liar, "simple ape shittabed," and "a fit grand juryman." John's attack on his mother was equally as vicious, labeling her a "gammar shithouse, gammar pisshouse, gammar two shoes, and ... the rankest sow in town." Upon appearing before the Essex County court for these offenses, Porter, Jr., admitted that he had "shamefully abused his father and mother contrary to the very light of nature and much more contrary to the little light of the word of God." However, soon after his apology to Magistrate William Hathorne (the former irreverent speaker of the House of Deputies) for "calling him a base, corrupt fellow" and that "he cared not a turd for him," Porter, Jr., attacked several of his father's servants, threatened a family member with a knife, destroyed fencing around his parents' farm, and attempted to set fire to the family home. By assisting a young man with obvious mental health issues, the commission had made mockery of its mission within the colony.[15]

The General Court realized both the threat to the colony's jurisdiction under the *Charter*, and an opportunity to discredit such a misguided extension of royal power. Magistrates and deputies objected that the commission's hearing of the Porter case infringed "greatly on the privileges of our charter," and was "derogatory to the majesty's authority here established." But the commissioners refused to withdraw their "warrant and protection" from young Porter. Colonists warned the quartet, by "weakening the hands of lawful authority in the preservation of the peace of his majesty's good subjects here" they were "emboldening and encouraging such notorious malefactors." The commissioners dismissed such charges as their authority derived from the King himself. Magistrates and deputies remained defiant, if "persons judicially prosecuted and sentenced for criminal offenses should have liberty to make their appeals" in England, it would "cause ... the whole colony to stand equal with them at the bar of another tribunal." Obviously, "if such malefactors had been suffered to pass unpunished, it had been impossible for his majesty to have had a colony

15 George Dow, ed., *Essex County Court Record* (Salem: The Essex Institute, 1912–1914), 2: 335–38; 3: 111; 4: 37. Nathaniel Shurtleff, ed., *MGCR*, 4 (Part 2): 216–18, 227. Several years after the departure of the royal commissioners Porter, Jr., appeared before the Essex County court on additional charges, after which he fled to Rhode Island. "Gammar" was defined as a "mean old woman." Robert Wall, "The Membership of the Massachusetts General Court," 520.

of people here." Next, the Court demanded to know whether the royal tribunal would proceed with a jury, and under what law did they intend to hear these cases? The commissioners replied, they "would have no jury," and obviously, their proceedings would abide by "the law of England." Magistrates and deputies erupted in protest, "of all the privileges of any the natural subjects of his dominions a chief one … is that no judgment shall pass on any man's person or estate but by the lawful trial of his peers, and that the rule of trial shall be the laws of the land," which colonists believed meant Massachusetts law.[16]

In an increasingly bitter contest, the royal commissioners conducted a point-by-point review of the General Court's submission to the King's demands. One addressed the colony's refusal to accord the royal commission authority of a supreme tribunal as Chares II had ordered. Colonists were reminded, "His majesty sent us with commission to sit as a court of appeals in these his majesty's dominions, but we are told that the inviolable observation of your charter seems inconsistent with our hearing and determining complaints." They demanded whether colonists "acknowledged his majesty's commission … to be of full force to all the intents and purposes therein contained?" Magistrates and deputies admitted, "we do freely own a non-concurrence on our part." Next, the commissioners cited colonists' repeated protests that they left England for "the liberties of your consciences." This being so, why did Massachusetts "deny the liberty of conscience" to non-congregants, only upon a "vain conceit … it will disturb your enjoyments." They disabused magistrates and deputies of any hope that allowing men who were taxed ten shillings or more annually to participate in elections would satisfy the King; upon being informed that "not one church member in a hundred pays so much, and that [in] a town of a hundred inhabitants scarce three such men are to be found, we fear the King will rather find himself deluded than satisfied by your late act." The General

16 Nathaniel Shurtleff, ed., *MGCR*, 4 (Part 2): 195–97, 217–18, 228 (No. 4). *Massachusetts Charter of 1629*, in *MGCR*, 1: 17–18. Massachusetts government was granted *"full and absolute power and authority to correct, punish, pardon, govern, and all such subjects of us, our heirs, and our successors, as shall from time-to-time adventure themselves in any voyage thither or from thence."* The General Court cited *Magna Charta's* due process clause (article 39) as the authority for the supremacy of its laws, making its claim manifest in a later entry, "His majesty's charter granteth to all his good subjects here all the immunities and privileges of his natural subjects within any of his dominions, whereof one principal is, that no man shall be diseised of his freehold, nor shall judgment pass upon any but by the lawful judgment of his peers, and by the law of the land." Jack Greene, *Peripheries and Center* (New York: W.W. Norton, 1986), 25, 35–36, 71. Such use of *Magna Charta* became increasingly commonplace in the colonies. Harry T. Dickinson, "*Magna Carta* in the American Revolution," in Lawrence Goldman, ed. *Magna Carta: History, Context, and Influence* (London: Univ. of London Press, 2018), 80–93.

Court remained defiant, "In all the propositions which were made unto us by his majesty's commissioners we have yielded as far as we could, ... as may clearly be seen in our orders about the oaths of allegiance, the enlargement of the body of freemen, and the issuing forth of warrants in his majesty's name." In 1670, just several years from now, the property requirement for participation by non-church members in town meetings was quadrupled from £20 to £80, making the colony's control over access to the franchise ironclad. Available voting records for colony level elections indicate that by the 1680's only twenty-five percent of men voted for standing counselors, while that figure fell to ten percent for the annual general elections held in Boston.[17]

Correspondence between two of the commissioners, colonels Cartwright and Nichols, reveals the significant impact that their initial visit to Boston had on them, as the experience led them both to anticipate resistance. Cartwright confided to Nichols, since Massachusetts was "the richest, greatest, most populated, and *inclinable to a commonwealth*, they ought to have the greatest circumspection about" the colony, especially as it improved its defenses around Boston harbor. Per "secret" instructions issued to them by the crown upon departure, they were instructed to proceed to Long Island if Massachusetts resisted their landing. Cartwright and Nichols decided to begin their inspection in Connecticut, as once another colony had cooperated with their inspections it would be a "strong inducement" for Massachusetts to do the same, avoiding any resistance and thereby denying "ill precedent" to the other colonies. Their plan would be aided by Connecticut's governor, John Winthrop, Jr., who had good relations with the crown. Meanwhile, Cartwright had received a copy of the General Court's amendment of qualifications for the status of freemen, but

17 Nathaniel Shurtleff, ed., *MGCR*, 4 (Part 1): 420, (May 31, 1660); 4 (Part 2): 199 (*Concerning the Use of the Common Prayer Book*), 204–5, 203, 219–23, 234–35, 464 (Oct. 12, 1670—raises property qualification for voting to eighty pounds); 5: 287–88, 301–3, 311, 321, 339, 464. *Hutchinson Papers*, 2: 212. William Whitmore, ed., *Laws and Liberties of 1660*, 76, title *Township*, §4. Stephen Foster, "Massachusetts Franchise in the Seventeenth Century," *William and Mary Quarterly* 24 (1967): 617–20. Timothy Breen, "Who Governs: The Town Franchise in Seventeenth-Century Massachusetts," *William and Mary Quarterly* 27 (1970): 468–72. Robert Wall, "Massachusetts Bay Colony Franchise in 1647," *William and Mary Quarterly* 27 (1974): 136–44. Charles Hilkey, *Legal Development in Colonial Massachusetts: 1630–1686* (New York: Columbia Univ. Press, 1910), 28–29, 50–53. William Pencak, *War, Politics and Revolution in Provincial Massachusetts* (Boston: Northeastern Univ. Press, 1981), 10–11. "Many ... second generation [colonists] could not obtain full citizenship ... By the 1680s no more than 1,800 men, about 25 percent of the adult male population, voted for [standing] councilors. In Boston itself, which had about 1,000 adult males, Samuel Sewall never recorded over one hundred ballots in any town election before the 1690's."

the Commissioners rejected the compromise as it failed to address the King's objections. Another secret instruction from Charles II urged the selection of a more friendly General Court in Massachusetts, but Colonel Cartwright had no expectations of "a good election for the next general assembly," as "none can elect or be elected but church members."[18]

Upon the commissioners' return to Boston several hearings were announced, including John Porter, Jr.'s, complaints of harassment by the magistrates and the Narragansett's claims of unjust seizures of land. Most importantly, they intended to try the colony's "entire leadership" for violations of the Navigation Acts. The General Court interdicted the proceedings before they could begin:

> The hour for the trial had arrived, when the sound of a trumpet was heard, and the voice of the crier, proclaiming to all the people of the colony, in the name of the King, and by the authority of the *Charter*, that the Court, in observance of their duty to God and to his Majesty, and to the trust committed unto them by his Majesty's good subjects, cannot consent unto, or give their approbation to the proceedings of the Commissioners nor countenance … their abettors.[19]

To ensure the commissioners received said notice, one of the three places in Boston the trumpet sounded happened to be adjacent to their Boston lodgings! Subsequently, in correspondence to Secretary of State Lord Arlington three of the commissioners—Carr, Cartwright, and Maverick—reported that

---

18 CSP, *Colonial Series (1574–1660)*, ed. W. Noel Sainsbury, (London: Longman, 1860), 5: 200–201 (#713) "Secret Instructions to the Commissioners" (April 23, 1664); 275–76 (#931) "Col. George Cartwright to Col. Nicolls" (Feb. 4, 1665). Richard Dunn, *Puritans and Yankees* (Princeton Univ. Press, 1962), 151–63.

19 Adrian Weimer, *Constitutional Culture*, 181–206. William Hubbard, *A General History of New England*, 726–29 (May 1665). Thomas Hutchinson, *The History of the Colony of Massachusetts Bay* (London: M. Richardson, 1765), 248–49 (1665). *Courts Declaration in ye Case of Mr. Deane*, in Nathaniel Shurtleff, ed., MGCR, 4 (Part 2): 218–19 (May 1665). *Declaration of the General Court of the Massachusetts General Court* (May 23, 1665), in CSP, *America and West Indies (1661–1668)*, 5: 299 (#996): "Declaration of the General Court of the Massachusetts. Protesting against the legality of the warrant of the King's Commissioners giving protection to John Porter, junr., a high 'offender against God, the King's authority and laws, and the peace of his good subjects here, who breaking prison, made his escape out of the hands of justice here.' With mem. that it was published 24th May by Oliver Purchas, one of the Deputies of the Court, with sound of trumpet in the market place in Boston, at the Dock head, and at the cross way by Capt. Breedon's." Adrian Weimer, *Constitutional Culture*, 168–72. Mark Peterson, *The City-State of Boston*, 67–71, 149–53.

as Massachusetts feigned its compliance to Charles II's demands, the General Court planned to continue dissembling "until the King ... and all his good subjects here lie weary of it." They urged revocation of the colony's charter, as his father Charles I had intended to do in 1636 or 1637. If Charles II failed to deal with the Bay colonists firmly, now that they had "declared themselves against his authority over them," his allies within the colony "will never dare hereafter to declare" their loyalty to him, because of "all the ill-consequences which must necessarily follow."[20]

In a follow-on report Sir Robert Carr relayed that upon the Commission's arrival, "Major Hawthorne made a seditious speech at the head of his company, and the late Governor [Endecott] another at the meeting-house at Boston, but neither were so much as questioned for it by their magistrates." On the commissioners' return to Boston, and attempt to hold a hearing on a number of controversies, the General Court "proclaimed by sound of trumpet that[it] was the supremist judicatory in that Province, and that the Commissioners pretending to hear appeals was a breach of the privileges granted by the late King and confirmed by his Majesty's own letter." Moreover, colonists had been "exceedingly cruel" to the Quakers, putting some to death, while beating others "to jelly." To aggravate matters, after being "entertained and feasted in every place after they were told they were traitors" the regicides, Whalley and Goffe, had mysteriously disappeared. As for the *Navigation Acts*, Massachusetts dominated regional trade and kept the profits for itself. Colonel Nichols added from New York, after reviewing the commission's materials, "his Majesty will read the sophistry of the Massachusetts ... They and all the other colonies are at a stand to see what reproof his Majesty will send over."[21]

---

20 *Sir Robert Carr, George Cartwright, and Samuel Mavericke to Sec. Lord Arlington* (Boston, July 26, 1665), in CSP, *America and West Indies (1661–1668)*, 5: 313–14 (#1024). Bailyn, *The New England Merchants in the 17th Century*, 2nd ed., 119–20. "The General Court declared their commission invalid on the ground that the authority it conveyed conflicted with that of the Massachusetts charter, and refused to authorize their activities within its jurisdiction. Denied access to the Massachusetts legislature, the commissioners announced their intention of holding a court of appeals in a private dwelling and summoned a number of litigants. To this the General Court replied with an official declaration ... published with 'sound of trumpet' in three centers of Boston [and] ... 'the Commissioners,' as one witness put it, 'gave up'."

21 *Sir Robert Carr to Sec. Lord Arlington* (Dec. 14, 1665), in CSP, *America and West Indies (1661–1668)*, 5: 344–46 (#1103). *Col. Nichols to Sec. Lord Arlington* (New York, April 9, 1666), in CSP, *America and West Indies, (1661–1668)*, 370–71 (#1169). Adrian C. Weimer, *Constitutional Culture: New England and the Struggle Against Arbitrary Rule in the Restoration Empire*, 1–2. Carr had a run-in with a local constable that led to a physical altercation. Despite the attempts by John Leverett to bring Carr to justice under colonial law, Carr stated he did not answer to Massachusetts law. Mark Peterson, *The City State of Boston*, 55–60. The

After the commissioners' final departure, Governor Bellingham pled the colony's case in correspondence to Charles II. Amongst many instances that the commission "steered a course so different from, if not contrary to, your majesty's … limitations in your royal letters and instructions," most outrageously, a "notorious malefactor" had been "protected from justice." He protested, "to be placed upon the sandy foundations of a blind obedience unto that *arbitrary, absolute, and unlimited power* which these gentlemen would impose upon us … is contrary to … the liberties of Englishmen." Meanwhile, the General Court was left to explain its deviation from English law as documented by the commissioners' review of its own law books. Upon their "perusal of the … *Book of the General Laws & Liberties*" they had identified twenty-six topics for "alterations and necessary additions," the primary one being the King must be "declared (in the title of the book) to be *the fountain* whence his colony of Massachusetts derive their laws and liberties"; second, legal processes be "issued out & performed in his Majesty's name"; third, "his Majesty's arms be set up in every court of justice" and the militia march under the English flag; fourth, the "*12th capital law*, 'if any conspire, etc., against our commonwealth,' 'commonwealth' may be expunged & 'against our peace of his Majesty's colony' be inserted"; fifth, on "page 21, title *Courts*, it may be expressed that the General Court, etc., is ye chief civil power of this colony (*not commonwealth*) under his Majesty"; and finally, "*indecent expressions and repetitions of the word 'commonwealth,' 'state,' and the like" must be deleted.*[22]

ultimate "success was born in fear: Boston's economic depression led many to believe that London-based ships would no longer bother to stop in Boston." George Beer, *The Origins of the British Colonial System: 1578–1660*, 176 (n. 1), 284–88, 312–16, 326–37, 344–46. Beer argued that the Navigation Acts intended to regulate not only Massachusetts' trade but dealt with the colony as a competitor in the West Indies trade. Bernard Bailyn, *The Barbarous Years* (New York: Vintage Press, 2012), 477–79, 489–94. Facing disaster, Massachusetts' leadership moved "to create a permanent self-sufficient economy" so that "native manufactures" would be able to "supply the two most vital imports: cloth goods and iron products."

22 *To the General Court of his Majesty's Colony of the Massachusetts, upon perusal of the book entitled the General Laws and Liberties concerning the Inhabitants of the Massachusetts, we find just reason … these ensuing alterations and necessary additions be made* (May 24, 1665), in Shurtleff, ed., *MGCR*, 4 (Part 2): 211–13. *Governor Bellingham to Charles II* (August 1, 1665), in *MGCR*, 4 (Part 2), 274–75. Mark Peterson, *The City-State of Boston*, 67–71, 149–53. "The General Court neither complied with the demand to revise its laws nor sent representatives to Whitehall." William Whitmore, ed., *Colonial Laws of Massachusetts. Reprinted from the Edition of 1660* (Boston: City Council of Boston, 1889), 100. Whitmore summarized the commissioners' demands: deferral to "royal authority," "recognition of the Church of England," and "citizenship" for non-congregants. Richard Bushman, *King and People in Provincial Massachusetts*, 2nd ed., (Chapel Hill: UNC Press, 1992), 11–13.

Upon review of these events Perry Miller concluded that the dissemblance with which the commissioners tried to co-opt the New England colonies, in lieu of a robust military campaign, prompted a colonial response of "pious misunderstandings, evasions, and half-truths." True enough. Yet, Bellingham's claim of the "liberties of Englishmen" had suggested a similar strategy to the crown. For years petitioners had made their way to the King's court to complain of Massachusetts' denial of their English liberties. Recently, on the eve of their execution, several Quakers demanded English justice, as others charged Massachusetts courts with obstructing seizures made under the *Navigation Act* recently enacted by Parliament. And after the General Court had regularly denied appeals to the King, fearing injury to its own jurisdiction, upon the appearance of a royal commission its members, in a stupefying reversal, claimed those same English liberties in its own defense! But no matter how fervent the General Court's objections, the commissioners' response to its incessant hectoring was sure to be embraced by Charles II: despite the Court's "false expositions" on the *Charter*, the King "has not granted his sovereignty away over them," that "supreme authority he has reserved for himself."[23]

In the short term, the magistrates' and deputies' strategy to wait the King out in hopes his attention would be drawn elsewhere did not work out well for them. In April 1666, Charles II addressed the following correspondence to all of his New England colonies:

> His Majesty has received full information from his commissioners of their reception in the several colonies of New England, in all which they have received great satisfaction, but in the Massachusetts, and is fully informed ... that those who govern the Massachusetts believe that the Commission is an apparent violation of their charter and tending to the dissolution of it, and *that his Majesty hath no jurisdiction over them, and no appeals against their judgments can be made to the King from their judgments, which would be a matter of such high consequence as every man discerns where it must end.* His Majesty therefore recalls his said commissioners, to the end he may receive a more particular account of his Plantations and of their differences with those of the Massachusetts; and he commands the Governor and Council of the Massachusetts forthwith to make choice

23 Perry Miller, *The New England Mind: From Colony to Province*, 126. Bernard Bailyn, *The New England Merchants*, 2nd ed., 122–23. *Part of the King's Instruction to Us—To Inquire how the Navigation Act is Attended To*, in Nathaniel Shurtleff, ed., MGCR, 4 (Part 2): 193–94; 218–19. *The King's Commissioner's Reply to the General Court and Council of Massachusetts* (July 1665), in CSP, *America and West Indies (1661–1668)*, 5: 311 (#1020).

> of four or five persons to attend his Majesty, whereof Richard Bellingham and Major Hawthorne to be two; and when all allegations or pretenses on behalf of said colony shall be heard, the King will make it appear how far he is from the least thought of invading or infringing in the least degree the Royal Charter granted to the colony.[24]

A royal public shaming in front of its sister colonies was perhaps only the initial comeuppance for the Bay colony. Upon receipt of the royal correspondence, the Massachusetts standing council convened in the Fall of 1666 to discuss the King's harsh response and demand that colonial agents be dispatched to Whitehall. A consensus began to emerge that the royal prerogative must compel their attendance, but others questioned whether they must answer such a summons, for their own "liberties were of concernment, and to be regarded for the preservation." *One council member noted the many recent treatises arguing that the King's "prerogative is not above law, but limited by it."* Another wondered, "If we shall refuse to answer here to the commissioners, and in England also, what will the King say?" Little did they imagine. When Charles II's chief minister, Lord Chancellor, the 1st Earl of Clarendon, forwarded the King's 1666 letter to Colonel Nichols, he was at a loss on "what to say of the demeanor of the Massachusetts colony," but "if they do not give Obedience, … we shall give them cause to repent it, for his Majesty will not sit down by the affronts which he hath received."[25]

By the Summer of 1666 the General Court had received notice that France and Denmark were allied with the Dutch against England in the Second Dutch War (1664–1667). The Court thanked Secretary Morrice for warning the colony of "our danger by the French and Dutch, and directing us to prepare for our defense," but its forces could not undertake an invasion of Canada; however, Massachusetts ships were raiding French ports as the Dutch harassed its own shipping. The colony followed this correspondence with a "gift" of two ship masts from its prodigious reserves of pine forests, a material the crown would covet in the next century. Only a week before, unbeknownst to colonists, the Great Fire of London had ravaged the city, burning for nearly a week. Ultimately, the General Court made a gift of twenty-four masts to his majesty's navy. Charles II received the gift as "expressions of their loyal and sincere affection," which

24 *The King to the Colonies in New England* (April 10, 1666), in CSP, *America and West Indies (1661–1668)*, 5: 372–73 (#1171).

25 *Lord Chancellor Clarendon to Col. Nicols* (April 13, 1666), in CSP, *America and West Indies, (1661–1668)*, 5: 376–77 (#1020). *Report of the Following Debate in Council*, in MHS *Collections, Second Series 1826*, 8: 99–100.

he found "exceedingly acceptable." The breech between King and colony had been sealed for now. However, according to Wim Klooster, by the early 1670's Charles II's councilors were warning of "extensive economic collaboration between the Dutch, with their low-priced, high-quality manufactures, and the New Englanders," who dominated "trade on the eastern seaboard and to the West Indies."[26]

In retrospect, the degree to which these events diverge from the established historiography of colonial Massachusetts is significant, to say the least. Perhaps this disparity could be downplayed if not for the colony's insistence on its legal autonomy. This is not only a retrospective interpretation however. As Boston emerged as an international port of call in the 1670's, as covered in the next chapter, even a member of the crown's Plantations Council, John Evelyn, acknowledged Bay colonists had become "'very independent as to their regard to old England, or his Majesty, rich and strong as they now were,' and seemed 'upon the very brink of renouncing any dependence on the crown.'"[27] Coupled with this external state of affairs was the freemen's embrace of the English Revolution's maxim *salus populi suprema lex*. As covered in Chapter 10, Winthrop's declaration that the freemen had adopted it as their "transcendent rule to walk by" is a profound testament to the colony's radicalism. It is certain that Winthrop viewed the Hingham case as a repercussion of the English struggle between King and Parliament over the militia, one that he derisively called the freemen's "common cause." As we saw at the beginning of this chapter in another remarkable exchange recorded by Winthrop, even though the leadership was cognizant enough to term the colony a "republic," in the course of debating the position it would take concerning Parliament's seizure of H.M.S. Mary, the decision was made that the time was not right to declare the colony an independent state; albeit the council reserved the right to invoke

26 *General Court to Secretary of State of the Northern Department Sir William Morice* (Sept. 11, 1666), in Nathaniel Shurtleff, ed., MGCR, 4 (Part 2): 316–17; *A Present for His Majesty, Two Large Masts* (Sept. 11, 1666) in MGCR, 318; *Further Order about ye Two Masts* (Oct. 10, 1666), in MGCR, 327–28; *Capt. John Pearce his Accounts relating to ye Court's Present of Masts to ye King's Majesty* (May 31, 1670), in MGCR, 461. CSP *America and West Indies, (1661–1668)*, 5: 590–91 (July 20, 1668; #1097–#1798). Barry Coward, *The Stuart Age: England, 1603–1714*, 2nd ed., (London: Longman, 1994), 298–303. Joseph Malone, *Pine Trees and Politics* (Seattle: Univ. of Washington Press, 1964). Wim Klooster, *The Dutch Moment: War, Trade, and Settlement in the Seventeenth-Century Atlantic World*, 108–109.

27 Council member Evelyn's remarks are quoted in Mark Peterson, *The City-State of Boston*, 67–71, 149–56. Peterson remarked on the colony's treatment of the royal commissioners, "The colony's response was remarkable for its effrontery, but characteristic of the depth of its commitment to autonomy."

self-defense if an appropriate threat presented itself in the future. And at the end of the English Commonwealth, with its persecution of the Quakers being attacked in London, that's exactly what the colony did in announcing in its broadside published there that only in self-defense and under salus populi, the "sovereign law," had it executed members of the sect. The wisdom not to separate from England in the early 1640's cannot overshadow the essential viewpoint manifested in the council's debate: that not only did the people's welfare represent the well-being of the colonists of Massachusetts, but the people's interest was worthy of defense if and when challenged as the sovereign entity of the state.

CHAPTER 13

# Sovereignty of the Law

Unchastened by the King's royal tongue-lashing over the treatment of his commissioners covered in the last chapter, and unaware of the colony's close brush with armed conflict, Massachusetts mocked the next royal official dispatched to the colony: Edward Randolph. In 1676, Randolph carried correspondence from Charles II demanding that the General Court finally dispatch agents to England per his earlier commands to settle claims upon its territory, amend its *Charter,* and acknowledge his kingship. Massachusetts had enjoyed a de facto independence for nearly half a century, restricted only by a tenuous bond of not passing laws "repugnant" to those of England. This phrase had been interpreted with great latitude, but upon the restoration of Charles II both King and Parliament were eager to resume international trade and collect new sources of state revenue. Massachusetts had been exceedingly fortunate since 1660, in so far as every time the crown had undertaken an initiative to impose royal authority upon the colony, one event or another had distracted its attention. By the mid-1670's the crown's patience had run out, and Edward Randolph was the chosen messenger of this state of affairs. Upon arrival, Randolph would embark on a tenacious crusade to enforce England's *Navigation Acts.* Unlike the itinerant commissioners of the last decade, his position as the crown's customs overseer would become a permanent feature of colonial life, even if it took him nearly a decade to decisively impose his authority by realizing the repeal of the colonial charter.[1]

---

1 Joseph Frese, "Early Parliamentary Legislation on Writs of Assistance," *Colonial Society of Massachusetts Publications* (1959), 38: 318–326. Michael Hall, *Edward Randolph and the American Colonies: 1676–1703* (New York: W.W. Norton, 1960), 9–52. Maurice Smith, *The Writs of Assistance Case* (Berkeley: Univ. of California Press, 1978), 9. Bernard Bailyn, *New England Merchants*, 2nd ed., (Cambridge: Harvard Univ. Press, 1979), 112–48. Oliver Dickerson, *The Navigation Acts and the American Revolution* (Philadelphia: Univ. of Pennsylvania Press, 1951), 7–10. By 1676 three Parliamentary statutes constituted the *Navigation Acts*. The *Enumeration Act* (12 Car. II ch. 18 (1660)) required all colonial imports or exports to be shipped in English "bottoms," which included American ships; the *Staple Act* (15 Car. II ch. 7 (1663)) required any product bound for the colonies from the continent "go first to a port in Great Britain and be reshipped from there"; and the *Plantation Act* (25 Car. II ch. 7 (1673)), intended to stem abuses of the Enumeration Act by laying a "duty on any enumerated commodity that was shipped [from one colony] to another colony." Nathaniel Shurtleff, ed., *MGCR*, 4 (Part 2): 193–94 (May 1665). The 1660's royal commissioners' instructions included direction to ensure repeal of any colonial laws interfering with the *Navigation Acts*.

 | DOI:10.1163/9789004706347_015

The *Plantation Act of 1673*, one of the three parliamentary statutes which then constituted the *Navigation Acts*, provided Randolph his most robust authority by taxing all listed goods (including sugar and tobacco) when shipped from colony-to-colony. While Randolph was eager to begin collecting revenues, no system of enforcement for parliamentary regulations existed beyond colonial authorities. In order to secure the seizure itself, and crown revenues that came with it, he had to initiate a court action of condemnation similar to the process of penal informers on English domestic goods covered in Chapter 9. If a court certified a seizure to be legally made, the proceeds from confiscated goods were split between the crown, the colony, and the informer. In Massachusetts, however, Randolph had to file his actions in colonial courts. With hostile colonial judges presiding over his cases, and colonial juries sitting in judgment on his attempts to seize their neighbors' property, Randolph's initial attempts to enforce England's trade laws were a colossal failure.[2]

While the King, Parliament, and Randolph all believed that the Navigation Acts to be in force in Massachusetts, the General Court consistently refused to acknowledge their authority. During Randolph's first visit Governor John Leverett disabused him of any hope that his royal appointment had jurisdiction in the colony, declaring that "laws made by your majesty and your Parliament obligeth them in nothing but what consists with the interests of that colony, that the legislative power abides in them solely to act and make laws by virtue of a charter from your majesty's royal father, and that all matters in difference are to be concluded by their final determination, without appeal to your majesty." The crown took such offense at the colony claiming the right of last appeal because this was the mark of ultimate sovereignty during this

2 Bernard Bailyn, *The New England Merchants in the Seventeenth Century*, 2nd ed., (Cambridge: Harvard Univ. Press, 1979), 149–64. Michael Hall, *Edward Randolph and the American Colonies: 1676–1703*, 53–78. The 1673 Act addressed complaints by English merchants of New Englanders shipping enumerated goods from one colony to another and then shipping them directly to Europe, and colonial merchants' claim that landing goods in another colony satisfied the Enumeration Act (1660). Thus, a requirement was enacted for duties to be paid when enumerated goods were shipped from one colony to another. Although Massachusetts did not produce any enumerated goods, its shipping dominated colonial trade, and those goods were present in ships in Boston harbor. Larry Sawers, "The Navigation Acts Revisited," *Economic History Review* 45 (May, 1992): 262–84. During the 1950s through the 1970s the *Navigation Acts* gained attention as a potential cause of the American Revolution. While that debate has passed away, the Acts illustrate Massachusetts' challenge to England's legal and political sovereignty during the latter's emergence as an imperial economic power; which in turn highlights Massachusetts struggle against a colonial status. Gurminder Bhambra, "Focus: Accounting for British History," *Discover Society* (July 1, 2020); (https://archive.discoversociety.org/2020/07/01/focus-accounting-for-british-history/).

era, as we have seen in earlier cases. To make matters worse, as Mark Peterson describes the scene, Randolph's steady-stream of reports to crown officials included Governor Leverett's refusal to act on his notification of the foreign shipping in Boston harbor "contrary to your Majesty's laws encouraging navigation and regulating the trade of the plantations":

> Randolph listed the many merchant ships recently returned to Boston from foreign ports in France, Spain, the Canaries, the Azores, the Netherlands, the Hanse cities in the Baltic, 'Scanderoon' (Iskanderun in the Ottoman Empire), various African ports from Madagascar to Guinea, and several Caribbean locations as well: "There is no notice taken of the act of navigation, planation, or any other laws made in England for the regulation of trade. All nations have liberty to come into their ports and vend their commodities without any restraint; … *that government would make the world believe that they are a free state and do act in all matters accordingly*."[3]

Meanwhile, in 1677, another review of the Massachusetts law book (this time the *Laws and Liberties of 1672*) was conducted by the King's Attorney General, Sir William Jones; after the dissolution of the Council of Trade and Plantations in 1676, Jones reported directly to the Privy Council. He identified the following topics to be "repugnant to the laws of England": "Civil privilege; liberty to dispose of estates; apparel; capital laws; power of courts; ecclesiastical laws; magistrates' election; freemen; dancing and gaming; observation of Christmas; marriages; coining of money; oaths; torture; drinking of healths; entertaining strangers; possession of lands, single women not to entertain lodgers; oppression in trade; [and] impressing soldiers." He concluded: "These laws are (1) defective: (a) in making no provision for High Treason [against the King], (b) in not requiring the oaths of allegiance and supremacy as the laws of England direct; (2) objectionable: (a) in the style, the word commonwealth being used, (b) in comprising under heresy several punishments disproportionate to the offences as by banishment and death." Since Charles II's Restoration in 1660, the crown had been reviewing and approving legislation enacted by the other English colonies in both North America and the Caribbean. Based on the Attorney General's findings, during a discussion "on the status of New

3 *"To the Kings Most Excellent Majestie"* (Sept. 20, 1676), in Robert Toppan, *Edward Randolph: Including his Letters and Official Papers* (Boston: Prince Society, 1899), 2: 216–19. Mark Peterson, *The City State of Boston: The Rise and Fall of an Atlantic Power, 1630–1865* (Princeton: Princeton Univ. Press, 2019), 152–56.

England as to royal control" the Privy Council's committee, Lords of Plantation, advised the King to demand the colony amend or repeal these laws, and dispatch a royal governor and customs officer to the colony so that "His Majesty would not suffer the abuse of the *Navigation Act* to continue."[4]

Stymied by the colony's refusal to render assistance, Randolph returned to England to convince his supervisors, the Customs Commissioners, that he needed additional powers pertaining to ships entering Boston harbor. English officials deferred on granting him sweeping powers of search and seizure, but awarded Randolph with a prestigious royal appointment under the "Broad Seal of England" and sent him back to New England. To Randolph's chagrin, upon his return to Boston he discovered that his new title had little effect in Massachusetts. On April 14, 1682, John Endicott and John Curtis barred a deputy of Randolph's from boarding their ship. Once before a colonial court, the pair testified they had resisted Randolph's assistant because he could not produce a "warrant from lawful authority for his going aboard and searching." Randolph provided the court his royal commission and its certification by Charles II as a lawful warrant, requesting it be read "for satisfaction of the people." Magistrate Samuel Nowell (1634–1688) not only forbid the "said patent to be read in court," he rebuked Randolph for presuming a royal commission could serve as a legal warrant rather than a colonial warrant. Ultimately, Nowell ruled that Parliament's trade regulations had "no force" in the colony. Governor Simon Bradstreet convened a special Court of Assistants of Admiralty to hear several condemnation cases and placate Randolph, only to see him lose three successive jury verdicts.[5]

4 Robert Toppan and Alfred Goodrick, eds., *Edward Randolph: Including his Letters and Official Papers*, 6: 101, 106. Bernard Bailyn, *New England Merchants*, 2nd ed., 163–66, 178. *Objections to the Laws of England by Mr. Attorney* (Aug. 2, 1677), in CSP, *America and West Indies (1677–1680)*, eds. W. Nowell Sainsbury, J.W. Fortescue, (London: HMSO, 1896), 10: 139–40 (#378); *Massachusetts Laws Repugnant to the Laws of England* (Aug. 2, 1677), in CSP, 10: 140 (#379); *Case on the Patent of Massachusetts Corporation* (Aug. 2, 1677), in CSP, 10: 140–41 (#380); *Journal of Lords of Plantation* (Aug. 2, 1677), in CSP, 10: 141–42 (#381). Elmer Russell, *The Review of American Colonial Legislation by the King in Council* (New York: Colombia University Press, 1915; reprint New York: Octagon Books, 1976), 19–34.

5 *Deposition of Randolph against Nowell* (May 3, 1682), in Robert Toppan, ed., *Edward Randolph: Including his Letters and Official Papers*, 3: 128–29. Michael Hall, *Edward Randolph and the American Colonies*, 69–75. Helen Crump, *Colonial Admiralty Jurisdiction in the Seventeenth Century* (London: Longmans, Green, and Co., 1931), 37–55. The unique powers of Massachusetts government under the *Charter* "tacitly gave the general court ... power to try admiralty cases." A unique admiralty jurisdiction evolved in which maritime cases were tried in a common law forum, and no formal civil admiralty proceedings ever took hold. The first admiralty case was tried in 1630, and in 1639 the General Court passed a law authorizing special "strangers" courts to hear these cases. By the 1640's the caseload showed a marked

Despite ever increasing pressure from the Privy Council, when Leverett's successor, Governor Bradstreet, sought compromise in the General Court, supported by a majority of assistants, he was enraged when the deputies enacted their own navigation law. In response, the magistrates passed a bill adopting Parliament's regulations verbatim, but the deputies refused its adoption by exercising their negative vote. Ultimately, the deputies' Naval Office bill became law in 1682. While adopting both Parliament's *Enumeration Act* (1660) and *Staple Act* (1663), its *Plantation Act of 1673* under which Randolph could confiscate goods shipped illegally from colony-to-colony was not included in the text. The deputies further undermined his office by "allowing any person with a warrant from the Governor or a magistrate" to be an informer, court filings must cover costs of convening judge and jury, and informers would be personally liable for illegal searches. Finally, the administrator of the new customs bureaucracy would not be appointed by the governor, as required by Parliament, because the deputies had retained this power in their own bill.[6]

Why couldn't Governor Bradstreet and the magistrates moderate the deputies' hardline on Randolph and his authority? Soon after the issuance of the *Laws and Liberties of 1672* the negative vote became a topic for amendment once again. No particular event appears to have prompted this action. The issue would remain controversial until the last days of Massachusetts government under the *Charter of 1629*. In 1673, the General Court again considered whether a negative vote should be exercised, if it was authorized by colonial law or the *Charter*, and how a deadlock between magistrates and deputies was best resolved. Since the last controversy over the veto power in the

---

increase "due to the growth of Boston." Eventually, these special courts, the General Court, and the court of assistants heard maritime cases. Bradstreet was empowered to convene the court of assistants to hear admiralty cases, and the odd process of commonwealth admiralty procedure allowed a jury to sit. Michael Hall, "The House of Lords, Edward Randolph, and the Navigation Act of 1696," *William and Mary Quarterly* 14 (Oct., 1957):. 494–15. Admiralty's usual process—in rem without a jury—is how it was administered in England. The 1696 amendments imposed this type of Admiralty jurisdiction on all of the colonies as a result of colonial resistance to the Navigation Acts. "A Few Notes Touching Strangers Courts," *Publications of Colonial Society of Massachusetts, Transactions (1889–1900)* (Boston: by the Society, 1904), 6: 282–86.

6 Elmer Russell, *The Review of American Colonial Legislation by the King in Council*, 19, 33–34. *Naval Office* (Feb., 1682), in Nathaniel Shurtleff, ed., *MGCR* 5: 337–338, 5: 383 (Feb., 1683). William Whitmore, ed., *Colonial Laws of Massachusetts: 1672* (Boston: City Council, 1887), 289–90. Michael Hall, *Edward Randolph and the American Colonies*, 69–75. William Pencak, *War, Politics, and Revolution in Provincial Massachusetts* (Boston: Northeastern Univ. Press, 1981), 13–14. Malcom Gaskill, *Between Two Worlds: How the English Became Americans* (New York: Basic Books, 2014), 312–16.

mid-1640's, when the General Court created itself a bicameral legislature and reaffirmed the requirement that majorities of magistrates and deputies must both approve legislation or judicial sentences, the House of Deputies passed a bill in 1649 making its majority vote decisive in Court votes on judicial matters. After several years of negotiation, in 1652 a veto was retained by the House of Assistants in matters of legislation, so that each house must still agree to a bill by majority vote, but in judicial cases the issue would subsequently be decided by the vote of "the major part of the whole Court"—or by magistrates and deputies voting together without distinction. The magistrates could no longer control the law's meaning by upholding judicial decisions on appeal in the General Court previously issued in their role as judges in inferior courts. Now, the deputies' greater numbers would determine the Court's final decisions in judicial cases. The magistrates' combined legislative and judicial power that Winthrop thought indispensable was severed; the *Laws and Liberties of 1660* included these amendments.[7]

Per Minister William Hubbard's (1621–1704) firsthand account, the deputies first use of their new judicial authority occurred during the trial of Ann Hibbins; the personage used by Nathaniel Hawthorne for the character Mistress Hibbins in *The Scarlet Letter* who befriends Hester Prynne (and is actually a witch in his fictional account). In real life, Ann suffered the horrible fate of being found guilty, condemned, and executed for witchcraft. Hubbard did not attribute her tragic fate to supernatural forces, however, but instead to

7 Nathaniel Shurtleff, ed., *MGCR*, 4 (Part 2): 559 (May 7, 1673). Members of the committee that deliberated on the negative vote were Deputy Governor Symon Bradstreet, Samuel Symonds, Esq., William Stoughton, Esq., Mr. John Oxenbridge, Mr. Vryan Oakes, Capt. Joshua Hubbard, Mr. John Richards, Mr. Henry Bartholomew, Capt. John Hull, and Mr. Samuel Torrey. William Whitmore, ed., *Laws and Liberties of 1660*, 22 (title *Courts*, §2). In matters of legislation, "no law, order, or sentence shall pass or be accounted an act of this Court without consent of the greater part of the magistrates on the one part, and the greater number of deputies on the other." But in judicial cases, "if the magistrates and deputies shall happen to differ in any case of judicature, either civil or criminal, such case shall be determined by the major vote of the whole Court met together." *MGCR*, 2: 58–9 (March 7, 1644), 285 (Oct. 17, 1649); 3: 179–80 (Oct. 19, 1649), 266 (May 27, 1652)—"It is ordered by the authority of this Court, that for time to come, if there fall out any difference betwixt the Magistrates & the Deputies, in any case of judicature, either civil or criminal, it shall be determined by the major part of the whole court."; *MGCR* 4 (Part 1): 3 (May 22, 1650), 14 (May 30, 1650), 82 (May 26, 1652)—"it is therefore ordered, that for time to come, if there fall out any difference betwixt ye Magistrates and the Deputies, in any case of judicature, either civil or criminal, it shall be determined by ye major p[ar]t of the whole Court.," *MGCR* 4 (Part 1): 381 (Oct. 18, 1659). Richard Dunn, ed., *Laws and Liberties of 1648*, 16 (title *Courts*, §4). Mark Howe and Louis Eaton, "The Supreme Judicial Power in the Colony of Massachusetts Bay," *New England Quarterly* 20 (Sept., 1947): 291–316.

"Vox Populi," as "she was condemned by the deputies." Hubbard provided some fascinating commentary considering his station as a church minister:

> The jury found her guilty, but the magistrates consented not, so the matter came to the General Court, where she was condemned by the deputies, (the first example in that kind), and executed. Vox populi went sore against her, and was the chiefest part of the evidence against her ... It fared with her as it did with Joan of Arc, in France ... Many times persons of hard favor and turbulent passions are apt to be condemned by the common people for witches, upon very slight grounds.

Apparently, the deputies were not proud of this populist outburst since their record of proceedings makes no mention of Hibbins' trial or sentencing; it is only recorded in the Assistants' record.[8]

The issue of the negative vote in matters of judicature endured. In 1667, and again in 1671, the House of Assistants sent the deputies bills reinserting a requirement for their own majority to accede to the decision of the General Court on any matter of appeal. The deputies refused both. In 1672, the ministers joined the magistrates in urging the deputies to compromise, again they refused; now the deputies could block changes to the status quo. Ultimately, the assistants charged both houses voting together in judicial cases was inconsistent with the colony's *Charter*, just as John Winthrop had, by arguing its provisions "cannot be contradicted or made null by any positive law, positive laws being superstructures which must not overturn the foundation." The deputies responded, just as Israel Stoughton had, that the *Charter* did not

---

8 William Hubbard, *A General History of New England* (Boston: Little & Brown, 1854), 574. "One Mrs. Hibbins, in the year 1656, was arraigned for a witch after her husband's death. The jury found her guilty, but the magistrates consented not, so the matter came to the General Court, where she was condemned by the deputies, (the first example in that kind)." *Mrs. Hibbins Trial*, in Nathaniel Shurtleff, ed., *MGCR*, 4: 269 (May 14, 1656). "The Magistrates not receiving the verdict of the jury in Mrs. Hibbins her case, having been on trial for witchcraft, it came, & fell of course to the General Court. Mrs. Anne Hibbins was called forth, appeared at the bar; the indictment against her was read, to w[hi]ch she answered not guilty, & was willing to be tried by God and this Court." Once the evidence was presented, and "parties witnessing present, her answers considered on, and *the whole court, being met together, by their vote*, determined that Mrs. Anne Hibbins is guilty of witchcraft, ... accordingly, ... she was to go ... from thence to the place of execution, & there to hang until she was dead." The House of Deputies record, volume 3 of Shurtleff's edited records of the Massachusetts General Court, makes no mention of Hibbins' trial. Justin Winsor, ed. *The Memorial History of Boston* (Boston: Ticknor & Co., 1881), 2: 138–41 (#3). Carla Pestana, *The English Atlantic in an Age of Revolution* (Cambridge: Harvard Univ. Press), 137–39.

contain "particular rules for the issuing of all causes of judicature." A committee appointed to settle the dispute, composed of three assistants, five deputies, and two ministers, reported that neither house possessed a negative vote. When the assistants realized this would allow deputies and magistrates to vote without distinction in matters of legislation as well as judicial cases, they dropped the issue. In the summer of 1685, after the General Court had been notified of the revocation of the *Charter of 1629*, deputies and magistrates still bickered over minute changes in the new (but never issued) law book, title *Courts*, sec. 2, the negative vote.[9]

In a searing condemnation of the *Naval Office Act*, or that "law made by a faction in the General Court," Randolph exposed the duplicitous strategy employed by the deputies to prevent him from collecting his Majesty's revenues. He noted that while the law was "repugnant" to English law in multiple respects, it contained a sinister intent to "maintain their law and right of making officers, [and] continue their customs and hinder any person from acting in their colony by a power not derived from themselves." Concerning search and seizure, Randolph rightly charged that Massachusetts' courts were obstructing his official duties contrary to the colony's own laws. In support he cited the General Court's 1645 excise upon wine by page number and year, which authorized colonial revenue officers to search without warrant with the assistance of a constable; a warrant being necessary only to seize goods, not to make a search. He also noted that the colonial warrant commanded colonists to lend assistance to constables. But on his request for a "governor's warrant" to perform a search, Governor Leverett refused on the laughable excuse that Parliament had not authorized "breaking open warehouses and suspected places of goods in the plantations." In sum, when Randolph confiscated goods under royal authority magistrates disallowed his seizures because they were made without warrant, but when he applied for colonial warrants he was refused because Parliament had not authorized such a request. Randolph returned to London to expose the shifting sands of colonial law as a blatant rejection of the prerogatives of King and Parliament. Several years

9 Mark Howe, and Louis Eaton, "The Supreme Judicial Power in the Colony of Massachusetts Bay," 305–16. On covering this disputed process, from which most of the content of this paragraph derives, Howe and Eaton describe the "tenacious radicalism of the deputies." William Whitmore, ed., *Colonial Laws of Massachusetts of 1660*, 107–110, 114–17. Barbara Black, "The Concept of a Supreme Court: Massachusetts Bay, 1630–1686," in Russell Osgood ed., *The History of the Law in Massachusetts: The Supreme Judicial Court, 1692–1992* (Boston: Supreme Judicial Court Historical Society, 1992), 43–79. Nathaniel Shurtleff, ed., *MGCR*, 3: 164, 179. Upon Winthrop's death in 1649 preservation of his "public writings" was ordered.

later the General Court informed the Lords of Trade, as "for the acts passed in Parliament for encouraging trade and navigation we humbly conceive, according to the usual sayings of the learned in the law, that the laws of England are bounded with the four seas, and do not reach America." Moreover, because colonists were "not represented in Parliament" they did not believe its statutory regulations "impeded ... our trade," as they would invade the "liberties and properties of the subject." Ultimately, Governor Leverett had sponsored a summarily concise ordinance (of two brief paragraphs) nominally ordering observance of England's Navigation Acts. After Randolph's return to the colony with his new royal credentials, he realized only two of thirty-six successful seizures from 1680–1682, with a jury sitting in every case acquitted. The *Massachusetts Charter of 1629* was annulled on October 23, 1684.[10]

It took several years for an official delegation to arrive in the colony, the event signaling the de facto end of colonial government under the first charter's authority. According to Randolph, the Congregationalists maintained control of the colony's government until the very end, "There is now no Government there, and the loyal party, which is always the majority, is in daily expectation of deliverance from the oppression that they have groaned under, but being

10 Nathaniel Shurtleff, ed., MGCR, 5: 200 ("To obj. 7"), 5: 155 (Oct. 10, 1677). *Mr. E.R.'s [Edward Randolph] Narrative, Sept. 20th and Oct. 12th 1676*, in *Hutchinson Papers*, ed. William Whitmore (Albany: Prince Society, 1865), 2: 210, 232. Barbara Black, "The Constitution of Empire: The Case for the Colonists," *University of Pennsylvania Law Review* 124 (May 1976): 1157–1211. Elmer Russell, *The Review of American Colonial Legislation by the King in Council*, 33–36. Michael Hall, *Edward Randolph and the American Colonies: 1676–1703*, 55–7. Robert Toppan, ed., *Edward Randolph: Including his Letters and Official Papers*, 3: 134, 138–40. The Governor refused Randolph's request on reference to the *Book of Rates*, which was a code of the *Navigation Acts* entitled, *The Act of Tonnage and Poundage and book of rates: With Several Statutes At Large Relating to the Customs*. Conrad Russell, *Politics and English Parliaments: 1621–1629* (Oxford: Clarendon Press, 1979), 228. The *Book of Rates* stipulated the "values at which goods should be rated for customs duty." Bernard Bailyn, *The New England Merchants*, 2nd ed., 178. Michael Hall, *Edward Randolph and the American Colonies*, 75–78. Before departing for England Randolph presented a list of questions to force the deputies to acknowledge parliamentary statute as law in Massachusetts. Shurtleff, ed., MGCR, 5: 383–84 (Feb., 1683). The deputies revised the *Naval Office Law* in February 1683 to protect their *Charter*. MGCR, 5: 339 (March 1682). The previous March the colony finally enacted a capital law penalizing any "invasion, insurrection, or public rebellion against the *king's* majesty." Philip Haffenden, "The Crown and the Colonial Charters, 1675–1688: Part I," *William and Mary Quarterly* 15 (July 1958): 298–311. Philip Haffenden, "The Crown and the Colonial Charters, 1675–1688: Part II," *William and Mary Quarterly* 15 (Oct., 1958): 452–66. The charter's revocation was not an isolated event; the crown had initiated a review of English borough and colonial charters several years before, with an intent to revoke them en masse.

kept out of the Government they cannot relieve themselves." Several days after the royal appointees' arrival the General Court held its final session under the first charter. It would not be in recess for very long, as a new royal charter was granted in 1691 by William III (1689–1702). Thereafter the colonial legislature would pass laws, although the governor would now be royally appointed, and the colony continued to issue its laws in print until the mid-1770's. But on May 20, 1686, the remaining members of the General Court were unaware of even the possibility of such future developments, and thoroughly used to governing themselves. After the order for the General Court's dissolution was proclaimed, as its last official act the Court petitioned the newly arrived crown officials. First, "as we conceive … there is no certain determinate rule for your administration of justice," and what did exist "seems to be too arbitrary." Moreover, the "whole unquestioned privilege of the subject" had been "transferred upon yourselves, there being not the least mention of an assembly." Under such a model of royal government colonists would be deprived of "their liberty as Englishmen, both in the matter of legislation and in the laying of taxes." Magistrates and deputies, finally united, issued this last warning, "we think it highly concerns you to consider whether such a commission be safe, either for you or us."[11]

Only several months after the royal delegation's arrival in Boston, an event Randolph had long labored relentlessly to realize, he was already firing off complaints to the Lords of Trade and Plantations. He warned the crown that the "great favor of liberty of conscience granted to this people may shortly appear to be of ill consequence to the government." Additionally, Bay colonists were proving to be quite resistant to the crown's new policy of replacing their practice of freehold land ownership with a new system of "quitrents," and

11 Nathaniel Shurtleff, ed., *MGCR*, 5: 515 (May 20, 1686); 5: 465 (Jan. 28, 1685). The General Court learned of the *Charter's* revocation in January 1685. *E. Randolph to Lords of Trade* (August 1685), in *CSP, America and West Indies (1661–1668)*, ed. W. Noel Sainsbury, (London: Longman, 1899), 12: 77 (#319); "More than nine months have passed since the judgment was entered for the late King against the charter of Boston, whereby the Government of the Colony is vested in the King; yet to this day disaffected persons, under cover of the vacated charter, pretend to exercise government there, and countenance breeches of the Acts of Trade and Navigation." *CSP*, 12: 188 (#674, May 16, 1686). Charles Hilkey, *Legal Development in Colonial Massachusetts* (New York: Columbia Univ. Press, 1910), 29. "In June 1683, Attorney-General Thomas Johnes filed an information in the nature of a writ of quo warranto. This having failed, the process of scire facias was resorted to, and the final decree abrogating the charter was entered October 13, 1684. But the Rose frigate, bearing the commission of Dudley, did not arrive at Boston until May 15, 1686. On the 20th the General Court held a meeting; the establishment of a new government was proclaimed."

the associated medieval system of land tenancy. These types of manorial-like arrangements had long been popular with the most powerful English colonial land proprietors, as they favored a hierarchal framework of governance instead of the troublesome colonial legislatures. Randolph also reported complaints about the lack representative government afforded to colonists, "I find the country dissatisfied for want of an assembly of representatives from the several towns … with power to raise money and make laws." With the revocation of their charter colonists' greatest hopes were for a "confirmation" of property holdings, and their "*establishment of independency by law*." In place of New England's chartered colonies, James II (1685–1688) created the Dominion of New England under Sir Edmund Andros. Despite Massachusetts' insistence that its "inhabitants … consent to such laws and taxes as shall be made," per James II's direction "no mention" of an "assembly" appeared in the new governor's commission. Both of the later Stuarts' policies sought to deny colonists representation, with New England being the last holdout by virtue of their status as chartered colonies.[12]

Luckily for Bay colonists, the Protestant champion William III (1689–1702) soon overthrew the Catholic James, and in a cascade of colonial revolts the Dominion's brief tenure toppled along with the rest. In April 1689, upon news of James II's flight from his capital, colonists rose in favor of the Protestant champion William of Orange. Although colonial ministers had lectured congregants earlier in the decade that "they may lawfully draw their swords in ye defense of their Charter," Congregational members had become a minority in the colony by that time, as membership had withered since mid-century despite the colony's continued deep religiosity; this made their call for resistance hollow as restriction of the franchise to church members had become

12 *E. Randolph to Lords of Trade* (Aug. 23, 1686), in *CSP, America and West Indies (1685–1688)*, ed. W. Noel Sainsbury, (London: Longman, 1899), 12: 230–31 (#824); "Commission for the Government in Massachusetts" (Sept. 27, 1685), *CSP*, 98 (#384); *CSP*, 12: 89 (#357, Sept. 9, 1685); *CSP*, 12: 81 (#333, August 26, 1685). Samuel Fullerton, "New England in the Royalist Imagination," *English Historical Review* 137 (Oct., 2022): 1375. Mark Peterson, *The City State of Boston*, 166–71. "Andros and the Dominion government threatened the practices … [of] political autonomy and self-governance, freehold land title that created equity throughout the commonwealth and encouraged market production, free trade throughout the Atlantic world for Boston's merchants, and the communitarian ethos grounded in the religion of the puritan churches." Jack Greene, *The Constitutional Origins of the American Revolution* (Cambridge: Cambridge Univ. Press, 2011), 108–18. Craig Yirush, *Settlers, Liberty, and Empire: The Roots of Early American Political Theory, 1675–1775* (New York: Cambridge Univ. Press, 2011), 64–69. Adrian C. Weimer, *Constitutional Culture: New and the Struggle Against Arbitrary Rule in the Restoration Empire* (Philadelphia: Univ. Pennsylvania Press, 2023), 126.

both unpopular and untenable. Merchants' demands for greater inclusivity and access to political power reflected the reality of the larger Atlantic World in which they must reside. Before the Dominion's tyrannical nature became clear, Boston held a celebration of James II's coronation featuring a "very fair appearance of a thousand-foot soldiers and about a hundred horse, and numbers of gentlemen and merchants." With the grant of a second charter to Massachusetts in 1691 came the long-threatened addition of a royal governor to oversee the colony's unruly inhabitants, but with a reconstituted General Court as well.[13]

In the end, the colony yielded to royal control in 1686, even though James II's sponsored Dominion government embodied that very arbitrary power to threaten their liberties and properties that colonists had long feared. If the story of the colony's self-government had ended here one could simply attribute its demise to Congregationalism's unyielding restriction of political participation, one that contemporaries of the American Revolution bewailed. Instead, with the grant of a new charter in 1691, the General Court reassembled and deliberated; although the governor was now royally appointed, and the General Court would be able to enact the colony's law, except now subject to Privy Council approval. Still, from the publication of the General Court's first collection of its capital laws in 1642, and its first book of colonial law, the *Laws and Liberties*

13 Steven Pincus, *1688: The First Modern Revolution* (New Haven: Yale Univ. Press, 2009), 224–53. Mark Peterson, *The City State of Boston*, 1. In April 1689, Bostonians and "crowds from the surrounding countryside, many of them soldiers experienced in colonial wars, confronted the king's troops stationed at Fort Hill and a Royal Navy warship in the harbor. They disarmed the royal governor, Sir Edmund Andros, ... and placed him under arrest." James II had intended to "destroy Boston's autonomy and fold it into an authoritarian mega-colony, the Dominion of New England, stretching from New Jersey to Maine," while Andros would deprive colonists of "their rights, properties, and liberties." Malcom Gaskill, *Between Two Worlds: How the English Became Americans*, 312–16. William Pencak, *War, Politics and Revolution in Provincial Massachusetts* (Boston: Northeastern Univ. Press, 1981), 10–11. "Many of the second generation [of colonists] could not obtain full citizenship ... By the 1680s no more than 1,800 men, about 25 percent of the adult male population, voted for [standing] councilors. In Boston itself, which had about 1,000 adult males, Samuel Sewall never recorded over one hundred ballots in any town election before the 1690's." Darren Staloff, "'Where Religion and Commerce Jump Together': Commerce and Piety in Puritan New England," *Reviews in American History* 27 (March 1999): 8–13. Boston merchants "with their direct contacts with the larger Atlantic world naturally reached out for an accommodation with that larger world in which they had of necessity to operate. Thus, their willingness to compromise with the metropolitan authorities, as well as their attempt to broaden participation in the churches." Emerson Baker, *A Storm of Witchcraft* (Oxford: Oxford Univ. Press, 2015), 54–57. CSP, *America and West Indies (1685–1688)*, ed. W. Noel Sainsbury, (London: Longman, 1899), 12: 31–32 (#137–138, April 1685).

*of 1648*, the Bay colony had been printing its official laws for almost a century and a half by the time of the American Revolution. The *General Court Record* of the first charter period along with the three major editions of the official colonial laws books, the *Laws and Liberties*, total eight volumes alone, while the nineteenth century publication of *Massachusetts Acts and Resolves (1692–1780)* of the second charter period through initial statehood tally twenty-one volumes; the very first enacted law of the new legislature in 1692 extended all laws passed by the previous Massachusetts General Court before the charter's revocation "not repugnant" to English laws or the new charter, a law the Privy Council vetoed in 1695. The *Massachusetts Constitution of 1780*, and its process of a special convention to ensure the public approved its contents, manifested this nearly century and a half period of enacting and publishing the colony's public law.[14]

While American colonists claimed an inheritance of "English Liberties" until the Revolution, as New England's representative Jeremiah Dummer reminded MP's earlier in the century, echoing his ancestors' claims, after

14 Richard Tuck, *The Sleeping Sovereign: The Invention of Modern Democracy* (Cambridge: Cambridge University Press, 2016), 181–95. Richard Bushman, *King and People in Provincial Massachusetts*, 2nd ed., (Chapel Hill: Univ. of North Carolina Press, 1992), 11–12, 101–8. Elmer Russell, *The Review of American Colonial Legislation by the King in Council* (1915; reprint, New York: Octagon Books 1976), 33–36. Nathaniel Shurtleff, ed., MGCR, 5: 244 (*Committee to revise ye laws* (August 15, 1679)), 5: 294 (Oct. 13, 1680), 5: 303–4 (Jan. 12, 1681), 5: 331–34 (Feb. 15, 1682); 5: 333 (*A true copie, compared.*—of Randolph's commission under the broad seal of England); 5: 339 (March 17, 1682—several capital laws were amended in response to complaints by the crown, including the enactment of a capital law for insurrection against the "kings majesty"), MGCR 5: 464 (*Lawes for the Press*, 15 November 84), 5: 473 (May 6, 1685), 5: 479 (May 27, 1685), 5: 484 (June 4, 1685). Upon its reassembly, the General Court continued supporting public education and distributing its laws in print although the next edition of *Laws and Liberties* did not issue in 1684 because of the charter's pending revocation; previously a new edition had occurred in twelve-year increments (1648, 1660, and 1672). Preparations of the new draft of the law book are noted in the General Court record from October 1679, through June 1685. John Cushing, ed., *Bibliography of the Laws and Resolves of the Massachusetts Bay: 1642–1780* (Wilmington: Michael Glazier, 1984), 2–29. *Acts and Resolves, Public and Private, of the Province of Massachusetts Bay*, 21 vols., (Boston: Wright & Potter, 1869–1922), 1: 27 (ch. 1, *An Act for Continuing the Local Laws*; this law was subsequently reenacted through 1695). *John Adams to William Gordon*, (May 26, 1780) in Greg Lint, et al., eds., *Papers of John Adams* (Cambridge: Belknap Press, 1996), 9: 342–43. Adams expressed great pride in his state's process of approving its constitution, as the citizens of "Massachusetts are exhibiting a Phenomenon in the political World that is new and Singular. It is the first People, who have taken so much time to deliberate upon Government." *State of Massachusetts Bay. In Convention, June 16, 1780, State Library of Massachusetts* (https://archives.lib.state.ma.us/handle/2452/43200).

landing on an "inhospitable shore and a waste wilderness" colonists had settled this New World at their own hardship and expense. Subsequently, New England's governments had come to be "celebrated for their excellent laws and mild administration, security of liberty and property, encouragement of virtue and suppression of vice, promoting of letters by the erecting of free-schools and colleges, and in one word for everything that can make a People happy." Great Britain remained far across the Atlantic, and as long as neither the crown nor Parliament pressed a clear statement of British sovereignty upon its North American colonies peaceful relations prevailed. But when Great Britain did attempt to tax its provinces rigorously beginning in the early 1760's, however, colonized Englishmen experienced a seemingly mundane policy of a now imperial world power as a cataclysmic event that undermined their very existence.[15]

By the time of the drafting of the *Declaration of Independence*, Thomas Jefferson claimed that the "circumstances of our emigration and settlement here" were achieved by "the expense of our own blood and treasure, unassisted by the wealth or the strength of Great Britain." So, in establishing "our several forms of government ... submission to their Parliament was no part of our constitution ... if history may be credited." On the eve of Revolution John Adams claimed it the "opinions of all the colonies" that "Parliament has no authority over them excepting to regulate their trade, and this not by any principle of common law but merely by the consent of the colonies":

> The truth is the authority of Parliament was never generally acknowledged in America. More than a century since, Massachusetts and Virginia both protested against even the act of navigation, and refused obedience, for this very reason, because they were not represented in Parliament and were therefore not bound; and afterwards confirmed it by their own provincial authority. And from that time to this, the general sense of the colonies has been that the authority of Parliament was confined to the regulation of trade and did not extend to taxation or internal legislation.[16]

---

15 Jeremiah Dummer, *A Defence of the New-England Charters*, 3rd ed., (London: 1721; reprint, 1765), 5–21. *Google Books* (https://www.google.com/books/edition/A_Defence_of_the_New_England_Charters/7uGrnkMLRrUC?hl=en&gbpv=0). Craig Yirush, *Settlers, Liberty, and Empire: The Roots of Early American Political Theory, 1675–1775* (Cambridge: Cambridge Univ. Press, 2011), 96–111.

16 *Declaration of Independence* (Congressional Committee's first draft), in Paul Ford, ed., *The Works of Thomas Jefferson* (New York: G.P. Putnam's Sons, 1904), 2: 199, @ 213. John Adams, *Novanglus* (1775), in Charles Adams, ed., *The Works of John Adams* (Boston: Little and Brown, 1851), 4: 33–48.

As we saw earlier in the chapter, this was not simply a rhetorical flourish by Adams, but instead a hard won right by Bay colonists to claim to have controlled their own early destiny, so that they perceived no debt owed to Mother England. Of course, Great Britain had just expended considerable treasure defending all of the colonies under threat during the French and Indian War.

Adams' argument in opposition to Parliament's attempt to tax the colonies is known as the "internal tax" argument—stipulating that while Parliament could tax trade between colonies and international ports, it had no authority to levy taxation within an individual colonies' boundaries because the respective colony's legislature had jurisdiction—seemed an absurdity to the British, and indeed to most present-day historians. Since the restoration of Charles II in 1660 parliamentary statute had become supreme by the 1760's, even in relation to the prerogative of King George III (1760–1820). To complicate matters, the titanic struggle between King and Parliament during the 1600's had not determined which entity had sovereignty over the colonies. Regardless, by 1775, as Pauline Maier has explained, "Jefferson and others in the vanguard of colonial resistance had moved beyond any desire to return to the situation of 1763. The Lords and Commons, they decided, had no right either to impose taxes or to make laws for the internal government of the colonies and, in fact, had never held the right, though the impropriety had long gone unrecognized." Maier identified the keystone of resistance: "For Americans to be bound by the edicts of a Parliament in which they were unrepresented ... denied them the right to participate in making laws that bound them, which the First Continental Congress called '*the foundation of all English liberty and of all free government.*'"[17]

As Richard Bushman recognized, in Massachusetts "parliamentary taxation bypassed the province's established line of defense and negated all the safeguards built up over the years," the chief fortification of which was the Massachusetts General Court. To lose control over taxation would jettison colonial interests into the infinite maelstrom of the affairs of Parliament, the crown, and ultimately the British Empire. What made this so threatening on the individual level was the seemingly omnipresent threat, with a lengthy historical provenance, of being cast back into a status of serfdom if the legislative branch was ever permanently dismissed from government. During John Hampden's trial for not paying the Ship Money tax during the 1630's, for

17 Pauline Maier, *American Scripture: Making the Declaration of Independence* (New York: Vintage Books, 1998), 21. Gordon Wood, "The Problem of Sovereignty," *William and Mary Quarterly* 68 (Oct., 2011): 573–77. Pauline Maier, "Whigs against Whigs against Whigs," *William and Mary Quarterly* 68 (no. 4, 2011): 578–82.

example, Oliver St. John explained his client's rationale signified far more than paying the tax itself: "It's not that Ship-Money hath been levied upon us, but it's that right whereby Ship-Money is claimed, which … makes [its] payment … [the] earnest penny of all we have. It's not that our persons have been imprisoned for payment of Ship-money, but that … our birth-right, our ancestral right, our condition of continuing as free subjects, is lost, that of late there hath been an endeavor to reduce us to the state of villeinage." To be taxed without representation was to be made a serf. And as colonists adopted this parliamentary sponsored ideology, "Revolutionary-era Americans also embraced the 17th-century republicans John Hampden and Algernon Sidney as heroic forefathers." As earlier generations of Bay colonists had shown, the primary way to avoid such a fate was to ensure that "the people" was the fount of all arbitrary power via grants of limited or ministerial authority, or those that could be rescinded and revert back to the people. Via such a process a legislature could control government's activities and safeguard the people's interests.[18]

The same rationale was employed by Massachusetts freemen as early as the 1630's in their opposition to taxation to build new military fortifications because these outlays had only been approved by the magistrates in the Court of Assistants, employing the same rhetoric of parliamentary resistance borrowed from their very own patron of their settlement, the Earl of Lincoln. In his own resistance to the Forced Loan in the 1620's, as covered in Chapter 3, Lincoln warned his fellow Englishmen: "Beware and consider what you do concerning these subsidies and loans which are now demanded of you lest you give away not only your money, but your liberty and property in your own goods … If this course be not withstood, but take effect, we shall be ourselves the instruments of our own slavery and the loss of the privilege we have hitherto enjoyed, that our goods cannot be taken from us without consent of Parliament." Similarly, as Maija Jansson described the "Addled" Parliament's 1614 session, "There was

18 Richard Bushman, *King and People in Provincial Massachusetts*, 2nd ed., 177. *St. John's Speech to the Lords in the Upper House of Parliament, January 7, 1640, concerning Ship-Money*, in *The Tryal of John Hambden in the Great Case of Ship-Money* (London: Browne, Mears, and Clay, 1719), 218–28. Sarah Covington, "Cromwell in America: As America Built a Vision of its Past Oliver Cromwell became both Angel and Demon," *History Today* 72 (Sept., 2022): (https://www.historytoday.com/archive/history-matters/cromwell-america). Caroline Robbins, "Algernon Sidney's Discourses Concerning Government: Textbook of Revolution," *William and Mary Quarterly* 4 (July 1947): 267–96. John Campbell, *The Lives of the Chief Justices of England* (New York: Cockcroft & Co., 1874), 2: 111–12. "In a few weeks' time the fame of this speech was spread all over the kingdom, producing a general resistance to the tax, which had hitherto been resisted by Hampden alone. St. John … was now celebrated by all mouths … as the great legal patron of the oppressed."

no question in the minds of MPs that the issue of impositions affected the commonwealth as a whole, and that … the rights of the Commons carried with them the liberties of the subjects generally. Everyone knew, 'If the King may impose by his absolute power then no man [is] certain what he has, for it shall be subject to the King's pleasure.'"[19]

According to John Phillip Reid, a leading charge made by colonists against Parliament's attempts to supplant colonial legislatures was its use of "arbitrary power." Indeed, the "principle of the balanced legislature was the very essence of the eighteenth-century notion of constitutionalism"; so much so that "in British legal theory avoiding arbitrary power was but another way of describing constitutionalism." The British people "feared arbitrary power," even "more than any other threat to liberty," because it lacked "balance" by concentrating the power of the state in the hands of a few. By the eighteenth century arbitrary had become the "measure of the difference 'between slavery and liberty,'" between "power and right," and between "unconstitutional and constitutional."[20]

A British takeover of colonial legislatures was the very definition of arbitrary power to colonists. Thereby, it was not taxation itself that was unconstitutional, but instead it depended upon whether taxation was enacted by a legislature duly constituted by the people to represent their properties and interests; while there could be protests against taxation in principle, if enacted by a representative legislature they could not be over questions of process. Such enactments were inviolable because they embodied a people's will, interests, and possessions. Adrian Weimer has recently described such a "constitutional culture" emerging in New England during this era: those colonists who opposed royal authority were "marked by a wariness of metropolitan ambition, a defensiveness about civil and religious liberties, and a conviction that self-government was divinely sanctioned … New Englanders forged a potent regional constitutional culture that would not easily succumb to an imperial metropolis intent on consolidating power."[21]

19 Earl of Lincoln, *To all English Freeholders from a Well-Wisher of Theirs* (Jan. 24, 1627), in Graham Seel and David Smith, eds., *The Early Stuart Kings: 1603–1642* (London: Routledge, 2001), 63 (source 1). Maija Jansson, ed., *Proceedings in Parliament 1614 (House of Commons)* (Philadelphia: American Philosophical Society, 1988), xxi–xxii.

20 John Phillip Reid, *Constitutional History of the American Revolution: The Authority to Legislate* (Madison: Univ. of Wisconsin Press, 1991), 134–41.

21 Adrian Weimer, *Constitutional Culture: New England and the Struggle Against Arbitrary Rule in the Restoration Empire*, 3.

Algernon Sidney was executed for his unpublished manuscript, *Discourses Concerning Government*, as a "seditious and traitorous libel" for what in future decades and centuries would become a famous paean to Republican government, and its assertion that the "power originally in the people is delegated to Parliament," and the monarch "must be content to submit his interests unto theirs." The great tragedy in Sidney's case was that with the succession of William III in just several years sovereignty was placed with the *King in Parliament*, and during his successor Queen Anne's reign (1702–1714) the crown made its last challenge to parliamentary enacted statute being supreme. Ironically, Bernard Bailyn attributed Henry Parker's theory of parliamentary supremacy to Parliament's unchallenged unitary sovereign power in British government that emerged during the following century, one the American Colonies would struggle mightily against. Many other English revolutionary principles had already been accepted over the decades, such as the supremacy of the House of Commons, periodic meetings of Parliament, parliamentary approval of government officials, an enacted *Bill of Rights* (1689), and by virtue of the inability of the crown to veto legislation the monarch had to endorse all legislation; all of these achievements were demands made by the Levellers or associated pro-democratic forces. The two demands that were not granted were apportioned representation based on population, and universal public education. Both would await nineteenth-century parliamentary reform.[22]

22 *Trial of Colonel Algernon Sidney* (1683), in T.B. Howell, ed., *State Trials* (London: Hansard, 1816), 9: 817 @ 819 (#300). Caroline Robbins, "Algernon Sidney's Discourses Concerning Government: Textbook of Revolution," *William and Mary Quarterly* 4 (July 1947): 267–96. Bernard Bailyn, *Ideological Origins of the American Revolution: Enlarged Edition* (Cambridge: Belknap Press, 1992), 200–1. Conrad Russell, *Causes of the English Civil War*, 142. "By the summer of 1642 the key point parliamentarians were trying to establish was that the King had no negative voice: they invoked 'the obligation that lieth upon the kings of this realm to pass such bills as are offered to them by both houses of Parliament'." Richard Overton, *An Arrow Against All Tyrants* (London: 1646), in Kevin Sharp, ed., *The Levellers* (Cambridge: Cambridge Univ. Press, 1998), 62. "The legislative power is not in the king himself but only in the kingdom and body representative, who has the power to make or to abrogate laws, statutes, etc., even without the king's consent." Charles Andrews, *The Colonial Period of American History* (New Haven: Yale Univ. Press, 1938), 1: 372. "This point has not been stressed sufficiently … though it is apparent enough to any one following the course of Puritan action from 1630 to 1684. The Puritans in America wished to establish a state of their own which should be independent of all alien control, … [including] the king and the Parliament. In this respect … they differed fundamentally from the Pilgrims, the latter of whom, though they rejected the Church of England, always recognized the higher authority of the king, Parliament, and the New England Council. The Puritan made no such acknowledgment. He recognized the existence of the king, but not the latter's authority over him."

# Conclusion

Reverend Edmund Hickeringill's *History of Whiggism* (1682) testifies to an enduring ideological continuity between the early 1640's, through the era of the Glorious Revolution (1688). His dialogue between a Whig and a Tory begins with the former boldly proclaiming the supremacy of Parliament in all matters of government, "If Kings of England would take advice of their great and best Council, the Parliament, there would be no grievances … It is a wonder to me, that ever any should dare to advise any King against his only interest, his People's Welfare, for which Kings were first invented." The Tory responded, "Oh, ho, you are for the old Whiggish maxim, salus populi, suprema lex, the People's Welfare is the supreme and chiefest law." "Yes, yes you have it right for once and for once speak true," the Whig confirmed, "that is my principle, and shall be all true English men's principles." Then, the Tory recalls, "[*t*]*his was the old plea in forty-one, in the late Rebellion*," infuriating the Whig, "Rebellion? There can be no rebellion against the King, but what is rebellion against his law; and laws he has none … but what are confirmed [by] … Parliament." Hickeringill concluded by declaring his version of parliamentary law as supreme, "I know that prerogative is part of the law, but sovereign power is no parliamentary word in my opinion, it weakens Magna Charta and all our statutes, for they are absolute without any saving of Sovereign Power … Magna Charta is such a fellow that he will have no Sovereign." The Earl of Bridgewater condemned the book's author as an "arrant Leveller," aiming "to do all the mischief to monarchy that he possibly can."[1]

1 Edmund Hickeringill, *History of Whiggism: or, The Whiggish-plots, principles, and practices (mining and countermining the Tory-plots and principles) in the reign of King Charles the First, … under the influence of the three great minions and favourites: Buckingham, Laud, and Strafford … to that fatal-year … 41* (1682), in *Works of Edmund Hickeringill* (London: 1709), 1: 43–4. Ibid., *Second Part of the History of Whiggism*, 4–5; *Early English Books Online* (https://quod.lib.umich.edu/e/eebo/A70223.0001.001/1:1?rgn=div1;view=fulltext). Tim Harris, "The Leveller Legacy," in Michael Mendle, ed., *The Putney Debates of 1647* (Cambridge: Cambridge Univ. Press, 2010), 220–221, 233. The "Levellers were deeply attached to the principle of popular sovereignty, … salus populi should be suprema lex, … the representative assembly should have supreme authority, and that the powers of government should be limited by principles of natural justice." Earl of Bridgewater quoted in Ibid., 221. Richard Ashcraft, *Revolutionary Politics and Locke's Two Treatises of Government* (Princeton: Princeton Univ. Press, 1986), 190–91. "The Whigs developed their position around three major tenets of natural law theory: (1) the Law of Nature was given by God to mankind in order preserve the common good; (2) natural law requires the keeping of agreements and contracts; and (3) the community and (secondarily) individuals have the right to preserve themselves against the unauthorized use

 | DOI:10.1163/9789004706347_016

Although John Locke's relationship to Leveller thought remains largely uncharted, the *Second Treatise's* section-title on representation, *Salus Populi Suprema Lex*, and content, "so that each place has a right to have its representatives," is a tell-tale of historical allegiance on his behalf. This allegiance was not ready-made, however, because Locke, like most other Englishmen before him, had been radically changed by the events of the 1640's and 1650's and sought a return to a more orderly and conservative nation. In the wake of a failed restored monarchy after James II had fled London, however, Locke reasoned, "it being the intention of the People to have a fair and equal Representative, whoever brings it nearest to that ... cannot miss the consent and approbation of the community." Nearly a half-a-century earlier Henry Parker's formulation of parliamentary sovereignty rested, in part, on its equitable representation of the people of England. Only five years after which, during the Leveller ascendancy at Putney, the Army's contingent led by Colonel Thomas Rainsborough proposed, "the election of Members of the House of Commons shall be distributed to all counties, or other parts or divisions of the kingdom, according to some rule of equality of proportion, in order to render the House of Commons as near as may be an equal representative of the whole body of the people that are to elect," consistent with Parker's original call for "geometrically proportionable" representation. At the time there were tens of thousands of soldiers in Parliament's now victorious armies playing an essential part in the life of the nation, regardless of their otherwise impotent political status as related to a lack of property ownership. Considering the hardships that England had endured during these political and religious upheavals, Locke believed that the royal "prerogative" must now be "nothing, but a power in the hands of the Prince to provide for the public good." Moreover, the pre-civil war model of parliamentary representation, of one Member representing the entire nation no matter his domicile, would be replaced by apportioned representation on a geographical model. In this new era, if scenarios which, "*depending upon unforeseen ... occurrences, certain and unalterable laws could not safely direct,* whatsoever shall be done manifestly for the good of the People, and the establishing the government upon its true foundations, is and always will be just prerogative." Setting the nation aright through a representative Parliament that could exercise its will must include "the power of erecting new ... representatives,"

of force ... 'This proposition', Edmund Hickeringill wrote in his *History of Whiggism*, 'is the meaning of the old Whiggish maxim, Salus Populi, Suprema Lex.'"

supposing that "in time the measures of representation might vary, and those places have a just right to be represented which before had none."[2]

Henry Parker's vision of a republic based on Cicero's "res publica," or the primacy of the public sphere in the state, as inspired by John Pym's parliamentary rhetoric, led his *Observations* to establish the English Commonwealth upon a popular sovereignty. Moreover, his pamphlet's strategy to undermine the King and his supporters required a rationale why Parliament was more suited to exercise arbitrary power, which Parker argued was by virtue of the many legislators who sat in the body could see the kingdom's needs in great detail. As Sir George More had described his role as a MP, he had been "sent hither from all the commons in the kingdom" with a "principal care to speak from the commonwealth that continually speaks to us." Therefore, Parker's solution was the election of representatives across the nation "geometrically proportioned." Concomitantly, however, the majority of the nobility and the gentry class opposed enlarging the electorate to satisfy the Leveller's and other radical parties' demands. Cromwell and his Council of State's attempts to set Parliament aright through purges and outright dismissals, such as his dismissal of one-hundred Members of the Second Protectorate Parliament, only highlighted this fatal flaw. To aggravate matters, besides a recalcitrant aristocracy that most every revolution has to deal with, the Protectorate's failure to reach

2 Richard Ashcraft, *Revolutionary Politics and Locke's Two Treatises of Government* (New Jersey: Princeton University Press, 1986), 75–76, 145–65. Locke's views on the powers of kingship, at the dawn of a new era of Restoration following a failed parliamentary state, provide an invaluable perspective for the historical observer; because they illustrate that his ideas, like anyone else's, were not immutable as a political philosopher and evolved over time as human events and experience suggested. By the early 1660s Locke granted the King "absolute and arbitrary power over all actions of individuals within society; he did not subscribe to a theory of natural rights; he was opposed to the toleration of religious dissent; he did not believe in parliamentary supremacy as an embodiment of the legislative power of society; … and he opposed the view that the people have a right to resist their rulers." Peter Laslett, ed., *John Locke, Two Treatises of Government* (Cambridge: Cambridge Univ. Press, 1988), 373 (*Second Treatise*, Ch. XIII, *On the Subordination of Powers in the Commonwealth*, §158). "158. *Salus Populi Suprema Lex.*, is certainly so just and fundamental a rule, that he, who sincerely follows it, cannot dangerously err … The power of erecting new … representatives carries with it a supposition that in time the measures of representation might vary, and those places have a just right to be represented which before had none." *At the Committee of Officers at the Quartermaster Generals* (Oct. 30, 1647), in C.H. Firth, ed., *The Clarke Papers* (UK: Camden Society, 1891), 1: 363 @ 365 (#5.1.) Richard Tuck, *Philosophy and Government: 1572–1651* (Cambridge: Cambridge Univ. Press, 1993), 229–33, 242–51. Mark Knights, "John Locke and Post-Revolutionary Politics: Electoral Reform and the Franchise," *Past and Present* 213 (Nov., 2011): 41–86. Rachel Foxley, *The Levellers* (Manchester: Manchester Univ. Press, 2013), 108–12, 177–79.

a religious settlement, even if based on a virtuous policy of religious toleration, left a plethora of religious sects running amuck in London's streets and across the nation as a constant specter of societal breakdown. In fairness, while apportionment of representation via the franchise is one of this era's most noteworthy ideas, even if unrealized, it was a problem not resolved by parliamentary reform until the nineteenth century.[3]

Meanwhile, across the Atlantic, the Restoration of Charles II negated any hope that Massachusetts might permanently separate itself from England over time, and confronted with this reality, the colony set upon a decades long campaign to resist the march of history. Indeed, it is a fair analogy to describe the colony as ensconced in a time-capsule of its own making, within which it suppressed inhabitants' petitions for a more inclusive government, while rebuffing royal emissaries. Despite Massachusetts' exercise of what Richard Bushman termed "virtually every privilege of Republican government" during its First Charter Period (1629–1686), when an opportunity to declare a Republic de jure arose upon the seizure of H.M.S. Mary in the mid-1640's (as reviewed at the beginning of Chapter 12), colonial leadership shied away from an outright declaration of independence. While Bay colonists clung stubbornly to a de

---

3 Christopher Hill, *God's Englishman: Oliver Cromwell and the English Revolution* (London: Weidenfeld & Nicolson, 1970), 206–7. "Underlying all the disputes between Oliver Cromwell, the Levellers and his Parliaments, was one fundamental problem: the problem of the electorate. After 1647, the Revolution had gone much further than the average MP, or the average gentleman or merchant … could approve. Religious toleration … was something which no Parliament elected on the traditional franchise would ever accept." George More cited in Maija Jansson, ed., *Proceedings in Parliament 1614* (Philadelphia: American Philosophical Society, 1988), xxi–xxii. Steven Pincus, *1688: The First Modern Revolution* (New Haven: Yale University Press, 2009), 99–102, 184–86. Barbara Shapiro, *Law Reform in Early Modern England* (Oxford: Hart Publishing, 2019), 158–59, 138. "Shortly after the dissolution of the Barebones Parliament, Cromwell, backed by the army, established England's first government with a written constitution [i.e., *The Instrument of Government*] … composed of a Protector, Cromwell himself, and a nominated Council of State" as well as a "single-house parliament. Together, the Protector and Council of State were empowered to make ordinances binding until approved or disapproved by parliament. The disputed legal status of ordinances lacking parliament's consent made legislation during the First Protectorate Parliament impossible. Parliaments summoned by Cromwell after the *Instrument's* issuance repeatedly objected that its Members had neither contributed to, nor approved its contents." Jonathan Scott, "What were Commonwealth Principles?," *Historical Journal* 47 (Sept., 2004): 591. To "invoke commonwealth principles was to subscribe to the Platonic or Aristotelian commonplace that whatever its constitutional form government must be directed to the common good. In a related sense, 'commonwealth' was the English rendering of the Latin *res publica*, meaning literally 'public thing,' and defined by Cicero as 'the concern of a people … through agreement on law and community of interest.'"

facto independence as illustrated throughout this work, they wisely remained within a colonial construct for preservation of their tiny state surrounded by hostile forces; if not subject to an English king or parliament, far less palatable choices of a French or Spanish Catholic monarch awaited them. Nevertheless, after several decades of fierce, if non-violent, resistance to Charles II, a stance that the King himself acknowledged in royal correspondence to the colony's government, once its options had run out at the end of the century, with the freemen's control of the franchise no longer legitimate, the General Court deferred to royal emissaries upon their arrival.[4]

In the end, the colony yielded to royal control in 1686, even though James II's sponsored Dominion government turned out to be the very embodiment of arbitrary power to threaten their liberties and properties that colonists had long feared. Nevertheless, if the story of the colony's self-government had ended there, one could simply attribute it to Congregationalism's unyielding restriction of political participation that contemporaries of the American Revolution bewailed. As David Ramsay recounted in his *History of the American Revolution* published in 1789, "The Puritans' … sufferings for non-conformity disposed them to reflect on the nature … of civil authority, and led to a conviction that tyranny, whether in church or state, was contrary to nature, reason, and revelation." However, their exclusion of non-congregants from the administration of church and state was "a matter of regret, that these noble principles of liberty ceased to operate … soon after they got power into their hands," so that in "a few years more, they had so far forgot their own sufferings, as to press for uniformity in religion, and to turn persecutors." The one mitigating factor Ramsay cited for this "inconsistent conduct" was, during their era, "the true grounds of liberty of conscience were then neither understood, nor practiced by any sect of Christians." Although hard to pin down, judging from the freemen's alteration of their loyalty oath in 1634 acknowledging the legitimacy of each man voting according to their own self-interest, as covered in Chapter 3, matters of religious conscience took considerably longer to gain legitimacy viz a vis the community because of the real fear of violent non-conformity. On the other hand, a "representative" public was achieved by excluding participation

4 Richard Bushman, *King and People in Provincial Massachusetts*, 2nd ed., (Chapel Hill: Univ. of North Carolina Press, 1992), 11–14, 101–8. Samuel Fullerton, "New England in the Royalist Imagination," *English Historical Review* 137 (Oct., 2022): 1354. Giuseppina Richard Lobo, "John Milton, Oliver Cromwell, and the Cause of Conscience," *Studies in Philology* 112 (no. 4, 2015): 774–97.

of a larger populace based on the criteria of gender, race, religion, or property holdings.[5]

Nevertheless, the colony's important legacy of representative government was initiated by a fifteen-year struggle over whether the magistrates led by John Winthrop, or the freemen represented by the deputies in the General Court, would control the enactment of legislation and its interpretation. Meanwhile, a Protestant impulse underwrote the liberal establishment of public education within the colony as it concomitantly legitimized an exclusive possession of the franchise in colonial elections by male church congregants. As noted in Chapter 7, although Winthrop's conception of the godly magistrate was derivative of the French Religious Wars and Calvinism, it also sounded very much like claims to divine right kingship as voiced by James I early in his reign. This may seem either hypocritical or, at the least, ill-conceived (as Puritans struggled against the crown's control of the English Church), but there are simpler explanations. Both French scholars like Theodore Beza, and later English churchmen including Hugh Peters, modeled the lesser magistrates on divine right monarchy because it was *the* era's model of executive/judicial power; similarly, Winthrop borrowed principles from pamphlets that were originally written to address English political events, ignoring the context and stripping out the general argument, such as Charles Herle's immutable fundamental law. All of these commentators shared the conception of arbitrary authority as a unitary whole, one that encompassed law-making and judicial interpretation. Ultimately, by the end of the century, John Locke believed that an "absolute arbitrary power, or governing without settled laws, can neither of them consist with the ends of society and government." According to John Phillip Reid, "there was no concept more dynamic, … or more useful for eighteenth-century politics and law than the concept of arbitrary power."[6]

5 David Ramsay, *The History of the American Revolution* (Philadelphia: R. Aitken & Son, 1789), 1: 8–9. John Coffey, "Puritanism and Liberty Revisited," *Historical Journal* 41 (no. 4, 1998): 962 71.

6 Peter Laslett, ed., *John Locke, Two Treatises of Government*, 359 (sec. 137). John Phillip Reid, *The Concept of Liberty in the Age of the American Revolution* (Chicago: Univ. of Chicago Press, 1988), 55. "The notion of arbitrariness appears in the polemical literature as frequently as any other concept except liberty, slavery, and constitution. For both constitutional law and non-constitutional public law it was … serving … to define law and set theoretical limits to governmental actions. There was no accusation against an official more serious than that he sought to impose arbitrary rule. It had been the first count in the attainder of the earl of Strafford, an article in the impeachment of judges who rendered the *Shipmoney* decision, one of the major charges justifying the execution of Charles I, and part of the indictment against George III in the American *Declaration of Independence*."

In the opening decade of the seventeenth century James I (1603–1625), followed by his son Charles I (1625–1649), attempted to incorporate a new concept of "reason of state" into the crown's government, to remedy not only a ramshackle approach to revenue collection, but to implement an empowered means of policymaking whereby expertise and more deliberative methods could replace royal courts dominated by personalities battling over feudal rights and privileges. Richard Tuck described a "new humanism" from which "reason of state" emerged, spreading across Europe with an accompanying wave of absolutism at the end of the sixteenth century, succeeding the earlier Ciceronian version of humanism that had initially animated England's Commonwealth reform movement. Tuck termed the new version both "anti-constitutional" and "often anti-ethical." As both of the first Stuarts embraced the idea that only a fully empowered executive could resolve contingent necessities of state, based on salus populi suprema lex, via royal consultations and advisory opinions concerning state revenue, the Stuarts, father and son, attempted to instill the authority for a new form of government over time through the common law courts and judges. The end-goal being, policymaking and enactment of revenue would be made as exclusive as possible to the crown. According to Maija Jansson, upon her review of the 1614 Parliament that foundered over impositions, ultimately "the argument ... was not about the petty sums extracted from merchants, but about who had the right to impose those taxes—the King or the Parliament—and the concomitant question, in whose power was it to define that right—the courts of law or the high court of Parliament?" In other words, was the "opinion in *Bates'* case ipso facto law?"[7]

Most historically significant, John Pym's concept of parliamentary supremacy, galvanized by the maxim salus populi suprema lex, gained revolutionary force via Henry Parker's distillation of the public good as the sovereignty of the people. Again, according to Richard Tuck, "in a European context the English rebellion was justified in extremely modern terms. All the key words of the new humanism were present in an astonishingly extensive pamphlet literature: 'necessity', 'salus populi', 'reason of state'." From this perspective, salus populi must qualify as an "*idea*" for "*fundamental change*," even a "*form*

7 Richard Tuck, Philosophy and Government: 1572–1651 (Cambridge: Cambridge Univ. Press, 1993), xii–xiv, 65–119. Geoff Baldwin, "Reason of State and English Parliaments, 1610–1642," *History of Political Thought* 25 (Winter 2004): 620–41. Tim Harris, *Rebellion* (Oxford: Oxford Univ. Press, 2014), 116–135, 186–222. Eric Lindquist, "The Failure of the Great Contract," *Journal of Modern History* 57 (Dec., 1985): 617–51. David Cressy, *Charles I and the People of England* (Oxford: Oxford Univ. Press, 2015), 177–85. Maija Jansson, ed., *Proceedings in Parliament 1614 (House of Commons)* (Philadelphia: American Philosophical Society, 1988), xxi–xxii.

*of revolutionary theory,*" as Christopher Hill originally articulated the issue, because of the populist agitation it excited on both sides of the Atlantic concerning universal public education, legal reform, and popular sovereignty. Upon his description of Charles I's final words from his execution scaffold "as uncompromising as ever," Malcom Gaskill noted, ironically, that he "echoed his political opponent, John Winthrop: the people's freedom consisted in the law, advised the king, 'not for having a share in Government,' which was none of their concern." After Charles's execution, his would-be prosecutor, John Cooke, briefed the state's intended case before that Court, which included his initial crime of being so "wedded to his own conceits and *private opinion*" in opposition to Parliament's "*publique judgment* and *reason of state.*" If only Charles had endorsed the *Militia Act* and utilized his prerogative for his people's "safety," rather than waging war upon their interests. For abandoning his primary responsibility, in favor of "shedding of so much blood for a pretended Prerogative," Cooke concluded that Charles I's intent was to "perpetuate an absolute tyranny."[8]

Once a public sphere of governmental policymaking had been demarcated by *Bates' Case* (1606), after which King and Parliament failed repeatedly to negotiate a shared jurisdiction, as Clarendon observed, each resolved to exclude the other from power. No matter if one side's spokesman or pamphleteer promised that they could be entrusted with an unfettered exercise of arbitrary power, each side's dominion had inevitably led to a despotic regime. To aggravate matters, during the entire span of this era both cavalier and roundhead seemed oblivious to how their respective declarations of absolute authority in the

8 Richard Tuck, *Philosophy and Government: 1572–1651* (Cambridge: Cambridge Univ. Press, 1993), 221–23. Christopher Hill, *God's Englishman: Oliver Cromwell and the English Revolution*, 211–12. The "English Revolution had no predecessors ... [and] in consequence lacked a revolutionary ideology: there was no Jean-Jacques Rosseau or Karl Marx. There were of course many intellectual, religious, and political discontents: but before 1642 they had not crystallized into the form of revolutionary theory, or even an idea that fundamental change might be required. The leaders of Parliament in the early 1640s believed themselves to be the true conservatives and traditionalists ... So, whereas the trinities of the later revolutions—liberty, equality, fraternity; peace, bread and land—demanded something new, something to be fought for and achieved in the future, the trinity of the English revolutionaries—religion, liberty and property—was intended to defend what already existed ... So when, in the early 1640s, men found themselves unexpectedly and unwillingly facing a revolutionary situation, a situation which demanded new thinking, they were ill-equipped for the task." Mark Kishlansky, "Charles I: A Case of Mistaken Identity," 189 *Past and Present* (Nov., 2005): 41–80. John Cook, *King Charles, His Case: Or an Appeal to All Rational Men, Concerning His Tryal before the High Court of Justice* (London: 1649), 6; *Early English Books Online* (https://quod.lib.umich.edu/e/eebo/A34423.0001.001?view=toc).

name of the people rang hollow, as if the actual public was unaware that its own interests were tertiary at best. A 1766 proclamation issued by Louis XV at the height of French divine right absolutism, shortly before its own collapse, articulates the culmination of absolute monarchy:

> [I]n my person alone lies that sovereign power whose very nature is the spirit of counsel, justice and reason. From me alone the courts receive their existence and authority. The fullness of this authority, which they exercise in my name only, remains permanently vested in me, and its use can never be turned against me. Legislative power is mine alone, without subordination or division. It is by my sole authority that the officers of my courts effect, not the creation of the law, but its registration, promulgation and execution ... Public order in its entirety emanates from me. I am its supreme guardian. *My people are one with me, and the rights and interests of the nation—which some dare to make into a body separate from the monarch—are of necessity united with my own and rest entirely in my hands.*[9]

The French monarch was no longer only "l'etat," he was the body politic itself: head, torso, and limbs. He was at one with the public because he was the public. He was unaccountable to any legal standard then in effect, because the law would accommodate whatever his actions required.

In reality, according to R.R. Palmer, during this era "French Parlements ... adopted the practice of formal remonstrances ... [that] were of great importance in the formation of public opinion," since the monarchy "insisted on the maintenance of administrative privacy ... [and] supplied no information." On the other end of the spectrum of an already failed English divine right absolutism, by the late 1680's Locke declared, "whosoever has legislative or supreme power in any commonwealth is bound to govern by standing established laws, promulgated and known to the People, and not by extemporary decrees." The people must be made aware of these enactments because the law had "no other end but the peace, safety, and public good of the people." On the other hand, after giving themselves up to an "absolute arbitrary power and will of a legislator" a people would inevitably find that "they have disarmed themselves, and armed him to make prey of them when he pleases." Therefore, under a commonwealth or republican form of government, "the ruling power ought to govern by declared and received laws, and not by extemporary dictates."

9 Louis XV quoted in François Furet, *Revolutionary France* (Oxford: Blackwell, 1988), 5–6.

Otherwise, “they shall have armed one or a few men” to govern them via their “sudden thoughts” or “unknown wills without having any measures set down which may guide and justify their actions.” Or, as Henry Parker had diagnosed such a dilemma a half a century before, in judging between “what prerogative the people’s good … will bear,” and the “King’s absoluteness or prerogative may admit,” one must “appeal to written laws [rather] than to the breasts of kings themselves.”[10]

While absolutism trended throughout early modern Europe, as the rising fortunes of parliamentary assemblies since the Middle Ages declined on the continent, with the Stuarts regularly proclaiming their divine right, English common law principles like habeas corpus hedged their ambitions. But it was Parliament’s steadfast opposition to imposts that prompted James I to circumvent his legislature by not recalling it for seven years. Similarly, after Charles I initially summoned Parliament frequently into session, upon a shortage of revenues granted during wartime, he also tried to outlast his legislature. Nevertheless, after Parliament’s forced return in the early 1640s, again on the issue of state revenue, with a Scottish army at the border, and a gathering of political enemies surfeit with grievances at his back, Charles held firm. He resolved to storm his legislative body with overwhelming force, and while only worsening his position, he persevered to field several armies. So, upon nearing his end, with a constitutional monarchy proposed, what was his response? That he ruled by divine right and his prerogative was absolute, as he answered only to God. Ultimately, per Henry Ireton’s dispatch to Edmund Ludlow, on the eve of Charles’ trial, the issue had finally come down to whether “the people of England [will] … be preserved in their just rights, from the oppressions of violent men?”; with the chief “question in dispute between the king’s party and us” being, should the king “govern as a God by his will, and the nation be governed by force like beasts, or, whether the people should be governed by

10 R.R. Palmer, *The Age of the Democratic Revolution* (Princeton: Princeton Univ Press, 1959), 1: 86–93. “French parlements … as the eighteenth century went on adopted the practice of formal remonstrances against actions taken by the royal government … [and] were of great importance in the formation of public opinion … The government … insisted on the maintenance of administrative privacy … [and] supplied no information.” Peter Laslett, ed., *John Locke, Two Treatises of Government*, 353 (sec. 131), 359–60 (sec. 137). Henry Parker, *The Case of ShipMony … Presented to the Censure and Correction of the High Court of Parliament, Nov. 3, 1640* (London: 1640), 4–5; *Google Books* (https://play.google.com/books/reader?id=m4NnAAAAcAAJ&pg=GBS.PP1&hl=en).

laws made by themselves, and live under a government derived from their own consent?"[11]

Consent itself took material form in instances like the traditional grant of supply for redress of grievances, when Parliament petitioned the monarch to address needful remedies for his kingdom's ills. It provided protection of his subjects' property so that they were not driven into abject poverty and villeinage, a villain or serf being historically bereft of any legal rights whatsoever. Similarly, John Winthrop initially denied the freeman an official role in Massachusetts government based on the *Charter of 1629* and their lack of a divine insight (as covered in Chapter 4) that Israel Stoughton objected to, charging the magistrates with pursuing an arbitrary "power ... over our persons, goods, and lives, without any law of ours." Stoughton accused Winthrop and the magistrates of instituting an arbitrary government without need of the approval (or consent) of male congregational members for their actions. Instead, based on his conviction of the necessity of the godly magistrate and its divine station, Winthrop initially denied the freemen an official role until they

11 Tim Harris, *Rebellion: Britain's First Stuart Kings*, 11–41. Peter Lake, "From Revisionist to Royalist History; or, Was Charles I the First Whig Historian?," *Huntington Library Quarterly* 78 (Winter 2015): 657–81. Jan Luiten van Zanden, Eltjo Buringh, and Maarten Bosker, "The Rise and Decline of European Parliaments, 1188—1789," *Economic History Review* 65 (Aug., 2012): 835–61. Edmund Ludlow, *Memoirs of Edmund Ludlow* (London: Millar, Browne, and Ward, 1751), 101–9. After the charges against him were read to the King, he objected, "'I am not entrusted by the people, they are mine by inheritance,' ... The king demurred to the jurisdiction of the court, affirming that no man, nor body of men, had power to call him to account." *The Trial of Charles Stuart, King of England: Before the High Court of Justice, for High Treason* (1649), in T.B. Howell, ed., *State Trials* (London: T.C. Hansard, 1816), 4: 990 @ 996 (#183); *At the High Court of Justice sitting in Westminster Hall, January 20, 1649*—Charles I at trial: "England was never an elective kingdom, but an hereditary kingdom for near these thousand years; therefore let me know by what authority I am called hither; I do stand more for the liberty of my people, than any here that came to be my pretended judges, and therefore let me know by what pretended authority I am seated here, and I will answer it; otherwise I will not answer it." Henry Robinson, *Certaine Proposals in Order to a New Modelling of the Lawes* (London: 1653), 3–4; *Google Books* (https://play.google.com/books/reader?id=OcJjAAAAcAAJ&pg=GBS.RA1-PA2&hl=en). "In the making of all our statute laws, the establishing [of] the King's Prerogative was more aimed at than estating [i.e., establishing] the people in freedom ... Now for a people redeemed out of the jaws of tyranny, and desirous to settle and establish themselves, and be made happy under a Common-wealth Government, with the self-same laws which were either wrung from their excluded Tyrants ... or in any ways indulged, ... is no more possible for a Tyrant to erect ... an usurped jurisdiction, while he governed by a body of laws that had been enacted by the free people of a Common-wealth. Let us therefore no longer idolize that thread-bare notion of fundamental laws, where perhaps the whole nation hath too much, too long hypocritized."

made their numbers felt. After which the magistrates fought a rear-guard action until Winthrop's impeachment that showcased the final showdown between the deputies and Winthrop's deep conviction that only the magistrates had the divinely endowed right to govern, after election, without constraint by any human entity. Whether monarch or lesser magistrate, a measure of divinity was required to rule. By the very end of the Commonwealth era a pamphlet enunciating the Levellers' "principles and maxims concerning Government and Religion" clearly rejected any such hierarchy. Their very first most "fundamental" principle was that "the Government of England ought to be by laws, and not by men." The law should be the means of protection and preservation, "under God, of all our persons and estates, ... and live under that protection, and safely, without fear of a redcoat, or a pursuivant from Whitehall."[12]

As John Adams attested in his 1766 article in the *Boston Gazette*, "Clarendon to William Pym, no. III," authored in response to recent anonymous attacks on the legitimacy of Massachusetts' chartered government in London papers: "The public good, the salus populi, is the professed end of all government, the most despotic as well as the most free. I shall enter into no examination which kind of government, whether either of the forms of the schools, or any mixture of them, is best calculated for this end. This is the proper inquiry of the founders of empires. I shall take for granted, what I am sure no Briton will controvert, namely,—that liberty is essential to the public good, the salus populi." According to his grandson and editor of his personal papers, Charles Francis Adams, "his letters clearly show how much he had studied the character of ... [Edward Hyde, 1st Earl of Clarendon], and of the age in which he lived"; the Earl being the author of a multi-volume *History of the Rebellion*. Adams' use of "salus populi" demonstrates his intimate knowledge of this history, recalling Clarendon's condemnation of both King and Parliament for their struggle over the public good, since neither of the two *London Evening Post* editorials had used the term. Although Adams did not attend the Constitutional Convention, owing to his appointment as the first US Ambassador to the Court of St. James, his authorship of the draft Massachusetts Constitution of 1780 that became a model for the US Constitution ensured that the English experience of the people's welfare enjoyed a prominent influence.[13]

12 *The Leveller; or the Principles and Maxims concerning Government and Religion which are asserted by those commonly called Levellers* (London: 1659), in *Harleian Miscellany* (London: 1810), 7: 36–46; *Early English Books Online 2* (https://quod.lib.umich.edu/e/eebo2/A88064.0001.001?view=toc).

13 Charles Francis Adams, ed., *Works of John Adams* (Boston: Little Brown & Co., 1865), 3: 477–83 @ 479. Ibid., 3: 469. Editor's Note: "On the 20th of August, 1765, there appeared in the *London Evening Post* an article, under the somewhat singularly-chosen signature

Meanwhile, an English pamphlet contemporary to Adams's essay quipped, "It is not to be expected that the spawn of the old Cromwellians will submit without a blow." According to Michael Hatton, "It was a common rhetorical move by Britons and some loyalists to argue that due to their Puritan origins in the period of the Civil Wars, New Englanders were by their very nature anti-monarchical, rebellious, and even seditious." Moreover, "during the imperial crisis, Cromwell appeared in New England literature as a popular counterpoint to Anglicans' commemoration of the Stuarts and to the moderate approach of most colonial elites ... In 1774, Nathaniel Low included a woodcut of Oliver

---

of Pym, the purport of which seems to have been to avow to the people of the Colonies a settled design in Great Britain to overthrow whatever they had been in the habit of regarding as safeguards to their liberties. The writer of this article is not known; but his style, which is clear and forcible, indicates confidence and connection with the sources of power. The drift of his argument may be gathered from the statement of his position in these words: 'Let me inform my fellow-subjects in America, that a resolution of the British Parliament can at any time set aside all the charters that have ever been granted by our monarchs.' Starting in this manner, it is not surprising his consequences should be, that the rights of the colonists were wholly at the mercy of Great Britain. This article was deemed of such importance as to gain immediate admittance into the columns of the *Boston Evening Post*, in which it appeared on the 25th of November following. It at once roused a host of writers on the colonial side, among whom the most conspicuous were James Otis, as Hampden, and John Adams, as Clarendon. However singular the assumption of this last title may appear in the latter, his letters clearly show how much he had studied the character of the man to whom the name had belonged, and of the age in which he lived." Also see, (http://www.masshist.org/publications/adams-papers/index.php/view/DJA01p296). Adams was not prompted by the original editorial to use "salus populi" because it had not been mentioned. "To the Printer, W: Pym," *London Lloyd Evening Post* (August 19–21, 1765), pg. 3; (https://newspaperarchive.com/london-lloyd-evening-post-aug-19-1765-p-3/): "The question now is, whether those American subjects are, or are not, bound by the Resolutions of a British parliament? If they are not, they are entirely a separate people from us; and the mere reception of officers appointed in this kingdom, is nothing but an idle farce of government, which it is by no means our interest to keep up, if it is to produce us no benefit but the honor of protecting them whenever they are attacked by their enemies." (https://newspaperarchive.com/london-lloyd-evening-post-aug-12-1765-p-3/). A week earlier "William Pym" opined on the issue of legislative sovereignty: "In the next place, instead of confining them solely to municipal laws, we have for a long time entrusted them with a kind of legislative capacity. We have empowered them to raise taxes, and levy forces, instead of keeping this power in our own hands; and filled their little assemblies with a notion, they were every whit as important as a British Parliament. This behavior has absolutely intoxicated them; and now they talk of their privileges with as great an air, as if they were the actual representatives of the Mother Country." Russell Osgood, "Early Versions and Practices of Separation of Powers: A Comment," *William and Mary Law Review* 30 (Feb., 1989): 279–86. Gordon Wood, "The Problem of Sovereignty," *William and Mary Quarterly* 68 (Oct., 2011): 573–77.

Cromwell on the front page of his almanac published in Boston, and two years later the first privateer sanctioned by the new Commonwealth was named the Oliver Cromwell." While akin to the age-old saying that the "victors write the history," despite the best attempts by English and British royalists to erase the English Commonwealth era (e.g., titling the period the "Interregnum," disinterring Cromwell's body to ceremonially defile it, and more recently labelling the Levellers as proto-communists), a good portion of colonial Massachusetts memorialized its own version of Cromwell as heroic.[14]

In conclusion, Massachusetts *Laws and Liberties*—in its format, content, and printing in the vernacular—was the result of the English Commonwealth's evolution spanning the sixteenth and seventeenth centuries, invigorated by the reform impulse of Protestantism, the same history that prompted the Levellers' agitation for public education and a comprehensive body of English law in print. As they so eloquently expressed in their pamphlets, the Levellers believed, fundamentally, that the combination of the law's publication joined with universal public education would empower an enlightened citizenry to suppress tyranny and arbitrary government, transforming the state itself. While the Levellers have been far more celebrated historically than Massachusetts freemen, the freemen shared their social and economic class, and labored under the same regulatory disabilities of English law and sought its reform. They also supported Independent church government, while utilizing salus populi ideologically to gain political advantage over the magistrates. Perhaps most revealing, the freemen's initial emigration anticipated their fellow commoners' war against the King a decade later, illustrated by their military service in Colonel Thomas Rainsborough's regiment; ultimately, the Rainsboroughs were at the center of Leveller radicalism in the New Model Army, and their multiple affiliations with the Bay colony serve as a testament to the colony's radicalism. The significance of these affiliations, while largely overlooked, should be of little surprise, considering the same culture and socio-economic environment produced both the freemen and the Levellers. As David Hall recently concluded, the "Levellers indictment of the English legal system was fully in keeping with reforms the colonists would undertake," and their subsequent "accomplishments ... became the fullest embodiment of the animus against arbitrary rule," and the "fullest realization of 'fundamental liberties,' the empowering of legislative representatives, and the principle of consent."[15]

14 Michael Hattem, *Past and Prologue: Politics and Memory in the American Revolution* (New Haven: Yale Univ. Press, 2020), 102–103.

15 David Hall, *A Reforming People* (New York: Alfred A. Knopf, 2011), 49–52. Samuel Glover, "The Putney Debates: Popular versus Élitist Republicanism," 57–60. "How probable was

Not only was the English parliamentary model of the House of Commons and its tradition of consent to taxation imported into the colony, a far more radical model of populism took root as ideology became tradition. Initially, a colony little more than a decade old, with only ten thousand inhabitants, required its towns to establish public schools, deputized townsmen to a colonial legislature, and founded town churches and governments to oversee local affairs. The Leveller popularized legacy of the importance of universal public education coupled with publication of the law bequeathed future generations the means to steel themselves when conflict came. Providing access to colonial legal administration to Bay colonists, via education and print, facilitated transparency in government and an exchange economy free of state surveillance, secured by a vote based on individual conscience to shape colonial government according to a collective will. Ultimately, however, the exclusion of colonists based on congregational membership, gender, or property ownership from the colonial franchise of voting destabilized the nascent commonwealth by undermining its creation of a durable public sphere of governance under law. Subsequently, when a newly created Dominion of New England imperiled all Massachusetts colonists, no matter their political status, a lack of unity dissolved a collective will to unite under a common banner; they were extremely fortunate that the Dominion was short-lived. With the second charter period (1691–1774) life returned to normal, as colonists artfully evaded imperial control until that arbitrary, absolute, and unlimited power manifested itself once more. Over those decades, the "widespread availability of land promoted the emergence of a yeoman society in which the majority of adult males could claim the security, identity, and liberty of freemen." This society came to embody an "idea: to live as his own master, unbeholden to lords, patrons, or creditors." A yeoman's simple "ownership of a farm" became a "publicly visible sign" of his "self-determination in economic, personal, political, and religious terms"; conversely, a freeman's loss of the family farm would ultimately reduce him to "tenancy," or rent-based habitation of the land, marking him as a "peon" or serf. Originally a parliamentary ideology, it steeled town freemen when the British regulars came.[16]

---

it that the Leveller leaders were familiar with republican political theory? Evidence of the leadership's education reveals that it would be surprising indeed if they had not been familiar with the republican ideas which formed the backbone of a contemporary humanist education." David Cressy, *Charles I & the People of England*, 26–32. "The 'common sort' constituted everyone below the gentry, perhaps 98 percent of the population of England. Their households were headed by merchants and tradesmen, artisans and shopkeepers, yeomen, husbandmen, laborers, and the vagrant poor."

16 Daniel Coquillette, "Radical Lawmakers in Colonial Massachusetts," *New England Quarterly* 67 (June, 1994): 203. The *Laws and Liberties* "was not just a 'theoretical' plan for reform. The Massachusetts colonists intended to put their legal ideas into practice, and they did.

In the popular imagination Lexington and Concord was "the shot heard round the world," with New England minutemen ever vigilant in defense of their communities. Who had fired the first shot setting the colonies on their path to independence? Long after 1775, at the age of ninety-one, Captain Levi Preston was asked to recount the hard fought and bloody battle, hardly a day out on the village green. "Captain Preston, what made you go to the Concord Fight?" Preston replied, "What did I go for?" Initially stymied, the interviewer took another approach, "Were you oppressed by the Stamp Act?" Preston had never seen "any stamps," and he didn't remember any being sold after the riots. Then it must have been the "tea tax." No, Preston "never drank a drop of the stuff, the boys threw it all overboard." Then he must have read "Harrington, Sidney, and Locke about the eternal principle of liberty." Preston had "never heard of these men. The only books we had were the Bible, the Catechism, Watts' psalms and hymns, and the almanacs." Exasperated, the interviewer gave up, "Well, then, what was the matter?" Preston responded, "Young man, what we meant in going for those Redcoats was this: we always had governed ourselves and we always meant to. They didn't mean we should."[17]

---

Bacon, in his *Advancement of Learning* (1605), castigated his English legal contemporaries: 'As for the philosophers, they make imaginary laws for imaginary commonwealths ... For the lawyers, they write according to the states where they live what is received law, not what ought to be the law: for the wisdom of the lawmaker is one, and of a lawyer is another.' Bacon became the Lord Chancellor of England in 1618, but could not effect his reforms. Even less successful were the 'Puritan' radicals who emerged in the context of the English Commonwealth. Their leaders were frequently executed, and the Restoration swept away their proposals." Mary Babson Fuhrer, "The Revolutionary Worlds of Lexington and Concord Compared," *William and Mary Quarterly* 85 (March 2012): 83–4. "Owning a farm provided more than material sustenance. In both Lexington and Concord, land ownership granted a man the right to participate in town meetings, a reasonable restriction given that town expenditures were financed from taxes on assessed property. Moreover, the colonists maintained, only individuals who depended on no other for their survival could exercise truly impartial judgment. Tenants, wage laborers, youth awaiting their farms, apprentices, women—all who relied upon a master for their daily bread—were subject to another's whim or susceptible to 'the financial temptations of designing men.'"

17 Captain Preston's interview quoted in David Hackett Fisher, *Paul Revere's Ride* (Oxford: Oxford Univ. Press, 1994), 163–64. Patrick Spiro, "The Revolution in Popular Publications: The Almanac and New England Primer, 1750—1800," *Early American Studies* 8 (no. 1, 2010): 61–66. Harvey Mansfield, Delba Winthrop, eds., *Democracy in America* (Chicago: Univ. of Chicago Press, 2000), 291 (Vol. 1, Prt. 2, Ch. 9, *Causes Tending to Maintain a Democratic Republic*). "The citizen of the United States does not acquire his practical science and his positive notions from books; the instruction he has acquired may have prepared him for receiving those ideas, but it did not furnish them. The American learns to know the laws by participating in the act of legislation; and he takes a lesson in the forms of government from governing. The great work of society is ever going on before his eyes and, as it were, under his hands."

# Works Cited

## Primary Sources

*An Abridgment of the Late Remonstrance of the Army* (December 1648); EEBO (http://name.umdl.umich.edu/A23670.0001.001).

*Abuses Discovered, whereby the Creditors are Meerly Cheated, the Officers of the Law, and Gaolers are Unjustly Inriched, and the Poor Debter and their Families Tyranically Destroyed* (June, 1649); *Thomason Tracts* 669 f14 (41), Reel 246.

*Accusation and Impeachment of John Lord Finch. (1640)*. In *Somers Tracts*. London: 1810; 4: 129–32.

*An Act for the Resignation of the Great Charter of New England. April 25, 1635*. In *Records of the Council for New England*. Cambridge: 1867: 75–78.

*Acts of the Privy Council: Colonial Series (1613–1680)*. 6 Vols. Hereford: HMSO, 1908.

*Acts and Resolves, Public and Private, of the Province of Massachusetts Bay*. 21 Vols. Boston: Wright & Potter, 1869–1922.

Adams, Charles Francis, ed., *Works of John Adams*. 10 Vols. Boston: Little Brown & Co., 1850–1865.

Adams, John. *A Dissertation on the Canon and Feudal Law. Boston Gazette* (August 1765). In *The Works of John Adams*. Edited by Charles Adams. Boston: Little and Brown, 1865; 3: 447–64.

Adams, John. *Novanglus* (1775). In *The Works of John Adams*. Edited by Charles Adams. Boston: Little and Brown, 1851; 4: 33–145.

Adams, Robert M., ed. *Desiderus Erasmus: The Praise of Folly and Other Writings*. New York: W.W. Norton, 1989.

*The Agreement at Cambridge*. August, 1629. In *Winthrop Papers*. Boston: MHS, 1931; 2: 151–2.

*Alexis De Tocqueville: Democracy in America*. Edited by Harvey Mansfield, Delba Winthrop. Chicago: University of Chicago Press, 2000.

*Animadversions upon those Notes which the late Observator hath Published* (1642); EEBO (http://name.umdl.umich.edu/A75367.0001.001).

*Answers to 28 Special Articles*. 1640. In *Rushworth Collections: Tryal of Thomas Earl of Strafford*. London: 1721; 8: 22–32.

Bacon, Francis. *Works of Francis Bacon*. 2 Vols. Edited by Basil Montagu. Philadelphia: 1841.

Bacon, Francis. *The Essays or Counsels Civill and Morall of Sir Francis Bacon (Baron of Verulam, Viscount St. Alban)*. 1597; reprint, New York: Heritage Press, 1944.

Bacon, Francis. *A Critical Edition of the Major Works*. Edited by Brian Vickers. Oxford: Oxford University Press, 1996.

Bagwell, William. *The Distressed Merchant.* (Aug. 25, 1645); *Thomason Tracts* E265 (1), Reel 44.

Ball, William. *The Rule of a Freeborn People.* (June 18, 1646); *Thomason Tracts* E341(1), Reel 55.

Ball, William. *The Power of Kings Discussed.* (Jan. 30, 1649); *Thomason Tracts* E540 (21), Reel 84.

*Bates' Case* (1606). In *Lane's Exchequer Reports: Being a Reprint of Reports of Cases in the Court of Exchequer from 1605–1612 by the Hon. Richard Lane.* London: 1884; 33–51.

*Bay Psalm Book.* Boston: 1640; *Library of Congress* (https://www.loc.gov/resource/rbc0001.2008amimp02405/).

Beza, Theodore. "Rights of Magistrates." In *Constitutionalism and Resistance in the Sixteenth Century.* Edited by Julian Franklin. New York: Pegasus, 1969: 100–35.

Blackstone, William. *Commentaries on the Laws of England: 1765–1769.* 4 Vols. Chicago: University of Chicago Press, 1979.

Blackwell, Elidad. *A Caveat for Magistrates.* (June 30, 1645); *Thomason Tracts* E 290 (120), Reel 48.

Bland, A.E., P.A. Brown and R.H. Tawney, eds. *English Economic History: Select Documents.* New York: Macmillan Co., 1919.

Bodin, Jean. *Six Books of the Commonwealth.* Edited and Translated by M.J. Tooley. Oxford: Alden Press, 1955.

Bradford, William. *Of Plymouth Plantation: 1620–1647.* Edited by S.E. Morison. New York: Alfred A. Knopf, 1953.

Breward, Ian, ed. *The Works of William Perkins.* Berkshire: Sutton Courtenay Press, 1970.

*Brief Collections out of Magna Charta.* (1643); *Thomason Tracts* E38 (12), Reel 7.

*A Brief Dialogue Between Creditor and Prisoner.* (Sept. 5, 1653); *Thomason Tracts* E713 (5), Reel 110.

Brodhead, John, ed. *Documents Relative to the Colonial History of the State of New York; Procured in Holland, England and France.* 3 Vols. Albany: 1853.

Bush, Jr., Sargent, ed. *Correspondence of John Cotton.* Chapel Hill: University of North Carolina Press, 2001.

*Calendar of State Papers (America and West Indies): 1661–1668.* 5 Vols. Edited by W. Noel Sainsbury. London: Longman, 1880.

*Calendar of State Papers (America and West Indies): 1677–1680.* 10 Vols. Edited by W. Noel Sainsbury and J.W. Fortescue. London: HMSO, 1896.

*Calendar of State Papers (America and West Indies): 1685–1688.* 12 Vols. Edited by W. Noel Sainsbury. London: Longman, 1899.

*Calendar of State Papers (Colonial Series): 1574–1660.* 1 Vol. Edited by W. Noel Sainsbury. London: Longman, 1860.

*Calendar of State Papers (Domestic Series): 1644–1645.* 20 Vols. Edited by William Douglas. London: HMSO, 1890.

*Calendar of State Papers (Domestic Series): 1654*. 7 Vols. Edited by Mary Green. London: Longman & Co., 1880.

Calvin, John. *The Institutes of the Christian Religion*. Geneva, 1559. Translated by Henry Beveridge. Grand Rapids [MI]: WM. B. Erdmann's Co., 1989.

*The Capitall Lawes of New-England*. London: 1643; *Thomason Tracts* 669f6 (99), Reel 245.

Carlyle, Thomas, ed. *The Letters and Speeches of Oliver Cromwell*. 3 Vols. London: Methuen & Co., 1904.

Carte, Thomas, ed. *A Collection of Original Letters and Papers Concerning the Affairs of England, from the Year 1641–1660, Found among the Duke of Ormond's Papers*. 2 Vols. London: James Bettenham, 1739.

*Case of George Giddings and Others of Ipswich, (Samuel Symonds' decision)*. 1657. In *Hutchinson Papers*. 2 Vols. Edited by William Whitmore. Albany: Prince Society, 1865: 1–25.

Chalmers, Alexander, ed. *Samuel Johnson's Dictionary of the English Language*. London: Studio Editions, 1994.

Chidley, Samuel. *A Cry Against a Crying Sin*. 1652. In *Harleian Miscellany*. Edited by T. Park. London: Robert Dutton, 1810; 6: 272–82.

Child, John. *New Englands Jonas Cast Up at London*. London, 1647. *MHS Collections (Second Series/1846)*; 4: 107–20.

Clinton, Theophilius (Earl of Lincoln). "To all English Freeholders from a Well-Wisher of Theirs." (Jan. 24, 1627). In *The Early Stuart Kings: 1603–1642*. Edited by Graham Seel and David Smith. London: Routledge, 2001.

Coke, Sir Edward. *The Reports of Sir Edward Coke*. 5 Vols. Edited by John Fraser. London: Butterworth and Son, 1826.

Coke, Sir Edward. *The Third Part of the Institutes*. London: 1797; reprint, Buffalo: William S. Hein, 1986.

Cole, William. *A Rod for the Lawyers*. 1659. In *Harleian Miscellany*. Edited by T. Park. London: Robert Dutton, 1810; 7: 25–35.

*Commission to Archbishop Laud, and Others, to Govern New England*. April 28, 1634. In *The New England Historical and Genealogical Register*. Boston: 1860; 14: 343–45.

*The Commons Declaration and Impeachment against the Duke of Buckingham* (May 1626). In *Historical Collections*. Edited by John Rushworth. London: 1721; 1: 302–335.

Cooke, John. *King Charles, His Case: Or an Appeal to All Rational Men, Concerning his Tryal before the High Court of Justice* (1649); *EEBO* (https://quod.lib.umich.edu/e/eebo/A34423.0001.001?view=toc).

Cooke, John. *The Vindication of the Professors and Profession of the Law* (Feb. 6, 1646); *Thomason Tracts* E320 (17), Reel 52.

Cotton, John. *How Far Moses His Judicials Bind Mass[achusetts]*. 1643. *MHS Proceedings (Second Series, 1902)*; 16: 280–84.

Craterus, Theophilus. *A Calm Consolatory view of the Sad Tempestuous Affairs in England* (April 19, 1647); *Thomason Tracts* E384 (13), Reel 61.

Cressy, David, ed. *Education in Tudor and Stuart England.* New York: St. Martin's Press, 1975.

Dalton, Michael. *Countrey Justice.* London: 1618; reprint, Norwood [NJ]: Walter J. Johnson Inc., 1975.

*The Debtors Act, 1869.* In *The London Gazette.* No. 23524. Aug. 10, 1869; (https://www.legislation.gov.uk/ukpga/Vict/32-33/62/enacted).

*A Declaration and Appeal to All the Freeborne People of this Kingdome in General … Humbly Craving their Assistance and Furtherance of this Just Request unto the High Court of Parliament. Made from all the Brethren the Poore Afflicted and Oppressed Prisoners (imprisoned for debt).* (November 1645); *Thomason Tracts* 669 f10 (40), Reel 246.

*A Declaration of the General Court holden at Boston 4 (9) 1646, Concerning a Remonstrance and Petition Exhibited at last Session of this Court by Doctor Child.* 1646. In *Hutchinson Papers.* Edited by William Whitmore. Albany: Prince Society, 1865; 1: 223–47.

*A Declaration of the General Court of the Massachusetts, Holden at Boston in New-England, October 18,1659. Concerning the Execution of Two Quakers. MHS Proceedings (October 1908-June 1909)*; 42: 203–4.

*A Discourse in Derision of the Teaching in Free-Schooles* (July 2, 1644); *Thomason Tracts* E53 (7), Reel 9.

Dudley, Digges. *An Answer to a Printed Book, Intituled, Observations upon some of his Majesties Late Answers and Expresses* (1642); EEBO (http://name.umdl.umich.edu/A35993.0001.001).

Dow, George, ed. *Records and Files of the Quarterly Courts of Essex County, Massachusetts.* 8 Vols. Salem: Essex Institute, 1911–21.

*Dr. Bonham's Case.* 1610. 77 *English Reports* @ 638–58.

Dummer, Jeremiah. *Defence of the New-England Charters.* 3rd ed. London: W. Wilkins, 1721; reprint, London: J. Almon, 1765.

Dunn, Richard, ed. *The Laws and Liberties of Massachusetts: Reprinted from the Unique Copy of the 1648 Edition in the Henry E. Huntington Library.* San Marino: Huntington Library, 1998.

Dunn, Richard S., Laetitia Yeandle and James Savage, eds. *The Journal of John Winthrop, 1630–1649.* Cambridge: Belknap Press, 1996.

Dury, John. *Israels Call to March Out of Babylon unto Jerusalem: Opened in a Sermon Before the Honorable House of Commons Assembled in Parliament* (Nov. 26, 1645); *Thomason Tracts* E310 (3), Reel 51.

*Eikōn Basilikē: The Pourtraicture of his Sacred Majestie in his Solitudes and Sufferings* (February 1649); *Google Books* (https://books.google.com/books?id=Pi1QAQAAIAAJ&source=gbs_similarbooks).

Eliot, Sir John. *The Grounds for Settling a Planation in New England.* MHS *Proceedings (1864–1865)*; 8: 413–30.

Emerson, Everett, ed. *Letters from New England: The Massachusetts Bay Colony, 1629–1638*. Amherst: University of Massachusetts Press, 1976.

*Emmanuel Downing to Sir John Coke.* December 12, 1633. MHS *Proceedings (Second Series/1892–1894)*; 28: 383–84.

*The Ethics of Aristotle: The Nicomachean Ethics.* Translated by J.A. Thompson. Edited by Hugh Tredennick and Jonathan Barnes. Harmondsworth [UK]: Penguin Books, 1976.

*An Exact Relation of the Proceedings and Transactions of the late Parliament, their Beginning and Ending.* 1654. In *Somers Tracts.* London: 1811; 6: 266–84.

*An Experimental Essay Touching the Reformation of the Laws of England* (August 17, 1648); *Thomason Tracts* E459 (20), Reel 73.

Ferne, Henry. *The Resolving of Conscience upon this Question whether upon such a Supposition or Case as is now usually made (the King will not Discharge his Trust, but is Bent or Seduced to Subvert Religion, Laws, and Liberties) Subjects may Take Arms and Resist* (1642); EEBO (http://name.umdl.umich.edu/A41219.0001.001).

Filmer, Robert. *The Anarchy of a Limited or Mixed Monarchy.* 1648. In *Patriarcha and Other Writings.* Edited by J.P. Sommerville. Cambridge: Cambridge University Press, 1991: 131–71.

Filmer, Robert. *The Free-Holders Grand Inquest.* 1648. In *Patriarcha and Other Writings.* Edited by J.P. Sommerville. Cambridge: Cambridge University Press, 1991: 69–130.

Firth, C.H., ed. *The Clarke Papers. Selections from the Papers of William Clarke, Secretary to the Council of the Army, 1647–1649.* 4 Vols. Camden Society, 1901.

Firth, C.H. and R.S. Rait, eds. *Acts and Ordinances of the Interregnum: 1642–1660.* 3 Vols. London: HMSO, 1911.

*Five Knights Case* (1627). In *State Trials.* Edited by T.B. Howell. London: T.C. Hansard, 1816; 3: 1–234 (#127).

Ford, Paul, ed. *The Works of Thomas Jefferson.* 2 Vols. New York: G.P. Putnam's Sons, 1904.

Fraser, John, ed. *The Reports of Sir Edward Coke.* 6 Vols. London: Butterworth, 1826.

*The Freeman's Oath* (1630); *Digital Commonwealth*; (https://ark.digitalcommonwealth.org/ark:/50959/f1881m213).

Frese, James. *Every Man's Right: Or, England's Perspective Glasse* (June 15, 1646); *Thomason Tracts* E340 (2), Reel 55.

Gardiner, Samuel, ed. *Constitutional Documents of the Puritan Revolution: 1625–1660.* Oxford: Clarendon Press, 1906.

Gardiner Samuel, ed. *Parliamentary Debates in 1610.* London: Camden Society, 1862.

*General Observations for the Plantation of New England.* 1629. In *Winthrop Papers.* Boston: MHS, 1931; 2: 111–21.

Goodwin, John. *Anti-Cavalierisme, or, Truth Pleading As well the Necessity, as the Lawfulness of this Present War, for the Suppressing of that Butcherly Brood of*

*Cavaliering Incendiaries*. London, Oct. 21, 1642. In *Tracts on Liberty*. Edited by William Haller. New York: Columbia University Press, 1934; 2: 219–69.

Greville, Robert (Lord Brooke). *A Discourse Opening the Nature of that Episcopacy which is Exercised in England*. 1642. In *Tracts on Liberty*. Edited by William Haller. New York: Columbia University Press, 1934; 2: 37–162.

Hale, Matthew. *The History of the Pleas of the Crown*. 2 Vols. Philadelphia: Robert H. Small, 1847.

Haller, William. *Tracts on Liberty in the Puritan Revolution, 1638–1647*. 3 Vols. New York: Columbia University, 1934.

*Harleian Miscellany*. 13 Vols. Edited by Samuel Johnson and William Oldys. London: Thomas Osborne, 1744–1753.

Harmar, Samuel. *Vox Populi, Or, Glostersheres Desire: With, The Way and Means to make a Kingdome Happy (by God's Help.) By Setting up of Schoole-masters in every Parish throughout the Land generally* (May 1642); *Thomason Tracts* E146 (2), Reel 26.

Harrington, James. *The Commonwealth of Oceana and a System of Politics*. Edited by J.G.A. Pocock. Cambridge University Press, 1992.

Harrington, James. *The Oceana and other Works*. 3rd ed. Edited by John Toland. London: A. Millar, 1747.

Harrison, William. *The Description of England*. Edited by Georges Edelen. Ithaca: Cornell University Press, 1968.

Hartlib, Samuel. *A Description of the Famous Kingdom of Macaria* (1641); *Thomason Tracts* E173 (28), Reel 30.

Hening, William, ed. *The Statutes at Large: Being a Collection of all the Laws of Virginia*. 11 Vols. New York: R.W.G. Bartow, 1823.

Herle, Charles. *A Fuller Answer to a Treatise Written by Dr. Ferne* (Dec. 29, 1642); *Thomason Tracts* E244 (27), Reel 42.

Hickeringill, Edmund. *History of Whiggism: Or, The Whiggish-Plots, Principles, and Practices (Mining and Countermining the Tory-plots and Principles) in the Reign of King Charles the First, … under the Influence of the Three Great Minions and Favourites: Buckingham, Laud, and Strafford, … to that Fatal-Year … 41*. 1682. In *Works of Edmund Hickeringill*. 2 Vols. London: 1709; 1: 1–170.

Hickeringill, Edmund. *Second Part of the History of Whiggism* (1682); EEBO (https://quod.lib.umich.edu/e/eebo/A70223.0001.001/1:1?rgn=div1;view=fulltext).

Hill, Don G., ed. *Early Records of the Town of Dedham, Massachusetts*. 5 Vols. Dedham: Historical Society, 1886–1899.

*His Maiesties Answer to the XIX Propositions of Both Houses of Parliament* (1642); *Google Books* (https://books.google.com/books?vid=BL:A0022003739).

*Hobbes: Leviathan (Revised Student Edition)*. Edited by Richard Tuck. Cambridge: Cambridge University Press, 2017.

Hobbes, Thomas. *De Corpore Politico, or, The Elements of Law, Moral and Politick.* London: 1640. In *The English Works of Thomas Hobbes.* London: John Bohn, 1840; 4: 200–20.

Hooker, Richard. *Of the Laws of Ecclesiastical Polity.* Edited by Arthur McGrade. Cambridge: Cambridge University Press, 1989.

Horne, Andrew. *Mirrour of Justices.* Translated by William Robinson. Washington, D.C.: John Byrne & Co., 1903.

Howell, Thomas Jones, William Cobbett and David Jardine, eds. *A Complete Collection of State Trials and Proceedings for High Treason and Other Crimes and Misdemeanors: From the Earliest Period to the Year 1783.* 11 Vols. London: T.C. Hansard, 1816.

Hubbard, William. *A General History of New England.* Boston: Little & Brown, 1848.

*Humble Petition of Divers Well-affected Persons Delivered the 6th day of July, 1659. to the Supreme Authority, the Parliament of the Common-Wealth of England* (1659); *Hathi Trust* (https://catalog.hathitrust.org/Record/102258555).

*Humble Petition of the Poor Distressed Prisoners in Ludgate* (December 20, 1644); *Thomason Tracts* E21 (33), Reel 4.

*Humble Remonstrance and Complaint of Many Thousands of Poor Distressed Prisoners* (February 3, 1643); *Thomason Tracts* E88 (8), Reel 15.

*Hutchinson Papers.* 2 Vols. Edited by William Whitmore. Albany: Prince Society, 1865.

Hutchinson, Thomas. *The History of the Colony and Province of Massachusetts-Bay: 1628–1691.* 2nd ed. 3 Vols. London: 1765.

Hyde, Edward. *History of the Rebellion and Civil Wars in England.* 8 Vols. Oxford: Clarendon Press, 1826.

James I. "A Speech to the Lords and Commons of the Parliament at White-Hall." 1610. In *King James VI and I: Political Writings.* Edited by Johann Sommerville. Cambridge: Cambridge University Press, 1994: 179–203.

James VI. "The Trew Law of Free Monarchies." 1598; reprint, 1616. In *King James VI and I: Political Writings.* Edited by Johann Sommerville. Cambridge: Cambridge University Press, 1994: 62–84.

Jansson, Maija, ed., *Proceedings in Parliament 1614 (House of Commons).* Philadelphia: American Philosophical Society, 1988.

Jewell, John. *An Apology for the Church of England.* Translated by Lady Anne Cooke Bacon and Stephen Isaacson. 1564; reprint, London: 1825.

Johnson, Edward. *Wonder-Working Providence of Sions Saviour in New-England.* London: 1654; reprint, Andover: Warren Draper, 1867.

Johnson, George, ed. *The Fairfax Correspondence: Memoirs of the Reign of Charles I.* 2 Vols. London: Richard Bentley, 1848.

Johnson, Robert C., Mary F. Keeler, Maija J. Cole and William B. Bidwell, eds., *Commons Debates 1628.* 4 Vols. New Haven: Yale University, 1983.

Jones, John. *Every Mans Case or, Lawyers Routed* (July 5, 1652); *Thomason Tracts* E1406 (2), Reel 181.

Jones, John. *Lawyers UnMask'd or, A Discovery of their Matchless Villanies* (1653); *Wing* J971A (1507), Reel 3.

Jordan, W.K., ed. *The Chronicle and Political Papers of King Edward VI*. Ithaca: Cornell University Press, 1966.

*Journals of the House of Commons: 1547–1629*. 1 Vol. London: HMSO, 1802.

*Journals of the House of Commons: 1642–1644*. 3 Vols. London: HMSO, 1803.

*Journals of the House of Commons: 1648–1651*. 6 Vols. London: HMSO, 1803.

*Journals of the House of Commons: 1651–1659*. 7 Vols. London: HMSO, 1813.

*Journals of the House of Lords: 1578–1614*. 2 Vols. London: HMSO, 1767–1830.

*Journals of the House of Lords: 1629–1642*. 4 Vols. London: HMSO, 1767–1830.

*Journals of the House of Lords: 1642*. 5 Vols. London: HMSO, 1767–1830.

Kent, James. *Commentaries on American Law*. 7th ed. 4 Vols. New York: William Kent, 1851.

Kenyon, J.P., ed. *The Stuart Constitution: Documents and Commentary, 1603–1688*. 2nd ed. Cambridge: Cambridge University Press, 1986.

Keyes, Clinton, ed. *Cicero: De Re Publica, De Legibus*. Cambridge: Harvard University Press, 1928.

*The King's Answer to the Nineteen Propositions* (18 June 1642). In J.P. Kenyon, ed., *The Stuart Constitution*. 2nd ed. Cambridge: Cambridge University Press, 1986.

Lambarde, William. *Eirenarcha: or the Office of the Justice of the Peace* (1619); *Google Books* (https://www.google.com/books/edition/_/o-A1AQAAMAAJ?hl=en&gbpv=0).

*The Laws Discovery*. 1653. In *Harleian Miscellany*. Edited by T. Park. London: 1810; 6: 322–4.

Leach, William. *Bills Proposed for Acts or Proposals Concerning the Principal Courts of England* (June 10, 1651); *Thomason Tracts* E632 (2), Reel 97.

Leach, William. *Propositions: For Recording and Registering of Deeds and Conveyances ... for Inabling Creditors to have the Benefit of Copyhold and Intalyed Lands ... for their Satisfaction* (June 20, 1651); *Thomason Tracts* E632 (5), Reel 97.

Lechford, Thomas. *Notebook*. Edited by Edward E. Hale, Jr. Boston: 1885; reprint, Camden: Picton Press, 1988.

Lechford, Thomas. *Plaine Dealing: Or, Newes from New England*. London, 1642. *MHS Collections (3rd Series/1833)*; 3: 55–128.

*The Leveller; Or the Principles and Maxims Concerning Government and Religion which are Asserted by those Commonly Called Levellers* (London: 1659). In *Harleian Miscellany*. London: 1810; 7: 36–46.

Lilburne, John. *England's Birthright Justified*. London, 1645. In *Tracts on Liberty*. Edited by William Haller. New York: Columbia University Press, 1934; 3: 257–307.

Lilburne, John. *The Peoples Prerogative* (February 17, 1648); *Thomason Tracts* E427 (4), Reel 67.

Lilburne, John. *A Worke of the Beast* (1638). In *Tracts on Liberty*. Edited by William Haller. New York: Columbia University Press, 1934; 2: 3–34.

Lilburne, John and Richard Overton. *The Out-Cryes of Oppressed Commons* (February 28, 1647); *Thomason Tracts* E378 (13), Reel 60.

Lint, Greg, Joanna Revelas, Richard Ryerson, Celeste Walker and Anne Decker, eds. *Papers of John Adams*. 9 Vols. Cambridge: Belknap Press, 1996.

Littleton, Thomas. *Lyttleton, His Treatise of Tenures*. 1481–82. Translated by T.E. Tomlins. New York: Russell & Russell, 1970.

Locke, John. "The Second Treatise of Government." In *John Locke, Two Treatises of Government*. Edited by Peter Laslett. Cambridge: Cambridge University Press, 1988.

*The Lord Deputy [Strafford] to Mr. Justice Hutton*. Sept. 13, 1639. In *The Earl of Strafforde's Letters and Dispatches*. 2 Vols. London: William Boyer, 1739: 388–89.

Ludlow, Edmund. *Memoirs of Edmund Ludlow, Esq; Lieutenant-General of Horse, Commander in Chief of the Forces in Ireland, One of the Council of State, and a Member of the Parliament which began on November 3. 1640*. London: A. Millar, D. Browne, 1751.

March, John. *Amicus Republicae* (May 19, 1651); *Thomason Tracts* E1360 (1), Reel 179.

Marcus, Leah, Janel Mueller and Mary Beth Rose, eds. *Elizabeth I: Collected Works*. Chicago: University of Chicago Press, 2000.

Maverick, Samuel. *A Briefe Discription of New England and the Several Townes therein, together with the Present Government thereof*. London: 1660; reprint, Boston: MHS, 1885.

*The Maxims of Mixt Monarchy* (Feb. 6, 1643); *Thomason Tracts* E88 (15), Reel 15.

Milton, John. *A Reply to the Answer (Printed by his Majesties Command at Oxford) to a Printed Booke Intituled Observations* (1642); EEBO (http://name.umdl.umich.edu/A50950.0001.001).

Milton, John. *A Soveraigne Salve to Cure the Blind, Or, A Vindication of the Power and Priviledges Claim'd or Executed by the Lords and Commons in Parliament* (1643); EEBO (http://name.umdl.umich.edu/A89494.0001.001).

Milton, John. *The Tenure of Kings and Magistrates*. 1649. In *John Milton: Complete Poems and Major Prose*. Edited by Merrit Hughes. New York: Odyssey Press, 1954: 750–780.

*Mock-Majesty: Or, The Siege of Munster* (February 24, 1644); *Thomason Tracts* E270 (50), Reel 145.

More, Thomas. *Utopia*. 1516. Edited by George Logan and Robert Adams. Cambridge: Cambridge University Press, 1989.

*Moses His Judicialls*. 1637. In *Hutchinson Papers*. Edited by William Whitmore. Albany: Prince Society, 1865; 1: 183–205.

*The Mournfull Cryes of Many Thousand Poore Tradesmen, who are Ready to Famish through Decay of Trade* (1648); EEBO (http://quod.lib.umich.edu/e/eebo2/A89397.0001.001).

Nedham, Marchamont. *A True State of the Case of the Commonwealth of England* (Feb. 8, 1654); *Thomason Tracts* E728 (5), Reel 112.

Nicholson, Benjamin. *The Lawyers Bane or the Laws Reformation and New Model* (1647); *Thomason Tracts* E401 (36), Reel 63.

Noble, John and John Cronin, eds. *Records of the Court of Assistants of the Colony of the Massachusetts Bay: 1630–1692*. 3 Vols. Boston: County of Suffolk, 1901–1928.

Norton, John. *A Small Treatise on the Negative Vote*. MHS *Proceedings* (*1912–1913*); 46: 279–85.

Notestein, Wallace, ed. *Commons Debates: 1621*. 7 Vols. New Haven: Yale University Press, 1935.

Notestein, Wallace, ed. *The Journal of Sir Simonds D'Ewes*. New Haven: Yale University Press, 1923.

Overton, Richard. *Appeale from the Degenerate Representative Body* (July, 1647). In *The Levellers in the English Revolution*. Edited by G.E. Aylmer. Ithaca: Cornell University Press, 1975: 82–87.

Overton, Richard. *An Arrow Against All Tyrants*. London: 1646. In *The Levellers*. Edited by Kevin Sharp. Cambridge: Cambridge University Press, 1998: 54–72.

Overton, Richard. *A New-found Stratagem Framed in the Old Forge of Machivilisme* (1647); *Thomason Tracts* E384 (11), Reel 61.

Overton, Richard and William Walwyn. *Remonstrance of Many Thousand Citizens*. 1646. In *The English Levellers*. Edited by Andrew Sharp. Cambridge: Cambridge University Press, 1998: 33–53.

Palmer, Herbert. *Scripture and Reason Pleaded for Defensive Armes: Or the whole Controversie about Subjects Taking Up Armes wherein … an Answer is Punctually Directed to Dr. Fernes Booke, Entituled, Resolving of Conscience* (1643); EEBO (http://name.umdl.umich.edu/A55033.0001.001).

Parker, Henry. *The Case of ShipMony … Most Humbly Presented to the … High Court of Parliament* (November 3, 1640); 4–5; *Google Books* (https://play.google.com/books/reader?id=m4NnAAAAcAAJ&pg=GBS.PP1&hl=en).

Parker, Henry. *The Contra Replicant* (1643); *Thomason Tracts* E87 (5), Reel 15.

Parker, Henry, *Observations upon Some of his Majesties Late Answers and Expresses*. 1642. In *Tracts on Liberty*. Edited by William Haller. New York: Columbia University Press, 1934; 2: 167–213.

Parker, Henry. *Reformation in Courts, and Cases Testamentary* (1650); EEBO (http://name.umdl.umich.edu/A91346.0001.001).

*Parliaments Power, in Lawes for Religion* (August 25, 1645); *Thomason Tracts* E298 (9), Reel 49.

Pegis, Anton, ed. *Introduction to Saint Thomas Aquinas*. New York: Modern Library, 1948.

Perkins, William. "Epieikeia: Or a Treatise of Christian Equity and Moderation." In *The Work of William Perkins*. Edited by Ian Breward. Appleford: Sutton Courtenay Press, 1970: 477–510.

Peters, Hugh. *A Good Work for a Good Magistrate* (June 17, 1651); *Thomason Tracts* E1364 (2), Reel 179.

Peters, Hugh. *A Word for the Army and Two Words to the Kingdom* (1647). In *Harleian Miscellany*. London: 1810; 6: 65–73.

*Petition of the Citizens of London, Feb. 26, 1641 Concerning the Election of Persons for the Militia of the City with the Government and Charters thereof: With his Majesties Message to both Houses of Parliament* (March 1642); *Thomason Tracts* E140 (12), Reel 25.

*Petition of the Greater Part of the Inhabitants of Hingham*. 1645. MHS *Collections* (*Second Series/1846*); 4: 108–9.

*Petition to the King on Impositions upon Merchandise*. July 7, 1610. In *Proceedings in Parliament 1610: House of Commons*. Edited by Elizabeth Read Foster. New Haven: Yale University Press, 1966; 2: 266–67.

*Petition to the King Respecting Impositions* (May 23, 1610). In *House of Commons Journal*. London: 1803; 1: 431–2.

*A Pittiful Remonstrance, or Just Complaint Made to all Free-Born True-Hearted Englishmen, Sensible of the Kingdoms Miserable Slavery. From All the Poor Afflicted and Miserable, Inslaved and Immured Prisoners for Debt*. (July 1648); *Thomason Tracts* 669 f17 (68), Reel 246.

*Polybius: The Rise of the Roman Empire*. Translated by Scott-Kilvert. London: Penguin Books, 1979.

*The Power of the Laws of a Kingdom*. (January 26, 1642); *Thomason Tracts* E86 (11), Reel 15.

*Proceedings in Parliament against John Lord Finch, Baron of Fordwich, Lord Keeper, for High Treason* (1640). In *State Trials*. Edited by T.B. Howell. London: T.C. Hansard, 1816; 4: 1–22 (#151).

*A Proclamation warning All his Majesties Good Subjects no Longer to be Misled by the Votes, Orders, and Pretended Ordinances, of … both Houses by Reason the Members do not Enjoy the Freedome and Liberty of Parliament* (June 20, 1643); EEBO (http://name.umdl.umich.edu/A79038.0001.001).

Prynne, William. *The Soveraigne Powers of Parliaments and Kingdomes* (August 2, 1643); *Google Book*; (https://www.google.com/books/edition/The_Soveraigne_Power_of_Parliaments_and/Lpg-AQAAMAAJ?hl=en&gbpv=0).

Pulton, Fedinando. *Collection of Sundrie Statutes Frequent in use* (1618); STC 9328, Reel 1515.

Pym, John. *A Declaration of the Grievances of the Kingdom*. 1641. In *Somers Tracts*. London: 1810; 4: 390–404.

Pym, John. *The Declaration of John Pym Esquire, Upon the Whole Matter of the Charge of High Treason against Thomas Earle of Strafford, April 12, 1641. London: by Order of the House of Commons* (1641); *Wing* P4260 (17), Reel 1512.

Pym, John. *Mr. Pym's Speech at the Delivery of the Charges against Dr. Manwaring*. 1628. In *Rushworth Historical Collections*. London: Newcomb for George Thomason, 1659; 1: 595–605.

Pym, John. *The Speech or Declaration of John Pym Esquire* (April 12, 1641). In *Rushworth Collections: Tryal of Thomas Earl of Strafford*. London: 1721; 8: 661–70; *EEBO* (http://name.umdl.umich.edu/A70881.0001.001).

*Questions of the Elders* (1643). *MHS Proceedings* (1912/13); 46: 275–6.

*Quo Warranto of 1635*. In *New England Historical and Genealogical Register*. Boston: 1884; 48: 209–16.

Ramsay, David. *The History of the American Revolution*. 2 Vols. Philadelphia: R. Aitken & Son, 1789.

Rastell, Johannes. *An Abridgment of the Statutes* (1527); *STC* 9518, Reel 6.

Rastell, Johannes. *The Great Abridgement of the Statutes* (1531); *STC* 9521, Reel 6.

Rastell, William. *Collection of All the Statutes from the beginning of Magna Carta* (1557); *STC* 9306, Reel 1686.

*Reasons against the Bill Entitled: An Act for County Registers* (August 1653); *Thomason Tracts* E708 (15), Reel 109.

*Reasons for the Continuance of the Process of Arrest, for the good of the Commonwealth* (June 10, 1659); *Thomason Tracts* 669 f21 (48), Reel 247.

*Records of the Suffolk County Court: 1671–1680*. In *Publications of the Colonial Society of Massachusetts*. Vols. 29 & 30. 2 Vols. Edited by S.E. Morison. Boston: CSM, 1933.

*Records of the Town of Cambridge, Massachusetts: 1630–1703*. 2 Vols. Cambridge: Cambridge City Council, 1901.

*The Remonstrance against Tonnage and Poundage* (June 25, 1628). In *Commons Debates of 1628*. Edited by Robert Johnson, et. al. New Haven: Yale University Press, 1977; 4: 470–71.

*Remonstrans Redivivus: Or An Accompt of the Remonstrance and Petition* (1643); *Google Books* (https://www.google.com/books/edition/_/tQpcAAAAQAAJ?hl=en).

*Report of the Following Debate in Council* 1666. *MHS Collections, Second Series* (1826); 8: 99–100.

*Rex v. Hampden* (1637). *State Trials*. Edited by T.B. Howell. London: 1816; 3: 826–1254 (#147).

Robinson, Henry. *Certain Considerations in order to a more Speedy, Cheap, and Equal Distribution of Justice throughout the Nation* (1651); *Wing* R1668, Reel 577: 1.

Robinson, Henry. *Certaine Proposals in Order to a New Modelling of the Lawes* (1653); *Google Books* (https://play.google.com/books/reader?id=OcJjAAAAcAAJ&pg=GBS.RA1-PA2&hl=en).

Rutherford, Samuel. *Lex, Rex: The Law and the Prince*. (1644); *Thomason Tracts* E11 (5), Reel 2.

Saunders, Trevor, ed. *Aristotle: The Politics*. Translated by T.A. Sinclair. London: Penguin Books, 1992.

Savage, James, ed. *The History of New England: From 1630 to 1649*. 2 Vols. Boston: 1825.

*Several Draughts of Acts Heretofore Prepared by Persons Appointed to consider of the Inconveniences, Delay, Charge, and Irregularity in the Proceedings of the Law. Printed by an Order of Parliament of the 12th of July, 1653*. In *Somers Tracts*. London: 1811; 6: 177–245.

Sharp, Kevin, ed. *The Levellers*. Cambridge: Cambridge University Press, 1998.

Shepheard, John. *Certain Proposals for Regulating the Law* (1652); *Wing* S3102 (10), Reel 1450.

Sheppard, William. *England's Balme, or Proposals by way of Grievance and Remedy towards the Regulation of the Law, and the Better Administration of Justice* (1657); *Thomason Tracts* E1675 (2), Reel 209.

Shurtleff, Nathaniel B., ed. *Records of the Governor and Company of the Massachusetts Bay in New England*. 5 Vols. Boston: William White, 1853–1854.

Smith, Joseph, ed. *Colonial Justice in Western Massachusetts, 1639–1702: The Pynchon Court Record*. Cambridge: Harvard University Press, 1961.

Smith, Sir Thomas. *De Republica Anglorum*. Edited by Mary Dewar. Cambridge: Cambridge University Press, 1982.

Spelman, John. *A View of a Printed Book Entitled Observations Upon his Majesties Late Answers and Expresses*. (1643); *Thomason Tracts* E245 (22), Reel 42.

St. John, Oliver. *An Argument of Law Concerning the Bill of Attainder of High-Treason of Thomas, Earle of Strafford: At a Conference in a Committee of both Houses of Parliament* (1641); *Google Books* (https://www.google.com/books/edition/_/-dhCAQAAMAAJ?hl=en&gbpv=0).

*St. John's Speech to the Lords in the Upper House of Parliament, January 7, 1640, Concerning Ship-Money*. In *The Tryal of John Hambden*. London: 1719: 218–28; *Google Books* (https://www.google.com/books/edition/The_Tryal_of_John_Hambden_Esq/48VCAQAAMAAJ?hl=en&gbpv=0).

Starkey, Thomas. *A Dialogue between Reginald Pole and Thomas Lupset*. Edited by Kathleen Burton. London: Chatto and Windus, 1948.

*State of Massachusetts Bay. In Convention, June 16, 1780. State Library of Massachusetts*; (https://archives.lib.state.ma.us/handle/2452/43200).

*The Statutes: Revised Edition. Vol. II. William and Mary to 10 George III. A. D. 1688–1770*. 2 Vols. London, 1871.

Steele, Robert, ed., *A Bibliography of Royal Proclamations of the Tudor and Stuart Sovereigns*. 2 Vols. Oxford: Clarendon Press, 1910.

Stoughton, Israel. *A Relation Concerning New England*. MHS *Proceedings (1860–1862)*; 5: 134–44.

*The Table Talk of John Selden*. Edited by Samuel Reynolds. Oxford: Clarendon Press, 1892.

*To the Right Honourable and Supreme Authority of this Nation, the Commons in Parliament*. March 1647. In *The Levellers in the English Revolution*. Edited by G.E. Aylmer. Ithaca: Cornell University Press, 1975: 75–81.

Toppan, Robert N., ed. *Edward Randolph: Including his Letters and Official Papers from the New England, Middle, and Southern Colonies in America, and the West Indies, 1678–1700*. 7 Vols. Boston: Prince Society, 1899–1909.

*Town Records of Salem: 1634–1691*. 3 Vols. Salem: Essex Institute Press, 1868–1934.

*Trial of Charles Stuart, King of England: Before the High Court of Justice, for High Treason (1649)*. In *State Trials*. Edited by T.B. Howell. London: T.C. Hansard, 1816; 4: 990–1194 (#183).

*Trial of Colonel Algernon Sidney* (1683). *State Trials*. Edited by T.B. Howell. London: Hansard, 1816; 9: 817–916 (#300).

*Trial of Dr. William Laud, Archbishop of Canterbury, for High Treason* (1640–1644). *State Trials*. Edited by T.B. Howell and T.C. Hansard, London: 1816; 4: 315–626 (#171).

*The Unlimited Prerogative of Kings Subverted*. (November 21, 1642); *Thomason Tracts* E 127 (32), Reel 22.

Walwyn, William. *England's Lamentable Slavery*. 1645. In *Tracts on Liberty*. Edited by William Haller. New York: Columbia University Press, 1934; 3: 311–18.

Ward, Nathaniel. *Nathaniel Ward to John Winthrop*. December 22, 1639. In *Winthrop Papers*. Boston: MHS, 1944; 4: 162–3.

Ward, Nathaniel. *A Religious Demurrer, Concerning Submission to the Present Power*. London: 1649: 1–7; *EEBO* (http://name.umdl.umich.edu/A97134.0001.001).

Ward, Nathaniel. *Sermon Preached before the Honorable House of Commons, at their late Monthly Fast, being on Wednesday* (June 30, 1647); *Wing* W785 (51), Reel 904.

Ward, Nathaniel. *The Simple Cobler of Aggawam in America. Willing to Help Mend this Country*. London, Jan. 29, 1647. *Thomason Tracts* E 372 (21), Reel 59.

Ward, Samuel. *Jethro's Justice of Peace*. Introduction and Postscript by Nathaniel Ward. (1618); *Google Books* (https://www.google.com/books/edition/_/A7FoAAAAcAAJ?hl=en).

Warr, John. *The Corruption and Deficiency of the Laws of England Soberly Discovered*. London, 1649. In *The Harleian Miscellany*. 6 Vols. London: 1811: 212–25.

Warr, John. *The Priviledges of the People*. (February 5, 1649); *Thomason Tracts* E541 (12), Reel 84.

Warren, Albertus. *The Royalist Reformed*. (1650); *Thomason Tracts* E582 (4), Reel 89.

*Watertown Records*. 6 Vols. Watertown: The Historical Society, 1894.

Whitelock, R.H., ed. *Memoirs of Bulstrode Whitelocke*. London: Routledge & Warne, 1860.

Winslow, Edward. *New-Englands Salamander*. 1647. MHS *Collections* (*Third Series/1830*); 2: 110–45.

Winstanley, Gerrard. *The Law of Freedom in a Platform*. 1652. In *Winstanley: The Law of Freedom*. Edited by Christopher Hill. Harmondsworth: Penguin Books, 1973: 273–389.

Winthrop, John. "Common Grievances Groaning for Reformation." 1624. *Winthrop Papers*; 1: 295–310.

Winthrop, John. "Defense of the Negative Vote." June 5, 1643. *Winthrop Papers*; 4: 380–91.

Winthrop, John. "Discourse on Arbitrary Government." July 1644. *Winthrop Papers*; 4: 468–82.

Winthrop, John. "Essay against the Power of the Church to Sit in Judgment of the Civil Magistracy." November 1637. *Winthrop Papers*; 3: 505–507.

Winthrop, John. "John Winthrop to Richard Saltonstall and Others." 1643. *Winthrop Papers*; 4: 402–10.

Winthrop, John. *A Short Story of the Rise, Reign, and Ruine of the Antinomians, Familists and Libertines, that Infected the Churches of New England*. (1644); *Thomason Tracts* E33 (16), Reel 6.

Winthrop, John. "Summary of the Case between Richard Sherman and Robert Keayne." *Winthrop Papers*; 4: 349–52.

Winthrop, Robert, ed. *Life and Letters of John Winthrop: 1588–1630*. 2 Vols. Boston: MHS, 1863.

*The Womens Petition*. (1651). *Thomason Tracts* 669 f16 (26), Reel 246.

## Secondary Sources

Adamson, John. *The Noble Revolt: The Overthrow of Charles I*. London: Weidenfeld & Nicholson, 2007.

Allen, David. *In English Ways: The Movement of the Societies and the Transferal of English Local Law and Custom to Massachusetts Bay in the Seventeenth Century*. Chapel Hill: University of North Carolina Press, 1981.

Allen, David. "Notes and Documents: The Zuckerman Thesis and the Process of Legal Rationalization in Provincial Massachusetts." *WMQ* 29 (1972): 443–68.

Alsop, J.D. "Ethics in the Marketplace: Gerrard Winstanley's London Bankruptcy, 1643." *Journal of British Studies* 28 (1989): 97–119.

Amory, Hugh. *First Impressions: Printing in Cambridge, 1639–1989*. Cambridge: Harvard University, 1989.

Amory, Hugh. "Printing and Bookselling in New England." In David Hall, ed. *History of the Book in America*. Chapel Hill: University of North Carolina Press, 2007; 1: 83–116.

Anders, H. "The Elizabethan ABC with the Catechism." *The Library* (Fourth Series) 41 (1936): 32–48.

Andrews, Charles. *The Colonial Period of American History*. 4 Vols. New Haven: Yale University Press, 1938.

Archibald, Steven. *English Civil War Flags: Cavalry Cornets and Guidons*. Hertfordshire: Redcrest Publishing, 2021.

Ashcraft, Richard. *Revolutionary Politics and Locke's Two Treatises of Government*. Princeton: Princeton University Press, 1986.

Ashton, M.E. "Lollardy and Sedition, 1381–1431." *Past and Present* 17 (April 1960): 1–44.

Ashton, Robert. *Counter-Revolution: The Second Civil War and Its Origins, 1646–8*. New Haven: Yale University Press, 1994.

Ashton, Robert. *The English Civil War: Conservatism and Revolution, 1603–1649*. 2nd ed. London: Weidenfeld & Nicholson, 1989.

Ashton, Robert. "From Cavalier to Roundhead Tyranny, 1642–9." In John Morrill, ed. *Reactions to the English Civil War, 1642–1649*. New York: St. Martin's Press, 1982: 185–207.

Aylmer, G.E. "Attempts at Administrative Reform, 1625–40." *English Historical Review* 72 (1957): 229–59.

Bailey, Gilbert. "The Promulgation of Law." *American Political Science Review* 35 (1941): 1059–84.

Bailyn, Bernard. "The Apologia of Robert Keayne." *WMQ* 7 (1950): 568–87.

Bailyn, Bernard. *The Barbarous Years: The Peopling of British North America—The Conflict of Civilizations, 1600–1675*. New York: Vintage Books, 2013.

Bailyn, Bernard. *Ideological Origins of the American Revolution: Enlarged Edition*. Cambridge: Belknap Press, 1992.

Bailyn, Bernard. *The New England Merchants in the Seventeen Century*. 2nd ed. Cambridge: Harvard University Press, 1979.

Baker, Emerson. *A Storm of Witchcraft: The Salem Trials and the American Experience*. Oxford: Oxford University Press, 2015.

Baker, J.H. "The English Legal Profession, 1450–1550." In Wilfred Prest, ed. *Lawyers in Early Modern Europe and America*. New York: Holmes & Meier Publishers, 1981: 16–41.

Baker, J.H. *An Introduction to English Legal History*. 3rd ed. London: Butterworths, 1990.

Baker, J.H. *Manual of Law French*. Amersham: Avebury Publishing, 1979.

Baldwin, Geoff. "Reason of State and English Parliaments, 1610–1642." *History of Political Thought* 25 (Winter 2004): 620–41.

Barth, Jonathan. "'A Peculiar Stampe of Our Own': The Massachusetts Mint and the Battle over Sovereignty, 1652–1691." *WMQ* 87 (September 2014): 490–525.

Beattie, J. M. *Crime and the Courts in England: 1660–1800*. Princeton: Princeton University Press, 1986.

Beer, George. *The Origins of the British Colonial System: 1578–1660*. New York: Macmillan Co., 1908.

Bellamy, John. *Criminal Law and Society in Late Medieval and Tudor England.* New York: St. Martin's Press, 1984.

Bennett, H.S. *English Books and Readers: 1580–1603*. Cambridge: Cambridge University Press, 1965.

Beresford, M.W. "The Common Informer, the Penal Statutes, and Economic Regulation." *Economic History Review* 10 (no. 2, 1957–58): 221–37.

Berman, Harold. *Law and Revolution: The Impact of the Protestant Reformations on the Western Legal Tradition.* 2 Vols. Cambridge: Belknap Press, 2003.

Bernard, G.W. "The Making of Religious Policy, 1533–1546: Henry VIII and the Search for the Middle Way." *Historical Journal* 41 (June 1998): 321–49.

Bhambra, Gurminder K., "Focus: Accounting for British History." *Discover Society* (July 1, 2020); (https://archive.discoversociety.org/2020/07/01/focus-accounting-for-british-history/).

Billings, Warren. *A Little Parliament: The Virginia General Assembly in the Seventeenth Century*. Richmond: Library of Virginia, 2004.

Bishop, Jennifer, "Utopia and Civic Politics in Mid-Sixteenth-Century London." *Historical Journal* 54 (December 2011): 933–53.

Black, Barbara. "The Concept of a Supreme Court: Massachusetts Bay, 1630–1686." In Russell Osgood, ed. *The History of the Law in Massachusetts: The Supreme Judicial Court, 1692–1992*. Boston: Supreme Judicial Court Historical Society, 1992: 43–79.

Black, Barbara. "The Constitution of Empire: The Case for the Colonists." *University of Pennsylvania Law Review* 124 (May 1976): 1157–1211.

*Black's Law Dictionary*. 5th ed. St. Paul: West Publishing, 1968.

Blatcher, Marjorie. *The Court of King's Bench: 1450–1550*. London: Athlone Press, 1978.

Bourke, Richard. "Review: Revising the Cambridge School, Republicanism Revisited." *Political Theory* 46 (June 2018): 467–77.

Bowen, Catherine Drinker. *The Lion and the Throne: The Life and Times of Sir Edward Coke*. Boston: Little, Brown and Company, 1956.

Braddick, Michael. *The Common Freedom of the People: John Lilburne and the English Revolution*. Oxford: Oxford University Press, 2018.

Braddick, Michael. "The Early Modern English State and the Question of Differentiation, from 1550 to 1700." *Comparative Studies in Society and History* 38 (January 1996): 92–111.

Breen, Timothy. *The Character of a Good Ruler: A Study of Puritan Political Ideas in New England, 1630–1730*. New Haven: Yale University Press, 1970.

Breen, Timothy. "Who Governs: The Town Franchise in Seventeenth-Century Massachusetts." WMQ 27 (1970): 460–74.

Bremer, Francis. "In Defense of Regicide: John Cotton on the Execution of Charles I." WMQ 37 (1980): 103–24.

Bremer, Francis. *First Founders: American Puritans and Puritanism in an Atlantic World*. Durham: University of New Hampshire Press, 2012.

Bremer, Francis. *John Winthrop: America's Forgotten Founding Father*. Oxford: Oxford University Press, 2003.

Bridenbaugh, Carl. *Vexed and Troubled Englishmen: 1590–1642*. New York: Oxford University Press, 1968.

Brigden, Susan. *London and the Reformation*. Oxford: Clarendon Press, 1989.

Brooke, John. *The Heart of the Commonwealth: Society and Political Culture in Worcester County, Massachusetts, 1713–1861*. Amherst: University of Massachusetts Press, 1989.

Brooks, C.W. *Pettyfoggers and Vipers of the Commonwealth: The "Lower Branch" of the Legal Profession in Early Modern England*. Cambridge: Cambridge University Press, 1986.

Brown, Leslie, ed. *The New Shorter Oxford English Dictionary*. 2 Vols. Oxford: Clarendon Press, 1961.

Bryson, W.H. *The Equity Side of the Exchequer*. Cambridge: Cambridge University Press, 1975.

Budziszewski, J. *Commentary on Thomas Aquinas's Virtue Ethics*. Cambridge: Cambridge University Press, 2017.

Burgess, Glenn. *British Political Thought: 1500–1660*. New York: Palgrave Macmillan, 2009.

Burke, Peter. "Reason of State." In J.H. Burns, ed. *Cambridge History of Political Thought: 1450–1700*. Cambridge: Cambridge University Press, 1991: 479–84.

Burnham, Michelle. "Samuel Gorton's Leveller Aesthetics and the Economics of Colonial Dissent." WMQ 67 (July 2010): 433–58.

Bushman, Richard L. *King and People in Provincial Massachusetts*. 2nd ed. Chapel Hill: University of North Carolina Press, 1992.

Byrom, H. J. "Richard Tottell —His Life and Work." *The Library* (Fourth Series) 8 (1927–28): 199–232.

Cahn, Mark. "Punishment, Discretion, and the Codification of Prescribed Penalties in Colonial Massachusetts." *American Journal of Legal History* 33 (1989): 107–36.

Calder, Isabel. "John Cotton's 'Moses His Judicials.'" *Publications of the Colonial Society of Massachusetts: Transactions* 28 (1933): 86–94.

Campbell, John. *The Lives of the Chief Justices of England*. 4 Vols. New York: Cockcroft & Co., 1874.

Campbell, Patrick F. "The Concept of Representation in American Political Development: Lessons of the Massachusetts Bay Puritans." *Polity* 47 (Jan., 2015): 33–60.

Capp, Bernard. *England's Culture Wars: Puritan Reformation and its Enemies in the Interregnum, 1649–1660*. Oxford: Oxford University Press, 2012.

Carlyle, A.J. and R.W. Carlyle. *A History of Medieval Political Theory in the West*. 5 Vols. 3rd ed. Edinburgh: William Blackwood and Sons, 1930–1950.

Carp, Benjamin L. "Edmund S. Morgan and the Urgency of Good Leadership." *Reviews in American History* 44 (March 2016): 1–18.

Chapin, Bradley. *Criminal Justice in Colonial America: 1606–1660*. Athens: University of Georgia Press, 1983.

Chapman, Alison. "Milton and Legal Reform." *Renaissance Quarterly* 69 (no. 2, 2016): 529–65.

Christianson, Paul. "Arguments on Billeting and Martial Law in the Parliament of 1628." *Historical Journal* 37 (September 1994): 539–67.

Clarkson, L.A. "The Organization of the English Leather Industry in the Late Sixteenth and Seventeenth Centuries." *Economic History Review* (2nd Series) 13 (no. 2, 1960/61): 245–53.

Coast, David. "Speaking for the People of England." *Past and Present* 244 (August 2019): 51–88.

Cobbett, William and Thomas Hansard. *Cobbett's Parliamentary History of England*. 36 Vols. London: R. Bagshaw, 1807.

Cockburn, J.S. *A History of English Assizes: 1558–1714*. Cambridge: Cambridge University Press, 1972.

Coffey, John. "Puritanism and Liberty Revisited: The Case for Toleration in the English Revolution." *Historical Journal* 41 (no. 4, 1998): 961–85.

Cohen, Morris L. "Legal Literature in Colonial Massachusetts." In *Law in Colonial Massachusetts*. Vol. 62. Publications of the Colonial Society of Massachusetts, 1984: 243–72.

Collins, John M. "The Long Parliament and the Law of Necessity in Seventeenth Century England." *Past and Present* 247 (May 2020): 3–35.

Collinson, Patrick. *The Reformation*. New York: Modern Library, 2004.

Como, David. "Making 'the Heads of the Proposals': The King, the Army, the Levellers, and the Roads to Putney." *English Historical Review* 135 (February 2021): 1387–1432.

Como, David. "Print, Censorship, and Ideological Escalation in the English Civil War." *Journal of British Studies* 51 (October 2012): 820–57.

Como, David. "Secret Printing and the Crisis of 1640." *Past and Present* 196 (August 2007): 37–82.

Cooper, Jr., James. *Tenacious of their Liberties: The Congregationalists in Colonial Massachusetts*. Oxford: Oxford University Press, 1999.

Coquillette, Daniel. "Past the Pillars of Hercules: Francis Bacon and the Science of Rulemaking." *University of Michigan Journal of Law Reform* 46 (no. 2, 2013): 549–92.

Coquillette, Daniel. "Radical Lawmakers in Colonial Massachusetts: The 'Countenance of Authoritie' and the Lawes and Libertyes." *New England Quarterly* 67 (1994): 179–211.

Corey, Deloraine. *History of Malden, Mass.: 1633–1785*. Malden: 1899.

Cotterell, Mary. "Interregnum Law Reform: The Hale Commission of 1652." *English Historical Review* 83 (October 1968): 689–704.

Coward, Barry. *The Stuart Age: England, 1603–1714*. 2nd ed. London: Longman, 1994.

Cowley, John D. *A Bibliography of Abridgments, Digests, Dictionaries, and Indexes of English Law to the Year 1800*. London: Selden Society, 1932.

Cramsie, John. "Commercial Projects and the Fiscal Policy of James VI and I." *Historical Journal* 43 (June 2000): 345–64.

Cramsie, John. *Kingship and Crown Policy under James VI and James I*. Woodbridge: RHS, 2002.

Cressy, David. *Charles I and the People of England*. Oxford: Oxford University Press, 2015.

Cressy, David. *England on Edge: Crisis and Revolution, 1640–1642*. Oxford: Oxford University Press, 2006.

Cressy, David. *Literacy and the Social Order: Reading and Writing in Tudor and Stuart England*. Cambridge: Cambridge University Press, 1980.

Cressy, David. "Revolutionary England 1640–1642," *Past and Present* 181 (November 2003): 35–71.

Croft, Pauline. "Fresh Light on Bates' Case." *Historical Journal* 30 (no. 3, 1987): 523–39.

Cromartie, Alan. "Parliamentary Sovereignty, Popular Sovereignty, and Henry Parker's Adjudicative Standpoint." In Richard Bourke and Quentin Skinner, eds. *Popular Sovereignty in Historical Perspective*. Cambridge: Cambridge University Press, 2016: 142–63.

Crump, Helen. *Colonial Admiralty Jurisdiction in the Seventeenth Century*. London: Longmans, Green, and Co., 1931.

Cunningham, W. *The Growth of English Industry in Modern Times*. Cambridge: University Press, 1892.

Currier, John. *History of Newbury, Massachusetts: 1635–1902*. Boston: Damrell & Upham, 1902.

Cushing, John D., ed. *A Bibliography of the Laws and Resolves of the Massachusetts Bay: 1642–1780*. Wilmington: MHS, 1984.

Cust, Richard. *Charles I and the Aristocracy: 1625–1642*. Cambridge: Cambridge University Press, 2013.

Cust, Richard. *The Forced Loan and English Politics: 1626–1628*. Oxford: Clarendon Press, 1987.

Cuttica, Cesare. "The English Regicide and Patriarchalism." *Renaissance and Reformation* 36 (no. 2, 2013): 131–64.

Dabhoiwala, Faramerz. "Summary Justice in Early Modern London." *English Historical Review* 121 (June 2006): 796–822.

Daniell, David. *William Tyndale: A Biography*. New Haven: Yale University Press, 1994.

Davies, Ebenezer T. *The Political Ideas of Richard Hooker*. London: SPCK, 1946.

Davies, Godfrey. *The Early Stuarts: 1603–1660*. Oxford: Clarendon Press, 1949.

Davies, Margaret. *The Enforcement of English Apprenticeship: A Study in Applied Mercantilism, 1563–1642*. Cambridge: Harvard University Press, 1956.

Davis, James. "Baking for the Common Good: A Reassessment of the Assize of Bread in Medieval England." *Economic History Review* 57 (August 2004): 465–502.

De Krey, Gary. "Amon Wilbee and Leveller Beginnings, 1647–8." *English Historical Review* 137 (April 2022): 416–44.

Dealy, Jonathan. "Coping with risk in the Seventeenth Century: The First Age of the English Old Poor Law." In Masayuki Tanimoto and R. Bin Wong, eds. *Public Goods Provision in the Early Modern Economy*. Berkeley: University of California Press, 2019: 100–17.

Dean, D.M. "Public or Private? London, Leather, and Legislation in Elizabethan England." *Historical Journal* 31 (1988): 525–48.

Dean, John W. *A Memoir of the Rev. Nathaniel Ward*. Albany: J. Munsell, 1868.

Dickens, A.G. *The English Reformation*. 2nd ed. University Park: Pennsylvania State University Press, 1989.

Dickerson, Oliver. *The Navigation Acts and the American Revolution*. Philadelphia: University of Pennsylvania Press, 1951.

Dickinson, Harry T. "Magna Carta in the American Revolution." In Lawrence Goldman, ed., *Magna Carta: History, Context, and Influence*. London: University of London Press, 2018: 80–93.

Dillon, John. "Bentham's Influence in the Reforms of the Nineteenth Century." In *Select Essays in Anglo-American Legal History*. Boston: Little, Brown, & Co., 1907; 1: 492–515.

Doe, Norman. *Fundamental Authority in Late Medieval Law*. Cambridge: Cambridge University Press, 1990.

Duffy, Eamon. *Reformation Divided*. London: Bloomsbury. 2017.

Duffy, Eamon. *The Stripping of the Altars: Traditional Religion in England, c.1400—c.1580*. New Haven: Yale University Press, 1992.

Duffy, Ian. "English Bankrupts, 1571–1861." *American Journal of Legal History* 24 (October 1980): 283–305.

Dugre, Neal. "Repairing the Breach: Puritan Expansion, Commonwealth Formation, and the Origins of the United Colonies of New England." *New England Quarterly* 91 (September 2018): 382–417.

Dunn, Richard. *Puritans and Yankees: The Winthrop Dynasty in New England: 1630–1717*. Princeton: Princeton University Press, 1962.

Dzelzainis, Martin. "History and Ideology: Milton, the Levellers, and the Council of State in 1649." *Huntington Library Quarterly* 68 (March 2005): 269–87.

Early Modern Research Group, "Commonwealth: The Social, Cultural, and Conceptual Contexts of an Early Modern Keyword." *Historical Journal* 54 (September 2011): 659–87.

Edling, Max M. "Review: William E. Nelson. *E Pluribus Unum: How the Common Law Helped Unify and Liberate Colonial America, 1607–1776*." *American Historical Review* 127 (March 2022): 497–98.

Eisenstein, Elizabeth. *The Printing Press as an Agent of Change: Communications and Cultural Transformations in Early-Modern Europe*. 2 Vols. Cambridge: Cambridge University Press, 1979.

Elton, Geoffrey. "Informing for Profit: A Sidelight of Tudor Methods of Law Enforcement." *Cambridge Historical Journal* 11 (1953): 149–67.

Elton, Geoffrey. *The Parliament of England: 1559–1581*. Cambridge: Cambridge University Press, 1986.

Elton, Geoffrey. "Reform by Statute: Thomas Starkey's Dialogue and Thomas Cromwell's Policy." *Proceedings of the British Academy* 54 (1968): 165–88.

Elton, Geoffrey. "The Sessional Printing of Statutes, 1484–1547." In E.W. Ives, et al., eds. *Wealth and Power in Tudor England*. London: Athlone Press, 1978: 68–86.

Elton, Geoffrey. *The Tudor Constitution*. Cambridge: Cambridge University Press, 1968.

Emmison, F. *Elizabethan Life*. Chelmsford: ECC, 1970.

Estep, William. *The Anabaptist Story: An Introduction to Sixteenth-Century Anabaptism*. 3rd ed. Cambridge: William B. Eerdmans Co., 1996.

Esturlid, Lee. "Where Everything is Weighed in the Scales of Material Interest: Anglo-Turkish Trade, Piracy, and Diplomacy during the Jacobean Period." *European Economic History* 22 (1993): 613–25.

Eusden, John. *Puritans, Lawyers, and Politics in Early Seventeenth-Century England*. New Haven: Yale University Press, 1958; reprint, Archon Books, 1965.

"A Few Notes Touching Strangers Courts." *Publications of Colonial Society of Massachusetts Transactions (1889–1900)*. Boston: 1904; 6: 282–86.

Firth, Charles and Godfrey Davies. *The Regimental History of Cromwell's Army*. 2 Vols. Oxford: Clarendon Press, 1940.

Fisher, R.M. "Thomas Cromwell, Humanism and Educational Reform: 1530–40." *Bulletin of the Institute of Historical Research* 50 (November 1977): 151–63.

Fitzgibbons, Jonathan. "Hereditary Succession and the Cromwellian Protectorate: The Offer of the Crown Reconsidered." *English Historical Review* 128 (October 2013): 1095–1128.

Fletcher, Anthony. *Reform in the Provinces: The Government of Stuart England*. New Haven: Yale University Press, 1986.

Forcellino, Antonio. *Michelangelo*. Translated by Allan Cameron. Cambridge: Polity Press, 2009.

Ford, Worthington. "Cotton's Moses His Judicials." *MHS Proceedings (Second Series/ 1902)*; 16: 274–84.

Foster, Stephen. *The Long Argument: English Puritanism and the Shaping of New England Culture (1570–1700)*. Chapel Hill: University of North Carolina Press, 1991.

Foster, Stephen. "The Massachusetts Franchise in the Seventeenth Century." *WMQ* 24 (1967): 613–23.

Foster, Stephen. "New England and the Challenge of Heresy, 1630 to 1660: The Puritan Crisis in Transatlantic Perspective." *WMQ* 38 (1981): 624–60.

Foxley, Rachel. "John Lilburne and the Citizenship of 'Free-Born Englishmen'." *Historical Journal* 47 (December 2004): 849–74.

Foxley, Rachel. *The Levellers: Radical Political Thought in the English Revolution.* Manchester: Manchester University Press, 2013.

Freer, Robert. "Imprisonment for Debt in Massachusetts before 1800." *Mississippi Valley Historical Review* 48 (1961): 252–69.

Frese, Joseph. "Early Parliamentary Legislation on Writs of Assistance." *Colonial Society of Massachusetts Publications* 38 (1959): 318–26.

Friedman, Lawrence. *A History of American Law.* 3rd ed. New York: Simon & Schuster, 2005.

Fuhrer, Mary Babson. "The Revolutionary Worlds of Lexington and Concord Compared." *WMQ* 85 (March 2012): 78–118.

Fullerton, Samuel. "New England in the Royalist Imagination." *English Historical Review* (October 2022): 1346–76.

Furet, François. *Revolutionary France: 1770–1880.* Translated by Antonia Nevill. Oxford: Blackwell Publishers, 1988.

Gardiner, S.R. *The Puritan Revolution: 1603–1660.* London: Longman, Green & Co., 1911.

Gaskill, Malcom. *Between Two Worlds: How the English Became Americans.* New York: Basic Books, 2014.

Gentles, Ian. "The Agreements of the People and their Political Context." In Michael Mendle, ed. *The Putney Debates of 1647.* Cambridge: Cambridge University Press, 2010: 148–174.

Glover, Samuel. "The Putney Debates: Popular versus Élitist Republicanism." *Past and Present* 164 (August 1999): 47–80.

Gooch, G.P. *The History of English Democratic Ideas in the Seventeenth Century.* Cambridge: University Press, 1898.

Gordon, Edward and Elaine. *Literacy in America.* London: Praeger, 2003.

Gorton, Adelos. *The Life and Times of Samuel Gorton.* Philadelphia: Historical Society of Pennsylvania, 1908.

Graham, Howard. "The Rastells and the Printed English Law Book of the Renaissance." *Law Library Journal* 47 (1954): 6–25.

Gray, Charles M. "Bonham's Case Reviewed." *Proceedings of the American Philosophical Society* 116 (February 1972): 35–58.

Gray, Francis C. "Remarks on the Early Laws of Massachusetts Bay; with the Code adopted in 1641, and called THE BODY OF LIBERTIES, now First Printed." *MHS Collections (Third Series/1838)* 7 (1838): 191–237.

Green, Ian. *The Christian's ABC: Catechisms and Catechizing in England, 1530–1740.* Oxford: Clarendon Press, 1996.

Green, Jack. *Peripheries and Center: Constitutional Development in the Extended Polities of the British Empire and the United States, 1607–1788*. New York: W.W. Norton, 1986.

Greene, Jack. *The Constitutional Origins of the American Revolution*. Cambridge: Cambridge University Press, 2011.

Grossman, George S. *Legal Research: Historical Foundations of the Electronic Age*. Oxford: Oxford University Press, 1994.

Gunn, J.A.W. *Politics and the Public Interest in the Seventeenth Century*. Toronto: University of Toronto Press, 1969.

Gunther, Karl and Ethan Shagan. "Protestant Radicalism and Political Thought in the Reign of Henry VIII." *Past and Present* 194 (February 2007): 35–74.

Gura, Philip. *A Glimpse of Sion's Glory: Puritan Radicalism in New England, 1620–1660*. Middletown, [CT]: Wesleyan University Press, 1984.

Hackett Fisher, David. *Albion's Seed*. Oxford: Oxford University Press, 1989.

Hackett Fisher, David. *Paul Revere's Ride*. Oxford: Oxford University Press, 1994.

Haffenden, Philip, "The Crown and the Colonial Charters, 1675–1688: Part I." *WMQ* 15 (July 1958): 298–311.

Haffenden, Philip. "The Crown and the Colonial Charters, 1675–1688: Part II." *WMQ* 15 (October 1958): 452–66.

Haigh, Christopher. *Elizabeth I*. London: Longman, 1988.

Hall, David. *The Faithful Shepherd: A History of the New England Ministry in the Seventeenth Century*. Cambridge: Harvard University Press, 2006.

Hall, David. *History of the Book in America*. Chapel Hill: University of North Carolina Press, 2007.

Hall, David. *The Puritans: A Transatlantic History*. Princeton: Princeton University Press, 2019.

Hall, David. "Readers and Writers in Early New England." In Hugh Amory, ed. *The Colonial Book in the Atlantic World*. Chapel Hill: University of North Carolina Press, 2007: 117–51.

Hall, David. *A Reforming People: Puritanism and the Transformation of Public Life in New England*. New York: Alfred A. Knopf, 2011.

Hall, David. "Review: Heads Must Roll—The Dynamics of Radical Puritanism in Stuart England and Early New England." *Reviews in American History* 42 (June 2014): 219–226.

Hall, David. *Worlds of Wonder, Days of Judgment*. Cambridge: Harvard University Press, 1989.

Hall, Michael G. *Edward Randolph and the American Colonies: 1676–1703*. New York: W.W. Norton, 1960.

Hallam, Henry. *Constitutional History of England*. 2 Vols. 6th ed. London: John Murray, 1850.

Haller, William. *The Rise of Puritanism: Or, the Way to the New Jerusalem as Set Forth in Pulpit and Press from Thomas Cartwright to John Lilburne and John Milton, 1570–1643.* New York: Columbia University Press, 1938.

Halliday, Paul and G. Edward White. "The Suspension Clause." *Virginia Law Review* 94 (no. 3, 2008): 575–723.

Harris, Tim. "The Leveller Legacy: From the Restoration to the Exclusion Crisis." In Michael Mendle, ed. *The Putney Debates of 1647*. Cambridge: Cambridge University Press, 2001: 219–240.

Harris, Tim. *Politics Under the Later Stuarts*. London, New York: Longman, 1993.

Harris, Tim. *Rebellion: Britain's First Stuart Kings*. Oxford: Oxford University Press, 2014.

Harris, Tim. "Revisiting the Causes of the English Civil War." *Huntington Library Quarterly* 78 (Winter 2015): 615–35.

Harrison, G.A. "Innovation and Precedent: A Procedural Reappraisal of the 1625 Parliament." *English Historical Review* 102 (January 1987): 31–62.

Harrison, Wes. "The Role of Women in Anabaptist Thought and Practice." *Sixteenth Century Journal* 23 (Spring 1992): 49–69.

Harvey, David. *The Law Emprynted: The Printing Press as an Agent of Change.* Oxford: Hart Publishing, 2017.

Haskins, George. *Law and Authority in Early Massachusetts: A Study in Tradition and Design*. New York: Macmillan Co., 1960.

Haskins, George L. "Codification of the Law in Colonial Massachusetts: A Study in Comparative Law." *Indiana Law Journal* 30 (1954): 1–17.

Haskins, George and Samuel Ewing. "The Spread of Massachusetts Law in the Seventeenth Century." *University of Pennsylvania Law Review* 106 (1958): 413–18.

Hattem, Michael D. *Past and Prologue: Politics and Memory in the American Revolution* New Haven: Yale University Press, 2020.

Hayes, T. Wilson. "The Peaceful Apocalypse: Familism and Literacy in Sixteenth-Century England." *Sixteenth Century Journal* 17 (Summer 1986): 131–43.

Herbert, Amanda. "Companions in Preaching and Suffering: Itinerant Female Quakers in the Seventeenth- and Eighteenth-Century British Atlantic World." *Early American Studies* 9 (Winter 2011): 73–113.

Herrup, Cynthia. *The Common Peace: Participation and Criminal Law in Seventeenth Century England.* Cambridge: Cambridge University Press, 1989.

Herrup, Cynthia. "Law and Morality in 17th Century England." *Past and Present* 106 (1985): 102–23.

Hilkey, Charles J. *Legal Development in Colonial Massachusetts, 1630–1686: Studies in History, Economics and Public Law Series*. 37 Vols. No. 2. New York: Columbia University Press, 1910.

Hill, Christopher. *The Century of Revolution: 1603–1714*. Edinburgh: Thomas Nelson & Sons, 1961.

Hill, Christopher. *The English Bible and the Seventeenth-Century Revolution.* London: Penguin Books, 1993.
Hill, Christopher. *God's Englishman: Oliver Cromwell and the English Revolution.* London: Weidenfeld and Nicolson, 1970.
Hill, Christopher. *The Intellectual Origins of the English Revolution.* 2nd ed. Oxford: Oxford University Press, 1997.
Hill, Christopher. *Liberty against the Law: Some Seventeenth Century Controversies.* London: Allen Lane, 1996.
Hill, Christopher. *Milton and the English Revolution.* New York: Penguin Books, 1979.
Hill, Christopher. *The World Turned Upside Down: Radical Ideas During the English Revolution.* New York: Viking Press, 1972.
Hilton, Rodney. *Bond Men Made Free: Medieval Peasant Movements and the English Rising of 1381.* London: Maurice Temple Smith, 1973; reprint, London: Routledge, 1993.
Hindle, Steve. "Dearth and the English Revolution: The Harvest Crisis of 1647–50." *Economic History Review* 61 (August 2008): 64–98.
Hirst, Derek. "Failure of Godly Rule in the English Republic." *Past and Present* 132 (August 1991): 33–66.
Hirst, Derek. "Of Labels and Situations: Revisionisms and Early Stuart Studies." *Huntington Library Quarterly* 78 (Winter 2015): 595–614.
Hirst, Derek. "Petitions and the English Republic." *Journal of British Studies* 45 (January 2006): 26–50.
*History of the Town of Hingham, Massachusetts.* Cambridge: University Press, 1893.
Hoffer, Peter. *Law and People in Colonial America.* Baltimore: Johns Hopkins University Press, 1992.
Holdsworth, William. *A History of English Law.* 16 Vols. Boston: Little, Brown, and Co., 1924.
Holdsworth, William. *Sources and Literature of English Law.* Oxford: Clarendon Press, 1925.
Hopkins, Neil and Will Coster. "The Levellers, Political Literacy, and Contemporary Citizenship Education in England." *Education, Citizenship, and Social Justice* 14 (2019): 68–81.
Horle, Craig. *The Quakers and the English Legal System: 1660–1688.* Philadelphia: University of Pennsylvania Press, 1988.
Howe, Mark. "The Recording of Deeds." *Boston University Law Review* 28 (1948): 1–6.
Howe, Mark. "The Sources and Nature of Law in Colonial Massachusetts." In George Billias, ed. *Selected Essays: Law and Authority in Colonial America.* Barre: Barre Publishers, 1965: 1–16.
Howe, Mark and Louis Eaton. "The Supreme Judicial Power in the Colony of Massachusetts Bay." *New England Quarterly* 20 (1947): 291–316.

Hoyle, R.W. "The Masters of Requests and the Small Change of Jacobean Patronage." *English Historical Review* 126 (June 2011): 544–81.

Hulsebosch, Daniel. "The Ancient Constitution and the Expanding Empire: Sir Edward Coke's British Jurisprudence." *Law and History Review* 21 (Autumn 2003): 439–82.

Iliffe, Rob. "Hartlib's World." In Matthew Davies and James Galloway, eds. *London and Beyond: Essays in Honour of Derek Keen*. London: University of London Press, 2012: 103–22.

Jenkinson, Matthew. *Charles I's Killers in America*. Oxford: Oxford University Press, 2019.

Jones, Douglas. "The Transformation of the Law of Poverty in Eighteenth-Century Massachusetts." *Publications of the Colonial Society of Massachusetts* 62 (1984): 153–90.

Jones, Whitney. *The Tudor Commonwealth: 1529–1559*. London: Athalone Press, 1970.

Jones, W.J. "The Foundations of English Bankruptcy: Statutes and Commissions in the Early Modern Period." *Transactions of the American Philosophical Society* 69 (no. 3, 1979): 1–63.

Judson, Margaret. *The Crisis of the Constitution: An Essay in Constitutional and Political Thought in England, 1603–1645*. 1949; reprint, New York: Octagon Books, 1980.

Judson, Margaret. *From Tradition to Political Reality*. Hamden [CT]: Archon Books, 1980.

Justice, Steven. *Writing and Rebellion: England in 1381*. Berkeley: University of California Press, 1994.

Kantorowicz, Ernst. "Mysteries of State: An Absolutist Concept and Its Late Medieval Origins." *Harvard Theological Review* 48 (1955): 65–91.

Kishlansky, Mark. "The Army and the Levellers: The Roads to Putney." *Historical Journal* 22 (December 1979): 759–824.

Kishlansky, Mark. "Charles I: A Case of Mistaken Identity." *Past and Present* (November 2005): 41–80.

Kishlansky, Mark. "Mission Impossible: Charles I, Oliver Cromwell and the Regicide." *English Historical Review* 125 (August 2010): 844–74.

Kishlansky, Mark. *A Monarchy Transformed: 1603–1714*. London: Allen Press, 1996.

Kishlansky, Mark. *Parliamentary Selection: Social and Political Choice in Early Modern England*. Cambridge: Cambridge University Press, 1986.

Klooster, Wim. *The Dutch Moment: War, Trade, and Settlement in the Seventeenth-Century Atlantic World*. Ithaca: Cornell University Press, 2016.

Knights, Mark. "John Locke and Post-Revolutionary Politics: Electoral Reform and the Franchise." *Past and Present* 213 (November 2011): 41–86.

Konig, David T. *Law and Society in Puritan Massachusetts: Essex County, 1629–1692*. Chapel Hill: University of North Carolina Press, 1979.

Korporowicz, Łukasz Jan. "George Harris and the Comparative Legal Background of the First English Translation of Justinian's Institutes." In William Eves, et al., eds. *Common Law, Civil Law, and Colonial Law: Essays in Comparative English Legal*

*History from the Twelfth to the Twentieth Centuries*. Cambridge: Cambridge University Press, 2021: 120–39.

Kulikoff, Alan, *From British Peasants to Colonial American Farmers*. Chapel Hill: University of North Carolina Press, 2000.

Kupperman, Karen. "Definitions of Liberty on the Eve of Civil War: Lord Saye and Sele, Lord Brooke, and the American Puritan Colonies." *Historical Journal* 32 (March 1989): 17–33.

Kupperman, Karen. "Errand to the Indies: Puritan Colonization from Providence Island through the Western Design." *WMQ* 45 (January 1988): 1–99.

Kupperman, Karen. *Providence Island, 1630–1641*. Cambridge: Cambridge University Press, 1993.

Kyle, Chris. "Monarch and Marketplace: Proclamations as News in Early Modern England." *Huntington Library Quarterly* 78 (December 2015): 771–87.

Lambert, Sheila. "The Opening of the Long Parliament." *Historical Journal* 27 (June 1984): 265–87.

Lake, Peter. "From Revisionist to Royalist History; Or, Was Charles I the First Whig Historian?" *Huntington Library Quarterly* 78 (December 2015): 657–81.

Langelüddecke, Henrik. "Law and Order in Seventeenth-Century England: The Organization of Local Administration during the Personal Rule of Charles I." *Law and History Review* 15 (Spring 1997): 49–76.

Lee, Daniel. *Popular Sovereignty in Early Modern Constitutional Thought*. Oxford: Oxford University Press, 2016.

Leng, Thomas. "Commercial Conflict and Regulation in the Discourse of Trade in Seventeenth-Century England." *Historical Journal* 48 (December 2005): 933–54.

Leng, Thomas. "A Potent Plantation Well Armed and Policed: Huguenots, the Hartlib Circle, and British Colonization in the 1640s." *WMQ* 66 (January 2009): 173–94.

Levy, Leonard. *The Origins of the Fifth Amendment*. 2nd ed. New York: Macmillan Co., 1986.

Levy, Leonard. *Ranters Run Amok*. Chicago: Ivan R. Dee, 2000.

Lewis, C.T., ed. *Elementary Latin Dictionary*. Oxford: Oxford University Press, 1891; reprint, 1995.

Lindquist, Eric. "The Failure of the Great Contract." *Journal of Modern History* 57 (December 1985): 617–51.

Lister, T.H. *Life and Administration of Edward, Earl of Clarendon*. 2 Vols. London: Longman, 1838.

Lobo, Giuseppina. "John Milton, Oliver Cromwell, and the Cause of Conscience." *Studies in Philology* 112 (no. 4, 2015): 774–97.

Lockridge, Kenneth. *Literacy in Colonial New England: An Enquiry into the Social Context of Literacy in the Early Modern West*. New York: W.W. Norton & Co., 1974.

Lockridge, Kenneth. *A New England Town: The First Hundred Years*. New York: W.W. Norton & Co., 1970; reprint, 1985.

Lockridge, Kenneth and Alan Kreider. "The Evolution of Massachusetts Town Government: 1640 to 1740." *WMQ* 23 (October 1966): 549–74.

Lucas, Paul R. "Colony or Commonwealth: Massachusetts Bay, 1661–1666." *WMQ* 24 (January 1967): 88–107.

Luiten van Zanden, Jan, Eltjo Buringh and Maarten Bosker. "The Rise and Decline of European Parliaments, 1188–1789." *Economic History Review* 65 (August 2012): 835–61.

MacCaffrey, Wallace. *Elizabeth I: War and Politics, 1588–1603*. Princeton: Princeton University Press, 1992.

Maclear, J.F. "New England and the Fifth Monarchy: The Quest for the Millennium in Early American Puritanism." *WMQ* 32 (April 1975): 238–58.

Maier, Pauline. *American Scripture: Making the Declaration of Independence*. New York: Vintage Books, 1998.

Maier, Pauline. *From Resistance to Revolution: Colonial Radicals and the Development of American Opposition to Great Britain: 1765–1775*. New York: Alfred A. Knopf, 1973.

Maier, Pauline. "Whigs against Whigs against Whigs." *WMQ* 68 (no. 4, 2011): 578–82.

Maitland, Frederick. "Introduction" to the *Mirror of Justices*. London: Seldon Society, 1895.

Malone, Dumas and Allen Johnson, eds. *Dictionary of American Biography*. New York: Charles Scribner's Sons, 1929.

Malone, Joseph. *Pine Trees and Politics: The Naval Stores and Forest Policy in Colonial New England*. Seattle: University of Washington Press, 1964.

Maloy, J.S. "Bodin's Puritan Readers and Radical Democracy in Early New England." *History of Ideas* 78 (January 2017): 1–25.

Mancall, Peter. *The Trials of Thomas Morton: an Anglican Lawyer, his Puritan Foes, and the Battle for a New England*. New Haven: Yale University Press, 2019.

Mandell, Daniel R. *The Lost Tradition of Economic Equality in America: 1600–1870*. Baltimore: Johns Hopkins University Press, 2020.

Mares, Henry. "Fraud and Dishonesty in King's Bench and Star Chamber." *American Journal of Legal History* 59 (no. 2, 2019): 210–31.

Martin, John. *Profits in the Wilderness*. Chapel Hill: University of North Carolina Press, 1991.

Martin, J.W. "Elizabethan Familists and English Separatism." *Journal of British Studies* 20 (Autumn 1980): 53–73.

Mathew, Theobald. "Law-French." *Law Quarterly Review* 54 (July 1938): 358–69.

Matthews, Nancy. *William Sheppard: Cromwell's Law Reformer*. Cambridge: Cambridge University Press, 1984.

Mayer, Thomas. *Thomas Starkey and the Commonweal: Humanist Politics and Religion in the Reign of Henry VIII*. Cambridge: Cambridge University Press, 1989.

Mayer, Thomas. "Thomas Starkey's Aristocratic Reform Programme." *History of Political Thought* 7 (no. 3, 1986): 439–61.

Mayville, Luke. *John Adams and the Fear of American Oligarchy*. Princeton: Princeton University Press, 2016.

McArthur, Ellen. "Women Petitioners and the Long Parliament." *English Historical Review* 24 (October 1909): 698–709.

McCusker, John. *Money and Exchange in Europe and America, 1600–1775*. Chapel Hill: University of North Carolina Press, 1978.

McLoughlin, William. *Soul Liberty: The Baptists' Struggle in New England, 1630–1833*. Hanover: Brown University Press, 1991.

McGrath, Alister E. *Reformation Thought: An Introduction*. 2nd ed. Oxford: Blackwell, 1993.

McIlwain, Charles H. *The High Court of Parliament and Its Supremacy: An Historical Essay on the Boundaries between Legislation and Adjudication in England*. New Haven: Yale University Press, 1910; reprint, New York: Arno Press, 1979.

McManus, Edgar J. *Law and Liberty in Early New England: Criminal Justice and Due Process, 1620–1692*. Amherst: University of Massachusetts Press, 1993.

McSheffrey, Shannon. "Heresy, Orthodoxy and English Vernacular Religion 1480–1525." *Past and Present* 186 (February 2005): 47–80.

Mendle, Michael. *Dangerous Positions: Mixed Government, the Estates of the Realm, and the Making of the Answer to the XIX Propositions*. Tuscaloosa: University of Alabama Press, 1985.

Mendle, Michael. "The Great Council of Parliament and the First Ordinances: The Constitutional Theory of the Civil War." *Journal of British Studies* 31 (April 1992): 133–62.

Mendle, Michael. *Henry Parker and the English Civil War: The Political Thought of the Public's Privado*. Cambridge: Cambridge University Press, 1995.

Mendle, Michael. "The Ship Money Case, the Case of Shipmony, and the Development of Henry Parker's Parliamentary Absolutism." *Historical Journal* 32 (no. 3, 1989): 513–36.

Merryman, John H. *The Civil Law Tradition: An Introduction to the Legal Systems of Western Europe and Latin America*. Stanford: Stanford University Press, 1969.

Miller, John. "'A Suffering People': English Quakers and Their Neighbours c. 1650-c. 1700." *Past and Present* 188 (August 2005): 71–103.

Miller, Perry. *The New England Mind: From Colony to Province*. Boston: Beacon Press, 1953.

Miller, Perry. *The New England Mind: The Seventeenth Century*. New York: Macmillan Co., 1939.

Monaghan, Jennifer. "Literacy Instruction and Gender in Colonial New England." *American Quarterly* 40 (March 1988): 18–41.

Moore, Susan. *Abandoning America: Life Stories from Early New England*. Woodbridge: Boydell Press, 2013.

Morag-Levine, Noga. “The Case of Proclamations (1610), Aldred’s Case (1610), and the Origins of the Sic Utere/Salus Populi Antithesis.” *Law and History Review* 40 (no. 3, 2022): 383–408.

Morgan, Edmund. *American Slavery, American Freedom: The Ordeal of Colonial Virginia*. New York: W.W. Norton & Co., 1975.

Morgan, Edmund. *Inventing the People: The Rise of Popular Sovereignty in England and America*. New York, W.W. Norton & Co., 1988.

Morgan, Edmund. *The Puritan Dilemma: The Story of John Winthrop*. 2nd ed. Boston: Little Brown, and Co., 1999.

Morgan, Edmund. *Visible Saints: The History of a Puritan Idea*. New York University Press, 1963; reprint, Ithaca: Cornell University Press, 1994.

Morison, Samuel Eliot. *Builders of the Bay Colony*. Boston: Houghton Mifflin Company, 1930.

Morison, Samuel Eliot. *The Founding of Harvard College*. Cambridge: Harvard University Press, 1935.

Morison, Samuel Eliot. *The Puritan Pronaos: Studies in the Intellectual Life of New England in the Seventeenth Century*. New York: New York University Press, 1936.

Morley, John. *Oliver Cromwell*. New York: Century, 1902.

Morris, Norval and David Rothman, eds. *The Oxford History of the Prison*. Oxford: Oxford University Press, 1995.

Morris, Richard. “Massachusetts and the Common Law: The Declaration of 1646.” In David Flaherty, ed. *Essays in the History of Early American Law*. Chapel Hill: University of North Carolina Press, 1969: 135–46.

Morris, Richard. *Studies in the History of American Law*. New York: Columbia University Press, 1930.

Mott, Rodney L. *Due Process of Law: A Historical and Analytical Treatise of the Principles and Methods Followed by the Courts in the Application of the Concept the “Law of the Land.”* Indianapolis: Bobbs-Merrill, 1926.

Muldrew, Craig. “The Culture of Reconciliation: Community and the Settlement of Economic Disputes in Early Modern England.” *Historical Journal* 39 (December 1996): 915–42.

Neem, Johann. “The Elusive Common Good: Religion and Civil Society in Massachusetts, 1780–1833.” *Journal of the Early Republic* 24 (no. 3, 2004): 381–417.

Nelson, William. *Americanization of the Common Law*. Cambridge: Harvard University Press, 1975.

Nelson, William. “The Utopian Legal Order of the Massachusetts Bay Colony, 1630–1686.” *American Journal of Legal History* 47 (April 2005): 183–230.

Nenner, Howard. “Loyalty and the Law.” *Journal of British Studies* 48 (no. 4, 2009): 859–70.

Newell, Margaret. “Robert Child and the Entrepreneurial Vision: Economy and Ideology in Early New England.” *New England Quarterly* 68 (no. 2, 1995): 223–56.

Ng, Su Fang. "Translation, Interpretation, and Heresy: The Wycliffite Bible, Tyndale's Bible, and the Contested Origin." *Studies in Philology* 98 (no. 3, 2001): 315–38.

Noble, Richard. "Lions or Jackals: The Independence of the Judges in *Rex. v. Hampden.*" *Stanford Law Review* 14 (July 1962): 711–61.

Norton, Mary Beth. *Founding Mothers and Fathers: Gendered Power and the Forming of American Society*. New York: Alfred A. Knopf, 1996.

"Notes: The History and Development of Qui Tam." *Washington University Law Quarterly* (no. 1, 1972): 81–115.

Nourse, G.B. "Law Reform under the Commonwealth and Protectorate." *Law Quarterly Review* 75 (1959): 512–29.

Orihel, Michelle. "All Those Truly Acquainted with those Times: John Adams and the Opposition Politics of Revolutionary England, 1640–41." *WMQ* 86 (September 2013): 433–66.

Orr, D. Alan. "A Prospectus of a 'New' Constitutional History of Early Modern England." *Albion* 36 (no. 3, 2004): 430–50.

Osgood, Russell. "Early Versions and Practices of Separation of Powers: A Comment." *William and Mary Law Review* 30 (February 1989): 279–86.

Palmer, Robert C. *The County Courts of Medieval England: 1150–1350*. Princeton: Princeton University Press, 1982.

Palmer, R.R. *The Age of the Democratic Revolution: A Political History of Europe and America: 1760–1800*. 2 Vols. Princeton: Princeton University Press, 1959.

Palmer, William. "Oliver St. John and the Legal Language of Revolution in England: 1640–1642." *The Historian* 51 (February 1989): 263–82.

Pasupathi, Vimala. "Mars Rising: Army Pamphlets and London Culture Post 1642." *Yearbook of English Studies* 44 (2014): 232–48.

Paterson, Ellen. "The Politics of Starch: Guilds, Monopolies, and Petitioning in Late Elizabethan and Early Stuart London." *The London Journal* (2022): 1–17; (https://www.tandfonline.com/doi/full/10.1080/03058034.2022.2038461).

Pawlisch, Hans. "Sir John Davies, the Ancient Constitution, and Civil Law." *Historical Journal* 23 (September 1980): 689–702.

Peck, Linda L. *Court Patronage and Corruption in Early Stuart England*. London: Routledge, 1993.

Pelikan, Jaroslav. *The Reformation of the Bible, the Bible of the Reformation*. New Haven: Yale University Press, 1996.

Pencak, William. *War, Politics, and Revolution in Provincial Massachusetts*. Boston: Northeastern University Press, 1981.

Perkins, Edwin. *The Economy of Colonial America*. 2nd ed. New York: Colombia University Press, 1988.

Pestana, Carla. "The City upon a Hill under Siege: The Puritan Perception of the Quaker Threat to Massachusetts Bay, 1656–1661." *New England Quarterly* 56 (September 1983): 323–53.

Pestana, Carla. *The English Atlantic in the Age of Revolution: 1640–41*. Cambridge: Harvard University Press, 2004.

Pestana, Carla. "The Quaker Executions as Myth and History." *Journal of American History* 80 (September 1993): 441–69.

Peterson, Mark. *The City State of Boston: The Rise and Fall of an Atlantic Power, 1630–1865*. Princeton: Princeton University Press, 2019.

Pincus, Steven. *1688: The First Modern Revolution*. New Haven: Yale University Press, 2009.

Pincus, Steven. "Rethinking Mercantilism: Political Economy, the British Empire, and the Atlantic World in the Seventeenth and Eighteenth Centuries." *WMQ* 69 (January 2012): 3–34.

Plucknett, T.F.T. *A Concise History of the Common Law*. 5th ed. Boston: Little, Brown, and Company, 1956.

Plucknett, T.F.T. "Some Proposed Legislation of Henry VIII," *RHS Transactions* 19 (1936): 119–44.

Pocock, J.G.A. *The Machiavellian Moment: Florentine Political Thought and the Atlantic Republican Tradition*. Princeton: Princeton University Press, 1975.

Pollock, Frederick and F.W. Maitland. *The History of English Law*. 2 Vols. 2nd ed. Cambridge: Cambridge University Press, 1968.

Poole, Austin. *From Domesday Book to Magna Carta: 1087–1216*. Oxford: Clarendon Press, 1951.

Popofsky, Linda. "Habeas Corpus and 'Liberty of the Subject': Legal Arguments for the Petition of Right in the Parliament of 1628." *The Historian* 41 (February 1979): 257–75.

Powers, Edwin. *Crime and Punishment in Early Massachusetts: 1620–1692*. Boston: Beacon Press, 1966.

Prall, Stuart. *The Agitation for Law Reform during the Puritan Revolution: 1640–1660*. The Hague: Martinus Nijhoff, 1966.

Prest, Wilfrid. "The English Bar, 1550–1700." In *Lawyers in Early Modern Europe and America*. New York: Holmes & Meier, 1981: 65–85.

Prest, Wilfrid. "Judicial Corruption in Early Modern England." *Past and Present* 133 (1991): 67–95.

Prest, Wilfrid. "Law Reform in Eighteenth-Century England." In Peter Birks, ed. *The Life of the Law*. London: Hambledon Press, 1993: 113–23.

Prest, Wilfrid. *The Rise of the Barristers: A Social History of the English Bar, 1590–1640*. Oxford: Clarendon Press, 1986.

Priest, Claire. *Credit Nation: Property Laws and Institutions in Early America*. Princeton: Princeton University Press, 2021.

"Printing of the Capital Laws in 1642." In *Publications of the Colonial Society of Massachusetts: Transactions (1927–1930)*. Boston: by the Society, 1932; 27: 112–15.

Reck-Malleczewen, Friedrich. *A History of the Münster Anabaptists*. Translated by George B. von der Lippe. New York: Macmillan, 2008.

Rees, John. *The Leveller Revolution*. London: Verso, 2016.

Reeve, L.J. "The Legal Status of the Petition of Right." *Historical Journal* 29 (June 1986): 257–77.

Reid, John Phillip. *The Concept of Liberty in the Age of the American Revolution*. Chicago: University of Chicago Press, 1988.

Reid, John Phillip. *Constitutional History of the American Revolution: The Authority of Law*. Madison: University of Wisconsin Press, 1993.

Reid, John Phillip. *Constitutional History of the American Revolution: The Authority to Legislate*. Madison: University of Wisconsin Press, 1991.

Reid, John Phillip. "'In our Contracted Sphere': The Constitutional Contract, the Stamp Act Crisis, and the Coming of the American Revolution." *Columbia Law Review* 76 (January 1976): 21–47.

Robbins, Caroline. "Algernon Sidney's Discourses Concerning Government: Textbook of Revolution." *WMQ* 4 (July 1947): 267–96.

Robertson, Geoffrey. *The Tyrannicide Brief: The Story of the Man who Sent Charles I to the Scaffold*. New York: Pantheon Books, 2005.

Rogers, Michael. "Gerrard Winstanley on Crime and Punishment." *Sixteenth Century Journal* 27 (Autumn 1996): 735–47.

Ross, Richard. "The Career of Puritan Jurisprudence." *Law and History Review* 26 (2008): 227–58.

Ross, Richard. "The Commoning of the Common Law: The Renaissance Debate over Printing English Law, 1520–1640." *University of Pennsylvania Law Review* 146 (no. 2, 1998): 323–461.

Ross, Richard. "Distinguishing Eternal from Transient Law: Natural Law and the Judicial Law of Moses." *Past and Present* 217 (November 2012): 79–115.

Russell, Conrad. *Causes of the English Civil War: The Ford Lectures Delivered in the University of Oxford, 1987–1988*. Oxford: Clarendon Press, 1990.

Russell, Conrad. *The Crisis of Parliaments: English History, 1509 1660*. Oxford: Oxford University Press, 1971; reprint, 1990.

Russell, Conrad. *The Origins of the English Civil War*. London: Macmillan Press, 1973.

Russell, Conrad. *Politics and English Parliaments: 1621–1629*. Oxford: Clarendon Press, 1979.

Russell, Elmer. *The Review of American Colonial Legislation by the King in Council*. New York: Colombia University Press, 1915; reprint New York: Octagon Books, 1976.

Rutman, Darrett. *Winthrop's Boston: A Portrait of a Puritan Town, 1630–1649*. New York: W.W. Norton & Co., 1965.

Sabbadini, Lorenzo. "Popular Sovereignty and Representation in the English Civil War." In Richard Bourke and Quentin Skinner, eds. *Popular Sovereignty in Historical Perspective*. Cambridge: University Press, 2016: 164–86.

Sabbadini, Lorenzo. *Property, Liberty, and Self-Ownership in Seventeenth-Century England*. Montreal: McGill-Queen's University Press, 2020.

Sachse, William. "The Migration of New Englanders to England, 1640–1660." *American Historical Review* 53 (January 1948): 251–78.

Samaha, Joel. "The Recognizance in Elizabethan Law Enforcement." *American Journal of Legal History* 25 (July 1981): 189–204.

Sawers, Larry. "The Navigation Acts Revisited." *Economic History Review* 45 (May 1992): 262–84.

Schmidt, Jeremy. "Charity and the Government of the Poor in the English Charity-School Movement, circa. 1700–1730." *Journal of British Studies* 49 (October 2010): 774–800.

Schweber, Howard. "Ordering Principles: The Adjudication of Criminal Cases in Puritan Massachusetts, 1629–1650." *Law and Society Review* 32 (no. 2, 1998): 367–408.

Scott, Jonathan. "What were Commonwealth Principles?" *Historical Journal* 47 (September 2004): 591–613.

Seel, Graham and David Smith, eds. *The Early Stuart Kings: 1603–1642*. London: Routledge, 2001.

Shagan, Ethan. "Protector Somerset and the 1549 Rebellions." *English Historical Review* 114 (1999): 34–63.

Shapiro, Barbara. *Beyond Reasonable Doubt and Probable Cause: Historical Perspectives on the Anglo-American Law of Evidence*. Berkeley: University of California Press, 1991.

Shapiro, Barbara. "Codification of the Laws in Seventeenth Century England." *Wisconsin Law Review* (1974): 428–65.

Shapiro, Barbara. *Law Reform in Early Modern England: 1540–1700*. Oxford: Hart Publishing, 2019.

Shapiro, Barbara. "Law Reform in Seventeenth Century England." *American Journal of Legal History* 19 (1975): 284–96.

Shapiro, Barbara. "Sir Francis Bacon and the Mid-Seventeenth Century Movement for Law Reform." *American Journal of Legal History* 24 (October 1980): 331–362.

Sharp, Andrew, ed. *The English Levellers*. Cambridge: Cambridge University Press, 1998.

Sharp, Buchanan. *In Contempt of All Authority: Rural Artisans and Riot in the West of England, 1586–1660*. Berkeley: University of California Press, 1980.

Sharpe, Kevin. *The Personal Rule of Charles I*. New Haven: Yale University Press, 1992.

Sheehan, W.J. "Finding Solace in Eighteenth-Century Newgate." In J.S. Cockburne, ed. *Crime in England: 1550–1800*. London: Methuen & Co., 1977: 229–45.

Shirley, F.J. *Richard Hooker and Contemporary Political Ideas*. London: SPCK, 1949.

Simpson, A.W.B. *An Introduction to the History of the Land Law*. Oxford: Oxford University Press, 1961.

Skeat, Walter W. *Dictionary of English Etymology*. 1884; reprint, Hertfordshire: Wordsworth, 1993.

Skinner, Quentin. "Classical Liberty and the Coming of the English Civil War." In *Republicanism: A Shared European Heritage; Volume 2. The Values of Republicanism in Early Modern Europe*. Cambridge: Cambridge University Press, 2002: 9–28.

Smith, David Chan. *Sir Edward Coke and the Reformation of the Laws*. Cambridge: Cambridge University Press, 2014.

Smith, Maurice H. *The Writs of Assistance Case*. Berkeley: University of California Press, 1978.

Sommerville, Johann. "English and Roman Liberty in the Monarchical Republic of Early Stuart England." In John McDiarmid, ed. *The Monarchical Republic of Early Modern England*. London: Routledge, 2007: 201–16.

Sommerville, Johann. "Ideology, Property, and the Constitution." In Ann Hughes and Richard Cust, eds. *Conflict in Early Stuart England*. London: Longman, 1989: 47–71.

Sommerville, Johann, ed. *Patriarcha and other Writings*. Cambridge: Cambridge University Press, 1991.

Sommerville, Johann. *Politics and Ideology in England: 1603–1640*. London: Longman, 1986.

Sommerville, Johann. *Royalists and Patriots: Politics and Ideology in England: 1603–1640*. 2nd ed. New York: Longman, 1999.

Staloff, Darren. *The Making of an American Thinking Class: Intellectuals and Intelligentsia in Puritan Massachusetts*. Oxford: Oxford University Press, 1998.

Staloff, Darren. "'Where Religion and Commerce Jump Together': Commerce and Piety in Puritan New England." *Reviews in American History* 27 (March 1999): 8–13.

Stearns, Raymond. "The Weld-Peters Mission to England." In *Publications of the Colonial Society of New England: Transactions, 1933–1937*. 32 Vols Boston: 1937: 188–246.

Stephen, James. *A History of the Criminal Law of England*. 3 Vols. London: Macmillan & Co., 1883.

Stephen, Leslie and Sidney Lee, eds. *The Dictionary of National Biography*. London: Oxford University Press, 1917.

Stoebuck, William. "Reception of English Common Law in the American Colonies." *William and Mary Law Review* 10 (no. 2, 1968): 393–426.

Stone, Lawrence. "The Educational Revolution in England: 1560–1640." *Past and Present* 28 (1964): 41–80.

Stone, Lawrence. "Literacy and Education in England: 1640–1900." *Past and Present* 42 (1969): 69–139.

Stone, Roy. "Bacon as Lawyer and Jurist." *Archiv für Rechts-und Sozialphilosophie* 54 (no. 4, 1968): 449–83.

Straumann, Benjamin. "Constitutional Thought in the Late Roman Republic." *History of Political Thought* 32 (no. 2, 2011): 280–92.

Surrency, Edwin. "The Beginnings of American Legal Literature." *American Journal of Legal History* 31 (no. 3, 1987): 207–20.

Taylor, Alan. *American Colonies: The Settling of North America*. New York: Penguin Books, 2001.

Thomas, D.L. and N.E. Evans, "John Shakespeare in the Exchequer." *Shakespeare Quarterly* 35 (1984): 315–18.

Thomas, Ernest. *Leading Cases in Constitutional Law*. London: Steven & Haynes, 1876.

Thompson, Roger. *Divided We Stand: Watertown, Massachusetts, 1630–1680*. Amherst: University of Massachusetts Press, 2001.

Tierny, Brian. *Religion, Law, and the Growth of Constitutional Thought: 1150–1650*. Cambridge: Cambridge University Press, 1982.

Tindall, William. *John Bunyan: Mechanick Preacher*. New York: Columbia University Press, 1934; reprint, Russell & Russell, 1964.

Todt, Kim. "Trading between New Netherland and New England, 1624–1664." *Early American Studies* 9 (Spring 2011): 348–78.

Tomlins, Christopher. *Freedom Bound: Law, Labor, and Civic Identity in Colonizing English America, 1580–1865*. Cambridge: Cambridge University Press, 2010.

Trace, Jamie. "The Only Early English Translation of Giovanni Botero's Della *ragion di stato*: Richard Etherington and Sloane MS. 1065." *Electronic British Library Journal, Art. #4* (2016): 1–27; (https://bl.iro.bl.uk/concern/articles/03d8040c-72c7-45d5-8c56-9b8456922439?locale=pt-BR).

"Trial of Mrs. Anne Hibbens." *MHS Proceedings* (*Second Series/1887–89*); 4: 315–16.

Trinterud, L.J. "William Haller, Historian of Puritanism." *Journal of British Studies* 5 (May 1966): 33–55.

Tubb, Amos. "Mixed Messages: Royalist Newsbook Reports of Charles I's Execution and of the Leveller Uprising." *Huntington Library Quarterly* 67 (March 2004): 59–74.

Tuck, Richard. *Philosophy and Government: 1572–1651*. Cambridge: Cambridge University Press, 1993.

Tuck, Richard. "Power and Authority in Seventeenth-Century England." *Historical Journal* 17 (March 1974): 43–61.

Tuck, Richard. *The Rights of War and Peace: Political Thought and the International Order from Grotius to Kant*. Oxford: Oxford University Press, 1999.

Tuck, Richard. *The Sleeping Sovereign: The Invention of Modern Democracy*. Cambridge: Cambridge University Press, 2016.

Tyacke, Nicholas. "The Puritan Paradigm of English Politics." *Historical Journal* 53 (no. 3, 2010): 527–50.

Tyacke, Nicholas. "Revolutionary Puritanism in Anglo-American Perspective." *Huntington Library Quarterly* 78 (December 2015): 527–50.

Underdown, David. *Fire From Heaven: Life in an English Town in the Seventeenth Century*. New Haven: Yale University Press, 1992.

Underdown, David. *A Freeborn People: Politics and the Nation in Seventeenth Century England*. Oxford: Clarendon Press, 1996.

Underdown, David. *Pride's Purge: Politics in the Puritan Revolution*. London: George Allen & Unwin, 1971.

Van Caenegem, R.C. *An Historical Introduction to Private Law*. Cambridge: Cambridge University Press, 1992.

Veall, Donald. *The Popular Movement for Law Reform: 1640–1660*. Oxford: Clarendon Press, 1970.

Vejnar, Robert. "The State of Education in Colonial Virginia." *International Social Science Review* 77 (no. 1/2, 2002): 16–31.

Vernon, Eliot and Philip Baker. "What was the First 'Agreement of the People'?" *Historical Journal* 53 (March 2010): 39–59.

Waite, Gary. "The Anabaptist Movement in Amsterdam and the Netherlands, 1531–1535." *Sixteenth Century Journal* 18 (Summer 1987): 249–65.

Wall, Robert. *Massachusetts Bay: The Crucial Decade, 1640–1650*. New Haven: Yale University Press, 1972.

Wall, Robert. "The Massachusetts Bay Colony Franchise in 1647." WMQ 27 (January 1974): 136–44.

Wall, Robert. "The Membership of the Massachusetts General Court: 1634–1686." Ph.D. Diss. Yale University, 1965.

Wallis, Patrick and Cliff Webb. "Education and Training of Gentry Sons in Early Modern England." *Social History* 36 (February 2011): 36–53.

Ward, Harry. *The United Colonies of New England: 1643–1690*. New York: Vantage Press, 1961.

Warden, G.B. *Boston: 1689–1776*. Boston: Little, Brown, & Co., 1970.

Warden, G.B. "Notes and Documents: Law Reform in England and New England, 1620–1660." WMQ 35 (October 1978): 668–690.

Warner, Jessica, Frank Ivis and Andree Demers. "A Predatory Social Structure: Informers in Westminster, 1737–1741." *Journal of Interdisciplinary History* 30 (no. 4, 2000): 617–34.

Webster, Charles. "The Authorship and Significance of Macaria." *Past and Present* 56 (August 1972): 34–48.

Webster, Charles. *The Great Instauration: Science, Medicine, and Reform, 1626–1660*. New York: Holmes & Meier, 1975.

Weimer, Adrian. *Constitutional Culture: New England and the Struggle against Arbitrary Rule in the Restoration Empire*. Philadelphia: University of Pennsylvania Press, 2023.

Weston, Corinne. "The Theory of Mixed Monarchy under Charles I and After." *English Historical Review* 75 (1960): 426–43.

White, Stephen. *Sir Edward Coke and "The Grievances of the Commonwealth": 1621–1628*. Chapel Hill: University of North Carolina Press, 1981.

White, William. "Sir John Eliot's *The Monarchie of Man* and Early Stuart Political Thought." *Historical Journal* 62 (no. 3, 2019): 639–62.

Whittle, Jane. "Lords and Tenants in Kett's Rebellion 1549." *Past and Present* 207 (2010): 3–52.

Wijffels, Alain. "Law Books at Cambridge, 1500–1640." In Peter Birks, ed. *The Life of the Law: Proceedings of the Tenth British Legal History Conference, Oxford 1991*. London: Hambledon Press, 1993: 59–87.

Williams, Ian. "James VI and I, Rex and Judex: One King as Judge in Two Kingdoms." In William Eves, et. al. eds. *Common Law, Civil Law, and Colonial Law: Essays in Comparative English Legal History from the Twelfth to the Twentieth Centuries*. Cambridge: Cambridge University Press, 2021: 86–119.

Williams, Ian. "Learning the 'New Law of the Star Chamber': Legal Education and Legal Literature in Early-Stuart England," *The Journal of Legal History* 43 (no. 3, 2022): 243–61.

Williams, Ian. "Perjury, Wager of Law, and Debt in the Elizabethan Star Chamber." *Legal History Miscellany* (October 15, 2019); (https://legalhistorymiscellany.com/2019/ 10/ 15/perjury-wager-of-law-and-debt-in-the-elizabethan-star-chamber/).

Willison, George. *Saints and Strangers*. New York: Reynal & Hitchcock, 1945.

Wilson, Douglas. "Web of Secrecy: Goffe, Whalley, and the Legend of Hadley." *New England Quarterly* 60 (December 1987): 515–48.

Winfield, Percy. *The Chief Sources of English Legal History*. Cambridge: Harvard University Press, 1925.

Winship, George. *The Cambridge Press: 1638–1692*. Philadelphia: University of Pennsylvania Press, 1945.

Winship, Michael. *Godly Republicanism: Puritans, Pilgrims, and a City on a Hill*. Cambridge: Harvard University Press, 2012.

Winship, Michael. *Hot Protestants: A History of Puritanism in England and America*. New Haven: Yale University Press, 2018.

Winship, Michael. *Making Heretics: Militant Protestantism and Free Grace in Massachusetts, 1636–1641*. Princeton: Princeton University Press, 2002.

Winship, Michael. *The Times and Trials of Anne Hutchinson*. Lawrence: University Press of Kansas, 2005.

Winsor, Justin, ed. *The Memorial History of Boston*. 2 Vols. Boston: Ticknor & Co., 1881.

Witte, Jr., John. "Right, Resistance and Revolution in the Western Tradition: Early Protestant Foundations." *Law and History Review* 26 (no. 3, 2008): 545–70.

Wolford, Thorp L. "The Laws and Liberties of 1648." In David Flaherty, ed. *Essays in the History of Early American Law*. Chapel Hill: University of North Carolina Press, 1969: 147–85.

Wood, Andy. *The 1549 Rebellions and the Making of Early Modern England*. Cambridge: Cambridge University Press, 2007.

Wood, Gordon. *The Creation of the American Republic: 1776–1787*. New York: W.W. Norton, 1969.

Wood, Gordon. *The Idea of America*. New York: Penguin Press, 2011.

Wood, Gordon. "The Problem of Sovereignty." *WMQ* 68 (October 2011): 573–77.

Wood, Gordon. *The Radicalism of the American Revolution*. New York: Vintage Books, 1993.

Woolrych, Austin. *Britain in Revolution, 1625–1660*. Oxford: Oxford University Press, 2002.

Woolrych, Austin. *Commonwealth to Protectorate*. Oxford: Clarendon Press, 1982.

Wooten, David. "From Rebellion to Revolution: The Crisis of the Winter of 1642/3 and the Origins of Civil War Radicalism." *English Historical Review* 105 (July 1990): 654–69.

Wooton, David, ed. *Divine Right and Democracy*. New York: Penguin Books, 1986.

Worden, Blair. "Cromwell and the Protectorate." In *God's Instruments: Political Conduct in the England of Oliver Cromwell*. Oxford: Oxford University Press, 2012: 230–59.

Worden, Blair. "The Levellers in History and Memory." In Michael Mendle, ed. *The Putney Debates of 1647*. Cambridge: Cambridge University Press, 2010: 256–82.

Worden, Blair. *The Rump Parliament: 1648–1653*. Cambridge: Cambridge University Press, 1974.

Wright, Louis. *Middle-Class Culture in Elizabethan England*. Chapel Hill: University of North Carolina Press, 1935.

Yirush, Craig. *Settlers, Liberty, and Empire: The Roots of Early American Political Theory: 1675–1775*. Cambridge: Cambridge University Press, 2011.

Zagorin, Perez. *A History of Political Thought in the English Revolution*. New York: Humanities Press, 1966.

Zagorin, Perez. "The Political Beliefs of John Pym to 1629." *English Historical Review* 109 (September 1994): 67–90.

Zagorin, Perez. *Rebels and Rulers: 1500–1660*. Cambridge: Cambridge University Press, 1982.

Zaller, Robert. "The Debate on Capital Punishment during the English Revolution." *American Journal of Legal History* 31 (April 1987): 126–44.

Zaller, Robert. "Henry Parker and the Regiment of True Government." *Proceedings of the American Philosophical Society* 135 (June 1991): 264–85.

# Index

www.ingramcontent.com/pod-product-compliance
Lightning Source LLC
Chambersburg PA
CBHW071327230926
51849CB00002B/330

* 9 7 8 9 0 0 4 7 0 6 3 3 0 *